Making Music

$39.95

ALEX BARRIS & TED BARRIS

Making Music

Profiles from a Century of Canadian Music

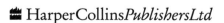 HarperCollins*PublishersLtd*

Making Music:
Profiles from a Century of Canadian Music
Copyright © 2001 by Alex Barris Enterprises Ltd.
and Ted Barris

For information address
HarperCollins Publishers Ltd,
55 Avenue Road, Suite 2900,
Toronto, Ontario, Canada M5R 3L2

www.harpercanada.com

HarperCollins books may be purchased for
educational, business, or sales promotional use.
For information please write:
Special Markets Department,
HarperCollins Canada,
55 Avenue Road, Suite 2900,
Toronto, Ontario, Canada M5R 3L2

First edition

Canadian Cataloguing in Publication Data

Barris, Alex, 1922–
Making music : profiles from a century of Canadian
music.

ISBN 0-00-200056-3

1. Musicians – Canada – Biography.
I. Barris, Ted.
II. Title.

ML385.B276 2001   780'.92'271   C2001-930140-5

WEB 9 8 7 6 5 4 3 2 1

Printed and bound in Canada
Set in Monotype Plantin Light

Contents

AUTHORS' NOTE:
Songs composed by the artist who is being profiled are in boldface. Album and CD titles for the profiled artist are in italic boldface. In some instances, it has been difficult to trace songwriting credits and we would be grateful for any correspondence that would assist us in correcting any errors or omissions.

Introduction

It's a frosty morning in January. In fact, it's the first frosty morning in January. The first in the year 2000. We two broadcasters, who happen to be father and son, are seated in a Toronto radio studio with a pile of notes, CDs, and vinyl albums, and a whole lot of anecdotes. Our CBC Radio producer, Mike Ewing, rolls the theme. As co-hosts, we look at the clock, lean toward the mikes and kick off the show.

"Good morning. I'm Alex Barris."

"Hi there. I'm Ted Barris."

"For the next few hours," Alex says, "some of our favourite music and some of our favourite anecdotes about the music makers."

"Anecdotes," Ted says, "like how Canadian country singer Hank Snow's famous song 'Movin' On' became a code phrase to soldiers in the Korean War ..."

"Or how Canadian Ruth Lowe, on the death of her husband, wrote lyrics and music that became Frank Sinatra's signature song ..."

"How the Guess Who played the White House, but not before the first lady warned them to censor their biggest hit ..."

"Why 'our pet' Juliette never claimed to be a pioneer, yet almost single-handedly created a star system in Canadian television ..."

"And how Edmonton pianist and conductor (now Senator) Tommy Banks steadfastly refused invitations for fame and fortune in the U.S. to keep on making music in Canada ..."

Thus began the latest Barris holiday special broadcast on CBC Radio. As in scores of other programs we've co-hosted, this one gave us the opportunity to go on-air, play some favourite recordings of Canadian artists, and tell stories about our encounters with them. The truth is, these shows are broadcasts of the kind of conversations we two have had in real life for a long time. We love the music Canadians have created and the lore that goes with it.

You see, for all the years we've been writers and broadcasters, we've also been incurable pack rats – collecting tapes, transcripts, published pieces, albums, press clippings, pictures, and bios. Our combined files of "stuff" constitute a library of musical Canadiana.

More importantly, over the years we've also accumulated stories by working first-hand with many of these same artists. We've sat in on recording sessions with the likes of Jack Kane, Buffy Sainte-Marie, Oscar Peterson, and Dr. Music. We've scripted television shows for performers such as Juliette, Long John Baldry, the Canadian Brass, k. d. lang, and Tommy Banks. We've emceed shows with artists such as Bobby Curtola, Peter Appleyard, Maureen Forrester, Stan Rogers, and Connie Kaldor. And we've covered concerts that featured Walter Susskind, Jeff Healey, Anne Murray, and Seiji Ozawa. As a result we've amassed an encyclopedia of personal musical memories. Which brings us to this book.

A few years ago, during a family dinner, which was punctuated by one or the other of us saying "That reminds me of the time …" somebody suggested we stop talking about the stories, but (in the family vernacular) "P.D.," that is, "put down" the anecdotes in a book. What a concept! We wrote up a proposal, submitted some sample stories to HarperCollins, and the rest is the history on these pages.

As professional chroniclers of Canadian music and music makers, we are immensely proud of these subjects. While the recordings of artists from the United States and Europe pepper our old vinyl and more recent CD collections, Canadians' music is the meat and potatoes on those shelves and racks. Not surprisingly, that pride leaps off the pages of this book.

We've written about a remarkable range of singers from Teresa Stratas to Diana Krall, from Ben Heppner to Raffi, and from Giselle MacKenzie to Burton Cummings. We've covered the bands Canadians danced to, including bands led by Cy McLean, Moxie Whitney, Guy Lombardo as well as the Carlton Showband, Downchild Blues Band, and Loverboy. We've included profiles of folk and country singers such as Susan Aglukark, Ian and Sylvia, Blue Rodeo, Joni Mitchell, Tommy Hunter, Rita MacNeil, and Stompin' Tom Connors. They're just a few of the music makers whose lives and anecdotes we've told here.

It's no coincidence, either, that many of the musical performers we've chosen to write about (like us) have a strong connection with the CBC. The CBC helped to launch many of their careers. In fact, long before there were Canadian-content regulations, CBC programmers showcased Canadian acts as part of the corporation's mandate to reflect Canadians to Canada. They and we owe much to the fulfillment of that mandate.

Broadcast licences aside, we also believe that music – Canadian-based or otherwise – is the only true global language, the one tongue that transcends borders, defies prejudices, unites people more completely than any solemn pact or well-intentioned organization can ever hope to do. It's in that spirit that we saw fit to assemble this candid collection of word portraits of some of the gifted music makers who have so enriched life in Canada and the world over the 20th century.

And so now, as we often said during those Barris holiday specials, "Sit back for the next while and enjoy some of our favourites …"

September 2001   ALEX BARRIS AND TED BARRIS

Bryan Adams

b. Kingston, Ontario, November 5, 1959

He may have that boy-next-door look about him, but Bryan Adams has toured farther afield than most A&R talent scouts, invested more time and effort in his career than many rock bands put together, and built as large an enterprise around him as any corporate CEO. Adams is a brand, worth millions of dollars, but it's no fluke. It's come as a result of many years of slogging in the rock 'n' roll trenches.

"Bryan's like Michael Jackson," a friend told *Canadian Business* magazine in 1987. "He knows all aspects of the business. He can talk about the record companies, publishing, agents' contracts. He understands all the elements of the business. He could have made it in any business."

In his heyday, when a Bryan Adams concert came to a venue such as Toronto's Maple Leaf Gardens, there would be hundreds of thousands of dollars in gate receipts and an equal amount in merchandise sales – including buttons, programs, T-shirts, and recordings. At the time his fifth album, *Into the Fire*, was released in 1987, Bryan Adams was the most successful recording star in Canadian history; that year he grossed $45 million from ticket sales and $15 million from merchandising alone.

All this could have been predicted. When he was 12, Bryan announced he was going to be a rock star. At the end of high school in Vancouver, he invested the $2000 his parents had put aside for his postsecondary education in a piano and then worked his way through several local bands, including Shock and Sweeney Todd. In 1978, he began collaborating with songwriter Jim Vallance (of the group Prism), an association that would eventually yield them both armfuls of awards.

At that point, however, Adams was so desperate to sign a recording contract that when an opportunity knocked, he signed with Irving-Almo of Canada (the Canadian publishing arm of A&M Records) and agreed to the payment of $1. A&M took his demo of a song titled **Let Me Take You Dancing**, released it as a single (on which Adams thought he sounded like a chipmunk) and watched it become a disco/R&B hit, selling 240,000 copies. In 1979, Adams signed with Vancouver-based manager Bruce Allen (who had handled Bachman-Turner Overdrive, Loverboy, and Liona Boyd). In 1980, A&M

1

financed Adams' first self-titled album, which was recorded in Toronto and mixed in Los Angeles.

Thus began his workaholic period. To help pay off the financing of the first album, Adams sang radio commercials for Canadian retailers. When his singles **Cuts Like a Knife** and **Straight from the Heart** were released in 1983, he hit the road in the United States, performing more than 100 dates in five months, followed by a six-week, 11-country tour of Europe.

The Canadian correspondent for *Billboard* noted that Adams "succeeded because he worked his tail off. ... He stayed out on the road incessantly. He played every little joint."

The breakneck pace paid off. Adams won the 1983 Juno Award, his first, for best male vocalist. The next year, his album *Reckless* came out and Adams hit the road again, this time for 250 days; by August 1985 the album was number one on *Billboard*'s Top 100 album chart, selling seven million copies worldwide, four million in the United States – and one million copies at home, a first for a Canadian artist.

"*Reckless* provided a soundtrack to the summer of 1985," wrote *National Post* reviewer Dan Brown. "[It] cemented his reputation as a straight-ahead rocker with an ear for a catchy riff. It also separated him from the pack ... [from] such outfits as April Wine, Loverboy and Trooper. It made Adams what he is today – a global star."

The popularity of *Reckless* saw his concert at the CNE Stadium in Toronto generate the largest gross by a Canadian artist in this country's show business history, over $914,000. It also yielded two Grammy nominations and six Top 10 singles, including **Run to You, Heaven, Summer of '69, One Night Love Affair**, and **It's Only Love**, this last a duet with Tina Turner. In fact, a live performance of the duet at the 1985 Junos capped a Bryan Adams night, in which he captured the top three awards – best album, best composer, and best male vocalist. The duet video later won the MTV award for best stage performance.

Also that year, as part of artists' response to the famine in Ethiopia, Adams co-wrote (with Jim Vallance and David Foster) **Tears Are Not Enough**, recorded at Toronto's Manta Sound under the name Northern Lights. The February session brought together a who's who of Canadian show business, including Adams, Carroll Baker, Salome Bey, Liona Boyd, John Candy, Robert Charlebois, Tom Cochrane, Bruce Cockburn, Burton Cummings, David Foster, Dan Hill, Tommy Hunter, Marc Jordan, Eugene Levy, Gordon Lightfoot, Loverboy, Richard Manuel, Murray McLauchlan, Frank Mills, Joni Mitchell, Kim Mitchell, Anne Murray, the 1985 NHL All-Stars, Catherine O'Hara, Oscar Peterson, Carole Pope, Paul Shaffer, Jane Siberry, Liberty Silver, Alan Thicke, Dave Thomas, Sylvia Tyson, and Neil Young.

Tears Are Not Enough propelled Adams onto the world stage. In 1987, he headlined the Prince's Trust Fund charity pop music concerts at Wembley

Stadium near London. Adams appeared on stage with Eric Clapton, Boy George, and Phil Collins, and then he joined former Beatles Paul McCartney, George Harrison, and Ringo Starr in renditions of "While My Guitar Gently Weeps," "With a Little Help from My Friends," and "Here Comes the Sun." Then in the summer of 1990, he joined Joni Mitchell and The Band in Roger Waters' performance of *The Wall* at the site of the Berlin Wall.

What some refer to as the second stage of Bryan Adams' career began in 1991, when he wrote and released **(Everything I Do) I Do It for You** for the movie *Robin Hood, Prince of Thieves*. With it, Adams became a creator of sure-fire ballads. It also sustained his reign atop the charts. **Everything I Do** became one of the best-selling singles ever. It stayed in the number-one spot on the British charts for 16 weeks, earning a mention in the *Guinness Book of World Records*. It won the 1991 award as *Billboard*'s number-one worldwide single and number-one adult contemporary single. It garnered the American Music Awards title for Song of the Year and a Grammy for Best Song Written for a Motion Picture.

Despite making his home in Britain in the 1990s, Adams never seemed to lower his profile in Canada. In 1990 he was named to the Order of Canada. In 1992, the CRTC ruled that his album *Waking Up the Neighbours* did not meet the "CanCon" – Canadian content – standards of the day, because some of its songs had been co-written by non-Canadian Robert "Mutt" Lange. The album sold 11 million copies worldwide, but to the CRTC, Canadian content means 100 percent or nothing at all. Adams and his fans objected so vociferously that the regulatory body changed the criteria to 50 percent, and on January 29, 1993 *Waking Up the Neighbours* was declared CanCon-eligible.

At the end of the 1990s, Adams toured Canada several times – once to promote his MTV album *Unplugged* and again to promote his book *Made in Canada* (with royalties going to Canadian breast cancer research). His musical appearances featured a scaled-down band – just Keith Scott on guitar, Mickey Curry on drums and Adams singing and playing bass – and a no-frills approach to his material. It marked a definite departure from what one critic referred to as "the white-guy, singer-songwriter arena tradition" that had also made stars of Bruce Springsteen and John Mellencamp.

After a more intimate Bryan Adams Massey Hall concert in January 2000, *Toronto Star* pop music critic Ben Rayner wrote, "Adams has never pretended to be anything but a hit-maker and a crowd-pleaser."

With 55 million albums sold to date, he's no slouch as a businessman, either.

Susan Aglukark

b. Churchill, Manitoba, January 27, 1963

It's one thing to represent one's community. It's another to become a role model and spokesperson for its people through lyric and song. This is the reality in which singer-songwriter Susan Aglukark has both prospered and struggled.

The middle child of seven, born to a travelling Inuit Pentecostal preacher and his wife, Susan Aglukark was influenced by the constant motion of relocating in Arctic communities and the music of the church's Glad Tidings choir.

Early on, she learned to play the guitar, bass, and piano. At age nine, she gave her first public performance of a song entitled **Happy, Happy, Happy**. The lyrics belied events in her early life – she was sexually abused (by a non–family member). Her grandmother was an alcoholic and tragically froze to death. A brother and sister both attempted suicide. These experiences, consciously and otherwise, would become the wellspring for her compositions and performances.

Show business would have to wait, however, because after her high school studies in Yellowknife, Aglukark moved to Ottawa and worked as a translator for the federal Department of Indian and Northern Affairs and then as an executive assistant for an Inuit lobby group.

In 1990, Les McLaughlin of CBC's Northern Service and Ottawa-based producer Randall Prescott heard a tape that Aglukark submitted in the network's attempt to assemble the work of northern artists. Said McLaughlin, "It was the clearest, finest voice I'd heard." In 1991, they put out her first solo album, *Dreams For You*, on the CBC label. The same year, the federal government, as part of its campaign to promote Inuit traditions, produced a video with Aglukark called *Searching*; it won for best photography in the Canadian Music Video Awards.

"That," said Val Haas, Aglukark's friend and manager, "was the turning point." Suddenly, Susan Aglukark was coming at northerners from several directions – on television screens, over the radio, and via live performances in hamlets across the Arctic. Then came her second compilation of songs, the album *Arctic Rose*, that launched in her hometown of Arviat in September of 1992. It sold 15,000 copies by mail order in the Northwest Territories alone.

"My audience is young people," Aglukark told *Billboard* magazine in 1994. "What I pass on to them are my experiences as a young person and the kind of things they relate to. Historically, Inuit people did not have conventional teen-age years. They married at 13 and didn't have experiences of peer pressure. Now, everything is new. This generation is realizing it's okay to have feelings of confusion, of not knowing what to do or where to go."

Embracing the rituals and values of her Inuit roots and singing in both English and Inuktitut, Aglukark addressed the tough social realities of life in the far North in song – friendship, suicide, abuse, and the struggle of fellow Inuit to reclaim a sense of self. By December of 1993, Aglukark had signed a contract with EMI, which then released her self-titled collection of Christmas carols sung in Inuktitut. Then, in 1994, EMI rereleased *Arctic Rose*; it went on to sell an additional 30,000 copies and earned her the Canadian Country Music Association's Rising Star Award and two Junos for Best New Solo Artist and Best Music of Aboriginal Canada Recording.

On her *This Child* album in 1995, Aglukark further illustrated a knack for bridging two worlds with her music. The recording demonstrated her ability to intertwine traditional Inuk chants with popular music. She used indigenous titles, such as **O Siem** (an exclamation of joy at seeing friends and family), **Hina Na Ho** (celebration), and **Shamaya** (a documentary of the traditions of the hunt) to capture elements of Inuit life. But she used contemporary pop music melodies and rhythms to project those images.

"She has a powerful presence, but it's quiet, hard to define," wrote Penny Williams in *Saturday Night* magazine. "Too poised and confident to be called humble, yet without affectation. Sweet, simple, but too tough, too realistic for sentimentality."

Her singing has taken her in front of MuchMusic video cameras, to command performances before the Queen, on the CBC network, and even to the Territories legislative building in Yellowknife. She travels, performs, prays, and speaks out for young people in the North, urging them to stay in school, avoid drug abuse, and get the skills they need to build the new territory of Nunavut and their own futures.

"My Inuit name is *Uuliniq*, 'Scarred from burns,'" says Aglukark. "When I asked my mother who this person was, why I bore this name, she'd only say, '[Your namesake] was someone very respected in the community.'"

It's a responsibility she carries well.

Lucio Agostini *b. Fano, Italy, December 30, 1913; d. 1996*

"His value as a composer," the editors of *Encyclopedia of Music in Canada* wrote of Lucio Agostini, "lies in his command of an orchestra and its colours,

his ability to satisfy the dramatic requirements at hand, his speed and precision, his effectiveness as a conductor, and his efficiency as a workman."

In 1983, the Alliance of Canadian Cinema Television and Radio Artists (ACTRA) added an important "Amen" to that description of this outstanding musician by awarding him the prestigious John Drainie Award for distinguished contribution to broadcasting. The significance of the award is that it went to a musician rather than to a performing ACTRA member.

Agostini was surrounded by music all his life. His father, Giuseppe Agostini, was himself a skilled composer, conductor, and arranger. Lucio's younger sister, Gloria, is a first-class harpist who had a successful career in New York and later taught at Yale.

The Agostini family emigrated to Canada when Lucio was a child, settling in Montreal. Lucio himself began studying music at the age of five and learned to play cello, tenor saxophone, and bass clarinet in his father's (Montreal) orchestra. By 1929, he was composing music for shows at McGill and soon after conducted his first radio show on CFCF. Next he began composing film scores for Associated Screen News.

He was destined to become one of Canada's busiest and most highly respected composers and conductors, operating in a great variety of musical venues. There was hardly a musician in central Canada who didn't, at some time or other, play under the Agostini baton.

After moving to Toronto in 1943 he completed scores for some 150 shorts, including monthly installments of the National Film Board's *Canada at War* series. Earlier, he had already begun conducting for the CBC and later composed and conducted for such dramatic programs as CBC's Sunday night *Stage* series and *CBC Wednesday Night*.

By the 1950s, he and his music were being featured on such CBC Radio series as *Strictly for Strings* and *Appointment with Agostini*. Next came *Music Album* and *Music to Remember*.

In 1958, he became music director for CBC-TV's *Front Page Challenge*, a post he held for almost a quarter of a century. He began with only five musicians under him, but as the program grew so did his orchestra. By the end, he had 12 musicians providing the music for the show. Then, in the program's last few years, CBC funding cutbacks also meant cutting down on the orchestra again.

Fred Davis, the moderator of that long-running series, said of Agostini: "Lucio is so brilliant. He was able to hand-tailor dramatic music for every guest, every story. We went through a period when the panelists would start out by saying, 'Well, that music sounds kind of mournful. Is it a sad story?' But sometimes he'd fool them. It was tailor-made music."

Speed was essential on *Front Page Challenge*. Lucio usually had a chance to look at the film representing the news event before writing the appropriate music. But on one occasion, things almost fell apart. The front-page story was the Bay of Pigs invasion. Because time was short, Agostini didn't have a chance to view the film of that story. He was aware only that the story had a Havana dateline. So he wrote some light, frothy rhumba music. Fortunately, he saw the film during the afternoon rehearsal and was able to come up with more appropriate music for that evening's show.

Agostini took a year off to go to Spain to work on an opera. "I didn't like Spain too much," he said later. "I liked it but not to stay. Too many parties there, I couldn't do any work. It was good getting back to *Front Page*."

During his long career, Agostini also provided music for such television shows as *Pick the Stars*, *The Tommy Ambrose Show*, *Chrysler Festival*, *Ford Theatre*, *Juliette*, *Take Thirty*, and many others.

Despite all this television work, Lucio Agostini found time to compose musical comedies, music for several films, a piano concerto, a flute concerto, and various other works, including the music for a radio adaptation of Robertson Davies' novel *Fifth Business*.

Lucio Agostini was a gifted, quiet, courtly, gentle man whose whole life was dedicated to composing, arranging, and conducting music. Long before his death, Andrew Allan paid him this handsome tribute: "All the *Stages* would have been impossible without the fine Italian hand of that beautiful, tireless, and enormously talented man."

Archie Alleyne   *b. Toronto, Ontario, January 7, 1933*

"Jazz," Archie Alleyne has long maintained, "is black classical music."

For several decades, Archie has been recognized as Toronto's premier jazz drummer. For more than a dozen years, he was the house drummer at the Town Tavern, then one of the city's top jazz clubs. During that time, he backed such stellar jazz artists as Billie Holiday, Lester Young, and Coleman Hawkins. He also toured in Canada and the United States with Marian McPartland, Teddy Wilson, Jim Galloway, Oliver Jones, and Peter Appleyard. With Jones he travelled to Cuba, Ireland, Spain, Egypt, the Ivory Coast, and Nigeria in his quest for jazz mastery.

He also used to play in such Toronto after-hours clubs as The House of Hambourg, Melody Mills, and The First Floor Club, venues where musical experimentation was not only tolerated but encouraged.

Alleyne is also a kind of self-appointed historian of jazz. He created a show called *The Evolution of Jazz* in 1991. It had a cast of 30 musicians and performers, and a somewhat smaller version of it has played in various schools in the Toronto area.

But one of Archie's fondest memories is having worked with Billie Holiday. "She came to sing at the Stratford Festival," he recalled many years later, "when they started staging jazz there, with the pianist Mal Waldron, and I was accompanying. After that, she came to the Town Tavern for a week. It could be a noisy room, but I remember one night when she just silenced the place. Even the kitchen staff stopped work and came out to listen to her sing. I've never known anything quite like it. That was less than three years before she died."

Archie was also with the Norm Amadio Quartet (with Ed Bickert on guitar) when it became the only Canadian band to play Birdland in New York.

After an automobile accident in 1967, Alleyne became a restaurateur (the Underground Railway in Toronto) and was inactive in music from 1970 to 1982. Then, he returned to the jazz scene with a quartet.

"I was born in the Cameron Hotel," he told an interviewer in 1990, "and raised in that area between Queen and College along Spadina, which was substantially the black area of Toronto in the 1930s. ... I left school when I was 16 and had a day job as a delivery boy in the fashion business."

That was when he began to teach himself to play drums, mostly at night. When he'd assembled a drum kit and could use it to play some gigs, he had a problem: "I didn't have a car, so I had to carry my drum kit on streetcars and the subway. I'd play from nine at night to one a.m., get home with my drums by three a.m. and would have to be up four hours later to go to my day job."

Over the years, Alleyne has been involved in several successful musical productions, including *Madame Gertrude: A Tribute to Ma Rainey*, *Lady Day at Emerson's Bar & Grill*, in which Montreal singer Ranee Lee portrayed one of Billie Holiday's last performances, and *Many Rivers to Cross*.

It was his insatiable hunger for exploring the roots of jazz that led to his most recent show, *The Evolution of Jazz*. After its initial presentation at the University of Toronto's Convocation Hall and then at Toronto's Limelight Dinner Theatre, Alleyne has concentrated on schools and also the Young People's Theatre.

"One problem," said Archie, "is that we do two or three shows and then stop, and to restart is tough. We'd like to be part of YPT's schedule over the long run. They approached us and it's an ideal location.

"We're also looking at touring, particularly in southern Ontario where a lot of black people settled after coming to Canada via the Underground Railroad, places like Dresden, Buxton, and Chatham. There's a lot of black history down there."

According to Alleyne, the work at schools has given his mission considerable help. "Students really listen and observe and ask intelligent questions afterward. We're hoping this message gets through, especially in the inner-city schools so that black students understand they're part of all this."

Norman Amadio *b. Timmins, Ontario, April 14, 1928*

"I never thought I'd get to play with all these people," Norm Amadio said a few years ago. "But in those days, all of the great singers and players came through town [Toronto]. I had a ball."

The comment is worth mentioning primarily because it reflects the innate modesty of this versatile pianist.

The "all these people" referred to range from jazz giants such as Lester Young and Miles Davis to diva Teresa Stratas, for whom he provided accompaniment for an aria during a TV special – without so much as a moment's rehearsal. He played it flawlessly the first time through. That was when his training at the Royal Conservatory of Music in Toronto proved its worth.

Albert Norman Benedict Amadio was born in Timmins, Ontario, of Italian-American parents and studied first in his hometown and then in Toronto. His parents wanted him to become a classical musician, and for a while he went along with their wishes. He began playing with a few local bands in and around Timmins. Soon he was attracted to jazz, particularly the more modern approaches to that form of music.

He made his professional debut at Rouyn, Quebec with a country music band. But, influenced mostly by pianists Lennie Tristano and Bud Powell, by the late 1940s Amadio was a familiar figure around some of Toronto's after-hours jazz clubs, most notably the House of Hambourg.

One thing that made Amadio so much in demand in the music business was his broad frame of reference. He could play bop or Dixieland, standard popular tunes that visiting jazz artists liked to improvise on, country music or rock. He could sight-read the arrangements of visiting performers and skillfully accompany them.

By the early 1950s he had become the principal house pianist at Toronto's Town Tavern, heading a trio that usually included drummer Archie Alleyne. He accompanied such famed artists as Roy Eldridge, Coleman Hawkins, Mel Tormé, Bill Harris, Zoot Sims, Dinah Washington, Carmen McRae, Stan Getz, and Bud Freeman, plus such Canadian artists as Moe Koffman, Tommy Ambrose, and Phyllis Marshall. One of his favourite musicians to play for was the great tenor saxophonist Lester Young. "He was so cool," Amadio later commented.

It was Bud Freeman who was so impressed by Norm's playing that he wanted to take him along on the road. Amadio resisted the temptation, but eventually he was lured to New York for what he later referred to as a "bad experience." He played at Birdland, a famous jazz club, sharing the spotlight with the Count Basie band, but for some reason he wasn't happy there. He preferred what he described as "the straight life."

After returning to Toronto, he told one interviewer: "Coming back to Toronto saved my life. In documentaries of Chet Baker, he's bragging that he's 54 and the poor guy looks 85." (Baker died in 1988 at the age of 59.)

Despite his preference for jazz, Amadio could make himself at home with almost any kind of music. In the 1960s, he was music director for a CBC-TV show called *Music Hop*, featuring pop music of the time. And in the Seventies he appeared frequently on a country show called *Nashville Swing*. Earlier in his career, he had played with Chicho Valle, who featured Latin music.

Making music has been Amadio's life, and whatever his personal musical preferences were, he never looked down his nose at any kind of music. Other musicians or singers always enjoyed working with him, because they were quickly aware that ego played no part in his work. From his earliest days in the business through the many years of playing for some of the most famous musical artists around, he remained a modest, soft-spoken, totally professional musician.

After more than half a century as a pianist, his only regret is that there are fewer and fewer venues for jazz. "It's sad to see this bunch of great musicians going to school and learning all this technique, then not being able to make a decent living. We were lucky in the old days."

Not one to rely on "personality" or showmanship, when Amadio sat down at the piano, he was all business and as solid as granite.

Tommy Ambrose

b. Toronto, Ontario, October 19, 1939

"When I was born and the doctor slapped me, I didn't cry – I sang," Tommy Ambrose wrote in the liner notes of his 1999 CD, **Songs Sinatra Taught Me**.

He actually began singing in public at the age of five – the youngest of the Ambrose Brothers – at a "Youth for Christ" rally in Toronto's Maple Leaf Gardens. He stayed with gospel singing until he was 16. Since the shift from gospel music to blues was not such a huge leap, he turned to rhythm and blues, jazz, and other forms of popular music, appearing in 1957 on CBC Television's *Cross-Canada Hit Parade*. Next came a summer series, *While We're Young*, in 1960 and 1961, after which he starred in *The Tommy Ambrose Show* for the same network.

After a couple of years of nightclub work, accompanied by pianist Norman Amadio, he was host for another CBC series, *Celebration*, first on radio and then on television, again featuring gospel music.

Blaik Kirby wrote of him in the *Globe and Mail*: "His lean-sounding voice is invariably in tune, his notes beautifully sustained and focused. There is a marvelous feeling of security as you listen."

During the 1970s, Ambrose performed in clubs and concerts, backed by a nonet led by pianist-organist Doug Riley. In this same period, he also became

connected with Trudel Productions, composing many commercial jingles, plus theme music for various TV programs. And, along with partners Larry Trudel and Doug Riley, he opened Jingles, a downtown Toronto bar which sometimes presented jazz musicians. A branch Jingles later opened farther up Toronto's Yonge Street.

His long association with Doug Riley was fruitful. Together, they turned out an LP (with Jackie Rae as producer) titled *Tommy Ambrose At Last*, which included some great standard songs such as "Night and Day," "Come Fly With Me," and "Get Out of Town." The Riley band had in its ranks such stalwarts as Guido Basso, Moe Koffman, and Rick Wilkins, all first-call studio musicians.

There was a period when Ambrose seemed to become remote and aloof. On one occasion, when he was supposed to perform at a large benefit, he sat outside the theatre in his limousine, refusing to enter until the moment when he was due to perform. Then, curiously, after his *Tommy Ambrose At Last* album, there was a long silence. Tommy Ambrose had not exactly retired, but he was certainly out of the public eye for close to two decades. His career seemed to have gone into neutral, as if he were waiting for the next wave to sweep him back into some kind of direction.

The silence was broken in 1999, with the CD titled *Songs Sinatra Taught Me*. He was guided on this effort by Frank Peppiatt, who had written and/or produced countless music-laden TV shows, including one (*Frank Sinatra: A Man and His Music*) which won Peppiatt an Emmy Award. The new CD was intended to be the framework of a concert show for Ambrose.

On the CD, Ambrose performs a dozen or so Sinatra classics – from "All or Nothing at All," which Sinatra recorded with Harry James in 1939, to a carefully chosen medley titled "A Very Good Year," featuring seven Sinatra hits of the past. On some of the songs, he was backed by a band led by super-arranger Rick Wilkins; on others, the band was led by veteran trumpeter Paul Grosney.

Ambrose at age 60 sounds a bit mellower, his voice a little deeper but still as sassy as two decades earlier. Only time will tell if the Ambrose appeal is strong enough to kick-start his career once again.

Paul Anka
b. Ottawa, Ontario, July 30, 1941

If there is any Canadian-born singer-songwriter who has been more successful financially than Paul Anka, his or her name does not easily spring to mind. The dynamic, endlessly energetic Anka, who traded his Canadian citizenship for an American one in 1990, has had an incredibly busy career, both as composer and lyricist and as performer of his own material.

If one had to choose a particular Anka song as being his most successful, it would surely have to be **My Way**, the lyrics of which he wrote to a French melody ("Comme d'habitude"). Anka wrote the song for Frank Sinatra, who transformed it into such a strong personal – and philosophical – statement on his own life that it soon became impossible to associate the song with any other performer – even though others (from Elvis Presley to the Sex Pistols) recorded it.

Anka's career started when he was young. He began performing in local amateur shows and on radio when he was 10. He formed a trio, the Bobby Soxers, in school. His formal music studies were brief: piano with Winnifred Rees and theory with Frederick Karam.

He appeared on CBC-TV's *Pick the Stars* and *Cross-Canada Hit Parade* and by 1957 had signed a recording and songwriting contract in New York. His first single **Diana**, which he wrote, became one of the top sellers in pop music history. That song, incidentally, landed Anka his first television gig: on the very first ABC telecast of Dick Clark's *American Bandstand*.

In a way, it was a good break, but it was mildly nightmarish, too. Paul was lip-synching to his recording of the song, but the needle got stuck, just as he was singing a long-drawn-out "o-o-o-o-oh." He mimed holding the note as long as he could, then burst into laughter.

But Anka was not a one-hit wonder. He followed **Diana** with such songs of his own as **Put Your Head on My Shoulder, You Are My Destiny,** and **Puppy Love**.

In December, 1957, he embarked on a 91-city tour of Britain, the United States, and Canada, attracting, understandably, huge and enthusiastic audiences of teenage girls.

Anka was as popular in Europe as in North America. A Parisian reviewer described him this way: "A finger of Johnnie Rae, a touch of Frankie Laine, the zest of Elvis Presley, several drops of The Platters – shake and serve. That's the Paul Anka cocktail."

But in the long run it was his ability as a composer and lyricist that made him the biggest money. For example, he wrote the theme music for *The Tonight Show* when Johnny Carson first took it over, in the fall of 1962. Over roughly the next quarter of a century, Anka's theme song was performed about 1,400,000 times – not only at the opening and closing of each show, but even into and out of commercials. Anka's royalties on that one tune alone, he told a *Toronto Star* interviewer, averaged out to "about" $100,000 a year. (When Carson retired and Jay Leno took over *The Tonight Show*, the program's new producers decided to drop the Anka-written theme.)

Another boost to the Anka aura came in 1960, when one of his current song hits – **Lonely Boy** – was used as the title of a National Film Board of Canada documentary about Anka. The film was widely acclaimed – and didn't do Anka's career any harm, either.

In 1962, Anka's drive for success went into overdrive. He wrote the title song for *The Longest Day*, Darryl Zanuck's hit movie about D-Day in the Second World War, and also managed to snag an acting role in the film. (Almost two decades later, Anka wrote the theme song for Louis Malle's movie *Atlantic City*.)

Over the years, Anka kept turning up in movies – usually in supporting roles. As early as 1959, for example, he was in a musical comedy called *Girls' Town*, as were such other performers as The Platters, Mel Tormé, and Ray Anthony. In 1992, he was in a Martin Short comedy, *Captain Ron*, and the following year he had a role in a sentimental movie titled *Ordinary Magic*, which was filmed mostly in Ontario.

Anka's songwriting continued. In 1971, for instance, singer Tom Jones had one of his biggest hit records with Anka's song **She's a Lady**.

During the 1970s, Anka was doing six to eight weeks a year at Caesar's Palace in Las Vegas. Among the original songs he recorded during the period were **Do I Love You, Let Me Get to Know You, You're Having My Baby,** and **Hold Me 'Til the Morning Comes**.

He also did a 12-week television series of musical variety shows for CBC-TV in 1972–73, shot in Vancouver. In the 1970s and 1980s, Anka made periodic appearances in Canada – at the O'Keefe Centre, the CNE Grandstand, Maple Leaf Gardens, and elsewhere.

For a time, Anka was part owner of the Ottawa Senators' NHL franchise, but he and the team's main owners had major differences, which were settled, more or less amicably, when the other owners bought him out.

Even though he lives in California, Anka still has warm feelings about his native city, and the feeling seems to be mutual. There's a street in Ottawa named Paul Anka Drive.

Louis Applebaum

b. Toronto, Ontario, April 3, 1918; d. 2000

By the time Louis Applebaum celebrated his 32nd birthday, he had already composed some 250 music scores for the National Film Board of Canada. In addition, he had written the music for two highly regarded Hollywood feature films – *Tomorrow the World* and *The Story of G.I. Joe*. The second of these earned Applebaum an Academy Award nomination for his music.

Then he was offered a third feature film – *The Stranger*, directed by and starring the formidable Orson Welles – but Louis turned down the opportunity. He gave three reasons for this decision: "I'm happy here [in Canada]. ... I think exciting things are ahead in the film, radio and television, and that Canada is in a position to play a leading part. ... I think money can be made in Canada as well as anywhere else, even in the arts."

But later, independent film producer Lester Cowan was able to convince Applebaum to score two feature films he had worked on. When he arrived in Hollywood, he was met at the train station in Los Angeles by an office boy in the Cowan organization. "So, you're from Canada," said the office boy. "That's a nice town, isn't it?" Although Applebaum never said so, that brief encounter may have had something to do with his decision to avoid Hollywood in future. In any case, he never worked there again.

On his first trip, Applebaum spent 10 weeks working in a small studio in the Hollywood Hills. Next door, in a studio whose windows faced his own, another young composer was at work. He was Leonard Bernstein, then writing *On the Town*, which was destined to become a Broadway hit. Applebaum later recalled that there was so much loud keyboard hammering on both sides that only by fierce determination were themes from *On the Town* kept out of *Tomorrow the World* and vice versa.

Applebaum left Hollywood and continued to work for the NFB, but not exclusively. He also composed incidental music for CBC Radio productions of *Hamlet, Peer Gynt, Antigone, Oedipus,* and *The Mad Woman of Chaillot.*

When the Stratford Festival opened, in 1953, Louis Applebaum became a kind of staff composer for this dynamic new theatrical venture. Indeed, visitors to the Festival were enticed by Applebaum's music even before they entered the tent (the Festival's first venue). It was Louis Applebaum who composed the various fanfares that were played outside the tent as curtain time approached. These "foyer fanfares" became a Stratford tradition, a way of getting the crowds to move into the theatre.

He also composed incidental music for the first two productions at Stratford that first season: *Richard III* and *All's Well That Ends Well.* Each year thereafter, he turned out at least one incidental score for Stratford – more than 50 by the early 1990s.

Two years after the Festival opened, Applebaum established its music wing, designing each new program – opera and jazz, folk music, etc. After seven years, Applebaum resigned from administrative duties at Stratford, but he continued for many years to provide incidental music for festival productions.

He was also music consultant for CBC Television (1960–63) and chairman of the music, opera, and ballet advisory committee for the National Arts Centre (1963–66). He later served as a juror for the Canada Council and as a consultant for the St. Lawrence Centre. During much of the 1970s and 1980s, he gave special courses on music for film, theatre, and television at York University.

Applebaum's compositions for concert and stage have been widely performed throughout the world and include large works for symphony orchestras, chamber music, vocal and choral pieces, and music for ballet and theatre.

In addition, he was commissioned to write original music for such occasions as the inaugurations of three Governors-General, the opening of Expo '67, visits by Queen Elizabeth II, the Massey Hall Centenary, and other special occasions.

During his busy career, he wrote many scores for plays produced by Esse Ljungh on CBC Radio, and for Tyrone Guthrie (*Tamburlane the Great*) and Michael Langham (*Andorra*) on Broadway, the Royal Shakespeare Company (*Much Ado About Nothing*), the Manitoba Theatre Centre (*Mother Courage*), and Theatre London (*Timon of Athens*).

He also wrote music for eight episodes of *The National Dream* and for numerous other CBC-TV projects. Two of his ballets were commissioned by the National Ballet of Canada and a third by the Janet Baldwin Ballet of Toronto. In 1988 he scored the mini-series *Glory Enough for All.*

In 1971, the Ontario Arts Council appointed Applebaum its executive director, which gave him a major role in the phenomenal acceleration of cultural development in Ontario. He held the post for a decade. Then he became chairman of the Federal Cultural Policy Review Committee, which later produced the famed *Applebaum-Hebert Report.*

In 1988–89, Applebaum was interim artistic director of the Guelph Spring Festival. He had previously worked in administrative capacities for PRO and SOCAN, organizations established to protect the interests of both composers and performers. He has also been the recipient of numerous honours and awards.

Applebaum once told an interviewer: "Essentially, I'm working to improve the lot of my colleagues and I have been doing that for many years ... at the same time staying on as a functioning artist."

After a long bout with cancer, Louis Applebaum died in April 2000 at the age of 82. A few months later saw the release of a CD titled *Fanfare* spotlighting a wide selection of Louis Applebaum's music for various Stratford Festival productions, from the first year (1953) onwards. Among the artists taking part in this CD (on the Marquis label) are the Elmer Iseler Singers, Richard Margison, Barbara Fulton, Steve Ross, Richard Monette, and Christopher Plummer. The music was arranged and conducted by Glenn Morley.

Peter Appleyard

b. Lincolnshire, England, August 26, 1928

Peter Appleyard started his career as a drummer with British dance bands and with Royal Air Force bands. In 1949, he moved to Bermuda and two years later settled in Toronto, where he began playing vibraphone, first with Billy O'Connor and then with Calvin Jackson. While with Jackson, he engaged in some crowd-pleasing duels, both on vibes, Peter's primary instrument, and on piano. Both men were masters of two-finger piano pyrotechnics and their lively workouts were invariably among the highlights of any evening at the Park Plaza Hotel in Toronto.

Peter formed his own group in 1957 and played at a new Toronto club (opened by Jackie Rae and called The Stage Door) playing for Steve Lawrence and Eydie Gorme. He was also co-host with singer Patti Lewis for CBC Radio's *Patti and Peter* in the early 1960s and with Guido Basso on CBC Television's *Mallets and Brass* in 1969. Later he fronted a syndicated TV series called *Peter Appleyard Presents*.

In the early 1970s he came to international prominence as a member of the Benny Goodman Sextet, with which he performed around the world. It's an indication of Appleyard's stature as a vibraphonist that he was preceded in the Goodman small groups by Lionel Hampton and Red Norvo. (Hampton himself said of Appleyard: "A great, great artist. My favourite vibraharpist.")

Jack Batten wrote in the *Globe and Mail*: "He's most reminiscent of Red Norvo in style, given the impeccable taste and easy rhythmic lift he displays as he glides over his vibes. He maintains wonderful control and fits every little passing nuance into perfect place."

He continued to work intermittently throughout that decade, playing three concerts in Carnegie Hall. In 1985, Appleyard formed the band Benny Goodman Tribute with clarinetists Abe Most and then Peanuts Hucko in Goodman's place. The ensemble, augmented by various veteran Goodman sidemen, appeared at several Canadian jazz festivals and then toured Britain.

On one occasion, CBC-TV planned a special program that was to feature a small group in tribute to Goodman. Pianist Teddy Wilson was involved and he wanted assurances as to who would be playing vibes on that show. He made it clear he didn't want Terry Gibbs to fill that role, but he enthusiastically endorsed Peter Appleyard.

Appleyard has also appeared at such noted events as the Dick Gibson Jazz Party in Denver in 1990 and 1991, and with singer Mel Tormé for a month at Michael's Pub in New York. In 1993, he toured Japan with Tormé. In one Tokyo concert, they recorded "Sing, Sing, Sing," again reflecting Appleyard's lifelong devotion to Benny Goodman's music. Tormé referred to Peter as a "world-class artist."

Peter Appleyard has also appeared with such noted musical artists as Ella Fitzgerald, Tony Bennett, Joe Williams, Buddy DeFranco, Buddy Rich, Maxine Sullivan, Ernestine Anderson, Tommy Dorsey, Duke Ellington, Count Basie, and Frank Sinatra – at Sinatra's request.

His performances at the Sarasota Jazz Festival in Florida earned him the title of "most popular musician" in the festival. He has also performed in Switzerland, Germany, and the Cork Festival in Ireland. He was both conductor and featured soloist with the Moncton Symphony and the New York Pops, plus the Ottawa Jazz Festival. With pianist Dick Hyman, he toured Japan in 1996 and played three concerts with Hyman in Florida.

On one of his trips to England, he got to know Robert Farnon and worked with him. Later, Appleyard arranged a musical tribute to Farnon during one of the famed composer-arranger's visits to Canada. This was a concert in Brantford, Ontario, where Farnon sat in the audience while a large orchestra (led by Skitch Henderson) and Peter's own small group played Farnon's music.

At the end of the concert, Appleyard persuaded Farnon to come up and take a bow. While Farnon stood by, Appleyard paid generous – and long – tribute to him. Farnon kept edging toward the wings as Peter talked. When Farnon had almost reached the wings, Peter looked about and saw him about to sneak off the stage. "I haven't finished yet," said Appleyard.

Replied Farnon: "Sorry, but I have to go to the bathroom."

In 1999, Appleyard virtually stopped the show at the Markham Jazz Festival, leading an exuberantly swinging big band in some superb Rick Wilkins arrangements. Peter, a dazzling soloist as well as a skillful leader, appropriately titled his Markham presentation *Swing Fever*. The band got a well-deserved standing ovation.

Appleyard, never at a loss for words, treated the audience to a lengthy dissertation on how he began his musical career back in England. One of his quirks has always been that he is a fussy eater. At one restaurant he frequented, the headwaiter became accustomed to Appleyard's endless complaints about this dish or that.

When he finished one dinner, the headwaiter approached Peter's table and asked: "Was *anything* satisfactory tonight?"

April Wine

formed 1969 in Halifax: Myles Goodwyn (b. Woodstock, N.B., June 23, 1948) lead vocals, guitar; David Henman (replaced in 1974 by Gary Moffet) guitar; Jim Henman (replaced in 1972 by Jim Clench, replaced in 1975 by Steve Lang) bass; Ritchie Henman (replaced in 1974 by Jerry Mercer) drums; Brian Greenway guitar

The road to success in Canadian popular music is often a marathon with enough detours and bumps to deter the most persistent musicians. Perhaps no other rock 'n' roll band of the 1970s endured more of those deterrents than the members of April Wine. Success eventually came, but not easily.

Originally a family act, bringing together brothers Ritchie and David Henman, cousin Jim Henman (all from the Halifax area), and Myles Goodwyn (from Woodstock, N.B.), the foursome had a very basic rock configuration in late 1969 – guitars, bass, drums, and vocals. The name was David Henman's suggestion, and because he was the one buying refreshment at a tavern in Halifax that day, "April Wine" stuck.

Quickly, the band recognized that Halifax did not provide immediate opportunities to play and record, so they sent a demo tape to the Montreal company that owned Aquarius Records, operated the club The Laugh-In, and promoted concerts through Donald K. Donald Productions in Montreal. Company managers Terry Flood and Donald Tarlton sent back a rejection note, but the band members mistook it for an invitation. On April 1, 1970 – April Fool's Day – April Wine went down the road to Quebec. They took with them their instruments, their few possessions, and $100 in cash.

Despite the misunderstanding, Flood and Tarlton helped the Maritimers get established. They put the band up in a Laurentians chalet, and they finally allowed them to play at The Laugh-In. By the summer of 1970, Aquarius signed April Wine and released a self-titled debut album the following year. It yielded a single that sold well in the Maritimes, but the album didn't sell. The band pressed on with a New York producer and a cover single from a British band, "You Could Have Been a Lady," became the band's first number-one hit in Canada. The single came from their second album *On Record*, which also featured "Bad Side of the Moon" (by Elton John and Bernie Taupin).

During the early and mid-1970s (after a number of personnel changes) April Wine became a touring band. They were the opening act for another Montreal pop group, Mashmakhan. They opened for T. Rex at the CNE. The recording of their album *Electric Jewels* kicked off their "Electric Adventure" tour, which saw the band play nearly every Canadian arena or concert hall that seated 2500 people or more in 1974.

April Wine (l. to r.): Steve Lang, Jerry Mercer, Myles Goodwyn, Brian Greenway, Gary Moffet

NAC/PA 207952

Touring not only cultivated a fan base; it put April Wine in touch with international artists. Two members of the American band The Young Rascals attended April Wine's 1974 Massey Hall concert in Toronto and offered to record a live album with the Canadians.

The one-night live recording session in Halifax proved a rushed enterprise. "It was at the beginning of a tour," Myles Goodwyn told Martin Melhuish in *Heart of Gold*. "We figured if we hurried everything along, the album would be out by the end of the tour. It was a good idea [but] the band was sick. The production and sound are not up to par. It sounds like a basement tape."

Still, *April Wine Live* went gold. Their 1975 album, *Stand Back*, sold 250,000 copies and their 1976 album, *The Whole World's Goin' Crazy*, shipped platinum (over 1,000,000 copies). That was a first by a Canadian group, and their subsequent 80-stop tour was the first to gross $1 million.

Another chance encounter produced one more unique session for April Wine in the late 1970s. The Rolling Stones' 1973 international tour included a concert at the Montreal Forum, promoted by Wine manager Donald Tarlton. When a bomb damaged a Stones equipment truck, April Wine lent the visitors their sound system. Tarlton even purchased cargo space on a flight from Los Angeles for additional gear. A few years later, when the Stones worked out details for a club concert in Toronto, April Wine got the nod as their opening act.

The resulting album, *April Wine Live at the El Mocambo*, in 1977, was not the band's greatest creative achievement, but that date and another with the Stones in Buffalo later that year gave April Wine additional cachet. Their 1978 album, *First Glance*, garnered notice in the United States and the band launched a U.S. tour that lasted a year. Their 1981 album, *Nature of the Beast*, produced the ballad **Just Between You and Me**, and oddly it became the biggest single ever for the group in the United States. Concert tours in Europe produced mixed results – unfavourable press in England but sold-out concerts in Germany, Holland, and the Benelux countries. April Wine completed a farewell tour in conjunction with a 13th album, *Animal Grace*, in the summer of 1984.

In 1992, April Wine enjoyed an onstage reunion as part of (no surprise) another cross-country tour.

"We were stars in Canada, where we would tour under good conditions," Goodwyn told Melhuish, "but in the U.S. we were bottom of the ladder, considered debutantes."

Debutantes to some, but like vintage wine, seasoned and well-travelled.

Jann Arden
b. Calgary, March 27, 1962

During the early moments of her one-night appearance at Toronto's Massey Hall, in 2001, Jann Arden opened with a couple of her quicker-paced songs, perhaps to fend off the butterflies. She accepted the welcoming applause of

her audience. Then she paused and announced, "Okay, all the up-tempo stuff is over now. It's all about my losses, my sorrows, my problems. Me." As flippant as it sounded, the comment was an honest assessment of her musical journey.

"I can try all I want to be trivial," she told the *Toronto Star*'s Greg Quill, "but I just can't do it. ... I'd rather write about things I'm thinking or seeing or doing."

Sometimes called "sad-eyed," "queen of mopey rock," or "the quirky diva of down," she experienced a troubled childhood in Calgary as Jan Richards. The family battled through substance abuse and run-ins with the law (her brother, Duray Richards, was convicted of murder in 1994). "Drugs and alcohol ruined his life," she told Jan Wong in the *Globe and Mail*. "It ruined all our lives, my parents' lives. We're all in recovery."

As a teenager, Jann sang in public for the first time at her high school graduation. She performed with local bands in Calgary, then in bars in British Columbia and battled a drinking problem herself. In 1983, while busking in Vancouver, Arden was beaten up. She stopped singing and worked in a fishery. Back in Calgary, two years later, her father got her a job managing a video store. In 1987, she returned to performing at night in lounges, nearby ski resorts, and bars; despite the work, she said she still had a drinking problem.

Nevertheless, A&M Records signed Arden to a recording contract in 1991, the same year her brother was arrested for murder. When her first album, **Time For Mercy**, was released in 1993, she took a year touring Canada, the United States, and Europe. (She used her middle name, Arden, to keep her albums at the front of record store racks.) Critics raved about the lyrical quality of her songs and the apparently effortless power of her voice. At the Juno Awards, the next spring, she won Best New Solo Artist and Best Video for her song **I Would Die For You**. Her first hit single was **Will You Remember Me?**

Arden's 1994 album, *Living Under June*, sold two million copies and earned her three more Junos – Female Vocalist of the Year, Songwriter of the Year, and Single of the Year for **Could I Be Your Girl?** The single, written just before she entered the studio, dealt with a recurring theme in her material – the uncertainties of romantic love. In a similar vein, the album contained **Unloved**, a song she wrote in the middle of the night and first recorded on her answering machine, "because my tape deck was busted and I had to get it down or I knew I would forget it."

The album also contained "Insensitive," a song written by Anne Loree and about which Arden said, "depending on how you look at [it], you'll either kill yourself laughing or feel terrible." The recording was a worldwide adult contemporary hit. Its video (directed by Jeth Weinrich) won awards. Just as importantly, the song revealed Arden's wicked sense of humour, something she began displaying at other public appearances.

"I did a speaking engagement for the Power of Women," she said. "They wanted me to talk about success and instead I talked to them about the benefits of failure. They loved it."

Arden hosted the 1997 Juno Awards, during which she said, "I almost missed [Céline Dion] … because she was standing sideways." Arden then stood at the mike stand and continued, "Can everybody see me okay behind this?"

That year, she released her album *Happy?* and in 2000 *Blood Red Cherry*, which contained all of her calling cards – innocence and passion, virtue and romance, more humour, and lust. The album earned her another Juno – Best Female Artist. She continued to tour in 2001 and while in Toronto appeared in Eve Ensler's award-winning play *The Vagina Monologues*.

The short distance between Jann Arden's personal life and her public one narrowed even more in 2000, when she opened a diary feature on her Web site. As her cyber-journal feature began, fans (the site registers 100,000 hits per week) learned about the death of her grandmother, the view from her window, and even her choice of underwear packed for her cross-country tour. In cyberspace, in life, or in music there's very little Jann Arden won't talk or sing about.

On the Massey Hall stage in 2001, Arden sang **Hangin' by a Thread**, a tribute to her imprisoned brother and a statement of her own struggle to cope with his actions. The song ended, the audience quiet; Arden cried, "I've lost so many things I so dearly love."

Carroll Baker

b. Port Medway, N.S., March 4, 1949

Back in the 1950s, nobody would have predicted that Carroll Ann Baker would win virtually every Canadian country music award in existence, least of all Baker herself. She grew up with music all around her, but she objected when her musical family launched into their repertoire of country songs. She preferred rock 'n' roll. She even objected to her father, an accomplished fiddler, suggesting that "one day, you'll love country music." She doubted it.

Growing up in a tiny east coast community, Baker was drawn immediately to singing and making music with her friends. For one thing, she recalled, "there was nothing else to do, except get into trouble, and we did our share of that too."

She made her first public appearance at age four, at a church concert, during which she squeezed the cat in her arms to yowl on cue. By the time she was in her early teens she was singing regularly, especially on Sundays.

"I worked every church in town," she claims, "the Anglican church in the morning, the Baptist church in the afternoon, and the Pentecostal at night."

Not everyone recognized her talent right away. When she went to high school in nearby Bridgewater, Nova Scotia, she was considered one of the "hicks from the sticks," and even the local glee club wouldn't let her sing. She says they did throw her a bone, since "they said I could play guitar for them though, as long as I stayed off stage."

When she turned 16, Carroll's family moved to Toronto. When she heard country music, it made her homesick for Nova Scotia. She made her stage debut in 1968, when her husband persuaded her to get on stage with a local band at a bar. Although the band members were initially impressed enough to ask her to join them, they soon became frustrated with her lack of progress, so they let her go.

Then, she was asked to perform on a radio station. An Oshawa sculptor named George Petralia heard her and thought she'd do a good job performing a song he'd written. He encouraged her to travel to Thunder Bay to record "Mem'ries of Home" for Gaiety Records. The owner, Don Grashey, was also a manager and offered to handle her career. Together they composed songs and recorded two albums with moderate success.

It was 1975, however, when she hit her stride with a recording of Conway Twitty's "I've Never Been This Far Before." That release and a sensational appearance on the telecast of the 1976 Juno Awards seemed to ensure her a path to success and stardom. The performance, in part, led to her subsequent signing with RCA Records. Thereafter, it seemed, hit followed award followed hit – **Tonight with Love, Little Boy Blue, Ten Little Fingers**, and **I'm Getting High Remembering**.

From 1975 through 1992, not a year went by when she didn't win something. She was nominated for the Juno Award for Country Female Vocalist every year between 1977 and 1986 and won 1977, '78 and '79. She had 14 consecutive singles that reached number one on the *RPM* magazine country music popularity charts. She received 10 Big Country Music Awards. Baker became a frequent guest, too, on nearly every television variety show on air during that same period. She hosted three *Superspecial*s of her own on CBC-TV.

It was clear from her momentum in the business that Baker had struck a chord with country music fans. Ken Waxman wrote about her in *Saturday Night* magazine: "She's brought a new sense of feminine sensuality to country music … the honest toughness of the songs she writes pinpoints the sometimes aggressive sexuality and determination of many women."

Whatever it was, Carroll Baker had it and her Canadian fans wanted more. In 1983, she decided to see if Americans wanted it too. She became Canada's representative at the International Country and Western Music Association showcase in Fort Worth, Texas, and began recording for Tembo. But the transition was never completely successful.

A great believer in charitable causes, Baker donated her time to numerous fundraisers, not the least of which was a "Baker's dozen" years as performer and host for the Easter Seals Telethon.

In the early 1990s, Baker returned to her musical roots and began recording gospel music. She hasn't recorded since 1992, but her impact on Canadian country music is still acknowledged. In 1991, she was presented with a Canadian Country Music Lifetime Achievement Award and in 1992 became the youngest performer to be inducted into the Canadian Country Music Hall of Honour.

At yet another award ceremony, held by the Ontario Country Performer and Fan Association in November 2000, Carroll Baker received the Career Achievement Award from her longtime friend and colleague Gordon Burnett, one of the founders of the Canadian Country Music Association. On accepting the award, which was presented in part for her contribution to the structure and success of the country music industry in Canada, Baker gave some advice to would-be country entertainers:

"Don't do it for the money or the awards, but because you love it. Then you'll do it with the passion and conviction you need to succeed."

Long John Baldry

b. Derbyshire, England, January 12, 1941

Long John Baldry physically towered above most friends and guests during a celebration of his 60th birthday at Vancouver's Commodore Ballroom early in 2001. At six-foot-seven, he literally stood head and shoulders above everybody present. So might it be said of his musical legacy, dubbed by one critic "the tallest footnote in the history of rock 'n' roll." Generally credited with discovering and/or boosting such rock stars as Rod Stewart, Elton John, Mick Jagger, Julie Driscoll, Ginger Baker, Brian Auger, Jimmy Page, and several of the Beatles, Baldry has always had a knack for recognizing talent and exhibiting his own.

An English choirboy from the age of eight, Baldry's voice broke early, about the time he discovered the 78-rpm rhythm-and-blues recordings of Big Bill Broonzy and Muddy Waters. He convinced his father to buy him a Grimshaw acoustic guitar and began playing in a school jazz and blues appreciation society.

In the mid-1950s, Big Tom Baldry (as he was originally known) began busking on the streets of London and playing in Bohemian coffeehouses. He regularly appeared with other folk singers and accompanied visiting American

blues singers. When the British rock and blues music explosion began in 1958, Baldry teamed up with Alexis Koerner and Syril Davis for weekly blues sessions at the Roundhouse, a pub in Soho. Eric Clapton admits being urged to take up guitar playing after seeing Baldry play – he is a virtuoso on 12-string guitar – and the Yardbirds were inspired by Baldry's singing style. Baldry was introduced to jazz by working with the Ken Sims Band, which performed in Liverpool at the Cavern Club, where the support act was a then-unknown band called the Beatles.

"In the early 1960s, in England," Baldry said in a *National Post* interview, "the blues spoke to a very narrow clique. We were all young – 17 to 22 – and a lot of people came out of art schools. I think we felt we were championing a cause."

In 1961, Baldry accepted an invitation to join Koerner's acclaimed Blues Incorporated, a band he feels was "the first white electric blues group ever in the world." They debuted in front of a score of people, but were soon packing in a thousand a week at the Ealing R&B Club. The band was occasionally joined by singer Mick Jagger, guitarist Brian Jones, and drummer Charlie Watts (all later of the Rolling Stones).

Within a year, Baldry had joined Syril Davis in another venture called the All Stars, which featured a 16-year-old guitarist named Jimmy Page (later of Led Zeppelin). When Davis died in 1964, Baldry led the band as the Hoochie Coochie Men, a name inspired by the Muddy Waters tune. The group was a microcosm of British society – ranging in age from 19 to 48 and from middle-class artists to working-class drifters.

"I happened to be on the platform of London's Twickenham railway station, around midnight on a night in January of 1964," remembers Baldry. "This guy was playing a very bluesy harmonica in an effort to keep himself company and fight off the chilling damp night air." Two days later, the soon-to-be rock star Rod Stewart joined the Hoochie Coochie Men at the Eel Pie Island Club.

Baldry's influence grew. In 1964, while costarring in a film production called *Around the Beatles*, Baldry turned John Lennon on to blues harmonica, which was featured on the Beatles' first hit, "Love Me Do." By 1965, Baldry had formed Steam Packet, a Motown-style revue, which debuted at the National Jazz and Blues Festival in Surrey; that appearance sparked the careers of band members (singer) Julie Driscoll and (pianist) Brian Auger. In 1966, at the London club Cromwellian, he tripped over another fledgling musician – Reginald Kenneth Dwight – who eventually struck out on his own (borrowing half his stage name from band sax player Elton Dean, the other half from Baldry) as Elton John.

The fact is, however, Long John Baldry was a star in England and later in North America before any of his protégés. By 1967, his single, **Let The**

Heartaches Begin, was a massive hit, one of the fastest-selling U.K. singles in the 1960s, racking up sales of more than a million in its first three weeks, staying in the Top 30 for nine weeks. His 1968 recording of the single "Mexico" was used as the theme for British television's coverage of the Olympic Games that year; it too was a chart-topper and generated overwhelming attention for Baldry's work.

With the 1971 release of his LP *It Ain't Easy* (coproduced by Rod Stewart and Elton John), Baldry travelled to North America. He released the album's single, **Don't Try to Lay No Boogie Woogie on the King of Rock and Roll**, which received extensive FM airplay and boosted the album to a million-seller worldwide, including gold status in Canada. Success in North America prompted the release of no fewer than eight Baldry compilation albums and more tours. His 1979 album, *Baldry's Out*, was partly recorded in Toronto. Its first single, **You've Lost That Lovin' Feelin'**, became an instant hit in the United States, Australia, and Canada. By 1980, Long John Baldry had shifted his base permanently because "I'd fallen in love with Canada," first living in Ontario until 1985 when he moved to Vancouver.

In addition to album production in Canada (four CDs with Stony Plain Records) Long John Baldry has taken full advantage of his baritone voice and plummy British accent to make a good living in voiceover work in commercials and children's cartoons (as the voice of Captain Robotnik in *Sonic the Hedgehog* and *The True Story of Winnie the Pooh*, which was nominated for a 1998 Grammy).

Another enduring contribution was his work on the production of the four-hour radio documentary *The History of British Rock*. In its creation, Baldry exhibited his encyclopedic knowledge of British rock 'n' roll and his interviewing skills in conversations with, among others, Paul McCartney, Keith Moon, Jeff Beck, Ginger Baker, Peter Frampton, and Marc Bolan. This audio archive remains a definitive testament to the music scene Baldry helped create and nurture.

Band, The

see The Band

Tommy Banks

b. Calgary, Alberta, December 17, 1936

During one of his infrequent nightspot engagements in Toronto, Tommy Banks was buttonholed by an enthusiastic fan who wanted to know "how" he achieved this or that jazz effect.

"Well," said Banks, "I'm not really a jazz musician."

What he really meant – but was, as ever, too modest to state – is that he isn't *just* a jazz musician.

The fact is Thomas Benjamin Banks has written, arranged, and conducted everything from pit bands for musicals to symphony orchestras – as well as leading a Juno Award–winning big band (1978 Montreux Jazz Festival) and playing for an impressive array of popular entertainers, including Vicki Carr, Charles Aznavour, Aretha Franklin, Jack Jones, Engelbert Humperdinck, Tom Jones, Rosemary Clooney, Carmen McRae, Robert Goulet, Patti Page, Tony Bennett, Ben Vereen, Maureen McGovern, Helen Forrest, and Ed Ames.

In his 40-odd years as a professional musician, he has played piano and written for and/or conducted orchestras for most of the popular musical artists of the past half-century.

What singers like most about Banks is his determination to go to any length to present every singer to his or her best advantage. Often, when a singer turned up as a guest on one of his countless radio or television shows with dog-eared or dated arrangements, Banks would somehow find time to write a whole new chart for the artist – and then give the arrangement to the artist, free of charge, to use in the future.

Another remarkable thing about Banks has always been his ability to get the maximum effort from all the musicians in his command – without ever igniting their enmity. He stands before his sidemen ramrod-like, all business, no nonsense, and somehow inspires their respect and faith in his considerable abilities as a leader.

If a singer/actor is unsteady, Banks will manage to reassure the artist. If the singer changes tempo or misses a cue, Banks will crack his whip and the band will instantly follow his lead. "Anything to avoid embarrassing a performer" seems always to be Tommy's guiding principle.

Ever the pro, Banks has voiced a pet peeve with television directors who devote their energies largely to the video aspect of a program at the expense of the audio. "If a television director misses a shot or catches another camera in his shot, he'll immediately stop tape and insist the number has to be done over. But if the poor first trumpet blows a 'crow,' it's too bad. They just keep right on going. 'Sorry, we haven't got time to do it over.'"

In the earlier days of television, this practice was so widespread that musicians eventually adopted their own method of combatting it. "We used to literally say 'shit,' very loud, on the microphone, to make them stop tape," Banks said.

The range of his musical experience is striking. Although he doesn't regard himself as a "classical" musician, he has been guest conductor of symphony orchestras in Edmonton, Regina, Saskatoon, Calgary, and Vancouver, as well as the National Arts Centre Orchestra in Ottawa.

In Hamilton, he conducted, arranged for, and played with that city's philharmonic orchestra for no less than 125 hour-long television variety shows in one four-month period in 1976–77. Each of these shows had six or seven guest performers, for whom Banks had to conduct – and sometimes rewrite arrangements to fit his endlessly versatile 12-piece band.

Banks has served as music director for various events, from Commonwealth Games to Winter Olympics. He has written and arranged music for such diverse musical enterprises as the musical fantasy *The Gift of the Magi* and a CBC production of Pierre Berton's *Klondike*. He has also worked with such jazz artists as P. J. Perry, Oliver Gannon, and Anita O'Day. Banks was music director for another series of television specials done in Montreal with Michel Legrand and the Montreal Symphony. In 1983, he led a quartet on a tour of Japan, Hong Kong, and Malaysia, and led the first foreign jazz group to do a tour of the People's Republic of China.

Banks was chairman of the Alberta Foundation of the Performing Arts (1978–86) and of the music program at Grant MacEwan College in Edmonton (1983–87). In 1989 he was appointed a member of the Canada Council.

Despite lucrative offers to move to Toronto and elsewhere, he has remained steadfastly loyal to Alberta – and especially to Edmonton.

"If you want to make something happen," Banks said, "you can. If I want to make a good living in Edmonton doing what I want to, I can work like hell to make it happen. Other people can do that, of course. Who ever heard of a great recording studio in Muscle Shoals, Alabama? But there is one, because somebody wanted to make it happen there. I want to make things happen in Edmonton so that I can stay here. It's as simple as that."

In the spring of 2000, he added yet another honour to his collection when he was made a senator. And by all accounts, he is taking that responsibility as seriously as he has every musical gig in his lengthy, busy, fruitful career.

*The Barenaked Ladies (l. to r.):
Kevin Hearn, Jim Creggan, Ed
Robertson, Tyler Stewart, Steven
Page*

Barenaked Ladies

*formed 1988 in Toronto: Steven Page (b. June 22, 1970) vocals, guitar; Ed Robertson
(b. October 25, 1970) guitar; Jim Creegan (b. February 12, 1970) acoustic bass; Andrew
Creeggan (b. July 4, 1971) keyboards, accordion (replaced by Kevin Hearn (b. July 3, 1969),
temporarily replaced by Chris Brown); Tyler Stewart (b. September 21, 1967) drums*

In the fall of 2000, when they released their sixth album, *Maroon*, few should
have been surprised that the maverick members of the group Barenaked
Ladies did it with an outrageous twist. Of course, it was issued on CD and
video, but in order to beat cyberspace bootleggers and pirates to the punch,
the band leaked their first single from the CD, **Pinch Me**, on the popular, but
now illegal, MP3 swapping Web site Napster. However, along with the free
music, computer downloaders also got the band members' criticisms of Napster users splicing into the song.

The stunt was pure Barenaked Ladies – a flouting of convention, wonderful
tongue-in-cheek satire, and, as always, doing things the different (and often
tougher) way. Indeed, that's the way it's been for the Ladies from the beginning. Originally a busking duo, Steven Page and Ed Robertson sang at summer camp and then as a warmup act for a travelling comedy troupe. It was

31

"during a giggling fit at a Bob Dylan concert" that the two arrived at the name. Apparently, when they approached two high school classmates, pianist Andrew and bassist Jim Creeggan – and later (at a buskers' festival in Waterloo, Ontario) drummer Tyler Stewart – they all got the joke and formed "Barenaked Ladies" as a five-man band.

In 1991, BNL amassed enough cash to fund a recording session which produced a five-song cassette, widely known as *The Yellow Tape*. Among the five songs were **Be My Yoko Ono** and **If I Had A Million Dollars**, which got enough airplay on alternative radio stations to boost sales and turn the cassette into the only independent release to ever reach platinum status in Canada. They drew audiences principally from among their peers in high school and college. They dressed in nerdy dime-store shirts, baggy shorts, white socks, and runners. They joked and sang about how much they loved Kraft Dinner, Mr. Dressup, counter girls at McDonald's, bungee jumping, and ice cream sandwiches.

"The group has an utterly charming folk sound," wrote *Toronto Star* pop critic Peter Howell, "with jazz flourishes, that harks back at least as far as The Weavers and Peter Seeger, although nowhere near as political." Their apolitical history changed, however, at the end of 1991.

Even though the Ladies had performed to large crowds at such Toronto venues as Ontario Place and Harbourfront, that year they were removed from the bill at a New Year's Eve concert scheduled for Nathan Phillips Square in front of city hall, because the band's name "objectifies women," said the city's event coordinator. "If your mother or my mother saw a headline saying, 'City of Toronto presents Barenaked Ladies,' they'd be really concerned."

The incident proved to be the band's biggest break. In 1992, while Toronto City Hall reviewed, dithered, and backpedalled on the ban, the Ladies signed their first recording contact with Sire/Reprise and released their first album, *Gordon*. Coined "Nakedmania" by the media, the Ladies' cult following translated into historic sales for the album – 900,000 copies in Canada and 400,000 in the United States.

The "five fat guys from Scarborough," as they called themselves, found the world beating a path to their door. *Gordon* (the album name derived from the name of the baby in the cut **Steven Page Is Having a Baby**) was soon released in the United States (selling 400,000 copies) and Europe. Within a year, the Ladies were being courted by Toronto-area promoters to perform – at the 14,000-capacity Kingswood Concert Theatre and at 3000-seat Massey Hall on April Fool's Day. Even Mariposa Folk Festival artistic director Richard Flohil had to eat his words; originally he had said, "I couldn't think of anything more ghastly" than booking a band by that name, but he gave BNL top billing the following year.

Fighting the novelty act tag, the Barenaked Ladies won the Juno for Best

Group of the Year in 1993. They planned a 65-stop tour, for which they all shed some excess weight. They also returned to the studio, suggesting "the next album will be almost certainly in a much more serious vein." The release, **Maybe You Should Drive**, fell short of expectations, but still went double-platinum with 200,000 sales in Canada. The band also faced new criticism for a line in the song **If I Had a Million Dollars** that went "I'd buy you a fur coat, but not a real fur coat – that's cruel," offending Dene and Métis trappers in Yellowknife. A meeting between the Ladies and trappers changed minds on both sides.

The middle 1990s were a struggle. Press and radio people who once fought for interviews now judged the Ladies uncool. The band members grew up and grew restless. They dismissed their manager, Nigel Best. There were marriages and children. Seemingly tired of it all, pianist Andy Creeggan departed. To make matters worse, the Toronto City Hall factor returned, when a Chicago writer criticized the city's "bad taste" for buying up tickets to a Barenaked Ladies concert.

Despite that bad press, by 1996 the band's fortunes were changing in the United States. It started when the Ladies engaged Terry McBride, Sarah McLachlan's manager. McBride sensed the potential of a strong live act with songwriting capabilities and he sent the band on the road for two years of solid touring, returning to some U.S. cities up to six times. This regimen was combined with the release of **Rock Spectacle**, a live album of greatest hits, and suddenly the Barenaked Ladies got airplay and big U.S. sales (800,000 CDs).

Their growing U.S. profile attracted actor Jason Priestley (*Beverly Hills 90210*) who directed the video of the Ladies' single **The Old Apartment** (from their other 1996 album release, **Born on a Pirate Ship**). In 1998, *Rolling Stone* magazine declared the Barenaked Ladies "the biggest new rock band in America" and when they released their CD **Stunt** the same year, it sold two million in the United States. As well, their single **One Week** topped the U.S. *Billboard* Top 100 singles chart that year, making BNL the first Canadian group to do so in a decade.

Making it big in the United States brought numerous spinoff benefits. There were appearances on Conan O'Brien's New Year's Eve show, CNN, *Late Night with David Letterman*, and even a guest spot on *Beverly Hills 90210*. In July 1998, a Ladies performance in front of Boston City Hall drew 80,000 spectators, closed four city blocks, and prompted the transit authority to provide free transportation for the day.

Still, for the two original Barenaked Ladies, there was a simpler benefit: a shopping spree at their record company's largest warehouse in Chicago. "They gave us shopping carts," Ed Robertson told the *Globe and Mail* in 1998, "and they let us take whatever we wanted."

"It was like those contests where you have 60 seconds to grab as much as

you could and throw it into a shopping cart," added Steven Page. "I kept waiting for my 60 seconds to be up."

In a short musical career of roadblocks and unexpected challenges, a shopping spree in a CD warehouse seems a fitting perk for the band that in 1991 was banned from performing on a hometown stage.

Guido Basso *b. Montreal, Quebec, September 27, 1937*

For a man in his mid-sixties, Guido Basso has quite a full, varied, rewarding career to look back on, one featuring warm associations, rich experiences, and generally happy memories.

He can recall, for instance, that his first jazz influence was Harry James, followed by Randy Brooks and the likes of Dizzy Gillespie, Chet Baker, Roy Eldridge, and Miles Davis. It was Miles who introduced Guido to the flugelhorn.

Born in Montreal, one of seven children of Italian immigrant (Protestant) parents, he recalls: "I spoke Italian at home, French at school, and English on the street."

"I wanted to play accordion," he admits, "but my older brother insisted on a trumpet." That brother was also Guido's first teacher, but the budding musician moved on to another teacher and later to the Conservatoire de Québec. He formed his first band at age 11. "We got experience and learned how to read."

He was with Maury Kaye's little band at El Morocco in Montreal when they played for such touring guests as Edith Piaf, Tony Bennett, the Will Mastin Trio (featuring Sammy Davis, Jr.), and Vic Damone.

Louis Bellson heard Guido play and promptly offered him a trumpet chair in his big band. Basso spent two-and-a-half years with Louis and his wife, Pearl Bailey.

In 1959, he met Darlene Anderson, that year's Miss Toronto, and they promptly fell in love. Once he began to tour with Bailey and Bellson, he used to fly back to Toronto periodically to visit Darlene. "Pearl took over the whole wedding," he recalled. "She was like Mom. She called me her alien son. She threw the whole wedding [in Las Vegas]. She was the matron of honour and Louis was the best man. Pearl hired my wife as a showgirl so we could be together wherever we went." (Unhappily, that marriage did not last.)

Once he tired of touring, Basso settled in Toronto where he felt the musical standards were higher. Besides television work, he played in small Toronto clubs. He was in Rob McConnell's first quintet at the First Floor Club and the House of Hambourg.

When McConnell formed the Boss Brass, Guido was a charter member. It was originally strictly brass and rhythm – no saxes. McConnell's arranging abilities rose above the pop tunes of the day. Says Basso: "We took 'Mrs. Robinson' to places she'd never been."

Soon the big band was attracting big crowds to the Savarin Club in Toronto. "Then the saxes were forced on Rob," Guido remembers. "We were picketed there one night. They came into the club carrying placards – 'Unfair to saxophone players.' Of course, it was a gag instigated by Moe Koffman, Jerry Toth, and Phil Nimmons. But the press picked it up, so Rob soon added saxes. But he was ready for expansion."

The one conflict in Basso's life has been musical: whether to play only jazz or to branch out into more commercial fields to survive financially. He walked that tightrope for many years. But along the way, he gained more valuable experience. He was music director for such series as *Nightcap, Barris and Company, Mallets and Brass* (with Peter Appleyard), and *In the Mood*, with Jack Duffy as host.

That last series was great, Guido said, because every week a famous leader would come in with his charts, and Guido's band would play them. "It was like playing with all the great big bands without having to go on the road."

He has the fondest memories of working with Charlie Barnet, Gene Krupa, Les Brown, Woody Herman, and Stan Kenton. The only one he "wasn't too crazy about" was Benny Goodman.

Long after hearing Miles Davis play flugelhorn, Basso took up the instrument and it virtually began a new career for him. He sticks by his oft-quoted dictum that one attacks a trumpet but makes love to a flugelhorn. "I've heard Maynard Ferguson attacking the flugelhorn. It's not pleasant," he said.

For some time, Basso led a dance band, playing private parties and social events, but he eventually felt moved to phase out that kind of work. "I've seen enough tuxedos already," he commented.

Basso notes a basic difference between his "golden age" and today's music scene. "We didn't have the school bands they have now. The youngsters today get a better musical education. But there are so few places to play. It's a pretty grim future."

Still, he hopes to keep doing what he has done. "The older I get, the more I enjoy playing jazz," was the way he summed up his feelings.

One more project he has in mind is a CD featuring himself on flugelhorn, a rhythm section, and strings. "But real strings," he adds, "no electronic gimmicks."

The (Five) Bells

formed 1965 in Montreal: Anne Edwards vocals (replaced by Jackie Ralph); Cliff Edwards vocals; Doug Gravelle drums; Charlie Clark; Michael Waye; Frank Mills keyboards (b. Montreal, June 27, 1942 [replaced by Dennis Will]); Mickey Ottier

Musical associations – bands, groups, or ensembles – sometimes are not just the sum of their parts, but apart become strong individual acts. From Three's a Crowd came solo performers Bruce Cockburn, Colleen Peterson, and David Wiffen. From The Guess Who came Burton Cummings and Randy Bachman. From Ian and Sylvia came Ian and Sylvia. Similarly, The Bells proved to be an incubator for several singing and songwriting talents. Nevertheless, to begin with, the members of the group were one for all and all for one.

"The Bells' ambition is to be the biggest group in North America," Cliff Edwards said in 1970. Initially, he and his wife Anne, along with Clark, Ralph, and Gravelle, were a touring band. The Five Bells (as they were originally known) spent 40 weeks per year on the road in night clubs.

An event in Manitoba changed the band's fortunes. Songwriter Rick Neufeld sat down and composed a tune about the sights and sounds around his home; he called it "Moody Manitoba Morning." His publisher sent a tape to Anne and Cliff Edwards and the Five Bells recorded it for Polydor Records. Initially, it sold only 3000 copies in Canada and consequently got little attention in the United States, although George Hamilton IV showed interest in the tune provided he could change the title to "Moody Mississippi Morning." Neufeld wouldn't allow it.

In the meantime, by 1970, Anne Edwards had left the group and it changed its name to The Bells. With a new configuration – Doug Gravelle (drums), Frank Mills (keyboards), and vocalists Charlie Clark, Michael Waye, Cliff Edwards, and his sister, Jackie Ralph – the Bells went into the studio to record again. It was Ralph's distinctive singing style on two new singles – "Fly Little White Dove Fly" and "Stay Awhile" – that seemed to catch fire on both Canadian and American radio playlists. Suddenly, there was new interest in their original track, "Moody Manitoba Morning," and sales took off – 35,000 copies sold in Canada alone.

"Stay Awhile" brought some fame to composer Ken Tobias (who later went on to a solo recording career). It was eventually a million-seller in the United States and gave the Bells an entrée to the American market, where they played not to clubs but at concert halls and on television – *The Tonight Show* and *The Merv Griffin Show*. When CRTC CanCon legislation forced Canadian radio stations to air more homegrown material, the Bells found they no longer had to tour the United States. There was enough work in Canada.

Frank Mills

The Bells disbanded, however, in 1973. Cliff Edwards pursued a solo career and Frank Mills went out on his own. Mills' first big solo hit was **Love Me, Love Me Love** that year, and in 1978 **Music Box Dancer**, which became an international hit. In 1980, his song **Peter Piper** earned Mills two Juno Awards – one for Composer of the Year and a second for Instrumental Artist of the Year; he repeated his win in the latter category in 1981.

Ultimately, the Bells had fostered no fewer than five successful individual careers – those of Neufeld, Tobias, Edwards, Ralph, and Mills – all in roughly eight years of existence.

Mario Bernardi

b. Kirkland Lake, Ontario, August 20, 1930

In his long and busy career, Mario Bernardi has conducted 75 different operas and no fewer than 450 other works with the National Arts Centre Orchestra alone. He has also conducted the CBC Vancouver Orchestra and Calgary Philharmonic.

Singers such as Frederica von Stade and Maureen Forrester accord him the highest praise. "He's a great conductor," said Forrester. "I admire him a lot. No matter what singer you talk to who has worked with Bernardi, they say, 'Boy, he makes you work hard.' But when you get the final product, you appreciate all the hard work."

NAC/PA 207956

Mario was born in Kirkland Lake, Ontario. When he was six his family moved back to Italy until he was 17. Consequently, his command of the Italian language has come in handy, particularly in conducting opera. The family had planned to stay "a few years," but the Second World War lengthened their overseas stay.

Young Mario began studying piano and organ with his uncle in Italy. He graduated from the Venice Conservatory with the highest possible marks. In Canada he continued his studies at the Royal Conservatory of Music in Toronto. By the 1950s he was making a name for himself, both as a concert pianist and as a conductor.

When he was studying piano and conducting at the Conservatory, the school's principal, Ettore Mazzoleni, asked Bernardi to become the Institute's opera coach. "I told him I didn't know the first thing about opera," Bernardi recalled. "You'll learn," Mazzoleni replied.

In 1963, he moved to London to become coach and assistant conductor for the Sadler's Wells. When he conducted *Madame Butterfly*, there were nine opening-night curtain calls. One critic, David Cairns of *The Financial Times*, wrote that Bernardi had the rare ability "both to lead and accompany the singers." Cairns also praised Bernardi's "most imaginative ear for the details of Puccini's very subtle scoring."

After three years, Bernardi was promoted to music director, and three years later (1969) he returned to Canada as music director of the newly created National Arts Centre Orchestra. He was 39 years old. He had to build the orchestra from the ground up, and also learn most of the repertoire from scratch – "mountains of music," as he put it.

In 1971, he began devoting his summers to opera as the artistic director of the National Arts Centre's Festival Canada (later renamed Festival Ottawa). He eventually conducted nearly all of Mozart's major operas, as well as Tchaikovsky's *The Queen of Spades* and Benjamin Britten's *A Midsummer Night's Dream*.

During Bernardi's 13-year tenure, the NACO made 21 Canadian tours, four U.S. tours, and two trips to Europe. One of the highlights of the first tour, in 1973, was a Moscow performance that included Prokofiev's *Classical Symphony*. The famed composer's widow led the audience in such enthusiastic applause that the orchestra was still playing encores half an hour after the official program had ended.

In 1984, after more than a decade with the NACO, he left Ottawa and became music director of the Calgary Philharmonic Orchestra, a post he held for nine years before stepping down in 1993.

Bernardi had great praise for the musicians of the Calgary orchestra: "Just an exhilarating group of people. They are very young, very enthusiastic.

They're ready to do anything. And I've worked them very hard. I realize that but they don't mind."

During Bernardi's reign, the orchestra travelled to Ottawa, Montreal, Washington, and Boston before concluding the tour at New York's Carnegie Hall.

Despite his busy schedule, he found time in the 1980s to appear as guest conductor for such companies as the San Francisco Opera, the New York City Opera, and the Houston Grand Opera, among others.

Calgary music critic Robert Everett-Green described him this way: "He is an intensely dedicated musician, and a rather shy man, for whom private engagement with a work of music seems more congenial than a large public experience."

Bernardi's reputation as a "tough" conductor was persistent. "He's tough," said Maureen Forrester. "He's a great taskmaster. But he's not tough because he likes to throw around his own weight. He's tough because he wants to serve the music."

When Bernardi stepped down as music director of the Calgary Philharmonic Orchestra, he was praised for his achievements during his tenure: "Bernardi has led the CPO for nine years," wrote Robert Everett-Green, "during which time it has broken from the pack of mid-level orchestras to challenge the best ensembles in the land."

In March 1997, Christopher Deacon, managing director of the National Arts Centre Orchestra, announced that Mario Bernardi had been appointed to the position of Conductor Laureate.

Ed Bickert

b. Hochfeld, Manitoba, November 29, 1932

Few jazz fans in Canada would argue with the notion that Ed Bickert is the best in his field. He is also probably the most modest.

For the second half of the 20th century, Bickert has proven himself, again and again, not only in Canada, but in the United States and Europe. In Toronto, in addition to fronting his own trio, he accompanied such jazz stars as Paul Desmond, Chet Baker, Red Norvo, Milt Jackson, and Frank Rossolino.

It was his work with Desmond, in 1974–76 at the Monterey Jazz Festival, that brought Bickert to international attention. *Down Beat* wrote of his "understated

Don Vickery

eloquence matched only by such masters as Jim Hall," and Jack Batten in the *Globe and Mail* praised his ability "to combine the logic of a mathematician and the grace of an angel."

Bickert was born in Hochfeld, near Winnipeg, and was raised in Vernon, B.C. He took up the guitar at the age of eight and first played with his parents. His father was an old-time fiddler and his mother a pianist with a country band. "Not country music as we know it today," he amended years later in a talk with author and jazz critic Mark Miller. "Just the kind of music that people in the country danced to: polkas, Viennese waltz-type things, fox trots; one-steps, two-steps, schottisches and I forget what all else."

He moved to Toronto at age 20, working first as an engineer at a radio station (CFRB) and playing at such after-hours clubs as the House of Hambourg. (For a time, Ed lived in Hambourg's attic.) His only formal training consisted of a few lessons from guitarist Tony Bradan.

When he first moved to Toronto, Bickert felt very insecure, even though he had been exposed to the work of some good guitarists. "I was really taken aback by the guitar players I heard [in Toronto]. I thought, 'Well, I'm not ready for this.' So I didn't play at all for a couple of years."

But he "gradually got fired up about music, met some musicians, played some sessions."

True to his cautious nature, he didn't quit his CFRB job until he had the promise of steady work – with reedman Jimmy Amaro, Sr. at the Silver Rail nightclub. In time, his credentials as a musician were substantial. He worked with Norm Symonds' jazz octet. It was from Symonds that he learned to extend his grasp of harmonics. He worked with Ron Collier, Phil Nimmons, and Moe Koffman. Starting in 1968, he was a member of Rob McConnell's Boss Brass.

He also worked in Toronto studios until the early 1970s and performed intermittently with groups headed by Peter Appleyard, Hagood Hardy, and Don Thompson. He formed his own trio in 1974 (initially with Thompson and drummer Terry Clarke). An album of duets he made with Thompson received a Juno award for the Best Jazz Recording of 1979.

That same year, he toured with Milt Jackson in Japan. During the 1980s he appeared on international stages with Koffman, Appleyard, and the Boss Brass. In 1987, he returned to Japan with the Concord All-Stars. By then, he was already recording for Concord. Also in the 1980s, he recorded in a quartet setting with tenor saxophonist Rick Wilkins or guitarist Lorne Lofsky and various bassists and drummers.

Bickert taught briefly at the Advanced School of Contemporary Music (the Toronto school founded by Oscar Peterson, Ray Brown, and Ed Thigpen), and also at Banff and the University of New Brunswick Chamber Music and Jazz Festival (in 1978 and 1982).

In the world of musicians, Bickert has long been a subject of discussion almost as much for his reticence – both on stage and off – as for his playing. "The way I play," he once told Mark Miller, sounding almost apologetic, "is the way I am as a person. I'm not an aggressive, adventurous type; I'm very traditional in a lot of areas of my life. I think that's pretty much how I play."

Yet his approach to music is not "traditional" in the sense in which that word is used in connection with jazz. As has been noted, his playing is (or, at any rate, was) "rooted in bebop and influenced by Tal Farlow, Barney Kessel," and other disciples of Charlie Christian – whom Bickert never saw or heard "live."

His low-key personal manner is very much a part of his approach to music. It is also akin to his concert stage style. At a Massey Hall (Toronto) concert in 1981, he and bassist Dave Young were the opening act for famed jazz violinist Stephane Grappelli. After one number, Bickert began to introduce the next one, when someone in the audience shouted out: "Can't hear you."

"Well," said Bickert, "you'll just have to listen, because I don't talk loud."

Blue Rodeo

formed 1985 in Toronto: Jim Cuddy vocals, guitar; Greg Keelor vocals, guitar; Cleave Anderson drums (replaced by Mark French, replaced by Glenn Milchem); Bazil Donovan bass; Bob Wiseman piano (replaced by steel guitarist Kim Deschamps, replaced by James Gray)

The history of bands in popular music is often the history of relationships, combinations of talent that gel to create extraordinary music, but then appear to disintegrate because of personality conflict. Sometimes the same qualities that bring band members together pull them apart. The phenomenal success of Canadian country-rock band Blue Rodeo has, like many bands of the 20th century, been buffeted by the volatility of the industry and the personalities of its individual players.

A cinema verité scene from the documentary *The Scenes in Between*, shot in New Orleans as Blue Rodeo rehearsed and recorded its ninth album, **The Days In Between**, depicted some of the tension that existed between the band's originals. Jim Cuddy and Greg Keelor disagreed about musical treatment.

"It's part of our work," Cuddy said after the incident. "The whole process of making a record, you have to stay emotionally connected to the material all the time. … I think it comes down to the two guys who think they're the leaders."

The two leaders – Cuddy and Keelor – knew each other in a Toronto high school in the 1970s. Cuddy was into songwriters (Lightfoot, Dylan, and the

Blue Rodeo (l. to r.): Glenn Milchem, Bazil Donovan, Jim Cuddy, Greg Keelor, James Gray

Beatles), while Keelor liked the San Francisco sound (Country Joe and the Fish and Quicksilver). After university, as friends got jobs and settled down, the two guitarists reconnected. It was the time of, as Keelor described it, "new wave amphetamine punk," and as Cuddy recalled, when "you didn't really have to play well to be in a band." They called themselves the HiFis, wrote their own material, and within six months had recorded a single.

They tried New York City, advertising in *The Village Voice* for new members to join them in a reggae, punk, and rock band they called Fly to France. They wrote and recorded with a variety of other players and bands, eventually returning to Toronto in 1984 with a demo tape. The record industry appeared to be interested in harder music than Keelor and Cuddy were playing and turned them down. Eventually, they were joined by pianist Bob Wiseman, drummer Cleave Anderson, and bass player Bazil Donovan, who answered the infamous 1984 *Now* magazine ad: "If you've dropped acid at least 20 times, lost 3 or 4 years to booze, are looking good and can still manage to keep time, call Jim or Greg."

"I remember walking into the rehearsal space," Donovan said. "We just started right in working on **Rose Coloured Glasses**. There was no audition, no meeting or anything. Back then the music came first."

The six-man band, now called Blue Rodeo, began appearing at Toronto clubs in 1984–85. By 1986, WEA Music (Warner Bros.) had signed them and released their debut album, *Outskirts*. One measure of their impact was the success of their single **Try**, which quickly found a following and went double platinum in Canada. Another was the 1988 year-end issue of *Rolling Stone* magazine, which wrote of Blue Rodeo, "The best new American band of the year, may very well be Canadian."

Another indication of their popularity was their invitation to the 1989 Junos to back up The Band as they (Robertson, Hudson, and Danko) were inducted into the Hall of Fame. At the same awards ceremony, Blue Rodeo received Junos for Single of the Year (**Try**), Group of the Year, and Video of the Year. Later in 1989, they released their second album, **Diamond Mine**, and at the Junos the next year they captured Group of the Year (the first of two straight in the category).

Blue Rodeo also began heavy-duty touring in a remarkable period of transition in Canadian music. Before them, bands unable to penetrate the United States were doomed, by economies of scale, to play the usual circuit of Canada's major centres and then wait until the next record before repeating the process. Blue Rodeo toured Canada's eight or ten major cities, then tried American touring, and when that didn't immediately succeed, they returned to the home circuit.

"We've played every inch of Canada," Cuddy told *Starweek* magazine. "Somewhere, somehow, that became the right thing for us to do and be. We're still out there doing it."

In the 1990s, Blue Rodeo lived hard, toured hard, and recorded hard. There was a string of albums – **Casino** (1991), **Lost Together** (1992), **Five Days in July** (1994), **Nowhere to Here** (1995), and **Tremolo** (1997). There were also lots of personnel changes. Drummer Milchem remembers album success but also that "things fell apart, people's home lives fell apart ... everything was intense, uneasy, traumatic ... all this buried frustration." In addition, Keelor had a brush with drug dependency while medicating a diabetic condition; his hospitalization scared the entire band, but remarkably caused only one tour-stop cancellation.

Rumours of breakup surfaced in 1996 as Keelor and Cuddy pursued solo album projects – **Greg Keelor: Gone** (1997) and **Jim Cuddy: All In Time** (1999). But also in 1999, Blue Rodeo released **Just Like a Vacation** and then in 2000 **The Days In Between**.

"Maybe this is a difficult band to be a sideman in," Jim Cuddy told the *Globe and Mail* in 1999 following another personnel change. "There's an inner sanctum that you don't get in. We share with each other. ... But we're not looking for blood brothers."

Liona Boyd

Courtesy Canapress

Beyond a doubt, Liona Boyd is one of Canada's most talented musicians – as well as one of the most glamorous.

The English-born Boyd was brought to Canada (by her parents, John and Eileen Boyd) and began studying guitar with Eli Kassner when she was 14. She made her New York debut at the Carnegie Hall Recital Hall in 1975 and the following year started to tour as an opening act for Gordon Lightfoot.

After establishing impeccable credentials as a classical guitarist (by the early 1980s she was being billed as "The First Lady of the Guitar") she moved to widen her audience by appearing with a broad variety of more popular musicians, from André Gagnon and Roger Whittaker to Chet Atkins and panpipist Zamfir.

That Boyd is also one of the country's most visible musicians in the media is something she has always insisted she doesn't plan – it just happens. But Boyd attracts publicity the way a light attracts moths.

In the couple of decades during which she has been famous virtually around the world, Boyd has gone from refined, genteel classical guitarist to champion namedropper and media tease. She once mentioned that she had slept in Mick Jagger's bed. Then, after just enough of a pause to allow for shocked reaction, she added: "It was all quite innocent. Mick wasn't even there. But his dog was."

Somewhat like an expert juggler, she enjoys switching from world-class namedropping to insisting she's happiest when she is alone. "I love my privacy," she once said, deadpan.

Liona has hobnobbed with the world's who's who: Ronald Reagan, Margaret Thatcher, Fidel Castro, Spain's King Juan Carlos, Julio Iglesias, Merv Griffin, Liberace, Yo-Yo Ma, Peter Ustinov, Eric Clapton, Placido Domingo, Queen Elizabeth, and Prince Philip. And she has no qualms about telling anyone within earshot of her various social encounters.

In 1998, she wrote her rather juicy autobiography, titled *Liona Boyd, In My Own Key – My Life in Love and Music*. A good deal of the book is devoted to the telling of her various romantic liaisons. One of these was with Dr. Carlos Payet, a young Salvadorian composer and professional psychiatrist.

"Payet developed a severe case of infatuation that inspired him to write 'Danza Nortena' and 'Brisas del Lempa,' which I recorded on my album *Virtuoso*," she wrote. "Sadly for him I was unwilling to reciprocate his affections; thus scorned by his Canadian muse, he became embittered and refused to write more music for me."

When Boyd worked with Roger Moore in the James Bond film *Moonraker*, she played a tune of Carlos Payet's during a break after which Moore commented that Payet must have been in love with her when he wrote the tune. Adds Boyd: "Roger was a most astute man."

In 1979 she was invited to play a short guitar piece at an upcoming Madison Square Garden show starring Julio Iglesias, and she was "intrigued" by the chance to meet the popular Spanish singer. A scheduled meeting with Iglesias was postponed (and the location changed) several times, but they finally met in Montreal, in his hotel room, with Julio "lying on a couch between two Latin beauties."

After she played a few guitar numbers for him, wrote Boyd, Iglesias said: "You play great. Come and be my special guest in tomorrow's concert. But tonight let's make love so we can get to know each other better." Boyd accepted his first offer (to play at the concert) but "declined the second as diplomatically as possible."

Not surprisingly, Boyd's prolonged association with Pierre Elliott Trudeau got considerably more space in her book. "Pierre Trudeau was a dashing and charismatic man," she wrote, rather superfluously. "His voice had a gentle resonance, with just the slightest French lilt to the phrasing."

The Prime Minister and Margaret Trudeau were still together (Margaret was expecting their third child) when Liona Boyd met them in the summer of 1975 at their country residence on Harrington Lake, outside Ottawa in the Gatineau Hills. According to the guitarist, Trudeau pursued her and their affair was in progress while the Trudeaus were still married, but separated.

"We shared bubble baths and champagne," she recalled, "while listening to classical music by candlelight." The Trudeau-Boyd affair lasted for eight years. In her account of it, barely a string is left unplucked. When Liona Boyd met Barbra Streisand, she told the singer that they once had a boyfriend in common. "You came before Margaret," she explained, "and I came after."

In 1992, Liona Boyd married John (Jack) Simon and they moved to California. She continues to play concerts, but not on as rigorous a schedule as in the past.

During her career, Liona Boyd won four Juno Awards and was named classical guitarist of the year by *Guitar Player* for four consecutive years, 1985–88.

Lenny Breau

b. Auburn, Maine, August 5, 1941; d. 1986

Guitarist Lenny Breau was always much easier to listen to than define. One critic described him as a modern-day Django Reinhardt. Yet, Breau had played at Nashville's Grand Ole Opry and loved playing with country and western guitarist Chet Atkins.

When Lenny was barely into his teens, people started telling Atkins about "this kid," and when Chet finally heard a tape of Breau he became a fan, a convert, a mentor, and eventually a friend. It was Atkins who brought Breau to the attention of the Grand Ole Opry in Nashville and Atkins who helped him get his first album recorded, *The Velvet Touch of Lenny Breau*.

The Breau family was from Auburn, Maine, where Lenny was born in 1941, but by the mid-1950s had moved to Winnipeg. There he grew up, learning to play the guitar along the way, without any formal training. He spent the next decade in Winnipeg, working both in clubs and on CBC radio programs. During that period, he also worked in Nashville.

Breau lists among his influences the paintings of Renoir and Gauguin, the piano of Bill Evans, and the guitar playing of Johnny Smith, Tal Farlow, Barney Kessel, Ed Bickert – and Andres Segovia.

But his earliest influences, actually, were his parents, Hal (Lone Pine) Breau and Betty Coty. He joined his parents' act while still in elementary school. By the time he was 15, he was recording on his own – literally. He accompanied himself, without any overdubbing tricks. Indeed, he later recreated the complex Les Paul version of "Tiger Rag" without any studio gimmicks.

During his roller-coaster career, he went through quite a range of musical experiences. He worked in Anne Murray's band. In the 1960s, having moved to Toronto, he worked with Don Francks in places like the First Floor Club. In the late 1970s, after having dropped out of music for some five years, he resurfaced with George Benson at a concert during a music convention in Georgia.

The reason Lenny Breau vanished for some years was, predictably, drugs. He had begun taking acid in Nashville during the 1960s, then was on methadone as a cure. "I took acid every day for three years," he commented in 1979, "but it didn't show in my playing. I was hiding it and doing TV shows, serious music where I played Bach. But I was out to lunch."

After a close call in New York in 1977, he had himself checked into a strict, quarantined drug rehabilitation program in a Brooklyn hospital and emerged drug-free for the first time in 12 years.

By the end of the 1970s, Breau was back impressing people with his playing.

By then, he had moved to California, where he was to live out the rest of his life.

Lenny's mind was open to all sorts of musical experimentation. He was attracted to jazz when he was still fairly young. Later he learned to love flamenco and classical guitar. There were critics who spurned him, charging that he was neither fish nor fowl, that he was not totally dedicated to one form of music. But to Lenny, there was room for more than one love in his heart.

"I'm not really a classical player," he said. "But I studied it, learned to understand it, and applied these techniques to jazz playing." In time he became aware of the dangers of being branded a jazz musician – "especially in Nashville, where if you were labelled a jazz musician you didn't work."

But wherever he played, he played with dazzling technique and deep passion. "I use all the fingers on my right hand. I have long nails. I use a thumb pick and my fingers. I'm using classical technique. I got the idea from listening to Bill Evans. What I'm trying to do is imitate a piano, really. I'm a self-taught musician."

So conscious was he of the importance of his hands that once, tripping and falling down in a street, he took the brunt of the fall on his face rather than risk damage to his fingers.

In 1998, Randy Bachman, a Breau fan from his childhood, issued a CD called *Lenny Breau, Boy Wonder*, which contains some of Lenny's earliest work. And in 1985, Guitarchives, started by Bachman, issued a double CD titled *Live at Bourbon Street*. This was a live recording from June 1983, and features the superb playing of Breau and bassist Dave Young. It offers some of Breau's (and Young's) most beautiful, lyrical work.

"I think of myself as a colourist, adding different colours and shades by using different techniques and touching the guitar in different ways," he is quoted on the liner notes of that CD. "I'd like to play sounds you can see if you've got your eyes closed; I'll always be a student, because I think of music as never ending."

When in 1986 Lenny was found dead, at the age of 43, in a Los Angeles swimming pool, the authorities said foul play was not suspected. The death was later ruled a homicide ("asphyxiation due to strangulation"), but no arrest was ever made.

Thus ended the short, turbulent life of one of Canada's most original musicians.

Boris Brott

b. Montreal, Quebec, March 14, 1944

The Brott dynasty is one of the most highly respected musical families in Canada, and Boris Brott is probably its most famous member.

His Montreal-born father, Alexander, was a composer, violinist, and teacher. His mother, Lotte (born Charlotte), was a cellist and music administrator, whose own parents were both musicians. Boris was their first son; cellist Denis was born six years later.

Boris studied violin with his father and was performing by the age of five. He took courses at McGill, and by the time he was 12 he was studying conducting at the summer school of Pierre Monteux. In 1959 he founded the Philharmonic Youth Orchestra of Montreal and led it in his conducting debut – at the age of 15.

By 1963 Boris Brott was serving as assistant conductor of Walter Susskind with the Toronto Symphony, and by the mid-1960s was conducting in England and also touring Canada and conducting concerts at Expo '67 in Montreal.

Next came posts as artistic director of orchestras in Thunder Bay and Regina. Then, from 1969 to 1990 he was artistic director and conductor of the Hamilton Philharmonic. Under his leadership, that orchestra made tremendous strides, increased its number of concerts, and toured.

In 1972, Brott was appointed conductor of the BBC Welsh Orchestra and three years later he assumed directorship of the CBC Winnipeg Orchestra. Next came three years as conductor of Symphony Nova Scotia, and in 1989 he was appointed associate director of the McGill Chamber Orchestra.

In addition to guest conducting for many major Canadian orchestras, he has fulfilled similar functions with numerous orchestras in England, France, Italy, and Germany. Over the years of his whirlwind career, he developed six orchestras in Canada – the Thunder Bay, Regina, Kitchener-Waterloo, CBC Winnipeg, and Nova Scotia symphonies and, of course, the Hamilton Philharmonic.

It was in the summer of 1987 that he launched the Boris Brott Festival as a two-week event that now stretches over seven weeks across Ontario, almost always backed by his Hamilton-based Festival Academy Orchestra.

For a man still in his 50s, Brott, a tireless promoter of the arts and, not incidentally, recipient of numerous awards, is zealous in his commitment to youth. "There are opportunities for young performers with the [Festival Academy] orchestra," he said in a recent interview. "Rehearsal time is limited, but they'll get to play a piece more than once, and that's always better because there's no surfeit of activity in the summer.

"Each year, around 350 young musicians apply for the 55 spots available in the orchestra, where they're guided by senior musicians from Toronto and Montreal. With the help of an apprentice conductor, I audition all of them."

About three-quarters of the apprentices find work in Canada and elsewhere. Brott came up with this idea after conducting an Ottawa concert in which National Arts Centre Orchestra players worked with members of his father Alexander's training orchestra, Montreal's Jeunes Virtuosos. The Boris Brott Festival, according to its founder, "must grow slowly and aim for the special magic that comes with sold-out houses."

In 1999, his orchestra was officially recognized as a national school by the Department of National Heritage. This put the orchestra on the same footing as the National Ballet and National Theatre schools, the first such designation outside Toronto or Montreal.

Brott never shuns travel – especially if there is a musical element involved. In the year 2000 he was in Rome for a political and theologically significant event. He conducted the late Leonard Bernstein's somewhat controversial "Mass" in the Vatican during Rome's 2000 Festival. There was an emotional aspect to the occasion, too; Brott had spent a year as assistant conductor of the New York Philharmonic under Bernstein in 1969. "It was very pleasant fulfilling Lenny's dream," he told the *Toronto Star*'s Geoff Chapman in an interview. "It was a tremendous experience, in a Catholic church with a work that, in parts, suggested faith was in crisis."

Between 1987 and 1989 he was national president of YMC (Youth and Music Canada), and not least among his numerous honours was his appointment, in 1986, as an Officer of the Order of Canada.

Jane Bunnett

formed 1988 in Toronto: Jane Bunnett (b. Toronto, October 22, 1955) soprano sax; Larry Cramer (b. Toronto, June 7, 1955) trumpet

Jane Bunnett has always done things a different way. Whether it was bucking authority back in high school or wading into Afro-Cuban musical culture

Jane Bunnett (seated) and Larry Cramer (with trumpet) with the Spirits of Havana 2000

Ivan Otis / EMI Music Canada

when it wasn't yet in vogue, she has rarely gone by the book. Her off-the-beaten-path route has established the jazz flutist and soprano saxophonist as a trailblazer, innovator, and award-winning performer on stage, on film, and often in out-of-the-way places.

"Life is a series of accidents," Bunnett says, "and I believe certain accidents are good."

Jane left an unrewarding school career at age 17 to study piano full time. But soon after, tendonitis in one hand stalled her concert piano career. She finished Grade 10 piano with her hand in a brace. Then, in 1977 she took a holiday in San Francisco and happened to catch the Charles Mingus band (including Don Pullen on piano) at the Keystone Korner club. She was instantly smitten by jazz.

"I came back and continued my piano studies," she says, "but I was supposed to have an operation on my hand – and I faced the fact that I was not going to be a piano player because I was always going to have this problem."

Instead she picked up the flute and began studying jazz first at the New School of Music in Toronto and then at York University. There she studied small-group jazz with John Gittins and met trumpeter Larry Cramer; they played jazz together and later married. Also at York, Bunnett broke her ankle on a set of stairs; she settled for $813, roughly equivalent to the price of a soprano saxophone.

During the late 1970s, Jane Bunnett overcame her fear of live performance and began playing flute and saxophone professionally in the cafes and Greek taverns along Danforth Avenue in Toronto. "I loved improvising," she told the *Toronto Star*, "the openness of sitting down and not knowing what you were going to play, though I didn't really know what it was about. That was always very exciting."

Meanwhile, that accidental meeting with Don Pullen in 1977 proved more than passing. In 1988, Jane Bunnett assembled Pullen and two other New York musicians – tenorman Dewey Redman and French hornist Vincent Chancey – with trumpeter Larry Cramer, pianist Brian Dickinson, bassist Scott Alexander, and drummer Claude Ranger in Toronto to record a debut album *In Dew Time*. The jazz press raved. She earned a Juno nomination. The recording and subsequent appearances with the band prompted *Down Beat* magazine to name Bunnett one of North America's most promising new players. In 1989, while appearing at the Greenwich Village Jazz Festival, Bunnett recorded with Pullen again on the album *New York Duets*.

Bunnett couldn't have chosen a tougher instrument than soprano sax.

"Intonation is a real bugger," she told *Down Beat*. "Getting a big sound with the tiny neck and mouthpiece is a problem. It sounds almost like an oboe, nasally." She also points out that being heard over the band on her other instrument, the flute, was just as tough, since "most of the truly great musicians know that there is an incredible strength in playing softly."

A major direction in Bunnett's musical journey occurred in 1982, when she and Larry Cramer escaped a Canadian winter for Cuba, where "we discovered the music is entirely integrated with people's lives. Their lifestyle (from the schools to the streets) revolves around folkloric music. It's a communication. It's a living, breathing life force."

Long before it became fashionable, Bunnett set out to explore the island's musical culture. In the fall of 1991, she and Larry Cramer assembled a band of Cuban musicians, put them in the state-owned Egrem Studios in Havana, and recorded their album *Spirits of Havana*. It earned Bunnett her first Juno award in 1992 for Best World Beat Recording and was named one of the top 300 jazz discs of all time by the U.S.-based *All Music Guide*.

Enjoying the best of both worlds, Bunnett continued to record – with her North American jazz friends *Live at Sweet Basil* (1991), *The Water Is Wide* (1994), and *Double Time* (1994), and as frequently with newfound Latin American players *Rendez-Vous Brazil/Cuba* (1995), *Jane Bunnett and the Cuban Piano Masters* (1996), *Chamalongo* (1997), *Ritmo+Soul* (2000), which won a Juno, and *Alma de Santiago* (2001).

During her subsequent visits to Cuba throughout the 1990s, "Havana Jane," as she was nicknamed, explored the Afro-Cuban folkloric music even further. In 1996, she and Larry Cramer were invited to visit a school to hear young music students play. Fourteen fully rehearsed students played for three hours.

"I was so impressed with the high level of communication between the teachers and students," Bunnett said. "[But] I was appalled by the condition of their instruments. One kid's flute had pieces of plastic bag where the pads should be. The kid played Mozart as beautifully as ever, despite her instrument falling apart."

Two months later, Bunnett and Cramer staged a benefit at Toronto's Senator jazz club auctioning off cigars, rum, and other Cuban collectibles; they raised $10,000. The couple formed the charity Spirit of Music, which in its first four years raised more than $30,000 to purchase and repair instruments for Cuban schools. Bunnett later chaired the music education committee of the Canadian Academy of Recording Arts and Sciences (CARAS) which allocated some of the royalties raised by the Canadian-content CD sets *Oh What a Feeling* to put 10,000 recorders into the hands of Canadian children. Every year Bunnett and Cramer travelled to a different Cuban music conservatory with Canadian technicians to record the music.

Their campaign, however, had a downside. At the time, the U.S. Helms-Burton bill prohibited trade relations with Cuba. Bunnett says the resulting backlash caused a cancelled recording contract, the loss of $40,000 in concert dates, and at least one bomb threat. Bunnett dubbed her subsequent appearances the "Come Helms or High Water" tour.

Defiantly, in November 1999, Bunnett and Cramer returned to Cuba, this time with a National Film Board crew, to document the country's musical legacy. With a date set at the Egrem Studios to record 40 of Havana's established musicians, the Canadians arrived to find 100 musicians waiting for them.

"All of them showed up, dressed in their best clothes, telling the NFB people, 'Jane invited me,'" Bunnett told *Maclean's* magazine. "When the producer asked us who this or that person was, we didn't have a clue."

The documentary *Spirits of Havana* and accompanying CD are a testament to Bunnett's persistence and passion for her work.

"I've always had big dreams," Bunnett says, "even if they aren't always based in reality."

Howard Cable

b. Toronto, Ontario, December 15, 1920

It would be difficult to find a music director/conductor who is more widely respected and admired by his colleagues than Howard Cable. This is partly because of his musical gifts, but also because of the genuine respect and affection he has always shown his musicians.

Cable began his musical studies early in life, learning to play piano, clarinet, and oboe. He played in the Parkdale Collegiate Institute orchestra under Leslie Bell. While leading a dance band in 1935–41, he studied with Sir Ernest MacMillan and Healey Willan. In that band, Fred Davis was a trumpeter. "I grew up with Fred. We went to Parkdale together. Leslie Bell got Fred involved in music, too," Cable remembered.

He began his radio career in 1936 and by 1941 was working as a composer of incidental music, soon succeeding Percy Faith as CBC Toronto's leading conductor-arranger-composer.

It was in 1941 that Cable first played at Dunn's Pavilion in Bala – "Where All Muskoka Dances." Denny Vaughan, a fellow musician Cable had heard of but never met, steered him to a job at the Beaumaris Hotel in Muskoka. This resulted in the job at Dunn's, where he led a six-piece band whose trumpeter was again Fred Davis. The Bala engagement helped enhance Cable's popularity among summer dance band fans.

"I'm very lucky. It's amazing how much luck plays in a person's life," he said years later.

"The joint was packed all the time – boats parked out at the back docks. We played every night, Sunday concerts and everything," Cable told trombonist and author Murray Ginsberg.

He was paid $36 a week, plus room and board. "The living conditions were bad, but not as bad as Beaumaris," Cable said. "We were the band that played the last year of the old hall – the old 1920s hall. I closed that hall in 1941 and came back and opened the new one in 1942. Dunn called it 'The Key to Bala.'"

In the 1950s, he was music director and arranger for various television shows and his concert band was the nucleus of his orchestra at the CNE

Grandstand, where he was music director and assistant producer to Jack Arthur, whom he succeeded in 1968.

During the 1960s he became a household word across Canada as conductor and arranger of over a thousand CBC radio and television shows, including such commercial series as *Canadian Cavalcade*, *O'Keefe Hi Time*, *Robin Hood Musical Kitchen*, and *Esso Happy Motoring*.

Nor did he confine himself to broadcast work. For 12 years he was music director of the Royal York Hotel's Imperial Room, in Toronto, working with such guest performers as Ella Fitzgerald, Tony Bennett, and Peggy Lee.

He also worked in New York as an arranger for Richard Rodgers and Meredith Willson. He served as conductor for the Broadway production *Man of La Mancha*.

By the 1980s he was appearing as guest conductor for various Canadian orchestras in concerts featuring his own arrangements. In 1987 he was music director of the Halifax Summer Pops Orchestra, and two years later, with co-director Alan Lund, he began a summer training program in musical theatre techniques and production at Dalhousie University.

Cable became a sort of mentor to the many young musicians who worked for him. That list included such outstanding musicians as Rob McConnell, Jack Kane, Teddy Roderman, Ross Culley, Ellis McLintock, Victor Feldbrill, Fred Davis, Ed Bickert, Johnny Cowell, Peter Appleyard, Gene Di Novi, Guido Basso, Laurie Bower, Erich Traugott, Phil Nimmons, Harry Freedman, Bobby Herriot, and John Weinzweig.

The bond between Howard Cable and his young musicians – many of whom got their first professional experience with him – has endured. More than half a century after those halcyon days, 20 veteran musicians who had worked for Howard Cable gathered in downtown Toronto for a luncheon to celebrate the leader's 76th birthday.

The invitation they received read: "Howard would be delighted if you would join him, along with some of the 'Golden Era guys,' as his guest." The "Golden Era" the invitation mentioned referred to the period from the mid-1940s to the 1970s when, according to Murray Ginsberg, "Musicians from all parts of Canada and the world at large enjoyed the good life, performing on CBC radio and television literally from morning to night.

"Most musicians who played those shows are gone, but those seated at the table joined Howard when he raised a glass to the memory of all those who were no longer with us. And he paid tribute to those lucky enough to be present when he said, 'You represent everything that made music work in Canada.'"

The wine flowed – as did the nostalgia – and at the end of the lunch Howard Cable announced that he would organize a similar reunion every year in December.

John Allan Cameron with the Cape Breton Symphony, CFCF TV Studios in 1975. (l. to r.): Wilfred Gillis, Jerry Holland, Angus Chisholm, John Allan Cameron, Winston "Scotty" Fitzgerald, John Donald Cameron (John Allan's brother)

John Allan Cameron

b. Glencoe Station, Nova Scotia, December 16, 1938

During the 1995 East Coast Music Awards, John Allan Cameron received the Lifetime Achievement Award. Three years shy of his 60th birthday, he responded, "Maybe you should get this when you're 70 years old, [because] if they think they're going to have John Allan go to a rocking chair, well, there's more energy in this man than a lot of youngsters."

The exuberance of this singer, songwriter, guitarist, and fiddler illustrates the point. John Allan Cameron has packed a lot of living into one performing career. It began in Cape Breton where, as Cameron points out, "the Bobby Orrs … in those days were the priests and the fiddlers."

His childhood was filled with the storytelling of his father, the fiddle-playing of his mother, brother, and uncle Dan Rory MacDonald, and music on Antigonish radio station CJFX. John Allan joined in at first on a jew's harp, then at age 12 on a guitar his father bought him. He regularly accompanied his brother John Donald Cameron at local dances, but was too shy to sing.

In perhaps a pivotal moment in his young life, about age 14, John Allan recalls making a trek on foot from his home at Glencoe Station 25 miles to Mabou where the famous fiddler Winston "Scotty" Fitzgerald and the Radio Entertainers band were performing at a dance.

"I stood at the bottom of the stage," Cameron said, "and watched Scotty from nine right through till one in the morning, just absorbing every second. At the end of the concert, at 1:20 in the morning, I was standing outside the hall when Scotty came out, saw me, and asked 'You like the fiddle?'

"'Sure do,' I said. And he asked my name.

"'You're Dan R. MacDonald's nephew? And you came all this way to see us?' … So they drove me the 25 miles back home. There I was in the back seat with my heroes, [fiddler] Winston 'Scotty' Fitzgerald, [guitarist] Estwood Davidson, and [pianist] Beatty Wallace."

Cameron gained the confidence he needed during his years studying for the priesthood with the Order of the Oblate Fathers in Ottawa. Seminary life from 1957 to 1964 taught him how to present his ideas through sermons, how to discipline himself, and how to deal with people. He also earned the nickname "Sports" as the seminary sports director organizing hockey games and arranging times to catch the pros on television.

"Living in a community of 80, with no contact with the outside world, you had to get along," recalled Cameron. "And you had to get permission for everything. So as sports director, I would go in to see the Superior to get permission for all of us to watch the hockey game on Saturday night. I'd negotiate."

Though he took his final vows of poverty, chastity, and obedience, six months before ordination Cameron decided against becoming a priest and received papal dispensation in 1964 to become a performer. As he made plans to attend St. Francis Xavier University in Nova Scotia, he began playing guitar professionally at dances, perfecting his own interpretation of bagpipe music on a 12-string guitar. CJFX radio broadcast one of his instrumental performances. Listeners responded. Meanwhile, at St. Francis Xavier, Cameron got a chance to sing at the winter carnival. He wowed the audience with both his playing and his singing. For the first time in his life he sensed "there really was potential here."

As Cameron continued his studies – a B.A. at St. Francis Xavier and a B.Ed. at Dalhousie – he agreed to appear on the Don Messer show and its summer replacement, *Singalong Jubilee*. After university he taught English and religion at a Catholic high school in London, Ontario; however, he kept up his appearances in folk clubs – Privateers Coffee House and the Monterey Lounge in Halifax, the Prince Edward Lounge in Charlottetown, and Wong's in Antigonish – and on television.

"[When] I came back to do *Singalong Jubilee*," Cameron said, "I made up my mind to give music a shot, because I love being on stage. That's where I was most comfortable, rather than having a regular nine-to-five job."

Signing on with Leonard Rambeau, Anne Murray's manager, proved to be John Allan Cameron's first breakthrough. He toured Canada as Murray's opening act. In a 1976 *Canadian Magazine* article, Dick Brown quotes Anne Murray's assessment of Cameron's unique talent on stage: "He's unique. He has great pitch. He sings the notes right on but … well, some people have a way of making notes sound so round and fat and perfect … John Allan is not one of them. He's a lot like Doug Kershaw, the Cajun fiddler, except that he's not as crazy and erratic. But he loves to perform.

"When he was doing concerts with me," Murray continued, "he used to have trouble keeping down the length of his performance. I remember one night I went to him and said, 'John Allan, you're an opening act, you've got to keep it to 40 minutes.'"

By the mid-1970s, television producers were pursuing Cameron to host his own program, first CTV in Montreal (1975–77) then CBC in Halifax (1979–81). Television allowed Cameron to explore and promote the music of his Cape Breton roots – Celtic melodies and rhythms. Guests included the Cape Breton Symphony (with fiddlers John Donald Cameron, Jerry Holland, Winston "Scotty" Fitzgerald, Angus Chisholm, and Wilfred Gillis, and pianist/accordionist Bobby Brown). Cameron went on to produce the Cape Breton Symphony's first album. He also brought Stan Rogers to national television for the first time in 1975; in fact, Rogers auditioned his legendary sea shanty "Barrett's Privateers" in John Allan Cameron's basement.

John Allan Cameron with son Stuart

Cameron loves to tell stories about the old-time fiddlers, in particular: "The night Wilfred Gillis was playing in Pictou, the band played one of the first tunes my uncle Dan R. wrote. Well, first Bobby Brown started the tune on the piano. Then Wilfred picked it up on the fiddle. Then right in the middle of the tune Wilfred sneezed and his false teeth flew right out of his mouth. … He didn't miss a note. He leaned over, picked up the teeth, and carried right on. At the end of the song, he acknowledged, 'That was a tune by the great Dan R. MacDonald … but I do apologize it included one extra bridge.'"

Cameron's itinerary during 30 years in show business is as disparate as the range of his music. He has not only toured across Canada, but also Japan, Egypt, Israel, Cyprus, Scotland, Ireland, and the United States. He has appeared in everything from the Newport Folk Festival to Mariposa to the Grand Ole Opry in Nashville. And his performances – now drawn from 10 recordings – encompass folk and rock traditions, while never leaving his Celtic roots too far behind. His CD *Glencoe Station* is an audio *ceilidh*, a musical gathering of musicians and material whose roots are closer to the kitchens and community halls of Cameron's home in Cape Breton than to his show business existence based in southern Ontario.

As attached as he is to his music and the performing stage, John Allan Cameron can be found nearly as often at a hockey arena. It's a part of his life he's maintained since seminary days. He regularly plays recreational hockey with such former NHLers as Pete Conacher, Bobby Baun, and Paul Henderson

(Cameron's son Stuart was born the day Henderson scored his historic goal against the Soviets – September 28, 1972). Unlike other performers who just appear at celebrity hockey games to sing the national anthem, Cameron finishes "O Canada," dons his hockey helmet and takes his regular shift on the Toronto Maple Leaf oldtimers team. Like performing on stage, for John Allan Cameron playing hockey is a lifelong pursuit.

James Campbell *b. Leduc, Alberta, August 10, 1949*

For a man of his age, James Campbell has certainly been around, in terms of musical activity. Called by music critic William Littler "the foremost Canadian clarinetist of his generation," Campbell once flirted with rock and roll and, more recently, has shown a serious interest in jazz. But there's no doubt that classical music is still his chief passion.

He grew up on a dairy farm near Edmonton. His parents and his brother, Bill, continued to live on the farm long after James moved east. When he was 15, he was "almost sidetracked into becoming a drummer in a rock band," as music critic Clyde Gilmour described it.

The band was first called J.C. and the Disciples, but Campbell's mother, who was also the church organist, objected on the grounds that some people might be offended. So the band's billing was changed to The Teen Tones.

But Campbell's interest in classical music soon triumphed and the rock world lost a drummer, although he still likes listening to some rock music, still admires what the Beatles recorded. Today, Campbell reveres Mozart above all other composers.

After getting his bachelor of music degree in Toronto, he studied at the Music Academy of the West in Santa Barbara, California, and later in Paris. He was a semifinalist in the Budapest International Clarinet Competition in Yugoslavia in 1970 and won the CBC Talent Festival the next year. He was a member of the Hamilton Philharmonic (1967–69) and the National Youth Orchestra in 1968–69.

He has performed widely throughout Canada and the United States and has played in major centres in Europe, South America, and China. In addition to appearing as soloist with many top orchestras, he was a founding member of the chamber group Camerata and also of the Arioso Trio.

He performed Aaron Copland's *Clarinet Concerto* with the Toronto

Symphony, with Copland conducting. Copland said of him: "He is a very sensitive musician with a natural musical gift."

When Clyde Gilmour asked him (in 1983) what classical clarinetist he most admired, Campbell said: "Harold Wright of the Boston Symphony. He can play anything. Wright certainly could be a big-name soloist if he wanted to."

As for jazz, Campbell chose Benny Goodman: "I own many of his albums, and I love them. He's not quite as good on the classics as he is on jazz, but he's a powerhouse in both fields. Goodman has probably done more for the clarinet than anyone else in our century."

That same year, Campbell's growing interest in jazz manifested itself in a series of concerts called *Jazz in a Classical Key*. He gathered together classical and jazz musicians. "Interesting things percolate when you're working with people who do jazz, like Eric Robertson and Gene Di Novi, as well as the classics," said Campbell. "There's a certain energy that gets born that doesn't come from either one or the other." In one of those concerts, Campbell featured music by Ravel, Debussy, Milhaud, Stravinsky, Scott Joplin, George Gershwin, and George Shearing.

One of his deepest satisfactions, he told one interviewer, was the fact that Glenn Gould used him five times in broadcast chamber recitals. "I remember that whenever I'm a bit depressed, and the thought cheers me up in a moment. Working with Gould was a heaven-sent opportunity. Each time I was on a musical 'high' for weeks."

Campbell and his wife, Carol, met in Paris, where he was studying clarinet and she French. Unlike most people, the Campbells have no television set. They prefer radio, records, reading, and conversation. But Campbell admits that he sometimes watches television – when he's in a hotel room, on the road. He likes to watch movies "but the commercials annoy me. I'm not opposed to the idea of commercials and I've played in some of them – musically, not on the screen. Yet I resent it when a sensitive scene in a worthwhile film is blatantly interrupted by a loud, tasteless sales pitch."

Campbell also confesses to another pet peeve: "Any music of the souped-up, switched-on variety. You know, Brahms to a disco beat. It's like defacing a Rembrandt."

Campbell is on the Faculty of Music at the University of Toronto and the Royal Conservatory of Music in Toronto. In 1985 he became artistic director of the Festival of the Sound (Parry Sound, Ontario) and in 1987 began teaching at Indiana University.

Campbell's recording **Stolen Gems** won a Juno Award for Best Classical Album (solo or chamber ensemble) in 1986.

The Canadian Brass at the Great Wall of China, 1977.
(l. to r.) Graeme Page, Ron Romm, Charles Daellenbach, Fred Mills, Eugene Watts

The Canadian Brass

formed 1970 in Toronto: Charles Daellenbach (b. Rhinelander, Wisconsin, July 12, 1945) tuba; Eugene Watts (Warrensburg, Missouri, February 22, 1936) trombone; Graeme Page (b. Toronto, September 8, 1947) French horn (replaced by Marty Hackleman 1983, replaced by David Ohanian 1986, replaced by Chris Cooper 1998, replaced by Jeff Nelsen 2000); Stuart Laughton (b. St. Catharines, August 19, 1951) trumpet (replaced by Ronald Romm, replaced by Ryan Anthony 2000); Bill Phillips trumpet (replaced by Fred Mills 1972, replaced by Jens Lindemann 1996)

For individual musicians playing in symphony orchestras, there is little or no choice about music, venue, or audience. While the rewards of performance are just as great for classical players, by comparison, popular musicians generally have more choice. The opportunity to have greater input was one of the forces that drew the original five members of the Canadian Brass together in 1970.

"Trombones sit in the orchestra and they play like 12 bars and then they rest for three movements," said Gene Watts, former trombone player with the Toronto Symphony Orchestra. "Twenty minutes later they play again. ... That was never really musically satisfying for me."

Watts had followed an orchestral path all his musical life, playing with symphony orchestras in North Carolina, San Antonio, and Milwaukee. Handpicked by Seiji Ozawa, Watts was first trombonist with the TSO when he met tuba player Chuck Daellenbach, who was teaching music at the University of Toronto. Together (with trumpet players Stuart Laughton and Bill Phillips and French horn player Graeme Page) they created the Canadian Brass Ensemble and consequently a new model for small brass groups interested in eclectic repertoire.

"The music must be satisfying," Daellenbach said, "and the format interesting and entertaining."

By 1971, the name was shortened to Canadian Brass and Ronald Romm had replaced Laughton. Soon after, renowned Chicago craftsman Renold Schilke designed and manufactured a set of gold-plated instruments for the group.

Even though the quintet quickly found a home as artists-in-residence with the Hamilton Philharmonic Orchestra in 1971, it set out on a unique course right away. The Brass found a way of combining extremely disciplined performance with levity and informality on stage, whether they chose to play music that was centuries old or days old. Consequently, the group earned wide appeal.

"We have what is known as a sitcom audience," said Watts, "everyone from the child of six or seven, who has seen us on *Sesame Street*, all the way up to the 80- and 90-year-old, blue-haired ladies and fine-tailored gentlemen."

Graeme Page remembers the quintet's first concert at Toronto's MacMillan Theatre being "particularly nerve-wracking … and sure enough the CBC recorded it. … We feel we've come a long way since then."

In 1972, trumpet player Fred Mills replaced Bill Phillips.

"I was playing in the National Arts Centre Orchestra [in Ottawa]," Mills remembered. "I thought it was too relaxed, playing in the orchestra and teaching at university. … I wanted to do something more exciting, some travelling."

Mills joined at the right moment. That year, the Canadian Brass toured with the Festival Singers across Britain. Then, in 1974, under the auspices of the Department of External Affairs, the ensemble played in Paris and debuted in the United States at the Kennedy Center in Washington, D.C. in 1976. During two weeks in 1977, the Canadian Brass became the first brass group to perform in the People's Republic of China; it gave 14 concerts, performed for 15,000 people, and did six broadcasts on Beijing radio. The visit left indelible impressions.

"[Chinese audience] applause builds over the performance," said Fred Mills. "It starts very calmly and politely in the beginning, but by the end of the performance they get very excited and loud."

"One lady, who was a conductor and worked with us," Gene Watts explained, "she said she had studied Bach, but she had never heard it performed. Bach had not been played since the [1960s] Cultural Revolution."

Mind you, Bach as the Canadian Brass performed it was like no other. Early on, the quintet incorporated additional business devised by Daellenbach and Watts. Witty exchanges between the two and plenty of onstage antics spiced every concert. One trademark routine involved playing Bach during a game of musical chairs, with four members of the ensemble keeping Watts from either taking a solo or a seat. By the time the frustrated trombonist finds a chair on which to sit, the rest of the group is standing and completing the piece without him.

"We treat things in our own fashion, very visually," Watts said.

On the one hand, the group members treated its instrumental reputation seriously; on the other, they took as many staging liberties as they could. The Canadian Brass approach to Bizet's *Carmen*, for example, was that an audience shouldn't have to commit four hours of listening time, so the ensemble came up with a 10-minute version. In addition, without a female member in its ensemble, the performance required a vital prop.

"There we were in Dayton, Ohio," Daellenbach remembered, "looking for a wig for Graeme to wear. You can imagine a bunch of guys going into a wig shop trying them on. Graeme looked so nice in the wig we chose, but they [Daytonians] still haven't figured that one out."

The Canadian Brass' repertoire has known no boundaries. Through scores and scores of recordings the group has tackled material from Scott Joplin to Erik Satie, from Bach to Broadway, from traditional Christmas songs to the novelty compositions of Ben McPeek, and from Olympic fanfares to Fats Waller. In addition to playing instantly recognized works, the Brass has been responsible for commissioning more than 40 new works from Canadian composers, including John Beckwith, Norma Beecroft, Walter Buczynski, Larry Crosley, Malcolm Forsyth, Harry Freedman, Srul Irving Glick, Gary Hayes, William McCauley, Oskar Morawetz, Eldon Rathburn, Norman Symonds, and John Weinzweig.

Neither has the group shied away from speaking out about the survival of its brand of music. In 1996, the quintet was invited to speak in the MacMillan Lecture series (sponsored by SOCAN, the musical performing rights organization) at University of Toronto's Convocation Hall. Following its trademark entrance – playing "A Closer Walk with Thee" in New Orleans funeral march fashion – the five musicians delivered a talk entitled, "What Your Music Teachers Don't Tell You – Doing It on Your Own."

In what *Toronto Star* music critic William Littler called their "active role as musical missionaries," the quintet spoke about preserving the classical music culture that was being upstaged by the profit motive. They argued for greater exposure of the classical heritage to children in school, and emphasized the need for more young people to play music more often and for a larger audience for classical music.

There is evidence of their success in this mission. The Canadian Brass continues to perform around the globe, playing an average 120 concerts per year. In honour of Gene Watts' homecoming, Sedalia, Missouri, declared December 3, 1999, "Canadian Brass Day."

In fact, the Canadian Brass has so helped the popularization of brass ensemble music that some of its current members actually grew up aspiring to become members of the group. Trumpet player Jens Lindemann, for example, who joined the Brass in 1996, remembered having his trumpet case signed by them in 1978 when he was 12. In turn, it was Lindemann's playing that inspired French horn player Jeff Nelsen, who turned down the first chair position in the Vancouver Symphony Orchestra to join the Canadian Brass in 2000. That same summer, trumpet player Ryan Anthony joined the ensemble; as a high school music student, he remembered sharing the stage with the Brass in a workshop performance.

"My first professional job was playing the Canadian Brass's repertoire, we so admired them," said Anthony. "It's a dream come true to be a member of the group that most influenced me as a student."

The *Washington Post* summed up the group's work this way: "The enthralling sound of a brass choir ... programs that feature virtuosic musicianship, masterful interpretations and flashes of humour ... repertoire that encompasses Bach to blues – all these ingredients make the Canadian Brass the world's leading brass ensemble."

Carlton Showband

formed 1964 in Brampton, Ontario: Chris O'Toole (b. Ireland, June 14, 1927) drums; Seamus Grew accordion; Christy McLaughlin accordion, harmonica; Sean McManus guitar, flute, harmonica; Freddy White guitar, banjo; Mike Feeney vocals; Johnny Patterson bass; Bob Lewis rhythm guitar

The trend didn't start with them, but few friendships have continued as long on- and offstage as those among the members of the Carlton Showband. Even stronger was the relationship the eight bandsmen developed with audiences who loved Irish music across Canada. For much of the latter half of the 20th century, the CSB maintained one of the highest profiles in Canadian show business on disc, on stage, and on television. The secret to their success was simple.

"We learned a lesson when we started out," said the group's founder Chris O'Toole. "There was a famous group around who were popular until they started playing only the music they enjoyed. Then they stopped being popular.

(l. to r.): Seamus Grew, Mich McCoy, Christy McLaughlin, Johnny Patterson, Freddy White, Chris O'Toole, Mike Feeney, Sean McManus

Arnott Rogers Batten

We always gear our music to the audience we play for. ... After the first four numbers we know what they want."

In effect, that same sentiment sparked the creation of the band in 1964. Recently arrived from County Wicklow, in Ireland, O'Toole attended a St. Patrick's Day do in Brampton, Ontario. While he wasn't then an authority on Irish music, he was aghast at the content of the party music, which included a rendition of "Knees Up Mother Brown." He sensed more authentic Irish music would be welcome in Canada.

A few nights later, at a step-dancing competition, O'Toole heard a young accordion player named Seamus Grew (also an Irish émigré from County Monaghan); the young musician was an accomplished player, having won the 1963 North American accordion championships.

Not long after that, O'Toole met another Irish immigrant (from County Tyrone). Christy McLaughlin was employed as a plasterer, but was also skilled at singing and playing harmonica and accordion. O'Toole organized the unnamed trio to perform at clubs during intermissions and local dances.

One day the trio, still without a name, got lost in downtown Toronto. When they got their bearings, they were outside Maple Leaf Gardens on Carlton Street. Someone suggested they adopt the name The Carltons Danceband, but they eventually settled on The Carlton Showband.

Within a year, a painter (from County Fermanagh) joined the group. Sean

McManus had learned to play the guitar and took great pride in performing the ballad "Mother," which became a standard in the CSB's repertoire.

Next, a Toronto automotive plant worker from New Waterford, Nova Scotia, joined the band; Freddy White regularly dazzled friends with his hobby banjo and guitar playing, and was a natural addition to the band. His large repertoire included "Nancy Whisky," "Finnegan's Wake," "Leaving Tipperary," and "My Old Man."

In 1966, a Toronto school caretaker, Mike Feeney (13 years an émigré from Galway City, in Ireland), added his singing and emceeing skills to the group. He contributed versions of "The Wild Colonial Boy," "Whisky in a Jar," and "Father Murphy," and closed every concert with a rousing rendition of "O Canada."

The next year, bass guitarist and singer Johnny Patterson (from Derry City, Ireland) added his powerful tenor voice to the group. He delivered such sentimental favourites as "I'll Take You Home Again Kathleen" and "My Wild Irish Rose."

Also that year, Bob Lewis, who'd known Freddy White in Cape Breton, joined as a singer-guitarist.

The next hurdle was getting the band some attention.

"We ran our own dances," O'Toole recalled, "here in Brampton at the Junior Farmers' Building and at the Parkside Tavern in Toronto. We'd open the windows, so people on the street could hear us and maybe come in. And we wore ridiculous things like green and gold boots."

By 1967, Canada's centennial year, the Carlton Showband was beginning to make an impact as a national musical ensemble. By that time, they had recorded a debut, self-titled album, and Quality Records had released two singles, "The Merry Ploughboy" and "Up Went Nelson."

It was the band's second album, *We're Off to Dublin in the Green*, that, in Freddy White's words, "got us in on the ground floor." That's when the group caught the attention of CTV and was signed to be the house band on a weekly, Irish music TV show, *The Pig 'n' Whistle*. The show lasted more than a decade and at its peak was second in ratings only to CBC-TV's *Hockey Night in Canada*.

In 1975, the CSB won the Juno as Country Group of the Year.

The group's schedule was hectic – recording four shows two days a month for seven months and then hitting the road in their $28,000 custom-built touring bus. With its growing repertoire of traditional, country and western, and even rock tunes – all done with an Irish twist – the band played across Canada at theatres, fairgrounds, universities, school auditoriums, nightclubs, and public halls. It also built a wider following by staging less visible concerts at hospitals, senior centres, and even prisons; the CSB performed rain or shine.

"During a trip to play for the Salmonier Prison Farm," wrote a member of the St. John's, Newfoundland Jaycees, "we managed to run into the worst storm of the season. ... A few people remarked that the band looked a little tired that night, so I guess pushing cars out of snowdrifts doesn't agree with them."

The Carlton Showband's trademark was not only music, but also a "paddy's love of mixing good times with jovial companions and a life on the road filled with practical jokes." Consequently, there were band members who found themselves locked out of hotel rooms with nary a stitch on, or tossed into a pool fully clothed. On one occasion, a band member stepped into a hotel swimming pool and watched the water turn a murky blue – his bathing trunks had been pre-dyed with blue-black ink.

"We're a band that's known for having fun," said Chris O'Toole, "and playing happy music."

Wilf Carter

b. Port Hilford, Nova Scotia, December 18, 1904; d. 1996

At Stampede time each summer in Calgary, everybody becomes a cowboy – dressing, talking, and even singing like one. Many emulate Wilf Carter, the country music singer who was always seen in his Stetson, string tie, and boots, often as the quintessential marshal for the Stampede parade. Truth is, Wilf Carter – Canada's first cowboy star, nicknamed Montana Slim – did not begin his singing career in the West, least of all in a saddle.

Born the son of a Baptist minister on the Atlantic coast of Nova Scotia, Wilf worked first as a boy lumberjack. At age 10, he attended a Chautauqua performance of *Uncle Tom's Cabin* and was inspired by a Swiss singer known as "The Yodelling Fool." Wilf developed his own style – a unique three-in-one or echo yodel. It wasn't until the mid-1920s that Carter migrated to Alberta to work as a cowboy.

First in bunkhouses, in work camps, and at local dances, Carter tested his yodelling style and built his repertoire of country music tunes. CFCN Radio broadcast his radio debut in 1930, when he appeared on the Friday night hoedown show, *The Old Timers*. Next, the Canadian Pacific Railway hired him to sing on trail rides into the Rocky Mountains and then invited him to perform on the maiden voyage of the SS *Empress of Britain* in 1933. En route to the ship's embarkation, Carter stopped at a tiny studio in Montreal to record **My Swiss Moonlight Lullaby** (which featured his yodelling) and **The Capture**

of Albert Johnson (his song about the mad trapper). By the time he returned from the voyage, the tunes had been pressed onto a 78-rpm disc and released by RCA Victor, and were well on their way to becoming the first hit record by a Canadian country music performer.

While on another trail ride, Carter was introduced to New York executives of CBS radio; they listened to his songs and yodelling style and offered him a contract to broadcast *The Wilf Carter Show*, so in 1935 he moved to New York to begin the broadcasts. There, in preparation for a program, Carter recited lyrics of his song **A Cowboy's High-Toned Dance** to a secretary. As she typed, she asked: "What name do I put on it?"

"Anyone'll do," replied Carter.

The woman thought a moment and typed: Montana Slim. The name stuck and that's how Wilf Carter is still known to millions of Americans. His straightforward singing voice, echo yodel, and simple guitar playing were his trademarks.

By 1940, Carter had returned to Canada, bought a ranch near Calgary, and appeared on CBC Radio for the first time (he still performed regularly on both CBS and NBC radio networks in the United States). That same year, an automobile accident left Carter with a severe back injury; though he continued to record, he didn't tour again until 1949. Carter wrote several hundred country songs on albums with such titles as **Cowboy Songs, Have a Nice Day,** and **Living Legend,** but he also recorded as many Maritimes folk tunes including "The Fate of the Old Strawberry Roan," which earned him the moniker "bluenose cowboy."

On tour again in the 1950s, he performed with his daughters Sheila and Carol in *The Family Show with the Folks You Know* across the United States and Canada. During one week at the CNE in Toronto, the show attracted 70,000 fans. His tours also introduced audiences to other country performers such as The Rhythm Pals and Orval Prophet. Calgary pianist David Steckenreiter, who played with Carter beginning in the 1970s, recalled a woman approaching Carter with a souvenir photo he'd autographed 40 years before; she wanted him to sign it again.

Wilf Carter was inducted into the Songwriters Hall of Fame in Nashville in 1972; in 1981 the Martin Guitar company named him Entertainer of the Year. For the years he had devoted to promotion of and performance at the Stampede, the directors presented Carter a trophy inscribed "Balladeer of the Golden West."

"They can give you all the awards in the world," Carter once said about his popularity. "It's the people. They've given me what I have today."

After Wilf Carter's death in December 1996, singer-songwriter Ian Tyson wrote in his tribute: "Wilf Carter was quite literally the sound of the west … the sound against which all others were measured."

Courtesy Canapress

Robert Charlebois is invested to the Order of Canada by Governor General Romeo LeBlanc in 1999

Robert Charlebois *b. Montreal, Quebec, June 25, 1945*

At a time when much of Canada was focused on the interminable "two solitudes" debate, most Quebec performing artists proudly proclaimed their commitment to separatism, especially in their music. Parti Québécois leader Jacques Parizeau once quipped that the Quiet Revolution was brought about by "three or four ministers, 20 civil servants, and 50 *chansonniers.*"

Prominent among them was *chansonnier* Robert Charlebois, once described by the *Globe and Mail*'s Blaik Kirby as "the frizzy-haired, pug-nosed darling of Quebec."

Writing about Charlebois' 1974 CBC-TV special titled *Outerplaces*, Kirby noted: "Charlebois sings about half the show's songs in English, the rest in French, but even if he were speaking Swahili he would be fun to watch. He is stunningly imaginative, sensitive, playful and full of fun. His show is first class, and surely is internationally saleable – even if the piqued CBC French network won't touch it."

As a youngster, he studied piano for six years, then attended the National Theatre School in Montreal (1962–65) to study acting. In 1965, CBC-TV's *Jeunesse oblige* named him discovery of the year in the *chansonnier* category and his first LP, on the Select label, received a special prize at the 1969 Festival du disque.

Soon he was putting to good use both his musical and his dramatic skills, working in revues and on television, and making records. In 1968, Charlebois represented Quebec at the fifth international Festival of French Song, at Spa, Belgium, winning the grand prize with "Lindberg," a brash, electrifying performance that became very popular and won him the Prix Felix-Leclerc in the Festival du disque.

But the restless Charlebois kept tripping over his need to reinvent himself. His albums were selling across the entire French-speaking world, but he couldn't crack the anglophone North American market. The solution was simple: in 1972, he decided to record in English. "The super-frog sells out," he said wryly in an interview. His new album would be called *Superfrog*.

He also said: "I'm a different writer in English. I'm a swooner – they came before crooners."

His 1972 concert at Toronto's Massey Hall was a considerable success. He made a point of switching from French to English in both his songs and his introductions. He also used a fair bit of *Joual*, a mixture of English and French slang. By now, he was Quebec's biggest international star, especially in France, where his use of *Joual* was first scorned, then became the "in" thing.

He worked pretty steadily during the 1970s, in festivals, in films, even in pops concerts with the Montreal Symphony Orchestra. Even when his popularity began to wane in Quebec it continued to grow in France, where he toured regularly during the 1980s.

"Everywhere I'm seen as being different – even in France itself, where I'm sort of an oddity," he said. "But everyone can still understand what I'm singing."

A year or so later, he told another interviewer: "I'm no French separatist; I'm an invader. I've decided to invade the whole English-speaking world disguised as a non-language exotic."

In 1974, he startled his fans with an announcement that he was going to retire. "I don't want to become an old singer," he explained. "I'll be 30 in a month and a half and you can't trust anyone over 30." (But that remark was merely mocking the old teenage cult cliché.)

Though he was of the rock era, his songs were not limited to it. Some of them have been notable for gentle feelings, not necessarily limited to love affairs. He became one of the few Quebec stars whose name was known in English Canada and who, in his heyday, shared stages with James Brown and Jimi Hendrix.

Like so many musicians of the rock era, he fell prey to both drugs and alcohol. But by the mid-1970s he knew he had to get away from them. "I cut down on drugs and alcohol too," he told an interviewer. "Alcohol is bad for your liver, and a singer sings with his liver more than with his heart or soul. ... Being an alcoholic is fun when you're 25. It's not fun when you're getting old and you start shaking."

In the early 1980s, he launched another comeback, spurred by the interest his own children showed in his old rock records. "The flash to perform came back from watching them dance," he said. "I should be doing more of this, too."

David Clayton-Thomas

b. Surrey, England, September 13, 1941

Music Ave Inc

Whoever said the greatest art results from tension, suffering, and living on the edge, may well have known Canadian singer, songwriter, musician, and Blood Sweat and Tears bandleader David Clayton-Thomas. On stage and off, the British-born wartime émigré to Canada, one-time prison inmate, and dogged performer has rarely seen things in show business come easily. Clayton-Thomas has battled demons, in the business and inside himself, to survive and succeed.

"I always believed in myself," says Clayton-Thomas, "the music I was writing and the bands I had," despite the number of wrong turns he experienced in life.

Born David Thomsett, the son of an English entertainer mother and a Canadian soldier en route to fight in North Africa and Sicily during the Second World War, the boy and his mother moved in with relatives north of Toronto in the 1940s. As a teenager, however, he ran away, began sleeping in parked cars, stealing food, and hotwiring cars. That landed him in a Guelph, Ontario, reformatory at age 14. Next came a labour camp, after that maximum-security prison. There seemed no road back, except that he found the inspiration to learn music. In prison, he planed down a cribbage board to make it look like a guitar, pencilled in frets and strings, learned music from a couple of Ojibwa inmates who got him a real guitar, and eventually David Thomsett put together a blues band of inmates.

Out of prison, in Toronto, as David Clayton-Thomas he worked at a manufacturing plant and as Sonny Thomas he played blues guitar at after-hours clubs, including the Bluenote where performers such as Doug Riley, Dianne Brooks, Domenic Troiano, Steve Kennedy, and Joey Hollingsworth debuted. About that time, Ronnie Hawkins, whose rock bands played the biggest clubs on Yonge Street, invited Thomas to sit in at Le Coq d'Or. Hawkins raved about Thomas as "a white boy [who] sings the blues like he comes from Mississippi. ... He's a white black man."

In the early 1960s Thomas was invited to join a band that included bass player Scott Richards (later a MCA record executive) and guitarist Fred Keeler (a friend of Robbie Robertson's). The group toured bars around Ontario as The Shays. Their first gig was nearly cancelled when the North Bay club owner found out Keeler was underage. They skirted the problem by hiding Keeler in a dressing room under the stage and piping his playing to an amplifier on stage.

The Shays toured for three years, had a hit single in 1964 called **Barbey Lee**, and released an album of rock 'n' roll standards on Roman Records called *Shays Au Go-Go* in 1965. The Shays were the first Canadian band to go on American network television, where Clayton-Thomas said "they surrounded us with dancers dressed up like hockey players." The Shays split up that year, but Clayton-Thomas persisted. His dream had always been to merge jazz and rock 'n' roll, so he assembled a jazz pianist (Tony Collacott) with a rock rhythm section (using two guitars) playing musical lines traditionally written for horns. The resulting band, the Bossmen, moved into Yorkville, where they played for two years and recorded a blues-based single, "Brainwashed," that spent 16 weeks at the number-one position in Canada in 1966.

Still, working in a band that never earned more than $25 a night two or three nights a week drove David Clayton-Thomas out of town and across the border. After playing backup guitar for John Lee Hooker at the Riverboat, he joined Hooker in New York. There he made connections with Charlie Musselwhite, the Paul Butterfield Blues Band, and Harvey Brooks (who later moved to L.A. to form Electric Flag), and in 1968, at the suggestion of Judy Collins, he auditioned for a sometimes fractious but avant garde jazz/rock aggregation known as Blood Sweat and Tears. With Al Kooper as lead vocalist, BS&T recorded its first album, *Child is Father to the Man*, but soon afterwards, Kooper left and the band called David Clayton-Thomas to take over as lead singer.

BS&T's subsequent self-titled album (1969) became the biggest seller in music history to date and in particular, cuts such as **Spinning Wheel, And When I Die**, and **You've Made Me So Very Happy** – all written by Clayton-Thomas – became million-selling singles within the year. The album also won a Grammy. More hits followed on each of the next three albums. The band toured widely in North America and Europe, including a US$40,000 eleven-concert tour through Yugoslavia, Romania, and Poland.

"The tour made us aware how repressive conditions are in Eastern Europe," Clayton-Thomas said. Then he remembered a Romanian manifesto that was issued to the band prior to the sellout concerts: "More jazz – less rhythm. Fewer body gestures. No removal of clothes. No technicians with long hair. If the audience should jump up, BS&T should stop playing and leave the stage. No encores and no throwing of instruments."

While *Down Beat* magazine reviewer Chris Albertson criticized the newly hatched band's "becoming a part of the U.S. [Nixon] administration's propaganda machine [in this] State Department tour of Eastern Europe," he still raved that "the embryo has grown into an imposing bird of dazzling plumage."

Ironically, the internal politics that had plagued BS&T from its beginnings reemerged to drive the band apart. The pace of performing (325 dates a year), while a boon to those making their living solely from concerts, was debilitating to others (especially Clayton-Thomas, who made supplementary income from songwriting). The impact of other abuses on the road took their toll on Clayton-Thomas too, but the band's infighting came to a head at the end of 1971; Clayton-Thomas made his last appearance with BS&T (for the moment) at the Anaheim Convention Centre on New Year's Eve.

Legal problems over recording labels hampered Clayton-Thomas in his pursuit of a solo career; nevertheless, he completed three albums on his own – *Magnificent Sanctuary Band* and *Tequila Sunrise* for Columbia (in 1972) and *David Clayton-Thomas* (in 1973) for RCA. In 1974, he rejoined BS&T and co-directed the band with Bobby Colomby, but then in 1976 assumed sole direction of BS&T; albums during that period included *New City, More Than Ever*, and *Brand New Day*. But the band dissolved again, leaving Clayton-Thomas to explore reggae, film score writing, club work, and commercials. Then in 1978, he re-formed the band in Toronto with local musicians for a cross-Canada tour and an LP in 1979 entitled *Nuclear Blues*.

For the next decade, David Clayton-Thomas slipped out of sight. Tough financial times and a problematic home life preoccupied him. But by the early 1990s, he was back with a CD, *Blue Plate Special*, that featured all his musical strengths – a reworking of his BS&T hit **Lucretia MacEvil**, a tribute to blues great Albert King, and numbers by Ray Charles, Willie Dixon, Freddie King, and others.

In 1996, David Clayton-Thomas was inducted into the Canadian Music Hall of Fame. There to introduce him was Ronnie Hawkins, who had once criticized BS&T as "smart-ass, big-city music," while reminding David Clayton-Thomas, "You're a blues singer, son. … Sing the blues."

Tom Cochrane and Red Rider

Tom Cochrane (b. Lynn Lake, Manitoba, May 14, 1953) vocals, guitar; Rob Baker drums; Peter Boynton vocals, keyboards; Ken Greer vocals, guitar; Jeff Jones bass

The enduring maxim "Write what you know" has guided scores of artists to compose some of the most successful tunes in Canadian music history. But few artists have taken that guiding principle to heart as regularly as singer-songwriter Tom Cochrane. He writes nearly everything on the basis of experience.

"I've worked at a lot of different jobs," Cochrane once told an Australian interviewer. "I drove a cab. I worked as a clerk. I worked packing meat. Then, when I moved to L.A. I was delivering phone books and washing dishes to make a living. ... Quite a few times, I've gone back to those original experiences ... for my songs."

It is no wonder that Tom Cochrane's signature song, **Life Is a Highway** (released in 1991), connected with so many people, shot up the international charts so quickly, helped sell two million copies of his album *Mad Mad World*, began a continuous run of Juno awards, and led to two world performance tours in the early 1990s.

Though he was born the son of a bush pilot in northern Manitoba, early in Tom Cochrane's life the family moved to Etobicoke, a west-end suburb of Toronto. At age 11, he bought his first guitar, and in the early 1970s divided his attention between studying music and journalism. Influenced by such Yorkville folk singers of the day as Bruce Cockburn and Murray McLauchlan, Cochrane performed in coffeehouses himself and in 1973 recorded a single, **You're Driving Me Crazy**, and then an album, *Hang On to Your Resistance*.

A move to Los Angeles opened a few doors, including a job writing the theme for Xaviera (the Happy Hooker) Hollander's movie *My Pleasure Is My Business*. Ironically, the use of the Mickey Mouse Club song on the movie soundtrack during an orgy scene generated more publicity and excitement than Cochrane's music, but the gig did pay some bills.

Back in Toronto in the late 1970s, Cochrane met a trio of musicians known as Red Rider – drummer Rob Baker, singer/keyboard player Peter Boynton, and singer/guitarist Ken Greer – and joined them. In 1978, the group added bass player Jeff Jones, and within two years Capitol had released the five-man band's debut album *Don't Fight It*, which included the single **White Hot**; it sold more than 50,000 copies in Canada. Red Rider generated three more albums in the early 1980s, but their 1986 album release, *Tom Cochrane & Red Rider*, indicated Cochrane's leadership role and its hit single, **Boy Inside the Man**, signified his emergence as lead songwriter in the band.

In **Boy Inside the Man**, Cochrane wrote about changes an individual experiences in life, how someone can be "a wild-eyed romantic" one moment and "a bastard trying to survive" the next. On stage Cochrane gave the tune a full range of interpretations – from a short acoustic poem to a 10-minute symphony. However, the song took on a whole new meaning the night Cochrane met an arena custodian, who told him **Boy Inside the Man** was his son's favourite song.

"I asked if [the son] was coming to the show that night," explained Cochrane. "He told me his son had died in a car accident. ... He said his son had a scholarship in the States and he was playing hockey with a bunch of his friends and he got hit by a truck. ... I knew that story had to be a song. ... I wrote it in 15 minutes." The song, titled **Big League**, was released in 1988.

73

Red Rider's 1989 recording *Symphony Sessions*, a collaboration with the Edmonton Symphony Orchestra, turned out to be the band's last. Soon afterwards, Cochrane undertook some charity work with World Vision and travelled to East Africa, where, despite the poverty and starvation, "I discovered something I wasn't prepared for – the resilience of the people, their ability to find joy in simple things and live for the moment. That was a big inspiration for me."

Cochrane's 1991 release **Life Is a Highway**, which author Nicholas Jennings describes as an "anthemic song, which perfectly captured a feeling of joyful abandon," roared up the charts that fall and into *Billboard*'s Top 10 the following summer. The song was even featured in an episode of Fox TV's *Baywatch* in the 1992 season. What's more, the song and the album *Mad Mad World* rejuvenated Cochrane's career, and led to more international touring and industry accolades.

In fact, Cochrane's 1992 harvest of four Juno awards – including Best Male Vocalist, Best Album, Best Songwriter, and Best Single – upstaged Bryan Adams' international smash hit "(Everything I Do) I Do It for You." That prompted show host Rick Moranis to quip: "Ian Tyson, would you please move your horse, so Tom Cochrane can get his U-Haul out of here."

Even Cochrane admitted his instant celebrity was "like living in a hurricane" as he began 30 months of nonstop touring, more writing, recording, and record-selling. (*Mad Mad World* eventually sold more than a million copies in Canada and more than two million around the world.) Though success took its toll on his physical and emotional health, nearly ruining his marriage, this too fuelled his creativity.

His 1995 album *Ragged Ass Road* explored long-term love, failed relationships, the wisdom of learning from mistakes, and life reaffirmation. In 1997, while Cochrane was touring to promote his *X-Ray Sierra* album, his private Cessna crashed at a small airport outside Montreal. He emerged uninjured but shaken; the crash, like so many other events in his life, vindicated his view of life and provided yet another experience for him to write about.

Bruce Cockburn   *b. Ottawa, Ontario, May 27, 1945*

Though many of his musical roots have developed in Canada and in the folk music tradition, Bruce Cockburn's melodies and lyrics have no nationality and his musical style defies categorization. He has always experimented. He has always looked for experiences beyond Canada. But he has always come home to share them.

Kevin Kelly

"It's true, I am a Canadian," Cockburn told an interviewer while seated under a tree at the Mariposa Folk Festival in 1971. "But in a sense it's more by default. ... I'm not really into nationalism. I guess I think of myself as a person of the world."

Born in Ottawa, Cockburn spent his earliest days on a farm outside Pembroke, Ontario. While still a teenager, Cockburn travelled to Europe and worked as a street singer in Paris. From 1964 to 1966 he studied theory, composition, and arranging at Boston's Berklee College of Music, where "we were constantly hearing every kind of music – mainly jazz – coming out of windows, even four and five blocks away from the school. There was a sort of down-your-nose attitude toward rock and roll and they didn't know anything about folk music at all."

Cockburn explored rock and folk when he returned to Ottawa – he played organ in a rock band called The Children, and guitar with The Esquires and later a psychedelic group called Flying Circus. Then he took to solo performing – singing and playing acoustic guitar – at coffeehouses and the Mariposa Folk Festival in 1967; although for a CBC-TV series (1968–69) he joined Colleen Peterson and David Wiffen in their folk-rock band Three's a Crowd.

While on his own, Cockburn encountered Gene Martynec, a former member of the Toronto-based band Kensington Market. It was managed by Bernie Finkelstein, who wanted to launch a record label. Cockburn and Finkelstein agreed on a contract and Cockburn became the first artist signed to Finkelstein's True North label, with Martynec as the producer. A single, **Musical Friends**, from his self-titled first album got Top 40 airplay and the team returned to the studio for a second album, *High Winds White Sky*, in 1970. That led to Cockburn's writing the score for Don Shebib's film *Goin' Down the Road* the same year. Cockburn undertook a first national tour and won Junos as folk singer of the year for 1970, 1971, and 1972.

Bryan Johnson, writing in the *Globe and Mail*, called Cockburn "one of the few folk guitarists with both a good-time bounce and amazing virtuosity."

During the 1970s, Bruce Cockburn's life and music entered what one reviewer called his "Christian dialogue" period. With his song **All The Diamonds**, on his *Salt, Sun and Time* album, Cockburn documented his conversion. He read the Bible, C. S. Lewis, Charles Williams, and Thomas Merton, and while they didn't motivate him to write gospel or evangelical songs, their images inspired spiritual poetry that he set to music.

Cockburn's experimentation with music returned to centre stage in 1979, when he recorded and released *Dancing in the Dragon's Jaws*. In this, his 10th album, Cockburn was being influenced by reggae, jazz, and African pop, while also discovering world politics. It went platinum in Canada and featured his only American Top 40 hit, **Wondering Where the Lions Are**. It was the "peak" of what Cockburn had to say about the spiritual side of things.

His songwriting in the next decade reflected a greater political awareness and a growing anger over exploitation, environmental destruction, and oppression. Songs on his *Trouble With Normal*, *Stealing Fire*, and *World of Wonders* albums were musical documentaries of the predicament of ordinary people in, for example, Africa and Central America. His 1984 song **If I Had a Rocket Launcher** included video that showed conditions in Central America and was regularly played on MTV.

"The songs I wrote in the Eighties," said Cockburn in an interview for *Third Way* magazine, "touched on issues because they had touched me personally, not because I had an axe to grind or an ideology. The songs in support of the aspirations of the Nicaraguan people, for example, were written because I was there and the situation touched me in a very personal way."

There were eight albums in the 1980s and seven more in the 1990s, culminating in his 25th album release in 1999 – *Breakfast in New Orleans, Dinner in Timbuktu*. While it contained one political piece – a humorous swipe at government corruption entitled **Let the Bad Air Out** – *Breakfast* brought Cockburn full circle, back to songs about friendship, love, sex, and destiny. It even contained a version of the Fats Domino classic "Blueberry Hill," as well as two instrumentals that showcased Cockburn's perennial guitar-playing talent.

Bruce Cockburn insists his career is not about record sales or awards. Still, the commercial successes and honours have been plentiful: 20 gold and platinum albums, 11 Juno Awards, SOCAN's prestigious William Harold Moon Award, the Order of Canada (1983), a Governor General's Performing Arts Award, and an honorary Doctor of Music from Boston's Berklee College of Music, where he had studied jazz composition in the 1960s. In 2000, while on a world tour doing benefit concerts for the Campaign to Ban Land Mines, Cockburn was informed he would be inducted into the Canadian Music Hall of Fame.

He responded by suggesting the award might have come "too soon. I think because I'm not dead yet," he said with a laugh. "It seems that goes with legendary status – with people who have been around long enough to become legends – and I sort of feel like I might be a little too active to qualify."

In 1987, *Musician Magazine* wrote: "All through his career, Bruce Cockburn has been plagued by a bad case of the hyphens. You know – folk-rock, folk-inspirational and now agit-rock-Latin-Afropop, or something to that effect. Such is the fate of anyone who confounds pop marketing categories as freely as Bruce Cockburn."

Leonard Cohen

b. Montreal, September 21, 1934

Leonard Cohen was a relative late bloomer in the music industry. First a poet and novelist, then a songwriter, Cohen didn't put his words to music professionally until 1966. In contrast, many of his contemporaries – Joni Mitchell, Gordon Lightfoot, Judy Collins, and even Bob Dylan (all still in their twenties at that time) – had learned to play guitar in childhood and begun making melodies of their innermost thoughts as teenagers. In the 1960s, the *Globe and Mail* quoted Cohen as saying "Everytime I pick up a pen to write something, I don't know if it's going to be a poem, a song, or a novel."

Leonard Cohen, photographed in 1995

Music, mostly country and western, did influence Cohen's early life. As a 15-year-old he began playing guitar, and a few years later, while studying English literature at McGill University, he played in a C&W band called The Buckskin Cowboys. His writing attracted interest first, however, with the publication of three collected works of poetry and two novels between 1956 and 1966. Ultimately, it was jazz that provided the first musical accompaniment to his writing in the 1960s when he gave his first poetry reading as jazz musicians played backdrop at a Montreal nightclub.

It was at the YMCA in New York in March of 1966 when, first he sang his poems **Stranger** and **Suzanne** (a poem/song about Suzanne Verdal, a dancer/model he'd seen on a nightclub dance floor in the early 1960s). Overnight, Cohen the songwriter got a lot of attention. In Toronto, the folk group Stormy Clovers performed his songs in coffeehouses and on the soundtrack of the NFB film *Angel*. Judy Collins included **Suzanne** on her 1966 album IN MY LIFE, and the next year, during a concert in Central Park, introduced Cohen on stage.

Columbia soon signed Cohen and he recorded his first LPs *Songs of Leonard Cohen* (1967), *Songs From a Room* (1968), *Songs of Love and Hate* (1971), and *Live Songs* (1970–72). Most were recorded in Nashville with producer Bob Johnston (who also produced Dylan and Johnny Cash). Music reviewers of the time called his poetically motivated material brilliant and universal. Rock critic Mike Jahn wrote in *The New York Times* that "Cohen appealed to the disaffected, professionally depressed and self-consciously tormented. ... Even his tender lyrics have an air of desperation."

Because of, or despite, that kind of assessment, Cohen struck a chord with many. His songs **So Long Marianne**, **Bird on a Wire**, **Dress Rehearsal Rag**, and **Sisters of Mercy** became required listening for fans, critics, and contemporaries. Artists as varied as Judy Collins and Joe Cocker, Jennifer Warnes and the Neville Brothers recorded Cohen songs. Moreover, media as varied as motion pictures and live theatre have presented Cohen material. In 1970, Harry Freedman wrote a score to Brian Macdonald's ballet, *The Shining People of Leonard Cohen*, based on Cohen verse, and in 1973 the Shaw Festival featured Cohen songs, poetry, letters, and unpublished snippets of manuscript in Gene Lesser's musical *Sisters of Mercy*.

As the 1970s wore on, Leonard Cohen's popularity faded. Fans turned away as his lyrics grew darker and more obsessive. Critics focused on Cohen's limitations. In 1977 he connected with Phil Spector (who produced the Beatles, the Righteous Brothers, and the Ramones in the studio). The collaboration generated Cohen's seventh album *Death of a Lady's Man*, described by poet and critic Judith Fitzgerald as "manic-depressive folk/doo-wop." Ken Waxman, looking at Cohen's early work, commented in a 1978 *Saturday Night* piece that "too often airborne imagery was shackled to a pedestrian tune, while Cohen compounded the problem by singing in an off-hand, droning monotone." Cohen even admitted to *Melody Maker* he was "doing it just for the money."

Cohen's 1979 album **Recent Songs** marked a comeback. He engaged a jazz-rock band, The Passengers, to provide backup on stage for a series of international concert stops, entitled the Field Commander Cohen Tour. Cohen was also fortunate that documentarian and friend Harry Rasky decided to capture the tour on film and (later, in 2001) as a book – *The Song of Leonard Cohen: Portrait of a Poet, a Friendship and a Film*. Following Cohen through six European centres, Rasky wrote of his friend's struggle to reconnect with his fans: "The crowd, the mass, the fans cheered for elegance, splendour ... and even more they cheered for blood," Rasky wrote. "Leonard's tour took him mostly to sports venues and occasionally majestified concert halls, a journey of exhaustion to the level of pain." Even if Cohen were never able to reinvent himself, new, younger listeners have always been drawn to his poetic artistry and romanticized gloom.

There were also peers who rejuvenated fan interest, not to mention record sales. In 1986, movie soundtrack diva Jennifer Warnes recorded the album *Famous Blue Raincoat: The Songs of Leonard Cohen*, which made much of Cohen's brooding material accessible; it included Warnes' treatment of many Cohen standards, as well as some memorable guitar work from Stevie Ray Vaughan on **First We Take Manhattan** and Cohen himself sitting in on **Joan of Arc**. Two tribute albums – 1991's *I'm Your Fan* and 1995's *Tower of Song* (with Cohen tunes covered by R.E.M., Elton John, Sting, and Billy Joel, among others) – revealed his influences on a new generation of songwriters. These generated further interest in Cohen's own albums **I'm Your Man** (1988) and **The Future** (1992). In 1988, CBS Records presented Cohen with an award to commemorate the sale of more than five million records outside the U.S. market.

Touring ended in 1993, when Cohen disappeared to a retreat at the Mt. Baldy Zen Center in California. But his contact with adoring fans did not.

Music videos and airplay of Cohen's songs on MuchMusic and Musique-Plus kept up his profile. Then, prompted by a ECW Press book of essays (edited by Cohen scholar Stephen Scobie) about Cohen, academics who also happened to be fans gathered for a Leonard Cohen conference at McGill University in May of 2001. Included among the essays was a testimonial by Canada's Governor General. "Everything Leonard Cohen says is a sleek embodiment of meaning coming down a corridor at you from the gilded rooms of a glittering palace you only dream about," Adrienne Clarkson wrote.

According to another Cohen scholar, UBC English professor Ira Nadel, in 1995 Leonard Cohen wondered about using the Internet instead of public appearances. He discovered a Web site created by Finnish accountant and computer wizard Jarkko Arjatsalo. Cohen gave his stamp of approval and the site became his link to what Nadel called the world's "Cohenists." He began posting new and unpublished poems, unrecorded song lyrics, original paintings, and sketches. He even posted one of the first manuscript versions of **Suzanne**.

"How Cohenesque," wrote Nadel in *Saturday Night*. "He is simultaneously here and not here, electronically available to his fans, but also private and elusive, travelling, writing and recording."

In 1991, at the 20th Annual Juno Awards ceremony, in response to his induction into the Hall of Fame, Leonard Cohen lived up to his original billing as poet by reciting the lyrics to **Tower of Song**.

Holly Cole
b. Halifax, Nova Scotia, November 25, 1963

In any other profession, the description "unpredictable" would be a recipe for disaster. Even in the entertainment business, not knowing where an artist is going can hurt a career, not boost it. For singer Holly Cole, however, keeping music promoters, reviewers, and fans slightly off balance has made the singer and her music that much more alluring.

"I look at the essence of a song," Cole told musicologist Rob Bowman. "If it's a great lyric I often love to slow it down, explore it, dissect it and deconstruct it. I love to … look at [it] in an entirely different way."

"A different way" sums up a lot of who Holly Cole is. Born into a musical family (both parents being concert pianists), she was a tomboy, more interested

Andrew MacNaughtan

in horses than music. As a teenager, she listened to the Grateful Dead and Frank Zappa and got thrown out of high school music for wearing a floppy hat in class. At 16, she visited her brother Allen, who was in Boston at the Berklee College of Music. Through him, she listened to jazz – singers such as Billie Holiday, Anita O'Day, Sarah Vaughan, and Betty Carter – and "dove into the music."

Part of that process was a two-year stint enrolled in a jazz vocal course at Toronto's Humber College. In the 1980s, the Queen Street music scene began hearing from Holly Cole, first as half of a drum-voice duo, then as a busker doing offbeat interpretations of Christmas carols and eventually singing backup for the Parachute Club, art songs at the Music Gallery, and late-night Brecht-Weill cabaret with her brother Allen Cole.

By 1985, pianist Aaron Davis had contacted Cole. They in turn hired bass player David Piltch, and the Holly Cole Trio resulted. Within a year, they had attracted a following at Toronto clubs such as the BamBoo, the Rivoli, Clinton's, and the Stage Door Café, while reviewers tried to pigeonhole her as "down-home siren," "sizzling chanteuse," "free spirit," or "jazz-pop diva."

Cole often appeared on stage in black, form-fitting gowns, elbow-length evening gloves, black hose, and spike heels. Describing her treatment of Gershwin's "The Man I Love," feature writer Ian Pearson wrote: "Cole is shy and dreamy at first, but then launches a fortissimo attack on the song, leaving no doubt that the man she loves will come along." C. Lee Crawford wrote that her "voice is akin to melt-in-your-mouth chocolate (and) looks deeper into the interpretation of a lyric." Reviewer Wilder Penfield III quoted Cole as saying, "Someone asked me, 'What's your favourite colour?' and I said, 'Dark.'"

It took three years of slogging to land a recording contract, but eventually her manager and Alert Music co-owner, Tom Berry, got the Holly Cole Trio into a studio. In 1989 they released a four-song CD called *Christmas Blues* and a year later their first full-length recording, *Girl Talk*, an album Cole described as "a feminist statement … with tongue-in-cheek" and which became the second-best-selling jazz record ever released in Canada. The trio's third album, *Blame It on My Youth*, demonstrated Cole's impact beyond Canada; in Japan (where CDs cost $60 each) initial sales were 500 copies a day, eventually hitting 200,000 copies worldwide. Her 1993 album *Don't Smoke in Bed* produced the band's first crossover hit, "I Can See Clearly Now."

The interplay among the three band members made the Holly Cole Trio an extremely saleable concert attraction – whether doing Christmas appearances in Toronto or regular stops in Japan. Bassist Piltch and pianist Davis, while equal partners in arranging the music and equally at ease with improvisation, never seemed to miss a single Holly Cole nuance on stage. Likewise, Cole never missed an opportunity to play with her audience or her two bandmates.

"Holly sometimes tries to trick me into playing a note just to see if she can," Piltch told *The Financial Post*. "She's only really caught me once. She thought

I was detecting her timing through her breathing, so she started without taking a breath and it worked."

Cole's 1995 album *Temptation* caught many off guard. She took 16 tunes by songwriting iconoclast Tom Waits. The album offered all the edge of a Waits lyric along with the moodiness of its melody and it established Cole as a strong musical interpreter onstage and in-studio. In a departure of a different kind, Cole's album *Dark Dear Heart* (produced by Larry Klein) marked her shift into popular music, as she presented adaptations of songs by Joni Mitchell, Mary Margaret O'Hara, and the Beatles.

"Cole has made the transition to pop," the *Globe and Mail* said, "without losing any of her trademark jazzy smokiness."

If doing a cover version of Mitchell's song "The River" didn't unnerve her, apparently nothing could. In the 1990s, she continued to tour (singing in French in Quebec, Spanish in Spain, and Japanese in Japan). She joined a tribute to Prince, doing "Purple Rain" and "The Question of You"; and she sang "Losing My Mind" in a recorded tribute to American composer and lyricist Stephen Sondheim. For complete changes of pace, she performed onstage with the Desrosiers' Dance Theatre and she became the voice of Venus in a Canadian cartoon, *The Adventures of Nilus the Sandman*. In 1999, she joined Sarah McLachlan's Lilith Fair tour.

In 2000, Holly Cole released a recording project that had been two years in the making. Her album *Romantically Helpless* offered a compendium of popular tunes, "representing a singer of vast gifts at the absolute pinnacle of her art," wrote Rob Bowman. The material encompassed works as diverse as Sinatra's "Come Fly with Me," Randy Newman's "Ghosts," and Paul Simon's "One Trick Pony."

"I don't think about my career in long-term goals," she told the *Toronto Star*. "I just think, 'Well, this is boring now and I want to change.'"

Like so many impulses in her career, every step marks a further step in Holly Cole's unmapped musical journey.

Stompin' Tom Connors

b. Saint John, N.B., February 9, 1936

If singing stars Wilf Carter and Hank Snow can be credited with putting country and western music on the musical map of Canada, it was Tom Connors

NAC/PA 207947

who put Canada on the musical map of country and western music. Consider the heart of the troubadour's song list. Not one pines for a Kentucky sweetheart. None celebrates Okies or even Billy the Kid. Nowhere is there reference to the Grand Ole Opry. Instead, Stompin' Tom Connors tunes celebrate a Sudbury Saturday night, pay tribute to Bud the Spud from P.E.I. and Big Joe Mufferaw from northern Ontario, and recognize institutions such as The Good Old Hockey Game and Canada Day. Stompin' Tom Connors, perhaps more than any other Canadian performer, is, on stage and off, staunchly nationalistic.

Born to an unwed teenager in New Brunswick, raised in an orphanage and a foster home in Prince Edward Island, Tom Connors spent his teen years on the run, and even on the high seas as an underage merchant seaman. Influenced by the careers of Hank Snow and Wilf Carter, he craved two things – to wander and to sing. At 14 he got his first guitar. At 15 he wrote his first song, **Reversing Falls Darling**. And for the next 13 years he indulged his Woody Guthrie fantasies and hitchhiked across Canada; he moved from job to job while writing songs and playing them, principally as an avocation.

Legend has it that in 1964 he arrived at the Maple Leaf Hotel in Timmins, Ontario, "a nickel short of a beer." Bartender Gaet Lepine offered to make up the difference if Connors sang for it. That command performance turned into more than a year's work singing at the hotel and weekly appearances on CKGB

Radio. In 1965, he recorded his first single, **Carolyne**, and began distributing it and other early recordings through the Revel label as he toured northern Ontario. Because he often performed in locations where amplification was limited, Connors began pounding the floor with his foot, both to establish the rhythm for his songs and to be heard over the din of the bar patrons. Audiences began referring to Connors as "Stompin' Tom."

In the fall of 1967 Connors wrote a song for his friend Bud Roberts from Prince Edward Island. Connors expected Roberts to record **Bud the Spud**, but when he didn't, Connors put it into his repertoire. Among the first audiences to hear the song was a crowd in Cobourg, Ontario.

"There must have been a lot of East-Coasters in the crowd," Connors later wrote, "because the whole house went wild." As he wrapped up his set, the audience screamed for "that potato song again." Coincidentally, Bud Roberts was there that night and none too pleased. He claimed to be saving **Bud the Spud** for his next album. Ultimately Connors recorded his composition before Roberts got around to it and it became his first national hit.

Stompin' Tom's recording career took off when he signed with Dominion Records in 1969. Over the next two years, he released six original albums, a compilation album, and a five-album set of traditional music. He left Dominion to help form Boot Records, who released his next 10 original albums. These albums are, in the words of *musicHound* writer Gary Pig Gold, "the Holy Grail of Canadian country. Rich in character studies as vivid as those of Hank Williams, but etched as always with Connors's fierce sense of Canadiana, the classic tone poems that fill these records – **Bud the Spud**, **Big Joe Mufferaw**, **Sudbury Saturday Night** and **The Hockey Song** – stand today as nothing less than national totems, part of the Canadian cultural lexicon, yet still perversely receive little if any radio play."

In 1971, the year the CanCon regulations for AM radio went into effect, Connors received his first Juno Award as Male Country Singer of the Year. It was the first of five straight wins in the category. In 1973 his album *To It and At It* won the Juno as top country album. The subject of two films, Connors also starred on CBC-TV's *Stompin Tom's Canada* in 1974–75. By 1977 he had written more than 500 songs, most based on actual events and people, others in honour of locales where he performed. By 1979 he had made 29 albums, four of which received gold-record sales awards from the Canadian Recording Industry Association: *Bud the Spud* (1969), *Stompin' Tom Connors Meets Big Joe Mufferaw* (1970), *My Stompin' Grounds* (1971), and *Live at the Horseshoe* (1971).

With the release of *Gumboot Cloggeroo*, however, Connors stunned everybody by returning his six Junos and announcing a year-long performance boycott. He condemned the Canadian music industry as one "that already reeks of unfairness" in dealing with its homegrown artists. He added that there's "nothing wrong with awards," but "in all good conscience," because of "the Americanization of the Canadian music industry," he could not remain part of the organization. "That's why I quit playing music altogether."

Connors never quit his dream, however, because in 1986 he reemerged by forming ACT Records, a label that would record and promote Canadian music. In 1988, he began touring and releasing records again, relaunching his career with a song paying tribute to his high-profile prodigy, k.d. lang. He kicked off the 1990s with a 70-date national tour and by signing with EMI Canada, which allowed for the complete rerelease of his entire catalogue.

In the spring of 2000, Stompin' Tom Connors arrived at Convocation Hall, at the University of Toronto, in his black cowboy hat, suit, and boots to receive an honorary doctor of laws degree; then-president Robert Prichard called him "a Canadian cultural icon … a great Canadian symbol." That fall, as he received the Performing Arts Award from Governor-General Adrienne Clarkson, she compared the country music icon's face and music to "a relief map of our country."

In her review of Part Two of his autobiography, *Stompin' Tom and the Connors Tone*, Judith Fitzgerald referred to the accolades and awards "in recognition of identifiably Canadian three-minute masterpieces [and] his uncompromisingly nationalistic public stand … which utterly delights his legion of fans."

Johnny Cowell   *b. Tillsonburg, Ontario, January 11, 1926*

Although he played his first trumpet solo at the age of six and later spent a couple of decades playing trumpet with the Toronto Symphony Orchestra, Johnny Cowell may be better remembered as a superior songwriter. By the late 1970s, some 150 of his 200 songs had been recorded by a remarkable variety of performing artists, from Vera Lynn to Al Hirt. His first hit, written in 1956, was **Walk Hand in Hand**, which was introduced by George Murray and subsequently recorded by the aforementioned Miss Lynn plus Denny Vaughan, Andy Williams, Tony Martin, and others.

Our Winter Love was recorded in orchestral arrangements by André Kostelanetz, Lawrence Welk, Bill Purcell, and Hugo Winterhalter. It was also a hit record for Anita Bryant.

Dick Clark featured Cowell's song **It's Just My Luck to Be Fifteen** on his show *American Bandstand* throughout 1957. Al Hirt recorded Cowell's **Strawberry Jam** and **His Girl**. **His Girl** was later recorded by the Guess Who and became a top hit for them.

Joyce Hahn had successful recordings of two other Cowell songs, **One Day Not So Long Ago** and **You've Got the Love**.

Another Cowell tune, **Stroll Along with the Blues**, was performed by an orchestra under Ted Heath on the soundtrack of the Peter Sellers movie *Two Way Stretch* from 1960. In 1963, Floyd Cramer recorded Cowell's **These Are the Young Years**.

By 1990, Cowell had made 10 albums and CDs of his songs and arrangements, for various record labels.

Back in 1969, Cowell composed **Roller Coaster**, commissioned by Seiji Ozawa, an encore piece performed by the Toronto Symphony, the New York Philharmonic, the Boston Symphony, and many other major orchestras in both Canada and the United States. In 1972, he was commissioned by the Canadian Broadcasting Corporation to compose **Anniversary Overture** for the Toronto Symphony's 50th anniversary.

Six years later, in 1978, Cowell premiered his own **Trumpet Concerto** with the Toronto Symphony at Ontario Place. The concerto was subsequently recorded on his CD *Carnival of Venice*.

Johnny Cowell came by his musical talent naturally. His father and three uncles were members of the Tillsonburg Town Band, with which Johnny played his first trumpet solo. Largely self-taught, Cowell did study briefly with Edward Smeale in Toronto when he joined the Toronto Symphony Band in 1941, at the age of 15.

After serving during the Second World War as a soloist with the Royal Canadian Navy band in Victoria, B.C., he studied composition with Oskar Morawetz and John Weinzweig. He also played first trumpet with the Victoria Symphony Orchestra from 1943 to 1945. In 1952, he joined the Toronto Symphony Orchestra.

In the mid-1970s, he resumed his solo work, appearing with the Toronto Symphony and other Canadian orchestras. A solo appearance with the Toronto Symphony in July 1991 was a special tribute concert to mark his retirement from that orchestra.

Over the years, he played trumpet with the dance bands of Stanley St. John and Art Hallman and with Jack Denton's Palais Royale Orchestra. He has also subbed for Doc Severinsen and sat in with Tex Beneke. Later, he played with the Spitfire Band and the Canadian Tribute to Glenn Miller.

But Cowell did not neglect his early background in classical music. He has arranged works for soloist and orchestra by such composers as Bach, Beethoven, Handel, and the 20th-century French composer Erik Satie.

By the early 1990s Cowell had received six BMI Canada (now known as

SOCAN, the Society of Composers, Authors and Music Publishers of Canada) Certificates of Honour for his most popular songs.

When he turned 65 in 1991, Cowell retired from the TSO, because that was the orchestra's policy. But within two weeks he was offered the Principal Trumpet chair with the Toronto Philharmonia and also became trumpet soloist with the Hannaford Street Band, alongside Toronto's best brass players.

In the spring of 2000, George Jonescu, the noted host of *Big Band Saturday Night* on Barrie's CHAY-FM and a regular contributor to the periodical *Big Band World*, paid handsome tribute to Cowell. "I do not know this quiet, unassuming genius," Jonescu wrote. "I don't know a great deal about this magnificent talent housed in a gentle man. I do know a bit about talent, and his is a major talent, and proudly a Canadian talent that must be heard and acknowledged."

The popular Barrie deejay further expressed his admiration of Cowell's "songs and melodies that covered my whole music awareness, pop to classic, all having the texture of a gentle, beautiful soul. I suppose I was hearing my life being played and sung. My emotion, which lingers yet, is the setting Johnny's music molded for my romantic and happy muse. Thank you, Mr. Cowell."

Crash Test Dummies

formed 1985 in Winnipeg: Brad Roberts (b. January 10, 1964) guitar, piano, vocals; Dan Roberts (b. May 22, 1967) bass; Mitch Dorge (b. September 15, 1960) drums; Ellen Reid (b. July 14, 1966) keyboards, accordion, vocals; Benjamin Darvill (b. January 4, 1967) mandolin, harmonica

There was probably no better name for a Winnipeg house band that originally had no designs on greatness than "Crash Test Dummies." They're a five-piece band that got into the mainstream of North American pop music entirely by accident ... and more than survived the impact.

The group began as a part-time venture for a group of University of Manitoba students, who came together to cover other people's songs at the Blue Note Café, a 50-seat after-hours club in Winnipeg in the mid-1980s. The principal driving force in the band was Brad Roberts (finishing his MA in English), who suggested to the others it might be fun to write a few songs and take the band on the road. The band laid down a demo tape and sent it to folk festival producers, including Richard Flohil, the artistic director of Mariposa.

"[They] sounded very fresh, different from anything else around at the time," Flohil told Nicholas Jennings of *Maclean's* magazine. "[Flohil] called

*Crash Test Dummies in 1996
(l. to r. Mitch Dorge, Ben Darvill,
Dan Roberts, Brad Roberts, Ellen
Reid*

me back," said Brad Roberts, "and said he couldn't book us that year, but suggested we show up for a record deal."

Following up on Flohil's suggestion, in 1989, the Crash Test Dummies played at Toronto's Albert's Hall, where no fewer than four major A&R label representatives caught the Dummies' act. Despite the fact that Roberts had begun studying composition (he even attended a Lyle Lovett workshop at the Winnipeg Folk Festival), the Dummies were still doing mostly cover material that included hits by Alice Cooper, TV theme songs, and traditional Irish tunes. Suddenly, offers started to come in and reality struck.

"I had only written five songs in my entire life," Roberts told Chris Dafoe of the *Globe and Mail*. "So I bluffed my way through it saying 'Oh, there's plenty more songs in the bag, just give us some money to record them.'"

The group signed with Arista in the United States and BMG Canada, who released the first album ***The Ghosts That Haunt Me*** (1989). The album presented a folk band with Celtic flavour, some country elements, an aggressive rhythm section, and the dynamism of Roberts' bottom-of-the-well voice. That unique vocal sound (what one critic called his "Bill-Medley-meets-Lee-Hazlewood-baritone") got greatest exposure on the album's emerging single, **Superman's Song**, the Dummies' tale of a failed superhero.

It got phenomenal radio airplay, just as much video play, won numerous industry awards, and became a number one hit in Canada. Carly Simon was so enamoured of the song that she contacted Roberts; she and the Dummies appeared together at the New York club Bottom Line in late 1991. *Rolling Stone* covered the gig, and told readers the Dummies were a Canadian band worth looking into. At the 1992 Junos, the Crash Test Dummies won Group of the Year Award.

The Dummies followed up their debut album success with **God Shuffled His Feet** (1993). It contained plenty of new elements, including sample sounds and synthesizers, but it too held a surprise in its quirky single **Mmm Mmm Mmm Mmm**, a thoughtful and humorous song about three young outcasts. What made the tune equally attractive was its construction: Roberts admitted his preference for writing melodies before lyrics; in the case of the **Mmm** song, he tried to fit his lyrics into a preconceived chorus, but couldn't. "A chorus is supposed to wrap things up," Roberts said. "I realized there wasn't much else to say, so I just left the lyric as Mmm Mmm Mmm Mmm to the melody. Funny thing is, it's probably the strongest chorus on the record."

The result was a hit single in the United States. The album was on its way to selling five million copies worldwide. It led to an American TV appearance on *Saturday Night Live* and three on *The Late Show with David Letterman*. There were also three Grammy Award nominations in 1995. Their song **The Ballad of Peter Pumpkinhead** was incorporated into the soundtrack of the movie *Dumb and Dumber*.

Back in Canada, despite some disparaging remarks Roberts made that "the Canadian music industry has to see its talent validated outside the country to feel comfortable in finally acknowledging it at home," the Dummies garnered three more Juno nominations.

Reviews for the Dummies' third and most offbeat album, *A Worm's Life* (1996), were mixed. Critics searched for the substance they had found in **Superman's Song** and **Mmm Mmm Mmm Mmm**. The album had a harder, noisier approach and featured songs that focused on such disparate subjects as household dangers mothers warn kids about, embalmed birds, road songs, writer's block, astronauts who throw up in their helmets, and a boy who (like Roberts) extracted his own teeth for fun.

"Their songs – quirky, literate and sometimes even existential – don't fit standard pop conventions," Nicholas Jennings wrote in *Maclean's*. "The hyperactive brain behind the Dummies clearly belongs to Roberts. ... *Rolling Stone* has dubbed him an 'egghead,' while *Billboard* ... dismissed him as an 'intellectual wanker.'"

The Dummies continued to push the envelope. They had sold in excess of six million records. In the spring of 1997, they negotiated an appearance (the first by any Canadian rock band) in Shanghai, China. Their video for **He Liked to Feel It** (about the teeth-extracting boy) drew demands for a re-edit from Hamburg to Hollywood. They opened for million-selling star Alanis

Morissette at Toronto's Air Canada Centre and clearly upstaged her; for an encore, the Dummies' Roberts stripped off part of his outfit to reveal a black bra and mimicked Britney Spears' "Baby One More Time." That same year, the Dummies released another album, *Give Yourself a Hand* (1999).

The frenetic pace of touring and recording was a long way from the haphazard life the band had known playing cover versions on weekends at Winnipeg's Blue Note Café.

"The whole idea of being in the music business seemed entirely inaccessible to me when I was younger," Roberts told Alan Niester of the *Globe and Mail*. "I never imagined that this would be remotely within the realm of what I would do."

The Crew Cuts

formed 1952 in Toronto: Rudi Maugeri (b. Toronto, January 27, 1931) baritone; John Perkins (b. Toronto, August 28, 1931) lead; brother Ray Perkins (b. Toronto, November 24, 1932) bass; Pat Barrett (b. Toronto, September 15, 1933) tenor

Just as Yorkville helped nurture Canadian folk and rock talent in the 1960s and 1970s, Toronto's St. Michael's Cathedral Choir School, the Catholic school for boys, was quite simply Canada's incubator for four-part, male harmony, doo-wop singing in the 1950s. The Toronto school, combining musical instruction with education for boys, was home to both The Four Lads and The Crew Cuts. In fact, they were all classmates in 1948.

Much like the Four Lads, brothers Ray and John Perkins, Rudi Maugeri, and Pat Barrett got together after class, experimenting with four-part harmonies of popular tunes. Maugeri and John Perkins originally began performing in a quartet called the Jordonaires (with two members of what would become the Four Lads) but by 1952 they had recruited Ray Perkins and Barrett into a foursome called The Four Tones.

The group changed its name again when a deejay Barry Nesbitt booked them on a teen music show, whose audiences dubbed them The Canadaires. The group appeared destined for a break, when it managed a booking on Arthur Godfrey's TV show *Talent Scouts* in New York. They placed second in the competition and returned to Canada. The group was performing at a frigid Sudbury booking in mid-winter 1953, when their agent Dave Bossin told them they had a guest spot on a Clevelend TV show. The group jumped in a 1939 jalopy that had no heat and drove the 1000 kilometres south to Ohio.

The Crew Cuts (clockwise from top left): Rudi Maugeri, John Perkins, Ray Perkins, Pat Barrett

They appeared on Gene Carroll's TV show and later met radio WERE disc jockey Bill Randle, who sent them to Mercury Records in Chicago. The group was promptly signed and renamed finally The Crew Cuts.

Their first single, **Crazy 'Bout You Baby**, was an original tune written by Maugeri and Barrett and was released that same year. The song was reasonably popular but their return visit to the recording studio produced a cover version of the Chords' song "Sh-Boom."

"What we did," John Perkins told *Globe and Mail* reporter Liam Lacey years later, "was take songs by black artists and redo them in our style ... In those days black artists weren't allowed on the charts. [It] had a different sound ... and we essentially made it palatable for the white audience, using conventional four-part harmony."

"Sh-Boom" wasn't a particular favourite of theirs, but the public loved it. It was number one on the charts for seven weeks and it won *Down Beat*'s poll as the best rhythm-and-blues song of the year. Upon their return to Toronto, to appear at the Casino Club, the Crew Cuts were welcomed with a tickertape parade up Bay Street.

Here were four skinny, fun-loving friends from school days not quite sure what all the fuss was about, but enjoying the crush of female fans, the public parades, the string of hit songs, and the performance paycheques of $5000 per appearance. Comedian Stan Freeberg recorded a version of "Sh-Boom" right after Crew Cuts' release. Freeberg's parody drew on elements heard on both the Chords' and the Crew Cuts' single; it also made reference to the R&B origin of both recordings. However, Freeberg didn't differentiate this new music as folk art or popular art, Negro or white music; he just presented it as senseless and incoherent. Unconsciously, Freeberg's parody pointed up an important aspect of the emerging rock 'n' roll idiom: in appealing to the puzzlement of adults, it marked the new sound as an expression of youth.

In a *Maclean's* magazine interview in 1954, Crew Cuts' manager Fred Strauss is reported to have said, "This outfit will go on forever." Years before the punk music scene was even heard of, he went on to say, "When we all get older, we'll just change the name. We'll call ourselves the Skinheads."

The Crew Cuts were one of the first R&B groups to tour Britain and Europe. Among their first few stops was Liverpool, where a 14-year-old Paul McCartney recalled lining up to see them. The group toured until 1963 and recorded another two dozen singles including such Top 10 hits as **Ko Ko Mo (I Love You)**, **Earth Angel**, and **Gum Drop**.

In 1977, the Crew Cuts reunited in Nashville, where they had recorded their original hits, then returned to their homes and retirement jobs – John Perkins to Louisiana where he edits a TV magazine, Ray Perkins to Denver and his investment business, Rudi Maugeri to California where he sells cars, and Pat Barrett to his car sales enterprise in New Jersey.

In 1984, the Juno Awards recognized the Crew Cuts, as well as Canada's two other 1950s four-man groups – the Four Lads and the Diamonds – with the Hall of Fame Award.

Crowbar

formed 1969 in Hamilton: Kelly Jay (Blake Fordham) vocals, keyboards; John "the Ghetto" Gibbard vocals, slide and lead guitar; Rheal Lanthier guitar; Josef Chirowski vocals, keyboards, flute, harmonica; Larry Atamanuik drums (replaced by Sonnie Bernardi); Roly Greenway vocals, bass; John Rutter vocals; Richard "King Biscuit Boy" Newell (b. Hamilton, March 9, 1944) vocals, harmonica

The late 1960s and early 1970s witnessed a golden era of pop music festivals. Whether indoors at Fillmore in New York and the Rock Pile in Toronto, or outdoors at Woodstock and Varsity Stadium, promoters reaped the benefits of parading marquee talent across those massive stages for hours at a time. Likewise, the bands that could enthuse an audience as well live as in a recording made musical hay on those stages. The big stages (indoors or out) brought out the best in one of Ronnie Hawkins' alumni bands, Crowbar.

"It was the second day of the hastily-arranged Strawberry Fields rock festival [at Mosport, near Toronto]," rock critic Ritchie Yorke wrote in 1970, "and the audience of about 50,000 had suffered through an afternoon of musical mediocrity. Just as the sun was setting, Crowbar climbed up on the massive stage with King Biscuit Boy. By the time they'd reached their usual set closer, the Biscuit's Boogie, the crowd was on its feet screaming for more."

The band had gotten the same rave reaction the year before, when it debuted at the club Fillmore East in New York. Then simply known as And Many Others, the group was playing backup for Ronnie Hawkins. They were on the same bill as Joe Cocker. The audience included Bob Dylan and a traditionally laid-back corps of New York music critics.

"These guys have everything," Dick Lupoff wrote in pop magazine *Crawdaddy*, "material, technique, stage presence."

Individually, the members of Crowbar had paid their dues in clubs and bars around southern Ontario. Kelly Jay and the nucleus of the band, for example, had picked up a young slide guitar player, John Gibbard, after putting out a call for a guitarist to help them back up a stripper and twin go-go girls at a bar in Pembroke, Ontario. Gibbard, or "Ghetto" as he was nicknamed, "looked like he should be playing with a Meccano set," Jay said, "but he picked up that guitar like a laser beam and shot through everybody in the club."

Like The Hawks and The Band before them, Crowbar learned in the tutelage of Arkansas-born rockabilly singer Ronnie Hawkins, whose strict rehearsing and lifestyle regimen were a powerful influence. Wrote Yorke, "Nobody had seen a band that tight in six years." However, as with so many of the Ronnie Hawkins' bands, And Many Others got tired of the long hours, rigorous road trips, and sleeping in cars to save money.

In May 1970, the band now called Crowbar reemerged with harmonica player Richard Newell. Originally, from Hamilton, Ontario, Newell had heard Little Walter play harmonica on a Nashville radio station about 1961 and immediately bought a harmonica and begun mimicking recordings. Newell bounced from band to band turning each one on to rhythm-and-blues music. In 1968, he joined Ronnie Hawkins, who nicknamed him King Biscuit Boy after the weekly KFFA radio show (from Helena, Arkansas) that featured harmonica player Sonny Boy Williamson and was sponsored by the King Biscuit Flour Co. Newell worked with Hawkins for two years, then departed with And Many Others to record an album.

Richard Newell a.k.a. King Biscuit Boy

Their collaboration, ***Official Music: King Biscuit Boy and Crowbar***, drew rave reviews and sold more than 10,000 copies within a few months of its release. "It's obvious that Crowbar could play circles around Canned Heat, Led Zeppelin and other equivalents," wrote Jim Beebe, then *Toronto Star* rock critic. "Crowbar should take the world by storm."

Crowbar was the first Canadian band to arrive on the rock music scene in the era of CanCon legislation. Its release of a single, **Corinna, Corinna**, hit the playlists in September 1970 and immediately gave the band a radio profile, hitting *RPM*'s Top 30 that fall. In January 1971, Crowbar released its second album, ***Bad Manors***, a play-on-words reference to the old farmhouse ($250 a month rent) on the Niagara escarpment where Crowbar and King Biscuit Boy lived and rehearsed their material.

"This is a good one," said the *Rolling Stone* magazine review. "This LP is one of the happiest, raunchiest, freshest emanations of a life energy to pin the grid in many moons." Critic Lester Bangs wrote in *Fusion* magazine, "I don't know anything about them [Crowbar] and I hardly ever like white blues bands, but I like these albums [***Bad Manors*** and ***Official Music***]."

Crowbar next signed with Paramount Records, which included tours of both the United States and Britain. Back in Ontario, the band developed a strong following on the bar and club circuit. It recorded three more albums, including ***Larger Than Life***, perhaps the best Canadian live-in-concert album of the decade. From the albums came six singles, among them **Oh, What a Feeling**, which became a CanCon rock music anthem (as well as the title of a Canadian Academy of Recording Arts and Science fund raising CD set in 1996), but because of its allusion to drugs was barred from the United States.

Before long, members of Crowbar began leaving: Atamanuik moved to Seatrain; Chirowski went to the Alice Cooper band; Greenway joined the band Next; meanwhile, Jay and Newell went off to record on their own. By the late 1970s, the group, once known as Prime Minister Pierre Trudeau's favourite band, was no more.

Bobby Curtola

b. Port Arthur, Ontario, April 17, 1944

In the era of Canadian popular music before national tours, major recording labels, and even Canadian-content regulations, there was only one musical artist who could claim to be an idol. His name is Bobby Curtola.

Teenagers in the Lake Superior community of Port Arthur (before it was amalgamated with Fort William into Thunder Bay, Ontario) knew but one rock 'n' roll band in the late 1950s. Bobby (Curtola) and the Bobcats performed their first professional gig at a high school assembly in 1959.

"Before then, I'd only sung for my family to earn a quarter now and then," says Curtola. "We did well at the assembly. I don't know whether it was fate or luck, but the kids seemed to like us. We got lots of newspaper space and we had a lot of work in the area."

Curtola quickly realized being in the right place at the right time was an essential ingredient for success in the music business even locally. He also sensed he needed his own material, songs he could call his own. Coincidentally, Curtola went to school with the son of local songwriter, Dyer Hurdon, who invited Curtola to record his composition "Hand in Hand with You." Using Hurdon's relatives as backup singers and recording at a local radio station on a one-track tape recorder (which meant the recording had to be done in one take – no overdubbing) Curtola says "after 25 tries, we had a good take … the sound was unbelievable."

Dyer Hurdon described Curtola's songs as "rock-a-ballads," while years later feature writer Frank Rasky said that Curtola sang "in a silvery tenor with a soft-sweet quality."

"We took that first recording to some of the record companies in Toronto," recalls Curtola. "But they weren't interested. We decided that the only way to get the record out was to start our own record company, which we did. It was called Tartan Records."

The Toronto industry gurus had also recommended Curtola not press more than a thousand copies of the recording. When it was released in February of 1960, "Hand in Hand with You" sold 1000 copies the first day it was available. In July, a few Toronto radio stations played it. But that didn't just happen. Curtola was forever on the phone trying to get his songs airplay. By the time he'd recorded his fifth song, **Don't You Sweetheart Me**, Curtola's persistence, and the angry phone calls of dedicated fans, were paying off. In 1964, two of his songs – **Fortune Teller** and **Aladdin** – made both the Canadian and U.S. charts.

Still there was little or no assistance from American distributors. So, with his next two records – **Indian Giver** and **Three Rows Over** – Curtola tried to handle the distribution on his own from Canada. Airplay began to pick up, but then the U.S. government put an embargo on Canadian record imports. Despite touring to American cities, the man who was now a teen idol in Canada with thousands of fan club members could sell nothing in major U.S. markets. Late in 1964, Dick Clark was about to sign Curtola to Capitol Records in the United States "when the Beatles hit. And that ended that."

The British invasion might well have killed Bobby Curtola, but then he tripped into a new promotional vehicle that rejuvenated his career. Jack Richardson, an advertising executive and producer of a nationally syndicated radio show sponsored by Coca-Cola, hatched a unique way of promoting his account and homegrown musical talent: Canadian pop artists would record a new brand of Coke commercial.

"We were the first people to record a jingle that didn't sound like a jingle, one that actually sounded like a song," says Curtola. "That started a world trend. Coke did all their jingles with artists after that."

As well as Curtola, Coke jingles were fronted by such artists as Boots Randolph, Chet Atkins, Petula Clark, and David Clayton-Thomas. The idea expanded and soon Coke was producing complete albums of these artists to be sold at a large discount with the presentation of eight Coke bottle-top liners. One such album, recorded by Bobby Curtola, sold an astonishing 117,000 copies.

By 1974, Curtola had 50 singles (including million-seller **Fortune Teller**) and 15 LPs to his credit.

Bobby Curtola's musical rise was full of firsts. In addition to being Canada's first teen idol, he was the first Canadian artist to receive a gold record, the first to host a teenage music show (*After Four* for CTV) in Canada, the first to travel the country as part of a magical show, and in the 1970s the first Canadian artist to sign an exclusive contract with the Hughes Hotel chain in Las Vegas, where he continues to perform into the 21st century.

Curtola's impact on the Canadian music industry wasn't limited to teen idolatry. He was among the first artists to speak out in favour of a Canadian star system that would recognize and promote homegrown talent. His vision was apparently recognized by the newly created Canadian Radio-television and Telecommunications Commission in 1969, because Canadian content regulations, requiring 30 percent Canadian content on air, soon followed.

Terry Dale

b. Vancouver, B.C., May 2, 1926

Terry Dale swings at the Shaughnessy Military Hospital, Vancouver, in a Wayne and Shuster Show *radio broadcast in March 1953.*

In the spring of 1949, a Winnipeg-based music publication called *Intermission* encouraged its readership to "get together on a national basis and support Canadian talent." Its Volume 1, Number 1 cover story featured what it described as a "vivacious, titian-haired, green-eyed, five-and-a-half foot, 120-pound … modern contralto" named Terry Dale. The article recounted her diverse entertainment background and quoted her responses to questions about a burgeoning career in show business.

"Oh, nothing exciting will ever happen to me," she joked, "unless I'm destined to be Artie Shaw's next wife."

In a career that spanned some 65 years performing in front of countless stage bands, radio microphones, television cameras, and audiences, Terry Dale can accurately say she has appeared in plenty of exciting roles, if not as Shaw's wife.

Born Iris Hatfull, she grew up with a healthy respect for the entertainment world, principally because her mother, Margaret Hatfull, had been an English concert and pantomime star and took her daughter to dancing, elocution, and classical singing lessons. When Terry was four, her mother got her in the door at Vancouver radio station CJOR, where she won a singing spot on a children's program called *Big Brother Bill*. She remembers wearing a pint-sized tuxedo, standing on a chair to reach the mike, and singing "Walking My Baby Back Home." The show's host was popular sportscaster Bill Nicholson, but also featured an 18-year-old pianist named Art Hallman, who would later play a vital role in advancing Terry's career.

During her teens, Terry sang in school music festivals, at church socials, at community revues, and (using the name Diane Sydney so her schoolmates wouldn't know) in shows at a Chinese nightclub for $10 a week. At 17, she heard that The Cave supper club in Vancouver needed a band singer.

"I kept bugging my mother to let me audition," remembers Dale. "So my mother contacted the bandleader, Earl Hill. I went in and auditioned. I knew all the songs, all the intros and all the key changes. And they said to my mother, 'She's a very talented girl. Could she start tomorrow night?' Could I start tomorrow night! I was there for three years and my mother was with me every single night."

W. G. Grant

The Cave exposed her to some big names in show business then – including vocalist Bonnie Baker, orchestra leader Johnny (Scat) Davis, and Jack Benny's comic character Schlepperman. During that time, composer/arranger/conductor Ricky Hyslop invited her to appear on a special CBC radio broadcast celebrating Canada's jubilee in 1947. Fine, but for Hyslop, neither her real name, Iris Hatfull, nor her earlier stage name, Diane Sydney, seemed appropriate.

"One of the chaps working at CBC was reading the comic *Terry and The Pirates*," she remembers. "He came across the name Terry and thought that it was a good name as was Dale from *Flash Gordon*. ... I thought, 'Oh well, it's easy to remember and no one will misspell it.' So Terry Dale it was."

The CBC broadcast fostered Dale's next break. Bandleader Mart Kenney happened to hear her jubilee appearance and recommended her to a then-Toronto-based bandleader in need of a female vocalist: Art Hallman, the young pianist with whom Dale had performed on CJOR in 1930. Dale immediately moved east and fronted the Art Hallman Orchestra on the CBC Dominion network series *Romance* and *Art Hallman Presents*. Hallman also included Dale on a Musicana label recording and hired her for the People's Credit Jewellers' *Sunnyside Sing Song*, a weekly open-air concert broadcast from the Sunnyside bandshell on CFRB Radio.

In 1950, after three years with the Hallman orchestra, Terry Dale got a call from Jackie Rae to join another broadcast institution, *The Wayne and Shuster Show*. Heard every Thursday night across the CBC's Trans-Canada network, comedians Johnny Wayne and Frank Shuster balanced their classic, self-deprecating gags and skit humour with Terry Dale fronting the Sam Hersenhoren orchestra. Occasionally, she would try to join the kibitzing that filled every show, but inevitably Wayne or Shuster would ask her to "Just sing, Terry, sing!"

In the summer of 1952, Terry Dale joined another groundbreaking show. Three nights a week, CBC's Dominion radio network caught up with the cast and crew of *Your Happy Motoring Show*. Sponsored, of course, by Imperial Esso, each 15-minute broadcast was live and sounded as if it came from a different Canadian vacation spot and featured Terry Dale with Wally Koster singing the songs of the countryside – sea shanties from the Maritimes, habitant music from Quebec, or western music from the Prairies. The supporting in-studio cast included announcer Alan McFee, conductor Howard Cable, producer Jackie Rae, and Doug Master (Mac, the on-air Esso guy).

Appropriately, when the first Canadian television viewers tuned into the CBC-TV launch in September 1952, they saw the *Happy Motoring* duet again.

"Wally and I were the first ones to sing on the opening-day show," recalls Dale. "We sang 'How About You,' but we were so nervous, it's a wonder we could open our mouths."

As if being part of Canada's first TV broadcast weren't adventure enough, in

Terry Dale at the CNE Grandstand show, 1953.

R.C. Ragsdale

1953, the Department of External Affairs invited the entire *Wayne and Shuster Show* (including its girl singer) to travel to the Far East to entertain Canadian troops fighting in the Korean War. Terry Dale said she was "thrilled to be able to go. … When you're young like that, you aren't afraid of anything."

During several weeks behind the lines, Dale and the rest of the entertainers performed concerts – nearly 40 separate shows – recorded their weekly radio show (to be sent back to Canada for broadcast), and visited troops in the trenches and in the field hospitals, where, she said, "I realized the seriousness of it all … all the killing that was going on … I grew up in a hurry over there."

Back in Canada, the pace of Terry Dale's show business career never let up. In 1953 she joined an all-star cast in the CNE Grandstand show, featuring Victor Borge, conductor Howard Cable, and a 60-piece orchestra. The show was produced by Jack Arthur, who, in 1954, invited Terry Dale to join the cast of another weekly CBC-TV show called *Mr. Show Business*. In this show, Arthur would describe highlights in a colourful show business career, while a chorus of 16 singers, including soloists Wally Koster, Billy O'Connor, and Terry Dale, accented each reminiscence with an appropriate number.

Though family illness demanded that she return to Vancouver in 1955, Terry Dale never found herself short of work. Guesting on the television show *Harmony House*, she worked with host Alan Millar, with whom she costarred on a network show *Terry and Me* and later *The Terry Dale Show*. They married in 1958. Daughter Sarah was born in Vancouver, and following the family's return to Toronto, son David was born in 1961.

Back on radio in the summer of 1964, Terry Dale found herself on-air with family, as it were, in a CBC show called *Thursday's Child*. Along with violinist

Albert Pratz, the show featured her old friend Ricky Hyslop conducting the orchestra and husband Alan Millar as host. The musical choices were their own and they were eclectic – from semi-classical to folk and jazz.

Appearances have been rare since those proud days of *Thursday's Child*. However, in 2000, when Toronto radio host and producer Glen Woodcock released a series of resurrected broadcast recordings (called *Swing Canada*) from the 1940s, he staged a musical launch. Along with a small band, he coaxed Terry Dale (who appeared on a number of the CD's singles with the Art Hallman Orchestra) to sing at a show in Toronto. It was like the old days for her.

"The adrenaline gets going," she said, "just like when you were performing every night with a big band. You could never get bored."

Trump Davidson

b. Sudbury, Ontario, November 26, 1908; d. 1978

Courtesy Harvey Silver

Beyond question, (Jimmy) Trump Davidson was among the first Canadian musicians to concentrate on jazz. His father was a grocer and a spare-time musician who played fiddle and, more importantly, imparted his love of music to his children.

"There was always somebody playing something at our place," Trump told author Mark Miller in 1976, "and even before I got an instrument, I'd be sitting with a rolled up piece of paper, maybe sheet music, and I'd be tooting away through that. When I got a cornet, it was just like I'd been practicing all the time; it was quite natural for me to start improvising right off."

At age 12, Davidson joined the boys' band of the Canadian Legion in Sudbury and got his first cornet. Naturally, he listened to recordings – of the Mound City Blue Blowers, Red Nichols and His Five Pennies and the Coon-Sanders Original Nighthawks. Another of his early idols was cornetist Bix Beiderbecke.

"The first time I got an instrument," he recalled, "I really didn't know how to play it properly and I wish – if I had it to do all over again – that I would have studied it. But there weren't any teachers in Sudbury, so I was more or less on my own." Even on his own, Davidson was proficient enough by the time he moved to Toronto, in 1929, to land a first trumpet chair with the legendary Luigi Romanelli – as a singer, originally, because he couldn't read music very well. But he soon noticed that the band's chief arranger (trombonist Red Ginzler) "wasn't always playing the notes that were written down either."

Thus, the idea of improvising – the very essence of jazz – was born in Trump Davidson's mind.

After five years with Romanelli and a short spell with Rex Battle's dance band, Trump organized his own 12-piece orchestra for Toronto's Esquire Club in 1936, broadcasting locally (CKEY) and in 1937 in the United States over NBC.

After a year with Horace Lapp's orchestra, Trump organized a big Dixieland-type band à la Bob Crosby, which played at the Palace Pier, a noted Toronto dance palace, for 17 years.

Even before that, Trump had a smaller Dixieland-type sextet, whose ranks included saxophonist Teddy (his brother), drummer Reef McGarvey, pianist Harvey Silver, and trombonist Murray Ginsberg.

Both as a singer and as a cornetist (and later trumpeter) Trump stood out. He and his band became so popular in Toronto that nightspots like the Colonial and the Edison, which usually brought in American bands, would book the Davidson group in for a week or two at a time.

Other musicians willingly expressed their admiration for Trump's talents. Saxophonist Lew Lewis said: "Trump could put more emotion into 16 bars than anyone I know. And working with him night after night for so many years, he never repeated anything, always in the best of taste, sheer utter music."

Lewis also recalled asking Phil Napolean, the renowned American trumpeter, which trumpeter he most admired. Napolean replied: "Trump Davidson. He's the boss. If he lived in the States he would be world-famous."

Virtually identical sentiments were expressed by yet another famous trumpeter, Charlie Shavers: "Do you folks realize what a great jazz musician you have in Trump Davidson? Had he been born in the United States, he would be world-famous, right up there with the best of them."

Trump's own pianist, Harvey Silver, told Murray Ginsberg: "Trump was just amazing. He would write his arrangements quite often when he was sitting in the car, while I was driving somewhere."

Trump's band had a well-earned reputation for drinking. And the leader sometimes set a fine example. In the spirit of fun, he liked to introduce numbers in an offbeat – usually risqué – manner.

Some examples: "The next number we are about to play is Duke Ellington's 'Black and Fat Testicle.'" Another time, he announced the band would play "Feel the Fluter's Balls," and then proceeded to sing: "Hennessy Tennessee played with hi'self while the music went round and round."

But despite the clowning, Trump's reputation as a musician never suffered. In 1937, the distinguished British bandleader Ray Noble toured the United States and Canada with a band of mostly American musicians (including Bud Freeman,

Claude Thornhill, and Charlie Spivak). Trump, then playing at the Club Esquire, met Noble and invited him to the club where he, Davidson, was playing.

At the time, Noble was about to launch a tour of the British Isles, but he had no band – except the Americans who had been touring with him. Once he heard Trump's band, Noble made him an offer: if Noble could use Trump's band for his tour – as the Ray Noble Orchestra – he would give Trump billing as a featured soloist. On that four-month tour, Noble and the Canadian musicians played to packed houses throughout the United Kingdom.

After the Palace Pier burned down in 1963, Trump went into semi-retirement, but he still did some jobbing around. In 1978, he was preparing to play the annual Easter Seal dance in Sudbury. But two days before the engagement, sitting in the sun at his sister's home, he started to get up, fell over backwards, and cracked his skull. He died in hospital two days later.

Canada has rarely again produced a jazz trumpeter of Trump Davidson's calibre.

The Diamonds

formed 1954 in Toronto: Stan Fisher (b. Toronto, July 26, 1935) lead vocal (replaced by Dave Somerville [b. Guelph, Ontario, October 2, 1933]); Ted Kowlaski (b. Toronto, May 16, 1931) tenor; Phil Levitt (b. Toronto, July 9, 1935) baritone; Bill Reed (b. Toronto, January 11, 1936) bass

The genesis of rock 'n' roll is often debated, but one of its undisputed Gardens of Eden was the campus of the University of Toronto in the early 1950s, when four undergraduate students plugged into the early rock 'n' roll phenomenon known as "blue-eyed soul." Musicologists call it "an imitation Negro sound." The Diamonds were not African-American rhythm and blues singers; they just sounded as if they were.

The Diamonds' story began during the summer of 1953, while baritone Phil Levitt and his buddy Stan Fisher were on holidays at a Lake Erie resort.

"One night Stan and I were walking down a darkened street in Crystal Beach," Levitt recalled. "We were just singing harmony on a Hilltoppers song, 'I'd Rather Die Young.' Suddenly, several girls came out of the shadows from between two cottages, saying 'Wow! That sounds great!' They fell all over us. ... What better motivation could there be? The idea for the Diamonds was born."

Initially the Diamonds, all fellow U. of T. students – Levitt, Fisher, Kowalski, and Reed – sang gospel music. But they learned how to sing it well one

The Diamonds (l. to r.): Ted Kowalski, Dave Somerville, Bill Reed, Phil Levitt

night in 1954 while attending a performance by the Detroit-based Revelaires.

"At that time, we had maybe three songs we knew how to sing," Levitt said. "And these guys came out and sang like nothing I'd ever heard in my life. They were marvelous. …They were singing spirituals with a gospel flavour. The four of us just sat there, laughing out loud every time they did something great. They noticed us and asked 'Are you laughing at us?' We said, 'No. We love it.' So we went to their room and sang together for three or four hours. The Revelaires took us under their wing and taught us how to sing spirituals."

The Diamonds' first gig was in a minstrel show, but the group (by now including Reed, a telephone installer, and Somerville, a CBC technician) soon found a Canadian disc jockey, Elwood Glover, who liked and promoted their music. This led to a meeting with Nat Goodman (who took them on as manager) and to an appearance on CBC-TV's *Pick the Stars*.

It was while they were performing at the Alpine Village Club in Cleveland, Ohio, however, that their big break came. They met radio WERE disc jockey Bill Randle (who had already assisted the Toronto-based Crew Cuts); Randle helped them land a contract with Mercury Records in Chicago. The group became known for its cover work, replicating the sound of American black artists of the day.

"We had a special, very distinctive sound," Kowalski told the *Toronto Star* in 1984. "Most vocal groups simply did four-part harmony and sang on the note. … We sang like a black group, a very dark sound for the time, with the anticipated vocal entries, vocal slides, doo-wapping background fills, the whole thing."

In 1956, the Diamonds did a version of Frankie Lymon and the Teenagers' hit, "Why Do Fools Fall in Love?" and later of the Willows' "Church Bells May Ring" and the G-Clefs' "Ka-Ding-Dong." Their recording breakthrough occurred in 1957, when manager Goodman directed the group's attention to a single, "Little Darlin'," recorded by a black group known as The Gladiolas.

"[Disc jockey] Bill Randle loved [the Diamonds' version of] 'Little Darlin','" said Kowalski years later, "and started playing it and playing it and playing it."

The song quickly climbed the *Cashbox* charts to become the sixth-most-popular single of 1957. That same year, they recorded "Words of Love," "Zip Zip," "Silhouettes," and then their own creation **The Stroll**, which started a dance craze on Dick Clark's TV show *American Bandstand*, while the song itself rose to become the thirtieth-most-popular single of 1957. By the time the original band broke up in 1961, it had recorded nearly 30 singles, including 16 hits, 10 of which were covers of black rhythm-and-blues artists.

Over the years, different versions of the Diamonds (with various personnel) have appeared. Dave Somerville continued singing, for a time with Four Preps' lead singer Bruce Belland, on television and concert stages. Singer Glen Stetson led a version of the group around the North American nightclub circuit into the 1970s.

The most celebrated reunion, however, occurred in the fall of 2000, when the original four Diamonds went to Pittsburgh's PBS-TV affiliate WQED as part of a special broadcast entitled *Doo Wap 51*. During the recording session, the Diamonds shared the stage with Maurice Williams, the composer of "Little Darlin'," their biggest hit. "That was God opening doors," T. J. Lubinsky, creator of *Doo Wap 51*, told a reporter.

In 1984, the Juno Awards recognized the Diamonds, as well as Canada's two other 1950s four-man groups – the Four Lads and the Crew Cuts – with the Hall of Fame Award.

Céline Dion

b. Charlemagne, Quebec, March 30, 1968

As the year 2000 began, the Canadian Recording Industry Association, the organization representing all the major recording labels, the independent

labels, and all the music manufacturers, took stock of a century of music in Canada. The association announced that Céline Dion was its choice as the artist of the century, principally because of album sales – nearly 120 million sold in Canada and abroad – more than previous leading sellers Bryan Adams, Anne Murray, and even Gordon Lightfoot. The sales figures – along with her numerous Juno and Grammy trophies – punctuated an extraordinary rise to success from quite extraordinarily modest beginnings.

Born into a show business family, Céline Dion grew up watching her four older brothers and sisters perform with their parents (father Adhemar, an accordionist, and mother Therese, a violinist) as part of a Quebec folk band – The Dion Family. At the family-owned piano bar, Le Vieux Baril in Charlemagne, Quebec, seven-year-old Céline sang the songs of Ginette Reno for the patrons. She demonstrated no less than a five-octave vocal range.

"I told my mom, that all I dreamed about was singing," Céline said. "I would run home from school as fast as I could to rehearse" in front of a mirror for hours on end. She confided to her mother that she would one day become a star.

Then in 1980, the family recorded Céline (singing a song written by her mother) to Ginette Reno's manager, René Angelil. So impressed was Angelil that he commissioned a Quebec lyricist to write the song "La Voix du bon Dieu" and signed her to his independent recording label T B S. About that time, Angelil lost Ginette Reno as a client and he was forced to mortgage his house to bankroll his new protégé.

Thus began an association between manager and singer that would eventually lead to courtship, marriage, and a family. In the beginning, however, Céline's relationship with Angelil was forcibly formal; not until she was 16 (when he had represented her for four years) was she allowed to address him as René. His management led to Dion's participation in the 1982 Yamaha World Song Festival in Japan; her performance of "Tellement j'ai d'amour pour toi" won a gold medal. Three years later, with Dion on the verge of becoming the biggest star in Quebec, manager Angelil took her out of the public eye. She signed with Sony and recorded her debut album *Incognito*. It yielded six Top 10 singles.

Meanwhile, behind the scenes, an army of beauty specialists began a radical makeover of Dion's image. They changed her hairstyle. They tossed out her wardrobe and replaced it with designs from Gucci, Chanel, Versace, and Dior. They immersed her in language training until her English was as fluent as her French. As far as her awkward teen look was concerned, a fan magazine reported that "her eyebrows were sleekened [and] the prominent canine teeth that had spurred cruel schoolmates to label her 'the vampire' were expensively capped."

For Dion's 1990 album *Unison*, Sony set aside $1 million, the largest promotional budget ever invested in a Canadian artist. The album, produced by David Foster, marked the launch of her singing career in English. It generated the single "If You Asked Me To," which Patti Labelle had recorded and pushed to the top of the R&B charts in 1989; Dion's version went to number five on the *Billboard* pop charts.

By 1991, the manager/client relationship between Angelil (who had divorced his wife in 1985) and Dion had changed. The two had fallen in love, but hesitated to make it public; in Dion's own words "I didn't want the world to think of him as my sugar daddy." When her 1993 album *The Colour of My Love* was released, however, the liner notes revealed her true feelings. The two were married in a $500,000 extravaganza – complete with 17 Rolls-Royce limousines, 500 guests, and a $25,000 wedding outfit – at Montreal's Nôtre Dame Basilica in December 1994.

Success begot celebrity begot success. In 1991–92, Dion teamed up with American singer Peabo Bryson to record the title song from *Beauty and the Beast*, which won that year's Academy Award for best song. There were numerous appearances on *The Tonight Show*. In 1991, she won her first Juno Awards for best album and female vocalist of the year. In total, Dion has won more than 115 trophies, including five Grammys, 33 Felix (French-Canadian music) Awards, 25 Junos, two Oscar-winning songs, and statues from the American Music Awards, *Billboard* Music Awards, World Music Awards, and People's Choice Awards.

In 1998, she appeared in the concert *Divas Live*, with such performers as Aretha Franklin, Carole King, Barbra Streisand, Gloria Estefan, Mariah Carey, and Shania Twain. She also was inducted into the Order of Canada that year. But in perhaps Dion's biggest "splash," she worked quietly with composer James Horner to record a song for the hit movie *Titanic* in 1998. James Cameron had refused to include a song in the film, but Angelil and Sony Records coaxed him into allowing "My Heart Will Go On" onto the soundtrack. It added an 11th Oscar to Cameron's Academy Awards sweep that year.

Following her receipt of five Junos at the 1999 awards ceremony, Dion told the audience, "You probably won't see me on stage receiving an award for a very long time. I'm planning to stop for a while, for a few years at least."

In the months that followed, Dion completed her autobiography, *My Story, My Dream* with the help of co-author Georges-Hebert Germain; she and Angelil renewed their wedding vows during a $1.5 million Las Vegas spectacle; she added an $8 million chateau north of Montreal to their collection of international properties and bought her own golf course; she announced the first Dion-endorsed products (sunglasses and a new breed of rosebush); and early in 2001, the couple announced the birth of their first child, René-Charles.

About this last, in a world exclusive published in Britain's *Hello!* magazine in March 2001 Dion said, "This is our biggest dream."

Downchild Blues Band

formed 1969 in Toronto: Donnie Walsh (b. March 24, 1947) guitar, harmonica; Richard "Hock" Walsh (b. Dec. 19, 1948) vocals (replaced 1973–77 by Tony Flaim); Cash Wall drums (later replaced by Bill Bryans, replaced by Paul Nixon, replaced by Jim Casson); Jim Milne bass (later replaced by Gary Kendall); John Witmer vocals (later replaced by Chuck Jackson); sax players Dave Woodward, Nat Abraham, James Warburton, Vic Wilson, and Pat Carey; Wayne Jackson trumpet; Jane Vasey piano (after her death replaced by Michael Fonfara)

The travels, encounters, and personnel lists of Canada's best-known blues group, the Downchild Blues Band, provide a veritable time capsule of blues music of the last 30 years of the 20th century. Concert dates took them from pubs, arenas, and prisons to some of the most celebrated festival stages in

Downchild Blues Band in 2001 (l to r.): Pat Carey, Jim Casson, Donnie "Mr. Downchild" Walsh, Chuck Jackson, Michael Fonfara, Gary Kendall

North America. They played warmup for and supported such acts as Muddy Waters, Buddy Miles, James Cotton, B.B. King, John Lee Hooker, and Howlin' Wolf. And many of the country's journeyman blues players have passed through the band's ranks.

At the core of the band were brothers Donnie and Richard Walsh, who got their early musical education clandestinely at their parents' resort hotel in northern Ontario.

"On Saturday nights, when they closed the bar there was always money left in the jukebox at closing time," Donnie Walsh said in a *Globe and Mail* interview. "So, on Sunday mornings, we'd get out of bed, plug it back in and play all the music that had been paid for the night before."

Donnie learned to play guitar and harmonica while Rick "Hock" (in reference to his girth) mimicked the voices of the greats. By the 1960s, when they were in their teens, the Walsh brothers had moved to Toronto to seek their fortunes. They borrowed the title of a Sonny Boy Williamson song, "Mr. Downchild," to give their six-man band a name and debuted at Grossman's Tavern on Toronto's Spadina Avenue.

"I remember we played on Monday, then on Tuesday, then on Wednesday," said Donnie Walsh. "Al Grossman gave us three jugs of draft for the band and we each got a meal. I guess that was around June 1969. Later, we got the idea of passing the hat, but I think the waiters took more money than we ever saw."

Their earliest fans were the clientele at public houses such as Grossman's and later the Forbes Tavern on Shuter Street. They were blue-collar workers, immigrants, hippies, poets, draft dodgers, hookers, and johns. They all drank hard while Downchild played the blues hard. The band's one-time publicist, Richard Flohil, remembers Hock Walsh's performances as "righteous and ribald. [He was] blessed with a fine sense of the absurd and a clown's natural ability to turn the laughter onto himself."

Flohil remembers one night, as the band played a late-night set at a downtown Toronto pub, that an impatient waiter (eager to close the place) began stacking empty chairs on the tables. Quick to take up the challenge, Hock Walsh launched into improvised lyrics of a song that poked fun at everybody in the room – including the owner, himself, and the impatient waiter. To the waiter's horror, Walsh managed to extend the song into a half-hour marathon.

In keeping with its humble beginnings, Downchild laid down its first recordings in the basement parking garage of Rochdale College, a Toronto cooperative apartment building. The studio, called "Sound Horn" because a sign with those words on it warned drivers of a blind spot in the parking garage, had a kitchen-sized control room separated from the recording area by a wall of glass bricks. Over two nights the band recorded 15 tracks in stereo and released the resulting album, *Bootleg*.

Soon after that, the band had a couple of brushes with history. Their old

Rick "Hock" Walsh and Donnie Walsh in 1969

Downchild on the road in the late Sixties (l. to r.) Jim Milne, Donnie Walsh, Hock Walsh, Nat Abraham, Cash Wall, Dave Woodward

tavern pal sponsored a unique concert – Al Grossman Presents Downchild – at Toronto's St. Lawrence Centre. It was the first-ever blues concert at that venue, and while the gig also featured Leon Redbone and Bobo Jenkins, Downchild saw no profits from the event. Then, during a live performance being broadcast on CHOM-FM in Montreal, the band got word the FLQ had occupied the radio station in Westmount – this was during the FLQ kidnapping crisis in Quebec. The band was told to keep playing while the station managers negotiated with the Quebec liberationists. Downchild performed for over two hours not knowing what was going over the air.

As the band hit its stride in the 1970s, it moved uptown. Downchild opened for ZZ Top at Maple Leaf Gardens, for B.B. King at Massey Hall, for Mike Bloomfield at the University of Toronto's Convocation Hall, and in Winnipeg for the legendary Muddy Waters. Despite being the backup to these headliners, Downchild kept writing and recording its own material. However, in 1973, when it released its second album, *Straight Up*, Downchild began pushing its version of a Big Joe Turner single. "Flip, Flop and Fly" sold more than 35,000 copies in Canada and won the band appearances at the New Orleans Jazz and Blues Festival and the Philadelphia Folk Festival.

While the performances of the Walsh brothers didn't always translate into large gate receipts, their blues stylings suddenly struck gold. In the mid-1970s, longtime Downchild fan and actor Dan Aykroyd borrowed the Walsh brothers' duet act when he and John Belushi created Jake and Elwood Blues for the television show *Saturday Night Live*. In 1978, the Blues Brothers recorded two Downchild songs – **Everything I Need Almost** and **Shotgun Blues** – on their LP *Briefcase Full of Blues*. The album went to number one on the charts and sold five million copies.

With the highs came the lows. Donnie Walsh recalls a drizzly morning after a late-night show in St. Catharines, Ontario. The band's van had just headed up the highway to the next night's performance in Ottawa, eight hours away. Walsh made the mistake of giving the band members an ultimatum: "If you don't want to do this gig in Ottawa you can get out of the van!" They did. Walsh had to cancel Ottawa and rehire everyone. Nor did Hock Walsh seem able to cope with the band's sudden stardom or its touring and recording schedule; heading into the studio to record Downchild's third album in 1974, Donnie Walsh fired his brother. And while Hock Walsh came back in 1977, he quit in 1985.

Downchild met with other challenges. In 1982, Downchild pianist Jane Vasey died of leukemia. And when seven-year veteran vocalist Tony Flaim left the band, John Witmer (formerly with Whiskey Howl) had to fill in until tensions eased. Then in 1999, when Rick Walsh failed to appear for a New Year's Eve show in Peterborough, Ontario, they found him dead of an apparent heart attack at his Toronto apartment.

The Downchild Blues Band, whether riding high or battling through adversity, has remained a mainstay of the Canadian blues scene. In most calendar years the band worked 150 dates. In addition to holding its own on the concert stage with the legends of the blues genre, the band has been home to many of the country's leading blues sidemen; some estimate that in 30 years, more than 130 different players have performed in the band.

Wray Downes   *b. Toronto, Ontario, January 14, 1931*

For a man who started out studying for a career in classical music, Wray Downes hasn't done badly as a jazz pianist.

"My first instrument was the piano and I loved it," he once told Greg Sutherland of *The Jazz Report*. "I was actually playing it before I could speak. I used to stutter and stumble over my words, but I could go to Sunday school and remember the melody or bass line of the hymn they had played and come home and repeat it with one finger."

He began formal study at the age of 12 in Toronto, and when he was 18 he was the first Canadian to receive the British Empire (Overseas) Scholarship in London. Next he studied at the Paris Conservatory. It was while he was in Paris in 1953 that a friend suggested they go out to hear some jazz. Oscar Peterson happened to be there, with Jazz at the Philharmonic, and they went to see him.

"Having attended lots of jazz concerts and dances with my parents, I was aware of who Oscar was," he recalled. "In fact, my father knew him personally. He was great that night. His performance really piqued my interest in jazz and started me on a musical journey I'm still continuing."

That journey has meant playing with a long list of jazz greats that has included Sidney Bechet, Buck Clayton, Bill Coleman, Roy Eldridge, Coleman Hawkins, Buddy Tate, Clark Terry, Milt Jackson, Zoot Sims, Lionel Hampton, Lester Young, Ed Bickert, Dave Young, Moe Koffman, and Ben Webster. Not a bad list of role models.

Wray returned to North America, spending six months in New York studying with Mary Lou Williams, then came back to Canada, settling first in Montreal. A couple of years later, he moved to Toronto and played piano with Peter Appleyard's quartet at the Park Plaza. He also worked at such other Toronto venues as the Town Tavern and Bourbon Street.

By the early 1960s he was attending Oscar Peterson's Advanced School of Contemporary Music. He also studied composition with Neil Chotem in Montreal. "Oscar has always been very supportive of me and a guiding light musically. Fortunately, I learned much, as they say, at the master's knee." Downes also received much encouragement from Rob McConnell, Dave Young, and Ed Bickert.

In 1973, Wray and Dave Young began playing as a duo, touring across Canada. "There were all sorts of duos around, but we were the ones who started it," Downes said.

Not long afterwards, Downes has said, "everyone jumped onto the duo concept. At the old Café des Copains, I was one of the first to try piano and saxophone with Eugene Amaro. Then I did piano and guitar, piano and trombone, and piano and drums, with Archie [Alleyne], in fact." (Another fascinating duo of the time was Dave Young with the versatile guitarist Lenny Breau, as witness the album they made in 1983 called *Live at Bourbon Street*.)

While based in Toronto, Downes has taken on engagements as music director of *Music Hop* in Halifax and also other musical assignments in St. John's and Ottawa.

Wray's career has taken him across Canada and beyond and led in time to teaching. In the late 1980s, during a Montreal appearance he was invited to do some teaching at Concordia University. He agreed to a three-year position, which stretched to four. In 1994 he was teaching at McGill University in Montreal.

Although he rarely goes out of his way to talk publicly about racial problems in North America, he has occasionally commented on the differences he has noticed between how European audiences regard jazz musicians and how these musicians are viewed on this continent. "I can well appreciate," he said in 1989, "why not only American musicians, black and white, but musicians from many, many countries have gathered in Europe, in Sweden and Switzerland, Holland and France, to live, play and work. It is truly an art form there. It's not, 'Oh, you play music? What do you do in the daytime?' You are an artist and you command respect over there, and I think you should command respect here, too."

He has also considered the relative merits of playing solo piano as against playing with other musicians.

"Nowadays," he said, "I feel quite comfortable playing the piano solo, or, as I did a week or two back, with a drummer such as Archie Alleyne, or, as I have done with piano, trombone, and guitar. The piano is an instrument complete in itself. I'll play the piano by myself, but I'm glad to be able to say today that I feel comfortable playing in any setting with any combination."

Dr. Music

formed 1969 in Toronto: Doug Riley (b. Toronto, April 24, 1945) keyboards; Laurel Ward vocals; Rhonda Silver vocals; Brenda Gordon vocals; Terry Black vocals; Dianne Brooks vocals; Trudy Desmond vocals; Michael Kennedy vocals, percussion; Steve Kennedy vocals, sax, flute; Brian Russell guitar; Terry Clarke drums; Kenny Marco guitar; Doug Mallory lead vocals, guitar; Don Thompson bass; Gary Morgan clarinet, sax, flute; Keith Jollimore vocals, sax, flute; Barrie Tallman trombone; Bruce Cassidy, trumpet; Wayne Stone, percussion

In the 1970s, television enjoyed an explosion of variety programming, that is, shows featuring various forms of entertainment in a single program. Variety shows produced in Canada at that time (by the CBC and CTV networks) were hosted by a recognized name – a singer, a comedian, sometimes an entire group. Musical guests on these shows were generally backed up in the television studio by a handpicked group of singers and/or musicians, who were

Courtesy Ken Marco

Dr. Music in concert in Hamilton, Ont., in 1970 (l. to r.): Rhonda Silver, Dianne Brooks, Don Thompson bass, Trudy Desmond, Brenda Gordon, Terry Clarke drums, Steve Kennedy, Kenny Marco guitar, Michael Kennedy, Terry Black, Gary Morgan sax, Brian Russell, Bruce Cassidy trumpet, Barrie Tallman trombone

there to help the featured acts shine. While it wasn't intended, sometimes the backup performers outshone the guest stars. One such studio group was Doug Riley's 16-member Dr. Music.

Put together to provide backup for a 1969 variety television show, Riley's ensemble quickly became a successful studio and touring band in Canada. The name of the group came simply from the initials of the D(oug) R(iley) Music publishing company. Initially, it featured the intricate and soaring harmonies of a three-woman and four-man chorus fronting a nine-piece rhythm and horn section, all driven by Riley's sophisticated jazz-rock compositions and arrangements.

Riley's musical skills were the natural progression of an accomplished career that began in 1950.

At age five, Doug Riley began learning the piano; at seven he'd entered the Royal Conservatory of Music in Toronto. His mastery of the keyboards came about almost grudgingly. Stricken by polio when he was young, Riley says he suddenly found himself unable to go outside to play with friends; consequently, hour after hour, he sat at the piano by the window watching his friends and banging out repetitious scales in frustration. Unaware of the notes he was playing and the fury with which he played them, Riley built up extraordinary speed and dexterity at an early age.

Riley's enrollment in the Music Faculty at the University of Toronto in the 1960s extended a childhood fascination for the classics. But along with a love of Bach, Bartok, and Stravinsky in class, he discovered an equal passion for the

Toronto street scene – jazz, blues, and rock 'n' roll. He began writing and performing commercial jingles. He played rhythm and blues (with the Silhouettes) at such Toronto clubs as the Bluenote Club and in 1968 got an offer to work as arranger and second keyboard player on Ray Charles' LP *Doing His Thing*.

"I was scared stiff," Riley told Ken Waxman for *AudioScene Canada* magazine. "There I was in Los Angeles for six months playing with some of the top studio musicians and even doing numbers for the Ray Charles show. Ray had always been one of my idols and was an early influence on piano ... we even got to play some duets together."

Doug Riley, photographed in 2001

Riley's studio splash in L.A. brought him to the attention of expatriate Canadian producers Chris Beard and Allan Blye, who hired Riley to put together a backup group for the variety television series *The Ray Stevens Show*, being shot in Toronto. Riley assembled musicians from his Bluenote days and singers from the Toronto production of the rock musical *Hair*. The group of eight singers and eight musicians was soon getting more attention than some of Ray Stevens' guests; it inspired Riley to make the impromptu group a permanent arrangement.

The band's convincing, high-energy performances precipitated more television variety work on such shows as *Rollin' on the River* (with Kenny Rogers and the First Edition). Dr. Music hit the road in 1971 – east to the Maritimes and across western Canada; then it recorded LPs for GRT Canada – *Dr. Music* and *Dr. Music II* – releasing several successful singles, including **Sun Goes By** and **Try a Little Harder** (both written by the group's Steve Kennedy) and Neil Sedaka's "One More Mountain to Climb."

The tough economics of keeping 16 performers working on the road and in the studio forced Riley to trim Dr. Music to a seven-piece, all-male group of singer/instrumentalists by 1973. There was another tour and a third album, *Bedtime Story*, before Dr. Music disbanded in 1974.

Meanwhile, Riley's own career flourished in many other directions. He composed two ballets for the National Ballet of Canada, worked as music director for Keith Hampshire's *Music Machine* on CBC-TV and *The Wolfman Jack Show*. He arranged music for, played piano or organ, or produced albums for such Canadian artists as Tommy Ambrose, David Bradstreet, Dianne Brooks, David Clayton-Thomas, Dan Hill, Klaatu, Moe Koffman, Sonny Greenwich, Gordon Lightfoot, Bob McBride, Anne Murray, Sylvia Tyson, Crowbar, and Boss Brass, and for such Americans as the Brecker Brothers, Dionne Warwick, the Supremes, and Bob Seger.

Doug Riley has always had a reputation, perhaps undeserved, of being silent and almost invisible. During those heyday-1970s, the Canadian media hardly noticed him. And yet, for much of his professional career, Doug Riley has juggled everything successfully – his jingle business, a Toronto recording studio, his music publishing business, management of Dr. Music, television music

113

direction, songwriting, and work as both a studio and club sideman. He's rightly been described as Canadian music's Renaissance man.

"I guess that's because I'm so busy," Riley told Richard Flohil in the magazine *Canadian Composer*. "The idea is to leave me alone as much as possible to write. Even then it gets pretty hectic and my only answer is to lock myself in the office, cut off the telephones and get to work."

Jodie Drake   *b. Detroit, 1919; d. Hawaii, January 25, 2001*

Priscilla Counsel was her real name, and Detroit was her birthplace, but she became Jodie Drake and made her considerable reputation as a blues singer in Toronto.

Before she crossed the border into Canada, she had been the warmup act for Billie Holiday, playing at the Club Conga in Detroit. She came from a hard-working, clean-living family. She never smoked, drank, or swore; but she made her living singing in bars and nightclubs.

Jodie's parents sent her to Northwestern University and then Wayne State. Her ambition was to be a journalist, but she got hooked on performing. The family legend was that she began performing on a wooden box to entertain neighbours when she was only three years old.

After leaving university, she began touring on what was called the "chitlin circuit." But in the 1950s, segregation was rampant in the United States and Jodie learned about racism first-hand.

In 1958, she landed a two-week booking at the Warwick Hotel in Toronto. That stretched into a 13-month run. She married and divorced in Detroit, before moving to Toronto with her young daughter, Judith. Both mother and daughter later became Canadian citizens.

Jodie played hotels across Canada, in Sherbrooke, Moncton, Val d'Or. Then she graduated to bigger cities and better bookings in Vancouver, Ottawa, and then Toronto, which became her home.

She looked like a star; she was 5 feet, 10 inches tall, with long, manicured fingers, a deep, throaty voice, and good looks that stayed with her late in life. Blues became her specialty, and she was the only Canadian in the New Orleans Jazz Hall of Fame.

Besides singing, she acted for a while, playing the leading role in *Born of Medusa's Blood*, a three-act play by John Herbert, best known for his searing

Rick Zolkower / Courtesy Toronto Blues Society

114

prison drama, *Fortune and Men's Eyes*. There were strong reviews of her acting, but the production closed after less than a month.

The dialogue contained a lot of coarse language, which prompted this outburst from Jodie: "The language! It was just awful. I thought I could never say those words. But I learned. I figured an actress had to be adaptable."

As an actress, she also appeared in the National Film Board production of *Fields of Endless Day*.

In her lengthy singing career, Jodie worked with such noted musicians as Tommy Flanagan, Kenny Burrell, Milt Jackson, Lucky Thompson, and Thad Jones. One time, she was spotted in the audience at a Duke Ellington concert and she was accorded an impromptu ovation by the Duke and his whole orchestra.

The *Toronto Star* named her the best "girl singer" in 1972, at a time when it was still acceptable to call a 43-year-old woman a girl. Two years later, she costarred with pianist/singer Gene Di Novi in *Gene and Jodie*, a variety series for CBC-TV.

She also appeared on television programs hosted by Elwood Glover and Bob McLean, and was featured in a musical special titled *In the Mood* with blues singer Joe Williams. Jodie was also featured in CBC's *Black Hallelujah* gospel special. But in her long career she recorded only two albums: ***I'm a Woman*** and ***Live at the Blues***.

Jodie was always outspoken, fighting for the rights of black people and for black performers in particular. She also did benefit performances for seniors, First Nations peoples, and many other groups.

Some people who worked with her remembered her as being unpredictable; after rehearsing one set of songs for a show, she would pick new ones when she went on stage.

In 1993, Jodie was the recipient of the "Blues with a Feeling" Award; she had appeared three times in the *Women's Blues Revue*.

Christine Brown, a friend of Jodie's and a television producer, got to know the singer while producing a documentary about Jodie for the CBC's series *Adrienne Clarkson Presents*.

"What I remember most about Jodie," Brown later wrote, "is her elegance and grace, the way she carried herself. She was the consummate star. Along with the elegance there was a certain raunchiness that surfaced only when she was belting out a low-down dirty blues tune. She sang the *real* thing as she punctuated the gutsy lyrics with her clenched fist. Jodie loved to laugh. We would spend most of our time together joking and laughing about something or other. Jodie also loved to eat. ... And I admired her beauty. Well into her seventies, Jodie was still as beautiful as ever."

Drake gave her last public performance in Toronto in 1995, at an annual jazz festival. She spent the late 1980s and early 1990s living at the Performing

Arts Lodge in Toronto. But in 1993 her diabetes worsened and she moved in with her daughter in Hawaii, where she died on January 25, 2001.

Jack Duffy

b. Toronto, Ontario, September 27, 1926

Jack Duffy can still remember the first "inspiration" that steered him toward music. The experience was at the Canadian National Exhibition in Toronto in 1940, when Jack was a mere 13 years old. He paid 50 cents to get into the "dance tent" to see the Tommy Dorsey band. Only eight years later he would be singing with that same band.

"But what really hooked me," he recalled, "was not so much the band but the sound of the vocal group – the Pied Pipers, with Frank Sinatra and Jo Stafford and the others."

Five years later he was part of a vocal group headed by Bill Brady and doing music jingles at Toronto radio station CKEY. "I had a good ear for third-part harmony," Duffy said. "I couldn't read music, but it worked out fine."

The Bill Brady group was working at the Club Norman when Tommy Dorsey and his band returned to Toronto. Dorsey heard about the group, auditioned them, and hired them. The Bill Brady group toured with Dorsey for a year. After that time, Dorsey asked Duffy to stay on as a solo vocalist, which he did for another year.

Duffy doesn't mention it, but there's little doubt his similarity in vocal style and slender appearance to Frank Sinatra was partly what interested Dorsey. For years afterward, Duffy did a pretty good tongue-in-cheek imitation of Sinatra, which his audiences always loved.

After leaving the Dorsey band, Duffy formed a vocal group called The Town Criers, performing first in Toronto and then on the road. Just when he had had enough of touring – "we were playing in Fargo, North Dakota" – he got a call from Billy O'Connor, inviting him to join his CBC television program, which he did for several years.

Next came a couple of seasons on *The Barris Beat*, after which he starred in his own TV series *Here's Duffy* for two years. On that series he sang and also made use of his comic flair.

Then he was called by Frank Peppiatt, who, with his partner, John Aylesworth, was writing *The Perry Como Show* on NBC in New York. He was invited to join the program's comedy group and appeared on that show for two years.

In the 1960s, Duffy was with the national tour of the revue *Spring Thaw*. He also played the title role in *Turvey*, a musical based on Earl Birney's book about a Canadian army private.

The 1970s brought him a job that was to last 10 years – *Party Game*, a variation on charades – at CHCH-TV in Hamilton, along with Billy Van, Dinah Christie, and Bill Walker.

He was also host and a frequent singer on CBC-TV's *In the Mood*, which featured Guido Basso and his big-band sound and such noted guests as Guy Lombardo, Benny Goodman, Gene Krupa, Charlie Barnet, and Count Basie.

Over the years, Duffy has appeared in straight dramatic roles in several movies, including *Silent Partner*, with Elliott Gould and Christopher Plummer, *Title Shot*, with Tony Curtis, and *Men with Guns*, with Paul Sorvino.

Although living in partial retirement, he still accepts the occasional gig, whether singing, acting, or clowning. With his wife, Marilyn, Jack Duffy lives at the Performing Artists Lodge (PAL) in Toronto, along with such other performers as Arlene Meadows, Frances Hyland, Ron Cullen, Roy Wordsworth, Paul Soles, Barrie Baldaro, and a distinguished recent arrival to PAL, Maureen Forrester.

In the summer of 1999, Duffy and many of the other PAL residents attended a party honouring Barbara Chilcott and her late brothers, Donald and Murray Davis, for their substantial contributions in developing Canadian theatre. Maureen Forrester did a little impromptu singing, and Jack sat with a friend, talking about one of his idols, Mel Tormé, who had just died.

Among other things, Jack Duffy has always had a solid appreciation of musical talent. That "good ear" of his – as well as his singing and acting talents – have taken him a long way from that summer of 1940 when he paid 50 cents to see Tommy Dorsey.

Charles Dutoit   *b. Lausanne, Switzerland, October 7, 1936*

For a man who spends so much of his time in public, Charles Dutoit has an impressive knack for keeping part of his life rather private. Even Georges Nicholson, a Montreal (Radio-Canada) broadcaster and Dutoit's official biographer, regards him as somewhat enigmatic: "Dutoit is Swiss. He will tell you he conducted this work here, or that work there, and he will tell you his father died. But he won't tell you how he felt about it."

The father in question was not musical. He was the custodian of a country estate; Charles's mother sang in a choir. Dutoit himself did not begin studying music until he picked up a violin at the relatively late age of 11. Even then, he showed little interest in the instrument until he saw a film about a young boy who hears Bach being played in a church. The boy is so smitten that he struggles to become a conductor and ends up reaping fame, glory, and riches.

The urbane conductor studied at Lausanne, Geneva, and Siena before becoming conductor of the Berne Symphony Orchestra at the age of 27. It was there that he met the dynamic Herbert von Karajan, of the Berlin Philharmonic, who profoundly influenced his conducting style, according to Nicholson.

Dutoit's brilliant musicianship is matched by administrative savvy. During a musicians' strike in the late 1990s, he met with Premier Lucien Bouchard and argued on behalf of the striking musicians – an act that earned him the grudging respect of the 98 members of the Montreal Symphony Orchestra.

Yet musicians are not totally enamoured of Dutoit. "Show me an orchestra that loves its conductor," one sage observed, "and I'll show you a lousy orchestra."

The MSO members have sometimes complained about Dutoit's autocratic attitude, his occasional bad temper, his long absences, and a sense of confusion during his stopovers in Montreal. Yet they give their all when they play under his baton.

The conductor is not shy when it comes to talking about his approach to his work. "My way of music making," he once told an interviewer from *Newsweek*, "is to clarify a score. An orchestra will play better if it understands the structure. It's not enough just to say 'This is too loud.'"

His workload is remarkable. In addition to the Montreal Symphony, he leads two other major orchestras: Tokyo's NHK Orchestra and the Orchestre Nationale de France.

"This man does not own five minutes of his time," Georges Nicholson said. "He's always studying, rehearsing, flying, conducting, attending parties, talking to the media. He just works and works. That's his hobby – work."

Nicholson's "authorized" biography of Dutoit was supposed to be published on October 7, 1986, to coincide with Dutoit's 50th birthday, but it had to be delayed because the image-conscious conductor didn't like the way he sounded in the book.

The biography was intended to provide a glimpse into the lesser-known sides of Dutoit's personality, but Dutoit would have no part of it. "He said my quotes were too literal," complained Nicholson, "and made him sound colloquial."

When the book finally came out, a Montreal critic commented that the book was "unequivocally an authorized biography, so readers expecting a romp through the maestro's underwear drawer or an independent assessment of his musical strengths and weaknesses will not be satisfied."

But no fair assessment of Dutoit's importance to the Montreal orchestra can deny his achievements. In 1981, he took the orchestra on a series of tours that led it first across Canada, then to the United States, Japan, Hong Kong, South Korea, and Europe. In 1982, the MSO performed in Carnegie Hall for the second time in its history, to sold-out houses. It continued its annual visits there with equal success. During the summer of 1989, the orchestra was invited to play five concerts at the Hollywood Bowl in Los Angeles.

Over the more than two decades of Dutoit's tenure with the Montreal orchestra, he has presented numerous Canadian guest artists, including pianist Louis-Phillipe Pelletier, soprano Marie-Danielle Parent, guitarist Michael Laucke, and baritone Gino Quilico.

Among the internationally renowned non-Canadian guest artists he has featured have been Jessye Norman, Isaac Stern, Pinchas Zuckerman, and Yo-Yo Ma.

It's understandable, in view of his record, that there are those who regard Charles Dutoit as the saviour of the Montreal Symphony Orchestra. It's true that the orchestra was debt-ridden and suffering from low morale when Dutoit arrived.

"But then," wrote William Littler, music critic of the *Toronto Star*, "along came Charles Dutoit, Swiss passport in hand, bringing to the shores of the St. Lawrence a combination of talent, energy and ambition that would soon set not only Montreal but the entire orchestral world on its ear."

Edward Bear

formed 1966 in Toronto: Larry Evoy (b. Toronto, February 19, 1946) vocals, drums; Paul Weldon (b. Toronto, March 4, 1936) keyboards (replaced in 1972 by Bob Kendall, replaced in 1974 by Barry Best); Danny Marks (b. Toronto, December 27, 1950) guitar (replaced in 1971 by Roger Ellis)

In 1995, at the annual awards night for the Society of Composers, Authors and Music Publishers of Canada, a slightly greying but fit-looking music publisher received a special award to acknowledge the airplay of three songs – **Close Your Eyes**, **Last Song**, and **You, Me and Mexico**. The recipient was Larry Evoy. The recordings, dating back to the 1960s and 1970s, were those of his former pop band Edward Bear. The award recognized that the tunes had each been aired on radio more than 100,000 times.

"It's wonderful to know our songs still have this life so many years after they were recorded," says Evoy, who started the band with architect and keyboard player Paul Weldon in 1966. Soon after, they were joined by guitarist Danny Marks.

Edward Bear (l. to r.): Paul Weldon, Larry Evoy, Danny Marks

Ann Carter

120

"There was an ad in the After Four section of the *Toronto Telegram*," recalls Marks. "It said, 'Blues Guitarist Wanted.' I met [Larry and Paul] in the basement of this architect's office where they were rehearsing. I distinctly remember saying, 'You can send the other guys home, 'cause I'm here.' I was 16 and accepted into the band."

With Marks' strong blues skills on guitar, Evoy's boyish ballad voice, and Weldon's skill at the keyboard, the sound they wanted was nearly there. Drummers and bass players were a problem, however; they auditioned 150 drummers and finally decided to have Evoy sing and play drums, while Weldon played both melody lines and bass on his electric organ (a Hammond B3 borrowed from Roy Kenner of the group Mandala). Their group would be a threesome called Edward Bear Revue.

"We were unusual because we split our talents three ways," recalls Weldon. "Not only were the three of us playing all the parts, but I looked after advertising and marketing, Danny did all the booking and Larry looked after the business; his mom was our bookkeeper. We even hired a lawyer friend of mine and we incorporated as a company, so we had equal shares. We were serious."

Edward Bear Revue (the name literally taken from the first lines of A.A. Milne's book *Winnie-the-Pooh*) began playing birthdays, high schools, hotels, and bars, and was the house band at the Night Owl coffeehouse in Toronto's Yorkville scene, "but we were only discovered and got a music contract with Capitol," says Evoy, "because [producer] Paul White accidentally saw us on a CBC television show. ... Right place, right time, I guess." Or, in music commentator Ritchie Yorke's words, "the band hit the magic circle of acceptance."

Capitol gambled. Edward Bear (they had dropped "Revue") had never recorded before. Nor had they registered a hit single, the usual prerequisite to laying down tracks for an album. Still, Capitol spent $12,000 to record and release their first LP, *Bearings*, in 1969. The album got plenty of airplay and strong sales response (10,000 units in Canada alone). Radio stations began focusing on a particular cut on the album, a song Evoy had written about an ex-girlfriend who had moved to Mexico and left him pining in Canada. Capitol released **You, Me and Mexico** as a single and it was an instant Top 10 hit in Canada and rose to number 68 on the American Top 100.

The success of **Mexico** made Edward Bear a commercial attraction. It paved the way for more albums – *Eclipse* in 1970 and *Edward Bear* in 1972 – and an international tour. The threesome bought an equipment truck and a renovated bus and hit the road. They engaged an opening act, a band called New Potatoes, and then incorporated them into their performances to produce a bigger sound.

Touring was not the band's forte. Danny Marks left the band and was replaced by guitarist Roger Ellis. The band kept clicking in the studio, however. Larry Evoy's next single, **Last Song**, became a smash hit in September

1972 in both Canada and the United States, selling over a million copies. The recording also earned Edward Bear the Juno for Outstanding Group Performance of the Year.

In spite of lacklustre moments during Edward Bear's touring history, a performance at the Rockpile (the Masonic Temple) in Toronto stands out. It was a hot summer night and people mobbed the concert hall to see the headline act, Led Zeppelin, from Britain. However, Zeppelin was detained from getting its equipment on stage because of a backstage disagreement over money. During the dispute, someone had removed a distributor cap from one of Zeppelin's equipment trucks. Stage setup came to a halt. Meanwhile, Edward Bear opened the concert.

"People were hanging off the rafters," recalls Paul Weldon. "It was the closest I think we got to the Haight-Ashbury atmosphere. People were sitting down with their legs over the balcony. And we played really well."

"Finally, negotiate, negotiate, Zeppelin said they would play," remembers Larry Evoy. "All of a sudden, here comes the distributor cap fired up from somewhere in the audience. So, Zeppelin whipped out its stuff on stage and played.

"Afterward people said we sounded way better than Led Zeppelin," says Danny Marks, "and that I played better than Jimmy Page. God knows I couldn't write or play like Page in the studio. But that night we were hot."

After 12 years, thousands of road trip miles, four albums, and at least four hit singles, however, Edward Bear packed it in.

"By the mid-70s," admits Weldon, "I was in my mid-thirties. My wife and I were expecting our first child," and he had an architectural career to tend to. Today, he's part owner of Stanford Design, a graphic art design and printing firm in Toronto. And just to keep his hand in music, "Saturday nights I play piano in a band called the Jazz Extension."

Even when he left Edward Bear, Danny Marks never stopped playing and learning about music, "because the real danger of being so big so young, was that it seemed too easy.

"I played every strip joint on Yonge Street … and learned from the ground up … I played in all kinds of bands … I did road shows for Datsun … I even did rock 'n' roll revival stuff and became the king of chicken wing bars," until a CBC radio producer, David Malahoff, put him on the air doing cover tunes and regular spots on *Basic Black* and *The Hum Line*, during which Marks and co-hosts Arthur Black and Dinah Christie try to solve musical mysteries based on partial melody lines or lyrics sent in by listeners.

In 1997, Marks' Cabbagetunes label released a labour of love – a recording called **Guitarchaeology** – a CD of his guitar playing "without the wawa pedals, without the fuzz-tones … just the pure tone and clean sound of electric guitar."

Meanwhile, the originator of Edward Bear, Larry Evoy, has left the playing of music behind. Today, he and his wife run a horse farm, and a music publishing business whose sole activity is "managing the copyright and re-packaging of Edward Bear songs.

"It's catering to the baby-boom bulge in the States, where all these oldie goldie stations keep playing our songs. It's almost a full-time occupation," feeding the apparently insatiable market for Edward Bear material into the 21st century.

Shirley Eikhard
b. Sackville, New Brunswick, November 7, 1955

Few performers have experienced both halves of the double-barrelled, popular music description – singer-songwriter – as fully as Shirley Eikhard has. Her exploration of each half has shaped who she is as an artist and a person.

She started early. In 1967, when she was 12, Shirley Eikhard debuted as a singer at a fiddlers' competition in Cobourg, Ontario. Given her mother June Eikhard's competitive talent as the first woman participant in the Canadian Open Old Time Fiddlers' Contest, and her father Cecil Eikhard's bass playing in the family band (called the Tantramar Ramblers), Shirley's presence at a music festival is no surprise. The next year, Shirley performed at the Mariposa Folk Festival and the next, 1969, on CBC-TV's *Singalong Jubilee*.

Courtesy Richard Flohil

"My family were on vacation [in Prince Edward Island]," she told arts writer Peter Feniak in the *Globe and Mail*. "My mother was playing in the bar there. I got up and sang at the party on Saturday night and [they] said, 'Who is this girl?'"

The tape was passed to *Singalong Jubilee* producer Manny Pittson at CBC-TV in Halifax. Soon afterwards, Pittson invited Eikhard to appear on the show. Then, he played a tape of an Eikhard composition for Anne Murray, who recorded it. **It Takes Time**, released in 1971, followed Anne Murray's breakthrough success with "Snowbird."

The resulting artist's contract for Eikhard led her onto a fast track of recording and performing. She recorded her first single, **Smiling Wine**, in 1972, and quickly became one of Canada's most visible stage acts, touring concert halls and coffeehouses (including a cross-Canada tour with Hagood Hardy). Her "dark alto" voice and widespread popularity won her back-to-back Juno Awards as Top Female Country Artist in 1972 and 1973, and she even travelled the world on Canadian Armed Forces tours. By 1976, Eikhard had made the transition from country to popular music and released her biggest hit, a version of Fleetwood Mac's "Say You Love Me."

The pace of being a performer, however, had robbed her of what she called a "normal" life. Hers was an existence of performing and travelling, not living close to home and school. Instead of being with her family or her peers, her acquaintances were promoters and some "dishonest, incompetent" agents and managers who booked her into impossible venues. She developed stage fright and later, on the hotel-lounge circuit, discovered an allergy to cigarette smoke. That's when Eikhard traded in her stage life for a songwriter's life; in 1985, she and Colleen Peterson swapped apartments – hers in Toronto for Peterson's in Nashville. During six weeks in Nashville, Eikhard wrote 16 songs, including **(Let's Give Them) Something to Talk About**.

Still, it took more than a creative surge to make her songwriting career a success. With words of encouragement from the likes of Anne Murray, Hal David, and even Leonard Cohen, Eikhard persisted. One by one, artists began performing and recording her songs – including Gary Buck, Donna Ramsey, Ginette Reno, Rita Coolidge, Emmylou Harris, Alannah Myles, and Chet Atkins (who recorded her instrumental composition, **Pickin' My Way**).

Still, Eikhard admits, while some took the chance and cut her songs, there were thousands of rejections and delays, including the seven years it took before **Something to Talk About** became a hit. But when Bonnie Raitt needed a radio-ready single for her *Luck of the Draw* album, Eikhard's demo tape had been sitting in a box at Raitt's office for seven months; it was just what the album needed, and in 1991, when it was released as a single, **Something to Talk About** became a Top 10 hit in both Canada and the United States. Raitt's recording was, in Eikhard's eyes, "the stamp of hipness, the stamp of approval."

The success of **Something to Talk About** (including Grammy Awards for both Raitt and Eikhard in 1991), coupled with the premature deaths of artist friends – Colleen Peterson and Diane Heatherington – sparked Eikhard to "get on with the projects I'd dreamed about," including jazz. Having grown up with the music of Chet Baker, Paul Desmond, Charlie Parker, and Cleo Laine, Eikhard now focused on learning to write in the jazz idiom. She also returned to the studio for the first time in eight years to record a jazz CD, *If I Had My Way*.

When Eikhard released her ninth album, *The Last Hurrah*, in 2000, critics suggested it was time to forget Eikhard the folkie, country singer, and hit-creator and to welcome Eikhard the jazz singer. The *Toronto Star*'s Geoff Chapman described "her natural ability with phrasing and versatile lived-in voice with its grainy tones [fitting] perfectly on a session of new songs crammed with wry sentiment."

Percy Faith *b. Toronto, Ontario, April 7, 1908; d. Los Angeles, 1976*

During his quarter of a century as music director of the popular music division of Columbia Records, Percy Faith recorded more than 45 albums for the label.

Among the recording artists indebted to Faith were Tony Bennett, who made three gold records with Faith: **Because of You, From Rags to Riches and Cold, Cold Heart**; and Guy Mitchell, whose career was launched with a Faith composition, **My Heart Cries for You**. Other performers whose careers were intertwined with Faith's were Rosemary Clooney, Johnny Mathis, Doris Day, and opera singer Eileen Farrell.

Faith's film scores included *Tammy Tell Me True, I'd Rather Be Rich, The Love Goddess, The Third Day, The Oscar,* and *Love Me or Leave Me.* The last-named, which was actually his first motion picture score, was nominated in 1955 for an Academy Award.

He composed piano, choral, and orchestral works during the 1940s and he won a $1000 prize in Chicago for his operetta *The Gandy Dancer.*

He began studying violin at the age of seven and piano when he was 10. He studied at the Toronto Conservatory of Music and made his debut at the age of 15 at Massey Hall, playing Liszt's *Hungarian Fantasia.* Even before that, when he was 12 years old, he was providing piano accompaniment to silent movies in Toronto movie houses. He was paid three dollars a night – plus car fare.

But an accident when he was 18, in which his hands were severely burned, ended his hopes of a career as a concert pianist. So he studied arranging and conducting and soon began arranging for the hotel orchestras of Luigi Romanelli and Rex Battle. He also wrote arrangements for the radio orchestra of Geoffrey Waddington. By the late 1920s he was arranging and conducting various radio shows, culminating in his own *Music by Faith* in 1938–40.

Although this series was primarily for Canadian consumption, the Mutual Broadcasting Company relayed it to the United States in 1938. The following year, *Variety*, the show business journal, held a poll to determine the most popular U.S. musical program. The Canadian *Music by Faith* was in fourth place.

Tommy Dorsey and Paul Whiteman, among others, urged Faith to move to the United States, but he remained in his native country until 1940. With the sudden death of Joseph Pasternak, conductor of the popular radio show of the day, *The Carnation Contented Hour*, Faith accepted a three-week engagement as guest conductor. So impressive were his appearances that the program's sponsor prevailed on him to continue in the post.

Later, he moved on to other U.S.-sponsored radio shows (Coca-Cola and Woolworth were among his sponsors in later years).

After conducting various musical radio shows he became conductor-arranger for Columbia Records. Next came the move to Los Angeles for film work. But Faith returned to Canada frequently, notably during the Second World War for Victory Bond drives and later conducting concerts and CBC television specials.

Winning awards became almost habit-forming for Percy Faith. His "Theme from *A Summer Place*" won a Grammy Award in 1960 and his "Love Theme from *Romeo and Juliet*" was chosen Best Performance by a Chorus in 1969. Among his 45 albums were three Gold Records: *Viva* (1957), *Bouquet* (1959), and *Themes for Young Lovers* (1963).

While concentrating primarily on his recording work, Faith also developed into a major concert conductor, both in North America and overseas. He conducted a special concert in Vancouver for then–Prime Minister Lester B. Pearson, an appearance in Salerno, Italy, conducting the La Scala Opera Orchestra, plus television specials for the BBC in London and a three-week tour of Japan.

Over the years he arranged and conducted orchestral settings for the scores of such Broadway musicals as *Kismet*, *My Fair Lady*, *Porgy and Bess*, *South Pacific*, *The Sound of Music*, *Camelot*, and *Subways Are for Sleeping*.

In 1974 he established the Percy Faith Award for music students at the University of Toronto as well as similar awards at the University of Southern California and the University of Jerusalem.

More than 29,000 pages of Faith's compositions and arrangements are on deposit at Brigham Young University in Salt Lake City, Utah.

Robert Farnon   *b. Toronto, Ontario, July 24, 1917*

Quite possibly Canada's most distinguished musical export, Robert Farnon began his musical studies with his mother when he was seven years old. By the middle of the 20th century he was widely regarded as the greatest living composer of light orchestral music in the world.

While still in his teens, Farnon became a household name across Canada through his many radio programs, especially the long-running series, *The Happy Gang*, of which he was a member from 1937 to 1943. He played lead trumpet in Percy Faith's orchestra, and when Faith decided to move to the United States Farnon took over the baton.

Farnon went overseas during the Second World War as music director for *The Army Show* and his name gradually became known throughout Britain and Europe. He arranged music for the English dance bands of Ambrose, Geraldo, and Ted Heath. He had his own radio series (*Journey into Melody*) and also served as choral arranger for Vera Lynn.

André Previn called Farnon "the greatest living writer for strings."

He was Captain Robert Farnon then, in charge of a large concert band, plus a 20-piece dance band. There was also a smaller jazz band that was allowed to take occasional civilian jobs to earn more money. (Trumpeter Fred Davis was one of these musicians.)

Normally, Farnon did not play with them, because he was an officer and they were not. But on one occasion, the pianist took ill and Farnon agreed to substitute for him. To disguise his rank, he wore his worst battle-dress jacket and darkened down his captain's pips.

At war's end, Farnon took his discharge in England, having decided the musical climate there was more suited to his talents. He continued to do radio and recordings, not only playing for various singers but introducing many of his own compositions, including such pieces as **Willie the Whistler**, **Portrait of a Flirt**, and **Jumping Bean**.

While still living in Toronto, he made frequent visits to New York and, despite his public association with "light music," he joined jam sessions with such jazz stars as Dizzy Gillespie and Oscar Peterson.

Since 1958, he has been a resident of the island of Guernsey in the English Channel, but for years he made periodic visits back home, partly to visit a sister living in Ontario.

Over the years, he has arranged and/or conducted recordings for such popular artists as Tony Bennett, Lena Horne, Peggy Lee, Frank Sinatra, Sarah Vaughan, The Swingle Singers, and jazz musicians such as George Shearing, Ben Webster, and Phil Woods. In 1963 he was in Copenhagen recording an album with Sarah Vaughan, *Vaughan with Voices*, which also featured the Danish Svend Saaby Choir.

Farnon's association with Tony Bennett has been long and fruitful. They made several albums together and have appeared in many concerts, notably in January 1971, when Farnon conducted the London Philharmonic for Bennett at the Royal Albert Hall as part of that institution's 100th-anniversary celebrations.

No fewer than 40 films have benefited from a Robert Farnon musical score, including *Spring in Park Lane, Maytime in Mayfair,* and *Captain Horatio Hornblower, R.N.*

The Farnon brand of humour is evident not only in some of his music but also in some of his comments. In 1962, Farnon was music director for *The Road to Hong Kong,* with Bing Crosby, Bob Hope, and Dorothy Lamour.

"They blamed me for killing off the series," he later joked. "It was the last 'Road' film they ever made!"

Farnon never lost touch with his Canadian roots; he has even composed pieces specifically for Canadian musicians he admired, including **Pleasure of Your Company**, for Oscar Peterson, and **Prelude and Dance** for harmonica and orchestra, written for and recorded by Tommy Reilly.

Over the years, Farnon made numerous return visits to Canada. He came home in 1961 for an appearance on the television program *Music Makers* with Jack Kane. He was back in 1969 for a television special titled *The Music of Robert Farnon.* The same year he did a concert at Maple Leaf Gardens with Vera Lynn. And in 1984, several Farnon works were played in his presence during a Toronto Symphony Christmas concert.

In 1997, he was in Brantford, Ontario for a concert of Farnon music organized by Peter Appleyard, with Skitch Henderson conducting a large orchestra. He also went to Ottawa, where Victor Feldbrill conducted a program of Farnon's music at the National Arts Centre. One of the highlights of that program was a performance of Farnon's **Rhapsody for Violin and Orchestra.**

Farnon has sometimes been portrayed as one of his native land's overlooked musical artists – most notably in Gene Lees' book, *Canada's Forgotten Musician,* published in 1974.

But the surge of interest in Robert Farnon's achievements, especially in the 1990s, belies that woeful appraisal. At age 84, Farnon remains one of Canada's most illustrious expatriates. In 1996 he received a Grammy for his arrangement of **Lament**, performed by J. J. Johnson and the Robert Farnon Orchestra.

Victor Feldbrill   *b. Toronto, Ontario, April 4, 1924*

Among other distinctions, Victor Feldbrill has probably conducted more orchestras than any other Canadian music director. He has also championed a great deal of work by Canadian composers.

The son of Polish-Jewish immigrants, he began studying violin at the age of 12 with Sigmund Steinberg, then theory with John Weinzweig, and conducting with Ettore Mazzoleni. At 18, he was conductor of the University of Toronto Symphony Orchestra and made his Toronto Symphony Orchestra conducting debut the following year.

Over the years, he was guest conductor for CBC orchestras in Vancouver, Edmonton, Winnipeg, and Montreal, and for various CBC-TV opera productions. He also appeared with the Atlantic Symphony Orchestra and the Calgary Philharmonic, and has conducted many times for the Canadian Opera Company. (Notably, he conducted the premiere of Harry Somers' opera *Louis Riel* in 1967.) He founded the Canadian Chamber Players in 1952 and conducted them for several seasons in Hart House Sunday concerts and elsewhere.

After studying in Salzberg in 1956, he was assistant conductor of the Toronto Symphony in 1956–57. Next, he conducted the Hart House Orchestra at the Brussels World's Fair, then became conductor of the Winnipeg Symphony Orchestra, a position he retained until 1968. During his years with the WSO, he expanded its repertoire to include pop and youth concerts and toured various Manitoba communities.

Feldbrill conducted the International Conference of Composers at Stratford in 1960 and the Vancouver International Festival in 1961. He was also the resident conductor for sessions of the National Youth Orchestra in six different years.

As part of an exchange program, he visited the USSR in 1963 and led orchestras in Ukraine – Lvov, Kiev, Odessa, and Zaporozhye. On a second visit, he conducted in the Soviet cities of Baku, Minsk, and Tbilisi. He has also appeared as guest conductor for the BBC and guest-conducted in Italy in 1972.

In 1979, he was the first Canadian guest conductor at the Tokyo National University of Art and Music, thus beginning an annual association with that institution that resulted in his appointment as a professor in 1981, and as principal conductor of the university's Geidei Philharmonic in 1982. Feldbrill did not pass up the chance to introduce Japanese audiences to some of the work of Canadian composers.

He was also the first Canadian invited to conduct the Philippine Philharmonic Orchestra in Manila in 1984; he also guest-conducted in China in 1987. In 1990, he was named music director and principal conductor of the Hamilton Philharmonic.

Victor Feldbrill, ever alert to the work of Canadian composers, has introduced the music of no less than 25 such artists, from Godfrey Ridout and Harry Somers to Howard Cable and Harry Freedman. During his decade as conductor of the Winnipeg Symphony, the orchestra played more music by Canadian composers than all other Canadian orchestras put together.

Victor Feldbrill's professional career began modestly enough, in 1943, when he was 19. Having been called up by the Navy, he became a violinist in the pit band of *Meet the Navy*, the Royal Canadian Navy's wartime project for entertaining Canadians in uniform. With a letter of introduction from Sir Ernest MacMillan, many doors opened for young Feldbrill.

Shortly after VE Day, the *Meet the Navy* troupe flew across the English Channel to do some shows in Europe. Feldbrill managed to get to Amsterdam and sneaked into a rehearsal of the famed Amsterdam Concertgebouw. Suddenly, the rehearsal was stopped when someone called him over. The orchestra's new conductor, Eduard van Beinum, was a heavy smoker and wanted a cigarette.

"I didn't smoke," Feldbrill recalled many years later, "but you needed cigarettes to buy stuff, so I gave him a package. He was going to give it back and I said, 'No, please keep it.' He asked me to wait and he said, 'Who are you?' I said I was with the Canadian navy but I was interested in conducting, and he said I could come to rehearsals. And later he gave me scores to read."

A decade after the war ended, the Amsterdam orchestra came to Toronto. "By that time," Feldbrill continued, "I was assistant conductor of the Toronto Symphony, and there was a big do for the visiting orchestra, and we were invited, of course. I thought, 'Oh, well, I'm not going to make a fuss about this. I walked past van Beinum, the conductor. We shook hands and he looked at me and said, 'You're the man with the cigarettes.' He had remembered!"

And it is a story Feldbrill likes to remember.

Maynard Ferguson

b. Montreal, Quebec, May 4, 1928

"There are few sights more impressive in animal physiology than the muscles in Maynard Ferguson's upper thorax straining for a top C. Unfortunately, on record there are no such distractions; putting a Ferguson disc on the turntable evokes sensations ranging from walking into a high wind to being run down by a truck." These uncharitable words about the Montreal-born trumpeter were penned by Richard Cook and Brian Morton in *The Penguin Guide to Jazz on CD* (1996).

A decade and a half earlier, Mark Miller, reviewing Ferguson's annual appearance at the Ontario Place Forum, mentioned a couple of the tunes he played – "Hit in the Head" and "Give It One" – and then said it was "no coincidence that these titles suggest physical aggression – that's the name of his game." Miller added that Maynard's version of "Take the 'A' Train" "goes 60 m.p.h. and screams around corners."

The following year, when Maynard played Ontario Place, a reviewer for the *Toronto Star* wrote: "Things haven't changed. Last night, Ferguson employed his patented stratospheric trumpet flourishes on every tune. Whether it was a ballad or something up tempo, he used the same approach; when in doubt, play high. On 'Birdland' this was exciting. On 'As Time Goes By' it was ludicrous."

The target of all these barbed comments came from a family in which one parent was a schoolteacher and the other a school principal. Maynard Ferguson began studying music at the age of four. His first instruments were violin and piano.

At age nine, he was so impressed by a cornet soloist at a Sunday social that "I said to my dad, 'Wow, that looks like fun. Could you get me one of those?'"

Like his fellow Montrealer, Oscar Peterson, Maynard was working professionally by age 14, spending eight hours a day studying at the French Conservatory while working the clubs six nights a week. Still in his teens, he worked with Montreal-area bandleaders Stan Wood, Roland Davis, and Johnny Holmes. While leading his own band in Montreal and Toronto in the mid-1940s, he came to the attention of U.S. bandleaders.

As pianist Paul Bley later recalled, "Maynard would always open the show and he played three octaves higher on trumpet than anyone else – you ought to have seen the jaws drop on the visiting musicians."

Predictably, by 1948 Ferguson moved to the United States, where he worked in the bands of Boyd Raeburn, Jimmy Dorsey, and Charlie Barnet during the 1950s. Next came a three-year stint with Stan Kenton. That was when he won the *Down Beat* readers' poll for trumpet in 1950, 1951, and 1952.

"When I was with Stan," he recalled many years later, "he used to introduce my feature every night by saying, 'Here's a guy who used to lead his own band up in Canada and I'm sure some day soon he will be leading his own group here, too.'" Those simple words of encouragement meant a lot to Ferguson and they have often been repeated to members of his own band. Yet, he doesn't like to look back too often.

In fact, he was responsible for some controversy in the 1970s, when he argued against nostalgia. An interviewer asked him if he thought the Big Band Era might come back. "I made a lot of enemies once when I said, 'Christ, I hope not!' I don't want it to come back as it used to be in a state of nostalgia and 'Remember this one folks when the B-49s were flying over London and the boys were dying at Dunkirk' and then we go into Glenn Miller's theme song ... that type of thing. No!"

Over the years, Ferguson led numerous groups of varying sizes, playing bop and even "fusion," always apparently striving for a different way to attract audiences. One reviewer said of his music: "Still, there probably isn't a trumpet player alive who can make more music-hungry teenagers stand on their seats with their jaws to the ground. And that must account for something."

Although he moved first to New York, in 1973, and to Ojai, California, in the early 1980s, he has often returned to Canada for appearances at Ontario Place, the Stratford Festival, and Toronto's Massey Hall, and for television appearances on such series as *Parade* and *In the Mood*.

By now something of an elder statesman in the music world, Ferguson, approaching his mid-seventies, devotes much of his time to nurturing promising young musicians. As he told *The Jazz Report*'s Greg Sutherland in 1997,

"It's very gratifying to assist these talented young musicians early in their careers just like so many others did for me."

Maureen Forrester

b. Montreal, Quebec, July 25, 1930

In 1965, when the opera singer Jan Peerce was 60, he was in the midst of an exhausting recording session in Vienna. But rather than grab a nap when he was on a break, he would slip into another recording studio to listen to a then 34-year-old singer.

"Sleep?" he commented. "Who needs it? One hour listening to Maureen Forrester is more refreshing to the spirit than three hours of slumber."

One American music critic called Forrester "Canada's greatest natural resource since gold was discovered in the Klondike."

After one of her performances, the New York *Herald Tribune* rhapsodized: "Miss Forrester has a contralto that one can only describe by comparing it to a stained-glass window with the midday sun pouring through it."

The object of these hosannas was then a young girl who dismayed her parents in Montreal by quitting school at 13 because she felt she wasn't learning anything. Despite a lack of formal education, Forrester learned to speak four languages and to sing fluently in nine.

The future queen of international contraltos was born in Montreal, the youngest of four children of a Scotsman and an Irishwoman who had met shortly after their arrival in Canada. Maureen began to sing in infancy, and although money was scarce in those Depression days, the Forresters sent Maureen to piano lessons at the age of five. She sang at a Sunday-school rally at eight. Later, she and her sister Jean used to harmonize in the kitchen while doing dishes. By the time she was 15, Maureen was singing regularly in a church choir. Although she was a soprano when she started singing, as she matured her voice deepened. When she was 16, virtually overnight her voice deepened to a throbbing contralto.

When she was 23 and singing in an Ottawa high school gymnasium, she saw, sitting in the audience, Eugene Kash, who was conductor of the Ottawa Philharmonic Orchestra. Forrester maintained, years later, that she said to herself: "There is the man I am going to marry."

They were married the following year and had five children. The youngest, a daughter, was temporarily referred to as "Opus Five." (Forrester and Kash were to separate in 1974.)

It was Forrester's good luck that her 1956 debut at Town Hall was the only musical event of any importance that day. Consequently, all the New York newspapers were represented by their senior music critics. "Voices of this order," wrote Howard Taubman in *The New York Times*, "make one feel that the fabled golden era is not gone forever."

In time, such praise was clearly justified. The famed conductors who kissed her hand in front of standing audiences ranged from Barbirolli to Walter, from Beecham to Szell, from Bernstein to Stokowksi, from Karajan to Ormandy, from MacMillan to Ozawa to Reiner and many more.

Most famous singers don't begin to teach until their careers are finished, or at least waning. Not Forrester. In 1965, when she was only 35 years old, she already had half a dozen regular voice pupils. "I know most of the pitfalls by now," she told the CBC's Clyde Gilmour in an interview, "and I love passing on the fruits of my experience to others. Besides, a few good pupils help to keep a teacher on her toes."

Keeping on her toes was never a problem for Maureen Forrester. In addition to the 120 concerts (on several continents) in her hectic schedule, it was announced that starting in 1984 she was to be the new chair of the 27-year-old Canada Council. When the idea was first proposed to her by Secretary of State Francis Fox, she had her doubts: "I said to him that I'm not sure I have the necessary amount of time, because I'm heavily booked for the next four years. But I told him I'd think about it for a couple of days. Then I called him back and said, 'Okay, I'll do it, but you must realize that I can't give up my career because I do have to make a living.'"

Nevertheless, she stayed as head of the Canada Council, a voluntary position, for five years, during which she travelled extensively, continuing to promote Canadian music and actively communicating to various levels of government the need for greater support and increased funding for the arts on behalf of Canadian musicians, artists, and cultural organizations.

Her immensely successful career resulted in her being awarded some 30 honorary degrees from universities across Canada. In addition to numerous other awards, in 1990 Forrester was inducted into the Juno Hall of Fame, the only classical artist besides Glenn Gould to be so honoured.

When she became head of the Canada Council, Forrester said: "I feel passionately about the arts in this country. I've had a great career, but I'm not on the upward swing of my career now; I'm on the other side of the mountain and I understand the needs of the artists in Canada."

Forrester was acclaimed not only in Canada and the United States, but throughout the British Isles and in France, Spain, Portugal, Italy, Switzerland,

Germany, Austria, Holland, Denmark, Norway, Sweden, Belgium, Russia, Australia, and New Zealand.

Although her sunny disposition became legendary among other singers, Forrester could, on occasion, display a bit of impatience – particularly when a rehearsal was delayed by another singer who arrived unprepared. "I do my homework," she said, "and I expect other people to do theirs."

In 1999, Maureen Forrester moved into the Performing Artists Lodge, in Toronto, mostly because the Lodge was home to other artists whom she had known over the years of her career. As it happened, her timing was perfect. The Lodge provides a certain amount of health care. Before the year was out, Forrester's memory was beginning to falter.

But she wasn't ready to give up. Before long, she had scheduled another recital for the following spring. Many years ago, she made a seemingly casual comment at a luncheon: "God gave me success young, because He knows I can't afford to retire early."

David Foster

b. Victoria, B.C., November 1, 1949

Although many Canadians are perhaps not familiar with the name David Foster, he has had more influence and more input into more popular recordings than anybody else in the music business.

Among those whose careers have been somehow enhanced by Foster's presence are Céline Dion, Kenny Rogers, Barbra Streisand, Rod Stewart, George Harrison, Tom Jones, Alice Cooper, Tina Turner, Cyndi Lauper, Michael Jackson, Kenny Loggins, Lionel Richie, Chicago, Hall and Oates, and Donna Summer.

When he was five years old, his mother realized David had a musical ear. While dusting the piano, she struck a key. Little David, in another room, called out, "That's an E." He was right. For the next eight years, he followed the Royal Conservatory program, which gave him a good technical foundation that would later prove valuable in recording studios.

He started out as a musician and eventually became one of the most successful record producers in the pop/rock music business. In his teens he was already working with a rock band called The Strangers (in England) and Ronnie Hawkins (in Toronto).

*David Foster (l.) with Richard Flohil
at the Juno Awards in 1989*

Foster became a protégé of Quincy Jones – and then one of his chief rivals as a producer in the early 1980s – at least in part due to his aggressive role at recording sessions.

He divides producing into two categories – "hands on" and "hands off." "I typically have been known to be a hands-on producer. You get in there, roll your shirtsleeves up, dig in real deep, rewrite the songs and play on a lot of the records, direct the thing from beginning to end."

In 1985, Foster received no less than six Grammy nominations – more than anyone else in the music business. By then, he had been nominated nine times and won twice.

In an interview for the *Vancouver Sun* that year, Foster said: "My experience with the Grammys in the past is that it's a great moment of recognition, and then it's kind of business as usual the next day."

But he knows that a "behind-the-scenes" person never gets the public recognition that performers do. "I read the *L.A. Times* the night the nominations came out," he said. "It just said, 'Tina Turner, Prince and Cyndi Lauper topped the Grammys with five nominations,' and I wasn't even mentioned."

As a writer/producer, he had his early disappointments, but his big commercial breakthrough came in 1979 with Earth Wind and Fire's *I Am* album. Foster produced, arranged, and co-wrote all the songs and it sold more than two million records in the United States alone.

His hands-on approach was a key to his success with the group called Chicago. "When I started with Chicago, I had their first five albums – I grew up on their first five albums," he said. "They were very inspirational to me, that group. They were the first group to show me that you could have jazz and rock and mix it."

Hired to produce records for them, he listened to their material and then told them bluntly, "Guys, you've got no songs here." The group challenged him to show them some good songs – and he did. "I co-wrote with all of them and we came up with hits."

He co-wrote eight of the ten songs on their next album, *Chicago 16*. On the next Chicago album, he co-wrote only four of the songs because the group came up with more good material. But, Foster said later, "I co-wrote three out of the four hits" on that album.

Foster wasn't shy in discussing his successes. "One plus," he said, "is the money's so good. If you take the Chicago album, I'll probably make three times as much as anybody in the band." (One published report said he made a million dollars from that album alone.)

Another plus, he added, was that "I can walk around on the street and nobody knows who the hell I am. I mean, Kenny Rogers, when he travels around, he's got six security guards, and they've all got walkie-talkies."

Apart from his more than two dozen Grammy nominations, Foster has won various awards and honours, including one for the soundtrack of the film *St. Elmo's Fire*.

He appeared in concert at Expo '86 in Vancouver and played with symphony orchestras in Vancouver, Toronto, and other cities. Two years later, his rousing "Winter Games," the theme of the Winter Olympic Games in Calgary, was a hit across Canada.

David Foster's great success as writer/producer/performer in pop music both in Canada and the world did not spoil him. "I would have to call myself a nice guy," he once told an interviewer. But then he added: "Ambition could possibly be my middle name."

The Four Lads

formed 1947 in Toronto: Jimmy Arnold first tenor; Bernie Toorish second tenor; Connie Codarini bass; Frank Busseri (b. Toronto, October 10, 1932) baritone

The first Canadian vocal group to attract wide public attention across the country – and across the border – were The Four Lads.

They first met in 1947 as students at St. Michael's Cathedral Choir School

The Four Lads (clockwise from top left): Jimmy Arnold, Connie Codarini, Frank Busseri, Bernie Toorish

in Toronto. After doing the mandatory Gregorian chants and scales and spirituals with other classmates, these four would get together on their own time and experiment with barbershop quartet songs and pop tunes. They got valuable experience performing at weddings, dances, and the like. They were soon good enough to be offered a booking at a local hotel, but Ontario's strict liquor laws of the time prevented the boys from accepting it – they were too young.

After several other tries, they decided to call themselves The Four Dukes and soon got an appearance on the popular *Arthur Godfrey's Talent Scouts* show, where they placed second in that evening's competition. But a phone call from Detroit – right after the show – informed them, rather forcefully, that there was already a group called The Four Dukes, so they had better find a new name.

The boys finished school at the age of 17 and decided to try singing professionally. Their first break came when Elwood Glover featured them on his CBC network radio show *Cross-Canada Cavalcade*.

In the spring of 1950, they got a double break: a chance to perform at New York City's Le Ruban Bleu and to receive a bit of sound advice from that club's legendary impresario, Julius Monk. He said: "You four lads need a new name." Monk inadvertently supplied it.

Their appearance in New York did so well that their two-week booking was extended to 30 weeks. They were reviewed favourably in *Variety* – "The Show Business Bible" – and next came an audition for Mitch Miller, then director of Artists and Repertoire for Columbia Records.

The Lads provided backup singing for Johnny Ray's biggest hits, "Cry" and "The Little White Cloud That Cried." They were also heard in the background on recordings by Doris Day, Jill Corey, Tony Arden, and Frankie Laine.

In 1952, Columbia released the first songs The Four Lads did on their own: **Istanbul (Not Constantinople)**, **Skokian**, and **Gilly, Gilly Ossenfetter by the Sea**. Three years later, they recorded their biggest hit, **Moments to Remember**, which sold more than four million copies and rode the pop charts for 26 weeks. It was to become their signature song.

Among their other hits were **No, Not Much**, **Put a Light in the Window**, **Happy Anniversary**, and "Standing on the Corner" from Frank Loesser's musical opera *The Most Happy Fella*. In March of 1956, The Lads went into the Columbia studio in New York to lay down a version of "Standing on the Corner." Frank Busseri remembers the unique occasion vividly.

"We generally recorded in the evening, between 7 and 9 o'clock," Busseri said. "The four of us walked in and the studio was all ready, with 40 musicians, the technical staff, and Mitch Miller all waiting. Mitch said, 'Okay, let's try a test, a run-through.' No overdubbing, nothing fancy, just the four of us singing the song. … When we finished, Frank (Loesser) came into the studio and said, 'That's it! We've got it!' One take."

The Four Lads' first take on "Standing on the Corner" reached number 3 on the charts two months before the show opened on Broadway. It too was a hit.

Three decades later, The Four Lads appeared at the Imperial Room of Toronto's Royal York Hotel, but they were only one-third of the show. Appearing with them were two other quartets from the 1950s, The Four Freshmen and The Four Aces, both American groups.

Writing in the *Toronto Star*, pop music critic Geoff Chapman said: "The silver-haired lads, led by original member Frank Busseri, were relaxed from the first note, their gentle stage presence providing the right atmosphere for some balanced harmony work."

At the studio in New York, The Four Lads' recording team listens to the first and only take of "Standing On The Corner." (l. to r.) Jimmy Arnold, Frank Busseri, Connie Codarini, (orchestrator) Ray Ellis, (composer) Frank Loesser, Bernie Toorish and (producer) Mitch Miller.

It was during this period that Frank Busseri talked about the group's early success: "The big thing that happened was when Mitch Miller decided to switch Jimmy [Arnold] from second tenor to lead, because he noticed a distinctive sound we had. We weren't great innovators. It was just good music – well arranged and well sung. We didn't sound as black as some of the subsequent vocal groups and, though we saw the rock thing coming, we couldn't see changing our style to sing that way."

But press clippings dating back to their initial success suggest Busseri was being a bit modest. All four had perfect pitch, and their conduct was exemplary. In keeping with a practice established by their choirmaster at St. Michael's, Monsignor J. E. Ronan, they made a practice of always praying together before singing.

While on the road, they collectively phoned home to their parents every Tuesday night. They even made a point of signing autographs together. When they were asked to sing at high school assemblies, they always obliged, even if they had been playing a club until very late the night before.

The Lads never hit the charts again after the 1950s. The group's career was effectively finished when lead singer Jimmy Arnold left in 1962. But Busseri kept the group alive until 1979 in one form or another. Living in Pasadena, California, he managed a version of The Four Lads, who performed the group's original material. He also became involved in handling the career of Connie Francis, whom he had known since the 1950s.

The original Lads keep in touch only sporadically. Jimmy Arnold became a schoolteacher in Sacramento, California, Connie Codarini went into the restaurant business in San Diego, and Bernie Toorish sold insurance in Cleveland.

In 1984, The Four Lads (together with their contemporaries The Crew Cuts and The Diamonds) received the Juno Lifetime Achievement Award. Canada's first vocal quartet to hit the big time certainly have moments to remember.

Ralph Fraser
b. New Glasgow, N.S., July 3, 1925

Anyone who didn't know him could be forgiven for thinking there are two Ralph Frasers. But that's just because there are two sides to him. The more serious side is most evident when he plays piano, as he does so skillfully on his CD titled *Welcome to My Dreams*. This CD was recorded at the Ontario Science Centre in February 2000 for Ted O'Reilly's CJRT-FM (now JAZZ-FM) station. On the album, Fraser plays solo piano, turning his talents to some 18 tunes, mostly familiar standards like "Skylark," "Little Girl Blue," a lively version of Jerome Kern's "Pick Yourself Up," and "Witchcraft," all of which he plays with his accustomed dash. Also well worth a listen are "Welcome to My Dreams," the album's title tune, which Ralph plays with admirable sensitivity, and Claude Thornhill's "Snowfall," a melody too often neglected.

Then, just for contrast, there's Milt Buckner's tune "Hamp's Boogie,"

which gives the Fraser inventiveness a chance to shine. There are also a couple of Fraser originals, **Go Train**, a light fling at boogie-woogie, and **Fat's Blues**, a pleasing salute to the great Fats Waller. And he also has fun giving that old chestnut "Canadian Capers" a boogie-woogie treatment.

He was just 16 when he moved from Nova Scotia to Toronto, but he continued his studies at the Royal Conservatory of Music. He learned to play organ and then vibraharp.

Fraser's career has been busy and varied. Over the years, he has played with Vic Centro, Cliff McKay, Billy O'Connor, Lucio Agostini, Jack Kane, Lloyd Edwards, and others.

One of his first record dates was an album featuring two pianists – himself and Carol Hughes – with an orchestra led by Bert Niosi. It wasn't until after they had begun playing together that Ralph discovered Carol was also from Nova Scotia.

In the 1950s he played in Toronto bars – the St. Charles, Dooley's, Duffy's Tavern – and also in the Jazz Unlimited Band appearing at Massey Hall. When he was a kid in New Glasgow, it was his dream to join the Toronto Maple Leafs. Well, he did eventually play at Maple Leaf Gardens, but not hockey – the organ. And his work at the Gardens also led to other sports-connected gigs. He played the organ for Blue Jays baseball games, for Argo football games, for soccer, basketball, and lacrosse matches, and even at Canadian National Exhibition horse shows.

Just for a change he played with the Dave Woods Band at Ontario Place – three shows a day for 220 days. Next came a two-month engagement at the Hotel Vancouver, followed by a jazz cruise with Jim Galloway.

"I began my career as a daredevil the day my brother Al and I made a death-defying flight down Kirk Hill in New Glasgow on one tricycle, through two busy intersections, across railway tracks, and managed to stop in time to avoid going down the bank and into the East River," he has said. "Al later became a Spitfire pilot while I kept on living dangerously by playing and writing music and in my spare time fishing, where hurting yourself is as easy as falling off a log."

Ralph always had an interest in playing jazz, but as most musicians know, playing jazz and making music don't necessarily go hand in hand. So Fraser played the field. And he was certainly well equipped to do that.

One of his early albums was titled *Variations on Popular Themes*; it included, among other things, his own variations on Edvard Grieg's "Anitra's Dance" from the *Peer Gynt Suite*.

In 1986, leading an eight-piece band, he played on the *Crown Odyssey* sailing the Mediterranean Sea and the Atlantic and Pacific Oceans. He played for all the acts, including Flip Wilson. Says Fraser: "Flip playfully accused me of hitting the black keys harder than the white ones."

He spent much of his playing life demonstrating his versatility – light classics, pops, country, jazz, show music, Irish songs. Name it, he could play it. And if he couldn't, he'd write it on the spot – music and lyrics.

Which leads to the "other side" of Ralph Fraser – the witty parodist. Exhibit A is a CD titled *Living Dangerously* on which he plays piano and sings 10 entertaining ditties of his own composition, more or less.

Time and a Half in Newfoundland has fun with the half-hour time difference between that province and the other Maritimes. One of the most clever is a parody about Hamilton (to the tune of "Camelot") in which he pokes merciless fun at that industrial city, its smog and other imperfections. Sample: "There's no legal limit to the smog here. ..."

Another irresistible item is **Dooley's Saturday Night**, a lighthearted salute to the many Saturday nights Fraser spent playing piano and singing at Dooley's – and the difficulties of trying to play all the songs requested.

Fraser retired – or tried to – in 1990, but he got bored, so he joined the band Canadian Tribute to Glenn Miller, led by Don Pierre, which has had considerable success in recreating the Miller sound.

At last word, Ralph Fraser was writing more songs and concert band arrangements, as well as planning an album of his own piano pieces.

André Gagnon

b. St-Pacome-de-Kamouraska, Quebec, August 1, 1942

Although he felt equally at ease in both, Quebec pianist and composer André Gagnon moved from the world of classical instrumental recital to that of the pop concert stage in the late 1960s. In the transition, he also grew from competent accompanist to internationally renowned entertainer.

"He captivates, he fills the stage," reported *La Presse* newspaper in 1976. "He is at ease and amusing and he exploits fully (unconsciously perhaps) the unsophisticated images he has always projected."

André Gagnon must have known very early in his life that there was more to the piano than scales and arpeggios. As a child, even before he attended school, he began taking lessons, and at age six even wrote several short pieces. At 10, he began studying theory and as a teenager André attended the Conservatoire de musique de Québec à Montréal – taking piano with Germaine Malépart and composition with Clermont Pépin. Throughout his classical study, however, André was also attracted to popular music.

In 1961, Gagnon went to Paris (on a Quebec government grant) to study accompaniment and conducting with Yvonne Loriod. When he returned to Canada the next year, he connected with Quebec singer-songwriter Claude Léveillée and served as his piano accompanist, arranger and music director. Their collaboration from 1962–1969 took Gagnon on tours across Canada, Europe, and into the Soviet Union. It also showcased Gagnon's keyboard talents on a half-dozen of Léveillée's LP recordings during that period.

Other artists who employed André Gagnon, the accompanist, included Jacques Blanchet, Pierre Calvé, Renée Claude, Claude Gauthier, Pauline Julien, Pierre Létourneau, and Monique Leyrac. In 1967, Gagnon appeared at Place des Arts in Montreal as principal soloist in a Mozart concert. He also recorded four albums for Columbia – ***Don't Ask Why***, ***Pour les Amants***, ***Notre Amour***, and ***Encore*** – all in 1968. These recordings whetted his appetite for the spotlight and in 1969, Gagnon left accompanying to work on his own career as a solo pianist, composer, and arranger.

First in England, Gagnon recorded with the London Baroque Orchestra; together they produced his four Vivaldi-like concertos, **Mes Quatre**

Saisons (1969). Then in Germany with the Hamburg Philharmonic Orchestra, he recorded a series of baroque-style suites, *Les Turluteries* (1972). Meantime, he represented Canada at Expo '70 in Japan and returned to Montreal to perform his own works with the McGill Chamber Orchestra at Place des Arts. By this time, his own compositions included more popular influences than ever before and he released two pop albums: *Saga* (1974) and *Neiges* (1975).

All nine tracks of *Neiges* were recorded in Montreal, including his composition up-tempo piece, **Wow**, which became an international hit, remaining on the *Billboard* charts for 24 weeks. The album itself earned Gagnon his first Juno Award for Best-Selling Album in 1976. The momentum of the single and the album carried him to concert dates in Europe and Mexico.

"Whether we like his music a little, a lot, or intensely," Pierre Beaulieu wrote in *La Presse* that year, "[Gagnon] makes sure that we enjoy ourselves. ... he is an excellent entertainer in the American sense of the word." The following year, 1977, he received a second Juno for Instrumental Artist of the Year.

As Benoit L'Herbier points out in the *Encyclopedia of Music in Canada*, Gagnon had mastered the knack of defying categories. "[His music] ranges widely and makes audacious combinations of elements from both sides of the barrier between the classics and pop music."

Following the immense success of *Neiges*, Gagnon found his composing talents in great demand. He scored Anne Ditchburn's ballet *Mad Shadows* (based on Marie-Claire Blais' novel), which the National Ballet of Canada premiered in Toronto in 1977. The same year, he composed ballet works premiered by the Compagnie de Danse Eddy Toussaint in Montreal. Meanwhile, he scored the NFB film *Games of the XXI Olympiad*, a CBS TV movie, and the feature film *Running*.

In 1979, André Gagnon was made an Officer of the Order of Canada.

For the theatrical stage, Gagnon wrote music for such Stratford Festival productions as *School for Scandal* and *Oedipus Rex*, directed by Robin Philips. He scored Michel Tremblay's opera libretto for *Nelligan*, performed by the Montreal Opera (which won a Felix Award for Best Show of the Year).

By the end of the 1990s, Gagnon had released more than 30 albums, some of which incorporated "new age" elements (such as *Saisons*) while others delivered a more traditional sound (such as his 1992 release *Noel*). In 1995, André Gagnon again received the Juno for Instrumental Artist of the Year. By that time, audiences in the Far East had discovered his music, so much so that he regularly played concerts in Japan and Korea. He apparently never tired of the art of performing his own works.

"I have played everywhere there is a piano," Gagnon once said, "and I'm still playing."

Jim Galloway

b. Ayrshire, Scotland, July 28, 1936

It took Jim Galloway two long voyages to get where he is – one a matter of geography, the other philosophy.

Galloway was born in Kilwinning, Ayrshire, Scotland, and began playing clarinet (then alto and baritone saxophone) while studying at the Glasgow School of Fine Arts. His earliest jazz influences were traditional – Louis Armstrong, of course, and such outstanding reed players as Johnny Dodds and George Lewis. Later, he was influenced, he freely admits, by Sidney Bechet and Johnny Hodges.

He played with a few Scottish bands before deciding to move to Toronto, where he chose to live because of the city's proximity to New York. He joined the Metro Stompers in 1966 and succeeded Jim McHarg as the band's leader two years later.

Galloway learned to play soprano sax after he moved to Canada. He had started on clarinet back in Scotland, simply because a friend of his had lent him a clarinet. "If he'd had a trumpet, I probably would have learned to play trumpet."

It was Galloway who moved the Metro Stompers from their traditional roots to a mainstream swing approach. The Stompers toured for several years.

And it was Galloway's experience of playing with such noted jazzmen as Buck Clayton, Wild Bill Davison, Vic Dickenson, and Buddy Tate that helped broaden Jim's musical horizons. "I really feel privileged," he once said, "that I managed to get in on the tail end of that era of jazz. No matter the direction the music has gone in, those were people who have been linchpins in the structure of it. I can't believe how lucky I've been to get to work with a lot of them, and to work with them when they could still play."

It was in 1979 that Galloway formed his Wee Big Band, a 17-piece aggregation that included some top Toronto sidemen and featured fresh, swinging charts that evoke Benny Goodman, Duke Ellington, and even Jimmy Lunceford.

Philosophically – as well as musically – it's quite a trip from the Metro Stompers to the Wee Big Band, from "South Rampart Street Parade" to "Don't Get Around Much Anymore."

By the mid-1980s, Galloway was becoming a big man on the Toronto jazz scene. He and critic/editor John Norris were booking pianists for the city's Café des Copains (and later the Montreal Bistro), and he was hosting a jazz radio show and leading the Wee Big Band in numerous gigs.

But it was in 1987 that Jim Galloway moved firmly into the centre of the jazz world's spotlight when he assumed the stewardship (as artistic director) of the Du Maurier Downtown Jazz Festival – after that festival had barely survived two earlier and ill-fated attempts.

Some years earlier, Galloway had told jazz writer Mark Miller: "I don't think I'm a particularly hard-sell kind of person. It's just that I really have a passion for the music, and if it's not happening anywhere, I got and make it happen. You've got to hustle. That's one of the reasons there's a jazz scene in Toronto – because there are a handful of people in this town who work at making it happen. ... If nothing's happening, I tend to try to make something happen. Most of these things have come about because there's some kind of void, and I wanted to create something to fill it, either for me or for what was happening in town."

Galloway tends to be modest about his musical talents. But over the years, he has managed to find a regular spot on the *Down Beat*'s International Critics' Poll among soprano saxophonists deserving of wider recognition.

"I still have trouble listening to myself; you always hear the things you don't want to hear and the things you wished you had done," he told Mark Miller. But that outward modesty masks a drive and determination that have helped make him a major figure on Canada's jazz scene.

Over the next dozen years, Galloway's energy and determination helped build the Du Maurier into one of the top jazz festivals on the North American continent. In addition to featuring such top Canadian musicians as Rob McConnell and the Boss Brass, Galloway lured many internationally acclaimed jazz figures to the Du Maurier Downtown Jazz Festival, including Toots Thielemans, George Shearing, Shirley Horn, Jay McShann, and the veteran trumpeter Doc Cheatham.

But Jim Galloway's greatest challenge was yet to come. In 1999 the Canadian government decided that arts and cultural events could no longer be openly sponsored by cigarette companies. That meant that after October of the year 2000, the Du Maurier Downtown Jazz Festival could no longer be sponsored by that company.

Yet Galloway's determination is such that he is confident he will find another corporate sponsor to put up the money so that his – and Toronto's – beloved downtown jazz festival will be able to continue.

Amos Garrett

b. Detroit, Michigan, November 26, 1941

A "who's who" of musicians is a well-worn phrase in most musical genres. When it's attached to blues performances or recordings, the name Amos Garrett usually appears on such a list. From the 1960s on, everybody from Ian and Sylvia Tyson to Maria Muldaur and from Anne Murray to Stevie Wonder has called upon his guitar versatility at one time or another. As the liner notes on his first live album *Amos Garrett Off the Floor Live* emphasize, "If Amos Garrett did not exist, it would be necessary to invent him."

An American by birth, Amos and his family moved to Toronto in 1946. In the mid-1950s, there was a brief move to Montreal, where the teenage Amos first studied piano and trombone at the Royal Conservatory. That's also where he first discovered R&B and jazz. As he would later describe in his song **Stanley Street**, Amos visited the Esquire Club in downtown Montreal.

"It was easy to get into the clubs in those days. Underage drinking was status quo," Garrett said. "I didn't drink. I didn't even like the taste of beer, but I'd have to order one just to sit at the show bar and watch the bands. I saw the R&B acts that were on the charts then, people like Fats Domino, Little Richard, Junior Walker. ... Then I taught myself to play guitar in 1954, the year rock 'n' roll was born."

Back in Toronto in the early 1960s, he began to explore Toronto's Yorkville and Yonge Street music scene. On that same live album (on a song called **Conversation with John**) he picks on his guitar and ad libs about his expeditions into downtown Toronto, doing "the Yonge Street crawl," to catch all the latest R&B acts there: "At Wellesley Street, I'd stop at the Bluenote and catch Dianne Brooks and the Silhouettes. ... At Gerard Street, I'd go to a little place called the Zanzibar and see David Clayton-Thomas and the Shays with a left-handed guitar player named Freddy Keeler. ... Pretty soon, I'd go down a little further to Dundas Street and I'd drop in on what they called 'the hip trip on the Yonge Street strip,' the Coq d'Or to see Levon Helm and the Hawks play blues ... they were my favourites."

While all that music history was going in, a lot of what Amos learned on guitar was coming out. By the mid-1960s he had worked his way into a popular Toronto band, called The Dirty Shames, consisting of Chick Roberts (kazoo and percussion), Jim McCarthy (12-string guitar), Carole Robinson (washboard and autoharp), and Garrett playing guitar and mandolin.

"It was a combination jug band and satirical revue show," Garrett said. "Carole and Chick came from an acting background, while Jim and I provided the music. ... But the Shames' comedy didn't translate to vinyl very well, which kind of limited our life span."

One story about the Dirty Shames from that era suggests they were so popular in Toronto that even on August 17, 1965, the night the Beatles were packing fans into Maple Leaf Gardens, the Shames still filled the Riverboat in Yorkville.

"No way," Garrett said. "I was in the 20th row dead centre at Maple Leaf Gardens, watching the Beatles."

Even so, Amos Garrett had a knack for being in the right place at the right time, a kind of Zelig of the pop music world. When Bill Langstroth and his primary client, Anne Murray, were looking for the right studio guitarist for their first session in 1969, they chose Garrett, who then played on all five of her first hit albums. Similarly, when Ian and Sylvia were preparing to take their folk music act into the electric era, they assembled a powerhouse rhythm section, with bass player Ken Kalmusky (later replaced by Jim Colegrove), drummer Ritchie Markus (later replaced by N. D. Smart II), pedal steel player Bill Keith, and electric guitarist Garrett. Their creation, The Great Speckled Bird, put Ian and Sylvia back in the public ear.

"When we recorded in Nashville," Garrett said, "our rhythm section was bigger and heavier-hitting than your average country band. It was the proto-typical country-rock approach. The only thing comparable at the time was the Byrds."

The Great Speckled Bird played the Atlanta Pop Festival and, in 1970, the Festival Express, a mobile Canadian rock 'n' roll tour. That summer Garrett and Great Speckled Bird travelled across the country in a dozen CNR train cars stopping to perform concerts in Toronto, Winnipeg, and Calgary. Also on board the train were The Band, the Grateful Dead, Janis Joplin, and Mash-makhan, 140 musicians in all. Garrett told Nicholas Jennings in his book *Before the Gold Rush*, the CNR had installed outlets in a couple of lounge cars so the musicians could plug in and play at will.

"People were almost reticent to get off the train to go out to the stadiums to play the show," Garrett told Jennings, "because there were so many amazing jams happening."

The United States beckoned Amos Garrett next. In the 1970s he moved to Woodstock, New York, and began touring and recording, first with Maria Muldaur, then Paul Butterfield's Better Days and the full stable of Bearsville Records acts. Then he moved to San Francisco where he spent thousands of hours in recording studios cutting tracks with more than 150 other artists, such as Stevie Wonder, Jesse Winchester, Bonnie Raitt, Todd Rundgren, Emmylou Harris, and even Martin Mull. Particularly memorable was Gar-rett's solo on Maria Muldaur's 1973 single, "Midnight at the Oasis," which became a number-two hit worldwide. As a result, Garrett got the job as Mul-daur's band leader for the next six years.

Garrett's reputation grew to be acknowledged by other greats on the instru-ment, Mark Knopfler and Chet Atkins to name two. Ian Tyson had said Gar-rett was Eric Clapton's equal. The magazine *Guitar Player* went so far as to say Garrett "is one of the most lyrical and original guitarists playing today ... his single note solos and melodic figures are so distinctive that it is virtually impossible to mistake them for anyone else's." Garrett's friend, science fiction writer Spider Robinson, said, "Amos Garrett plays guitar like God when He's drunk."

The trouble with studio work, however, was that Garrett spent what seemed a lifetime with a beeper on his belt, expected to pick up and play wherever, whenever, and with whomever. In the early 1980s, he decided to form his own band and create his own material – *Go Cat Go* (1980), *Amosbehavin'* (1982), and *Return of The Formerly Brothers* (1987), which won a Juno Award.

"The transition from sideman to band leader was immense," Garrett admit-ted. "I had no idea of the responsibility and headaches involved, but having the freedom to choose the music made it worth it."

By this time, his band, The Eh Team, had evolved into an all-Alberta band.

He had signed with Stony Plain Records, an Alberta-based company, and his manager was Holger Petersen, who lived in Edmonton. So he moved north and then released *Home in My Shoes* (1989), *Live in Japan* (1991), *Third Man In* (1992), and *Off the Floor Live* (1996), recorded at Edmonton's Sidetrack Café.

"My guitar playing is constantly changing," Amos Garrett said as he made plans for his first ever jazz recording in 2001. "I don't think I've done my best work yet."

Bobby Gimby *b. Cabri, Saskatchewan, October 25, 1918; d. 1998*

Few Canadian popular music instrumentalists achieved the star status of Bobby Gimby, especially as he did in the last two decades of his life.

Born in Cabri, near Moose Jaw, Saskatchewan, he played in the Cabri Boys' Band and other western Canadian boys' bands of the time. By the time he was grown up (age 23) he was playing lead trumpet with Mart Kenney and His Western Gentlemen. Many years later, in his own book, Kenney still had fond memories of Gimby's "exciting" version of the trumpet classic, "Flight of the Bumblebee."

In the mid-1940s Bobby formed his own orchestra and led the Rodeo Rascals in 1949 on CBC Radio's *Bobby Gimby Show*, which featured mostly country music. Next he was a featured soloist and raconteur for four years with *The Happy Gang* on CBC Radio and then joined the *Juliette* Show on CBC TV in 1956.

Although he stayed with the program as a featured performer for several years, Gimby and Juliette never became friends. In fact, it was quite the opposite: the coolness between them was palpable. Bobby got it into his head that she was trying to get him off the show. If Juliette, on the other hand, felt threatened by Bobby, she never showed it. But Gimby was often heard to complain about Juliette's treatment of him. His billing was as "Bobby" Gimby, but he complained that she sometimes referred to him (during a rehearsal) as "Bob," which he regarded as an intentional attempt to diminish his importance.

It all came to a loud explosion one day when the cast and production crew of the program were watching a tape of the previous week's show. Bobby's feature number was playing when a brief whispered conversation between

Juliette and one of the show's staff could be heard. Bobby erupted in anger, accusing her of deliberately sabotaging the screening of his feature number.

He rose and left the room, never to return. The next day, the show's producer was informed that a doctor had instructed Gimby to take a long rest.

It was not long after this that Bobby Gimby went to Singapore, where he wrote and recorded (with a girls' choir) **Malaysia Forever**, dedicated to the idea of a Malaysian federation. That was when he was nicknamed "The Pied Piper of Canada." He also wrote centennial songs for Manitoba and British Columbia.

Bobby returned to Canada in 1963 and led hotel orchestras and occasionally Dixieland groups in Toronto.

It was in 1967 that he wrote **Ca-na-da**, which quickly became the most popular song of Canada's centennial celebrations. He toured the country – and later the United States, Germany, and Japan – leading groups of school children in performances of this and other songs. That year, Bobby was made an Officer of the Order of Canada.

Over the next few years, the recording of **Ca-na-da** sold half a million copies. There were some 50 different recordings of the song, and some 250 school choirs and bands recorded it. In 1971, Gimby presented the original manuscript and all future royalties to the Boy Scouts of Canada.

Ca-na-da was not Bobby Gimby's first hit song. A decade earlier, he had co-written (with comedian Johnny Wayne) **The Cricket Song**, which was recorded by several performers. The biggest hit was the version done by Ray Bolger.

No musician's life is ever free of toil and trouble, and Gimby's was no exception. Mart Kenney recalled an incident when Bobby was still one of his Western Gentlemen. This was in 1941, when the Kenney band was about to move from Calgary to a playing engagement at Lethbridge, Alberta. Gimby's wife, Grace, went to Calgary to spend a little time with her husband before going back east.

"Our railway car was at the rear of the train," Kenney wrote in his own book about his big band days, "and as Bobby was kissing her [Grace] goodbye the train slipped quietly out of the station. Instead of grabbing a cab to chase the train to its first stop, Bobby thought, 'Okay, I'll have a few more hours with Grace and then I'll fly down to Lethbridge.' So he made a plane reservation, but when he got out to the airport, he found he'd been bumped by a Canadian Forces officer, and wound up taking a taxi all the way from Calgary to Lethbridge, about 150 miles. It cost him a fortune, and he arrived just in time to play 'God Save the King.'"

In his later years, Gimby led a band called the Leisure World Retirement Band in North Bay, Ontario. He died in June 1998, in his 80th year.

Murray Ginsberg *b. Toronto, Ontario, October 4, 1922*

It would be difficult to find a musician in Canada – or perhaps anywhere else – whose experience has covered a broader range of musical genres than Murray Ginsberg.

The Toronto-born musician took his first trombone lesson in 1937, when he was 14 years old. Within two years, he was playing professionally. Over the next quarter of a century, he played with such diverse leaders as Trump Davidson (Dixieland), Bert Niosi (swing), Lucio Agostini, Howard Cable, and Jack Kane, in various radio and television studio orchestras.

He took time out during the Second World War to join up and played in the Royal Canadian *Army Show*, first across Canada and then in Britain and Europe.

In 1955, when the CBC Symphony was organized under Geoffrey Waddington, Murray Ginsberg was a charter member. He was still playing trombone in that orchestra when Igor Stravinsky guest-conducted a performance of some of Stravinsky's own works.

In 1961, Murray decided to audition for the Toronto Symphony Orchestra. He was to meet Walter Susskind, the TSO's suave music director, at Massey Hall. Feeling a bit nervous, he stopped at the nearby Silver Rail for a bit of liquid fortification. It was there that he ran into Susskind. The two had a couple of drinks together before making their way across the street to Massey Hall to proceed with the dreaded audition.

Ginsberg first played a standard trombone exercise, to demonstrate his basic abilities.

"Fine," said Susskind, at the conclusion of the piece. "Can you play Ravel's 'Bolero'?"

"No, sir," Murray was forced to admit.

"Good!" exclaimed Susskind. "You've got the job."

Murray stayed with the TSO for the next 17 years. During that time, he played under three other conductors following Susskind's departure in 1965: Seiji Ozawa, Karel Ancerl, and Andrew Davis. With Ozawa, the TSO toured Japan in 1969 and China in 1978. Ginsberg made both trips.

Then, in September 1978, Ginsberg left the orchestra, feeling he could no longer play trombone well enough to meet his own exacting musical standards. The following year, he was hired by the Toronto Musicians' Association as its business representative, a position he held for 15 years. In 1995, he was elected secretary of the union, but by that summer decided on retirement instead.

But he didn't exactly retire. In 1980, he began writing a monthly column titled "Canadian Scene" for *The International Musician*, a monthly publication of the American Federation of Musicians of the United States and Canada. He continued writing that column for almost two decades.

In his spare time, he also managed to author an engaging book titled *They Loved To Play*, in which he chronicled leading figures on the Canadian musical scene, starting roughly with the First World War and covering musicians and their careers up to 1998, when his book was published.

In his book, he touched on virtually every aspect of the musical panorama in Canada – from The Dumbbells and the Romanelli dynasty, through the birth of music on CBC Radio, the "society" dance bands of Stanley St. John and Frank Bogart, the renowned expatriates like Robert Farnon and Percy Faith, the swing bands of Bert Niosi and Ellis McLintock, the enduring Mart Kenney and Howard Cable, the giants like Oscar Peterson and the forward-looking Phil Nimmons, and many more.

He even touched on the Casino Theatre, Toronto's last authentic burlesque house. The theatre's bandleader, Archie Stone, recalled to Murray the stripper who "complained she couldn't walk in the key we played. We played too high for her."

Ginsberg's own background with the Toronto Symphony Orchestra also gave him a healthy respect for the likes of Glenn Gould, harpist Judy Loman, violinist Albert Pratz, horn player Mary Barrow, and conductors Victor Feldbrill and Sir Ernest MacMillan.

For *They Loved to Play*, Ginsberg researched and/or interviewed dozens of the instrumentalists, composers, arrangers, and vocalists who, as a group, represented and justified the title of his book. One of the most touching of Ginsberg's tales is about Ruth Lowe, who wrote "I'll Never Smile Again" after her husband, Harold Cohen, died. Although Tommy Dorsey heard and liked the song, a year went by before he recorded it – and helped make Frank Sinatra a star.

Murray Ginsberg has not only been one of those musicians who "loved to play." He has, particularly in his so-called retirement years, also become a reliable and eminently readable chronicler of the Canadian music scene for most of the 20th century. The respect and affection Murray Ginsberg feels for these musicians is evident on every page of his absorbing book.

In November 1999, after 19 years on the job, Murray Ginsberg wrote his final "Canadian Scene" column for *The International Musician*, and the paper ran a little news item in the same issue, announcing Murray's retirement – again.

The Good Brothers

formed 1972 in Toronto: Bruce Good (b. Toronto, January 27, 1946) vocals, autoharp, dobro; Brian Good (b. Toronto, January 27, 1946) vocals, guitar; Larry Good (b. Newmarket, Ontario, December 25, 1952) vocals, banjo; Travis Good (b. April 10, 1968); Dallas Good (b. May 22, 1973)

The family that plays together stays together. The homily perhaps applies to no other family band more than to the original three members of the singing Goods. As a country pop band, the Good Brothers were officially formed when invited to perform at Toronto's legendary folk club, the Riverboat, on May 14, 1972. They have continued with the original twins – Bruce and Brian – as well as younger brother Larry for the better part of 30 years. It all began at the family home in Richmond Hill, Ontario.

"It started in the kitchen with our Acadian mother and our Irish–Scottish father," Brian Good says. "We were exposed to the music of all three of these cultures at an early age."

It was Brian and Bruce who launched the professional edition of the family in performance when they were just teenagers. In fact, one their first appearances, at a bar in Collingwood, nearly landed the two in jail for performing underage in a drinking establishment. A $28 fine perhaps gave them pause, but not for long. In the early 1970s Bruce Good's wife Margaret joined the twins in a Celtic folk band called Kinfolk, performing traditional Irish and Scottish material as well as bluegrass classics.

The Good Brothers (l. to r.): Brian, Larry, Bruce

The Good brothers next met Winnipeg musician James Ackroyd and that trio performed as James and the Good Brothers. Their repertoire shifted to accommodate the rock 'n' roll of "the psychedelic era" and the band joined the Festival Express on a continent-wide tour with such acts as Janis Joplin, The Band, and the Grateful Dead. That connection helped generate a recording session in San Francisco with Columbia Records. Not long after that, however, the trio disbanded.

"We decided to come home," Brian Good said, because the West coast "wasn't our lifestyle."

Again, the Goods turned to the family environment at home in Ontario. Younger brother Larry had reached his final year of high school. More to the point, he'd studied ukulele at the Toronto Conservatory of Music and become proficient on the banjo in a local band, the Country Rebels. When the Riverboat gig came along, the Good Brothers' sound had evolved to bluegrass. Recording reps seemed little interested in their brand of music and recommended they abandon bluegrass and focus on a more commercial rock sound. The Goods might have quit then were it not for a mentor, fellow Canadian Gordon Lightfoot, with whom they had performed in 1972.

"He encouraged us, first of all, to continue in our folk-bluegrass style," Brian Good explained. "He even rehearsed us, helped us do a demo, and provided the opportunity to open some of his shows."

Joined by American bassist Mike Love and fiddler John Allen (later of Prairie Oyster), the Good Brothers made their debut recording in mid-1974. The album (distributed by RCA), self-financed and again not well received among industry moguls, still generated 20,000 sales in Canada. They seemed to hit their stride with a second recording, done in Nashville. That album, *Pretty Ain't Good Enuff*, helped them earn a Juno in 1977 as Best Country Group, the first of eight straight in that category.

"The Goods are purveyors of every shade of wheatfield music, from bluegrass to country to country-pop," wrote Paul McGrath in a 1976 *Globe and Mail* article.

The Juno recognition affirmed the band's original decision to keep on the country side of rock music. From then on the Good Brothers left the critics and the local bars behind. It was concert stages only, in such venues as Massey Hall, Hamilton Place, the National Arts Centre in Ottawa, as the band crisscrossed the country piling up over 100,000 miles in just two years.

"Some of those big halls we were playing, I'd never been in them," Bruce Good remembered, but suddenly "we were standing on those stages."

The Good Brothers' third album, *Doin' the Wrong Things Right*, in 1978, sold 32,000 copies within seven weeks of its release. In 1980, the brothers recorded a live album, which incorporated recordings at Ontario Place and the CNE Grandstand in Toronto, as well as the Coronet in Kitchener. It included such favourites as **Fox on the Run**, Dylan's "Mr. Tambourine Man," and Lightfoot's "Alberta Bound."

In 1985, the band was among the first North American artists to tour the former Czechoslovakia. Larry Good left the band for a short time in the early 1990s and was replaced by Bruce's son Travis. Today, it's not uncommon for a Good Brothers concert appearance to include the original three brothers, Bruce's wife Margaret, and their sons, Travis and Dallas. Recently, as well, older brother George (living in Los Angeles) has taken on the role as executive producer of the family's recordings.

NAC/PA 207955

Glenn Gould   *b. Toronto, Ontario, September 25, 1932; d. 1982*

So much has been written about the eccentricities of Glenn Gould that it would be easy to forget what an incredibly gifted musician he was. And yet his genius was recognized early in his all-too-brief life. He made his debut at the age of 13 – not on the piano but on the organ – at an Eaton's Auditorium recital.

His musical talents preceded that debut by years: at the age of three, Glenn was able to read music even before he could read words. He also knew that he had absolute (or perfect) pitch. By the age of five, he was writing piano pieces and playing them for friends in the east Toronto neighbourhood where he was raised.

A Toronto reviewer wrote of Gould's Eaton's Auditorium debut: "Not only astonishing technique but interpretive intuition is his in full maturity." A year later, when Gould first played the piano publicly (accompanied by an orchestra and playing Beethoven's *Fourth Piano Concerto*) the same critic wrote: "He showed the music lover that scale passages and arpeggios on the humble piano may have spiritual as well as technical beauty and character. His phrasing was eloquent as poetry chanted by the poet himself."

He made his network broadcast debut on the CBC in 1950 at age 18 and later referred to the occasion as the start of his love affair with the microphone.

But it was primarily his piano playing that had critics raving – and rave they did.

"Mr. Gould, at his best, is a pianist of divine guidance," wrote one critic, "and even at his worst is a musician so far in advance of most of his contemporaries that there is no legitimate basis for comparison."

Another called Gould "the foremost pianist this continent has produced in recent decades."

Even in the Soviet Union he was described as "a tremendous talent, a great master, a lofty spirit, and a profound soul."

A decade later, Gould was enough of a celebrity to warrant the full treatment from *The New Yorker*: a 7500-word profile by Joseph Roddy that not only traced his meteoric rise to fame but allowed the reader a glimpse into Gould's off-concert stage life and even sample his prankish humour.

Once, in the early 1960s, Gould was to appear with the New York Philharmonic at Carnegie Hall, playing Beethoven's *Second Piano Concerto* – with Leonard Bernstein conducting. Bernstein walked into Gould's dressing room and greeted him warmly – "Glenn, baby …"

After a few moments of lighthearted banter, Gould said: "I have an idea – thought of it last night. Let's walk out there together, and you play the piano part and I'll conduct the orchestra. It will be the surprise act of the season."

"Oh, no," Bernstein said and went on to say (while, according to Roddy, "affecting a pompous manner"), "the Beethoven *Second* is not one of the five glorious concertos in my solo repertoire this season."

"It's been in mine, sir, since I was 13," said Gould, bowing low to the conductor.

Yet it was not Beethoven but Bach who was to help propel Gould to global stardom. Gould's 1955 recordings of Bach's *Goldberg Variations* led to his becoming considered perhaps the most important interpreter of Bach of the 20th century – surpassing even the venerable Wanda Landowska. Gould's speedy flight through the *Goldberg Variations* was described as being "as close to a smash hit as a chamber-music record ever gets."

As for his highly publicized "eccentricities," one of the most public has been his inability to refrain from uttering a kind of vocal accompaniment to his own piano playing. (He is not, however, alone in this. The revered Toscanini sang his way through a recorded broadcast of *La Bohème*, and Pablo Casals "grunted out an ad lib self-accompaniment for an album of Bach suites for unaccompanied cello," according to Joseph Roddy.)

During one recording session, the Columbia engineer Howard Scott complained: "Glenn, we can hardly hear the piano because you're singing so loud."

Gould said it was the fault of the piano – which he had earlier in the recording session proclaimed inadequate. Then, his mood suddenly lighter, he added: "Suppose I wear a gas mask while I play. Then you won't hear me sing."

He was also criticized for his "behaviour" on the concert stage – his distracting habit of bending down so close to the keyboard that he was almost obscured by it.

Gould was also ridiculed – quite possibly unfairly – for his apparent inability to tolerate cold. According to Roddy's profile: "For a Canadian, he is extraordinarily sensitive to low temperatures – or even to what New Yorkers consider comfortable room temperatures."

Roddy went on to mention that at the first meeting he had with Gould the musician kept a portable heater going "full blast, close to his left side" and a piece of Oriental carpeting under his feet. While Gould talked, he soaked his hands in a basin of hot water. He often wore gloves – with the fingertips cut out – for public performances.

Another of Gould's frequently reported eccentricities was his endless searching for pianos worthy of his talents. He preferred a Steinway piano, but rarely found one he really liked. Either the action wasn't up to his standards or there was some other flaw not evident or audible to mere mortals.

While most travellers tend to judge cities on the basis of hotels, restaurants, climate, and such, Gould went about the globe concerned almost totally with the quality of pianos he had to use. After a while, he rated cities on that basis: Moscow, Berlin, and Tel Aviv were fairly good places, but St. Louis, Missouri, for some reason, had not one but two acceptable pianos. San Francisco ranked even higher in Gould's book, for the quality of the piano in that city's opera house.

When Gould had made his debut at that Eaton's Auditorium performance – at the age of 13 – sitting beside him and turning the music pages was his friend, neighbour, and schoolmate, Robert Fulford, destined to become one of Canada's most respected journalists.

Shortly after Glenn's death, in 1982, Fulford wrote a piece for *Saturday Night* magazine in which he recalled his friendship with the renowned pianist: "... until our early twenties we were friends," Fulford wrote, and during much of childhood and adolescence we were each other's best friend. In the 1950s we drifted apart, toward different interests, different passions. But knowing him that long was a unique experience. Glenn's soaring talent, his limitless ambition, his rich humour, his marvellous quick understanding of everything and everyone – these constituted my first meeting with genius."

The Gould genius manifested itself in other ways, too. He became a composer, a conductor, and a writer of a variety of articles – some 50 in all – mostly, but not exclusively, related to music.

In his mind, performing in public was not the best way to demonstrate his talents. In a sense, he was as distracted by the presence of spectators as they were by his sometimes bizarre concert stage behaviour. And so, it should not have been a great surprise when he decided to stop playing concerts and devote his time to playing for radio broadcasts, writing, and making films. And yet the music world was stunned by his withdrawal from public performance.

His best-known television film was called *Glenn Gould's Toronto*, which he wrote and narrated. It was a tribute to his native city and a fine example of his odd sense of humour. It was part of John McGreevey's *Cities* series, and was shown on CBC-TV in 1975.

In Fulford's warm tribute to his childhood friend, he wrote: "Gould seemed never to doubt his value as a musician, and early in adolescence his imagination was soaring toward that distant world he would soon occupy so triumphantly. In his mind the great musicians of Europe and North America were already his peers, even if they hadn't yet heard of him."

Robert Goulet   *b. Lawrence, Mass., November 26, 1933*

Courtesy Canapress

In the early 1950s, a regular summer theatrical attraction in Toronto was called *Melody Fair*. It was a series of Broadway musicals presented in the round, first in a kind of circus tent, then in the cavernous Mutual Street Arena.

The producer of these musicals was a crusty Brooklynite named Leighton K. Brill. Before the opening one season, Brill allowed a group of visitors (mostly press) to visit an early rehearsal. At one spot during the rehearsal, he pointed to a dark-haired, handsome young man in the chorus and said: "You see that kid up there? His name is Bob Goulet, and he's gonna be a big star."

Although he was born in Lawrence, Massachusetts, he moved with his mother to Edmonton, Alberta, when he was in his early teens. He studied voice with Herbert G. Turner and Jean Leturneau, and in 1950 he became a radio announcer at radio station CKUA, but continued his voice training for two years at the Royal Canadian Conservatory in Toronto on a scholarship.

He was a semifinalist on CBC-TV's *Pick the Stars* and also competed on *Opportunity Knocks* and *Singing Stars of Tomorrow*. Next came the job in the chorus at *Melody Fair*.

It did not take too long for Mr. Brill's seemingly rash prediction to prove true. While appearing in *Melody Fair*'s summer musicals, Goulet, aged 20, made his television debut in a walk-on role in the CBC production of Menotti's *The Consul*. He was also featured in the annual Canadian revue *Spring Thaw*. Within a couple of years, he was being seen fairly regularly on Canadian television, as well as in such theatrical productions as *Gentlemen Prefer Blondes*, *Finian's Rainbow*, and *South Pacific*.

By 1957, he was costarring with Joyce Sullivan on CBC Television's *Showtime* and also sang the part of Macheath in the Stratford Festival production of *The Threepenny Opera*. His matinee-idol looks and strong, almost operatic baritone voice were ideally suited to such roles.

But it was in 1960 that he achieved international stardom. Cast as Sir Lancelot in the Lerner-Loewe musical *Camelot*, he all but stole the show from its billboarded stars, Richard Burton and Julie Andrews, when the musical began its out-of-town previews at Toronto's brand-new O'Keefe Centre. He repeated that success when the show moved to New York. His rendition of "If Ever I Would Leave You" was a showstopper.

The musical did not get uniformly good revues. Actor Lou Jacobi, a friend of Goulet's, had this consoling advice: "Worse comes to worst, you got a two-year flop."

After the long *Camelot* run, Goulet continued to work in Broadway theatre, winning a Tony Award for his performance in *The Happy Time*. He had already won a Grammy Award as the Best New Recording Artist of 1962.

He also worked in such movies as *I'd Rather Be Rich*, *Naked Gun*, and *Honeymoon Hotel*, as well as television productions of *Carousel*, *Kiss Me Kate*, and *Brigadoon*. In 1962, he and Judy Garland recorded the singing voices for the animated film *Gay Purree*. He also starred in the television adventure series *Blue Light*. (In 1980, Goulet played himself in the Louis Malle film *Atlantic City*.)

Goulet's recording career was somewhat more successful than his straight acting. He made more than 30 albums for Columbia, including **Robert Goulet's Greatest Hits**, plus the original-cast albums of both **Camelot** and **The Happy Time**. He also made various theme albums, devoted to Christmas, Broadway, and Hollywood. Among his biggest hit singles were "What Kind of Fool Am I?" and "My Love Forgive Me."

In 1975, while living in Los Angeles, he and his then wife, singer Carole Lawrence, appeared in a new production of *Camelot*, directed by Douglas Campbell. But this time Goulet played the role of King Arthur, in which he was clearly wasted. What he did was a carbon copy of Richard Burton's performance in the original production, which meant that he "talked" his songs – as Burton had done simply because he couldn't sing. And the man who played Lancelot only served to remind audiences of how much better Goulet had been in the original production – 15 years earlier.

Goulet's later career saw him appearing in Las Vegas, singing in hotels and nightclubs across the United States and Canada, and participating in tours of revival productions of such evergreen musicals as *South Pacific*, in which he sang the leading role of Emil de Beque. That production played both the

O'Keefe Centre in Toronto and the Place des Arts in Montreal. He also gave a "homecoming" performance in Edmonton in 1985.

Great Big Sea

formed 1991 in Newfoundland: Alan Doyle guitar, keyboards; Séan McCann bodhran (Celtic drum), tin whistle, guitar; Darrell Power bass, acoustic guitar; Bob Hallett fiddle, accordion, mandolin, concertina, bouzouki

No matter how far from their home, wherever Great Big Sea performs, it seems the four band members are always greeted by rowdy cheers from expatriate Newfoundlanders waving provincial flags. In turn, singer/guitarist Alan Doyle usually welcomes his audience to "the biggest kitchen party in the country" and launches a concert that combines 400-year-old Celtic music with modern rhythms.

"The tradition of people making their own entertainment is still strong in Newfoundland," says Doyle. "There are lots of folk around who know the original versions of the old tunes, [but] with the younger players getting into it, the scene in Newfoundland has never been more lively. The geographic isolation helps keep the home music strong. The coldness of winters keeps the kitchen parties alive, because the kitchen's always the warmest place in the house."

Great Big Sea (l. to r.): Darrell Power, Séan McCann, Bob Hallett, Alan Doyle

Andrew MacNaughtan

Each of GBS's foursome discovered music early in life – if not in the kitchen, certainly close to home. Alan Doyle's mother taught piano to the local children in Petty Harbour; Darrell Power's father played traditional music in a group The Quidi Vidi Celi Band based in Outer Cove; originally from Carbonear, Séan McCann picked up an assortment of stringed instruments and the tin whistle; and in St. John's, Bob Hallett's grandmother inspired him to play the button accordion, while the legacy of his great-grandfather prompted his decision to pick up the fiddle.

"I hate electronic music," Hallett told a newspaper reviewer in 1999. "It just doesn't have the same feeling as live instruments." Not only is Hallett's choice of music slightly unorthodox, so is his playing – he plays the accordion left-handed, which is in effect playing the instrument upside down.

Hallett met McCann at Memorial University, where the two organized several bands, culminating with Rankin Street, a pub act that focused on live, spontaneous performances. As Hallett remembers it, "Rankin Street's open-ended approach led to a revolving door membership and a reputation for over-the-top showmanship. ... [I] recall evenings when the audience was invited to participate on-stage, the night the band swapped instruments (unsuccessfully) and the night when a tempo dispute led to on-stage fisticuffs."

The band still relies on that spontaneity. Whichever folk format it chooses – a single, reel, jig, strathspey, or sea shanty – Great Big Sea works at interpreting the traditional tunes by adding harmonies, choruses, and contemporary rhythms. Séan McCann calls it "reinventing" centuries-old traditional folk songs. However, as Darrell Power points out, "it's still folk-based and played on traditional instruments, so you're never straying too far from what's expected."

"We're a live band," says McCann, referring to the band's breakneck schedule of 270-plus shows a year. "That's our bread and butter. It's all well and good to be purists and artistes, but ... we're entertainers."

The formula has translated into platinum status for each of the band's first three albums – *Up*, *Play*, and *Rant and Roar*. At the 2000 East Coast Music Awards, the band's *Turn* was voted album of the year, while the band garnered top group and top entertainer of the year honours as well.

The music of GBS appears to make as many friends backstage as on stage. In 1996 the band inaugurated a summertime concert series, they called "Great Big Picnics" at several locations in Atlantic Canada. The band's version of an outdoor kitchen party attracted an impressive array of performers – including the Philosopher Kings, Colin James, and Blue Rodeo among others. The first picnic in St. John's drew 6000. Two years later – in July 1998 – 20,000 fans descended on Grand Falls–Windsor, Newfoundland (population 5000), to see and hear Chantal Kreviazuk, Wide Mouth Mason, Philosopher Kings, the Rankins, and GBS. When the picnic arrived in Halifax that fall, the godfathers of Celtic music, the Chieftains, had joined the event.

"These guys have been playing this kind of music for 35 years," said Bob Hallett. "They've done every gig on the planet. When they say they're looking forward to [playing with us] that's a real compliment."

On tour in the summer of 2000, Great Big Sea were the lead act for Sting's Toronto appearance. As usual, Newfoundland flags were unfurled by fans throughout the sold-out amphitheatre on the city's waterfront. It was a high-water-mark for the band. Commented Alan Doyle: "It says a lot when a band that sings 400-year-old traditional music from Newfoundland can be as successful as this."

The Guess Who

formed 1965 in Winnipeg: Allan Kowbel replaced by Burton Cummings (b. Winnipeg, December 31, 1947) vocals, piano; Randy Bachman (b. Winnipeg, September 27, 1943) vocals, guitar (replaced in 1970 by guitarists Kurt Winter and Greg Leskiw, Leskiw replaced in 1972 by Don McDougall, replaced in 1974 by Domenic Troiano); Jim Kale bass guitar (replaced in 1972 by Bill Wallace); Garry Peterson drums

Canada's most storied and internationally acclaimed rock band began its musical life with a question mark and ended with an exclamation mark.

In 1957, Allan Kowbel, Jim Kale, and Allen Sufoe assembled a Winnipeg high school band called Al and the Silvertones. The next year, the group expanded to include Randy Bachman and Garry Peterson and then recorded a tribute to the memory of Buddy Holly called **We'll Always Remember**. The group was still in flux in 1962, when it changed its name to Chad Allan and the Reflections (until the American group, the Reflections, recorded its hit "Just Like Romeo and Juliet," when the Winnipeggers became Chad Allan and the Expressions). In 1964, the band signed with Quality Records and released its version of "Shakin' All Over" in 1965.

Revealingly of both the band's circuitous evolution and the inferiority complex of the Canadian music scene at the time, Quality executive George Struth felt the disc could be a national hit only if radio stations did not know the recording artists were Canadian. Thus, under the song title on the label of the 45-rpm disc, the band byline read "by the Guess Who?" Struth even hoped some DJs might mistake the band for England's The Who. At any rate, the gimmick worked, and the disc hit the Top 40 charts in Canada, the United States, England, and Australia. The name stuck.

Despite a moderately successful U.S. tour that same year, Chad Allan decided

Randy Bachman and Burton Cummings at the Crescentwood Community Centre in Winnipeg

to leave the group. Randy Bachman contacted the lead vocalist of Winnipeg's next most popular band, the Devrons. He was a punk singer named Burton Cummings, whose act included jumping on pianos in his high-heeled boots. Bachman invited Cummings to join the Guess Who. At the end of the meeting, Cummings simply looked at Bachman and said, "Thanks for the offer, but the Beatles just called me this morning and I'm joining them," and he walked out. Bachman was stunned. But this was just Cummings's characteristic wry humour at work; moments later, he returned, said "Wow," and joined the band.

With its new lead singer, the band toured and recorded, but kept in touch with home by appearing regularly on television rock shows such as *Let's Go*, *Music Hop*, and *Where It's At*. The Guess Who recorded Neil Young's "Flying on the Ground Is Wrong" in 1967 and "His Girl," which was a bigger hit in England than at home. In 1968, the band caught the attention of advertising executive and producer Jack Richardson; he approached the Guess Who about recording one side of an album called *A Wild Pair* (which also featured Ottawa band the Staccatos), and it sold 85,000 copies. The same year, Quality sold the group's contract to Richardson's newly formed Nimbus 9 Productions for a mere $1000.

In a situation also symptomatic of the Canadian pop industry of the day, the Guess Who found greater acceptance earlier in the United States than at home in Canada. Accordingly, Richardson took the band to New York's A&R Studios in September 1968 to record its debut album *Wheatfield Soul*; he mortgaged his home for the $9800 in recording fees. Then he hired PR men (at $500 per week) in New York, Chicago, Washington, and L.A. to launch a

165

single from the album – a ballad co-written by Bachman and Cummings – **These Eyes**. Within weeks the song reached the top of three American best-seller charts, sold a million copies, and returned about $35,000 in production royalties to Nimbus. In 1969, the Guess Who performed the flip-side hit, **Undun**, on Dick Clark's *American Bandstand* and were presented with a gold record for **These Eyes**. The following year, their single **American Woman** hit the *Billboard* Hot 100 chart and stayed there for three weeks, making them the first Canadian group to have a number-one record in the United States and the first to have a Top 10 album, which was also titled *American Woman*.

After listening to a 16-minute, live version of **American Woman**, U.S. rock critic Lester Bangs wrote: "The Guess Who is God."

"This kind of stuff is exactly what makes The Guess Who great," Bangs wrote in *Creem* magazine. "They have absolutely no taste at all, they don't even mind embarrassing everyone in the audience, they're real punks without even working too hard at it. ... Play this loud and be the first on your block to become a public nuisance!"

Released at the height of the war in Vietnam, the song resonated as a metaphor for the low regard many young Canadians had for anything American. The lyrics and tone of the song were so critical of the American way of life, that at a command performance at the White House in front of Prince Charles and Princess Anne in May 1970, First Lady Pat Nixon asked the band not to perform the song.

Ironically, by the middle of the same month, irreconcilable differences between Cummings (the dark, rakish, hard-drinking, high-living pop star) and Bachman (the heavyset, introspective, Mormon family man) pushed the two apart. In fact, one Toronto critic reported that to get their story, he had to interview each band member individually in a single day, because they weren't talking to each other. At any rate, just as **American Woman** became the band's biggest-selling single to date and the group played the famed Fillmore East music hall, Bachman announced it would be his last appearance with the Guess Who, and after the performance he left the band.

Despite what looked like a bleak creative future, Cummings and band manager Don Hunter found two new singing/songwriting talents in Winnipeg – Kurt Winter and Greg Leskiw, who had just written **Hand Me Down World**. Nevertheless, the bulk of the Guess Who songwriting burden shifted to Cummings. The flow of singles continued – 20 of them released between 1969 and 1976 were million-sellers – and three LPS – *American Woman, Share the Land*, and *Best of Guess Who* – received awards certifying sales in excess of $1 million. The band won Juno Awards as the Best Vocal-Instrumental Group in 1965 and annually between 1967 and 1970. The band toured extensively, including a command performance in London in 1973 and annual concerts before audiences of up to 20,000 at the CNE

Domenic Troiano with Jack Richardson at Nimbus 9 Studios in 1974, the year Dom joined The Guess Who

from 1971 to 1975. The Cummings-led band gave its final performance at the Montreal Forum on September 13, 1975.

Randy Bachman left the group in 1970, but not the music business. Clearly blessed with the capability to create and perform rock 'n' roll hits, he simply built a new band around his talent. The first was Brave Belt, comprising Bachman on guitar, his younger brother Robbie on drums, Fred Turner as a second guitarist, and singer Chad Allan. Brave Belt produced two albums, then replaced Chad Allan with Bachman's older brother Tim and renamed itself Bachman-Turner Overdrive. The band's self-titled album, which debuted in May 1973, was the first of four successful albums, which included the hit singles **You Ain't Seen Nothin' Yet** and **Takin' Care of Business**.

By 1976, BTO's so-called "big bad sound of blue-collar rock" had established loyal followings in Canada and the United States, but musical differences the next year sent Randy Bachman packing again; he formed new groups – Ironhorse and Union – but neither repeated the success of either the Guess Who or BTO. He briefly reunited with BTO in 1989, but then went back on his own and produced solo albums *Survivor*, *Any Road*, and a mini-CD titled *Live in Seattle*. His autobiography, *Takin' Care of Business*, co-authored with music writer John Einarson, was published in 2000.

Going solo for Burton Cummings was more than a musical change. It was a life change since, from the age of 13, he'd performed only in bands. Even he admitted, "I didn't know how to be a solo artist." Nevertheless, in 1976, CBS Records released his first solo album containing the anthem-like, million-selling hit single, **Stand Tall**. Two albums later, in 1978, Cummings released his album *Dream of a Child* (containing the Top 10 hit **Break It to Them Gently**); it marked his debut as a producer and was the first Canadian album to be certified triple-platinum (300,000 copies). *Dream of a Child* won Best Album of the Year at the Juno Awards, earning Cummings his ninth Juno.

From his new base in Los Angeles, he worked as guest artist on albums by Leo Sayer and Bette Midler. He was considered for the lead in the movie version of *The Buddy Holly Story*, but then costarred in the movie *Melanie*, for which he also composed and performed the musical soundtrack. Cummings also appeared in CBC-TV specials, including *Portage and Main*, which earned him an ACTRA Award, making him the first musician to win a Canadian television award. For Cummings, however, the thrill of singing and recording are still most important.

"When I was a kid in my first band," Cummings says, "I dreamed about having one hit record. Now I've got a wall full of gold records and it still overwhelms me. It's never become boring. I've never become jaded. I'm just as excited about every new release as I was 25 years ago. In some ways more, because I've been lucky enough to last."

Perhaps the most poignant moment of Burton Cummings's post–Guess Who career occurred after the release of his first solo album.

Among other cuts, the album contained a laid-back, lounge-like version of Randy Bachman's raucous tune **You Ain't Seen Nothin' Yet**. Considering the rancour that had existed when Bachman had left the Guess Who, many felt the interpretation was a slam at Bachman. The two hadn't spoken in seven years. Then one night Bachman attended a Burton Cummings concert in Vancouver.

"He stopped in the middle of the show," says Bachman, "and apologized in front of 6000 people for the bad stuff he had said about me. He dedicated the next part of the show to my wife and me. The lights got real low and sitting at the grand piano he [played] "The Way We Were" and then went into **These Eyes, Laughing, No Time, Undun**, and **American Woman**. I was sitting there in tears. Everyone else was going nuts. I went backstage and it was like nothing had ever happened."

In the summer of 1999, the premier of Manitoba invited the original members of the Guess Who to the closing ceremonies of the Pan-American Games in Winnipeg. It was the first time (since a concert reunion in 1983) that the band had performed together and according to Bachman it was "the spark that showed us we still had the fire to go out and play the songs."

On a Saturday night in late May of 2000, the Guess Who (with Bachman, Cummings, Kale, and Peterson reunited) launched its *Running Back Thru Canada* tour. That night, for an early-1960s price of $4.99 a ticket, the Guess Who played to 250 fans (chosen by lottery) at the Crescentwood Community Centre in Winnipeg, one of the venues the band had played in its earliest days. The 24-date tour entertained 160,000 fans, grossed $8.5 million, and produced a 22-song, retrospective CD and one more CBC-TV documentary. The papers called the Guess Who "the quintessential Canuck band."

Joyce Hahn

b. Eatonia, Saskatchewan, January 31, 1929

One of the ironies of Joyce Hahn's life is that while she was something of a television star, albeit way back in the medium's infancy, her virtually unknown brother, Bob Hahn, made far more money through music than she ever did.

For five years (1955–59), Joyce costarred with Wally Koster on CBC Television's popular weekly show, *Cross-Canada Hit Parade*. She started at $300 a week and whatever raises she got during her run on the show were not spectacular.

Television may have been rather new to Joyce, but singing in public certainly was not. She and her siblings were singing publicly from the time the diminutive Joyce was but five years of age. Organized by their father, Harvey Hahn, and billed as The Harmony Kids, they toured Saskatchewan, then Montana, New Jersey, and even New York.

Harvey had been a farmer, but the Depression forced him off the land. His own interest in music moved him to form the family singing group. Before too long, the Hahn Harmony Kids had won first prize on the *Major Bowes Amateur Hour* and turned professional.

The Hahn family spent some years on the road. They lived, drove, sang, danced, and played a remarkable odyssey of some 50,000 miles of Canadian and American roads, doing sometimes one show a day in one town and as many as ten in another. In 1985, it was brother Bob who wrote a book about the Hahn families. It was titled *None of the Roads Were Paved*, and however fanciful the book may have been, the title was almost surely literally correct.

It was Bob, too, who had figured out a way to earn far better money than any other member of the Hahn family. During the Second World War, Bob Hahn served in the RCAF, then lived in Hamilton, Ontario and Montreal, Quebec, where he again formed a family vocal group which included Joyce.

But it was in the early 1950s that Bob Hahn landed in the musical field that would make him both successful and relatively rich by writing musical jingles for commercials. By the time he was 60, Bob Hahn had written some 1500 of them. The most famous of them was "Mainly Because of the Meat," which he wrote for Dominion Stores, Ltd. Over the eight-year period that this

Joyce Hahn and Wally Koster

NAC/PA 207949

catchy jingle was used by Dominion, Bob Hahn earned some $64,000 for his effort.

Having grown up in a family of musical gypsies, Joyce Hahn had virtually no formal education. During the time that she was a popular television performer, a musician on the program said he had often seen Joyce perusing a dictionary or studying a book titled *30 Days to a More Powerful Vocabulary*.

During that period, Helen Kirk wrote a profile of Joyce for *Canadian Home Journal*. This is part of what she wrote: "At 27, she is two women. One is calmly and determinedly on her way to the very top in show business. The other is searching unconsciously for the childhood she never had and in imminent danger of missing her chance at adult happiness and fulfillment."

Kirk also quoted Stan Harris, who was the producer of *Hit Parade* during that time: "She doesn't act like a star. Joan Fairfax and Phyllis Marshall, for instance, drive up for rehearsal in mink and big cars. Joyce comes to work on the streetcar wearing old slacks and looking like a schoolgirl. She doesn't mix socially with the cast, either. She might come to an end-of-the-season party, but that's all."

In 1959, Joyce quit *Cross-Canada Hit Parade* – and, for the most part, show business in general. It was a time of nothing but bad news for Joyce.

That same year, she lost her husband, who was a CBC technician. During a business trip to the Bahamas, he was stung by a scorpion and died hours later – at only 39 years of age.

Not long after that, her only son, Graham, barely a toddler, was diagnosed as autistic. (Joyce also had an older daughter, Beverlee, who was raised in Montreal, mostly by her grandparents.) That was when Joyce gave up singing professionally for good.

From then on, her time was devoted to looking after Graham and working on behalf of societies which raise funds for research into the causes and treatment of autism. In the late 1970s, she was living with a new husband in Calgary, "delighted to be just a housewife, busy with cooking, handicrafts, and volunteer work."

One interviewer asked if she was still recognized by people on the street.

"Yes," she replied, "even though my hair is shorter now, I still get stopped on the street now and then. But it's also nice to be accepted for myself at places where they don't know my background, like the ladies' quilting club."

Bobby Hales

b. Avonlea, Saskatchewan, August 9, 1934

Not the least of the accomplishments that could be claimed by Bobby Hales is that he composed, arranged, and conducted the theme and background music for the most successful dramatic television series ever produced for the CBC – and also seen in England, Australia, and New Zealand – *The Beachcombers*, which ran for more than 400 episodes. His assignment didn't end there. Hales continued to write background dramatic music for the show for the next 16 years. In a later interview, he shrugged off any suggestion that this was some sort of achievement.

"It was one of those things," he said. "It has nothing to do with planning. It's all luck."

Hales, who was born in Avonlea, Saskatchewan, began taking trumpet lessons as a child. When he was 15, his family moved to Chilliwack, B.C., where "there was a little more music to do."

That brought him a step closer to Vancouver, the city where he made his name. He has ever since been associated with that west-coast city. But it was the 19-piece band he formed in 1965 that made Bobby Hales a household name in British Columbia and, eventually, beyond.

It was just four years later that Hales took his big band into Vancouver's best-known nightclub, The Cave, where he remained for several years. The list of performers that Hales and his band played for at The Cave sounds like a Hollywood phonebook: Bob Hope, Sammy Davis, Jr., Sonny and Cher, Mitzi Gaynor, Shirley Maclaine, Ann Miller, Ginger Rogers, Natalie Cole, Mickey Rooney, Yul Brynner, Richard Harris, Liberace, Engelbert Humperdinck, Pat Boone, Eartha Kitt, Jack Jones, Stevie Wonder, Billy Eckstine, Maynard Ferguson, Mel Tormé, Liza Minelli, Frankie Laine, Steve Allen, Jack Carter, Joan Rivers, Harry Connick, Jr., and more.

Hales and his band also played for numerous Broadway stars in shows that played Vancouver's Queen Elizabeth Theatre. Among these were *Cabaret* with Joel Gray, *The Unsinkable Molly Brown* with Debbie Reynolds, *Sugar Babies* with Mickey Rooney and Ann Miller, *Camelot* with Richard Harris, *Zorba* with Anthony Quinn (based on the film *Zorba the Greek*), *South Pacific* with Robert Goulet, and *The King and I* with Yul Brynner.

Originally, Bobby wanted to become a music teacher, but he left school in Grade 12 and worked in a bank for a couple of years. When the bank wanted to transfer him to Prince George, Hales quit and decided to go to Hollywood, California to study music. While studying modern music at Westlake College in Los Angeles, he spent his summers playing at a resort hotel in Sylvan Lake,

Alberta. That was where he met his wife, Marj. They married and moved to Vancouver.

"I just had to pay my dues," he recalled. "You have to establish yourself. At the time there were oodles of musicians around. I'm just a trumpet player – you have to establish what you could do, what is different."

For a while, things didn't go well, until he mentioned to a fellow musician that he had trained in Hollywood. This inadvertently started a rumour. "I started it quite accidentally," Hales said later. "It got around that I was from Hollywood. All of a sudden, I started getting calls."

For six years, Bobby was the bandleader at Isy's nightclub in Vancouver. "It gave me a good base so I could support my family. They used to produce Las Vegas spectaculars. They were well-constructed shows with dancers. I used to write the music for them. A steady paycheque for a musician is almost unheard of."

He started his own big band in 1965, a 19-piece jazz ensemble chosen from Vancouver's top instrumentalists. The Bobby Hales Big Band stayed together for more than a quarter of a century. Among the musicians in that band were Don Clark, Oliver Gannon, Bob Doyle, Stew Barnett, Wally Snider, Dave Quarin, Jack Stafford, George Ursan, and Fraser MacPherson.

In 1969, Hales moved his band to The Cave, where they stayed for several years.

In 1976, Bobby formed his company, Center Line Music Productions Ltd., which produces records, music tracks for advertising, film scores, and music for TV shows.

Among many other generous acts, in 1977, he became music director for the annual *Timmy Christmas Telethon*, raising funds to aid disabled children in British Columbia.

From 1978 to 1984, Hales was acting musical director for the Pacific National Exhibition, Canada's second-largest annual exhibition. It was during that period that Bobby Hales had one of his most satisfying experiences. His big band plus 25 strings provided the accompaniment for Frank Sinatra when that legendary singer appeared at the PNE. It was the first and last time a Canadian orchestra was privileged to accompany Sinatra on any of his engagements in Canada.

In 1995, Hales was elected president of the Vancouver Musicians' Association.

Bobby Hales has always been realistic enough to recognize the difference between the general public's taste and that of, say, jazz fans. But he doesn't turn up his nose at any form of music – not even waltzes or polkas.

Still, he recognizes the difference. In 1980, while playing a "Tea Dance" in Vancouver, Bobby Hales articulated it: "This is music for the feet. Jazz is music for the head."

Art Hallman
b. Kitchener, Ontario, January 11, 1910; d. 1995

The singer, arranger, saxophonist, pianist, bandleader and vocal coach, Art Hallman – born Arthur Garfield – was to become one of Canada's most popular bandleaders of that era (mostly the second half of the 20th century) when dance bands were drawing big crowds at various locations across the country.

He began studying piano at age 10 and saxophone at 18. A year later, he took a job in a hardware company in Vancouver, but he was so consumed by his interest in music that he quit the job and spent the summer on a ship – but as a musician. He played on CNR steamship cruises to Alaska. "That summer," he recalled, "I made 14 round trips to Alaska, and then I joined CJOR in Vancouver as a staff pianist." It turned out to be a lucky move for young Hallman.

In 1932, Hallman joined Mart Kenney and His Western Gentlemen. Many years later, he recalled the circumstances of his joining Kenney: "The station [CJOR] was above the Alexandra Ballroom [in the Hotel Vancouver] where Mart Kenney's band played. Mart wanted a singer who could play piano and made me an offer. That's how I became the seventh Western Gentleman in the Kenney orchestra." Many years later, Hallman's warm memories of his time with Kenney had not cooled: "The Mart Kenney band was *the* band," he told Helen McNamara.

During the war Kenney's band toured army camps and war plants and presented a series of half-hour broadcasts known as the *Victory Parade* on the CBC English and French radio networks. Said Hallman, with justifiable pride: "We went across Canada 14 times in three years."

The job with Kenney turned out to be a 13-year gig. In 1945, he formed his first band in Toronto – a band that was to remain active for 45 years. He started with a 15-piece band, opening at Casa Loma in 1945. He did a lot of singing, but he also had an unerring knack for picking good, talented female vocalists and featured a succession of them – Terry Dale, Joan Fairfax, Shirley Harmer, and Marilyn Kent, the last-named going on to become Miss Canada of 1952. (Dale, Harmer, and Fairfax went on to successful singing careers on their own.)

Hallman also had the ability to coach vocalists. "I took advanced people only," he said many years later. "They were usually singers who had problems, perhaps in intonation or phrasing, or perhaps the quality of their voices needed changing." For example, Hallman remembered that he helped Joan Fairfax bring her semi-legitimate soprano voice into a contralto range.

However, he gave up hiring female singers. "I dropped all the girl singers eventually," he commented. "They all got married."

But Art's career as a bandleader continued to flourish. (One of his sidemen was Johnny Cowell, who later became a prolific songwriter.) After working at Casa Loma and Toronto's Royal York Hotel, the band appeared at the popular Palais Royale, along the shore of Lake Ontario. It also played for various conventions and appeared elsewhere in Ontario (including Oshawa's Jubilee Pavilion for 35 years). The band was featured for many years on CBC Radio and during the 1950s and 1960s on CFRB's *Saturday Night Sing-a-Long*. Hallman's theme song was one he wrote himself, titled **Just a Moment More with You**, which became familiar to generations of dance band fans.

During the 1940s especially, Art was one of Canada's most popular tenors. But he also had the qualifications – and the good sense – to become a vocal coach, devoting his time to students.

Yet another sideline kept Hallman busy. Along with such eminent sidemen as Bobby Gimby, Joe and Bert Niosi, Jimmy Coxson, Hank Monis, singer Dorothy Deane and her husband, drummer Jimmy Cooke, he recorded dozens of radio commercials – which at least meant money, if no glory. And for three years (1963–66) he served as choral director for CBC Television's *Juliette* show, which featured the Art Hallman Singers.

His recordings include several 78 rpms with Mart Kenney and His Western Gentlemen (1938–45) and others with his own band (circa 1947). He made the LP **Turn Back the Pages of Time** in 1973.

During the late 1980s and early 1990s, Art Hallman was reunited with the Mart Kenney orchestra on several occasions. He died early in 1995.

The Happy Gang *first aired, 1937; final show, 1959*

Sound effect: Knock, knock.
One voice: "Who's there?"
Voices: "It's the Happy Gang!"
Voice: "Well, come on in!"

That opening was familiar to a whole generation of radio listeners across Canada. For 22 glorious years and nearly 4000 broadcasts, The Happy Gang entertained Canadians from coast to coast with their daily CBC Radio show.

The names of Bert Pearl, Robert Farnon, Blain Mathe, Kathleen Stokes, and announcer Herb May became known and beloved to listeners across the

The Happy Gang (l. to r.): George Temple, Bert Pearl, Cliff McKay, Blain Mathe, Eddie Allen, Kathleen Stokes, Bobby Gimby, Hugh Bartlett, Bert Niosi, Jimmy Namaro

country, as did those of Eddie Allen, who joined the cast the following year, plus such later additions as trumpeter Bobby Gimby, clarinetist Cliff McKay, pianists Jimmy Namaro, Lloyd Edwards, and Lou Snider, and multi-instrumentalist Bert Niosi.

From the very beginning, the public responded positively. "The mail started to pour in," Bert Pearl recalled years later. "In 10 days we knew we had something, but we didn't know what it was." They were destined to become Canada's first radio stars. Their pleasant music and lighthearted banter held a loyal audience from St. John's to Victoria from 1937 to 1959.

The Happy Gang was formed – almost by accident – by Bert Pearl, who recalled: "I played piano for Percy Faith and one day someone [at the CBC] said they needed to fill a half hour. So I took Robert Farnon out of the brass, and a few others – and we were off and running." (The other original Happy Gang members were violinist Blain Mathe, organist Kathleen Stokes, and announcer Herb May.)

Spontaneity was the key to their success. Only the several daily musical numbers were rehearsed. Everything else was ad lib – no script. "All you had to do in arranging then was to write an introduction and an ending," said Pearl. "In the middle part it was every man for himself."

Once the show became a big hit, tourists visiting Toronto often made a point of visiting the CBC studios, to peer in through plate-glass windows at their favourite radio entertainers at work. Many years later, Pearl recalled: "The show grew like Topsy. It became a habit. People would tell friends, 'Don't call while we're listening to the show.'"

During the Second World War, they played and sang "There'll Always Be an England" on the air every day, at the beginning of each show. And Canadians never tired of it. Eddie Allen, who played accordion as well as singing, introduced Ruth Lowe's haunting song "I'll Never Smile Again" to Canadian

175

audiences. When Bert Pearl moved to Los Angeles in 1955, it was Allen who took over running the show.

But it was in 1950 that June Callwood, one of Canada's leading journalists, wrote an eyebrow-raising article for *Maclean's* titled "The Not-So-Happy Gang," in which she revealed some of the cracks in the smiling faces of Canada's most popular radio entertainers. (Sample: "With one or two exceptions, the gang feels nothing warmer than respect for the boss, Bert Pearl, and in the other department it is possible one half the Gang would cheer happily if the other half was fired. ... Bobby Gimby and Cliff McKay are as close as any two on the Gang ever get but they are a great deal less than buddies.")

One CBC producer was quoted by Callwood as saying that Pearl was a first-rate orchestra leader and "without parallel in his good taste. It's killing him to slosh around with that always-smiling routine."

To which Pearl reportedly replied: "If I'm any better than this, why hasn't someone given me a better show?"

It was the strain and pressure of keeping the show's cast smiling that sent Bert Pearl into severe depression and eventually led him to quit the show and head west. There, he became pianist for singer Gisele MacKenzie, among other performers, but his career never again approached the level of success he had enjoyed as the harried boss of The Happy Gang.

In 1963, the group held a kind of reunion (for an appearance on the CBC television show *Flashback*) and some of the Gang felt more inclined to let their hair down a bit. They remembered the practical joke they once played on Pearl – setting the studio clocks ahead a quarter of an hour, pretending they were on the air. Farnon remembered that Bert – thinking the show was on the air – asked Eddie Allen to sing something and Eddie told him, "I don't want to sing that damn song."

Kathleen Stokes: "Bert almost had a heart attack from it. The joke was almost on us."

Stokes also had fond recollections of Farnon: "He was the fun of the program. When he left [to join the Army in 1943 and then settle in England] we became serious."

During that 1963 reunion, Pearl remembered: "In the early years particularly there was never a trace of personality difficulties. But the larger a thing grows the less of an intimate unit it becomes. Something was lost later on. We became big business."

Few of the Happy Gang cast members are still alive. Blain Mathe died in 1967, Kathleen Stokes in 1979, Bert Pearl in 1986, and Cliff McKay and Bert Niosi in 1987. As of this writing, Eddie Allen, Robert Farnon, and Jimmy Namaro are still alive.

But the Canadian public still has a warm spot in their hearts for The Happy Gang. In 1975 – 16 years after the Gang's last broadcast – entertainer Billy

O'Connor, who had never been associated professionally with The Happy Gang, organized a reunion of the troupe for two concerts in one day at Toronto's CNE Grandstand. Each of the two shows attracted 15,000 fans.

Prolonged applause followed the entrance of Bert Pearl. "I've waited 38 years for this occasion," said Pearl – he was harking back to the day in 1937 when The Happy Gang first went on the air – "but right now," he added, "I feel as if it was only yesterday."

Organist Kathleen Stokes got two standing ovations that day: one for playing "Amazing Grace" and another after she played "Now Is the Hour."

Between the two concerts, hundreds of fans managed to crash the backstage area to get autographs of the legendary performers. After the first show, O'Connor was so moved that he was weeping backstage. All choked up, he said: "And Bert was afraid people wouldn't come!"

Hagood Hardy

b. Angola, Indiana, February 26, 1937; d. 1997

Hagood Hardy lived for only 59 years, but they were years packed with music and drama – success as a musician and composer, fighting an ugly lawsuit that dragged on for two years, and taking a fling at politics.

In a way, he sort of backed into fame and fortune. His Canadian father and American mother moved to Canada when Hagood was an infant, settling in Oakville, Ontario. He began studying piano when he was nine, but switched to vibraphone at 15. "I was mesmerized," he recalled. "I just thought it was a smashing instrument." He saved money from a summer job and laid out $375 for a set of vibes.

In his college days he couldn't practise enough on the vibraphone. "He used to drive us nuts," said a school friend who lived in the same residence. "Night after night, we'd be trying to sleep, and all we could hear was Hagood, tinkling away somewhere in the building. I think he was down in the laundry room. At three in the morning, for God's sake."

Hardy defended himself: "I had to develop my wrists. You need strong hands to play the piano, but you need very strong wrists for the vibraphone – you play it with mallets, you know."

He had planned to study architecture at the University of Toronto, but he kept getting distracted by his love of music. At 19, he was finishing his second

year of university, but spent much of his time sitting in with musicians like Moe Koffman at the House of Hambourg, at that time a favourite Toronto jazz spot. By the time he graduated in 1958, he had already been playing the Town Tavern, then one of the city's top jazz venues.

In 1961, he moved to the United States and played with various groups, including one headed by George Shearing. Hardy said later: "People who played with Shearing used to say, 'Six weeks with George is like two years at the Juilliard.'"

But it was after returning to Canada in 1966 that Hagood Hardy literally struck it rich. He formed a trio and landed a choice gig at Stop 33, atop the new Sutton Place Hotel. In 1969 he formed a new group – adding two female vocalists – and called the ensemble The Montage.

He also got into commercial work, composing jingles for such products as Dole Pineapple, Kellogg's cereals, and Benson and Hedges cigarettes. In 1972, he wrote **The Homecoming** as a jingle for Salada Tea. "To be honest," he said later, "it wasn't until people began writing in to the [advertising] agency that I realized how much they liked it."

Hardy revised and recorded the tune. It was released in 1975 as a single on the Isis label and became a runaway smash. It was also an international hit, selling about a quarter of a million copies in Canada alone, and won him several prizes – a Juno Award as Composer and Instrumentalist of 1975,

Instrumental Artist of the Year by *Billboard*, and the William Harold Moon Award from BMI Canada.

He began doing concerts – usually sold out – and getting lavish praise from critics. A Winnipeg critic said his work was "music that is as soft and shimmering as silk." Another critic from the east coast [in Halifax] wrote: "Much of Hagood Hardy's music is like shuffling through leaves on a wet November day, hands dug deep into pockets, eyes dreamy, and the mind full of teasing, nostalgic thoughts."

But one evening, he came in for work at George's Spaghetti House and found a plain brown envelope awaiting him. Inside it was a letter informing he was being sued for $100,000. The suit charged that Hagood had stolen the melody for **The Homecoming**.

Hardy's reaction was as smooth as his music. "In Nashville," he commented, "they say you don't have a real hit until you've been sued seven times." But the case dragged on for two years before it was dismissed. "For two years," said Hagood, "my life was in someone else's hands."

Then, in 1995, Hagood Hardy became interested in politics – seriously interested. He was nominated by the Ontario Liberal Party to run against then-Premier Bob Rae in the riding of York South. In nominating Hardy, Liberal John Nunziata said: "Bob Rae, your days are numbered."

He was wrong. In fact, two years later, it was Hagood Hardy who lost a battle against cancer. At his funeral, Bob Rae said of Hagood Hardy: "Of all the opponents I've had running in nine elections, he was without question the most decent and the warmest."

Also at the funeral services, Tom Williams, a friend of Hardy's, said: "Will Rogers said that he'd never met a man he didn't like. Hagood never met a person who didn't like him."

Ofra Harnoy
b. Israel, January 31, 1965

"My parents didn't know if they were going to have a boy or a girl, but they knew they were going to have a cellist," said Ofra Harnoy, a decade ago.

Her family moved to Toronto in 1971, and she became a naturalized Canadian in 1977. Ofra had begun taking cello lessons from her father when she was six. She studied in England, then in Canada. Among her teachers have been Pierre Fournier, Jacqueline Du Pré, and Mstislav Rostropovich. By

179

1979, when she was 15, she had already appeared as soloist with numerous orchestras, including the Montreal Symphony Orchestra, the Boyd Neel Orchestra, and the Toronto Symphony.

She has received a number of music awards, even as early as 1982 when she won the New York Concert Artists' Guild Award – the youngest first-prize winner in the history of that award.

"Many critics have commented that when I play it looks as if my arms and legs are growing out of my cello," she once said, laughing. "It really is a part of my body."

Her cello is her constant companion: "My cello flies full fare and gets seat-belted in, just like me. It doesn't get a meal, though. Yet sometimes, when I'm lugging this big cello case down those skinny aisles in airplanes, or waiting with it in those long lines at Customs, I really do wish I played the flute."

On her way up, Harnoy had her detractors as well as her admirers. William Littler, music critic for the *Toronto Star*, wrote that she was "not in the front ranks with Rostropovich or Yo-Yo Ma," and other, lesser-known critics, called her "overrated."

But Placido Domingo, who performed (and dined) with her in Toronto, told her she played like a tenor – which is the ultimate compliment, coming from one of the world's leading tenors. And Prince Charles sent her handwritten notes to entice her to play at his Salisbury concert. The Japanese royal family, who are very serious musicians, are friends who love to play with her when she's in their country.

"Playing the cello is not the only thing I do," she told one interviewer. "My friends are from different fields. I don't just sit around and analyze sonatas all day."

Her other interests include nature, books, cooking, and shopping. "I'm a fanatical shopper," she confessed. "That's why I don't have a credit card. I'd go crazy. I love clothes, paintings, furniture, books."

Ofra Harnoy is anything but the stereotypical "classical" artist. Perhaps because of her youthful start, perhaps because of her glamour and outspokenness and independent spirit – quite possibly all of these – her musical interests are catholic. She plays Bach and Vivaldi and Mozart and Haydn, and she also "digs" a good deal of contemporary music. But here, too, she is selective.

"I don't like heavy rock and deep country and western. I like jazz, rhythm and blues, and funk. I got into reggae from listening to Bob Marley and 'rap' to the dirty macho stuff. It becomes like your heartbeat."

Harnoy's meteoric career has been breathtaking – even to her. Her recording of Vivaldi concertos was one of the best-selling classical albums in the world in 1990. Other Harnoy recordings have won numerous prizes, including three Juno Awards, the Canadian Music Council's Grande prix du disc, and record of the year or critics' choice awards from *Gramophone, High Fidelity, Ovation*, and *CD Review* magazines.

One critic, reviewing Harnoy's recording of Haydn cello concertos, wrote: "She has approached these war-horses with fresh vision, a superb technique and flawless instinctive musicianship – not to overlook her excellent intonation."

Because she is talented and attractive and possesses a dynamic personality, Harnoy's personal life has sometimes been troublesome. Her admirers have occasionally turned into fanatics. "They go from love letters to threatening letters to suicidal letters," she said in 1993. "They leave things for me in my car.

"One guy sent pictures of cut-up body parts and roses."

During a holiday in Dubrovnik she met a "local hero," a water polo star revered by women. He had no idea who she was – he simply was attracted by her beauty. They married in haste and the marriage ended in a year. "It was a major mistake," said Harnoy. "I was so paranoid. I had male friends and I didn't think I needed a boyfriend because I was travelling all the time. I didn't trust the men who fell in love with me in my career. They don't know me. There are men who fall in love with my picture and pursue me and all these wealthy men following me and sending me flowers. I don't trust this; it's not real. So I put up barriers for a long time."

The barriers were lowered when she met someone "who understands" the place her career has in her life, someone she declined to identify. They were married and in 1996 Ofra took a 14-month maternity leave, after which she returned to the concert stage at Toronto's Ford Centre for the Performing Arts.

But, being the unpredictable Harnoy, she featured a selection of songs by the Beatles and Simon and Garfunkel, mostly arranged for solo cello and string quartet.

Corey Hart

b. Montreal, May 31, 1961

During the 1980s, the Canadian hard rock music industry enjoyed a boom. Bands such as Loverboy, April Wine, Rush, and Triumph, or solo acts such as Carole Pope, Kim Mitchell, Bryan Adams, and Corey Hart, rockers with an edgy, provocative, sexy, and brash sound, found favour and plenty of audiences in the decade. For a time, the genre was dominated by Corey Hart, the

so-called "heartthrob" originally from Montreal, who wanted to be heard as much as fans wanted to hear him.

"I aspire for my music to be heard everywhere," Hart told the *Toronto Star*. "I'm not happy if it just stays within the four walls of the control room. I feel incomplete."

For a time, when he was young, Corey rarely had four walls he could call home, his family moved so frequently. From Corey's birthplace, Montreal, the Hart family moved to Spain in 1966 (when he was four), then to Mexico (when he was nine), and eventually, in 1974, back to Canada. As a youngster (he's the youngest of five children), Corey had ambitions to sing; he enjoyed the vocal stylings of Smokey Robinson, and the writing style of the Police and Sting.

A connection through Tom Jones to Paul Anka proved to be Corey's entrée to the business. Anka financed a recording session for Corey (at age 12) in Las Vegas. A Corey Hart version of Anka's song "Ooh Baby" for United Artists Records in 1974 did not make it on the charts and UA did not renew his contract. Hart tried his luck in the L.A. scene for a while, then returned to Montreal. In 1983, Hart signed with EMI (Aquarius) Records and recorded an album's worth of material in England (Eric Clapton guested on the song "Jenny Fey"). What propelled this debut album *First Offense* up the charts in the United States and later Canada was the single **Sunglasses at Night**, which was actually a last-minute addition to the recording.

"I heard about this sunglasses-at-night idea when I was over in England," Hart told *Canadian Composer* magazine. "I had an idea ... the George Orwell and 1984 thing ... it was a takeoff, where everyone in society had to wear sunglasses at night and I didn't want to do it. I would go against the rule, be a James Dean."

Hart wrote the song in Montreal, went back into the British recording studio and added it to the album. **Sunglasses at Night** (and its followup single, **It Ain't Enough**) both reached the Top 20 on the *Billboard* charts. Television exposure of its accompanying video moved **Sunglasses** into the Top 10 and earned Hart his first Juno Award for Best Video. With a half-dozen performances to prepare, Hart made his professional debut with Culture Club in Toronto, in 1984. He toured North America, Europe, and Australia to promote the single and album.

Oddly, while on tour, more than any other single item, he lost countless pairs of ... sunglasses.

In 1985, Hart released *Boy in the Box*, an album that sold more than one million copies in Canada (a feat only he and Alannah Myles had achieved to that time). The single **Never Surrender** did equally well, hitting number three on the U.S. charts and number one in Canada; it earned a Grammy nomination and a Juno Award for Best Single of the Year. He and Bryan Adams seemed to be jockeying for Canadian teenagers' attention at awards ceremonies, on the concert circuit, and on MTV. They both appeared (with dozens of other top Canadian names) in the Northern Lights for Africa fundraiser "Tears Are Not Enough."

More touring, with such acts as Hall and Oates and Rick Springfield, followed. There were two more albums in the 1980s – *Fields of Fire* (1986) and *Young Man Running* (1988) – and more television appearances. There was a string of nine Top 40 hits. Hart's face appeared on magazine covers everywhere, including *TV Guide* to promote a CBC concert special.

"You [can't] turn on a radio without hearing Corey's voice or click on a TV video show without seeing his trademark pout," said the *Toronto Star*.

Hart's workaholic pace overtook him, however, and in 1987, after performing in Sudbury, he collapsed and had to cancel the remainder of his planned cross-Canada tour. The celebrity, whether in the manufactured rivalry with Bryan Adams or simply because of overexposure, took its toll too.

"I tended to want to be too protected from going out and doing regular things," Hart told the *Globe and Mail*'s Elizabeth Renzetti later. "Sometimes it was so frenetic and I felt uncomfortable. You end up not going through the front door of your hotel."

By the early 1990s, despite having racked up an amazing 10 million albums sold, Hart was dropping out of the commercial picture. His albums *Bang* (1990) and *Attitude and Virtue* (1991) didn't register on the *Billboard* charts at all. Relations with his record label soured. As well, Hart's marriage to Erika Gagnon ended and he considered retiring from show business entirely.

By the late 1990s, Corey Hart was making a comeback. He was living in Nassau, Bahamas, having struck up a new relationship with Quebec singer Julie Masse (they were married in July 2000 with three daughters). He recorded a seventh, self-titled album which quickly reached certified gold in Canada. He also made a return to the touring circuit – not to the CNE Grandstand or the Saddledome, but to small venues such as the Danforth Music Hall in Toronto and the Jack Singer Concert Hall in Calgary.

In 1998 he wrote two songs for Céline Dion's album *Let's Talk About Love* and then composed material for his own 1998 release, *Jade*. The album was recorded at Nassau's Compass Point Studios, which had previously hosted such performers as the Rolling Stones, the B52s, and Roxy Music. The process appeared to rejuvenate his passion for music.

"I love writing songs," Hart commented on his Web site, "all at once cathartic, consuming, frustrating, life affirming, humbling."

Ronnie Hawkins

b. Huntsville, Arkansas, January 10, 1935

Before international recording labels set up branch plants in Toronto, before A&R scouts began perusing pubs and bars in the Great White North, and even before Canadian radio stations discovered there was talent north of the 49th, an expatriate American pop band leader was grooming and promoting it.

In fact, most veterans of the Canadian popular music scene agree that no single entertainer has done more to develop, encourage, and showcase new Canadian talent than Rompin' Ronnie Hawkins, either before or since the CRTC rules on Canadian content.

"He was a genuine rockabilly superstar when he came to the musically arid desert that was Canada in the late 50s," wrote Earl McRae. "And clubs were desperate to book him. Hawkins was only too glad to oblige – if those same clubs would also promise to give young and struggling and talented Canadians a break."

There was, however, no sugar daddy in Ronnie Hawkins' career.

Born just two days after Elvis Presley, Ronald Cornet Hawkins, as a boy, was allowed to listen and watch as a small blues band rehearsed in the back of the barbershop where his father worked. The experience triggered his interest in music, and Ronnie tried pulling together high school bands until 1952 when he was drawn to the music mecca of the south – Memphis, where black blues music and country music were crossing paths. Back home he formed the Ron Hawkins Quartet mimicking that rockabilly sound. He'd open his act by shouting, "It's *rrr*racket time with Mr. Dynamo!" And he'd perform in rowdy, local roadhouses for beer and a few bucks.

"Those places were rough," recalls Hawkins, "and one of those big old microphones … was a good weapon to defend yourself. I got better than Zorro with the mike stand."

After a short stint at the University of Arkansas studying physical education, Hawkins served six months in the army; he never once carried a weapon, but often held a mike and sang with a band called the Black Hawks, which earned him a "soldier of the month" award and was, in Hawkins' words, "the first mixed and desegregated band my part of the south had ever seen."

In 1957, Elvis Presley was taking the radio and the country by storm with his rockabilly sound. Hawkins wanted to get in on it and presented himself to Sun Records' legendary star-maker Sam Phillips at about the same time that Buddy Holly did. The meeting did not yield a recording contract, so Hawkins returned to Arkansas to form Ronnie Hawkins and the Hawks, but fate turned him northward.

Hawkins' friend Harold Jenkins and his band the Rock Housers had borrowed equipment and followed up an invitation to play in Buffalo, New York, where a Canadian booking agent was recruiting bands to play in southern Ontario. The Rock Housers played the Golden Rail club in Hamilton and Hawkins and the Hawks followed. While in Hamilton, Jenkins penned "It's Only Make Believe," changed his name to Conway Twitty, and became a country music star. Hawkins chased that elusive recording dream north to Canada and decided to stay. First, he felt he could sell his Memphis sound to new audiences in Canada. Second, he felt he could help talented musicians in Canada gain the recognition they deserved.

"Most of them were starving to death," Hawkins told Martin Melhuish in his book *Heart of Gold*, "because agents wouldn't book a Canadian group. ... club owners felt that a Canadian band wouldn't draw in Canada. ... I used to loan different bands my car which still had American plates on it, and fool the agents and club owners by saying the band came from [the United States] ... They'd tell them they were from Scarborough ... Tennessee."

Hawkins finally did cut a disc for Quality Records. They released **Bo Diddley** in the summer of 1958. With airplay on both sides of the border, Hawkins was approached by American label Roulette Records (who were still looking for their own version of Elvis Presley). Two singles followed in 1959. **Forty Days** spent 80 days on the *Billboard* 100 chart, while **Mary Lou** climbed to number 25 in the summer of 1959. It seemed the perfect time to resettle in the United States: Elvis was in the army, Jerry Lee Lewis was embroiled in a child bride scandal, and Ritchie Valens, the Big Bopper, and Buddy Holly had recently died in that fabled plane crash. Instead, Hawkins returned to Canada, or, as he described it, "the promised land."

Part of that promise was steady work for Hawkins and the Hawks. At a time when few Toronto downtown nightspots sold both liquor and entertainment, Hawkins became the house band at Le Coq d'Or Tavern on Yonge Street where he introduced his brand of Memphis blues and Ozark rock 'n' roll to captive audiences night after night.

"It was a pretty good mix," said Hawks drummer Levon Helm, "a mix of southern-flavoured music and the wildest showman they had ever seen."

Soon, however, the call of home tugged at many of Hawkins' band members and they began to depart the Toronto scene, a pattern that would continue in Hawkins' bands throughout the 1960s. That meant the band needed replacements. They came from local ranks, not from Arkansas.

First recruited was guitarist Robbie Robertson, 16 and, in Hawkins' words, "a street greaser like Sal Mineo ... who wanted to be somebody." In the spring of 1961, a rhythm guitarist named Rick Danko joined the band at a gig in Simcoe, Ontario; he later replaced a departing bass player. That summer, Richard Manuel, a rocker with a distinctive voice, joined the band on keyboards. And finally by Christmas of 1961, classically trained pianist Garth Hudson had joined.

"We were probably the best white rhythm-and-blues band by far," said Hawkins in a CBC-TV documentary.

The truth was Ronnie Hawkins whipped every band (the *Globe and Mail* described him as "the drill sergeant of Canadian rock 'n' roll) into the best by far. As band leader, he was a no-nonsense disciplinarian. He shouted. He swore. He handed out stiff fines for drunkenness, drug abuse, or showing up late. He rehearsed the band seven days a week. But he praised, coaxed, and cajoled too. Perhaps apocryphal, it's said he forced a guitarist to the breaking point over squeaky strings on his chord changes. "Dammit, Ronnie," the guitarist objected, "not even Segovia plays without a little string noise." To which Hawkins replied, "That's why Segovia ain't in my band."

"My god, what a talent, what a teacher he was," commented Levon Helm. "Everybody wanted to play in his bands."

From such expert tutelage, not surprisingly, came the need to grow and move on. About the time Ronnie Hawkins got married (in the early 1960s) both the lives and the musical directions of the Hawks and their leader began to diverge. Suits and choreographed routines were a thing of the past. Individuality was the calling card of the 1960s, and it seemed fame and fortune was just sitting there for the taking. Then, in the summer of 1965, a secretary working for Bob Dylan's manager suggested the Hawks might be ideal for Dylan's first electric tour. They signed a four-month contract as "the band" backing up Dylan. About a year later, Hawkins' Hawks had flown the coop to become legendary as The Band.

Quipped Hawkins in *Rolling Stone* magazine: "I don't change my music, I just change bands."

Though the musicians came and went, Hawkins' influence on Canadian rock music persisted. In the early 1960s, Hawkins introduced the Twist and go-go girls to the Toronto bar scene. He openly invited up-and-coming performers to sit in and learn tricks of the trade; among them was John Kay, lead singer of The Sparrow (later Steppenwolf). Hawkins worked with Robbie Lane, who went on to host *It's Happening*, a national TV show in 1967. He worked with Richard "King Biscuit Boy" Newell, who often fronted Crowbar. He tutored (Jim) Atkinson, (Terry) Danko, and (Duane) Ford. And countless sidemen worked under Hawkins' wing – guitarists: Fred Carter, Terry Bush, John Till (who left Hawkins to join Janis Joplin's Full Tilt Boogie Band; Joplin raved about his musicianship), Pat Travers, and Dom Troiano; pianists: Scott Cushnie, Ricky

Bell, and David Foster (whom Hawkins once fired for putting too many notes in his song **Bo Diddley**); and singers: Bobby Curtola, Beverly D'Angelo, Jackie Gabriel, Tobi Lark, Jay Smith, and David Clayton-Thomas. And Hawkins struck up a friendship with Gordon Lightfoot, which yielded Lightfoot's song "Home from the Forest" in 1967.

In 1969, *Rolling Stone* commissioned a feature article on the Canadian rock music scene; the writer discovered Hawkins with lots to say about his own career as well as The Band's. When the article was published in August, Hawkins' stock soared. With his Roulette Records contract expired, the bidding began (Hawkins claims Paramount was offering a three-year contract for $300,000). He signed with Atlantic, who flew him to Muscle Shoals to cut an album. Before long Hawkins found himself in the middle of another rock groundswell – John Lennon and Yoko Ono's world peace campaign. The campaign recruited Hawkins both to provide haven for the outspoken performers and to be an ambassador for their cause. The relationship also helped Hawkins' single, **Down in the Alley**, become a hit simultaneously in Canada, the United States, and Australia.

Hawkins revelled in the deserved attention and success. He and his wife, former Miss Toronto Wanda Nagurski, bought a house in Toronto and 198 acres of farmland near Stoney Lake, Ontario. He began collecting classic cars (17 in all, including Porsches, Karmann Ghias, a gull-wing Mercedes, a Lamborghini, and three Rolls-Royces) and raising a family. He became a millionaire, an ex-millionaire, and a millionaire again by going back on the road singing **Bo Diddley**, **Mary Lou**, **Forty Days**, and all the rest of his repertoire.

In the late 1970s and early 1980s, Hawkins was in and out of hospital for exhaustion and hiatus hernia attacks numerous times. Despite that, he still met the demands of a scaled-down performance schedule and formed a new band with bassist Ken King and lead guitarist John Lewis, as well as Hawks alumni Jerry Penfound (sax), Dave Lewis (drums), and Stan Szelest (keyboards). He landed his third movie role as Major Wolcott in Michael Cimino's film *Heaven's Gate*. In 1981, he renovated the old city hall building in London, Ontario as a 350-seat honky-tonk called Johnny Finebone's and also began hosting *Honky Tonk*, a weekly show on CTV. He even found time to release several compilation albums including **The Hawk**, **Sold Out**, and **Legend in His Spare Time**, and in 1984 he toured England and recorded his first-ever live album, **The Hawk and the Rock**.

Two books were published on his life – a 1989 autobiography, *The Last of the Good Ol' Boys*, assisted by Peter Goddard, and Ian Wallis' 1996 publication *The Hawk: The Story of Ronnie Hawkins and the Hawks*. In 1994, a musical 60th birthday celebration at Massey Hall in Toronto produced a TV special and yielded Hawkins' first gold-certified recording **Let It Rock**. Then in 2000, another TV documentary, *Tall Tales from the Long Corner*, celebrated Hawkins' 65th. Says Hawkins, "They told me in 1952 the big time was just around the corner. It's a long corner, but I'm still hoping."

Ronnie Hawkins' career path took him away from the source of the music he has played for half a century. Some suggest that path to Canada led him away from fame and fortune. During a phone call he once made from Sturgeon Falls, Ontario to his friend Levon Helm in Arkansas, Hawkins reported, "I'm so far north that Admiral Byrd turned back 50 miles south of here." Whether he himself achieved greatness or not, his impact on the music scene in Canada was great.

Sylvia Tyson once commented, "Ronnie Hawkins took young Canadian talent and made them believe in themselves, if only because he believed in them. He told them they could be just as good as anybody in the world with hard work and dedication and he proved it."

Jeff Healey Band

formed 1985 in Toronto: Jeff Healey (b. Toronto, March 25, 1966) vocals, guitar; Joe Rockman (b. Toronto, January 1, 1957) bass; Tom Stephen (b. Saint John, N.B., February 2, 1955) drums

Under different circumstances, Jeff Healey might have picked up a cornet and played in a traditional jazz band or walked into a radio station and become a full-time broadcaster. But because playing guitar was in vogue when he was three, "I asked for a guitar for Christmas and got one."

Blinded by eye cancer as an infant, Jeff taught himself to play the guitar cross-lap style (like blind Halifax singer Fred McKenna), so that he could use all five fingers of his left hand for notes, chords, and vibrato. One Saturday afternoon in 1976, at a flea market west of Toronto, 10-year-old Jeff picked up a guitar at a music stall, turned it over on his knees, and started playing a blues tune. A crowd gathered to listen. He played all afternoon. The music store owner had him back every weekend for a year. It was Jeff's first paying gig.

"Most people figured that I'd descended out of space," he told Mark Miller in the *Globe and Mail* in 1986. "Such is not the case."

Jeff had been playing since his teens, working semiprofessionally in bands playing country, rockabilly, jazz, blues, and rock. His first challenge was to master his guitar. Evidently, he succeeded. By the early 1980s, Healey began jamming with players in Toronto clubs. During a session at Albert's Hall,

Jeff Healey Band (l. to r.): Jeff Healey, Tom Stephen, Joe Rockman

visiting blues guitarist Stevie Ray Vaughan saw Healey and predicted he would "revolutionize the way the guitar can be played." Soon after, at Grossman's Tavern, Healey teamed up with bass player Joe Rockman and drummer Tom Stephen, ultimately forming the Jeff Healey Band (JHB).

The JHB recorded an independent single, **See the Light**, on its own Forte Records in 1985. Then using the demo, a video, and a lot of upbeat press clippings, Tom Stephen began knocking on doors in New York and landed a contract with Arista Records. By 1988, the band had released its *See the Light* album and coincidentally was cast in a movie, *Road House*, starring Patrick Swayze. While the film got mixed reviews, the album got raves. It produced two hit singles. The album went double-platinum in Canada and platinum in the United States. Meanwhile, within a year, the band got a Grammy nomination, a Juno nomination, and several international awards, and was featured on *The Tonight Show* with Johnny Carson, *The Late Show with David Letterman*, and *Arsenio Hall*.

"The three years following *See the Light* were a whirlwind," Healey said, "non-stop touring, press and radio interviews [and] talk shows."

Tom Stephen often told the story about learning to play drums later in life (in his late twenties) by jamming with friends at a bar in Toronto. At the time, not a virtuoso on the kit, Stephen was routinely dismissed from the sessions.

In the late 1980s, with the band tight, successful, and all over the media, his old jamming partners would say, "I saw you on Carson the other night and I still don't regret throwing you off the stage."

Despite its fame, the Jeff Healey Band felt the pressure of the sophomore jinx on its second album. **Hell to Pay** featured six original pieces, included both live performance and studio playing, and incorporated some notable cameos: Mark Knopfler, Paul Shaffer, Bobby Whitlock – and an ex-Beatle. The JHB had just finished a version of "While My Guitar Gently Weeps" in a Montreal recording studio. Someone suggested adding the song's composer, George Harrison, to the track. The band approached him; he agreed; the tape was sent to L.A. and Harrison played and sang backup. The album sold two million copies worldwide.

In 1990, the Jeff Healey Band won its first Juno Award for Canadian Entertainers of the Year. Just as importantly, *Guitar Player* magazine published a readers' poll that named Jeff Healey Best Blues Guitarist and Best New Talent of the year. Reviewers began describing Healey as "the seventh wonder of the guitar world." Ironically, neither Healey nor JHB considered themselves a blues band.

To make the point, at the end of the 1992–93 tour promoting the album **Feel This**, what it called "a jumped-up fusion of blues, rock, ballads, and rap," the JHB went back to its roots. As it prepared to record its fourth album, the band made an appearance at Grossman's Tavern (where everything had started), as the opening act for an unannounced Rolling Stones Voodoo Lounge tour stop. The subsequent **Cover to Cover** (1995) was a concept album full of rock 'n' roll standards and blues classics. It garnered another Grammy nomination.

Then, after 12 years of recording, touring, and racking up awards, the band went on hiatus. Jeff Healey didn't rest, however. He reverted to pursuing an equally deep passion – listening to and talking about traditional blues and jazz music. Along the way, he had inherited a record collection begun by his great-grandfather, which in 1990 consisted of 10,000 78s, thousands of 33s, and as many CDs. Since 1988, the University of Toronto radio station had put Healey on the air every week playing his discs and taking calls. In 1991, the CBC put his radio show, *My Kinda Jazz*, in a summer broadcast slot and then extended it year-round.

"Louis Armstrong is my all-time favourite artist both instrumentally and vocally," Healey told audiences. "He was the first performer to capitalize on the art of improvisation … and revolutionized popular music and performance. He was a big influence on me."

A capable broadcaster/host, Healey also lobbied the major recording companies for more and better CD compilations of his jazz favourites, in particular jazz artists of the 1920s and '30s. In 1995, he assembled and issued *The*

Complete Recordings of Fletcher Henderson on CD. He also began playing jazz frequently, but not on guitar, with the band Hot 5 Jazzmakers.

"I had more or less taught myself to play the trumpet and often sat in with traditional jazz bands," Healey said. "When I went out to Los Angeles in 1988 to do our first album and the movie, I had the good fortune to play in a jazz band with ... Dick Miller. I came in with a trumpet. He used to kid me about it, saying I wasn't really playing a horn and that I should play the cornet. So a 22-year-old kid up against a great cornet player who's 50, I took it personally and went out and rented a cornet. And I've not stopped playing cornet since."

In 2000, the Jeff Healey Band returned to the studio and the circuit promoting its album *Get Me Some*. Fans welcomed the JHB back with open arms, during an inaugural New Year's Eve show at Niagara Falls Park (broadcast to North America on CNN). Then, in 2001, adding something completely different to his résumé, he opened Healey's, a music club in Toronto.

Sheila Henig *b. Winnipeg, Manitoba, February 19, 1934; d. 1979*

Canadian apathy regarding Canadian artistic achievements has long been an unfortunate byproduct of that long-cherished Canadian characteristic: reluctance to display enthusiasm, at least when it comes to gifted Canadians. It isn't that we don't enjoy Canadian artists, but that we tend to reserve our enthusiasm for "world-famous" artists.

No doubt, the typical Canadian lack of self-confidence was at play here: we don't really believe anything Canadian is worthwhile until somebody outside our country tells us it is. The awful irony in the case of Sheila Henig is that she was, in fact, a world-famous artist, but the "world" in this case didn't include Canada.

Sheila was taking dancing lessons before she was two years old. At three-and-a-half she signed her first contract as a singer. At four, she was taken to Hollywood, where Eddie Cantor wisely advised her mother to let her grow up normally.

But it was not to be. Her parents scrimped and saved to buy a piano for her, and instead of playing games with other children, Sheila spent her childhood indoors, playing scales.

When the Henig family moved to Toronto, Sheila enrolled at the Royal Conservatory and later graduated at the top of her class from the University of Toronto's Faculty of Music.

It was Walter Susskind, the urbane music director of the Toronto Symphony, who introduced Sheila Henig to Toronto audiences early in 1960, and for a time she managed to garner some share of acclaim. But that did not last – at least in Canada.

By the early 1960s, she had triumphed in her American debut with the Houston (Texas) Symphony. "This reviewer," wrote that paper's music critic, "has not heard more brisk, accurate, clean-cut management of the keyboard by an artist of her years in a long time." Another Houston critic wrote: "Miss Henig is destined to become one of the great keyboard artists. Her technique is dazzling, and she pours in a great affection for her music which is welcome after seeing so many mechanical musicians who play as if they were calculating mathematical equations."

When she performed with the Concertgebouw in Amsterdam, the critic there wrote of Henig: "A great musician from whose fingers come a very colourful attention-capturing expression." Another Amsterdam critic wrote: "The name of Sheila Henig is one to remember. A great musician … she showed a virtuosity and flawless technique. An unforgettable experience."

The *London Times* referred to "the heroic, the poetic – a nobility of utterance near the grand manner – energetic and expressive."

A Vienna critic wrote: "Tenderness and sensitivity – she played with a power which one would not expect from her fragile appearance."

She became a Laureate at the Geneva Competition and twice toured Europe, bringing back a pile of laudatory reviews.

In 1971, she performed a recital at the National Gallery in Washington, D.C., and the *Washington Post* gave her a rave review. In 1976, she toured Brussels, Rotterdam, Vienna, and Salzburg, earning more favourable reviews.

Yet her success went unrecorded in Canadian newspapers.

In 1978 she made her Carnegie Recital Hall debut in a dazzling triple-threat capacity: singing, playing the piano, and joining oboist Senia Trubashnik in chamber music, prompting *The New York Times* to describe her as "a richly satisfying artist in all three capacities."

But even this high praise was not enough to persuade Toronto Arts Productions to allow her to repeat the performance at the city's St. Lawrence Centre.

Her father, Harry Henig, wrote an understandably bitter book about his daughter's frustrating career and its consequences. In an epilogue, Henig interviewed several prominent Toronto musicians, allowing them to speak freely. One of them, Stuart Hamilton, founder of Opera in Concert, commented: "The Canadian trait is to keep everything on the same mundane level. There is a fear of excellence."

And yet Sheila Henig herself seemed to have some misgivings about the whole music world. "You may not even want fame, if you get it," she said in 1969. "You can't have all the glory and not have the travelling, the fatigue, the miserable halls – all the uncomfortable, unglamorous parts of it."

Somewhere along the way, it seems that Sheila Henig began to weigh the advantages of stardom against the disadvantages. And, quite possibly, the absence of critical and public acclaim in her native country might well have been a factor. In any case, Sheila Henig's tortuous roller-coaster of a life came to a sudden, shocking, and mystifying end in May of 1979. She was found slumped over the steering wheel of her family car in a garage reeking of exhaust fumes.

"But why?" wrote one dismayed Toronto journalist. "Why would a 45-year-old woman in the prime of her life, with a husband, two children and a beautiful Bayview home suddenly take it into her own mind one warm spring day to end it all?"

No suicide note was ever found; no acceptable reason for suicide – if that's what it was, rather than an accident – could be offered. Unless, perhaps, it was the Canadian apathy that she could not quite understand or accept.

Ben Heppner   *b. Murrayville, B.C., January 14, 1956*

It's quite a long trip, both geographically and philosophically, from a Mennonite community in Dawson Creek, B.C. to the leading operatic stages of Vienna, Milan, London's Covent Garden, and New York's Metropolitan Opera, but *heldentenor* (literally, "heroic tenor") Ben Heppner seems to have made it without ever running out of breath.

"My whole family sang, partly because of church but also at home," he recalled. "Most of us play the piano well enough to accompany a song or hymn and we'd often sing popular songs in the car or after supper. It wasn't quite the Trapp Family, but we sang a lot."

Not long after arriving in Toronto, where one of his teachers was the tenor William Neill, he was accepted by the Canadian Opera Ensemble. "I was already married and had a child, so the idea that the ensemble would pay me to learn proved irresistible," he said. "Among other things I learned was that if you can finish two years with the Ensemble program and still have a voice, you can have a career. I had to be able to sing at the drop of a hat, even if it meant at ten in the morning. In one of my first roles at the O'Keefe Centre in *The Magic Flute*, I wore a costume that made me look like an artichoke."

When he made his La Scala debut a decade ago in Wagner's *Die Meister-*

193

Courtesy National Post

singer, one critic gushed that Canadians should "slap a protected-species order on him because he is already on the way to turning into one of the great talents of the world."

And *La Stampa*, the newspaper in Turin, Italy, called him "a superb performer, capable of extreme gentleness" whose performance "merited applause before the entire world."

In 1999, when Heppner and English soprano Jane Eaglen starred in the Met's production of Wagner's *Tristan und Isolde*, Bernard Holland of *The New York Times* declared that "opera has found its new Tristan and Isolde and I wonder if we have ever had better ones."

Heppner studied first at the University of British Columbia and then at the University of Toronto's Opera School. After winning first prize at the CBC Talent Festival, he sang in Australia and Sweden and in 1988 was one of 11 winners of the Metropolitan Opera Auditions and was awarded the Birgit Nilsson Prize. He made his U.S. debut at Carnegie Hall at a state concert commissioned by the King and Queen of Sweden.

Although he has sung works by Verdi, Mozart, Meyerbeer, Massenet, Puccini, Dvořák, and Britten, Heppner is still primarily identified with the music of Wagner, of whose music he has by now become perhaps the world's leading interpreter. And his singing is in such demand that managers have to begin negotiating for him three and four years ahead.

For all his success, some of Heppner's humble, religion-based background still shapes his values. He has been quoted several times as saying that wife, family, and faith matter more to him than fame and fortune. His wife, Karen, is herself a musician. Indeed it was she who actually accompanied Heppner at the piano when he won the CBC Talent Festival in 1979. She is the person he credits with minimizing any swelling of the Heppner head.

When he is at home, he's usually up at 7:30 to get their three children off to school. He also makes it a point at least once every season to take each of the children on the road with him.

"I take each [singing] offer seriously," he said to a music journalist a few years ago, "but family life comes first. You need time to recuperate at home or you use yourself up."

He is very conscious of trying to keep a reasonable balance between the demands of his career and his responsibilities as a husband and father. "If you lose the tension between family and career," he once told music critic William Littler, "the career has won. I want the tension. It's not very pleasant. Dad is away a lot. When my youngest son sang a solo on Father's Day last year, I wasn't there; I was in Vancouver doing a recording. But I believe that if there isn't some kind of sacrificial element in everything you do, you'll come out of it on the wrong side."

Heppner the *heldentenor* may not always seem heroic to his children, but he certainly earned their enthusiastic approval a few years ago when he sang "O Canada" at a Toronto Maple Leafs hockey game. And while his "fee" was somewhat below his usual stipend for singing in public, it was somehow appropriate: he was given a Felix Potvin sweater.

Dan Hill

b. Don Mills, Ontario, June 3, 1954

He didn't really enjoy celebrity. There just wasn't enough time.

At the height of his singer-songwriter career – after releasing his most successful song to date, **Sometimes When We Touch**, in 1977, Dan Hill was only 23. He was travelling constantly, doing half a dozen interviews a day, one or two concerts a night, flying (aboard a Concorde) to England to do *Top of the Pops*, flying back in time to play New York or Los Angeles. There were television shows, interviews, performances, marketing meetings, studio sessions, and the pressure to repeat the success.

"It was like a blinding light," says Hill. "I'm not saying I wasn't happy. I'm saying I was so consumed with everything. It was just like this wild blur of activity. It just never stopped."

Life didn't begin that way. Born of an interracial marriage, Hill was raised in middle-class suburban Toronto where, he remembers, "there was a feeling of ordinariness." To break a trend where most kids knew what they wanted to be in life by age 13, Hill began singing and writing folk songs as an antidote.

He travelled along the U.S. performing circuit where a couple of opportunities – José Feliciano expressing interest as manager and Harry Belafonte showing interest as a producer – looked promising but didn't pan out. He continued to write and returned to play at Toronto's folk club, Riverboat, whose owners, Bernie Fiedler and Bernie Finkelstein, signed Hill as co-managers. In 1975, Hill recorded **You Make Me Want to Be** on a self-titled album for GRT Records, which earned him a first Juno as best new male singer. Soon a new album, *Hold On*, followed.

The true breakthrough, however, happened in 1977 when a publishing company representative introduced Hill to songwriter Barry Mann. Then in his mid-thirties, Mann had written such hits as "You've Lost That Lovin' Feelin'" for the Righteous Brothers, "On Broadway" for George Benson, "Kicks" for Paul Revere and the Raiders, and "We've Got to Get Out of This Place" for the Animals.

"I felt intimidated when he started playing me one killer melody after another," wrote Hill. "This was my first time collaborating and I felt like I was clearly in over my head. So as a last resort I reached into my pocket and pulled out the typewritten lyrics to **Sometimes When We Touch**. I left the room to call for a taxi. Barry had the chorus melody written before the taxi arrived. … The next day we used a $25 tape deck to record the song. Everyone who heard it went crazy."

The single went number one in a dozen countries. It sold over a million copies worldwide. The album *Longer Fuse* eventually went platinum and that year, 1977, Hill won Juno Awards for Best Composer, Best Male Singer, and Best-Selling Album (his producers also won for Single of the Year and Album of the Year). The sweep at the Juno ceremonies prompted Alex Lifeson (whose band Rush captured best group of the year) to say, "We'd like to thank Dan Hill for not being a group."

Clearly, the song changed Hill's life. In addition to the writing and performing success, **Sometimes When We Touch** opened many other doors. Suddenly there was a fan base. There were those who described the song's lyrics as the best ever written. Tina Turner heard the song about the time of her breakup with Ike and was so moved that she recorded it. (In the 1980s, Tammy Wynette and Mark Gray recorded it and took it to number five on the country charts; as recently as 1999, it was covered by Rod Stewart and Barry Manilow.) In 1978, Hill set out on a U.S. tour with Art Garfunkel and an Australian tour with John Sheard, to great acclaim. That year, the American trade papers *Cashbox* and *Record World* named Hill Best New Male Vocalist of the Year. He was truly a pop star.

As quickly as his star rose, however, Dan Hill's career imploded. The next album, *Frozen in the Night*, with another Hill/Mann single **Let The Song Last Forever**, did well but not up to label expectations. Two subsequent albums were ignored. As Greg Quill wrote in *Canadian Composer* years later, "[Hill] was anathema, the butt of industry jokes, the quiet, sensitive suburban kid whose only fault it seemed, was having succeeded too well." Promotional staff were soon fired at the 20th Century label and Hill was forced to buy himself out of the contract, "because the label wasn't effective anymore. … $300,000 US to get out of a record deal. So there I was. … I had already made and lost a million dollars. A has-been at age 25."

It was Dan Hill's natural gift, ultimately, that guaranteed his survival. Just as it had been the way he phrased his desperate efforts to hold onto a love affair in the lyrics to **Sometimes When We Touch**, it would be his ability to capture disappointment, a lifelong promise of love or fear of death in poetry, that would make him successful again. Hill drifted away from the singer in himself and closer to the songwriter.

"It's a liberation, frankly," says Hill. "You'd like to think that your work is appreciated or valued for the sake of its worth rather than for any kind of baggage that people have associated with you or what they imagine your persona to be."

One of the first successful steps came in 1987, when he wrote and recorded a duet called **Can't We Try** with Vonda Shepard; it became *Billboard*'s Adult Contemporary Record of the Year. And while his own version of **Never Thought That I Could Love** was climbing the charts to number one, Hill was also writing Céline Dion's first English hit in Canada, **Can't Live Without You**.

The songs of collaboration moved to centre stage for Hill. In 1982 he worked with Michael Masser to create **In Your Eyes**, the hit title song on a George Benson album. In the 1990s Hill teamed up with producer Keith Stegall; the first song they wrote together, **Love of My Life**, roared up the country charts when sung by Sammy Kershaw and a second song, **I Do Cherish You**, became a hit for Mark Wills. In 1997, Hill received a Grammy for his production and songwriting contribution to Céline Dion's album *Falling Into You*.

Dan Hill continues to travel, but not on the concert circuit (he hasn't performed a public concert since a benefit for the homeless in Calgary in 1999). He splits his time between Nashville, where he regularly writes for country performers, and his home in Toronto; there he waits to find out if demoed songs for Céline Dion, the Backstreet Boys, and even Britney Spears will be recorded, pressed, and released.

"I'm able to put into words what people feel all the time, but rarely can say in quite the way that I can say them," says Hill of his strength as a songwriter. "I just have a way of saying things that connect to the human heart and it's just something I was born with. It's magic, it's not hard work."

Tommy Hunter

b. London, Ontario, March 10, 1937

For many years, his billing proclaimed him "Canada's Country Gentleman." It would be difficult to come up with a more accurate description of Thomas James Hunter.

In a 1966 interview, he was quoted as saying that he really wanted to offer a "middle-of-the-road approach ... something that's just as much pop music as it is country and western."

And yet the biggest battle this hugely popular entertainer ever had during his long and relatively hassle-free television career was precisely over that: the fight to keep his program from moving too far away from its country and western roots and closer to "pop" music.

Actually, Hunter's roots were neither country nor western, at least geographically speaking. He was born in London, Ontario, where his father worked for the Canadian National Railway. His parents bought Tommy his first guitar (for $49) when he was 13 years old. He had already shown a strong interest in music – and, more specifically, country and western music.

When Tommy was nine years old he saw a newspaper ad announcing a concert in London featuring Roy Acuff and his Smoky Mountain Boys and Girls. Acuff was one of country music's earliest icons.

"I don't know why I wanted to go so badly," Hunter later confessed in his autobiography, "but I remember pestering and begging and pleading with my dad until he agreed to take me." It proved to be a seminal incident in guiding Tommy Hunter toward his future. "From the moment Roy Acuff and the other performers came onto that stage," Hunter recalled, "I was completely and totally mesmerized. My ears were ringing with a sound unlike anything I'd ever heard before, and a beat that filled me with such excitement that I could hardly stay in my seat."

The day after the Acuff show, Tommy began to plead with his working-class parents to let him begin studying the guitar. After he had nagged them into submission, he enrolled in the Edith Hill Adams Academy in downtown London. The guitar lessons cost one dollar each.

By the time he was 16, he was performing regularly on Gordie Tapp's *Main Street Jamboree* on Hamilton radio station CHML. Next came appearances with the Golden Prairie Cowboys, from Wingham, Ontario. In 1956, he joined CBC-TV's *Country Hoedown* as rhythm guitarist with King Ganam's Sons of the West. Ganam was an authentic westerner, having been born in Swift Current, Saskatchewan, albeit of Syrian-English parents.

The Tommy Hunter Show, heard weekdays on CBC Radio (1960–65) succeeded *Country Hoedown* as a weekly CBC-TV program in 1965. By then, Tommy was using **Travellin' Man** as his theme song. The song had originally been presented to him by a man he remembers (vaguely) as "Al Rain." He isn't even sure of the spelling. But the song was first called "Gamblin' Man," to which Tommy objected.

"I'm not a gambling man. I hate gambling," he said. He asked the song-writer if he could rewrite it. Aware that Tommy did (and still does) a lot of touring, he came up with the idea of changing the title to "Travellin' Man," and that's how Tommy Hunter's theme song was born.

Five years later the show was extended to an hour's length and was introduced to American viewers in the early 1980s.

Hunter also built his audience during the summers (1963–70) by appearing at the Academy Theatre, in Lindsay, Ontario, in a concert series broadcast by CBC Radio as *Country Holiday*.

Tommy was part of several Canadian performing troupes put together by the CBC to travel to Europe (and Cyprus) to entertain Canadian troops stationed there.

The country gentleman won three successive Juno Awards (1967–69) as Best Male Country Singer, and other and even greater awards were to come his way.

Wisely, he surrounded himself with a supporting cast that suited his style – The Rhythm Pals, fiddler Al Cherny, Donna and Leroy Anderson, the Allen Sisters, and Maurice Bolyer. The writer he felt most comfortable with was Les Pouliot. He also managed to attract such big-name country and western guests as Hank Snow, Kris Kristofferson, and Charley Pride.

The show was at the top of its popularity – as was Hunter – when friction developed between Tommy and his then-producer, David Koyle. It happened in 1975 when Hunter had decided to add Donna and Leroy Anderson

Tommy Hunter (right) enjoys visit from Ronnie Hawkins during the Tommy Hunter Show on CBC-TV that ran weekly for 27 years.

to his cast. Hunter got a frantic call from Leroy, complaining that Koyle had informed him he and Donna were to perform rock music on the Hunter show. That crisis was resolved: Hunter won. There would be no rock music on his show.

Three years later, Hunter and his producer David Koyle were at loggerheads. Koyle was determined to add different, broader "values" to the Hunter show, such as comedy sketches. Tommy preferred not to fix something that wasn't broken.

At the start of the 1978 season, Koyle informed Tommy that he was going to add eight professional dancers and a choreographer to the show. Hunter felt this was wrong for a country music show; he suggested they hire square dancers, but the producer disagreed.

Neither man would budge, but it was Hunter who was determined to clarify – at the network level – who was truly in charge: the star or the producer. Hunter and Koyle went to Jim Guthro, then the head of CBC-TV Variety, asking him to arbitrate the dispute. Guthro wasted no time in siding with Hunter, and Koyle promptly resigned his post. Tommy chose Les Pouliot to become his new producer.

Tommy's personal life has always been remarkably free of strife or scandal. In 1963, he married Shirley Brush, whom he had known for years, and they raised three fine sons.

In 1974, Hunter received a citation from the Country Music Hall of Fame in Nashville. In 1984, he was inducted into the Canadian Country Music Association Hall of Honour, and in 1986 he was appointed a member of the Order of Canada.

Ian and Sylvia

formed 1961 in Toronto: Ian Dawson Tyson (b. Victoria, B.C., September 25, 1933) vocals,
guitar; Sylvia Fricker Tyson (b. Chatham, Ontario, September 19, 1940) vocals, mando-cello,
accordion, guitar; each went solo 1975

Along with the natural flavour of acoustic instruments, a harmonic blend of voices, and a wide range of rhythms and percussion, at the heart of any folk-singing tradition is credible delivery. Perhaps the most consistent and successful (both as a duet and individually) practitioners of that approach to music are Sylvia Tyson and Ian Tyson.

Whether it was "All those things that don't change, come what may," in Ian's landmark song **Four Strong Winds**, or the lyrics "When I woke up this morning, you were on my mind," that reveal the title of a song from Sylvia's early repertoire, the two captured the experience of everyday life and love in words and music. They made every song their own. They built a following on that credibility. As a result, they changed the landscape of folk music.

"Although they weren't nearly as well known as some of their peers in the early '60s urban folk movement," wrote rock music historian Dave Marsh, "Ian and Sylvia were both a major force within it and deeply influential on the

Courtesy Mascoli Entertainment

generation of rock and folk singers who followed them out of Canada."

Ian Tyson's first passion was rodeo. As a young man studying at the University of British Columbia, he spent summers competing on the rodeo circuit around British Columbia. When an injury sidelined him, Tyson started playing guitar and in 1956 he joined an imitation Elvis Presley band called Jerry Fyander and the Sensational Stripes as its rhythm guitarist. Wilf Carter's flat-picking guitar technique and the music of Big Bill Broonzy, Merle Travis, and Flatt and Scruggs were more Tyson's style; so, while attending the Vancouver School of Art, he began playing and singing solo at the local Heidelberg Café. By 1957, Tyson had moved to Toronto and worked in commercial art by day, while keeping his music up at night, singing blues with Don Francks at the First Floor Club.

Sylvia Fricker's early musical education came from listening to Detroit R&B radio stations from her home in Chatham, Ontario. She sang in the Anglican church choir and, playing a $25 mail-order guitar, she taught herself English folk songs she found in books at the local library. Periodically, she made what she described as "field trips" by train to Toronto, taking to the stage at the Bohemian Embassy on breaks between poetry readings by Margaret Atwood, Milton Acorn, and John Robert Colombo. She eventually appeared at the First Floor Club, where Ian Tyson performed and hosted an open mike session on Wednesday nights. Accompanying herself on mando-cello or auto-harp, Fricker sang with a high vibrato voice that caught Tyson's attention.

The two became a duet act in Yorkville cafes and clubs in 1961.

To begin with, they were only singing partners, Tyson providing folk songs influenced by the rockabilly scene then hitting Toronto's Yonge Street and Fricker offering ballads from those English folk songbooks she'd studied. Within a year they'd moved to New York's folk club and recording scene. They met and signed with Albert Grossman, Bob Dylan's manager, and connected with Vanguard Records. They recorded an album of traditional folk tunes at the Masonic Temple in 1962, hit the U.S. college singing circuit and were married in 1964.

"The magical blend of their voices – Tyson's warm and smooth as leather, cool as the night air – set them apart from the dozens of other folk acts playing on the coffeehouse circuit," wrote author Nicholas Jennings in *Fifty Years of Music*. "The pair's song selection was equally striking. They were the first on the scene to perform traditional Canadian songs, ballads like 'Mary Anne' and 'Un Canadien errant.'"

Their choices of storytelling songs, their first album with Vanguard, and getting caught up in the folk revival of the early 1960s helped propel Ian and Sylvia to the forefront of the North American folk movement. As they began writing more of their own material, they became influenced by others in the New York folk scene, including Bob Dylan.

NAC/PA 207943

"I remember when Dylan wrote 'Blowin' in the Wind,'" Ian Tyson told author Martin Melhuish. "I was in a bar with him and I thought at the time, 'Boy, if this guy can write a song like that, I can too.' The next day I went to my manager's (Albert Grossman's) apartment and wrote **Four Strong Winds**."

Every step of their career together Ian and Sylvia blazed new trails. Their second album, *Four Strong Winds*, came out in 1963 and established Tyson's reputation as a songwriter; it also included a cover of Dylan's "Tomorrow Is a Long Time." In 1964, on their third album, *Northern Journey*, they included Sylvia's most famous song, **You Were on My Mind**; the Australian group We Five parlayed the song into a massive hit in 1965. Meanwhile, the same year, Ian and Sylvia released a fourth album, *Early Morning Rain*, which illustrated their fascination for both country and Canadian roots; they were the first to showcase songs by a then-unknown songwriter, Gordon Lightfoot. Later that year, even before Dylan and The Band outraged traditional folk audiences by "going electric," Ian and Sylvia "went electric"; and while others contemplated recording in Nashville, Ian and Sylvia had already adopted the Nashville sound.

"We were looking for something different, a new sound, a new feel," recalls Sylvia. What they came up with was what she called "country folk," which galvanized country, folk, and rock music. To deliver the sound, in 1969, they assembled a backup band – Amos Garrett (guitar), Bill Keith (pedal steel guitar), Ken Kalmusky (bass), and Ritchie Markus (drums) – which the Tysons named The Great Speckled Bird (after Roy Acuff's classic song). Like Dylan's transition to electric folk, Ian and Sylvia's shift to electric country folk in the early 1970s met with mixed success. In the early 1970s they recorded three Nashville-sound LPs.

About that time, Sylvia cut back on the touring to be with their son, Clay (born in 1966), at home in Canada. Ian did some solo work and was invited to host the CTV variety program *Nashville North*. Sylvia appeared sporadically on the show, but in 1973 she signed a CBC Radio contract to host the weekly roots and folk music program *Touch the Earth*. Ian continued to perform with The Great Speckled Bird, until the band broke up. Sylvia looked at recording some of her own material and signed with Capitol Records. Despite releasing 13 notable recordings together, clearly their paths were diverging. They performed their final concerts together in 1975. The band broke up in 1976; their founders broke up a year later.

After a brief stint in Nashville, Ian Tyson returned to western Canada. He used his royalty money to buy a quarter-section of Alberta prairie and began raising cattle and cutting horses at his ranch, the T-Bar-Y. For a while he experimented with a so-called "outlaw-style Texas band" called North-West Rebellion, but then settled into a comfortable solo role performing at resorts, conventions, and small-town halls and writing for what he called "North America's last 700 working cowboys." He embarked on a series of six "cowboy culture" albums, spiced with plenty of country and western jargon, but essentially based on stories of cowboys (the most successful one, *Cowboyography*, sold 100,000 copies). In 1996, he selected 17 songs from an inventory of more than 60 he'd written and released a greatest-hits CD called **All the Good 'uns**.

Although dedicated to her evocative style of songwriting, Sylvia Tyson never stopped experimenting. In 1975, during International Women's Year, she released **Woman's World**, a compilation of 10 of her own songs celebrating the independence of women. The album earned a Juno nomination, while a single, **Sleep on My Shoulder**, won an *RPM*-sponsored Big Country Award for Outstanding Performance by a Female Country Singer. Following an Olympic benefit show in 1976, she recorded a second solo album, *Cool Wind From the North*, which included the single **River Road** that Crystal Gayle turned into a cover hit.

Quartette (clockwise from bottom left): Sylvia Tyson, Caitlin Hanford, Cindy Church, Gwen Swick

In 1993, Sylvia Tyson teamed up with three sister singer-songwriters – Colleen Peterson, Cindy Church, and Caitlin Hanford – to form Quartette. The four were thrown together for a one-time concert at Toronto's Harbourfront Centre. Following that hot August afternoon concert, as the audience gave them a standing ovation, all four women realized "something special had happened." When Colleen Peterson died in 1996, Gwen Swick joined the group.

In 2000, Sylvia Tyson returned to community halls and theatres across Canada to sing and to play instruments, but also to act in her one-woman stage production called *River Road and Other Stories*. Inspired by a stage adaptation of Timothy Findley's *The Piano Man's Daughter*, *River Road* featured Sylvia portraying several characters from her rich repertoire of folk songs.

"I've always believed in the dramatic possibility of songs," she told the *Toronto Star*'s Greg Quill. "I learned that from folk music when I was a teenager. Folk music was a great training ground for this."

Since their split in the 1970s, Sylvia Tyson and Ian Tyson have reunited on stage several times: in 1979 at a benefit, in 1982 during the videotaping of the Canadian music television retrospective *Heart of Gold*, and in 1987 for The Ian and Sylvia Reunion (which won a Gemini Award). Between them, Sylvia Tyson and Ian Tyson have accumulated a remarkable list of accolades. Ian was named Canadian Country Music Association's Male Vocalist of the Year in 1987, 1988, and 1989. He's been inducted into the Canadian Country Music Hall of Honour. What is perhaps equally rewarding, his **Four Strong Winds** was named by *Country Music News* the All-Time Favourite Canadian Country Song.

"What counts with us," Ian Tyson explained in the liner notes for their very first album in 1962, "is how emotionally involved we get with a song. ... Whether it's a blues number or an English ballad ... each song becomes personal."

In 1996, Sylvia Tyson compiled and edited the book *And Then I Wrote: The Songwriter Speaks* while Ian Tyson published his autobiographical *I Never Sold My Saddle.*

At the Juno Awards ceremony in 1993, they were inducted into the Canadian Music Hall of Fame. Both are members of the Order of Canada.

The Irish Rovers
formed 1964 in Calgary: Will Millar guitar, banjo; George Millar guitar; Joe Millar accordion, bass; Jimmy Ferguson vocals; Wilcil McDowell, accordion

The Irish Rovers were formed in 1964 in Calgary by musician Will Millar and his brother George, along with a cousin, accordionist Joe Millar, and singer Jimmy Ferguson. All the group members were born in Northern Ireland between 1938 and 1947. (Cousin Joe left the group in 1967 but returned two years later.)

From the outset, Will was the leader. They began their professional career at a coffeehouse called The Depression in Calgary and appeared at other coffeehouses throughout North America, notably the Purple Onion in San Francisco and the Ice House in Los Angeles.

It was at the Ice House that they recorded their initial album, *The First of the Irish Rovers*, on the Decca label. They moved into concert halls and nightclubs on the 1968 success of Shel Silverstein's children's song "The Unicorn."

That album was a remarkable success, selling some eight million copies worldwide, and was followed by a less successful song, "Whiskey on a Sunday." The group subsequently toured Australia in 1969 (and again in 1974) and appeared at the Canadian pavilion at Expo '70, in Osaka, Japan.

Between 1971 and 1975 on CBC, Vancouver's television series *The Irish Rovers* was one of the most popular variety shows of the day, and thereafter appeared in many CBC specials.

The Rovers performed for audiences in many parts of the world and in 1979 received the PRO Canada William Harold Moon Award for international achievement.

The group had a second substantial hit record, **Wasn't That a Party?**, in 1980 and was seen in the CBC-TV miniseries *The Rovers' Comedy House* in 1981. They were billed simply as "The Rovers" during this period; later they reverted to "The Irish Rovers."

By the mid-1970s, Will Millar was reported (by Frank Rasky in the *Toronto Star*) as being "fed up to the teeth with the stereotyped blarney that his five Celtic folksingers are a bunch of stage Irishmen and are not to be taken seriously."

Rasky added: "The next time a fan calls him 'wee,' 'elfin,' 'pixyish,' or 'head leprechaun' of the Irish Rovers, Will Millar thinks he'll scream."

Nevertheless, over the years, they balanced their repertoire of traditional and novelty material with contemporary songs by Will Millar, Gordon Lightfoot, Joni Mitchell, and others.

In 1966 Peter Goddard suggested (in the *Globe and Mail*) that they "whistle, hoot and sing through songs with the subtlety of a shillelagh" but in 1978 he noted that they "are only Irish in passing these days and we're to think of them now as singers of international songs."

Their album for Attic called *Hardstuff* reflected this duality with titles by Bryan Adams, Jim Vallance, Randy Bachman, and Tom Northcott, on the one hand, and several tunes featuring Ireland's Chieftains as guest performers on the other.

Leader/spokesman Will Millar has never been too shy to speak his mind, preferably with media people present. On one occasion, he sounded off about "hoodlums" in his homeland.

"I'm so disgusted with my country I don't know why I'm living there," he told journalist Blaik Kirby. "Last Saturday afternoon I was taking a walk through the heart of Belfast and a gang of hoodlums tried to pick a fight with me. I ducked into a shop and they picked on someone else. I saw them beating him, with cuts all over his face, and not a policeman to be found. That would never have happened before. Law and order have completely broken down."

Millar has usually signalled the group's periodic switches of emphasis – away from purely Irish music, back to it, and so on.

And it seems unlikely he wasn't aware that the outburst just referred to came on the eve of a CBC-TV special.

The album *Hardstuff* took another verbal shot at his homeland. Included was a Millar song titled **Paddy on the Turnpike**, aimed at expatriate Irishmen who insisted on being more Irish than the Irish.

"It deals with the subject a bit maliciously, I suppose," Will told Chris Dafoe of the *Globe and Mail*, "but I'm tired of being the little green person. And the way some of these people behave is demented. I was in an Irish pub in New York City and there was a guy walking around collecting money in a tin can. And the sign on the side of the can said 'Kill a British Soldier.' It's like Belfast, what a strange city. At home the Catholics and Protestants fight each other. But if they're overseas, they'll fight anyone who tries to put down Belfast."

This sly verbal jousting – along with the Rovers' undeniable musical gifts and high spirits – helped keep the public interested in the group for a quarter of a century.

When that 25th anniversary came along, Will and the other Rovers got busy organizing a tour that started in North Bay, included a western Canada swing, and ended with a concert at Roy Thomson Hall in Toronto.

Elmer Iseler *b. Port Colborne, Ontario, October 14, 1927; d. 1998*

The Canadian musical community lost a valued artist with the death (from cancer) of conductor Dr. Elmer Iseler, for 38 years the artistic leader of the Toronto Mendelssohn Choir. Tributes to Iseler poured in, from critics, colleagues, and admirers alike.

"Elmer tuned the Mendelssohn Choir perfectly, so that the sound became light and flexible," said Ken Winters, coeditor of *The Encyclopedia of Music in*

Canada, in an interview for the *Globe and Mail* a few days after Dr. Iseler's death. "It could take on any colour and dynamic and still keep its lovely, lucid tuning. It was a sound of incredible transparency and lightness that, at the same time, could become vigorous and strong."

Jean Ashworth Bartle, who sang in the Choir before founding the Toronto Children's Chorus, said, "Iseler got the music off the page." Singer Susan Cooper recalled that when she sang in the Elmer Iseler Singers she watched Iseler's eyes and face intently. "He would bring out the real musician in you," she said.

Iseler was also associated with the Toronto Symphony Orchestra for many years, conducting more than 150 performances of Handel's *Messiah*.

Born in Port Colborne, near Niagara Falls, he studied piano and organ as a youth, got his bachelor's degree in Toronto, then studied organ and church music while a freshman at Waterloo Lutheran (now Wilfrid Laurier) University.

He continued at the University of Toronto, and in 1950–51, while attending the Ontario College of Education, conducted the University of Toronto Symphony Orchestra and the All-Varsity Mixed Chorus. He apprenticed (1951–52) as assistant rehearsal conductor of the Toronto Mendelssohn Choir, and taught orchestral and choral music in Toronto high schools.

In 1954 Iseler helped found the Toronto Festival Singers, and during 24 years as their conductor was credited with developing and maintaining a choir of rare excellence.

Iseler taught choral music (1965–68) at the University of Toronto and in 1968 began to edit Gordon V. Thompson's *Festival Singers of Canada Choral Series* (later the *Elmer Iseler Choral Series*), which included a number of his own arrangements and by 1990 comprised some 180 titles.

In 1978 he formed the Elmer Iseler Singers, a professional choir with which he participated in events such as the Toronto International Festival of the Arts, the Seoul Olympics, the 1983 TriBach Festival in Edmonton, and the 1989 International Choral Festival in Toronto.

Iseler was often described as the outstanding Canadian choir conductor of his generation. He brought to the Festival Singers and the Mendelssohn Choir fresh discipline and versatility, eliciting stylistic resilience, fine tuning, and a healthy sound adaptable to music of all periods.

A one-time member of Healey Willan's St. Mary Magdelene Church Choir, he was an authoritative interpreter of Willan's choral music. Iseler also made a significant contribution to Canadian choral music by commissioning and programming new works, whose exposure through touring and broadcasts later became part of the standard choral repertoire.

But in May 1978, the board of directors of the Festival Singers dumped Iseler. When the story leaked out, according to William Littler, music critic of the *Toronto Star*, board chairman Barbara Heintzman said: "The singers are so elite, they have almost 'elited' themselves out of the business. They have to be seen through their smiles as people who can sing carols as well as *Palestrina*."

She added, "I feel awful about Elmer (Iseler). My heart aches for him. He is hurt and confused. We wanted to give him time to respond so we could put the new direction forward together, as positively as possible." It was no secret, according to William Littler, that Iseler and the Festival Singers board of directors had locked horns over the years.

In any case, the following year, Elmer Iseler formed the Elmer Iseler Singers, a smaller group – 20 voices as opposed to the 36 in the Festival Singers. A year later, in William Littler's words, "the organization learned the error of its ways." The Festival Singers – minus Iseler – filed for bankruptcy.

On October 14, 1997, Iseler turned 70. It might have been a happy birthday but for the problems he had been having with the Mendelssohn Choir for the past several months. Like many professional athletes, Iseler was working under a 12-month contract that had to be renewed annually. But that year, the board of directors of the Mendelssohn Choir, led by president Irene Bailey, decided not to renew Iseler's contract. In other words, he was fired.

Asked in an interview with the *Globe and Mail* why that decision was made, Bailey bristled at the question and replied: "We felt it was time to move on. It was new energy required there. Thirty-three years is a long time in any job. You need a new outlook on things, a new look. ... We wanted to make our choir relevant to the millennium."

Since Iseler was viewed by many as an icon on Canadian choral music and was the recipient of numerous honours and awards, his firing caused some consternation in the musical community – especially since the story leaked out before it was supposed to be announced.

Sadly, Iseler's last years were packed with disappointment. At the very time his succession was being considered, he became a victim of cancer, a brain tumour. He died on April 3, 1998, at his Caledon home. George Pannie, his long-time friend and president of the Elmer Iseler Singers, said: "All the world conductors looked up to him."

Wrote William Littler: "Elmer Iseler was the single greatest influence on the maturation of both the Canadian choral conductor and the Canadian choral art."

Colin James

b. Regina, Saskatchewan, August 17, 1964

Despite the geographical and historical reality that blues music was born in the American south, it's fair to say that the genre found one of its more fervent and contemporary disciples on the Canadian Prairies in Colin James. As *Canadian Composer* magazine pointed out in 1990: "Colin James is blessed with talent to burn. … He looks like a cross between Marlon Brando and James Dean, has a fabulous voice, plays guitar like it's a part of him and writes songs that are obvious classics from the first time you hear them."

Born Colin James Munn, this son of Quaker parents got his first electric guitar when he was 10, but as a teenager he had also learned the mandolin and pennywhistle; he played Irish and bluegrass music with groups such as Sod Hut and the Buffalo Chips. Blues guitar was, however, Colin's primary interest, to the extent that his school work suffered.

His stepfather, a full-blooded Cree, got Colin a job teaching guitar to other youngsters on a nearby reserve and introduced him to the music of Stevie Ray Vaughan. By Grade 10, having decided to pursue music, Colin left school.

"My first band, The Hoodoo Men," James says on his Web site, "played their first show at a coffee house in Winnipeg when I was about 16. I was badly hooked on the blues and I wouldn't listen to anything else."

That same year, 1980, his band opened for George Thorogood and John Lee Hooker and he received favourable reviews. Back in Regina in 1984, he got a break to open onstage for Stevie Ray Vaughan and his band Double Trouble.

"I had no band and no manager," James told the *Toronto Star*, "so I called up some musicians I knew … and turned up at the concert hall without even a rehearsal. … I broke two strings in the first song, walked behind one of the speaker columns and just screamed. Stevie Ray was watching from backstage and handed me one of his guitars."

Vaughan became Colin's mentor and proxy godfather. The next year, when Vaughan came to the Canadian west, he rehired Colin and his band to be his opening act again, and then Colin joined the popular blues guitarist on the road from Texas through the Midwestern United States.

By 1984, James (even though he called Vancouver home) was still living hand-to-mouth and constantly on the move – in 1986 he performed more than 300 shows. His dedication to touring and creating a distinctive blues sound began paying off in the late 1980s. There were return engagements, lined-up crowds to see him, and finally a Virgin Records contract to record his first album.

Colin James (1988) got good reviews and generated two Top 10 videos and a Top 10 single in Canada; James received two Juno nominations and won for Most Promising Male Vocalist in 1989. There were also good sales in the United States and a tour with Steve Winwood and Keith Richards. James's followup album *Sudden Stop* (1990) was described by one reviewer as "a highly charged blend of rock, blues and pop smarts." The album went platinum in Canada and he won two more Junos – Male Vocalist of the Year and Single of the Year for **Just Came Back**.

By this time, the early 1990s, popular music was shifting to grunge and alternative rock. James took the opportunity to make an about-face and recorded some early rock 'n' roll chestnuts, jump blues, and swing tunes. The CD, *Colin James and the Little Big Band* (1993), was an album even he admits "surprised, bewildered, but pleasantly pleased some people enough to keep us on the road."

It was a risk worth taking, because it demonstrated James's commitment to his art and not to a commercial agenda. The material was musically uncompromising, while it anticipated a revival in swing; it chalked up strong sales and earned James a Juno nomination in the Best Blues/Gospel Album category in 1994. There was a second swing album, *Colin James and the Little Big Band II* (1998).

During that period, James made another intriguing side trip. About 1990, James happened to mention to a New York publicist his longstanding interest in Celtic music and in particular an interest in the Irish traditional band the Chieftains. A short time later, when James was about to do a showcase at New York's Cat Club, the band's Paddy Maloney met James backstage.

They hit it off, and when the Chieftains came through Vancouver they invited James to join them onstage at the Queen Elizabeth Theatre. When he arrived at the theatre, James had left behind his blues guitar (with the trademark lightning bolt on the strap) in favour of a mandolin and a pennywhistle. The relationship grew from there. In time for St. Patrick's Day 1992, James joined the Chieftains on the bill at Roy Thomson Hall and then joined them in a Toronto studio to record a track together.

Colin James' next two albums also proved unique. *Bad Habits* (1995) prompted David Henman to write in *Network*, "Welcome the new Colin James, multifarious roots, influences and styles melded into a voodoo stew of sultry vocals, feverish guitar solos and spooky rhythm 'n' blues compositions." On *National Steel* (1997), James teamed up with Colin Linden for an exploration of Delta blues classics. Critics said James had settled comfortably back into his first love – rhythm and blues. It seemed so. At about that time, Colin James commented to David Howell of Southam News: "A career in the blues is something you have to kind of nurture. It takes a lot longer than something that's going to come out and be a huge hit right off the bat. It's something you want to work at."

Oliver Jones

b. Montreal, Quebec, September 11, 1934

Oliver Jones is that all-too-familiar figure in the music business: the "overnight star" who spent 20 years paying his dues. He made his debut as a pianist at the age of five in a Montreal church. His teacher for six years was Daisy Peterson Sweeney, the older sister of Oscar Peterson. But he was 50 years old before much of Canada (apart from Montreal) or the rest of the world knew much about him.

After working in various Montreal clubs, he spent some 15 years as music director for pop singer Kenny Hamilton, whose base of operations was Puerto Rico. Jones returned to Montreal in 1980 and finally began to attract some attention with Canadian fans and critics.

He likes to joke about the background he shares with Oscar. At a Toronto nightclub engagement, he picked up a pile of notes, looked them over, then announced: "We have a request for 'Hymn to Freedom.' This was written by an up-and-coming young pianist named Oscar Peterson."

After the laughter died down, he played Peterson's famous piece, paying proper respect to Oscar's melody but in no way imitating Oscar's style.

Rather than avoid the possibility of comparisons with Peterson, Jones apparently has gone out of his way to perform and/or record with several musicians Peterson already worked with, including Clark Terry, Herb Ellis, and Ed Thigpen.

After one New York appearance by Jones, John S. Wilson, critic for *The New York Times*, commented: "One hears light-fingered reminders of the facility of Tatum and Peterson, but it is done in a context that is reminiscent of the big, buoyant melodic structures that were created by Errol Garner."

In one Montreal concert, which was also filmed for television, Jones featured a lengthy version of "Hymn to Freedom," accompanied by his own group plus a gospel choir and a full orchestra.

Peterson is nine years older than Jones and first heard Oliver at the insistence of his own teacher – his sister, Daisy. In the liner notes to one of Oliver's albums, Peterson wrote that he thought Jones was on the road to "music genius."

Even then, in the mid-1980s, Jones' range was impressive. He could excite the audience with a rollicking stride version of "Cheek to Cheek," soothe them with a lyrical interpretation of "All the Things You Are," dazzle them with an extended Duke Ellington medley, and move them deeply with a bluesy Thelonius Monk composition.

Jones never takes any engagement lightly. Whether playing in a small club or a large concert hall, in a recording studio or on a bandstand, he always shows his remarkable energy and endless inventiveness.

Jones and Peterson grew up within a few blocks of each other, in the St. Henri district of Montreal. Oscar's younger brother, Chuck, was a friend of Oliver's, and Jones wrote a melody dedicated to his friend titled **Something for Chuck**.

Once Jones had "arrived," the nightclub and concert engagements piled up. By the mid-1980s, he was playing at Café des Copains in Toronto, then flying off to the Jazz City Festival in Edmonton, the Coastal Jazz Festival in Vancouver, and the Greenwich Village Jazz Festival in New York, where one critic described him as "a swinging, two-fisted pianist, updating the style of Art Tatum, with just a few nods to bebop harmony."

He also appeared in Moncton, Sydney, Halifax, Edmonton, Calgary, Vancouver, Victoria, Regina, and Brandon – all on one tour.

Jones appeared at Boris Brott's Autumn Festival in Hamilton for six consecutive years, soon after making successful appearances at the Montreal Bistro (in Toronto) and also in Markham, Ontario.

And the awards came, too, including a Juno for the album *Lights of Burgundy*, plus a Felix Award in 1989 and the Prix Oscar Peterson the next year. And then, late in 1999, Oliver Jones announced he would soon be retiring – at the age of 65. After his final Ontario appearance, in Hamilton, critic Geoff Chapman wrote in the *Toronto Star*: "Though notes flew like streaking strobe lights, Jones was always in control, as relaxed when tearing through 'Sweet Georgia Brown' with playful stride as when teasing beauty from ballads like 'What a Wonderful World,' 'Somewhere Over the Rainbow' and emoting with a gorgeously detailed Gershwin medley that conquered the intricate challenges of seven of the master's tunes."

Whether it was the constant drudgery of touring or the arthritis in his hands making playing more difficult, Jones wound up his spectacular career at a New Year's Eve concert, appropriately enough, in his native Montreal.

Juliette

b. Winnipeg, Manitoba, August 26, 1927

Juliette Augustina Sysak's Polish-Ukrainian parents moved the family to Vancouver when she was 10 years old. Three years later, she sang with Dal Richards' orchestra at the Hotel Vancouver.

At 15, she made her CBC Radio debut. After spending a year in Toronto (1943–44) on Alan Young's CBC Radio show and with Lucio Agostini's orchestra, she returned to Vancouver and sang on numerous programs, including *Burns Chuckwagon*, a country and western series with The Rhythm Pals.

Juliette grew up singing. She was a child when Shirley Temple was the rage. She was a pretty blonde singer when Alice Faye was a star. She was a popular Vancouver entertainer when Betty Grable was everybody's favourite pinup girl.

She returned to Toronto in 1954 and costarred with Gino Silvi on *Gino and Juliette*. Next came a regular spot on television's *The Billy O'Connor Show*. Two years later, she succeeded O'Connor to create one of the CBC's most popular television shows – *Juliette*. It ran for 11 years.

"Our Pet Juliette," the term coined by one of her producers, was arguably Canada's first television star, and she did it with her own talent and determination. During her years on television, she fought for every inch of progress – a bigger budget to have better lighting, a bigger orchestra, more glamorous gowns.

She was a star because she believed she was a star and she behaved like a star. Nobody ever saw her wearing anything but what a star is supposed to wear in public – even a mink coat for a trip to the supermarket.

Humourist Mort Sahl once observed that a true conservative is "someone who believes nothing should be done for the first time." To a considerable degree, Juliette fit that description. She could not be persuaded to sing a song on her show unless it was already an established hit. "I'm no pioneer," she argued. "Let Sinatra and Peggy Lee do that. I'll do the songs the public know."

Despite the platinum hair, toothy smile, and aura of glamour, Juliette was always meticulous about her public image. Once, when singer George Murray was her guest on the show, they did a love duet. At the end of it she felt compelled to tell the television audience that she and George were "only kidding" – they weren't really in love.

She was married to musician Tony Cavazzi, who played in the orchestra on her show. He was a soft-spoken, shy man, but Juliette always told people that she relied totally on Tony's advice about her career.

As her show expanded and improved, a vocal quartet called The Romeos was added, and then came trumpeter Bobby Gimby. In little time, there was no love lost between Juliette and Gimby. He bristled when she referred to him as

"Bob." He was billed as "Bobby" and wanted to be known only that way. Their mutual dislike fired a public disagreement that ended with Gimby promptly leaving the show, never to return. (The producer later received a note from Gimby's doctor saying Gimby was unable to return to the program.)

Juliette always felt she knew best what her public expected of her: glamour cloaked in propriety. She had pretty well created her image and was relentlessly protective of it. Her viewers saw only the sweet smile and heard only the most civil words from her mouth.

Only once did she stretch out during the long run of her television series. That was when Gordie Tapp was a guest. They did an uninhibited number in clown outfits. Juliette really unbent and had fun with it. It was a revelation. But the explanation was simple, as even she admitted. She was "being someone else," not the glamorous, neatly dressed, impeccably coiffured Juliette – she could clown around without fear of criticism.

She had the reputation of being difficult to work with – which was true only if she didn't like someone or distrusted a person. But she could also be warm and considerate. When Marg Osborne, of the program *Don Messer's Jubilee*, was a guest, Juliette went to great lengths to make her feel at ease. "I know what it's like," she said, "coming to Toronto to do a show. You're scared stiff."

Like any star, she was always at her best when she was the centre of attention. She enjoyed entertaining occasionally at the immaculate apartment she and Tony shared. The end of a television season usually meant a big party with Juliette happily playing the gracious hostess. But she was also thoughtful enough to look after her television crews. After a season closer, she would supply cases of beer and fried chicken or pizza for everyone – camera crews, sound men, lighting crew, stage hands, and the rest.

After her Saturday night television show was cancelled in 1966, she did some television specials and then became host of the CBC talk show *After Noon*, which ran for another three years. Then *Juliette and Friends* ran for another two years.

She and Tony moved to Vancouver, where she continued to do occasional CBC specials. But her life had become difficult. Her beloved Tony was stricken with Alzheimer's disease and Juliette looked after him as best she could. But he eventually had to be hospitalized and later died.

In the 1990s, Juliette began appearing in public again, but only occasionally – such as an interview with Pamela Wallin. She had put on weight, had undergone knee surgery, and suffered other ailments. But her spirit was still in fine shape.

When being interviewed by Peter Gzowski on *Morningside*, she said: "The nice thing about being a senior is that you can say whatever the hell you think."

Connie Kaldor

b. Regina, Saskatchewan, May 9, 1953

In 1981, singer-songwriter Connie Kaldor created her own record label, called Coyote Records. She couldn't have chosen a more appropriate name. Like the company's independent namesake, Kaldor works essentially alone. Like the logo, she can't be pinned down either by peers or by her audiences. And, while the coyote is comfortable in most North American environs, it, just like Connie Kaldor, comes from western Canada.

As a kid living on the outskirts of Regina, Saskatchewan, Kaldor remembers always singing. Her father was choir director at a local Lutheran church. Her mother insists Connie sang in the cradle. And the only rule at mealtime was "no singing at the table." While she hated the mandatory piano lessons of her youth, they sharpened her ear for music, and the deal was if she got Grade 8 piano she could buy a guitar. Not surprisingly, she got the guitar.

"I was raised to think for myself," Kaldor says. "I've always been a very independent person ... initiating projects ... getting out there. ... Nothing struck me as insurmountable."

From the start, Connie Kaldor recognized she was working in a male-dominated industry – from Beatles records to folk festivals and television shows – so she looked to role models such as Patsy Cline, Laura Nyro, Carole King, and Joni Mitchell. In 1970 she auditioned for the Regina Folk Festival, which featured Humphrey and the Dumptrucks, Don Freed, and others, and made the most of her appearance.

"I felt out of it," Kaldor remembers, "because I was new and young and I think I was the only woman. I felt like an outsider, [but] it was also fun and exciting. It helped me to develop my own style."

In the 1970s, Kaldor attended university intent on becoming a professional actor. She worked with Newfoundland's Mummers and Toronto's Theatre Passe Muraille, and even co-wrote and costarred in a musical production called *The Last Best West Show* which celebrated the cowboy traditions of hard work, heartbreak, and the music of open spaces. By the end of the decade, however, she had recognized the lifetime commitment acting required and how much music had touched her life. She quit theatre and focused completely on her music – practising, writing, and performing everywhere from small festivals to clubs. In 1981 she invested $15,000 of her own into Coyote Records and her debut album *One of These Days*. It was well received.

"[But] at the time nobody wanted to touch me," Kaldor told Pieter Hofmann of *Dirty Linen* magazine. "The record companies were more concerned with pop music and they didn't know what to do with me. If they can't pigeonhole you, they just scratch their heads. I've done so many different things that it's difficult to find a phrase that sticks."

An Edmonton reviewer said "her country tunes are as good as Dolly Parton or Emmylou Harris. Her comic routines rival Carol Burnett. Her love songs pull tears from stones." A Vancouver writer said her voice was remarkable "ranging from a Dory Previn sound to Judy Collins, from the simple quavering of a young Joan Baez to the pure *a capella* joy of Patsy Cline." Still another suggested she was closer to Woody Allen than to Woody Guthrie.

However they described her, Connie Kaldor's audiences in Canada and the United States were growing and her work gained recognition. Her second album, 1984's *Moonlight Grocery*, earned a Juno nomination for Most Promising Female Vocalist and in 1988 *Lullaby Bercuese*, recorded with Carmen Campagne, won the Juno for Best Children's Album and was a U.S. Parents' Choice gold award winner.

Settling in Montreal, Kaldor and her husband Paul Campagne began to raise a family. The nature of her brand of music allowed Kaldor to bring her family with her and to use every trick in her musical bag; during a 1992 tour of China, India, and Europe, her son became "a little ambassador" and she remembers a show in Beijing, during which "I sang my western music and the crowd went mental. I thought I was at a Van Halen concert. Back then, they didn't get to hear that type of stuff. I went out there and played the most ripsnorting material in my repertoire and it was like I was some guitar god."

In 1997, Kaldor signed a recording contract with Boston-based Rounder Records and they released her 1996 Coyote album *Small Café* in the United States. Her eighth album, released in 2000, *Love Is a Truck*, about love, life, and liars, earned another Juno nomination in the Best Folk-Roots Album category.

What keeps reviewers and fans from pigeonholing Connie Kaldor is her ever-growing repertoire and her ease in slipping from one musical category to another. Whether she sings **Jerks**, her putdown of catcalling men, cowboy songs from *The Last Best West Show*, a lullaby from her children's material, or songs about moonlight and coyotes, hers is the music of experience.

"I grew up with [coyotes] in the back of my mythology," Kaldor said. "They survive against all odds, whether it's in the city or in the country. They travel a lot. And I guess they are a voice calling in the wilderness. Being in this business, sometimes I feel like a coyote – a voice howling at the moon."

Jack Kane
b. London, England, November 29, 1924; d. 1961

A decade before Rob McConnell formed his justly famed Boss Brass, Jack Kane was leading Canada's best-known big band – to the evident glee of music fans across the country – via the CBC-TV show *The Jack Kane Hour*.

Courtesy the Kane Family

At the same time Kane was also making a name for himself in the United States, largely as the result of the success of his arranging and conducting albums for Steve Lawrence and Eydie Gorme, Andy Williams, Steve Allen, Dorothy Collins, and a television special featuring Ethel Merman.

Kane's father was the British music-hall entertainer, Barry Kane. Jack was brought to Toronto by his parents as a child and by the age of nine was singing with his father in vaudeville shows. He studied clarinet for three years at the Toronto Conservatory of Music and made his radio debut in 1941 as a member of The High Timers.

After serving in the Royal Canadian Signal Corps Band (1942–45) and leading the Khaki Kollegians in *The Army Show* during the Second World War, he studied composition with John Weinzweig, then worked on CBC Radio shows and became assistant arranger-conductor to Howard Cable. In 1950, he was chief arranger for the radio show *Startime*.

Next came arranging and conducting for such CBC-TV shows as *On Stage*, *The Jackie Rae Show*, and *Summertime '57*. But Kane came into his own on *Music Makers* and ultimately in 1960 with his own show, *The Jack Kane Hour*. At the time, other big-band shows on television had flagging ratings. Not the *Kane Hour*, because, as he told *Liberty* magazine, "Kenton, Lombardo, the Dorsey Brothers – they all lack showmanship. … My show has it because I present music people want, then give it a little twist. … I'm brash, uninhibited, just like my personality."

What was unusual about the Kane approach to television was that it was the first television series in which a jazz-tinted band was presented as the focal point. There were guest vocalists, of course, but fans tuned in mostly to see and hear Kane's group of instrumentalists execute his increasingly fascinating arrangements.

Kane had gusto too, or as critic Jack Miller put it, "He was boyish, bouncy, and enthusiastic in front of the cameras [which] tended to endear him more than ever to his fans."

Not everybody enjoyed Kane's innovative approach. One time, some fan letters arrived suggesting "he conduct … more like a band leader and less like an Olympic gymnast." Kane tried it for several weeks but noticed the band wasn't swinging. So did TV critic Gordon Sinclair, who encouraged

Jack Kane (l.) conducts an orchestra that includes pianist Steve Allen

the boisterous bandleader in his column: "Jack, to thine own self be true."

But it was Eydie Gorme and Steve Lawrence who widened Kane's appeal. Eydie commissioned him to write the arrangements for her act at the Palace Theatre in New York, and Steve brought him to New York to arrange and conduct his album, *Here's Steve Lawrence*. Then Kane was signed as music director for the Gorme-Lawrence television show, set to replace Steve Allen for the summer on NBC.

Trombonist Murray Ginsberg, who worked with Kane in the early days of their careers, likes to tell about young "Jackie" Kane – all of two years younger than Ginsberg – whose playing at the time left something to be desired.

Kane worked in Frank Bogart's society dance band, and one of the sidemen, Benny Winestone, was forever complaining about Jack's alto saxophone playing and urging him to take some lessons. Apparently, Kane's clarinet work was fine, but on the sax he played out of tune. Fed up with the razzing, Jack went to New York and took a lesson (one) from Hymie Schertzer, who had played lead alto sax with Benny Goodman.

Several years later, Jack Kane was in New York again – this time as arranger and music director for the Steve Lawrence–Eydie Gorme television series. The musicians in the show's band had been hired by a New York contractor. Playing lead alto was Hymie Schertzer and Kane reminded the veteran musician of their one previous meeting: "I took a lesson from you six years ago."

Schertzer could hardly believe that his out-of-tune alto saxophone player from Canada was now the leader of the band on one of America's top television shows.

But Kane had long since proved himself as a skilled and imaginative arranger and music director. Even while he was studying with Weinzweig, young Jack composed a number of concert works, including works for a string quartet, **Suite for Orchestra**, and **Concerto for Saxophone**. He later began writing a symphony, but that was never completed.

But Kane had his light side, too. One of the albums he wrote and recorded was titled *Jack Kane Salutes the Comics*, in which he paid tribute to various famous comedians – Jimmy Durante, Bob Hope, Jack Benny, the Marx Brothers, Phil Silvers, Charlie Chaplin et al., with appropriate versions of their theme songs or music somehow associated with them.

Ironically, this recording was made in 1959, less than two years before Jack Kane's death from cancer of the esophagus. His illness was sudden and swift. He was still doing his popular television show, although he could barely talk. Tragically, he died in March of 1961, at the age of 37.

Two years later, a tribute album called *The Jack Kane Band Conducted By Bert Niosi* was released.

In a reflective piece in 1999, Ian G. Masters referred to Jack Kane as a "godfather of Canadian music" and recalled *The Jack Kane Hour* because "the quality was so high that the program attracted numerous international big guns. But I think I was typical in that I tuned in for the band and for Kane's pull-out-all-the-stops arrangements rather than the guests."

Mart Kenney   *b. Toronto, Ontario, March 7, 1910*

It would be unthinkable for any book about Canadian musical artists to omit Mart Kenney. He pretty well represents the history of dance band music in Canada. For seven decades, "Mart Kenney and His Western Gentlemen" has been a familiar appellation from one end of this country to the other.

Oddly enough, despite the "Western Gentlemen" tag, Mart Kenney was born in Toronto. Equally remarkable is the fact that as of March 7, 2000, Mart (born Herbert Martin) Kenney was 90 years old – and still leading a band.

Kenney's parents separated while he was an infant. By the time he was a year old, he was living on a B.C. island near what later became the Vancouver Airport. His interest in music – and, more particularly, the saxophone – began

NAC/NL 14465

in childhood. But it wasn't until he was 15 that Mart bought his very first alto saxophone, borrowing five dollars from a friend to make a down payment on the instrument.

Kenney had little formal training, but by his middle teens he was playing with various local Vancouver bands. "We knew only four tunes," he wrote in his autobiography, "and kept repeating them all evening and nobody seemed to mind." He formed his five-piece band – the Western Gentlemen – in 1931, for an engagement at Vancouver's Alexandra Ballroom. A year later a sixth musician joined. He was the saxophonist-pianist-vocalist Art Hallman, who was to go on to considerable fame of his own, after he formed his band in 1945.

Mart Kenney and His Western Gentlemen soon became popular favourites and were to remain so for the rest of the 20th century. In 1973, Hallman recalled for jazz journalist Helen McNamara his days with Kenney: "The Mart Kenney band was *the* band. We went across Canada 14 times in three years."

Stuart Keate, publisher of the *Vancouver Sun*, said of Kenney's orchestra: "They were to Canada what Ambrose was to England and Guy Lombardo to the United States." (It's interesting that Keate used the past tense – "were" – when he made the above statement, which was in 1981 – almost two decades ago. Yet Mart Kenney and His Western Gentlemen still "are.")

The Kenney legend simply never stopped growing. The band made records and performed on network radio in Canada, the United States, and Great Britain. In 1934, the orchestra appeared at the Hotel Saskatchewan in Regina, Chateau Lake Louise, Banff Springs Hotel, the Hotel Vancouver, the Forum in Montreal, and the Royal York Hotel in Toronto. The Western Gentlemen also appeared in such Ontario landmarks as the Brant Inn, Casa Loma, the Palace Pier in Toronto, Oshawa's Jubilee, and Dunn's Pavilion in Bala.

In 1938, Kenney's became the first Canadian orchestra to record for RCA Victor. In 1940, it was the only band to perform regularly for Canadian Armed Forces and international radio networks.

It was in 1949 that Kenney bought a piece of property (108 acres) at Woodbridge, Ontario, and developed what became "Mart Kenney's Ranch," an open-air nightclub with a western motif. Things went well at the Ranch for a while, with Jack Fowler leading a small band two nights a week and Kenney and a 15-piece band (including Norma Locke) on Fridays and Saturdays, plus such guest acts as harmonica whiz Larry Adler, singers from Giselle MacKenzie to Mel Tormé, and the Oscar Peterson Trio.

But in 1951, the Ranch fell victim to provincial liquor laws. Vaughan Township, where the Ranch was located, was "dry" and all Mart's efforts couldn't accomplish the desired end: the legal sale of drinks at the Ranch. Still, Mart Kenney kept the Ranch operating. It wasn't until 1966 that a plebiscite held in

Vaughan Township resulted in the opening of (Ontario) government liquor stores, and "banquet permits" became available. Kenney modernized his Ranch, which then was able to accommodate up to 1000 persons and in a position to compete for the banquet business.

In 1969, Kenney decided to retire to Mission, B.C., so he broke up the band and closed the Ranch. But he resumed his musical activities in British Columbia, with occasional trips to spots elsewhere in Canada.

Over the years, many fine musicians passed through the ranks of Kenney's orchestra, among them Rob McConnell, Al Harris, Ron Collier, Ross Culley, Carne Bray, Percy Cutts, Phil Antonacci, Herbie Helbig, Bobby Hales, and Bobby Gimby. Featured vocalists, at one time or another, besides Art Hallman, included Wally Koster, Roy Roberts, Judy Richards, and Veronica Foster. It was Foster's departure, late in 1943, that made way for Norma Locke, who was to become Mrs. Mart Kenney in 1952. She remained as vocalist with the band until her death in 1990.

The occasion of Mart's 90th birthday was well and truly marked. In Mission, B.C., the town declared March 7 (his birthday) "Mart Kenney Day," with a week-long party celebrating the occasion. Festivities culminated on March 12 with a special afternoon dance at the newly restored Commodore Ballroom in Vancouver. Kenney performed with another music legend, Dal Richards, and his orchestra.

Another "Mart Kenney Day," March 12, was proclaimed by the mayor of Vancouver, and Bobby Hales, president of the Vancouver Musicians' Association, wrote a letter nominating Kenney for the Order of B.C. In 1980 Kenney received the Order of Canada; in 1992 he was named British Columbia's Senior Citizen of the Year; and the next year was honoured by the Toronto Musicians' Association and inducted into B.C.'s Entertainment Hall of Fame.

And still Mart Kenney does not rest on his laurels. In the summer of 2000, he finished a new CD called *Swingin'* that offers three new compositions of his.

Andy Kim (Baron Longfellow) *b. Montreal, December 5, 1952*

If ever there was a popular music performer who learned the business from the ground up, it was Andy Kim (also known as Baron Longfellow). From songwriting to demo production to landing a label to getting product in the door and on the air, here was one singer who, despite countless setbacks, refused to give up until he was a star. Somehow his story is very Canadian.

"I had never written a song in my life," Kim said in 1971. "I didn't know a thing about the music industry, but I knew I could do it."

Growing up in Montreal, Andrew Joachim listened to Elvis Presley and Buddy Holly. He wondered how he could be like them. A disc jockey warned him the public wasn't interested in Canadian singers, but wanted a California or Nashville sound. So Andy announced to his parents that he was moving to New York. He took a week off school, bought train tickets, and went to New York to figure out the music business. He quickly discovered he needed to be able to play his music, write songs, and present them on a demo tape.

Andy spent the next several years commuting between New York and Montreal, making demos, handing them in to record companies and producers and then working at odd jobs to make enough money to repeat the process. Meanwhile, his brother Joe was starting to play the guitar.

"I asked him to teach me to play because I was going to write a song," Kim said. "He laughed and then taught me two chords – C and F – and with that I sat down and wrote **How'd We Ever Get This Way?**"

Back in New York, Kim called a producer acquaintance, Jeff Barry. He told Barry if he wanted to make a million dollars to sign him up. For months the Montrealer hounded Barry until he listened to the demo and liked it. Just before Christmas in 1967 Barry took Kim into a studio to record **How'd We Ever Get This Way?** on the Steed label. It ended up selling more than 800,000 copies.

Right away, Kim figured out that his territory was love won, love lost, and the way young people felt happy or sad. "I wasn't the kind of writer that was out to save the world," he said. "I decided to leave that to Bob Dylan. ... I think they should have closed the book after he wrote 'Blowin' in the Wind.'" With that in mind, Kim wrote and recorded a song about going out and having a good time; it was called **Shoot 'Em Up Baby**. The timing was all wrong. American cities were enduring race riots and enough radio programmers thought Kim was encouraging drug use that it got limited airplay. It still sold 500,000 copies and earned Kim his first Juno as Top Male Vocalist in 1968.

A couple of tries later, in 1969, he struck gold again with **Baby I Love You**. It sold 1.5 million copies. He was on a roll. Despite the growing interest in longer-playing album cuts on FM radio, at the time Kim and his producers (Jeff Barry and his wife/partner Ellie Greenwich) believed that Top 40 AM stations catered to the crowd he was writing for, the so-called "teenyboppers." They were right. They soon connected with the bubblegum group, the Archies. In 20 minutes over the phone, Andy Kim composed a song for the group called **Sugar, Sugar**. It was *Billboard*'s 1969 record of the year and sold more than 13 million copies.

Not content to sit on the strength of a couple of teen hits, Kim looked beyond the immediate singles buyers, to what he called "the Pepsi generation, the ones who want to think young," he said at the time. "Show business in the States has zoomed down to one-nighters and concerts. So I'll do my records but I think my audience will grow."

In the early 1970s, Andy Kim and his brother, Joe, formed their own label, Ice Records, and in 1974 released a third album **Rock Me Gently** that contained a single by the same title. It zoomed up both the British and the American chart and stayed there for four months. It was another million-seller.

When the Kims' father died, in the mid-1970s, the brothers pulled back from the music business for several years. When Andy Kim reemerged in the 1980s it was under new management. He'd signed with Gordon Mills, the manager of Engelbert Humperdinck (Arnold Dorsey) and Tom Jones (Thomas Woodward). Kim began recording under the name Baron Longfellow. He released a new single, **Amour**, which became one of the top-selling singles in Canada. It also earned a Juno nomination for Single of the Year in 1980. As Longfellow in 1991, he released a single, **Powerdrive**, but then began looking for collaborative work and producing opportunities.

At last count, Andy Kim had sold 30 million records worldwide.

Moe Koffman *b. Toronto, Ontario, December 28, 1928; d. 2001*

In many cases, it's the musician of limited talent who tries to mask his deficiencies by clowning or leaning on "novelty." (Kay Kyser, Ben Bernie, Cab Calloway, and Shep Fields spring to mind.) But that's not the case with Moe Koffman. For several decades he was arguably the best jazz flautist to be found anywhere.

Moreover, there is a tendency to overlook the fact that Moe was equally impressive on alto saxophone. (For evidence of this, listen to the Boss Brass' 11-minute version of "All the Things You Are" on the CD titled **The Brass Is Back**, on which Moe blows chorus after blistering chorus.)

By his own admission, Moe Koffman was always something of a workaholic. "It's always been that way," he once commented. "Years ago, in the studio days. Everybody is playing poker or having a taste, and I'm practising. I'm always working or on the phone. I always enjoyed it, that's my makeup. I've always been a busy player, and in order to stay a professional musician, you've gotta practise your buns off, so I still practise a helluva lot."

Yet there was a puckish side to his nature which cannot resist such comic

Tom Robe

gestures as recording bopped-up versions of classics **Back to Bach**, which features such oeuvres as **Canned Daddy** (i.e., Cantata) and **Bad 'n' Eerie** (badineire). His off-the-wall humour also emerges in far-out musicians' jokes, not all of which work except when Moe tells them.

His flair for pun-ny album titles continued through *Tales of Koffman*, then *One Moe Time* and *Moe-Mentum*, the latter two with Bernie Senensky at the keyboards.

Moe started studying violin at the age of 9, and alto saxophone at 13. In his mid-teens he was playing in dance bands led by Horace Lapp, Leo Romanelli, and Benny Louis. He was one of the first Canadian jazz musicians to embrace the then-new bop movement.

He moved to the United States in 1950 and worked with the bands of Jimmy Dorsey, Charlie Barnet, Tex Beneke, and Sonny Dunham, among others. But this was the tail end of the big band era, so Moe tried moving to studio work, but that proved to be a long, long waiting line.

He returned to Toronto five years later and soon became booking agent for George's Spaghetti House, then a leading jazz venue. He held that post for 35 years, during which he appeared with his own group one week each month. "Eventually," he quipped in typical Koffman mode, "it will become a steady job."

In 1958, he recorded **Swinging Shepherd Blues**, which became an international hit – and also helped to popularize the flute as a jazz solo instrument.

His next big challenge came when Garth Drabinsky hired Moe to contract the musicians for his various musical productions, beginning in the fall of 1989. Koffman booked the musicians for the Toronto productions of *Phantom of the Opera, Joseph and the Amazing Technicolor Dreamcoat, Aspects of Love,* and *Kiss of the Spider Woman.* All of them did well, but *Phantom* was the mega-hit. Moe referred to it as "the cash cow."

An interviewer asked him, at about that time, if his job got a bit easier after a show opened and was running smoothly. "It never runs smoothly," he answered. "There's always problems that I have to be at the end of a phone for."

When Drabinsky's Livent opened the North York Performing Arts Centre (later the Ford Centre), Koffman was the theatre's contractor of musicians for its opening attraction, *Showboat,* another huge hit.

Becoming something of a big wheel via hiring musicians did not change Moe's realistic outlook on the music business. "I remember myself as a kid in New York," he mused in 1993, "calling up these contractors like they're calling me now, bugging them, driving them crazy every day. So I can see where they're coming from, I know exactly how they feel, so I'm able to deal with them in a more humane manner."

Much as he enjoyed being busy as a contractor of musicians for various big stage productions, his heart was still in jazz. Whether he's playing alto sax or flute, audiences still marvel at his remarkable musicianship, the fluidity of his ideas, the skill of his execution, and the energy that informs all his playing.

Moe Koffman's career suffered something of a jolt when Drabinsky's Livent went belly-up in 1999. For Drabinsky, of course, it was a major financial disaster. For Moe it meant an end to all that entrepreneurial work of supplying musicians for Livent's various activities.

But the mighty Moe was never a man to be kept down for long. With his flute and his sax – and his endless determination – he was soon back gigging, swinging, inventing, having fun playing, and surprising listeners with his remarkable skills.

There is ample evidence of how highly he is regarded by his fellow musicians. In 2000, Moe was seriously ill and out of action for some time. When he returned to work, he wore a hat to cover his bald head – bald because of the chemotherapy he had undergone. The night he started a gig in Toronto, all his sidemen also wore similar hats, as a gesture of support for Moe.

But not even serious illness could daunt the invincible Koffman. In the summer of 1999, he put together a group with organist Doug Riley, bassist

Andrew Hermant, Rob Piltch, and a few others for an exciting CD called *The Moe Koffman Project*, which serves to prove, yet again, what a priceless treasure this amazing musician is.

As this book was being prepared, Moe Koffman died of cancer in March 2001. His friends, fellow musicians, and the jazz world at large will miss him.

Wally Koster

b. Winnipeg, Manitoba, February 14, 1923; d. 1975

Nobody who ever watched him on television would have guessed it, but what Wally Koster really wanted to be was a hockey player. "I hear skates on ice and I want to be out there," he once admitted in an interview.

He was born of Polish-Russian parents "on the wrong side of the tracks" in Winnipeg. He used to say there were only two ways to cross the tracks – as an athlete or a musician. He did both. He was a dance band singer at 16, in Winnipeg and in Jasper, Alberta. Soon he was singing on local radio shows.

The young Wally also played semi-pro hockey and was once third-string centre for the Winnipeg Blue Bombers. He still did some singing while he played hockey in North Sydney, N.S. and was invited to try out for a professional team.

But music offered better opportunities – although sports were involved at first. It was at a football team's victory dance that the bandleader heard Wally sing and promptly hired him as a singer and trombonist. As both singer and instrumentalist, he was self-taught.

Nobody could ever accuse Koster of letting success go to his head. When he was a television star in the 1950s and 1960s, he still played his trombone at nightclub dates to augment his income.

Nor could anyone suggest that he had no sense of humour. It was always near the surface, ready to be used. One day he was trundling a cart around a supermarket and couldn't help overhearing the chatter of two teenage girls behind him.

"It can't be him," one declared. "He wouldn't be in here shopping."

"I tell you it is," argued the other girl. "I'd know him anywhere."

They kept up their half-whispered argument until Wally Koster stopped in his tracks and turned to face them.

"You're right, girls," he announced. "It's me – Robert Goulet."

After serving as a bandsman in the Second World War, he returned to civilian life and worked for such bandleaders as Ellis McLintock and Mart Kenney. It was Kenney who gave him his first Toronto job.

Koster sang on the CBC's inaugural telecast from Toronto and within two years was being heard on *Trans-Canada Hit Parade* (on radio) and then *Cross-Canada Hit Parade* (on television).

For five years, he appeared regularly on the latter show, featured along with Phyllis Marshall and Joyce Hahn. In 1960, he became the singing host of *The World of Music*, also on CBC-TV.

He was also active in musical theatre – especially in the summer, when his television schedule permitted. He starred in such shows as *Guys and Dolls* and *Carousel* at Winnipeg's Rainbow Stage, *The Most Happy Fella* at Toronto's O'Keefe Centre, and *Oklahoma!* in Sydney, N.S., where he played to packed houses and received standing ovations. He also starred in *Paradise Hill* at the Charlottetown Festival.

Koster's big, warm baritone was easily identifiable to radio listeners, and his pleasant, informal personality made a quick impression whether on stage or television.

In a world where monogamy is rare, Wally wooed and won Myra Symes, an attractive blonde from the better part of town. They were still married in 1975, when Wally died at the age of 54.

The Kosters had one son, Wally, Jr., who soon became his famous father's biggest fan and protector. At age five, he used to bawl out teenagers who would phone the Koster home "just to hear Daddy's voice." He would ask Tuesday visitors to his parents' home if they had watched the previous night's *Hit Parade* – and if not, why not.

Wally (senior, that is) took boyish delight in the byproducts of his success. On his and Myra's 10th anniversary, he arrived home with a grin like a bright sunrise, unable to stand still in his excitement of surprising his wife with a blue mink stole. At the height of his popularity, he and Myra lived on a 50-acre farm near Stouffville, Ontario, and they farmed the place themselves.

He took his work seriously, but not himself. Once, for a roughhouse sequence on his television show, he urged the dancers to be tough on him, "make it look real." Delighted with the realistic results, he limped home covered in bruises.

Because he wasn't afraid of physical challenges, he was regarded as being "strong as a bull." But with all the hard work, the long hours, the physical effort involved in so much of his life, Wally's health began to deteriorate. He suffered a collapse from exhaustion in 1970 when he was working a 19-hour day combining farm chores, a daily carol concert, rehearsals at the CBC, and a nightclub booking.

He underwent open-heart surgery, which led to complications. There was an infection following the surgery in July 1975, and by December he was back in a Toronto hospital, where he died.

Diana Krall

b. Nanaimo, B.C., 1964

It's a pretty long journey from Nanaimo, B.C. to the White House. But Diana Krall made it in less than 35 years – and without an election. The sexy, saucy, savvy singer/pianist from Vancouver Island managed, between other gigs, to squeeze in a performance for U.S. president Bill Clinton.

Her rise from obscurity to international stardom seems, at first glance, to have been meteoric. But, in fact, Krall's, like every other "overnight stardom" story, hasn't been all that swift. It just seems that way.

It was, after all, in 1993 that Diana caught the attention of the *Toronto Star*'s jazz critic, Geoff Chapman. His review of her first album was headlined: "Canadian Makes Impressive Debut."

Jane Shirek

A year later, Chapman was again praising Krall in print: "Diana Krall has discovered a devastating jazz formula. Keep it simple. Keep it swinging. Keep it bluesy. Stir, simmer and serve – and you can't miss with her deadly dual armory of succulent singing and peerless piano-playing."

The following year, the *Globe and Mail*'s Mark Miller was predicting great success for her, even quoting a *Wall Street Journal* profile: "... you can't help but feel sure that Diana Krall is bound for glory; and that glory will be a much nicer place once she gets there."

She lived in a home surrounded by music. "I grew up with a father who collected 78 [rpm] records and old newspapers and listened to old radio shows," she recalled. "I was immersed in nostalgia. My dad had very eclectic tastes, so I heard Fats Waller at home and started playing boogie-woogie in the third or fourth grade."

"I sound like my grandmother," she told one interviewer. "She'd sing 'Hard-Hearted Hannah' and the family would join in at home."

Her father, Jim Krall, who works as a chartered accountant, put himself through college by playing piano in a dance band. He started his two daughters (Michelle is the younger one) on piano lessons before they began kindergarten. Jim has said that Michelle sang as well as Diana but never showed "the same focus" as her sister.

It was, in part, that "focus" that landed Diana her first gig at the Nanaimo Harbour Lights restaurant – at the age of 15. At 18, she won a scholarship to Boston's Berklee College of Music. At 19, she moved to Los Angeles to study with the great jazz pianist Jimmy Rowles. "I think because she left so early," said her mother, Adella Krall, "she learned to keep her compass set to home."

But visits home sometimes had to take second place to the demands of her studies and growing career. She spent much of the 1980s between Los Angeles and Toronto, studying with Rowles in L.A. and Don Thompson in Toronto.

By 1997 Krall had no trouble packing the small Top o' the Senator, one of Toronto's top jazz clubs. She took what seemed a big gamble by scheduling her next appearance for the 2765-seat Massey Hall; but it wasn't really that big a risk. Her CD titled *All For You*, a tribute to Nat King Cole, had already sold 300,000 copies and garnered a Grammy nomination for Jazz Vocal Performance.

"I think the Nat King Cole tribute was a real stepping stone for me," she said later, "in terms of realizing what I do – which is not to shout. ... I'm able to sing very quietly in this trio [with guitarist Russell Malone and bassist Ben Wolfe] and play with a sense of spareness and simplicity – just play what's necessary and not try to prove anything pianistically, not try to burn down the rafters."

Some combination of her home environment, that steady focus, hard work, and the talent she was born with seemed inevitably to lead to Krall's success. In 1996, Greg Sutherland wrote a profile of Krall for *The Jazz Report* which started out: "It seems that every time you pick up a magazine these days, the name Diana Krall appears."

The next year Mark Miller wrote about her upcoming Massey Hall appearance – and the fact that she had just performed at the Monterey, California Jazz Festival to an audience of 6000.

By 1998, the Saskatoon *Star Phoenix* ran a piece that started out: "Yes, that is the slinky, sexy Diana Krall doing the come-hither thing on the cover and inside the package of her latest CD release ***Love Scenes***, but she's quite happy with that."

In 1999, in the *Toronto Star*: "Canadian Diana Krall's reputation as a leading jazz artist has been cemented in a significant manner – she's just been voted Female Vocalist of the Year by readers of the prestigious *Down Beat* jazz magazine."

And in March 2000, Diana Krall was back in Toronto – at the huge Sky-Dome this time – to perform with her quartet at the Juno Awards, fresh from winning a Grammy for Best Vocal Jazz Performance on her hit CD, ***When I Look in Your Eyes***.

Krall's experiences with interviews and critics have ranged from warm to icy. Usually, she plays it cool, but she's been known to flare up, as in one instance when she was asked why she thought she had "broken through" when other jazz artists hadn't. Her response was, "I don't really want to sit around trying to figure it out. I'm too busy trying to find the right B-flat chord. I get up at four-thirty in the morning and play music, and travelling and getting on planes and doing concerts. Do you think I have time to ponder why I'm successful? Nor would I want to."

k. d. lang

b. Edmonton, Alberta, November 2, 1961

It's likely that k. d. lang (born Kathryn Dawn Lang) would have succeeded simply on the strength of her voice. It's just as likely that her magical relationship with audiences is what has propelled her to stardom. In one of her earliest stage performances, in a 1982 show entitled *Country Chorale*, lang played the part of a famous country and western singer – modelled on Patsy Cline – who is idolized by a small-town girl hoping to follow in her footsteps.

"She had such a strong presence," remembered Raymond Storey, then associate artistic director of Theatre Network in Edmonton, "that people couldn't take their eyes off her."

The Patsy Cline alter ego seemed to ignite lang's onstage persona. Storey gave the then-20-year-old performer a stack of Cline records to listen to. He urged her to stand with hands on hips, side-on to the audience. Indeed, lang says she began to remember a childhood dream about a plane, a storm, and a fiery crash (Cline was killed in a Tennessee plane crash in 1963); lang even called her backup band of the day The Reclines ("Re-Clines") in the country star's honour.

k.d. lang in concert at Molson Park, Barrie, Ont.

It also didn't hurt her unique stage presence in those formative years that she wore cowboy boots cut off at the ankles; a black, calf-length skirt decorated with bright felt cutouts of cowboys and Indians; a black cowboy shirt with pearl snaps and "Moore Trail Riders" stencilled across the back; and a pair of cat's-eye glasses with no lenses in them. With her thick black hair shorn in a punk-style buzz-cut, k. d. lang would roar around the stage, as one critic wrote, like "a riderless motorcycle." She would dash in and out of washrooms, dance on the tables, and eventually return to the microphone to swivel her boyish hips à la Elvis Presley.

"Because I'm taking the first step in making myself look stupid," she told *Alberta Report* magazine in 1984, "it frees people up. They get addicted and they keep coming back for more."

Born in Edmonton in 1961, k. d. lang and her family soon moved to the dryland prairie town of Consort, Alberta, where her mother taught school and her father established a drug store; residents still remember k.d. whizzing around the pharmacy aisles on roller skates imagining she was a roller derby queen.

While she watched *The Beverly Hillbillies* on television, drove a grain truck for spending money, and worked out as a track and field athlete (she was ranked eighth in Canada in the javelin throw in 1979), music wasn't very far away.

Once a week, her mother drove k.d. and her brother to a nearby convent where k.d. took piano lessons; she says "I got my ear" listening to John practise scales. While mom favoured Broadway show music and dad liked Percy Faith tunes, at night k.d. and her sister Keltie listened to the music of Creedence Clearwater Revival, Eric Clapton, Maria Muldaur, and Joe Cocker on a Seabreeze record player. Then, at age 13, k.d. bought her first guitar – a 12-string Yamaha – and wrote her first song, **Hoping My Dreams Come True**.

Performing was always part of the picture – at weddings, school functions, and talent contests; once, returning with her high school team on a bus, k.d. convinced the driver to detour to Coronation, Alberta, where a talent contest was under way. "I just walked in, still with my bright yellow track suit on, sang a song, won, and left." She enrolled in the Red Deer College music program, but left without getting the diploma; she felt suffocated by the rules, the formal instruction, and little recognition for the musical experimentation she was doing.

In 1983, k.d. answered an ad from a band looking for a female country vocalist for a studio recording. Lars Wanagas, of Edmonton's Homestead Recorders Ltd., realized her talent and signed her to a management and publishing agreement. The manager of Edmonton's Sidetrack Café, Geoffrey Lambert, also took a chance on her; before long k. d. lang and the Reclines were packing them in. Next, lang borrowed $2000 from her mother and produced her first album, *A Truly Western Experience*; it immediately sold 1500 copies. She appeared at the Edmonton Folk Festival that year and got rave notices from promoter Richard Flohil; he booked her into Toronto's Brunswick House for a week.

"There was a lineup on a Monday night," said Flohil. "I don't think I've ever seen a lineup on a Monday in Toronto. She got incredible attention. She was everywhere – in the *Globe*, on CBC Radio, in the *Star*. She was so busy she turned down *Canada A.M.*"

In the 1980s, lang's campy garb, rhinestone spectacles, and off-the-wall cow-punk music stylings found plenty of favour in a pop culture that seemed eager for anything and everything new. Writes Jeff Breithaupt (in *Saturday Night*), "Her fine-featured androgyny underscored the crossover appeal of her country music, which quickly entered regular rotation in the homes of people who, until she came along, had been sure that they hated country music."

In 1987 she debuted on a major label with the album *Angel With a Lariat*. Next, she brought legendary Patsy Cline producer Owen Bradley out of retirement for *Shadowland* (1988), a triumphant album that proved she could take on Nashville on its own terms and succeed; she even teamed up with Roy Orbison in a duet version of his 1961 hit "Crying." With her album *Absolute Torch and Twang* (1989), lang and the Reclines invented the perfect tag for their brand of music.

With the 1992 release of *Ingenue*, her three-million-selling album of mournful lost-love songs (including the single *Constant Craving*, her first Top 40 hit), k. d. lang broke through. The work, she jokingly called her "stalker" album, won a Grammy and found its way onto the playlist of every cafe, restaurant, and pop radio station in North America. With it she successfully moved from country to adult-contemporary and became a celebrity. She hit the movie screens with Percy Aldon's film *Salmonberries*, and wrote the soundtrack for Gus Van Sant's film *Even Cowgirls Get the Blues*.

In 1992, lang also went public with her political and social views – announcing her homosexuality in an interview with *The Advocate* and promoting her vegetarian lifestyle in the "Meat Stinks" ads for People for the Ethical Treatment of Animals (PETA). She was dubbed the queen of "lesbian chic" by *New York* magazine and then appeared on the cover of *Vanity Fair* with Cindy Crawford in a barbershop photo by Herb Ritts. Her next album, *All You Can Eat* (1995), however, met with critical and commercial indifference; her vegetarian views prompted cattle-country radio boycotts of her music in her home province and the U.S. Midwest. Even *Drag*, a 1997 concept album built around the theme of love as an addiction, also came up short. She described the times as "the down period" as she retreated to the family home in Alberta.

In 1998, k. d. lang moved to Los Angeles and rejuvenated her career. On a suggestion from friend Madonna, she contacted techno-minded producer Damian LeGassick for a new concept album. In 2000 she released *Invincible Summer* – a collection of breezy, sun-drenched songs in celebration of the calendar's most carefree season.

During the tour to promote *Invincible Summer*, k. d. lang appeared in Toronto. During the love-in between fans and their pop idol at the Hummingbird Centre, lang sang favourites from all phases of her career. The adoring audience called out questions, comments, and requests to her as she chatted between songs. When a fan in the balcony asked, "Will you sing 'Happy Birthday' to me?" lang asked for her name. "Dusty!" the fan called back. Laughing with the audience, lang prepared herself and then sang a Marilyn Monroe–style version of the tune, ensuring an unforgettable birthday for Dusty.

"Live performance is everything to me," she told a *Globe and Mail* reviewer that summer. "It's my ultimate purpose. It's why I was placed here. It's when I feel the most comfortable and satisfied and peaceful."

It helps that k. d. lang has a stunning voice. But without that special relationship with her audience, she'd just be a remarkable singer instead of the international star she now is.

Horace Lapp   *b. Uxbridge, Ontario, March 3, 1904; d. 1986*

Having started his music studies in childhood, Horace Lapp became a church organist in Beaverton, Ontario at the age of 13. Next he played the organ at Port Hope before studying piano under Alberto Guerrero, and organ under Healy Willan. He went on to play piano with Luigi Romanelli's orchestra in Toronto. In 1923, he was accompanist to the Toronto Mendelssohn Choir on tour.

In the early 1970s, Lapp recalled his time with Luigi Romanelli: "I worked for Luigi when he was musical director at the Allen Theatre, which later became the Tivoli. We'd play the afternoon show, then go on to the King Edward Hotel to play the dinner dance with Luigi's trio."

For a dozen years (1924–35) he played piano with one or another of Jack Arthur's various theatre orchestras and conducted music for stage shows at Shea's Hippodrome and the Imperial Theatre (both in Toronto). For two years, he led a dance band at the Royal Muskoka Hotel, near Port Carling, Ontario, and then at Toronto's Royal York Hotel. Also in the 1930s, his band appeared in a 12-minute *Screen News* film titled *Music from the Stars*.

For 19 years, Lapp was the organist on Kate Aitken's public affairs program, first on CFRB, then on CBC Radio. "Mrs. A. liked to smoke," Lapp told Helen McNamara for her 1973 book, *The Bands Canadians Danced To*, "and this day she had accidentally dropped her lit match on her script. ... Cy Strange, our announcer, ran in carrying a bottle of seltzer water. Me? I was playing 'There'll Be a Hot Time in the Old Town Tonight.'"

When Horace organized his first orchestra, the first thing he did was have his men learn to tap-dance. "I was all show business," he told McNamara. "We'd announce, 'Ladies and gentlemen, the floor show!' and the musicians would get out on the floor and dance. It was terrible."

But he had some fine musicians with him, including Trump Davidson, Cliff McKay, Bobby Gimby, Moe Koffman, and William McCauley, who was to become the music director of the O'Keefe Centre in the 1960s. Another Lapp sideman was Denny Vaughan, who went on to considerable fame as a bandleader (in both Canada and Great Britain), and a Canadian television star.

He was the pianist, arranger, and sometime conductor of CBC Radio's "Opportunity Knocks" for seven years in the 1950s and the conductor for the Eaton Operatic Society for three years. During the 1960s he served as producer of shows at the Canadian National Exhibition Bandshell in Toronto.

Over and above Lapp's musical abilities, he had a great sense of showmanship. According to Helen McNamara, "Lapp's fine theatrical touch even extended to the band's appearance. Before intermission the men came out wearing white suits. After intermission they appeared in red jackets. Some evenings they wore tails. But it was worth the effort. The average-size crowd was 700 to 800 dancers nightly, with a minimum of 1000 on Friday and Saturday evenings."

The Horace Lapp orchestra played close to nine years in the Royal York Hotel and never, according to Lapp, went into the red. The best time, he recalled, was during the Second World War, "when the place went mad, filled with soldiers and airmen out for a good time. They were a marvellous audience." A bit wistfully, he added: "Yes, after I went to the CBC I made a lot of money, but it was never quite as much fun."

It was in the 1960s that Horace Lapp was recognized as one of the last surviving silent-film accompanists in Canada. He played for screenings of historic movies at the Ontario Film Institute in Toronto, and also at the Stratford (Ontario) Film Festival and in Ottawa.

Lapp also recorded soundtracks for CBC Television's 1969 series of the 37 extant Laurel and Hardy short movies. In 1978, for a Film Institute screening of the 1928 silent movie *Carry On Sergeant*, Lapp played Ernest Dainty's original accompanying score.

From 1962 to 1973, Lapp wrote a music column for the Toronto-based Arts and Letters Club monthly letter. His unpublished autobiography was deposited at the National Library of Canada.

Horace Lapp died in Toronto in January 1986.

Gordon Lightfoot

b. Orillia, Ontario, November 17, 1939

One day, if CBC television, Group of Seven paintings, or Pierre Berton history books disappear, Canadians who listen to the songs of Gordon Lightfoot will still get a strong sense of who they are, where they've come from, what life in their country looks and feels like, and what makes it distinctive. Lightfoot's straightforward yet compelling melody lines and his evocative lyrics about relationships, wanderlust, and historic moments are universal, yes, but their resonance echoes more sympathetically among fellow Canadians.

"Is there such a thing as balladeer laureate of Canada?" one newspaper reviewer asked. "Gordon Lightfoot should be it."

Balladeer – laureate or otherwise – was not Gordon's initial intention. He

took the requisite piano lessons, but later gave them up in favour of guitar and drums. He sang in the church choir and he credits the choirmaster, Ray Williams, who taught him the art of vocalization. Equally eclectic as a teenager, he was attracted to jazz and in 1955 placed second in an Ontario-wide competition of barbershop quartets. When he was 17, Gordon tried his hand at composition and wrote a novelty song called **The Wise Old Owl**. He even studied orchestration for a year at Westlake College in California and then worked in Toronto as a studio musician/choral singer and on CBC-TV's *Country Hoedown*.

"In 1960, I was starting to listen to folk music," he told Ritchie Yorke, "things by Pete Seeger and Bob Gibson. ... I started playing guitar and singing in various folk clubs [and] in bars."

In Toronto, Lightfoot played such Yorkville clubs as the Village Corner and the Purple Onion. During that time he teamed up with Terry Whelan, and the duo, known as The Two Tones, recorded an album on Chateau Records. However, it was during a solo Lightfoot appearance at the Steeles Tavern that newly established folk singers Ian and Sylvia heard several of his compositions – **Early Morning Rain** and **For Lovin' Me**. By 1963, he was being drawn to the urban folk movement led by Bob Dylan and had composed 75 songs of his own. In 1965, he debuted in New York City and *Times* critic Robert Shelton suggested, "with a little more attention to stage personality, he should become quite popular."

Meanwhile, Peter, Paul, and Mary had recorded **For Lovin' Me**, and Ian and Sylvia had helped Lightfoot get into a studio to record an album of his own. The material, like Dylan's, featured a more personal reflection of his own identity and it triggered the release of singles **I'm Not Sorry, Go Go Round, Spin Spin**, and (Bob Dylan's) "Tom Thumb's Blues," which all made the Canadian Top 10.

"I guess I'm so Canadian," Lightfoot said at the time, "that I got everybody involved."

The essence of that remark was borne out in a landmark song he created initially for a television show. In 1966, during a chance meeting between Prime Minister Lester Pearson and CBC-TV producer Bob Jarvis, the prime minister mused about a television extravaganza on the occasion of Canada's centennial the next year. Somehow the idea of depicting construction of the Canadian Pacific Railway came up and Jarvis immediately thought of Lightfoot.

"A month later Gordon came back," Jarvis said, "and asked to play what he'd created, to see how we reacted. We were absolutely blown away. He had produced **The Canadian Railroad Trilogy**."

Jarvis took the work into a CBC-TV studio, with Lightfoot singing in front of actors, Yonge Street panhandlers, and even members of the Toronto Argonauts football team portraying the navvies wielding sledgehammers and living in bunk cars in 1885. Broadcast within the program *100 Years Young* on New Year's Day 1967, Lightfoot's composition was a musical dramatization, perhaps Canada's first music video, depicting the arduous but vital building of a national dream.

"I never had the slightest concern that Gordon would produce something that was memorable," said producer Jarvis. "What I didn't know was that it would be such a jewel. I believe **The Canadian Railroad Trilogy** will be sung a hundred years from now. It's that important a piece of music."

In 1967 Lightfoot made his first cross-country tour (including Expo '67), leaving the bars and lounges behind for sold-out concert halls wherever he went. By this time, singers of nearly every stripe were picking up on Lightfoot's writing genius and contacting his publishing firm, Early Morning Productions (established in 1969), for the rights to record. Both Chad and Jeremy and the Johnny Mann Singers covered **For Lovin' Me**; Leroy Van Dyke recorded **I'm Not Sayin'**; Marty Robbins' version of **Ribbon of Darkness** went to the top of the country music charts. Eventually, Lightfoot's songs would be recorded by artists as diverse as Richie Havens, Judy Collins, Elvis Presley, Harry Belafonte, Barbra Streisand, the Kingston Trio, George Hamilton IV, the Carter Family, Ronnie Hawkins, Johnny Cash, and Bob Dylan.

A glimpse of Lightfoot the writer at this stage of his career revealed an artist torn between the demands of touring, moving his wife and two children into a Toronto home, and squeezing in as much writing time as possible. In 1969, as he prepared to record a new album (originally titled *Sit Down Young Stranger* but later released as *If You Could Read My Mind*), he wrote in the empty house, every day for a month, up to 12 hours a day. That way he completed most of the material for the album, about a song a day, in a four-week period in July that year. The recording yielded the best sales numbers of his career to that point – 350,000 albums sold and 750,000 singles of **If You Could Read My Mind** sold – and catapulted him onto the international scene. (Since its 1970 release, **If You Could Read My Mind** has been covered by more than five dozen other artists.)

In 1970, at age 32, he received the Order of Canada, but barely had time to stop at Rideau Hall for the ceremony. During the 1970s, Lightfoot performed an average of 70 concerts a year in the United States (with multiple concerts in New York and L.A. and one in Las Vegas). He toured Europe every spring and Australia twice. At home he continued to grind out dazzling compositions, including **Summer Side of Life**, **You Are What I Am**, **Sundown** (which went to number one), **Carefree Highway**, **Rainy Day People**, and yet another landmark historical ballad, **The Wreck of the Edmund Fitzgerald** (which registered on both the country and the rock music charts). In 1976, he also headlined a benefit for Canada's Olympic athletes at Maple Leaf Gardens in Toronto.

Enviable sales numbers continued, too – by 1976 eight gold albums and one platinum for *Sundown*. In 1978 he performed an unprecedented series of nine sold-out Massey Hall concerts in as many nights. By 1979 he had written more than 500 songs and earned 15 Juno Awards (as best folk singer, best male singer, and best composer, and for album of the year).

Riding high, however, had come at a price. "Lightfoot's is the voice of the romantic," noted Geoffrey Stokes in *The Village Voice* in 1974. "For him (as for Don Quixote, one of his chosen heroes) perfection is always in view and always slipping from his grasp." Years later, he told the *Globe and Mail* that during the 1970s he needed alcohol to relax and help him to perform on stage, and that "I knew my work, my craftsmanship was going to fail. It was ruining my health." An additional health problem emerged in the 1970s – Bell's Palsy, a facial paralysis – and the medication combined with alcohol consumption nearly destroyed him.

Lightfoot said he quit drinking in 1982, but for a while, declining interest in folk music and his own creative blockage brought the singer-songwriter once dubbed an "oral Pierre Berton" down hard. As well, during the 1980s, Lightfoot's voice seemed to change (some critics said for the worse) from supple and resonant to nasal and less warm. In 1986, Lightfoot was inducted (by presenter Bob Dylan) into the Canadian Music Hall of Fame. That same year, however, in response to the commercially disappointing album *East of Midnight*, Lightfoot announced his recording days were over. He felt he was all dried up and had nothing more to say.

Suddenly in 1993, a reinvigorated Gordon Lightfoot appeared on a concert bill with Simon and Garfunkel and Blue Rodeo at Toronto's SkyDome. At the same time, a new "back-to-basics" album *Waiting For You* was released, containing up-tempo material, new ballads, a cover of Bob Dylan's "Ring Them Bells," and something topical and Canadian – **Drink Yer Glasses Empty**, about Canadian troops preparing for their role in the Persian Gulf War in 1991. By that time too, Lightfoot had married for the second time, had two new young children in his life (there are six in all), and was a grandfather to his daughter's two children.

In 1997, Lightfoot received the highest official arts honour in the country, the Governor-General's Award for the performing arts. He, like fellow recipient Joni Mitchell, was recognized for raising the profile of Canadian culture.

The following year, when he turned 60, Lightfoot released *A Painter Passing Through*, his 19th album, which, he noted on his Web site, was "very autobiographical. ... I've settled down now and I'm in this wonderful position of being allowed to make my own albums. As usual, the songs ... paint pictures." That year he took those musical paintings (and fan favourites from the past) to his traditional springtime Massey Hall concerts, an event he called "a milestone." Lightfoot must also have been buoyed by the fact that his music was in vogue again: The Rheostatics had covered **The Wreck of the Edmund Fitzgerald**; **If You Could Read My Mind** had been resurrected as the signature tune for the soundtrack of *54*, the film about New York's notorious disco palace, Studio 54; and in 2000, **Sundown** (Lightfoot's song about his relationship with super-groupie Cathy Smith) was recorded by New York hip-hop artist Elwood.

Noting Lightfoot's versatility as a songwriter in 1966, Jack Batten wrote in *Canadian Magazine* that he filled the role of "journalist, poet, historian, humourist, story-teller and folksy recollector of bygone days."

Five Grammy nominations and 17 Juno Awards later, Lightfoot himself reflected on the inspiration of his work this way: "I simply write the songs about where I am and where I'm from. I take situations and write poems about them."

Lighthouse front four (l. to r.): Paul Hoffert, Skip Prokop, Bob McBride, Ralph Cole, during the 1982 reunion.

Fred Phipps

Lighthouse

formed 1968 in Toronto: Skip (Ronn) Prokop drums, vocals; Paul Hoffert (b. Brooklyn, N.Y., September 22, 1943) keyboards; Ralph Cole (b. Mt. Clemens, Michigan, May 13, 1947) guitar, vocals; Grant Fullerton bass (replaced by Louis Yacknin); Pinky Dauvin vocals (replaced by Bob McBride); Paul Armen violin; Myron Moskalyk violin; Don Dinovo viola; Dick Armin cello; Leslie Snider cello; Paul Adamson trumpet; Bruce Cassidy trumpet (later Pete Pantaluk, John Naslen, and Mike Malone); Howard Shore, Keith Jollimore, and Dale Hillary sax, flute; Russ Little trombone (replaced by Larry Smith); other players: Arnie Chycoski, Freddy Stone, Rick Stepton, Don Englert, Joe Ambrosi, John Capon, Dave Tanner, Sam Alongi, Rick Waychecko, Simon Wallis, Steve Kennedy

The single greatest criticism any popular music band (with more than a few members in it) faces is: "Why don't you sound, in person, the way you sound on the recording?" The answer, of course, is that the electronics of a recording studio can take any small group into a studio and make it sound like a symphony orchestra. But trying to replicate that orchestra sound live, in front of an audience on the road, is a different story. It was that musical challenge that the Toronto-based band Lighthouse was created to meet.

"I got this great idea," drummer Skip Prokop remembers telling keyboard player Paul Hoffert on the telephone in 1968. "Could you conceive of a band, a big band, with like strings and brass and everything? So that when we record and go on the tour, we actually sound like we do on record?"

At the time, Paul Hoffert was putting the finishing touches to an off-Broadway musical he'd written. His background in orchestration, jazz arrangement, and performance on keyboards and vibraphone meant he could tackle the problem of instrumentation. Prokop had played drums for six years – first in a group called The Riverside Three, then in the mid-1960s with Bill Misener, Chuck Beale, and Denny Gerrard as The Paupers – so he was a natural onstage showman. Hoffert and Prokop approached guitarist Ralph Cole and bass player Grant Fullerton to round out the rhythm section. By early spring of 1969, this idea of a live, big-band with jazz horns, symphonic strings, and a rock 'n' roll rhythm section was off and running. They'd taken on vocalist Pinky Dauvin. All they needed was an engagement.

Lighthouse debuted at the Rock Pile (Toronto's Masonic Temple) on May 14, 1969. The bill had Lighthouse opening for Super Session, a band of all-star musicians including Mike Bloomfield, Al Kooper, and Skip Prokop. Prokop would play for both bands.

"Problem was nobody showed up from Super Session," recalls Prokop. "We [Lighthouse] were prepared to play about a half an hour. Nobody showed up except Lighthouse and 1500 people in the Rock Pile."

Oddly enough, the band was introduced by Duke Ellington, who announced, "I'm beginning to see the light ... house."

"Nine tunes," says Hoffert. "That's all we had. And three hours to fill. ... So there was a lot of jamming [which] helped the band. It helped build our reputation as a band with a lot of solos."

"And a lot of stamina," added Prokop.

Literally overnight, Lighthouse's high-energy fusion of rock, strings, and jazz caught audiences' attention. Immediately following the Rock Pile gig, Lighthouse appeared at the Boston Pop Festival on May 25th at Carnegie Hall, later at the Newport Jazz Festival, and then back home in front of 20,000 fans jammed into the square at Toronto City Hall. Also in 1969, Prokop and Hoffert took the band into the studio and produced their first self-titled album, then two more the same year – *Piecing It All Together* and *Suite Feeling*, all for RCA Victor.

The festival invitations kept coming. Lighthouse went to Monterey, Atlantic City and the Isle of Wight Festival, but turned down an invitation to play in South Africa and one to join the festival at Woodstock in 1970. Prokop, instead, focused on the sound he'd been trying to create on stage since organizing the band.

"I sat down around Christmas of 1970," Prokop told Ritchie Yorke, "and I listened to all the records I'd made with the Paupers, Lighthouse, even an old demo of the first songs I'd written. The earliest songs had a certain original essence, a simplicity, which wasn't coming through on the Lighthouse records. … We had to change the approach."

In 1971, Lighthouse signed with a new label, G R T (the Canadian subsidiary of General Recorded Tape of California), and hired a new producer, Jimmy "Teeth" Ienner, as well as a new lead singer. Bob McBride had worked on the road with Ronnie Hawkins and had even taken voice lessons from Johnny Mathis to help develop his style. The resulting album, *One Fine Morning*, came out in May that year, and became the fastest-selling album in Toronto that summer – 25,000 copies by August 1971.

"It was one of the biggest turnarounds for the band," remembered Prokop. "We'd made a big mistake by thinking we had all these people in the band and we had to use them all. It became more of an arrangement than a song. So instead, we let the song be the essence of what Lighthouse was doing. No matter how much we wanted to write a fancy brass lick, we didn't put it in if it wasn't apropos of that piece of material."

That was also the year that Canadian content regulations on AM radio came into effect (requiring that 30 percent of all musical compositions played between 6 a.m. and midnight be Canadian).

Several successful singles emerged from the album – **Hats Off to the Stranger** and **One Fine Morning**. The combination of skillfully conceived horn and string arrangements by Paul Hoffert, Howard Shore, Keith Jollimore, Larry Smith, and Skip Prokop, with McBride's powerful voice soaring overhead, gave Lighthouse the sound it was searching for. Another G R T album, *Thoughts of Movin' On*, came out with more successful singles, **Take It Slow** and **I Just Wanna Be Your Friend** the same year. The following spring Lighthouse won the Juno Award for Outstanding Performance of the Year.

In 1972 Lighthouse released two more albums, *Lighthouse Live!* and *Sunny Days*; that year they won the Juno for Vocal Instrumental Group and in 1973 for Group of the Year. The band played in hockey arenas, high school auditoriums, and concert halls indoors and out. It performed with the classical symphonic orchestras in Toronto, Montreal, Edmonton, Cincinnati, and Philadelphia. Its band members received the keys to the city of Winnipeg, were made honorary members of the Cree nation, and toured with the Royal Winnipeg Ballet in a production of *Ballet High*. In addition to the three Junos, Lighthouse produced nine gold and platinum records.

In 1973, both Paul Hoffert and Bob McBride left Lighthouse. Skip Prokop left in 1974, while Ralph Cole kept the band together until the end of a farewell tour in 1976. In 1982, many of the original members of Lighthouse reunited for four shows at the Ontario Place Forum in Toronto. They augmented the band with some well-known rock and jazz musicians, including bass player Dennis Pendrith, trumpeter Arnie Chycoski, and sax player Steve Kennedy. Lighthouse played to 35,000 fans during those One Fine Weekend concerts.

After his days with Lighthouse, reed player Howard Shore became music director for NBC-TV's *Saturday Night Live* in 1975. Grant Fullerton, playing guitar, led a new band called Fullerton Dam from 1974 to 1977, then one called Madcats. Ralph Cole continued to write and produce music through his own company. Paul Hoffert returned to composing orchestral, theatrical, and dance music, wrote several books, and became a professor of music at Toronto's York University. Meanwhile, Skip Prokop continued writing and performing music in film scores and commercials, and for charitable causes. In February 1998, former Lighthouse lead singer Bob McBride died of complications from his lengthy battle with substance abuse.

Russ Little

b. Toronto, Ontario, December 13, 1941

It is one of Russ Little's happy gifts that his in-your-face style of trombone playing is so easily recognizable that the listener has no trouble identifying his sound.

This in itself is somewhat remarkable when you consider the wide range of bands he has played with – Woody Herman (in the United States and Europe), Slide Hampton (in Belgium), Ted Heath (in England), Lighthouse and the Boss Brass (in Canada and the U.S.), another big band led by Fred Stone, and a rhythm-and-blues band, The Silhouettes (in Canada).

In 1983, Russ made an album with the Spitfire Band, titled ***Flight III***. On one tune in the album, Little was showcased in a romping, lively version of "Cherokee," the Ray Noble tune that became a favourite with jazz musicians years ago.

Music critic Peter Goddard wrote of his playing: "Its roots lie somewhere in bop by way of rhythm and blues, with a funky, edgy tone that bites little phrases out. With a small group, his solos swarm with notes, looping in and around the melody line."

Russ Little studied trombone under George MacRae at Malvern Collegiate and later studied conducting and composing at the University of Toronto.

Along with the bands already mentioned, he wrote and arranged for such diverse singers as Salome Bey, Paul Anka, Dusty Springfield, and Patsy Gallant. He was also music director for numerous television series and specials, including *Canadian Express*; *The Patsy Gallant Show*; *The Gene Taylor Show*; *Shake, Rattle and Roll*; *Circus*; and the Miss Canada and Miss Teen Canada pageants – each of those last two for 15 years.

His compositions include **Black Hallelujah** (in collaboration with Norm Symonds) and **Cosmic Orpheus**, the latter commissioned and performed by the New York City Ballet. He has also written music scores for film and television documentaries and features, plus numerous pieces of incidental music, jingles, and special material songs for specific singers.

Little is a big, good-natured, outgoing guy whose personality matches his seemingly loose, breezy style of playing. As he developed and matured, he learned the value of gaining different kinds of experience – jazz, rock, pop, whatever. He spent a year with Lighthouse and has long maintained that he "loved every minute of it." Years later, he still remembered that Paul Hoffert, the Lighthouse leader, had written a tricky trombone part for Russ and he loved responding to the challenge.

On the bandstand or off, Little exudes great energy and enthusiasm, and musicians who work with him tend to respond positively to his dynamic personality. He was once quoted as saying that a musician has a continuing battle with himself, between what he would like to do and what he has to do to make a living. But when he is reminded of this, he will shrug it off lightly, indicating that he declines to be spooked by the demands of the music business.

Another indication of Russ Little's professionalism and maturity is the way he can slide quietly into the background when he is in the role of composer/arranger/accompanist to a singer, rather than a featured trombone soloist.

For example, in 1980 he did his second album with Salome Bey. For this one, Russ and Rick Wilkins collaborated on the arrangements. In addition, Russ wrote four original songs for the session. Typically, there is little audible evidence that Russ Little was on the record date. He was there as a composer/arranger/leader – not as a trombonist. Russ had no trouble adjusting to that reality.

Russ Little's little brother, Michael Stuart, is seven years younger. Michael, who plays tenor and soprano saxophone, was born in Jamaica, but did not move to Toronto until he was 21 years of age. Michael toured Europe in the summers of 1977 and 1978 with the American drummer Elvin Jones, but he has also worked in Canada, with such musicians as Sonny Greenwich, Hagood Hardy, and Doug Riley – and, of course, with his big brother, Russ.

Perhaps the difference in age between the two Little brothers partially accounts for Michael's preference for the fusion style of blending jazz with rock. He has also done a recording called **The Blessing**, which documents the influence of John Coltrane.

Judy Loman

b. Goshen, Indiana, November 3, 1936

As she approached her 65th birthday, Judy Loman made it known that when she reached that date she would retire from playing her harp – but not from teaching it.

Judith Ann Leatherman began her musical education as a child, studying with Carlos Salzedo at the Salzedo Harp Colony in Camden, Maine, and at the famed Curtis Institute in Philadelphia. She became Salzedo's assistant in the Salzedo Harp Ensemble in 1957, when she was not quite 21.

Loman moved to Toronto that same year and two years later became the principal harpist with the Toronto Symphony Orchestra, a position she was to hold for the next four decades.

Her many appearances as soloist with the TSO have included performances of John Weinzweig's *Concerto*, which was written for her, and of Harry Somers' *Suite for Harp and Chamber Orchestra*, which she played with the orchestra on its 1965 European tour.

The TSO commissioned Murray Schafer's *Concerto for Harp and Orchestra* for Loman and they premiered the work in 1988. Loman appeared as soloist with the orchestra on its 1979 Canadian and United States tour, and on its 1987 tour to northern Canada and the Arctic. She has also appeared as soloist with the Calgary Philharmonic, the Edmonton Symphony Orchestra, and the CBC Vancouver Orchestra. She has given many recitals and performed on CBC radio and television, with the Festival Singers at the Festival of the (Parry) Sound, and at the Elora and Stratford Festivals.

Her recording of Schafer's **Crown of Ariadne** received a Juno Award as Best Classical Album of 1979, and in the same year the Canadian Music Council's *Grand prix du disque*. She gave the premieres of Schafer's *Theseus 28* in 1986 with the Oxford String Quartet, of Weinzweig's *15 Pieces for Harp*, also in 1986, and of Glen Buhr's award-winning *Tanzmusik* the following year in Pittsburgh as part of the American Harp Society's annual composition competition.

When she appeared again at the Parry Sound festival in 1982, the *Globe and Mail*'s music critic, John Kraglund, wrote that her performance was "first-class Loman, which is to say superb harp-playing."

Judy Loman became a board member of the World Harp Congress in 1985. She has adjudicated at the 1985 Israel International Harp Contest, the American Harp Society's annual harp composition competitions, and the 1989 International Harp Competition.

She also became a member of the Faculty of Music at the University of

Toronto in 1966 and established a summer school for harpists in Fenelon Falls, Ontario, in 1977.

When she arrived in Toronto, she met Joseph Umbrico, who was already principal trumpeter at the TSO. Umbrico, born in Thorold, Ontario, in 1934, had studied at the Curtis Institute. He was also principal trumpet of the CBC Symphony Orchestra, and had taught privately, and in 1979 he joined the teaching staff of the Royal Conservatory of Music in Toronto. Loman and Umbrico married and raised three daughters and a son.

Their son, Joey, an autistic child, needed special education. "We're not oversensitive about it," Loman once said. "The more people realize the problems involved – the more educated they become about it – the better it is for parents like ourselves. If they know about it maybe they'll start to rethink priorities concerning education."

She has always loved playing the harp, despite the problems and costs it involves. Her instrument weighs 250 pounds and cost $7000. What worries her most is cold weather – because large temperature variations make its nylon strings expand and contract, putting them out of tune. "I always have to make sure it's tuned," she told an interviewer. "That's what I'm thinking about most of the time when I'm not playing."

Lawrence O'Toole wrote a piece about Loman and Umbrico for the *Globe and Mail* back in 1977. The title (not likely devised by O'Toole) was "A Harp and Trumpet and a Melodic Marriage," but in the article Loman made it clear she and her husband "don't serenade each other to sleep with heavenly plucks and glorious fanfares." Then she added: "Of course it depends on the piece of music being played and whether you get wrapped up in it. Otherwise, there's a certain professional attitude that always remains."

Loman looked forward to the day when harps would be available in schools, but she was resigned to the forbidding transportation costs. Airlines apparently charge by cubic foot instead of just by weight. As she pointed out to O'Toole, it costs as much to fly her harp to Edmonton as her own return ticket between Toronto and Edmonton. That's the main reason why Loman, considered one of the finest of all harpists, doesn't tour very much. (Of course, her husband has far less trouble travelling with his instrument.)

But Judy Loman takes all life's slings and arrows in stride.

Guy Lombardo

b. London, Ontario, June 19, 1902; d. 1977

Nobody understood the appeal of Guy Lombardo's music better than Lombardo himself. "The big trick," he once said, "is to be recognized without an announcer telling you who it is."

Arguably, no other dance band leader ever mastered that trick as well as Lombardo. From the very first strains of "Auld Lang Syne," the Lombardo theme, there was no doubt the band was none other than that of London, Ontario–born Guy Lombardo.

For more than half a century Guy Lombardo – born Gaetano Lombardo, Jr., in 1902 – led the world's most successful dance band. Understandably, he also became one of dance music's wealthiest practitioners. Guy Lombardo and his Royal Canadians sold many millions of recordings – well over 300 million – arguably more than any other dance band. Their music swept through much of the century. They played at more U.S. Presidential Inaugural Balls than any other band – from Franklin Roosevelt through Ronald Reagan.

As a kid growing up in London, one of his pals was Georgie McCullagh. Both boys had paper routes for the *London Free Press*. McCullagh eventually became publisher of the *Globe and Mail* and Lombardo became an incredibly successful dance band leader, with best-selling records and a weekly television show. Lombardo was also the impresario of musical/aquatic extravaganzas at New York's Jones Beach. (In 1955, a featured guest was Marilyn Bell, the girl who, the year before, had swum across Lake Ontario into sports history.)

All four sons of the Italian immigrant family studied music, beginning with Guy, the oldest. The others were Carmen, Lebert, and Victor. Guy started on violin but soon switched to baton. (A sister, Rose Marie, sang with the band for a few years in the 1940s.)

Despite the Lombardo family's reverence for music, there was a practical side to their thinking. In the 1950s, when Guy, by this time a multimillionaire, would go home to London to visit his aged mother, she would ask him: "When are you going to settle down and get a real job like Georgie McCullagh?"

The Lombardo Brothers' Orchestra was formed in 1917, and by 1922–23 was playing at the Winter Garden in London in the winter and at Port Stanley in the summer. (The annual summer engagement at Port Stanley became so much a part of the Lombardo legend that the band played there up to and including the summer of 1977, only a few months before Guy's death.) It was late in 1923 that they crossed the border for their first job in the United States, at Cleveland. In 1924, they were first billed as Guy Lombardo and His Royal Canadians. In 1927, they were lured to Chicago's Granada Café. A local radio station there (WBBM) offered to air the Lombardo orchestra one night for 15 minutes.

"The place was so empty," Lombardo later told music historian George Simon, "we had to get four waiters and a guy out of the kitchen to applaud."

When the short broadcast was about to finish, Guy was told to keep on playing. This order was repeated – this time by the radio station's president – with the added instruction to keep playing until signoff time at 1 a.m.

The following year, Ashton Stevens of the *Chicago Tribune* conferred upon the Lombardo orchestra the description that would last as long as the band did: "The sweetest music this side of heaven."

The Lombardo orchestra began playing at New York's Roosevelt Hotel in 1929, a gig that was to last several decades. It was there that a regular CBS radio broadcast helped make the band nationally known. And it was on these broadcasts that Guy played "Auld Lang Syne" every New Year's Eve – although he had been using it as his theme even before moving from London to Cleveland.

By 1934, the Lombardo name was so well known that he and the Royal Canadians appeared in their first movie, *Many Happy Returns*, along with the comedy team of Burns and Allen. They later appeared together in several more films.

From the beginning, Guy was the boss. The other brothers would have ideas and suggestions, but Guy's word was final. And it was Guy who resisted any marked change in the style that made the band famous.

Conversely, when it came to Lombardo's other passion, speedboat racing, he was always looking for the latest improvements in design and speed capability. Over the years, he owned a number of such boats, all of them called *Tempo*. In 1942, he entered 22 races and won 21 of them.

Guy's staunchest ally was Carmen, just a year younger than Guy and the orchestra's music director. Carmen's wide vibrato, both vocally and in his saxophone playing, helped establish the orchestra's style. He was also a prolific songwriter. Among the Lombardo hits he wrote were **Boo-Hoo, Coquette, Sweethearts on Parade**, and **Seems Like Old Times**.

The greatest friction in the Lombardo clan was caused by Victor, the fourth brother. As the youngest, he joined the band in 1930, more than a decade after it was formed. Victor was always suggesting ways of modernizing the Lombardo sound. But while recognizing Victor's talents, Guy invariably rejected change.

Since Victor's musical tastes clashed with Guy's, Victor left the band in 1947 and formed his own band. His timing was not good. The popularity of big bands was waning, and a Lombardo band that wasn't Guy's had scant chance of success. Victor returned to the fold in 1951, but things had changed.

The Lombardo empire was growing. Soon to come – besides making records and playing at the Roosevelt Grill and later at the Waldorf Astoria – were a weekly television series and the Jones Beach extravaganzas. But when Victor returned to Guy's orchestra, he came in as just another sideman (albeit a brother) and had no financial stake in the burgeoning Lombardo enterprises.

Victor was to leave and return again several times. Indeed, when Guy died, in 1977, and Lebert became "boss" of the band (Carmen had died in 1971), Victor was sent for again, to "front" the band. And, in time, he and Lebert were at odds, so Victor left yet again.

It was Lebert's son, Bill, who took over the band when Victor departed. (While all of the brothers married, only Lebert had children.) Although Lebert, the oldest surviving brother, owned the band, he didn't want to front it so he appointed his son to that post.

The Lombardo orchestra continued to tour under various leaders well into the 1990s – four decades after the big-band era was supposed to have ended. But it was still called Guy Lombardo and His Royal Canadians.

Benny Louis   *b. Niagara Falls, Ontario, 1915; d. 1984*

There was a time when Benny Louis had one of the most popular dance bands in or around Toronto. The light, understated piano played by leader Benny was typical of his approach to music. His music was mostly for people who wanted to dance.

He was in his twenties when he moved to Toronto to study composing and arranging with the noted Canadian composer John Weinzweig. Before forming his own band in 1946, he had played with the bands of Don Romanelli, Ellis McLintock, and Bobby Gimby. His band was soon playing at Montreal's Belmont Park.

Over the next 30 years, he played for many social events. His band was also a breaking-in forum for young musicians and vocalists. Margo McKinnon, Diane Stapley, Anne Gable, and Ann Marie Moss all worked for Benny at one time or another, as did Moe Koffman, Fred Stone, and Norman Symonds. The jazz trumpeter Herb Spanier worked with Benny's band at Casa Loma in Toronto.

Despite his respect for Glenn Miller and other American bands, Louis avoided stock arrangements, preferring to write his own. During his career, it was estimated he wrote more than 10,000 arrangements – a phenomenal feat for a man plagued by physical frailties. He did not copy the Miller style, but he shared Miller's desire for a clean sound, precision in playing, and an attractive, danceable mood.

Benny's life was not an easy one. An old lacrosse injury came back to haunt him and plagued him the rest of his life, in the form of crippling arthritis that made it virtually impossible for him to sit on a piano bench. Even in public, he barely perched on the edge of the bench, unable to bend his back. Yet this did not stop him from playing and leading his smooth dance band.

For many years, his wife, Ann, drove him to and from engagements – one-nighters, conventions, hotel bookings, high school dances, whatever. And the band wasn't always booked in Toronto – they travelled to Sudbury, Crystal Beach, Montreal – wherever.

In 1964, Benny succeeded in getting the city of Toronto to sponsor dance band concerts in city parks – he wanted people to enjoy themselves with free dance music. Until then, park concerts had featured mostly military bands.

He never did much work on television. According to his wife, this was because producers felt uncomfortable about his evident disability and they felt it was not the "right image" to present. (Odd that the matter of "image" never hurt Art Tatum or George Shearing or even Alec Templeton.)

Blessed with a remarkable memory, Benny could remember perfectly arrangements he had written long before, without reference to the written score. He was also a great sports fan and had an equally impressive recall for sports trivia – final scores, batting averages, etc.

For years, Benny and his band were featured at events sponsored by Simpson's, where Ken Watts was in charge of promotion. Ken always had an appreciation of Benny, both as a person and as a musician.

In the 1970s, when his son, David, began playing guitar, Benny began to change the style of his music, to make it more contemporary. (However, the son drifted away from music and ended up as a tax lawyer.) Benny Louis' daughter, Charmain, became a violinist with the Toronto Symphony.

Benny's ability to get around was severely limited in 1980 when his wife died. After that, he was forced to cut down on the amount of work he could undertake – especially work that required him to go outside Toronto. This gentle, much-loved man died in September of 1984, at 69 years of age.

Loverboy (l. to r.): Paul Dean, Doug Johnson, Mike Reno, Matt Frenette, Scott Smith

Loverboy

formed 1980 in Vancouver: Paul Dean (b. Vancouver, February 19, 1946) guitar; Mike Reno (b. New Westminster, B.C., January 8, 1955) vocals; Matt Frenette (b. Calgary, March 7, 1954) drums; Doug Johnson (b. New Westminster, B.C., December 19, 1957) keyboards; Scott Smith (b. Winnipeg, February 13, 1955, d. California, 2000) bass

No rock 'n' roll band is an overnight success. Most are the result of members acquiring a skill elsewhere and then coming together with the right chemistry at the right time. Such was the pedigree and relatively short life of Loverboy. The band had a half-dozen origins that ultimately contributed to its 1980s success.

Singer Mike Reno came to Loverboy following stints with such Canadian acts as Moxy and Hammersmith. Keyboard player Doug Johnson had worked with a band called Fosterchild. Scott Smith was a journeyman bass player. Meanwhile, the two principals – guitarist Paul Dean and drummer Matt Frenette – emerged from a highly successful rock 'n' roll band from Regina, Streetheart.

"Matt and I went down to see [Streetheart] one night," Paul Dean told author Martin Melhuish. "They were doing just what we wanted to do."

By that time, Dean had pinballed from Vancouver to Toronto and back, working in the ranks of numerous bands, ranging from psychedelia in the 1960s to hard-driving rock 'n' roll in the 1970s. Dean met Frenette, the drummer of an Edmonton-based band, Great Canadian River Race, when the two heard about Streetheart. At first, Streetheart management wasn't interested in

253

their overtures to join; then in 1976, things changed and Dean and Frenette were invited to join a revamped Streetheart and the band's fortunes took off.

The Winnipeg-based band (also featuring singer Kenny Shields, keyboardist Daryl Gutheil, and bass player Ken Sinnaeve) impressed Warner Bros./Atlantic enough to win a recording contract; their debut album, *Meanwhile Back in Paris*, sold 100,000 copies in 1977. While it filled most venues in the West with the up-tempo treatments of Van Morrison, Small Faces, and Rolling Stones material, Streetheart's music approach ultimately did not appeal to Dean and Frenette. By 1980 they had left Winnipeg for Vancouver where they first connected with singer Mike Reno.

"When Mike and I got together," Dean said, "the stuff we wrote was commercial, and a lot of people liked it." Dean, Frenette, and Reno added bass player Smith and keyboard player Johnson to complete the quintet.

One additional factor proved timely for the launch of Loverboy in 1980: the arrival of new wave music and its various technologies. Widening acceptance of the compact disc (CD) as a durable source of music and the increasing popularity of music video became catalysts for emerging groups. First it was MTV in the United States, then MuchMusic in Canada, that became the ultimate promotional tool. The band also hooked up with Bruce Allen, who had managed the careers of such Canadian successes as Bachman-Turner Overdrive, Prism, and Bryan Adams.

In January of 1981, Loverboy released its debut, self-titled album and appeared with Kiss at a packed Vancouver Coliseum. It was the first of a 250-day tour, orchestrated by manager Allen. Within two weeks of its release, *Loverboy* jumped 85 places up the *Billboard* music chart, in spite of the fact the magazine's rock music editor, Roman Kozac, dismissed their music as bland franchise rock 'n' roll.

That spring Loverboy released its first single, **Turn Me Loose**, in time to feature it during TV appearances on *Solid Gold* and *American Bandstand*. During a tour with the band Kansas, the Americans paid tribute to their opening act by closing their set with a version of **Turn Me Loose**. Later in the year, the band completed a second album, *Get Lucky*, and was honoured by Columbia Records with a party in the streets of New York; their first album had gone gold in the United States (with more than 500,000 copies sold) while sales in Canada were over 300,000.

"No fey new-wave keening here," wrote Thomas Hopkins in *Maclean's* magazine in 1982. "The Canadian invaders play knee-capping rock forged in the legion halls and among the backed-up toilets and sour-smelling alleys behind Toronto's Gasworks, Vancouver's Body Shop and Halifax's Misty Moon."

Success in the United States continued. Loverboy opened for ZZ Top on a two-month U.S. tour. In 1982, the band appeared in a segment of the television soap opera *Guiding Light*. The next year, Loverboy became the first international artists in CBS recording history to sell over three million albums in the United States. In the fall of 1983 the citizens of Shreveport, Louisiana declared October 16 "Loverboy Day" in their city and in November, Loverboy appeared as musical guests on *Saturday Night Live.*

Still the critics accused Loverboy (and similar bands such as Rush, April Wine, and Triumph) of dishing up hollow forms of old-time rock while sucking the danger out of it to please programmers. "The rocker once saw his role to intimidate," wrote rock critic Peter Goddard. "These rockers want to ingratiate."

Nevertheless, Loverboy's rocketing CD sales and popularity continued. The band's sophomore album, **Get Lucky**, became the biggest-selling LP ever to come out of Canada, and by that time the band had begun collecting Juno Awards by the armful: in 1982, Group of the Year, Album of the Year, and Single of the Year; in 1983, Group of the Year and Album of the Year; and in 1984, Group of the Year. There were also Junos for their composers (Mike Reno and Paul Dean), producers (Paul Dean and Bruce Fairburn), and engineers (Keith Stein and Bob Rock).

The heyday ended in 1987, when Loverboy performed a farewell concert with Def Leppard in Europe and broke up. The band reunited periodically in the 1990s – a benefit in 1991, a western Canadian tour in 1993, a 90-concert tour in 1998 (which grossed US$1.5 million), and 50 dates in 2000 (at US$25,000 per show). To date, Loverboy has sold 23 million records.

The band was working on touring and recording schedules in December 2000 when bass player Scott Smith disappeared, apparently swept from a sailboat in waters off the California coast.

Ruth Lowe   *b. Toronto, Ontario, August 12, 1914; d. 1981*

It was probably inevitable that one of the most soulful popular ballads of the 20th century was written by one of the most unhappy songwriters who ever had a hit. The song was **I'll Never Smile Again** and its composer and lyricist was an attractive young Canadian musician named Ruth Lowe. She was born in Toronto in 1914, but moved with her family to California when she was still a child.

She was a grown-up by the time she returned to Toronto and had been studying music. Her first job was playing piano in a music store – luring

potential buyers to purchase sheet music of the latest Tin Pan Alley ditties.

In the mid-1930s, Ina Ray Hutton and her all-female band (billed as the Melodears) were playing in Toronto and needed a pianist. Lowe auditioned for the job and got it. She toured North America with the Hutton band for a couple of years. In her travels she met a music publicist named Harold Cohen. They soon married and settled in Chicago. Then tragedy struck; Cohen died suddenly, leaving the 24-year-old Ruth a grieving widow.

She moved back to Toronto and tried to start life fresh. She managed to get a job at CBC Radio, playing piano and writing songs. She replaced Percy Faith, who moved on to conduct an orchestra on his own radio series before emigrating to the greener fields south of the border.

Before he left, though, Faith heard Ruth playing the song she wrote after her husband died. It was **I'll Never Smile Again**. He got Ruth's permission to perform her song on his radio series.

In September 1939, the Tommy Dorsey Orchestra arrived in Toronto to perform at the Canadian National Exhibition's "big band tent." Every day, after every show, a young woman appeared with a demo recording in hand, asking Dorsey to listen to it. Dorsey wasn't that anxious to hear yet another demo recording – he used to have them shoved at him by the hundreds.

But Carmen Mastren, who was Dorsey's guitarist, heard Ruth's song and reportedly flipped over it. He and others in the Dorsey organization kept trying to get the bandleader to listen to the song. Finally he did listen to the off-the-air demo recording of the Percy Faith performance, with Louise King doing the vocal. Dorsey promptly arranged for his publishing company to acquire the rights to the song. Eight months later Dorsey recorded the song with Frank Sinatra, Jo Stafford, and the Pied Pipers.

Dorsey was present when Sinatra, Stafford, and the Pipers were trying to figure out the best way to approach the song. He suggested they sing it as if they had just gathered around the piano. They took his suggestion and the result was not only a lovely intimate performance, it also launched Frank Sinatra's career.

Frank's confidence in Ruth Lowe shot way up. When he decided to leave Dorsey and launch a solo career, he chose Ruth's song **Put Your Dreams Away** as his radio show's theme. It became his signature song for the next two decades.

Lowe's name was now well known, not only in popular music circles but also to the public. She wrote the songs for a big MGM musical, *Ziegfeld Girl*, which starred Judy Garland, Hedi Lamarr, and James Stewart. Her best song in that flick was **Too Beautiful to Last**.

In 1943, Ruth returned to Toronto, where she met and married Nat Sandler, an enterprising stockbroker and financial consultant. Among other things, he owned the Club Norman, and Ruth booked the performing talent for the club.

(l. to r.): Frank Sinatra, Ruth Lowe, Tommy Dorsey

Nat and Ruth had two sons: Stephen, who is an investment broker, and Tommy, now a highly regarded photographer. (Tommy has also been working on a television documentary of his mother for the History Channel.)

Over the years, Ruth Lowe received many accolades for her contribution to music – all in the United States. In 1955, she was the subject of a *This Is Your Life* episode hosted by Ralph Edwards. The Dorsey-Sinatra version of **I'll Never Smile Again** was picked in 1958 as one of the best pop songs of all time. A year after Ruth Lowe's death the song received Grammy honours as it was inducted into the American Recording Hall of Fame.

In the more than half-century since she wrote the song, it has been recorded by more than 100 artists – including Fats Waller, Joe Williams, Count Basie, George Shearing, Billie Holiday, and the Platters.

Ironically, even though her most famous song was written when she was still living in Toronto, the Canadian music world has largely ignored Ruth Lowe's achievements. Perhaps her son's documentary will bring her the recognition she deserves in her home country.

Galt MacDermot *b. Montreal, Quebec, December 16, 1929*

There are probably worse things that can happen to a composer than being remembered primarily for a 30-year-old musical score – not being remembered at all, for example.

But that is the cross Galt MacDermot has to bear. No matter that he has created several other noteworthy musical scores and even won a coveted Tony award for one of them (*Two Gentlemen of Verona*), MacDermot will always be remembered primarily for writing the music for *Hair*, just over three decades ago. *Hair* was one of the most controversial and sensational musical hits ever to land on Broadway – and in top theatres in England, France, Germany, Sweden, Japan, Israel, Holland, and Australia.

The Montreal-born MacDermot was raised in several Canadian cities, attended Upper Canada College in Toronto, and then continued his musical studies in Cape Town, South Africa, where his father was posted as Canadian high commissioner. He returned to Montreal in 1954 and played piano in jazz clubs and wrote the music for the successful McGill revue *My Fur Lady*. He settled in New York in 1963, playing in studios and with rhythm-and-blues bands.

In 1970, MacDermot told jazz critic Helen McNamara that since he spent time in South Africa the only music that interested him was rock and roll. "I played jazz in Montreal from 1954 to 1961," he said, "but jazz lost all its importance to me about the time rock came in."

Years later, MacDermot recalled the impact on him of his first exposure to African music: "It was a mindblower. I would go to the mines over in Johannesburg every Sunday and watch these guys dance, and it was unbelievable. The dancing was so good. The emotion of it was phenomenal. I tried in *Hair* to get some of the feeling of African music."

After returning to Montreal he relocated in New York and landed a job making demonstration records for publishing companies. Looking for more work to make ends meet, he came across a fledgling Broadway producer named Nat Shapiro. It was Shapiro who steered him to two American writers, Gerome Ragni and James Rado, who had written the book for *Hair*, later described as a "Tribal Love-Rock Musical," which dealt with the character of the hippie culture in North America during the 1960s. It was produced by Joseph Papp for the New York Shakespearean Festival Public Theatre. MacDermot was taken aboard to compose the music.

After an off-Broadway tryout, *Hair* opened at the Biltmore Theater and ran for 1729 performances. MacDermot's music was instrumental in giving the show several hit songs, including **Aquarius**, **Let the Sunshine In**, **Good Morning Starshine**, and **Easy to Be Hard**.

Both on Broadway and in its various other productions, *Hair* proved a phenomenal success. For instance, the Toronto production at the Royal Alexandra Theatre was rewarded with a standing ovation on opening night. It grossed $1,000,000 in its first three months.

The *Globe and Mail*'s Herbert Whittaker, dean of Canadian theatre critics, recognized *Hair* as a landmark show. He predicted it would be "as much a signpost in musical theatre as was the Theatre Guild production of *Oklahoma!* back in 1943. Before *Oklahoma!* musicals were different; after *Hair* it is unlikely they will be completely the same as before."

Galt MacDermot was the toast of Broadway – and other theatre centres throughout much of the world. In the next few years, he composed the music for several other shows, including *Hamlet, Troilus and Cressida,* and *Two Gentlemen of Verona*, all for Papp's New York Shakespeare Festival.

But the only success among these was *Two Gentlemen of Verona*, which won a Tony Award as the best musical of the 1971–72 season.

Although he had several more kicks at the can, MacDermot did not again attain the heights of *Hair* or even *Two Gentlemen of Verona*. He had two Broadway flops (*Via Galactica* and *Dude*) and the musical scores for such films as *Cotton Comes to Harlem* and *Rhinoceros*.

In 1985, MacDermot wrote the music (25 songs) for the musical called *The Special*. It was an unmitigated failure. Sniffed *The New York Times*: "To call *The Special* a trivial evening is to overdramatize its achievements."

In the spring of 2000, at age 71, by which time *Hair* had grossed $120 million worldwide, MacDermot turned up at Nashville's Vanderbilt University for a fundraiser and was greeted with cheers as he pounded out (for 40 minutes) funky versions of his songs from *Hair*.

"I found them delightful," he said afterwards of his attentive audience. "I was quite astounded by the way they responded, and especially that they recognized certain phrasings of my music."

He looked back on his musical career philosophically, but with candour: "It's nice when it works, but it's a drag when it doesn't."

Ashley MacIsaac

b. Antigonish, Nova Scotia, February 24, 1975

While *ceilidh* is the Gaelic word for pilgrimage, sojourning, and visiting, its most popular usage defines a musical gathering, in which musicians share tunes and dances with an audience that joins in by singing, clapping in tempo, and dancing to the music. The *ceilidh* owes much of its current global popularity to such Cape Breton artists as John Allan Cameron, the Rankin Family, and Ashley MacIsaac. For, while the controversial fiddler's onstage antics and offstage lifestyle have drawn much criticism, his passion for the music of Cape Breton has beamed through.

Like many young people on Cape Breton, Ashley MacIsaac grew up fiddling. The difference was that while his peers played, Ashley practised – mostly four hours a day, but eight hours on days he had fiddle lessons. When he was nine, Ashley step-danced for the Pope and was spotted by CBC broadcaster Peter Gzowski during a *ceilidh* at the MacIsaac family home in Creignish. In 1992, Gzowski featured the young fiddler on his show *Morningside* and commented, "when he has that instrument in his hand, it's really a very special creative event."

That same year, MacIsaac recorded his first independent album, ***Close to the Floor*** (1992), and immediately demonstrated his clarity and proficiency on the fiddle. Then, at a now-infamous Cape Breton square dance, MacIsaac was spotted by a visiting New York theatre director. Quoted in *The New Yorker*, JoAnne Akalaitis said, "I appreciate all the talent that is on the island, but … nobody plays in such a physical, demonic way. Nobody engages his body the way Ashley does. There's a kind of harshness, a volcanic ambience to his performance. … I was in a state of meltdown. I thought, this is a great performance."

Despite the concerns of his parents – Carmelita and Angus MacIsaac – Ashley went to New York, and, in the words of *New Yorker* writer Rebecca Mead, was "transformed from a folk-music prodigy into a rock star." In New York, while teaching Akalaitis' cast to step-dance, MacIsaac stayed with musician/composer Philip Glass, met and played for Paul Simon (MacIsaac would perform on Edie Brickell's next album), and immersed himself in New York's club, drug, and gay community culture.

After four months in New York, MacIsaac returned to Nova Scotia and signed with Halifax-based manager Sheri Jones, who figured if she put a rock band behind MacIsaac's quicksilver fiddle-playing, the result might attract a young audience. She was right. In 1994, MacIsaac performed at an industry event in Newfoundland and was immediately signed to an A&M Records contract and a tour with such popular artists as Sarah McLachlan and the Chieftains.

MacIsaac's second album, *Hi How Are You?* (1995), was a bizarre blend of traditional and modern sounds. He combined punk guitars, pounding dance beats, and samples (à la MTV) with his rollicking fiddle-playing. (MacIsaac said, "Celts were the original punks.") The album included a makeover of the traditional tune "Sleepy Maggie" (using Gaelic vocals by Mary Jane Lamond surrounded by MacIsaac's fiddle work) and it became a hit single. His sometimes ragged, off-key singing on the album raised the ire of some music purists, but still sold 300,000 copies and earned him two Juno Awards for Best New Solo Artist and Best Roots and Traditional Album. As a kind of response to criticism, however, MacIsaac returned to the studio and recorded a more traditional-sounding album, *Fine Thank You Very Much* (1996), which soon sold 45,000.

The pop music world, which *The New Yorker*'s Mead said "relies upon putting onstage young people whose talent exceeds their maturity and whose very rawness and inexperience constitutes much of their appeal," couldn't get enough of the Cape Breton prodigy. On stage, MacIsaac wore his hair in a Mohawk cut and performed in combat boots and a kilt, appealing to young fans of alternative music and hip-hop, while still selling records to their grandparents.

MacIsaac's exhibitionist approach to performance and outspoken views of his lifestyle, in the view of some, went over the top in 1996–97. During an appearance on *Late Night with Conan O'Brien* he flipped his kilt, exposing his genitalia, and in response to his being named to *Maclean's* magazine's honour roll, he volunteered details of his sex life with a teenage boyfriend; the magazine withdrew his name from the list. Apparently bored with touring, MacIsaac smashed his violin apart onstage in Cleveland and cut short the rest of the U.S. tour. In 1998, at an appearance back in Cape Breton, instead of playing, MacIsaac ranted at the audience and at a later festival trashed his backstage trailer.

Meanwhile, the media turned against him. In a major feature, *The New Yorker* published stories of his hard drug use. The *Toronto Star* headlined a story "Manic MacIsaac fiddles while career burns." Corporate bookings dried up. His manager, Sheri Jones, stopped representing him. MacIsaac campaigned for a release from his A&M Records contract; he even went into their office demanding $1 million and when he was refused he trashed the office. Nevertheless, he signed a three-album deal with Loggerhead Records (owned by the food company McCain family). His public antics came to a head in 1999, during a Halifax New Year's Eve rave which featured invitations to sex onstage and racial slurs.

The year 2000 witnessed an abrupt change in Ashley MacIsaac's attitude and fortunes. He chatted with confused fans via his Web site. Despite declaring bankruptcy, his lone Loggerhead Records release *Helter's Celtic* (1999) began to sell. In support of the album, he performed 120 dates in smaller venues, drawing good audiences and favourable reviews. He joined the Chieftains for part of the tour, as a kind of symbolic return to his Celtic roots. He sold out shows at Your Father's Moustache in Halifax, the Horseshoe Tavern in Toronto, the Chrysler Auditorium in Windsor, and Hurley's Irish Pub in Montreal.

"Mark this down about his musical felicity," wrote *Montreal Gazette* music critic Mark Lepage. "Given all the pressure that has come down on him as the result of his now-legendary New Year's Eve rant at a Halifax rave, MacIsaac was the soul of professionalism. … His brow knit in concentration, straight as an arrow despite all the drug talk, it was easy to understand that the world outside matters not at all when the man is playing the music he was born to play."

Late in 2000, he released another independently produced album, *Fiddle Music 101*, marking his return to more traditional fiddle instrumentals. During a *National Post* interview, sensing he was again at home with his music, MacIsaac said, "It is fiddle music. Celtic music. Happy, sad, angry music without a lot of violence. It's clean, friendly music. And that's been at the forefront of what I was trying to sell when I started. It's what has given me the freedoms I had over the last few years."

Giselle MacKenzie

b. Winnipeg, Manitoba, January 10, 1927

At first, she was known simply as "Giselle," one of the relatively few popular entertainers with enough courage to risk single-name billing – well before Juliette, Valdy, or Madonna came on the scene. (Actually, before any of the above-named, there was Hildegarde, a Milwaukee-born daughter of a delicatessen-store proprietor, whose singing career began in the early 1930s.)

Although she had studied violin and music theory (the latter with the famed musician Godfrey Ridout), Giselle turned away from a promising career as a concert violinist to become a successful popular singer. She could sing in both English and French, which came in handy from time to time when she was working in the more sophisticated nightclubs.

She played violin and sang with the dance band of Bob Shuttleworth (her first husband) in 1946, and for four years starred in CBC Radio's *Meet Giselle*. During that period, she moved to Toronto and was signed by Oscar Berceller to sing and play at his elegant (and snobbish) restaurant known as Winston's, where she built a following of loyal and admiring fans. She usually accompanied herself at a baby grand.

It was while Giselle was performing at Winston's that a road company of the hit Lerner and Loewe musical *Brigadoon* played at Toronto's Royal Alexandra Theatre. At the time, Winston's was a regular after-the-show hangout for musical theatre performers appearing in the city, and the cast of *Brigadoon* was no exception.

On this particular night, Susan Johnson, road company star of such hit musicals as *Oklahoma!* and *The Most Happy Fella,* sang a number of songs and also served as an impromptu mistress of ceremonies at Winston's. She took advantage of the opportunity to focus attention on Giselle, whose work she truly admired.

Giselle took over the spotlight and proceeded to knock out the audience. Indeed, a member of the *Brigadoon* cast who caught her performance was moved to comment that Giselle was in the class of the then reigning American nightclub chanteuse, Hildegarde.

Yet, in 1950, she added "MacKenzie" to her billing. It wasn't merely invented, but was her father's second given name. Apparently, she sensed that the single-name billing – "Giselle" – would not work in the United States where she was bound.

It didn't take Giselle long to find work below the border. In New York, she sang with Percy Faith's orchestra on CBS Radio, then joined Bob Crosby on CBS Television's *Club 15*.

The fact that Giselle had perfect pitch soon attracted the attention of America's favourite comedian, Jack Benny – also a violinist, a fact he shrewdly turned to comedic use. Giselle was the perfect foil for Benny and she made numerous radio and television appearances with him. They usually played duets, the point of which was always to show off Giselle's flawless playing – and Benny's carefully choreographed imperfections. They also became good friends.

Benny was not above making some use of Giselle's gift of perfect pitch. On one occasion – at least, the story goes – Giselle was in Paris and he was in Los Angeles. He telephoned her while he was tuning up and asked for a favour: "Give me an 'A.'"

But there was more to Giselle's career than comedic appearances with Benny. From 1953 through 1957, she appeared on NBC-TV's *Your Hit Parade*, at first sharing the spotlight with yet another Canadian singer, Ontario-born Dorothy Collins. Then, she starred in her own NBC television series. MacKenzie also played leading roles in summer stock productions of *South Pacific, Annie Get Your Gun,* and *The King and I,* and other musicals of the 1960s.

Having begun to reach a wide audience, Giselle also did a good bit of recording, both in New York and Los Angeles. Two of her LPs in this period were **Giselle Mackenzie at the Empire Roof of the Waldorf Astoria** and **Giselle Mackenzie Sings Lullaby and Goodnight**.

By the mid-1960s, she was appearing in public less frequently, but she turned up for television specials with Jack Benny or Sid Caesar.

After her divorce in 1966 from bandleader Bob Shuttleworth, she stepped out of the limelight. In 1975, Giselle married a California banker, Robert Klein. She returned to Toronto for an Ontario Place concert in 1976, where her warmth, charm, and musically impeccable renderings of all the old favourites earned her a standing ovation.

The musically perfect lady from Winnipeg achieved fame through a distinctive blend of cool-headed, cheerful candour and an easy, pleasant voice of medium range, always in tune and handled with a disarming lack of affectation.

Sir Ernest MacMillan

b. Toronto, Ontario, August 18, 1893; d. 1973

One of the major figures in Canada's musical history, Sir Ernest MacMillan was a conductor, composer, organist, pianist, educator, writer, administrator, and world traveller – and occasionally a figure of controversy.

He began to study the organ at the age of eight and soon began appearing in public. When he was ten, he appeared in the *Festival of the Lilies* at Toronto's Massey Hall. "I admit," he said years later, "I found it thrilling to play to so many people."

His father, Alexander, was both a clergyman and a musician. When the elder MacMillan went to Edinburgh to fulfill an engagement in his native city in 1905, Ernest went along. He stayed for three years, continuing his musical studies. He developed a special fondness for Scotland and his speech occasionally took on a noticeable burr.

At age fifteen, he took his first appointment as organist at Knox Presbyterian Church. After two years, he returned to Edinburgh to complete his musical studies. Back in Canada, he studied modern history at the University of

Nor Baker Limited

Toronto and served as organist at St. Paul's Presbyterian Church in Hamilton.

In 1914, MacMillan went to Paris for further piano study. As a visitor to the Bayreuth Wagner Festival that summer, he was detained by the Germans for several months. After the outbreak of the First World War, he became a prisoner of war (at Ruhleben) for the remaining war years.

He returned to Canada early in 1919, when he embarked on a lecture tour of the west, his program usually consisting of a short organ recital and a talk on his experiences as a POW. Later that year, he became organist and choirmaster at Timothy Eaton Memorial Church in Toronto, a position he held for almost six years.

Soon after his appointment as dean of the University of Toronto's Faculty of Music, he formed the Conservatory Opera Company. In 1924, he conducted the Toronto Symphony Orchestra at the invitation of Luigi von Kunits. Seven years later, aware of his grave illness, von Kunits suggested that MacMillan succeed him as the TSO's conductor. In view of the leadership qualities MacMillan had already displayed, the TSO's board of directors accepted the nomination.

Sir Ernest's own reign at the TSO was to last for 25 years (except for a leave of absence in 1952), but it was not to be without its controversies. The most widely publicized of these was in 1951–52 and came to be known as the affair of the "Symphony Six." The TSO was about to play its first concert in the United States, in Detroit. But this was the time of "McCarthyism," the label pinned to the tactics of Wisconsin Senator Joe McCarthy, whose zealous red-baiting had suspicious Americans looking under their beds for communists. As a result, six members of the TSO were denied entry to the United States by that country's immigration officials, who termed the musicians "unacceptable." The orchestra's board meekly accepted the U.S. ruling and Sir Ernest refused to comment on the debacle. Rather than jeopardize the orchestra's American debut, the TSO went to Detroit without the "Symphony Six." Worse yet, the contracts of the six unjustly smeared musicians were not renewed the following year, so that the TSO could fulfill engagements in Boston, New York, and Philadelphia.

It was after this trying incident that Sir Ernest took his extended leave of absence, travelling to England, Scotland, and other parts of Europe. But the conductor was so highly regarded that this messy skirmish did not detract from his standing in music circles.

As far back as the late 1930s, he had gained fame as a guest conductor in the United States, appearing in such prominent series as the Hollywood Bowl concerts and with symphony orchestras in Chicago, Philadelphia, and Washington, D.C. He also did considerable conducting on various radio programs.

He resigned his post as conductor of the TSO at the completion of his 25th year there. Tribute was paid publicly to the great strides the orchestra had made under his command. The orchestra had lengthened its season, increased dramatically its number of annual concerts, branched out into recording and broadcasting, and otherwise solidified its claim to status among major North American orchestras.

It also introduced Canadian audiences to a new repertoire (sometimes over the objections of board members), including the works of Bartok, Copland, Holst, Sibelius, and others.

In his later years, MacMillan became recognized as a musical elder statesman – not only as a conductor but also as a composer of numerous orchestral and other works.

Perhaps understandably, his musical boundaries did not extend beyond what is usually called "classical" music. Once, at a party in the 1950s, he was asked his opinion of Bing Crosby. Sir Ernest said he had never heard of Crosby, who was then at the peak of his fame. In fairness, it's entirely possible that Bing Crosby had never heard of Sir Ernest MacMillan, either.

In 1971, Sir Ernest suffered a stroke, and after a second stroke he died in 1973. He was knighted by King George V in 1935, "for services to Canada" – the final year of such honours and the last of King George V's reign.

Rita MacNeil

b. Sydney, Nova Scotia, May 28, 1944

It's not very often an entertainer can sit in an audience and see herself perform. Rita MacNeil had that opportunity on an August night in 2000. On that summer evening she attended the Live Bait Theatre in Sackville, N.B., for a performance of *Flying on Her Own*. It told MacNeil's life story through her songs. And while she enjoyed the attention the production gave her career, she said, "I didn't think the story was earth-shattering, just something you could pretty well put anyone into. It was about one person, but so many of us could be there."

Playwright Charlie Rhindress couldn't have said it better. MacNeil's songs are about conversations, friends getting together, community roots, believing in dreams, both good and bad times, working people, taking risks, home, and paying tribute to a loving family – things that ring true for everybody. "MacNeil's artistry lies in the way she can turn the events of her life into something with which many people can identify," said Rhindress. "[What's] remarkable is that she can touch on the specific, but it becomes universal."

Truth is, not many could weather what she did and achieve what she has. *On a Personal Note*, her book written with Anne Simpson, detailed most of her struggle to succeed as a singer in spite of personal difficulties. Rita grew up in Big Pond, Cape Breton, with three brothers and four sisters. Often chaotic, her youth included the physical and psychological trauma of surgery for a cleft palate, molestation by an uncle, a first love affair that left her with a child and a broken heart, a second marriage breakdown, and numerous frustrating attempts to kickstart a musical career.

Rita's shyness, even during childhood singing lessons when "the teacher did most of the singing," thwarted her first attempts to express herself musically, so she only sang to her mother in the kitchen. As a teen, however, Rita loved to listen to music – Celtic, country, folk, rhythm and blues, and rock – on the radio. Her mother Renee "was a great encouragement," Rita said. "She believed in the singing and wanted me to be able to perform, one day, because she knew that's what I loved." Renee MacNeil did not live to see her daughter's success, but Rita's song **Reason to Believe** acknowledges the gift.

After a number of unsuccessful attempts to find work in the music business, Rita MacNeil found inspiration in the women's movement (the Toronto Women's Caucus). In 1971, she wrote about women having a voice and called it **Need for Restoration**; the next year she wrote a song protesting a beauty pageant, called **Born a Woman**, which became the title of her first album, recorded in 1974. Picked up by Boot Records, *Born a Woman* launched

MacNeil into the folk music circuit – from the Riverboat and Mariposa to Northern Lights (in Sudbury) and the Kootenays Folk Festival in British Columbia. Despite a troublesome marriage, having to care for her two children, and a disappointing career thus far, "whenever I sang I felt strong," she wrote. "Music … was really the best medicine for me."

Back in Cape Breton in 1979, she found work and more inspiration to write. The songs came fast and furious – **Black Rock**, **Troubadours**, **My Island**, **Brown Grass**, and **Old Man** (for her father), and **Working Man** (about the coal miners in Sydney Mines). Suddenly, people paid attention to her work. There were press interviews, radio appearances, and calls for concert appearances. She even got an invitation to sing **Working Man** with Men of the Deeps, an all-male choir of miners that had been singing since 1966; it was the beginning of a beautiful relationship. "The song became like an anthem when the men sang with me," she wrote.

Flushed with new successes, the MacNeil family and friends financed her second album in 1980. *Part of the Mystery*, while a creative success, stumbled at the start. The first 250 albums were flawed in the pressing. The family's Big Pond Publishing and Productions Limited was operating on a shoestring and sales were conducted on consignment. Nevertheless, Rita MacNeil's fan base grew, more media appearances resulted, and the first royalty cheques rolled in.

The turning point, however, was Expo '86 in Vancouver, where, despite her normal misgivings about the gig, "I was on cloud nine when I discovered the first show was sold out, 350 people were in the audience and … the audience

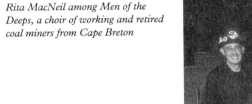

Rita MacNeil among Men of the Deeps, a choir of working and retired coal miners from Cape Breton

stayed. ... People wanted to listen to the music," she said. Meanwhile, the *Vancouver Sun* said, "for God's sake, you must hear Rita MacNeil. See her at Expo this month so you can talk knowledgeably when she becomes a star." Later that year, her album ***Flying on Your Own*** was recorded and then released in 1987. The album soon went gold and helped earn MacNeil her first Juno Award for Most Promising Female Vocalist, at age 42.

She sang in Britain, opening for Steeleye Span. Her album ***Reason to Believe*** went platinum in 1988, the same year it was produced. She went to Australia to sing with André-Philippe Gagnon. In 1989, at the Juno Awards, she and Men of the Deeps performed **Working Man** and brought down the house; right after, with tears in her eyes, k. d. lang came on stage to accept her Country Female Vocalist Juno and commented, "It's tough standing up here after listening to that."

MacNeil was on a roll. In 1990, she sold more records in Canada than Garth Brooks. In 1991 she was invited to play at Royal Albert Hall in England. There were honorary doctorates from the University of New Brunswick, St. Mary's University, Mount St. Vincent, St. Francis Xavier, and University College of Cape Breton. In 1992, she was inducted into the Order of Canada. Her television appearances broke records – her 1993 CBC-TV Christmas special, *Once Upon a Christmas*, drew two million viewers, and her musical variety show *Rita & Friends* (winner of the 1996 Gemini Award) attracted one million viewers a week over three seasons. There were two more Junos, four Canadian Country Music Awards, and seven East Coast Music Awards in the 1990s.

No longer subject to the flawed pressings and shoestring budgets of the early 1980s, Big Pond Publishing and Productions was modernized, but it was still operated by Rita MacNeil's family. Her son Wade Langham managed her career (under Lupins Productions), while her daughter Laura Lewis handled another MacNeil enterprise, Rita's Tea Room, the former schoolhouse turned into a restaurant in 1982 in Big Pond. From June to October visitors began arriving by the busload to enjoy a meal, buy Rita MacNeil souvenirs, and sign the three-ringed binder that serves as a guest book.

In spite of the confidence so much success might have instilled, MacNeil still doubted herself. During the recording of a Christmas 2000 special, the prospect of performing a duet with Patti LaBelle left MacNeil petrified. When promoting the songs on her 14th album, ***Music of a Thousand Nights***, she would periodically sing "Snowbird" (written by Gene MacLellan and made famous by Anne Murray) on stage. "I was terrified to do that song," she admitted. "I said backstage, 'I think they're going to throw tomatoes.'"

After all these years, even Rita MacNeil found it difficult to recognize what her playwright biographer, Charlie Rhindress, saw in her. "She has a very shy personality, but is a very strong person on the inside."

Fraser MacPherson

b. Winnipeg, Manitoba, April 10, 1928; d. 1993

When young Fraser MacPherson arrived in Vancouver in the early 1950s, he faced a major decision: whether to continue his academic pursuits as a budding economist or spend his life as a musician. He opted for music – but with limited enthusiasm. "I never had stars in my eyes," he once said. "I was always realistic about my talents."

Despite his modesty, MacPherson's talents eventually triumphed over his self-doubts. While in his twenties, he was playing at the few clubs Vancouver offered at the time – the Palomar, The Cave, and the Mandarin Gardens in Chinatown. Then he went to New York for a while, working in various clubs and resort hotels. But 18 months later he returned to Vancouver to take over as bandleader at The Cave.

But the Vancouver scene in those days was still iffy. MacPherson, like most other musicians, made his living via recording commercial jingles. "Jazz," as he told author and critic Mark Miller, "was something we did on CBC Radio. There weren't any clubs to speak of, just a few after-hours places that would come and go, like the Cellar, where the younger guys – the Don Thompsons, Terry Clarkes, Bill Boyles, Al Neils, and Dave Quarins, who weren't doing commercial work – would hang out all the time. We'd go down, have a few drinks, and play."

Clubs that featured jazz in Vancouver included the Penthouse, the Espresso Coffee Shop, and Basin Street. MacPherson said of Basin Street: "I worked it once. It was like getting jet lag without leaving town."

Fraser MacPherson was never what might be called progressive in his approach to jazz. A conservative man by nature, he was content to play the tunes he liked – usually old standards – in his own way, ignoring fads or trends. But he made his own way, at any rate. "A friend offered me a six-week series on CBC Radio. It kind of snowballed from there," he recalled many years later.

Still, making a living still depended largely on commercial jingle work. MacPherson, as ever, viewed things philosophically. "The guys who did the commercial stuff," he said, dryly, "found that I could read, show up on time, and play the melody if I had to."

Eventually, he was to become one of the most sought-after musicians west of Toronto. But his cynicism and dry humour still survived. When he made his record debut in 1971 with a pop group called The Shadow, he commented: "I expect it will go over big in elevators."

Looking back on his struggles to survive, he said: "It's curious. When I was doing shows and radio work, I was serious about the clarinet, so I went to New York to take lessons on the alto sax, and I took up the flute there, too. I practised them all every day. But the tenor? Nothing. It was a fun horn. If you wanted me, this is the way I played; if you didn't like it, you could get somebody else."

Ironically, it was MacPherson's tenor sax playing that was to make his name well known and highly respected across Canada. He also established a reputation for being independent in his thinking.

"I lost interest in going to sessions," he once said, "when drummers started playing the melody." In the early 1970s, he formed a group with guitarist Oliver Gannon and bassist Wyatt Ruther, but had no drummer. "The sort of thing I was interested in," MacPherson recalled, "came on the market again. The group I loved was the Ruby Braff/George Barnes Quartet – no drums, playing tunes. That's lovely. The other thing, I was reading in *The New Yorker*, as I always do to see who's playing where, and Zoot Sims and [guitarist] Bucky Pizzarelli were playing in a Greek restaurant. I thought 'What a great idea!'

"I wondered whether I was at the age when I was too old for this – it had passed me by. That, and the fact that I wanted to play standards, which in Vancouver is not the hippest idea. Then I thought, 'What the hell, it's what I want to do.' So I called Oliver. He said, 'Sure.'"

The businessman in MacPherson helped him parlay the tape of a 1975 CBC broadcast into an international release on the prestigious Concord label. Another broadcast, *I Didn't Know About You*, released on the Sackville label, featured duets (MacPherson and guitarist Gannon) and won a Juno Award for Best Jazz Album of 1982.

In the 1980s, MacPherson had some success with recordings. First came *Indian Summer* on Concord. Next was *Jazz Prose*, also on Concord, on which he used a drummer, Jake Hanna, after a long spell without one. In 1987, he did an album for Justin Time Records titled *Honey and Spice*. That same year, he was made a Member of the Order of Canada.

It was in 1983 that he looked back at his career in a conversation with Mark Miller: "Here I am, doing at 55 what I started out doing at 16 – only, with any luck, a little better. I'm playing those good tunes, having fun – and getting around a little. It wasn't part of my long-range plan at all; it's just the way it turned out."

Fraser MacPherson died in September 1993 at the age of 65. The following year the Pacific Music Association began raising funds in support of a permanent scholarship program in his name.

Lois Marshall   *b. Toronto, Ontario, January 29, 1924; d. 1997*

By any yardstick, Lois Marshall was a remarkable woman – one of Canada's most gifted singers, who sang under the batons of such renowned conductors as Toscanini, Stokowski, Beecham, and Sir Ernest MacMillan. She also performed with artists Glenn Gould, Anton Kuerti, and many more. But perhaps the most remarkable thing about her was her courage.

"I was more or less laid up in and out of hospital between the ages of two and 12 [with polio], and while at home, lying on my back, I heard music all the time," she told music critic William Littler. "It was the most important thing in my brother's life. He had records of everything. I developed a natural response to it from hearing so much. People seemed to like to hear me sing. Even when I was in the Sick Children's Hospital, every time a new nurse or doctor came on the floor I'd have to sit up in bed and sing something."

By the time she was 13, Lois was no longer confined to hospitals and taking singing lessons. Her recovery, however, was not total. The effects of her bout with polio made a full stage career impossible. But her outstanding vocal abilities demanded recognition.

She sang Puccini and Wagner, Mozart and Handel, but although she disliked suggesting her favourite composers, she had a special affinity with Bach, whose music, she said, "is something I really need – like oxygen."

This feeling for Bach dated back to 1947, when she was 23 years old.

Sir Ernest MacMillan handed her the score of Bach's *St. Matthew Passion* and invited her to try out for his annual Massey Hall performance of it.

"Four days later," Sir Ernest recalled, "she returned with every note of that taxing role not merely learned but so completely inside her, so deeply and personally understood, that I could only say to her, 'My child, you have won the engagement.'" MacMillan reengaged her for the part in Toronto for many seasons and also for the New York performances in 1954, plus his recording of it.

According to *The Encyclopedia of Music in Canada*, Lois Marshall's "dramatic acuity, immaculate musicianship and extraordinary communicative gifts and vocal powers (at their peak able to meet authoritatively a wide range of soprano challenges, dramatic, lyric and coloratura) have tempted producers to stage works especially for her."

The range and versatility of the vocal challenges she faced – and conquered – is further testimony of her determination not to be restricted by her physical limitations. In 1982, in a reminiscent mood, she told John Kraglund, of the *Globe and Mail*: "I often wished opera directors had been more aware of the importance of singing in opera. I know it would have been impossible for me to appear in some of the most active roles, but some roles, like Donna Anna in Mozart's *Don Giovanni*, which I sang in a semi-staged performance, do not require a great deal of action – preferably less than some directors require because it does not occur to them (or, sometimes, to the singers) that a role can also be acted with the voice. The operas I have attended have been memorable for the singing, not the visual appearance of the singers, the sets and the costumes."

In 1982, when she was 58 years old, she decided to retire – sort of. That same year she was named artistic director of the TriBach Festival to be held in Edmonton three years later. And in a farewell benefit concert at Toronto's Roy Thomson Hall (for the Parkinson Foundation of Canada and the Canadian Rehabilitation Council for the Disabled), she shared the stage with a number of younger colleagues whose cause she championed. "They are the future," she explained.

At the time, she said, "My friends say everything sounds fine. It's not true. I'm not what I once was. Sometimes the singing feels wonderful still, but sometimes it doesn't and if I'm in trouble vocally I'm in despair. It has been so many years. It's enough."

Still, for the next several years, she continued to sing – in recital with pianist Greta Kraus, at the Royal Conservatory of Music in Toronto's centennial concert in 1987, with the Toronto Mendelssohn Choir, with the London Fanshawe Symphonic Chorus, and, in 1990, in the Scotia Festival of Music, giving master classes and performing as narrator in Walton's *Facade*.

Even in retirement she continued to speak out on behalf of people with disabilities. "Having to deal with my own disability for 55 of my 57 years," she said at the time of her official farewell concert, "I feel I can speak very well for my fellows who happen also to have a handicap."

When she died early in 1997, there were great outpourings of regret by her fellow artists and eloquent tributes. Among those who paid tribute to her were Jon Vickers, Ben Heppner, and Maureen Forrester. Forrester said: "I treasure first of all her glorious voice which brought me to tears many, many times; and then how often she broke me up with her infectious laugh and a healthy smack on the back. She proved that she was not frail."

David Beach, dean of the faculty of music at the University of Toronto, announced the creation of the Lois Marshall Memorial Scholarships to "honour the memory of a great singer and teacher and enable young singers to realize their talents and ambitions."

Phyllis Marshall

b. Barrie, Ontario, November 4, 1921; d. 1996

Helen McNamara

Having studied piano as a child, Phyllis Marshall made her singing debut at the age of 15 on radio station CRCT, then performed for Jack Arthur – known across Canada as "Mr. Show Business" – and with orchestra leader Percy Faith on CBC Radio.

By 1943, when she was just 22 years old, she was a strong enough performer (and attraction) to open at Toronto's classy Park Plaza Hotel. Her engagement there was successful enough to last for 16 months.

She found a strong and powerful supporter in CBC Radio personality Byng Whitteker, who encouraged her to sing more blues and jazz. She sang with various Toronto dance bands and her own trio, as well as touring (1947–48) with the Cab Calloway Orchestra.

Calloway's career as a bandleader hit its zenith in the early 1930s, when he was chosen to succeed Duke Ellington at New York's famed Cotton Club, then and for years to come the top nightspot in Harlem. Although Calloway himself was more a showman than a musician, he certainly had a knack for spotting and hiring good sidemen, mostly then unknown, such as Dizzy Gillespie, Tyree Glenn, Jonah Jones, Hilton Jefferson, and Danny Barker.

He also had a flair for finding – and employing – good singers. Among those who sang with him during his long career were Lena Horne, June Richmond – and Phyllis Marshall.

Phyllis appeared in the late 1940s and early 1950s on such radio series as *Blues for Friday* and *Starlight Moods*. She gained further prominence on television via such shows as *The Big Revue* (1952–54) and *Cross-Canada Hit Parade* (1956–59). On this latter show she was seen every week, sharing the spotlight with Wally Koster and Joyce Hahn.

In 1959 and again in 1964 she performed in England over BBC Radio and in nightclubs. Also in 1964, she was featured on a successful LP titled ***That Girl***, with such noted sidemen as Buck Clayton, Buddy Tate, and Norm Amadio. That recording later won a Juno Award.

Byng Whitteker wrote of her, in the album notes for ***That Girl***: "Phyllis Marshall the person is gentle, kind and sensitive. Phyllis Marshall the singer is tenacious, tireless and, with herself, utterly ruthless. … I first met Phyllis when I was beginning a series of radio programs called 'Blues for Friday' and I thought then, as I still do, that she sings as well as anyone I have ever heard. In my view she is one of those rare singers with the innate ability to take the subject matter of any song and live it completely."

Her acting career began in 1956 with Toronto's Crest Theatre and included both dramatic and musical roles in stage, radio, and television productions, such as the revue *Cindy-Ella* and CBC Radio's *The Amen Corner*.

For a time she went into a kind of semi-retirement, to devote more time to her family. But on New Year's Day, 1964, she returned to work, as Byng Whitteker wrote, unable "to resist any longer the desire and the need to entertain."

At the time, Marshall's return to performing was hailed in a *Weekend Magazine* article titled "Phyllis Marshall's Swinging Comeback." The article was written by jazz critic Helen McNamara.

Through the rest of the 1960s and into the 1970s, Phyllis made various singing appearances, at the ACTRA Awards ceremonies in 1977, for example, and for *Freedom Fest* at Toronto's Harbourfront in 1988. But the years were catching up with her. When Phyllis died, in February 1996, she was approaching her 75th birthday.

Phyllis Marshall was a pioneer among black Canadian performers. So beloved was she by Toronto's jazz community that a huge tribute to her was staged in the CBC's Atrium in its Toronto studios on March 24 of that year. The music director for the occasion was her longtime friend, drummer Archie Alleyne (who has spent much of his time over the past decade researching the history of black Canadian musicians for his production *The Evolution of Jazz*).

Among the musicians and performers who agreed to appear at the tribute were Rob McConnell, Norman Amadio, Eugene Amaro, Guido Basso, Russ Little, Bob Price, and Joe Sealy. Jackie Richardson coordinated the vocalists who were scheduled to appear at the Marshall tribute, among them Salome Bey, Dianne Brooks, Dinah Christie, Michael Danso, Joey Hollingsworth, Don Francks, Bobbie Sherron, and Almeta Speaks.

The sketch here was rendered by the same Helen McNamara referred to above, the revered (and now ailing) jazz critic for the *Toronto Telegram* and a longtime friend and admirer of Phyllis Marshall.

Rob McConnell   *b. London, Ontario, February 14, 1935*

By any yardstick, Rob McConnell is a man of many talents. He is a trombonist, a composer, an arranger, a clinician, and the leader of what is arguably the best big band in existence anywhere on this planet. On top of all that, he has an irrepressible and irreverent sense of humour.

Barbara McDougall

McConnell played slide trombone in high school. He worked with saxophonist Don Thompson and Alex Lazeroff. He switched to valve trombone and, while studying with Gordon Delamont, worked with Bobby Gimby and with Maynard Ferguson before returning to Toronto and studio work. He formed the Boss Brass in 1968.

You can't totally separate his sense of humour from his other, more utilitarian, gifts. It is, in part, the unruffled, easy way he has with his sidemen that is perhaps the key to his effectiveness as a bandleader. The atmosphere at a McConnell rehearsal is relaxed, apparently free of pressure, totally devoid of any hint of ego or temperament. And yet the professionalism of the musicians is unfailing. The work always gets done, with no evidence of ill will or frayed nerves.

Rob's good humour is contagious. He likes to play with language, just as he plays with harmonics. When he wants to rehearse a coda, he usually refers to it as "the deadly cobra." Song titles demand a play on words. "If You Could See Me Now" is called for (in rehearsals) as "F. U. Could See Me Now."

If he hears a wrong note, he bellows a two-sour-note phrase on his valve trombone and the band, familiar with this signal, promptly stops.

The McConnell humour is everywhere. The Boss Brass's CD titled *Even Canadians Get the Blues* has a cover picture of Rob in a Mounties uniform, slumped over and snoozing over a piano whose top is crammed with empty liquor glasses. In the album notes, McConnell wrote: "I hope you realize the tremendous depths of acting ability I had to draw on for the cover shot of a Mountie gone wrong."

Beneath the brassy, breezy exterior there's a kind of modesty that manifests itself in self-mockery. When he won a Grammy in 1984 (after five earlier consecutive nominations), McConnell typically downplayed its importance, referring to the award as merely an excuse to visit friends on the west coast. "You know," he said, "you get a rate at the hotel, so that's a good deal."

But three years later, when he suffered a heart attack, he made no attempt to hide the gratitude he felt for the many expressions of concern he received from members of the jazz community throughout North America. "I was very touched and honoured by a lot of the response I got," he said. "People I didn't even know – really nice people – and I didn't know they cared."

In April 1999, when he was made an Officer of the Order of Canada, he toyed with the idea of presenting to Governor-General Roméo LeBlanc, upon receiving his medal, a copy of that CD, its cover photo showing McConnell in a drunken stupor. But after bouncing his idea off a couple of colleagues he reluctantly suppressed the urge.

He likes to grouse about what he regards as a worrying lack of work for trombonists, as opposed to, say, guitarists or flute players. He quotes this definition of an optimist: "That's a trombonist with a beeper."

McConnell is not averse to making fun of himself. Not long ago, he had two side-by-side pictures of himself printed. One shows Rob wearing a suit and tie; the other has him in a sort of hunter's windbreaker. The picture on the left is marked "Tie." The one on the right is marked "No Tie." He doesn't mention that the two pictures are different in yet another way: they are separated in time by perhaps 30 years, and about the same number in pounds of weight.

But the humour is one thing – and one thing McConnell simply cannot (or will not) resist – and the music is quite another.

Musically, what it all boils down to is a profound mutual respect between the leader and the sidemen. He knows he has the best musicians available – and they know they have a leader who relies on them.

When he isn't otherwise occupied, he might dash off to Norway or Sweden or Denmark or Germany or Brazil for a jazz clinic – and a few playing gigs. As if all this weren't enough to keep him from getting stale, Rob organized yet another band. At first he referred to it as "The Baby Brass" or "The Not So Boss Brass" or "The Cheap Boss Brass." But he finally settled on "The Tentet," since it involves ten musicians, himself included.

They made their debut in a one-nighter at Toronto's Top O' the Senator late in 1997. They didn't assemble again until the following June when, after one three-hour rehearsal, they played a week at the same club. Rob took this same group back for another engagement at the Top O' the Senator the following summer.

With sidemen like Guido Basso, Steve Wallace, Alex Dean, Mike Murley, and Barry Elmes, you knew this band is going to sound great. Their debut CD finally came out on the Justin Time label in November 2000. In addition, the Tentet, like any group McConnell forms, has the benefit of his skillful, imaginative, distinctive arrangements. He can take a rarely heard standard like "I'll Be Around" by Alec Wilder, and find in it rich and arresting harmonies that you never suspected were there.

"We might not play any originals at all," he said.

McConnell's thinking was that he might use the Tentet to showcase some long-forgotten – but well worth recalling – "old standards" by the likes of Alec Wilder, Kurt Weill, Richard Rodgers, and Ray Noble. This suggested the possibility that Rob may be thinking of phasing out the Boss Brass in favour of the Tentet.

Rob admitted there were some tempting reasons to consider such a possibility. Not the least of them, of course, is financial. It is, after all, less costly to find more frequent gigs for a 10-piece band than for one that totals 21. Also, he has "more fun" with the smaller group and he admits he's always supported having more fun.

By late 2000, McConnell had pretty well decided to scrap the Boss Brass for the Tentet. But whatever band he leads, McConnell, at 65, wants most to stay active. "That's my goal," he said. "To keep on playing and playing well."

John McDermott *b. Glasgow, Scotland, March 25, 1955*

One of the greatest success stories in the music world during the last decade of the 20th century has been the rise to stardom of John McDermott, the Scottish-born balladeer.

His life sounds like a true-to-life Horatio Alger story. He was the ninth of 12 children brought to Toronto from Scotland by their parents. He developed his talent at the famed St. Michael's Choir School in Toronto (he was an altar boy, too) and began a working life that had him parking cars for less than two dollars an hour. He graduated to factory jobs, getting promoted to sales positions where he succeeded partly because of his warm personality and a readiness to work as many hours as necessary to get the job done right.

McDermott was "discovered" while singing at a private party, at a time when he was moonlighting from his job as a circulation manager with a Toronto newspaper. He was befriended by tycoon Conrad Black, who helped finance the first McDermott recording – which was originally intended as a collection of family favourites for his parents' 50th wedding anniversary.

Andrew MacNaughtan

Danny Boy, released in 1992, became one of the most successful debut albums ever released by a new artist in Canada. It sold more than 200,000 copies and, in a slightly different version of the album (with some tracks from his second Canadian release, *Old Friends*) sold more than 400,000 in the United States.

The CBC's veteran radio personality Peter Gzowski described McDermott as "the owner of one of the world's most glorious voices." In the next six years, McDermott released half a dozen CDs, all of which reached either gold or platinum status.

McDermott's concert schedule was soon booked solid and audiences and critics around the world hailed John McDermott as North America's finest lyric tenor. Said the *Chicago Sun Times*: "John McDermott is the real thing. … A sound as pure and achingly beautiful as the ancient countryside."

In December 1995, the *Toronto Star*'s Mitch Potter wrote of McDermott: "He is quite possibly the most sentimental singer in Canada, and that suits the 1,486 people who bought every seat for tomorrow night's show at the Royal Alex just fine."

In his story, Potter also discussed McDermott's apparent willingness to tackle unfriendly critics head-on. "Don't waste my time and don't take a seat you don't want to be in," Potter quoted McDermott as saying. "Give it to someone who wants to be there because I really don't give a shit what your review says."

Evidently, singing is in McDermott's Celtic blood. Saturday night gatherings invariably turned to song. There might be a political argument and when it got too heated, some member of the family would say, "Give us a song."

"My mother's voice is magnificent," John McDermott told the *Toronto Star*'s Leslie Scrivener. "Just thinking about her singing can give you goose bumps. I can just see her cupping her hands, standing against the wall, singing."

In the same article, John's mother, Hope McDermott, is quoted: "When you listen to John, you're listening to my husband. Lots of folks say it's his father's voice, really. But we never ever thought a professional singer would come out of these home gatherings."

McDermott has been known to react angrily to critics' accusations that he deliberately manipulates his audience by selecting sentimental material designed to make them emotional. "Ultimately," he told Mitch Potter, "it's a question of taste. Maybe if I were an only child, I would be very cynical of me. The way I interpret songs is in direct relation to the way I grew up among 11 kids and the wonderful family that gave me this music."

Apart from the occasional angry outburst, McDermott has gone his way, turning out album after album, winning award after award. His second album *Old Friends* earned two Juno Awards. It was followed by *Christmas Memories*, which became another platinum hit. Next, in 1995, came *Love Is a Voyage*, which earned him a 1996 nomination for a Juno Award as Male Vocalist of the Year.

He spent the last couple of months of 1997 on a tour, from St. John's, Newfoundland, to Victoria, B.C., with side trips to Washington, D.C., Boston, and Chicago. The next year, almost all his concerts were planned for the United States. "I'm just visiting the neighbours," was the way he described it.

The following year's highlights included John McDermott's Remembrance Tour, presented in conjunction with the War Amps of Canada. Commemorating the 80th anniversary of the 1918 Armistice, his tour began in Halifax and also took him to Saint John, N.B., St. John's, Ottawa, Kingston, Ontario, Hamilton, and Montreal.

"The thing about all these songs," McDermott said, discussing his repertoire, "is that they all fit together so nicely. They push you, to some degree, to memories of the past, some fond, some not so fond. But these are romantic songs, and *When I Grow Too Old to Dream* is a romantic album. And I'm a romantic, sentimental man, and I'm proud of that."

Ian McDougall *b. Calgary, Alberta, June 14, 1938*

"An artist with great technical skill" is how some dictionaries usually define the word "virtuoso." You can also find a few synonyms for it, such as "master" and "expert." All of these are apt ways to describe the distinguished Victoria, B.C.–based trombonist Ian McDougall.

His father, George McDougall, played banjo and guitar in Calgary dance bands in the 1920s. Ian took up the trombone at the age of 11 and it seems as if he never put it down again.

At age 22, he went to England, where, for the next two years, he played with bands led by John Dankworth and Ted Heath – two of England's top orchestra leaders. Upon his return to Canada he settled in Vancouver to become a member of the Vancouver Symphony. He was also a member of the house band at The Cave, playing with Chris Gage and Fraser MacPherson.

After attending the University of British Columbia, he was for a brief time a member of the Woody Herman orchestra. He led various jazz groups in Vancouver. In 1970 he formed the group Pacific Salt, whose ranks also included Oliver Gannon and P. J. Perry.

McDougall moved east to Toronto in 1973 and stayed for a dozen fruitful years. His credentials were such that he was soon established as a first-call musician.

"I came to Toronto for two reasons," he recently told Greg Sutherland of *The Jazz Report*. "One [was] to play with the Boss Brass at Nathan Philips Square. It was kind of a reunion with … Terry Clarke, Don Thompson, Steve Wallace … and, very importantly, Moe Koffman, who has been sick recently. It was really great to see the guys."

It was Rob McConnell, boss of the Boss Brass, who invited McDougall to make the trip east. In addition to the gig at Nathan Philips Square, McConnell asked Ian if he'd like to go to the Montreal Jazz Festival to play with guitarist Jim Hall, that festival's honoree for the year 2000. McDougall couldn't refuse.

Understandably, McDougall loves his instrument. "The trombone is a *vocal* instrument. What better way to explore this quality than by playing songs?" is the way he put it a few years ago on the liner notes of his double-CD titled *Songs & Arias*, as engaging a collection of his gorgeous playing as you are likely to find.

And the title is absolutely perfect. On the first record, Ian plays 11 familiar standard songs by Harold Arlen, Irving Berlin, the Gershwins, Cole Porter, and Jerome Kern, including "Where or When," "If I Loved You," "I Loves You Porgy," "My Heart Stood Still," and the exquisite "All the Things You Are." He is accompanied beautifully by pianist Ron Johnston.

But it is the second record on the CD that really makes you sit up and listen. Again accompanied only by a pianist, Robert Holliston, Ian McDougall plays a dozen operatic arias, most of them familiar. Included are "The Toreador Song" from Bizet's *Carmen*, Rossini's Neapolitan Tarantella "La Danza," plus arias by Puccini, Mascagni, and Donizetti.

Again, there's a standout – Bizet's "Au fond," from *The Pearl Fishers*. What makes it so enjoyable is that this is a duet by McDougall and McDougall. If anything could be better than one McDougall, it's two McDougalls.

Then there is McDougall the composer. Among his works are several written for big band – **The Jazz Suite** (1967), **The Vancouver Suite** (1971), **Pellet Suite** (1976), and **Blue Serge Suite** (1983). The first two works were commissioned by the CBC; the others were written for the Boss Brass. **Pellet**

Suite was recorded by the Boss Brass. He was also commissioned by the Boss Brass and the CJRT Orchestra to write his **Symphonic Suite for Jazz Band and Orchestra** (1984).

Among his other compositions are **Tidelines** (1970), commissioned by the Vancouver Symphony Orchestra, **Minuet for the RCMP** (1979), **Concerto for Clarinet and String Orchestra** (1984), written for and recorded by Stanley McCartney with the CBC Vancouver Orchestra, and **Three Pieces for String Quartet** (1986), composed for and recorded by the Vancouver Chamber Choir.

If Ian McDougall has a beef it is over the lack of respect shown Canadian musicians by jazz festival organizers. "I don't do too many festivals," he told Greg Sutherland, "and although I'm on record with my complaints about the various organizations, I would rather take some action with my colleagues across the country to see what we can do as a collective to make the life of the Canadian jazz musician a little easier, a little nicer, and a little more respectful. Especially when you are on the road – I would like to see Canadian musicians treated with a little more respect and given the credit they deserve."

And who could argue with that?

Kate and Anna McGarrigle

Anna McGarrigle (b. December 4, 1944), Kate McGarrigle (b. February 6, 1946) both at St-Sauveur-des-Monts, Quebec

Randy Saharuni

Family and music. The two have been at the core of Canada's most creative and its most celebrated family duet, the McGarrigles. From their beginnings in a Laurentian Mountains village in the 1950s to their celebrated family get-togethers in-studio and on stage, known as *The McGarrigle Hour*, these two artists have brought laughter, tears, and much entertainment to audiences and family members.

As children in rural Quebec, Kate and Anna enjoyed the warmth of a house full of music. Whenever they weren't part of singsongs drawn from their parents' Irish and French-Canadian heritage, they brought home piano lessons from the nuns who taught them at the village convent. They sang in both French and English, and beyond the piano, they learned to play guitar, banjo, and accordion.

While Anna studied art and Kate took engineering at Montreal universities in the 1960s, they also sang in coffeehouses, principally in the folk group Mountain City Four (with Peter Weldon and Jack Nissenson). Eventually, their own material caught other artists' attention – among the first, in 1972, the Canadian foursome McKendree Spring recorded Anna's **Heart Like a Wheel** (using it as their album title) and in 1974 Linda Ronstadt did the same. The same year, Anna's **Work Song** and Kate's **Cool River** were recorded by Maria Muldaur.

In 1975, Muldaur's producer Greg Prestopino helped sign them with Warner Bros. and the sisters' self-titled debut album was released the same year.

"Here were two intelligent, whimsical and decidedly quirky women, who wrote often witty, often wrenching songs that shot straight for the heart-strings without a hint of cheap hamming," wrote music critic Gil Asakawa.

Following a Montreal concert in 1976, Knight-Ridder reviewer John Lehndorff wrote, "It seemed to me I was hearing truly timeless music, that poetic songs such as **Heart Like a Wheel** would become standards that would resonate a generation later."

Similar reviews followed the McGarrigles through the 1970s in the United States, Canada, Ireland, Belgium, Holland, and Britain, where *Melody Maker* magazine called their music "a holy marriage of strong sentiment and brilliant pure singing. … Anna's lilting and airy, Kate's deeper and fiercer – these are amongst the very best voices to be heard in popular music today."

Albums continued to flow – *Dancer With Bruised Knees* (1976), *Pronto Monto* (1978), *French Record* (1982), *Love Over and Over* (1982), and *Heartbeats Accelerating* (1990). The latter was considered a "comeback" recording, since several cuts were successfully marketed as singles, including a version of the title track which became a hit for Linda Ronstadt in 1994.

The McGarrigles' continuing popularity with other artists reflected a widening circle of audiences and artists with like tastes in music. They appeared on Ashley Hutchings and the Albion Band's *Rise up Like the Sun* (1978); the Chieftains' album *The Bells of Dublin* (1991); Richard and Linda Thompson's *Sunnyvista* (1992); Emmylou Harris' *Wrecking Ball* (1995) singing **Goin' Back to Harlan**; Joan Baez' CD *Ring Them Bells* (1995) singing **Willie More**; and Gilles Vigneault's single "Charlie Jos."

On stage, the sisters have headlined the Newport Folk Festival, appeared on Garrison Keillor's National Public Radio show *Prairie Home Companion*, participated in the Harry Smith Project (a concert series celebrating the American artist's film and music collection), and starred in Canada Day celebrations in Toronto. Elsewhere on television, they have guested on *Saturday Night Live*, *The Late Show with David Letterman*, a PBS fundraiser (*Songs of the Civil War*), and costarred on a PBS special with Linda Ronstadt and Maria Muldaur.

In 1994, Anna and Kate McGarrigle were inducted into the Order of Canada.

They have also won two Juno Awards, in both the Best Roots and the Traditional Album category, for *The McGarrigle Hour* and *Matapedia*.

Perhaps the most gratifying of their creative achievements was their studio recording, *The McGarrigle Hour* (1998). The session assembled the McGarrigle sisters with "honorary McGarrigles" Linda Ronstadt and Emmylou Harris, Loudon Wainwright III (formerly Kate's husband), Kate's son Rufus Wainwright, daughter Martha Wainwright, and some old Montreal musical friends – Chaim Tannenbaum, Joel Zifkin, and Michel Pepin. The gathering of friends and family worked its way through material as diverse as Cole Porter's "Allez-vous en" and the 1960s drug anthem "Green Green Rocky Road" and included McGarrigle favourites **Mendocino**, **NACL**, and **Cool River**.

"*The McGarrigle Hour* started off as a tribute to Gaby [the McGarrigles' mother]," Kate McGarrigle told the *Globe and Mail* in 1998, "but it almost immediately turned into a summoning of the family."

The studio performance was repeated on video during a concert at the Monument National Theatre in Montreal and then aired on television in Canada and the United States.

Cliff McKay

b. Seaforth, Ontario, 1908; d. 1987

If ever a musician lived a double life, it was certainly Cliff McKay. The clarinetist was long regarded as one of the best jazz players on his instrument. He worked with such noted Canadian jazzmen as Trump Davidson, Jimmy Reynolds, and Rex Battle.

Critic Peter Goddard remarked that McKay, whether playing clarinet or soprano, "develops a warm, round tone which is used with little fuss and few frills. He seems to avoid complexity as much as may other players develop it."

Cliff McKay, whose father was a fiddler, started studying piano at the age of 10 and began playing saxophone when he was 15. He moved to Toronto in 1926 to work with Harry Rich's orchestra, who were billed as the "Versatile Canadians." The band played at the Palais Royale on Toronto's lakeshore. Cornetist Morris London received featured billing, but he didn't exactly steal the show: McKay, then still a teenager, was attracting attention, too.

"I started playing and listening to jazz in Guelph [Ontario] when I was only 14," he told jazz historian Mark Miller, many years later. "First I listened to

Cliff McKay on Holiday Ranch

Phil Napolean, then Joe Venuti, and then Miff Mole. A bunch of us formed a band in high school. But a rather strict bandmaster wanted us to change things, so we went professional, playing at a local YMCA on Saturday afternoons. I finally got a job with a bigger band in Galt. My grandfather even bought me a little Ford roadster to get around in and I thought I had made the big time. I made five dollars a night, three nights a week."

When he joined the Versatile Canadians, he was paid $100 a week and stayed with that band through an engagement at the Hotel St. Charles in Winnipeg during the winter of 1928–29, but he left the band by next fall. After playing in Joe DeCourcy's dance band in Ottawa and leading his own orchestra at the Seigniory Club in Montebello, Quebec, he returned to Toronto, working in radio, theatre, and hotel orchestras under Percy Faith, Horace Lapp, and others.

But McKay's broadcasting work – and his other "identity" – still lay in the future. He was a soloist on CBC Radio's *The Happy Gang* from 1941 to 1952, and he also performed on *Starlight Moods* for four of those years.

Then, in 1952, he was music director and host of CBC Television's weekly show *Holiday Ranch*. Almost overnight, his standing as a jazz clarinetist was forgotten – replaced by the folksy image required for the country and western milieu of *Holiday Ranch*. But it was on this show – whose type of music was anathema to jazz buffs – that Cliff McKay reached a far bigger audience. He stayed with this program for six years, during which he attracted hundreds of thousands of country music fans who had never heard him play jazz clarinet.

His duties as the show's host naturally involved considerable talking, which Cliff did quite capably, despite a lifelong lisp that *Holiday Ranch* fans apparently didn't even notice, or at least did not heed. McKay's standard closing on the Saturday evening show was: "Remember, wherever you are, tomorrow is Sunday." Due to his lisp, his last two words came out: "ith Thunday."

Bernie Orenstein, a writer and friend of McKay's, commented: "One thing about Cliff McKay – he always calls a spade a thpade."

Despite the continued success of *Holiday Ranch*, McKay was not ready to sacrifice his jazz heritage lightly. He was heard frequently as a soloist on CBC Radio's *Jazz Unlimited* and other shows. In 1958, with several Toronto jazzmen, including Hagood Hardy, he made a jazz LP titled ***The Other Side of Cliff McKay***.

In 1959, he returned briefly to *The Happy Gang*, but this was that program's last year on radio after 22 years on the air. After that, he led orchestras and small groups in Toronto nightclubs. In the late 1960s, he played Grandpa Schnitzel on the CHCH-TV [Hamilton, Ontario] children's program *Schnitzel-House*. With his options somewhat limited, McKay began teaching music in different Toronto separate schools, which he did for many years.

In 1978, Cliff's [old] sidekick, Trump Davidson, died. Harvey Silver, Trump's pianist, took over the band, renaming it the Harvey Silver Dixieland Band. In 1980, that band played a two-week gig at a Toronto club called the Chick'n Deli. In the band for those two weeks were two veteran musicians and friends – Jimmy Reynolds and Cliff McKay. By this time, Cliff was in his early seventies and had only recently returned to performing after his years of teaching music in high schools.

"You can call it a comeback," he quipped to writer David Lancashire, "but I call it a resurrection."

In March 1987, while motoring through Yugoslavia, Cliff McKay was killed in an automobile accident.

Perhaps it was because so many television viewers had that *Holiday Ranch* image of him that Cliff McKay titled his album ***The Other Side of Cliff McKay*** – to remind us of what a skilled jazz musician he was.

McKenna Mendelson Mainline

formed 1968 in Toronto: Mike McKenna (b. Toronto, April 15, 1946) vocals, guitar; Joe Mendelson (b. Toronto, July 30, 1944) vocals, harmonica, piano, slide guitar (replaced by Rick James); Timothy O'Leary bass (replaced by Denny Gerrard, replaced by Michael Harrison (b. Brampton, Ont., November 15, 1949), replaced by Frank "Zeke" Sheppard); Tony Nolasco (b. Sudbury, Ont., July 9, 1950), drums

McKenna Mendelson Mainline (l. to r.) Tony Nolasco, Joe Mendelson, Mike Harrison, Mike McKenna

Perhaps it is illustrative of the Toronto music scene of the late 1960s that this rock 'n' roll band began as a result of an advertisement in a newspaper. Mike McKenna – a quiet, unassuming guitar player (formerly with the group Luke and the Apostles and later The Ugly Ducklings) – placed the ad. Joe Mendelson – a brash and gifted slide guitarist and singer – answered it. In that instant, one of the original, hard-driving, but short-lived blues bands got its start in Toronto.

Its co-founders might have sensed the bumpy road ahead when it took most of the first summer for McKenna and Mendelson to find a bass player who would fit in. For a first recording, in 1968, they settled on Denny Gerrard (formerly of The Paupers), whom Mendelson called "a genius." Typically of those early days in the rock music business, however, the band recorded a demonstration tape that strangely disappeared only to resurface a couple of years later as a bootleg album. Even today it exists as a CD – *McKenna Mendelson Blues* – and the original band doesn't make a penny in royalties.

For the next six months McKenna Mendelson played blues clubs in England, built up a faithful following, and (in the spring of 1969) recorded a new album, *Stink*. "Our album *Stink* broke big in New York and Chicago," McKenna said years later. "At the time, there was some talk of touring with the Allman Brothers [blues band]. We had no idea how popular we were. But we were from Toronto, Canada. Nobody really cared. If somebody had just slapped us, we would have realized. We had a chance to be huge."

It was the relentless touring around Britain, however, and coping with a small equipment truck and even smaller gate receipts, that nearly drove the band members out of the business. One night, Mendelson, who was a bearded, imposing motorcycle enthusiast, travelled home with the pub owner to make sure the band got paid for its performance.

Back in Canada within a year, the band rode *Stink* (which sold over 30,000 copies) and a single, **Better Watch Out**, to a Top 10 hit. McKenna Mendelson Mainline, as they began to promote themselves, became one of the most successful concert groups in Ontario. In fact, at the time, rock journalist Ritchie Yorke reported, "the group could command higher gig prices than almost any other Canadian band (upwards of $2,500 a night) without the obvious benefit of U.S. success." Yorke went on to say that when Mainline

Night Owl '68. "Though the photo does not show the face of the drummer Tony Nolasco, the energy of the performers appears intense (we were always intense)." — *Mendelson Joe*

toured Australia with Frijid Pink in 1970, "the Pink had a lot of trouble following Mainline."

"Our music is like nothing you've ever heard," Mendelson said at the time. "[It] covers a lot of ground. It has evolved into something very political and very weird." Mendelson had been strongly influenced by Little Richard, Jimmy Reed, and Elvis Presley. But they were never as daring as Mendelson's band would be.

In 1972, Mainline staged a concert at the Victory Theatre, a strip club west of Toronto's downtown. The concept was simple enough. The band played its music and the strippers took off their clothes to it – it was a wild combination of electric blues and old school vaudevillian burlesque entertainment as the strippers strutted their stuff in (and out of) costume.

"One girl came as a nurse," Mendelson told author Nadia Haim in their book *Alien*. "She rode a little tricycle out on the stage. There was one woman (I made her a leather S & M kind of costume) and she performed to the motorcycle song. The star of the Bump 'n' Grind Revue was known as Mother Superior, so she had a nun routine."

The revue attracted a lot of attention in Toronto at the time. TVO, the provincially run educational network, sent comedian Michael McGee and a video crew to the Victory Theatre as part of a television show called *Mean Business*. Meanwhile, Mendelson had convinced the owner of CITY-TV and

Thunder Sound, Moses Znaimer, to take the only 16-track recording console in Canada from his Thunder Sound recording studio and set it up at the Victory. The recording of the show became the band's fourth album, *The Mainline Bump 'n' Grind Revue – Live at the Victory Theatre*, but not before the police raided the theatre because one of the strippers was simulating sex with a stuffed beaver.

"I thought it was the most interesting eclectic show you could ever go to in your life," said dyed-in-the-wool Mendelson fan, Stan Joskowitz. "It was a historical event in Toronto."

Personality differences drove the band apart after that. Later in 1972, Joe Mendelson recorded his first solo album, *Mr. Middle of the Road*, and Mainline only appeared in a kind of reunion format from time to time, including a *Bump 'n' Grind Revue Two* at the Victory, on New Year's Eve 1975. That year Mendelson recorded another solo album, *Sophisto*, and a reunion album with McKenna called *No Substitute*. But that was the end of the musical association between the two.

That same year, 1975, Joe Mendelson changed his name to Mendelson Joe and began painting and exhibiting, as well as playing the blues. He recorded albums for Stompin' Tom's Boot Records label with such titles as *Not Homogenized*, *Jack Frost*, and *Let's Party*. But by the 1980s, Mendelson Joe was recording for a variety of labels; he recorded *The Name of the Game Ain't Schmaltz*, *Born to Cuddle* (with the Shuffle Demons), and *Addicted*.

Like a Frank Zappa, or, as he himself suggests, a Captain Beefheart character, Mendelson Joe communicated his criticism of the world's politics, pollution, greed, and racism on canvas and in his music. His next album titles reflected that attitude: *Women Are the Only Hope*, *Humans Bug Me*, *Spoiled Bratland*, and *Everyone Needs a Pimp*. Rightly, Mendelson Joe fits no category, and even denies being "cast as a blues guy. ... It's not that I have any disrespect for blues musicians ... the thing is I'm not from Chicago. I'm not black."

Post-Mainline, Tony Nolasco got together with Mike McKenna briefly in a group called Diamondback (which had a single hit, **Just My Way of Loving You**, in 1974). McKenna never stopped playing blues and rock 'n' roll, appearing with the Downchild Blues Band, Diamondback, and even the Guess Who. In 1997, McKenna rejoined bass player Denny Gerrard (who, in the interim, had played with Jericho and Great White Cane) and sax player Ron Jacobs (who had played with Downchild, David Clayton-Thomas, and Kelly Jay) to form Mike McKenna and Slidewinder, who released a self-titled CD that year.

Loreena McKennitt

b. Morden, Manitoba, February 17, 1957

Richard Haughton

Just as landlocked-plains people often have a better sense of the open sea than Maritimers, so an artist from the middle of the Canadian Prairies, while not directly linked to Celtic culture, can relate to its traditions and voices. So it has been for Loreena McKennitt, born on the Prairies, but today recognized as one of the world's greatest interpreters of Celtic music.

"Although my family's ancestors for the most part came from Ireland," McKennitt said in 1997, "there was very little overt Celticness to my upbringing in the sense of music or storytelling."

Growing up in rural Manitoba, Loreena was nonetheless exposed to a mosaic of cultures, ranging from Scottish and Irish to German and Icelandic immigrant traditions. That cultural diversity is illustrated if only by the names of her earliest music teachers – Olga Friesen her piano teacher and Elma Gislason her voice instructor. Her one overt connection to Celtic culture was her passion for highland dancing.

In the 1970s, she moved from rural Manitoba to Winnipeg and discovered folk music at a city club near the girls' school she attended. Even though she "dreamed of becoming a veterinarian" and studied the science for a time, she began singing traditional folk ballads and discovered the music of Celtic harpist Alan Stivell, in particular his recording of "The Celtic Harp Renaissance." Eventually, she bought a second-hand harp to incorporate into her performances.

McKennitt's fascination for the lyric poetry of William Butler Yeats and for the Celtic music of Stivell, Planxty, and the Bothy Band drew her to Ireland in 1982. When she returned home (by that time Stratford, Ontario), she had composed a musical interpretation of Yeats' poem "The Stolen Child." She had also read a book by Diane Rapaport called *How to Make Your Own Recordings*, and by 1985 had incorporated her own record company, Quinland Road, and recorded **Elemental**, an independent cassette containing nine songs. Wherever she busked, McKennitt brought along a trunk full of cassettes to offer curious fans.

"I think coming from a farming and rural background gave me the insight into being self-sufficient," McKennitt said. "You become familiar with creative problem-solving. If you want something badly enough you'll roll up your sleeves and start chipping away."

As "new age" music grew to become a commercial force in the music industry, so Loreena McKennitt's soaring voice and ability to turn traditional folk songs into angelic hymns proved popular and marketable. In the mid-to-late-1980s she also found work scoring movie soundtracks – *Boyo* (1985), *Heaven on Earth* (1986), and the National Film Board documentary series *Women and Spirituality*.

Back into recording mode, McKennitt assembled an album of Christmas carols, **To Drive the Cold Winter Away** (1987), recorded on location at a church in Canada and at an artists' retreat and a monastery in Ireland. Another recording, **Parallel Dreams** (1989), integrated native and Celtic musical roots and included a piece called **Breaking the Silence**, which was written for Amnesty International.

In 1991, McKennitt's wanderlust took her to Italy, where she encountered an exhibition of international Celtic artifacts. It proved to be a turning point in her creative career.

"Until I went to that exhibition, I thought that Celts were people who came from Ireland, Scotland, Wales, and Brittany," McKennitt said after seeing Celtic art from Asia Minor, Spain, Ukraine, and Hungary. "I felt exhilarated. It was like thinking that all there was to your family are your parents, brothers, and sisters, and then you realize there's a whole stretch of history that is an extension of who you are."

The resulting recording **The Visit** (1991) began with the drone of a primeval-sounding tamboura and proceeded into musical interpretations of William Shakespeare, Alfred Lord Tennyson, and a distinctive treatment of the ballad "Greensleeves." Once again, McKennitt's word-of-mouth popularity attracted crowds, and sales from the trunk of her car hit 50,000. That's when Warner Music noticed, signed her, reissued **The Visit** (1992), and saw the recording go gold in Canada and the United States. The album also earned McKennitt her first Juno Award for Best Roots/Traditional Album.

For the next album, **The Mask and Mirror** (1994), McKennitt explored the Celtic traditions of 15th-century Spain and its exposure to the cultures of Judaism, Christianity, and Islam. It sold more than a million copies worldwide and garnered McKennitt a repeat Juno for Best Roots/Traditional Album. The extraordinary fan growth and sales momentum continued with **The Book of Secrets** (1997). The music, conceived while she travelled aboard the Trans-Siberian Express, reflected more of McKennitt's interpretations of poetry, her narratives of history, and her interest in epic journeys.

"The actual process of recording **The Book of Secrets** took place over a year at Real World Studios in England ... Peter Gabriel's wonderful, rural residential recording facility," McKennitt said, "which feels at times like a cross between a commune and a kibbutz ... with access to a rather eclectic assembly of instruments and players."

The album sold more than four million copies worldwide. It spawned **The Mummers' Dance**, a single that climbed to the *Billboard* Top 20 and became an MTV video hit as well. The album also topped the *Billboard* World Music chart and became the chart's most successful crossover album ever. It debuted at number one in Greece and Turkey, number three in Canada, and reached the Top 10 in Italy, New Zealand, and Germany and the Top 20 in the United States, Spain, and France.

In 1999, McKennitt released a two-CD set recording *Live in Paris and Toronto* featuring sessions recorded at the Salle Pleyel and Massey Hall. McKennitt assigned proceeds of the album to a memorial fund for water search and safety, a Canadian-based agency founded by the artist and the families of Ronald and Richard Rees and Greg Cook after all three men perished in a boating accident on Georgian Bay in 1998.

Not only has McKennitt sold more than 10 million albums; her work has also been in demand for movie and television productions. She has composed for, or had songs featured in, such Hollywood movies as *Jade*, *Highlander III*, *The Holy Man*, *Soldier*, and *The Santa Clause*, and such TV series as *Northern Exposure*, *Due South*, and *Boston Public*. Then, after a 17-year absence from the Stratford Festival stage (in 1984 she appeared in *Two Gentlemen of Verona*), McKennitt agreed to score music for the 2001 production of *The Merchant of Venice*.

"I feel extraordinarily lucky," McKennitt has said, "to be able to marry the vehicle of my talents with the fuel of my curiosity and imagination."

Catherine McKinnon

b. Saint John, New Brunswick, May 14, 1944

When she began her career, Catherine McKinnon was perfectly at ease covering songs on coffeehouse stages. As she and the music moved on, she was equally comfortable on a musical theatre stage, out on a hotel nightclub floor, in a television studio, and in front of a symphony orchestra, covering songs in every musical genre.

"I interpret songs," she once told Melinda McCracken of *The Globe and Mail*. "That's all I can do, sing the beautiful things other people have said, change it enough to make it mine, but keep the beauty the author intended."

Catherine's interpretation of songs began early – at age eight on radio in Saint John and when she was 12, on television in London, Ontario. (Her father was a career soldier, so Catherine, her sister Patrician Anne, and her brother René grew up in the neighbourhood of military bases in the Maritimes, Ontario, and the north.)

"My singing career actually began on the way to the bathroom," she told Noah James in the *Star* magazine. "I was in Grade 1, and on the way to the little girls' room I was singing a song. When I returned to class, my teacher asked me if I'd repeat the song for my classmates. I did. She then asked me if I'd sing it for the other kids and she ended up taking me from classroom to classroom with me singing 'I've Got a Lovely Bunch of Coconuts.'"

Catherine studied music at the Mount St. Vincent College in Halifax, where, in 1963, she joined the TV show *Singalong Jubilee*, the summer replacement for *Don Messer's Jubilee*. Three years later she became a regular on the year-round show, shooting 40 television programs each season and appearing in summer concert tours every year through 1966.

During that time, she recorded several albums – *Voice of an Angel I* (1964), *Voice of an Angel II* (1965), and *The Catherine McKinnon Christmas Album* (1966) – the first of which sold 175,000 copies and made her the best-selling female recording artist in Canada at the time. Arc Records also released her cover version of Buffy Sainte-Marie's "Until It's Time for You to Go," which became a hit single in Canada.

In the summer of 1966, her obligations to *Don Messer's Jubilee* took McKinnon to Prince Edward Island. In Charlottetown, she met actor/writer/comedian Don Harron, who was there for the production of *Anne of Green Gables* (his script). That year, Harron had also written music and skits for the annual production of *Spring Thaw*, a revue of topical and satirical songs, dances, and skits on Canadian subjects. Harron invited McKinnon to join the cast in Toronto.

So she left the Maritimes (reportedly turning down $35,000 worth of concert touring) and prepared for a 40-date, cross-Canada tour of *Spring Thaw*, but not before making a quick flight to Cyprus as part of a Canadian contingent to entertain U.N. troops in the Middle East. She and Harron were married in the spring of 1969, not surprisingly between the matinee and an evening performance of *Measure for Measure* on the road in Chicago.

"We wouldn't have seen each other for months otherwise," McKinnon said, "because Donald left the next day for London. So we had our honeymoon on the phone."

Having made the move to Toronto to further her acting interests, McKinnon quickly acclimatized her career to the surroundings. Before long she was singing folk material in Yorkville coffeehouses and then starring on CTV's show *River Inn* (1968–69) and that network's *Catherine McKinnon Show* (1970–71).

Neither the folk clubs nor television shows seemed enough. During the fall and winter of 1969–70, for example, Catherine McKinnon was the headline act at The Riverboat, the featured soloist (performing Debussy and Fauré) with the Saskatoon Symphony Orchestra, and the attraction at both the Queen Elizabeth Hotel in Montreal and the Royal York Hotel in Toronto. Though he disliked the idea of her shifting to nightclub singing, critic Blaik Kirby, reviewing McKinnon's appearance at the (Royal York's) Imperial Room, called her "a thoroughly-schooled pop singer."

"The first time I played the Imperial Room," McKinnon said, "I told the conductor midstream that I was going to incorporate folk material into my act. 'You'll die out there,' he warned me. The next night they asked me to add even more."

In the 1970s, McKinnon broadened her scope yet again, when she co-hosted Global Television's variety show *Everything Goes*. The show required that she take on the role of interviewer as well as performer of some 12 to 16 new songs every week (180 songs over the three-month run of the show). That year she was taping two editions of the variety show every Monday, Tuesday, and Wednesday in Toronto, then flying to Ottawa to tape the satirical TV show *Shh! It's the News*, and then back to Toronto to record a TV quiz show, *What's His Name*, with Don Harron and publisher Jack McClelland guessing the identity of famous Canadians.

In the midst of her breakneck appearance schedule onstage, in concert, and on television during the succeeding years, McKinnon found time to record several more albums for Arc Records – **Both Sides Now** (1968), **Everybody's Talkin'** (1969), **Catherine McKinnon** (1980) with the Jimmy Dale orchestra, **Explosive** (1980), **Patrician Anne** (1984), and a second Christmas album in 1992.

Since 1997, she has owned and operated a restaurant, Catherine McKinnon's Spot o' Tea in Stanley Bridge, Prince Edward Island. Two years later, next to the restaurant she built what she called "a theatre barn," in which she has performed each year in the summer months.

Among her proudest moments as a singer/performer came in 1989, when she played the role of Marg Osborne in John Gray's musical history, *Don Messer's Jubilee*. News of Osborne's death (in 1977) had hit McKinnon hard, so she felt honoured to be part of the commemorative show. It also marked a temporary return to the music she had learned to interpret first in her career.

"It was truly Canadian," she told the *Toronto Star*, "based in the traditional folk and country music of this country."

Sarah McLachlan

b. Halifax, Nova Scotia, January 28, 1968

Courtesy Canapress

They said it couldn't be done. Promoters said a bill with just women on it wouldn't sell. Radio programmers, conditioned never to air two female vocalists back to back, cringed. Media dismissed it as Chickapalooza or Girliepalooza. Nevertheless, Lilith Fair succeeded, not just once when it premiered in 1997, but three summers in a row. It succeeded artistically, bringing to the stage recognized and emerging women singer-songwriters. It succeeded financially, since the three tours netted US$60 million.

"I wanted to try and break that attitude down," Sarah McLachlan said in Lynne Stopkewich's documentary, *Lilith on Top*, "to show that it's not just about women. It's about music and if it's good music … it should prevail."

And prevail she has, despite numerous obstacles, man-made or otherwise.

According to biographer Judith Fitzgerald (in *Building a Mystery*), Sarah was born to Judy Kaines James, a Newfoundland art student attending college in Halifax. Adopted there, by Jack and Dorice McLachlan, Sarah fell in love with music at age four. Unable to hold a full-sized guitar à la Joan Baez, she transposed the notes to a more manageable ukulele. Despite being picked on at school, Sarah excelled in music, winning scholarship and festival prizes both singing and playing guitar or piano. She listened to Baez and Cat Stevens, but then as a teen to new-wavers Kate Bush and the Cocteau Twins.

In the early 1980s, she developed her talents, academically by attending the Maritime Conservatory of Music and practically by playing with a band called October Game that regularly played student clubs and pubs. One night, after a concert at the Dalhousie Student Union building, where Sarah and the band played warmup for another band, two Nettwerk Records owners – Terry McBride and Mark Jowett – invited her to sign a contract. It took two years of convincing, but in 1987 she signed with the Vancouver-based company and then relocated to British Columbia to begin assembling material for a first album. Brought in to assist were After All keyboard player Darren Phillips and ex-54-40 drummer Darryl Neudorf.

"I was really lazy … for the first little while," she told Chris Dafoe of the *Globe and Mail*. "When I tried to write, I kept writing songs with too many notes. … I guess I was trying to cram everything into one song."

Her debut album *Touch* was released in 1989. Reviewers made references to the "mystical waif with the angelic voice." They also compared her to one of her influences, Kate Bush, but *Billboard* predicted critical success and good sales (it would go gold in Canada within two years). Chicago critic Joshua

Zarov wrote of "her stunning, dramatic vocals that tiptoe between her normal range, a throaty push and a soprano falsetto … a unique sound that's allowed McLachlan to stand apart from scores of female singers."

McLachlan immediately hit the road to tour Canada (including a successful homecoming in Halifax) and then dates in Europe. By that time, Nettwerk Records had hooked up with Arista/BMG for eight record releases in the United States.

Concurrently with her second album **Solace**, in 1991, McLachlan also released a video for the single **The Path of Thorns (Terms)** during which she shed her clothes, and that turned many heads. However, the strength of the album – its poetry and music – came about partly because of an additional ingredient, Pierre Marchand (who had produced Kate and Anna McGarrigle's *Heartbeats Accelerating*). He encouraged McLachlan to sing more conversationally and less oratorically. It worked. By the time she had earned two Juno nominations, **Solace** had sold 200,000 copies.

In 1993, McLachlan created her third album, *Fumbling Towards Ecstasy*, "as a metaphor for life," she told the *Calgary Herald*, "because we're continually making mistakes, but we're also always striving for that ecstasy." It debuted in the United States at number one on the *Billboard* Heat-Seekers Chart and within two years had sold 1.5 million copies. In addition, a video representation of her single **Possession** caught people's attention. Based on her experience of being stalked by fans, McLachlan is depicted both as a strong woman and conversely as the victim of a rapist's attack.

Her sense of vulnerability heightened the next year when a fan attacked her via the Internet with accusations that she had used his letters for the lyrics of **Possession** (in 1997 the man was found dead apparently having committed suicide). At the same time, members of her former band – Darryl Neudorf and Jeff Sawatzky – filed a suit claiming they had contributed to four songs on her album *Touch* without credit or royalty (in 1999 their claim was dismissed).

During the same period, McLachlan released the CDs *The Freedom Sessions* and *Surfacing* but not with nearly the same groundswell of fan response. McLachlan needed a hit.

It was on the road in 1996 that, as biographer Fitzgerald notes in her book *Building a Mystery*, McLachlan conceived the idea of an all-woman concert "in an effort to right the wrongs of women's place in the testosterone-based world of rock and pop." As an experiment that June in Detroit, McLachlan booked a concert featuring Lisa Loeb, Paula Cole, Aimee Mann, and, one of her heroes, Patti Smith. The experiment was repeated in California, where the name "Lilith Fair" first appeared. By August, the *L.A. Times* reported her plan to unveil Lilith Fair in Vancouver the next year.

Despite criticism that Lilith was a political statement, a feminist platform excluding men, McLachlan saw Lilith (the first independent woman, Adam's first wife) as a family affair. The 1997 concert tour ran from July 5 at the George Amphitheater in Washington state to the Thunderbird Stadium in Vancouver on August 24. It consisted of 35 concert dates and included 50 artists – a who's who of women performers. In hot pursuit were the media. *Rolling Stone* referred to it as "Vulvapolooza." *Ottawa Sun* reporter Ben Rayner tired of the event and "the newly potent grrl-power [McLachlan's] brainchild supposedly unleashed across the land." Elsewhere – *Time, Elle, Maclean's,* and *People* – there appeared glowing quotes from audiences and participants, such as Emily Saliers, who said McLachlan's "spirit and sensibility are inspiring."

Lynne Stopkewich, the director of the documentary *Lilith on Top,* shot 400 hours of Lilith Fair footage. The film catches McLachlan (back to the camera) flashing her breasts to co-performer Chrissie Hynde to prove she could be a bad girl. Said Stopkewich, however, "I was waiting for some rock-star tantrums, or some ego battles ... but there were no cat fights, no crazy gossip, no dirt."

Through three summers, Lilith was one of the largest-grossing tours of the 1990s – it generated US$60 million. Tour proceeds raised $2 million for women-related charities. It spawned a double CD set *Lilith Fair: A Celebration of Women in Music.* And while it left its creator drained for a time, Sarah McLachlan soon released a new album *Mirrorball,* a kind of greatest-hits package from her 1998 tour, including such songs as **Angel, Building a Mystery, Adia, Possession,** and her first single **I Will Remember You**.

With four Juno Awards, two Grammy Awards, the Order of Canada, and even a cookbook to her credit, said Sarah McLachlan's biographer Fitzgerald, "the high-profile Goddess of All Things Grrlish [has] clearly earned her bragging rights."

Murray McLauchlan

b. Paisley, Scotland, June 30, 1948

Whether in a concert hall, on a radio or television show, or in conversation on the street, Murray McLauchlan has a knack for telling stories. Most come from being there. They generally include a patented McLauchlan twist. And they always leave a lasting impression. He once described climbing a mountain near

Banff. Some distance up the mountain he spotted a sign prohibiting passage without a permit.

"I figured, 'Hey, this mountain's been here 10 million years and some mother's put up a sign saying I can't go up the mountain.' So I wrote a song."

That's tended to be Murray McLauchlan's reaction to much of what he's experienced. The people, places, and events he's encountered (most often in Canada) have made their way into his music much the way painters' mind's-eye images make their way to canvas.

McLauchlan's first artistic exploration was, in fact, painting. After the family emigrated from Scotland to north Toronto, in 1953, he showed an aptitude for art, sketching everything from aircraft to nudes to derelict ferryboats on the Toronto Islands. Beginning in 1962, he attended Central Technical Institute and studied with Bob Ross and Doris McCarthy. At the same time (having heard Bob Dylan recordings on radio), he developed a fascination for the guitar, the harmonica, and singing. Hanging out at the Bohemian Embassy, he met singer-guitarist Jim McCarthy, from whom he learned the Merle Travis picking style. He first sang professionally (admitting he was "as nervous as a cat") at a small Yorkville club called Rive Gauche (Left Bank) in 1965. Feeling the urge to be "a rebellious and iconoclastic young folk poet" he finished art school and left home to cross the country. He later wrote about the parting in **Child's Song**.

When he returned McLauchlan pursued his music more seriously – playing at folk clubs in Stratford, Hamilton, Ottawa, Montreal, and Toronto. He married Patty Sockwell in 1967 and began performing at the Mariposa Folk Festival (he even designed its posters), first appearing on the main stage in 1968. That Mariposa, he met Tom Rush, who promised to record McLauchlan's **Child's Song** and **Old Man's Song**. McLauchlan says it was a crucial break.

After an unsuccessful stint in New York, in 1970 McLauchlan signed with Toronto manager Bernie Finkelstein (and his new label, True North Records) and was invited by Bernie Fiedler to perform at his premiere Yorkville club, the Riverboat. The next year, McLauchlan recorded his debut album *Song From the Street*, which received favourable reviews and plenty of airplay on FM stations.

"The FM jocks would just drop on a whole side of one of my new records," McLauchlan wrote in his autobiography, *Getting Out of Here Alive*. "It would be up there along with Jethro Tull or The Band and ... damned if people didn't come to the conclusion that it was important!"

McLauchlan's appeal proved to be much wider than FM playlists, when in 1973, country radio stations began playing his **Farmer's Song**. It sold 70,000 45s and earned him three RPM Gold Leaf (predecessor to the Juno) Awards – for best country single, best folk single, and composer of the year. Again, Tom Rush picked up on it and it became an entrée to many more American clubs and folk festivals; Neil Young hired him to open during his Tonight's the Night tour. Also that year, McLauchlan recorded his album *Day to Day Dust* with backup musicians Amos Garrett and Dennis Pendrith, who regularly played bass for McLauchlan and his friend Bruce Cockburn. The success on FM and AM continued, in 1974, with the release of *Sweeping the Spotlight Away* and its hit singles **Linda Won't You Take Me In**, **Shoeshine Working Song**, and **Down by the Henry Moore**.

The year 1976 was a watershed. McLauchlan formed a country rock fusion band, the Silver Tractors (named by his bass player in keeping with the original name of the Beatles – the Silver Beatles) with Gene Martynec (guitar), Ben Mink (violin), Jorn Andersen (drums), and Pendrith (bass). In addition to their first album *Boulevard*, McLauchlan and the Silver Tractors appeared at the largest venue to date, Maple Leaf Gardens for the (Gordon-Lightfoot-initiated) Olympic benefit that raised $100,000 for Canada's athletes. That year, McLauchlan also started taking flying lessons.

While it began upbeat, his 1977 tour to promote his album *Hard Rock Town* was disastrous. However, McLauchlan rebounded with *Greatest Hits* in 1978 and in 1979 *Whispering Rain*, whose title track included background vocals (à la "The Wayward Wind") recorded by Elvis Presley's backup group the Jordanaires in Nashville. He returned to touring, this time (because he was licensed) flying from gig to gig. Carole Pope did backup vocals in 1980 on *Into a Mystery*, and, perhaps more importantly, producing his 1981 album *Storm Warning* was Bob Ezrin (who had just coproduced Pink Floyd's album *The Wall*). While the album was not as successful as others, its song **If the Wind Could Blow My Troubles Away** became the theme song for the 1981 International Year of Disabled Persons. And he continued to win Junos as best male country singer in the 1970s and 1980s.

"That was the end of my being a force to reckon with," McLauchlan wrote in his autobiography. Other music industry forces – a new British invasion, Punk, and New Wave music – effectively ended his 10-year run and "the era of the singer-songwriter in the sense of what that used to mean was over."

That didn't mean Murray McLauchlan's career was over, not by a long shot. In the 1980s he reinvented himself. Among the ingredients in his change of focus were the stories he began to weave into his songs; they were about events, characters, and places he'd experienced; they were about Canada. His song **Out Past the Timberline** yielded the idea of travelling by float plane and documenting the stories of Canadians. First on a CBC Radio series, then on television as *Floating over Canada*, McLauchlan the storyteller took audiences to Muskoka with Gordon Lightfoot, Montreal with Edith Butler, Yellowknife with Max Ward, etc.

In 1988 he switched from Bernie Finkelstein's True North to Capitol Records and released *Swinging on a Star*, on which he tackled such social issues as racism, domestic violence, and environmental destruction; proceeds from the song **Let the Good Guys Win** (with Paul Hyde and Tom Cochrane) go to the United Nations for reforestation projects and feeding children. The album title was also used as the title of a CBC Radio show, in which he interviewed, sang with, and promoted other Canadian performers.

In 1996, Murray McLauchlan put down his guitar, gave up touring, started painting again, wrote his autobiography, appeared for a time on a TV talk show, and began spending time with his wife (record company executive and former MuchMusic chief Denise Donlon) and their son. In 2000, when taking a physical for renewing his pilot's licence, doctors found a blood clot and conducted an emergency angioplasty. In the spring of 2001, however, he began rehearsing for yet another concert tour (exactly 30 years after a similar tour) with the Everly Brothers – on stage alone performing his (now well-known) song stories, just the way he started.

But "the pressure's off. I'm no longer goal driven," he told Greg Quill of the *Toronto Star* at the start of the tour. "This is not about fame and glory. Hokey as it sounds it's about art, the imagination, giving life to ideas."

Cy McLean

b. Sydney, N.S., 1916; d. 1986

Perhaps inadvertently, Cy McLean was something of a revolutionary figure in the evolution of jazz music in Canada. He was a black man at a time when blacks were excluded from membership in the Toronto Musicians' Protective Association. Walter Murdoch, the imperious president of the musicians' union, ruled: "Niggers are not allowed here."

McLean had started his musical education – first on violin, then piano – at an early age. When he was 12, he was spotted by Sax Hector, a touring leader of a group called The Jubilee Singers, and hired to play piano for them.

McLean brought his own swinging little band to Toronto in the 1930s and bumped into Murdoch's racist dictum. Murdoch wasn't the only racist in town, either. In those days, in "Toronto the Good," even world-famous bandleaders such as Duke Ellington and Cab Calloway were not allowed to stay at the top hotels. Only certain (usually less elegant) hotels offered accommodations to blacks.

"In those days," Murray Ginsberg later wrote in his book, *They Loved to Play*, "even though visiting black musicians from the U.S.A. drew large crowds

Courtesy Frank Wright

The Cy McLean Band (front row, l. to r.): Bobby Brown, Lloyd Salmon, Wilfred Williams; (middle row, l. to r.): Albert Marson, Roy Whorl, unidentified, Henry Wright; (rear row, l. to r.): Sam Richardson, Viviene Roberts, Cy McLean

in places like the Palais Royale and the Silver Slipper, it was understood that black audiences were usually barred from Toronto entertainment venues."

Since work for black musicians in Toronto and elsewhere in Ontario was rare, most of them worked for the railroad – if they were lucky. Cy McLean worked as a courier for Imperial Oil between gigs.

Guitarist Henry Wright, a contemporary of Cy McLean's, said: "We had more dry spells than pay days. I couldn't earn enough money as a musician playing in non-union halls."

The veteran musician Murray Ginsberg recalled going to the Universal Negro Improvement Association Hall in 1941: "Pat Riccio, his brother Jimmy and I were invited to the U.N.I.A. Hall. ... We saw Cy McLean and his musicians playing Count Basie tunes on a small stage. Almost everyone in the packed room – men and women, boys and girls – participated in the entertainment. They came out of the audience to sing, tap dance, or tell funny stories. Even in the very small Toronto black community of the day, the wealth of talent we saw on stage that night was extraordinary."

In 1944, Cy and his band opened at the Club Top Hat and played there, on and off, for three years. As Ginsberg described it, "That job was a turning point for black musicians in the city because, at last, due to pressure brought by the Top Hat management on the musicians' union, Cy McLean and his band were allowed to join the Toronto Musicians' Protective Association – Local 149 of the American Federation of Musicians of the United States and Canada."

In 1946, the Scholes Hotel on Toronto's Yonge Street was purchased by three businessmen – "Goodie" and Harvey Lichtenberg and Mike Lawrence. They changed their property from a so-so bar/hotel into an attractive jazz club named The Colonial Tavern. In 1947, Cy McLean brought a trio into the Colonial and the club did well enough to follow McLean with a parade of U.S. musicians – Muggsy Spanier, Jack Teagarden, Phil Napolean, Bobby Hackett, Red Norvo, and others.

Goodie Lichtenberg recalled: "Cy and his musicians were decent guys whose music attracted a lot of nice people to the club. Cy was always cheerful and displayed a positive attitude about life in general. A wonderful guy."

That was a turning point, not only for McLean but for other black musicians in Canada. Cy's reputation as one of Canada's most talented jazz pianists is best illustrated by an incident involving the world-famous pianist Earl "Fatha" Hines. When Hines was appearing at the Colonial Tavern in Toronto, he had to fly back to New York for a television appearance. The pianist Hines chose to take his place was Cy McLean. But despite McLean's growing popularity, it would still be a long while before conditions for black musicians in Canada would change.

Cy McLean died in 1986, at the age of 70, after a heart attack in his Port McNicoll, Ontario, cottage. And even though his music may be lost to present-day listeners, his legacy as a kind of antiracism pioneer has been of immense benefit to a younger generation of black musicians. Consider the number of outstanding Canadian black jazz musicians whose acceptance by white audiences was helped in part by the bold invasion of Toronto by Cy McLean: Oscar Peterson, Oliver Jones, Wray Downes, Sonny Greenwich, Joe Sealy, Archie Alleyne, Russ Little, and Frank Wright, and such jazz-influenced singers as Phyllis Marshall, Eleanor Collins, Ranee Lee, Jackie Richardson, Almeta Speaks, and Rudi Webb.

Ellis McLintock   *b. Toronto, Ontario, November 18, 1921*

As the *Hamilton Spectator* once said of Ellis McLintock: "musician, big band leader, broadcaster, teacher – he did it all. And did it well."

Ellis was born in 1921 to musical parents – his father played the euphonium professionally and his mother was a pianist. By the time he was 13, Ellis "played the cornet in a finished style" and had won many awards, including 19 first prizes.

At 14, he was one of four Canadians selected from about 4000 applicants and became a part of the British Empire Boys' Band, a 60-piece band made up of boys from all over the British Empire. They sailed to London for rehearsals in anticipation of a European tour but the tour was cancelled. "Just as we were about to start the tour, the [Spanish] Civil War began in Europe. They thought this was the beginning of the big one," McLintock recalled.

The next few years were a whirl of activity as Ellis won a scholarship to the Royal Conservatory of Music, played in the Conservatory orchestra, did various live CBC programs, and was hired by the Toronto Philharmonic Orchestra and then the Toronto Symphony where, at age 17, he was appointed first trumpet. The first trumpet player traditionally heads up the Brass Instrument Department at the Conservatory. "So here I am a professor of brass and I'm still going to high school," McLintock recalled.

He studied music and arranging in New York in the early 1940s and wound up as one of the only two Canadians in the All-American Youth Orchestra under the direction of Leopold Stokowski.

During the war he played in the RCAF Central Band in Ottawa and was discharged for medical reasons, due to psoriasis. After the war, he established the Ellis McLintock Orchestra, but his activities during the next two decades involved both playing dance music and leading a concert band. The dance band played everywhere, from Hamilton's Royal Connaught Hotel to Toronto's Casa Loma and The Old Mill. In 1967, he was the music director for the Canadian Pavilion Concert Band at Expo '67.

McLintock's sense of humour shows through clearly in a tone poem he put together for the opening night of the Alcoholics Anonymous world convention in the late 1950s. As a finale to the overture, McLintock's band played a medley dedicated to the members of his alcoholics audience. It included "How Dry I Am," "There Is a Tavern in the Town," "Drink, Drink, Drink," "Little Brown Jug," and "Comin' Through the Rye." The music was greeted with howls of laughter. "It took them five minutes to settle down before we could start the show," Ellis remembered.

During Expo '67, McLintock lived a hectic life. He would lead the band in Montreal from 2 p.m. to 6 p.m., then rush across the grounds to a waiting helicopter, fly to Toronto, catch a private plane to Kitchener, and then hop into a waiting limousine that would take him to his evening gig at Bingeman Park Lodge. The next day, he would make the same trip in reverse.

After Expo, the pace didn't slow up much for Ellis. He and his band were in demand. He continued a seven-year engagement at the Old Mill in Toronto, plus CBC performances and other work.

Then disaster struck. A trip to the dentist for cosmetic work exposed seven cysts on his gums, two of which were malignant. After the operation which removed teeth and bone, he could never play to his usual standard again. McLintock continued to lead his band at the Old Mill, but found it heart-breaking to make excuses when people continually requested songs featuring him on trumpet.

He gave up playing – but not music. Most of the 1970s and half of the 1980s were spent teaching music, first at Thornlea Secondary School in Thornhill, Ontario, and then at Orillia High School in Orillia, Ontario. "I never was able to play the way I had again. I felt it was silly to have all that experience and not pass it on."

He was proud of his students but wondered how they would do professionally. "I wouldn't want to be in the music business today," he commented. "There isn't the work around like there was in the days that I was young." He's also on record as saying he doesn't like contemporary music because it lacks "sub-tlety." "Maybe I'm an old fudd," he said, "but I'm glad I was born in the era of the big band."

Ellis McLintock retired to Delhi, Ontario in 1986. Since retiring, he began spending his time woodworking and selling antiques with his wife, Edna. He remarked that he doesn't miss the old days, that he wouldn't have the energy to get all dressed up in a tuxedo and work so hard again.

Don Messer

b. Tweedside, N.B., May 9, 1909; d. 1973

Among the more mystifying decisions ever made by the CBC was, in 1969, to cancel the television series that starred Don Messer and His Islanders.

Messer began his radio career in 1929 over CFBO, in Saint John, N.B. Although the personnel (and the show's name) varied over the years, the mainstays, in addition to country fiddler Messer, were singers Charlie Chamberlain and Marg Osborne. In 1934, the band began a radio show for CBC. Five years later, Messer joined CFCY, in Charlottetown, P.E.I., as music director and began calling his band The Islanders. By 1944, the band was being heard three times a week on the CBC's national network.

Messer began playing the violin at the age of five, learning country tunes from his uncle, Jim Messer, and traditional Scottish and Irish tunes from his

Don Messer with Marg Osborne and Charlie Chamberlain

mother. In his teens, he spent three years in Boston, where his studies with Henry Davis and Edith Hurter constituted his only formal training.

By 1954, *Don Messer's Jubilee* was being seen on CBC Television. Bill Langstroth, the show's original producer/director (and later the husband of singer Anne Murray) recalled years later: "When they first aired, the switchboard just lit up. I just had the feeling that the rest would be growth and evolution. It was well-done entertainment that represented the pioneer spirit of the country."

Combining a down-East style fiddle music from Messer and the Islanders, the swirling skirts and fast footwork of the Buchta Dancers, and standards and hymns sung by Marg Osborne and Charlie Chamberlain, the show found a very special place in the hearts of Canadians across the country.

Once the show was established as one of Canada's most popular, first on radio and then on television, Messer and the Islanders began to appear outside the Maritimes, making their first tour of Ontario in 1949. By 1969, they had made 18 tours, including a centennial trip in 1967 that lasted three months and played to 61 venues.

Regular performers added during the television era included the Buchta Dancers, led by Gunter and Irma Buchta, and the Scottish accordionist-singer Johnny Forrest, who joined in 1966. Frequent guest performers included Stompin' Tom Connors, Myrna Lorrie, Catherine McKinnon, Fred McKenna, and Graham Townsend.

Messer began recording in the days of 78s, but went on to make some 30 albums, issued (and reissued) by labels such as Apex, MCA, and Rodeo. A compilation LP called *The Good Old Days* (MCA) was issued in 1979 to some 100,000 advance orders.

Don Messer was credited (by folklorists Dorothy and Homer Hogan) with a synthesis of many and varied fiddle traditions, influencing other fiddlers with a style "as clean, straight ahead and neat as a well-tended farm" and marked by its "down-to-earth simplicity."

The program's cancellation in 1969 brought many complaints from outraged viewers and even led to questions raised in the House of Commons. As proof that Messer fans were many, a syndicated version of *Don Messer and His Islanders* was launched by CHCH-TV in Hamilton, Ontario, the same year CBC cancelled the show – and remained on the air until Messer's death in 1973.

Messer always insisted that his music was not Western or cowboy music. "Our tunes," he said, "have been around for two or three hundred years. They're folk tunes passed from generation to generation." In addition to traditional hornpipes, jigs, and reels, the Islanders played many Messer compositions, as well as pieces by such Islanders musicians as Al Cherny, Andy DeJarlis, Jim Magill, and Graham Townsend.

At the height of its popularity, the program received widespread critical approval. One critic remarked that the show was "breaking new ground in its use of a cast of real people – as opposed to those glittering, superbly-posed, make-believe characters we normally associate with Television Land."

All the regulars are gone now: Messer in 1973, Charlie Chamberlain in 1972, and Marg Osborne in 1977. But their fans linger on.

A stage musical titled *Don Messer's Jubilee*, described by its composer, John Gray, as "a fan letter," was premiered in 1985 by the Neptune Theatre in Halifax and subsequently toured in Canada. In 1989 a Theatre Plus production offered Catherine McKinnon playing Marg Osborne.

Joni Mitchell   *b. Fort Macleod, Alberta, November 7, 1943*

For a time, the road to folk music venues and success was clogged with male troubadours. In Canada, in the late 1950s and early 1960s, Neil Young, Leonard Cohen, Bruce Cockburn, Murray McLauchlan, David Wiffen, and Gordon Lightfoot seemed to command the stages of coffeehouses and small

concert stages as they sang about lust, love, and losing. Joni Mitchell was the exception. From the beginning, she worked as a singer, songwriter, musician, and producer, when such a combination, for a woman, was unheard of. She has always done the unexpected and succeeded on roads apparently dominated by others.

"Women's songs were written by men 99 per cent of the time; they carried old feminine values," she told *Entertainment Weekly* in 2000. "My songs began to reveal feminine insecurities, doubts, recognition that the order was falling apart."

Joni Mitchell (born Roberta Joan Anderson) began that reshaping process early. The family moved from its original home in Pierce, Alberta, to several Saskatchewan locations in search of opportunities, while Joni searched for a favourite form of expression – initially festival singing and four years of piano lessons, but then an interest in art. At an elementary school in Saskatoon she was inspired by her literature teacher to write poetry (she paid tribute to Michael Kratzman, "who taught me to love words," in a song from her first album, **Michael from Mountains**).

In the early 1960s, when Joni finished high school, she got a job waiting tables in Saskatoon at the coffeehouse Louis Riel. Along with her wages she took home a new appreciation for folk music and enough cash to buy a baritone ukulele. By 1963, she had enrolled in an art course in Calgary, but continued to practice on her ukulele with the help of a Pete Seeger instruction book and persuaded the Depression Club in Calgary to let her perform.

"Joni … just out of art school, came with her uke and tormented us all with a shrill 'Sloop John B' and 'I With I Wath an Apple on a Twee,'" remembered Will Millar, who later founded the Irish Rovers.

Strumming her way onto local coffeehouse stages was only one of the battles Joni waged. Another was the pull of art school versus singing and songwriting. By 1964, the music was clearly winning. She travelled to Toronto in time to take in the annual Mariposa Folk Festival and to find work in Yorkville at the Penny Farthing coffeehouse. She made a lasting impression on Mariposa organizer Martin Onrot.

"She had a soft, beautiful voice and an easy melodic style," Onrot said, "but I had no idea she would become a superstar."

In Yorkville, Joni met roving singer Chuck Mitchell. They soon married and made his home in Detroit their home base for tours to the U.S. east coast. But as she grew musically into a solo act onstage, Joni Mitchell also grew out of the marriage; within six months the two parted ways. The club and coffeehouse circuit soon led her to New York. During an appearance at Café à Go Go she met David Crosby, who offered criticism of her work and who would eventually produce her 1968 debut album, *Joni Mitchell* (also known as *Song to a Seagull*).

It was Mitchell's songwriting, however, that made the biggest first impression. From her earliest days in New York, other established folk artists gravitated to Joni's songs. George Hamilton IV recorded **Urge for Going**, Tom Rush did **The Circle Game**, and when Judy Collins was assembling her album *Wildflower* in 1967, she included Mitchell songs **Michael from Mountains** and **Both Sides Now**. The latter became a Top 10 hit in 1968.

A move to the U.S. west coast put Mitchell in closer touch with the L.A. scene and with another circle of musical friends. Through her close association with James Taylor, Neil Young, David Crosby, Stephen Stills, and in particular Graham Nash, Mitchell generated plenty of interest in her material. In 1969, her album *Clouds* sold 100,000 copies in advance of its release and her anthem to the youth movement, **Woodstock,** was recorded by CSN&Y on their 1970 album *Déjà Vu*. But those same friendships soon overshadowed her creative output and innuendoes about her promiscuity (printed in pop music journals) drove her from the limelight and back to Canada for a time.

Despite being a recluse in British Columbia, Mitchell continued to write some of her strongest autobiographical material. The success of her early albums attests to that quality: her first gold album *Ladies of the Canyon* (1970); *Blue* (1971), which reached number 15 on the charts; *For the Roses* (1972); and *Court and Spark* (1974) – commercially her most successful album, described by one critic as "the highly personal, confessional standard by which many ambitious young artists still set their watches."

While the albums netted Mitchell her Grammy nominations, during this period she also enjoyed success with singles such as **Big Yellow Taxi, You Turn Me On (I'm a Radio), Help Me,** and **Free Man in Paris.**

Just when it seemed the recording world and her fans had her figured out, in 1975 Joni Mitchell fooled them again by releasing *The Hissing of Summer Lawns.* On the recording she abandoned standard guitar tuning. "In the same way that Van Gogh searched for his own color schemes," she said, "I searched for my own harmonic voice, found it, and spent a career being dismissed as too jazzy."

One label she no doubt enjoyed that year (1976) was her Juno Award as Female Vocalist of the Year.

Her so-called "jazzy" material was, more accurately, roots or worldbeat music, something she explored long before others got on the bandwagon. In fact, however, her affection for jazz was always close to the surface. In high school she had listened to Lambert, Hendrix, and Ross and later Miles Davis. The trend to jazz continued with her album *Hejira* in 1976 and most notably in 1979 with her tribute to Charles Mingus, recorded shortly before he died. *Mingus* includes the jazz bassist's concept of a composition based on T. S. Eliot's *Four Quartets* (but because Mingus was ill and couldn't play, Jaco Pastorius played bass).

Throughout the 1980s and 1990s, Joni Mitchell continued to explore new sounds and rhythms. In 1982, she released her first of several albums with Geffen Records, **Wild Things Run Fast,** with jazz guitarist Pat Metheny, and in 1994 she recorded *Turbulent Indigo* (on Reprise Records) and finally won her first two Grammy Awards, one for Album of the Year. She toured infrequently; and even when she did, her concerts rarely dwelled on the past, because, she said, "I will not be a living jukebox."

Joni Mitchell allowed herself and her fans to look back in 2000, when she released the album *Both Sides Now,* a compilation of cover material (including some of her own) as "a commentary on romantic love in the 20th century." The idea originated with her more recent concerts, in which she sang versions of "Stormy Weather," "Comes Love," and "You're My Thrill," and was the first of a planned trilogy.

Having once described her music as "audio paintings," Mitchell also began to return to her one-time passion for visual art. Her first showing – an 87-work exhibit in Saskatoon – depicted, in reviewer Robert Enright's words, "who and what she likes with no concessions to either art fashion or market pressure."

In recent years, she has been honoured with some of the most prestigious awards in the business: the Order of Canada, *Billboard*'s Century Award, the ASCAP Founders Award, the National Academy of Songwriters' Lifetime

Achievement Award, and induction into the Rock and Roll Hall of Fame.

In true Joni Mitchell style – doing the unexpected – the night she was inducted into the Canadian Hall of Fame by Prime Minister Pierre Trudeau, in 1981, she got into the spirit of fun that co-hosts John Candy and Andrea Martin had established through the evening and commented, "The Hall of Fame … Makes me feel like Boom Boom Geoffrion!"

Kim Mitchell

b. Sarnia, Ontario, July 10, 1952

The rock 'n' roll industry remains the domain of young performers. Programmers can almost plot the rise and fall of a career on the same curve as the rocker's age. Part of that reality is dictated by the rigours of touring and recording. Another is the performer's ability to come up with songs that connect with the generation of younger concertgoers and record buyers. As Kim Mitchell approached his 50th birthday he described what he called "the bugaboo of rock 'n' roll."

"It's virtually impossible for any artist to keep re-inventing himself," he told Dan Brown of the *National Post*, "and hone his appeal to the prime buying demographic, which is people under the age of 25."

In the mid-1960s, Kim Mitchell was a teenager playing guitar in a Sarnia-based band called Zoom. The band's move to Toronto proved unsuccessful, but Kim pressed on as a musician doing studio sessions, lounge dates, and commercial jingles. Following a working trip to Greece, Mitchell connected with a childhood friend, Pye Dubois, and the two co-wrote some songs. They then assembled some Sarnia friends (drummer Paul Kersey, bass player Mike Tilka, pianist Terry Watkinson, and Mitchell on guitar) into a new band, Max Webster (the name came from a phone book). Anthem Records heard the original quartet and signed them up in 1972.

The band's first two albums – *Max Webster* and *High Class in Borrowed Shoes* – established Max Webster's penchant for unpredictable musical progressions, abstract lyrics, and flamboyant stage antics. The four were such a powerful draw in person that one of their contemporaries, Rush, invited them to open concerts on their 1977 tour. Max Webster finally got radio airplay with a single **Let Go the Line** (1979) and **Paradise Skies** (1980). However, it was lack of promotion and insufficient product that (at

the end of another Rush tour in 1981) forced Mitchell to leave the band to work on his own.

In 1984, he moved to Tom Berry's Alert Records and released his first full-length solo LP, *Akimbo Alogo*, which launched Kim Mitchell's party-rock persona. It went double-platinum in Canada (more than 200,000 copies sold). He won his first Juno Award as Most Promising Male Vocalist. From the album came **Go for Soda,** which went Top 5 that same summer. The single's lyrics by Pye Dubois – "Might as well go for a soda / Nobody hurts and nobody cries / Might as well go for a soda / Nobody drowns and nobody dies" – were not meant to be an anti-alcohol protest, but the U.S. chapter of Mothers Against Drunk Driving (MADD) used it as their theme song.

Nevertheless, Mitchell's blue-collar rocker image grew. His next album, *Shakin' Like a Human Being*, came out in 1986. It went triple-platinum and earned him another Juno for Album of the Year. Meanwhile, singles such as **Alana Loves Me, Easy to Tame,** and **Patio Lanterns** immediately went Top 40. *Music Express* named Mitchell "Working Class Hero" and he played three sold-out concerts at Kingswood Music Theatre (north of Toronto), surpassing the previous attendance record set by ZZ Top and Sting. His 1989 album, *Rockland*, kept pace and he won the 1990 Juno for Male Vocalist of the Year.

"I think of myself more as a white boy yelling," Mitchell said in accepting his trophy. He also performed his hit **Rock 'n' Roll Duty** at the awards ceremony that year. There were additional albums in the 1990s and a *Kim Mitchell Greatest Hits* package went platinum, but that would be his last album for a while.

By 1999, his everyman symbol of the Ontario Provincial Police cap was gone, and the locks had been trimmed and he'd moved away from Toronto. Still, Kim Mitchell was back with his first original material in five years on an album entitled *Kimosabe*. He put up the $100,000 to record it himself. He was proud of the new content, but he faced one important question: Was there still an audience for his brand of rock 'n' roll party music? He described the state of his career this way: "If I was a blues or a jazz musician and I was 60," he told Alan Niester in the *Globe and Mail*, "people would be saying, 'Oooh, he's got depth.' With rock or pop, it's like you can't have depth."

The public perception is, unless you're Mick Jagger or Tina Turner, you can't be old and be a rock musician.

Alanis Morissette   *b. Ottawa, June 1, 1974*

At a pub in Toronto, in 1995, some recreational hockey players (guys in their forties) arrived to quench thirsts. Their post-game bravado drowned out the music playing in the background. Suddenly, the pub speakers carried the rhythmic intro to a familiar song. In an instant a group of 20-something women across the room began singing word-for-word the angry lyrics of Alanis Morissette's **You Oughta Know**. They swayed, clapped, and mimicked together the stretched-out syllables of the chorus: "And I'm here to remind you/Of the mess you left when you went away." Their loud unison singing took control of the room, as if in defiance of every other patron, particularly the hockey players. It was the kind of outburst, no doubt, repeated by many young women, that first year of Alanismania.

"With the ... Morissette of 'You Oughta Know,' a whole new palette of female emotions hitherto confined to college and alternative audiences has become acceptable," wrote *New York* magazine's Kim France, "even admirable."

More than acceptable, since the CD (*Jagged Little Pill*) containing that

312

single sold 30 million copies and became one of the best-selling albums of all time. All the more extraordinary, since between her first recording and the monster album, Morissette transformed her image from dance pop teen to alternative rock terror.

Alanis Nadinia Morissette, born a twin with her brother Wade, grew up with two teacher parents. A devoutly religious couple, Alan and Georgia Morissette raised Alanis and her two brothers with plenty of encouragement. They were clearly a family of achievers – brother Chad was a teenage entrepreneur and Wade was a superb athlete. Alanis expressed a fascination for music early; at three she memorized every song in the musical *Grease*; at seven she was taking piano and dance lessons.

By the mid-1980s, Alanis was appearing on CJOH-TV's *You Can't Do That on Television*, an Ottawa children's show, which gave her enough money to privately record a single called **Fate Stay with Me**. In high school, according to *Ottawa Citizen* writers Carolyn Abraham and Norman Provencher, Alanis "hung out with the fashionable, big-haired girls in frosted pink lipstick. She led a lunch-time aerobics class, sang at assemblies and in Grade 12 she and (her brother) Wade lip-synced to her favourite musical, Alanis as Newton-John, Wade as Travolta." She even sang with a local cover band known as The New York Fries.

About that time she also met choreographer/producer Stephan Klovan, who helped market the young singer's (and her brother Wade's) talents at a national entertainment extravaganza in Ottawa. The twins became models for a line of youth clothing. Alanis sang the national anthem so often at sporting events that she became known as "Miss O Canada." And in order to secure a recording contract, Klovan and musician Leslie Howe took Morissette to Paris to shoot a video of the song **Walk Away**. It worked. She signed with MCA Records in 1988.

By 1991, Morissette had collaborated with Ottawa songwriter Serge Cote and Leslie Howe to record her first album *Alanis*, consisting of pop numbers, usually with a pronounced dance beat. Not surprisingly, critics and fans made comparisons of her work with that of dance artists Tiffany and Debbie Gibson, referring to Morissette as a "pop princess" and "teenybopper artist."

When the album approached platinum status in Canada (100,000 copies sold) and its single, **Too Hot**, hit number four on the charts, suddenly she was being mobbed in Ottawa as a pop idol. By year's end she had been nominated in three Juno Awards categories; ultimately she won Most Promising Female Vocalist of the Year. Her second album, *Now Is the Time*, went gold (50,000 copies sold) but, despite her efforts, did not put distance between her and her dance tunes image.

"There was an element of me not being who I really was at the time,"

Morissette told David Wild in *Rolling Stone* later. "The focus for me then was entertaining people as opposed to sharing any revelations I had at the time. I had them, but I wasn't prepared to share."

By 1992, her recording company had convinced Morissette not to attend university but to pursue a musical career. MCA also terminated her association with Klovan and Howe, in favour of a new manager, Scott Welch, who moved her away from Ottawa. She lived in a small apartment in Toronto, worked seven days a week, hosted a CBC-TV show called *Music Works* and attempted a number of creative collaborations; however, according to Barry Grills, author of *Ironic: The Story of Alanis Morissette*, "Morissette called the two years she lived in Toronto, the lowest time of her life. It was here where Morissette admits she endured a number of unhappy relationships with men which would eventually find a point of release in some of [her] songs."

In 1994, living in Los Angeles, Morissette met keyboard-player-turned-producer Glen Ballard, who had been producer for the likes of Quincy Jones, Aretha Franklin, Natalie Cole, George Benson, Chaka Khan, The Pointer Sisters, and Paula Abdul. He had also written and arranged Michael Jackson's song "Man in the Mirror" and he was credited with nearly 100 million album sales. An MCA executive invited Ballard to a meeting with Morissette. Ballard almost didn't go.

"As it turns out, I did," said Ballard, "and within an hour we were writing a song," a tune called **The Bottom Line**, which didn't make it on the first album. They worked for two months solid at Ballard's Encino, California, home, setting Morissette's lyrics to Ballard's music. Next, they found a new label – Madonna's Maverick Records – and by 1995 had recorded Morissette's groundbreaking album, *Jagged Little Pill*.

Maverick shipped out the record with very little fanfare. Morissette's manager, Scott Welch, predicted the album would be successful, selling perhaps over 100,000 copies. Even Morissette herself did not have huge expectations for the album. Plans were made for a low-key, but continuous tour so that Morissette could get comfortable with her touring band – she would perform 250 concerts in 18 months around the world.

"Barely older than the high school girls who flock to her concerts, Ms. Morissette sings to her fans as someone with fresh memories of teen-age betrayals and identity crises," wrote Jon Pareles in *The New York Times*. He quotes her as saying, "I didn't have high self-esteem when I was a teenager … I used to think I was alone in that. Oh, man, I wish I had me to listen to when I was 14."

In the United States, *Jagged Little Pill* zoomed up the *Billboard* charts and stayed there for a year. It was the best-selling American debut album ever. As well, *Billboard* magazine observed that the success of the album "was a complete groundswell. It was from the public up, not the company down." Record producers referred to the CD's popularity as "scary." By June of that spring, one of the singles from the album, **You Oughta Know**, was the most requested song in Los Angeles. Morissette was so popular that, that summer, when Sinead O'Connor bowed out of the Lollapalooza tour, producers invited Morissette to replace her; she declined – wary of repeating the too-fast climb that had hurt her as a teenaged pop star. During the same week in November 1995, Morissette was featured on the covers of both *Spin* and *Rolling Stone* magazine.

"She dismissed skeptics who doubt the authenticity of her music, her image as Miss Female Rage '96 and her Grammy-nominated, multi-platinum album, *Jagged Little Pill*," wrote Marisa Fox in *New York Daily* in 1996. "And she let her fans know that she – like them – is no mere rebel without a cause."

In the United States Morissette was a brand-new artist. Manager Welch confidently aimed her work at fans of alternative rock; however, the American press did pick up on Morissette's past as a teenybopper diva and referred to her first two albums as "dirty little secrets." In Canada, divorcing the past was even tougher. "Is Alanis Morissette bogus?" mused Toronto's weekly magazine *eye*. Maverick's distributor, Warner Music Canada, said "she might be up against prejudices because of her background as a dance artist. But we also knew that she had to answer for her past."

Neither reviewers' putdowns nor distributors' fears dissuaded her fans. In February 1996, she won four Grammys, for Best Rock Song, Best Rock Album, Best Album, and Best Female Rock Vocalist. A month later, at the 25th annual Juno Awards, she was nominated six times and took five Juno Awards for Best Album, Best Rock Album, Best Single (**You Oughta Know**), Best Songwriter, and Best Female Vocalist of the Year. She also shared a Juno International Achievement Award (the first ever awarded) with Céline Dion and Shania Twain for bringing "honour to themselves [and] to the whole Canadian music industry." In 1997, she won Junos for Best Songwriter and Best Single (**Ironic**).

The seemingly overnight success of *Jagged Little Pill* launched Morissette's career into the stratosphere. In 1996 the Prince's Trust invited her to perform (along with Bob Dylan, The Who, and Eric Clapton) for 150,000 in London's Hyde Park. *Rolling Stone* recognized her (with fellow Canadian Neil Young) as Artist of the Year. On the World Wide Web, cyber-chat about her music, her taste in liquor, and her sex life became a feeding frenzy; by December of that year, an average of 1000 new information sites and Web pages per month were being built on the World Wide Web in her honour. Meanwhile, back home in Ottawa, Morissette's high school contemporaries were making small fortunes selling their old Glebe Collegiate yearbooks containing Alanis Morissette photos and sayings.

Following the whirlwind of 1996, Morissette stepped back, travelling to

India and Cuba, competing in triathlons, collaborating with artists (such as Dave Matthews and Ringo Starr), doing some acting (playing God in the Kevin Smith movie *Dogma*), writing songs while hanging out in Toronto, and developing her own Web site on which she posted poems and photographs. She contemplated letting *Jagged Little Pill* be her last album.

Eventually, however, she returned to Glen Ballard's Aerowave Studio in California. Using keyboards, computers, and guitars the two fashioned the music to which Morissette attached lyrics from what Ballard called "this duffel bag full of her thoughts, poems, ruminations." Ballard told John Pareles of *The New York Times* that "every word for her is like giving blood. As she writes, she eliminates all the things that don't work for her emotionally. But once she's satisfied … she sings it once, maybe twice and she walks away from it."

The resulting album *Supposed Former Infatuation Junkie* debuted in November 1998 at number one on the *Billboard* album chart. Unlike her first album, which lashed out, the second dealt with reconciliation: with parents, lovers, and weaknesses she saw in herself. By the new year, *Junkie* had sold four million copies and Morissette was back on tour. For all her reconciliation, Morissette still had a penchant for the controversial. Her second album video featured images of her naked, and in an episode of the TV series *Sex and the City* she was seen in a passionate kissing embrace with the show's star Sarah Jessica Parker. During a 26-city fall tour, Morissette's handlers announced they were posting live versions of her concerts on MP3.com, a Web site offering thousands of songs for free.

Despite any lost income from free downloading on the Internet, by the summer of 2001, the *National Post*'s business supplement reported that Alanis Morissette was still among the 40 wealthiest Canadians, worth more than $33 million.

Anne Murray   *b. Springhill, Nova Scotia, June 20, 1945*

In the 1960s and 1970s, when Canadian popular music enjoyed both an explosion of talent and the enforcement of Canadian-content regulations, the performers who succeeded were as credible in front of an audience as they were on those CanCon records. That's one of the reasons Anne Murray became the most successful female performing artist in the history of Canadian entertainment. Throughout her career – on disc, on television, and in person – Anne Murray could deliver a song from the heart.

"I've always said you could put an Italian aria in front of me or Glen Campbell," Murray told the *Globe and Mail*'s Liam Lacey, "and we could sing it. A good singer is a good singer."

Andrea Eccles / Courtesy Palmer Publicity Ink, Ltd.

Music and song surrounded the young Anne Murray at home, if only because both she and her five brothers all took music lessons – Anne studied piano for six years and voice lessons with Karen Mills in Tatamagouche for three years. Anne debuted on local television in 1962, singing "Moon River" with an all-female chorus; even then she knew her voice was different and that "I was always able to move out of myself and become the other person" to perform.

While a physical education student at the University of New Brunswick, Anne appeared in campus revues, and did an audition in Halifax for the CBC-TV show *Singalong Jubilee*, a summer replacement show for *Don Messer's Jubilee*. In 1964, producer Bill Langstroth turned her down, but later invited her back; she sang the folk standard "Oh, Mary Don't You Weep."

"She sat on a stool and played a baritone ukulele," Langstroth told *The Toronto Star*. "She had a little porkpie hat on her head. … She opened her face and out came that voice – she was startling to me."

Langstroth booked her for two appearances and by 1967 she had become a regular on the *Singalong* summer series. Murray began teaching phys-ed at Summerside, P.E.I., but made the fateful decision to pursue a career in the music business in time for the autumn season of another Halifax CBC-TV show, *Let's Go*. Producer Brian Ahern called her about making a record and by 1968 she had recorded an album, **What About Me?**, for Arc Records. Capitol Records noticed her and in 1969 sent Murray and Ahern into the studio to produce a second album, **This Way Is My Way**. The same year, Langstroth and Murray met Gene MacLellan, a Maritime songwriter who played several songs for them. One caught her ear.

"I thought 'Snowbird' was hot from the moment I first heard it," Murray told Ritchie Yorke in 1970. "Later on I found out that Gene had written the song a year before with my voice in mind. At the time we hadn't even met."

Though it was the B-side in some markets, Murray's single version of "Snowbird" began moving on both Canadian and American music charts in 1970. Capitol sent her on a promotional trip to nearby American cities and the single took off in Pittsburgh and Cleveland. By July it was number 45 in the United States and by November its sales had passed one million. Soon there were television appearances on CTV's *Nashville North* and CBC-TV's *Tommy Hunter Show* (CBC also signed her to an exclusive contract – the first in the Corporation's history), and in October 1970 she debuted on U.S. TV on *The Glen Campbell Goodtime Hour*.

The Anne Murray voice, what *New York Times* critic John Rockwell called "a conversationally husky, womanly mezzo soprano," got a lot of attention. The story goes that when producer Ahern, Capitol Records (Canada), and Murray pitched the idea of releasing another Gene MacLellan song, "Put Your Hand in the Hand," Capitol Records (USA) executives balked, saying it wasn't enough like "Snowbird." The truth was, they felt Murray's voice sounded too masculine on the recording and "Put Your Hand in the Hand" was shelved. Ironically, a version of the song recorded soon after by Canadian group Ocean sold two million copies.

The early 1970s belonged to Anne Murray. She appeared at important concert venues (including the Imperial Room at the Royal York Hotel in Toronto, The Cave in Vancouver, the Bottom Line in New York, and Las Vegas nightclubs) and on mass-market television programs (such as CBC-TV's *Wayne and Shuster Show* and *The Merv Griffin Show*, where she received a gold record, the first by a Canadian female singer to exceed a million sales in the United States).

In 1971, she sang at the Grammy Awards (being nominated in two categories), and at the inaugural Juno Awards ceremony that year she received Top Female Vocalist honours (while Ahern won two for Best Single and Best Album and MacLellan won for Composer of the Year). During the presentations Murray referred to her management team as "the Maritime Mafia." That year she set up her company – Balmur (B for Bill Langstroth, A for Anne, L for her manager Leonard Rambeau, and MUR for her childhood nickname) – and relocated to Toronto.

Balmur now searched for a followup to "Snowbird." The string of singles that followed – "Sing High, Sing Low" (1970), "A Stranger in My Place" (1971), "It Takes Time" (1971), "Talk It Over in the Morning" (1971), "Cotton Jenny" (1972), "Danny's Song" (1972), "What About Me?" (1973), "Love Song" (1974), "The Call" (1976), "Walk Right Back" (1978), "I Just Fall in Love Again" (1979), and "Shadows in the Moonlight" (1979) – performed well, particularly on country music charts.

Her image as a crowd-pleaser, which she periodically played up (appearing barefoot on stage), was later hard to shake. Murray says she got pigeonholed as a country singer in the United States because she was a ballad singer. While her cover of the Beatles tune "You Won't See Me" (1974) prompted John Lennon to say she was his favourite interpreter of their music, she kept winning Junos in the country category. At one point in 1974, Murray had each side of a single riding the number-one spot – "You Won't See Me" atop the easy listening chart and "He Thinks I Still Care" atop the country chart. On the heels of "Love Song," she won her first Grammy for Best Country Vocalist.

Her U.S.-based management team (Shep Gordon and Allan Strahl) tried playing down her girl-next-door image and marketed her as a Hollywood superstar. There were parties, photo opportunities, and encounters with the press; one prompted U.S. rock critic Lester Bangs to comment that Anne Murray was "God's gift to the male race."

The pace was gruelling. There were times, she admitted to the press, when she would get sick before every performance and want desperately to escape the relentless cycle of touring, recording, and public appearances. By the mid-70s, Murray was in need of a rest. After marrying her friend and business partner, Bill Langstroth, in 1975, she slipped into semi-retirement; that same year, she was inducted into the Order of Canada.

In 1978, she recorded a new album, *Let's Keep It That Way*, which contained "You Needed Me," a ballad by Randy Goodrum. EMI Music's Deane Cameron attended the mix in Toronto and told author Nicolas Jennings, "I stood there and shivered as I listened to that track. Anne's voice was so moving." In November "You Needed Me" was number one on both the *RPM* and the *Billboard* chart. The album sold more than two million copies, but perhaps more satisfying was Murray's winning a second Grammy (over Barbra Streisand, Carly Simon, Olivia Newton-John, and Donna Summer) for Best Female Pop Vocalist.

"That was a real coup for me," she told writer Lynn Saxberg. "They were always in a quandary every year when they tried to figure out what category to put me in. I like that. I like to be able to sing whatever I want."

Into the 1980s, the Anne Murray frenzy didn't let up. Between 1980 and 1984, Murray spent 52 weeks in Las Vegas nightclubs and while there maintained a routine of two shows a night, off at 2 a.m., up with her infant children (William Jr. and Dawn) at 6 a.m. In 1980, her star was embedded into Hollywood's Walk of Fame. The hits continued to come – "A Little Good News" (1983), "Nobody Loves Me Like You Do" (1984), "Now and Forever You and Me" (1986) – and they rose to the top of the country charts. Her song "Could I Have This Dance?" became a multimillion-seller, was featured in the movie *Urban Cowboy*, and earned her another Grammy for Best Female

Country Vocalist. By the end of the decade, Springhill, Nova Scotia, had opened the Anne Murray Centre in honour of "Canada's Sweetheart."

In the early 1990s, Murray (then in her late forties) had no intention of quitting. In 1991, at a concert with the Boston Pops Orchestra, Murray ran into singer/producer Tommy West (who'd often said he detected a Patti Page influence in her sound); he suggested that she record a 1950s album. They took the idea into a Toronto recording studio; the result was *Croonin'*, an album of songs made famous by Rosemary Clooney, Eddie Arnold, Peggy Lee, Jo Stafford, and Doris Day. West called Murray's recording a "fantasy come true." The album went double-platinum.

The decade proved emotionally tumultuous. In 1992, Murray ended her 22-year relationship with the American arm of Capitol Records (who still viewed her as principally a country music star). That year she was inducted into the Canadian Music Hall of Fame. In 1995, the year she turned 50, Leonard Rambeau, her manager of 25 years, died of cancer. Gene MacLellan, her Maritime friend and the composer of "Snowbird," also died that year.

By December 1995, she had signed Bruce Allen, the manager who'd handled Bachman-Turner Overdrive and Bryan Adams; he assessed Murray's career by saying, "The broad needs a hit." The next year Murray released her 30th album, *Anne Murray*, and put her career total album sales over 26 million worldwide. Early in 1996, after 25 years of declining invitations, she hosted the Juno Awards and in December played Toronto's Massey Hall for the first time since 1973; she joked, "Twenty-three years … and I haven't changed a bit."

In 1998, Murray separated from her husband, Bill Langstroth. Then in 1999, Murray and her daughter Dawn Langstroth talked publicly about the 19-year-old's battle with anorexia nervosa and staged a benefit for Sheena's Place (a Toronto eating-disorder help centre).

At the turn of the millennium, the Anne Murray success story continued. Her company concentrated on media convergence. Picking up on the motion-picture model, Balmur Entertainment Ltd. became a vertically integrated firm encompassing music, television, and books. Her 2000 album of inspirational songs, *What a Wonderful World*, coincided with a CBC-TV special and a book of inspirational phrases and lyrics by the same name. Balmur joined forces with an animation firm to produce a series based on Murray's 1977 multi-platinum album *There's a Hippo in My Tub*.

By 2001, Canada's "songbird" had sold more than 40 million albums around the world; she had earned 31 Juno Awards, four Grammy Awards, and three American Music Awards; and she'd become a Companion of the Order of Canada. Of perhaps greater importance was the knowledge that her voice still had what it takes.

"When I'm singing," she told Liam Lacey in the *Globe and Mail*, "I get into a zone … [like] playing golf or tennis. … I know where I can take it and I can lose myself. The best way I can describe it is total, complete concentration."

Boyd Neel

b. London, England, July 19, 1905; d. Toronto, Ontario, September 30, 1981

"I've never made a record I didn't want to do over again," said Boyd Neel, in discussing some recordings of his orchestra that were reissued (by London Records) 20 years after they were made. "They aren't real stereo," he complained. "They've jazzed them up, boiled them in oil or something," the then 67-year-old conductor said.

Although he technically retired in 1970, he continued his usual practice of keeping several balls in the air at the same time. In 1974, when he spoke to the *Globe and Mail*'s John Fraser, Neel was about to run off to conduct the Winnipeg Festival Orchestra, then immediately return to Ontario to take over directorship of the first annual Blue Mountain Summer School at Collingwood.

Neel had started out planning a career in the British navy, then turned to medicine, specializing in surgery. He was once the resident surgeon at St. George's Hospital at Hyde Park Corner.

On the side, he was a pianist and amateur conductor; he went on to study theory and orchestration at the Guildhall School of Music in 1931, even though he still considered music a hobby. Yet, in 1932 this "hobbyist" formed the Boyd Neel Orchestra, consisting of 17 young string players, some of whom were Canadians living in London, a coincidence which may have had some bearing on his decision, later, to move to Canada.

Neel's orchestra was in the vanguard of the baroque revival, and over the next two decades committed to disc for the Decca label much of the chamber orchestra repertoire.

During the Second World War he served as a medical officer, but he also did a lecture tour of the Mediterranean and, with the Sadler's Wells orchestra, gave several hundred concerts for troops in England.

Both before and after the war, he was a guest conductor with many English orchestras, including the Royal Philharmonic, the London Philharmonic, the London Symphony, and the BBC Symphony Orchestra. Neel conducted the first Glyndebourne Festival at Sadler's Wells. In 1948–49 he was conductor for the D'Oyly Carte Company.

With his orchestra, he visited Canada in 1952, touring in Quebec, Ontario, and the Maritimes.

In 1954, he founded the Hart House Orchestra at the University of Toronto, which he conducted until 1971. A year after starting the Hart House Orchestra, Neel conducted eight concerts at the Stratford Festival, which featured such luminaries as Glenn Gould, Lois Marshall, and Elisabeth Schwarzkopf.

He became a naturalized Canadian in 1961. He was a leader in the campaign to build a new home for the faculty, a campaign that resulted in the Edward Johnson Building. It was also his persistent urging that resulted in new buildings for the Royal Conservatory, the faculty of music, and the opera school.

Never one to keep his opinions to himself, he got into a major battle over Toronto's "blue laws," proponents of which insisted that no musical performances could take place on Sundays. "I had an important ally, though," recalled Neel, "and that was Sydney Smith, the president of the university. He told me he was damned if anyone was going to tell him how to run his university. I then went on Nathan Cohen's *Fighting Words* and had it out with all those fools. It came down to the single fact that it was somehow sinful to employ musicians and give them pay for working on a Sunday.

"It was a United Church minister [possibly the Rev. Gordon Domm] who claimed this and when he said it I knew I had him. I asked him if it wasn't just as sinful to make his organist and choirmaster work on Sunday for pay. And what about all the people on television and radio? Were they all sinners on Sunday, too? Well, the point was too ridiculous to last much longer and the law was changed shortly afterwards."

A calm and self-assured after-dinner speaker and radio commentator, Neel was heard nationally on such CBC radio programs as *Sunday Concert*, *Tuesday Night*, *Concerts from Two Worlds*, and his own *Opera with Boyd Neel*. His writings have appeared in various music journals. In 1979 Neel was the subject of a CBC-FM series titled *The Boyd Neel Memoirs*.

No new job or title or challenge ever fazed him. When he was offered the post of artistic director of yet another music festival – this time in Sarnia, Ontario – he reacted typically, referring to it as "a very grand title" but added he thought of it as "a hobby."

"But then," he added, "for that matter, medicine seemed like a hobby, too, and so does music. Nothing I've ever done has felt like work."

Phil Nimmons

b. Kamloops, B.C., June 3, 1923

The achievements of Phil Nimmons over a long, busy, and varied career are considerable, and his standing among his peers is at the highest possible level. Yet, he scowls when he is referred to as an elder statesman.

Music has been a vital part of his life since his childhood in Vancouver. His parents were both musical, but not professional. His father paid his way through dentistry school by playing the violin; Phil's mother was a pianist. Both earned extra money by providing music that accompanied silent movies in the early 1920s – "chase" music, dramatic punctuation, romantic moods. Nimmons and his pianist sister, Arlene, inevitably absorbed some of this music. Years later, they would have "musical evenings," playing some of that same music with their father.

Phil began playing clarinet in high school. His idol was Benny Goodman, but he also liked Barney Bigard, Buster Bailey, and Irving Fazola.

Although his early musical background ranged from light operettas to dramatic scoring, he drifted toward jazz, playing with the bands of Stan Patton and Dal Richards, and with Ray Norris, Vic Centro, Bud Henderson, and others – all while studying at the University of British Columbia.

Nimmons spoke highly of Ray Norris. "Ray was ahead of his time," he said. Norris encouraged young Phil, not only as an instrumentalist but also as an arranger for the Norris quintet. "I was in seventh heaven," Nimmons recalled. "I just wrote what I wanted to write. I used to come in with eight chord changes in a bar and dear old Bud Henderson would snap out – 'Come on, there aren't that many chord changes in life.'"

Despite his obvious musical gift, Nimmons' mother wanted him to be a doctor, and he started out studying medicine. His mother never got over the "loss" to medicine. "She used to say it was a pity because I had the perfect hands to be a doctor," Phil remembers.

His later, more formal studies included three years at Juilliard and another three at the Royal Conservatory of Music in Toronto. In 1953 he formed his famous group "Nimmons 'N Nine," which included such stalwarts as Erich Traugott, Jerry Toth, Roy Smith, Ross Culley, Murray Lauder, Ed Karam, Butch Watanabe, and his old Vancouver cohort, Vic Centro.

This fine band was later expanded to Nimmons 'N Nine Plus Six. The band's recording of Nimmons' four-part *Atlantic Suite* won the 1976 Juno Award – and the inaugural award – for Best Jazz Album.

While he was arranger for the television series *The Barris Beat*, he worked with producer/director Norman Jewison. He was kept so busy that he missed the birth of his second child. "Norman went to stay with Noreen [Phil's wife] and told her I was fine," Phil said, "which didn't thrill Noreen too much."

It was in 1956, the same year, that the Nimmons band made its concert debut at the Stratford Festival, and later played with the Toronto Symphony.

The following year marked the beginning of an association with CBC Radio that was to last 20 years. The Nimmons band also toured Canada and twice in the 1960s went overseas to play for Canadian Armed Forces in Europe.

Over the years, Nimmons has written more than 400 original contemporary classical or jazz compositions for stage, television, radio, musicals, and film. But lurking under the facade of the composer, arranger, and instrumentalist was Nimmons the teacher. In 1960, he and Oscar Peterson and Ray Brown started the Advanced School of Contemporary Music, which operated for three years.

He was director of jazz studies at the University of New Brunswick; he was the first director of summer jazz programs at the Banff School of Fine Arts; and he helped to establish the Jazz Studies Program at the University of Toronto, and became Director Emeritus there. He also taught at several other Canadian universities, including York, Wilfrid Laurier, and Western, and the Courtney Youth Music Centre.

Nimmons felt that the greatest hope for the future of jazz is in the high schools, where the teaching and practice of big-band jazz flourished over the past two decades or so. "I believe in the country," he told an interviewer in 1998, "in the talent that's here." Ever aware of the uphill struggle musicians in Canada face, he always tried to improve the circumstances in which they work.

When he performed in 1997 at a benefit for the beloved, ailing jazz critic Helen McNamara, the *Globe and Mail*'s critic Mark Miller wrote: "Nimmons, who's always been ahead of his time in this country, offered the most modern tune on the program."

In June 1999, Nimmons brought a quartet to the Toronto club The Montreal Bistro. One critic called Phil's choice of tunes "impeccable" and said the quartet "blew the crowd away."

An accurate appraisal, but hardly unusual for Phil Nimmons.

Bert Niosi

b. London, Ontario, February 10, 1909; d. 1987

Since Benny Goodman, who played the clarinet, was called "The King of Swing," it was probably inevitable that Bert Niosi, who also played clarinet, would be nicknamed "Canada's King of Swing."

In fact, the clarinet was only one of the many instruments Niosi played. He was equally proficient on the alto saxophone, the trumpet, the trombone, and the piano.

Bert Niosi was the middle one of three musical brothers – bass and tuba player Joe was three years older than Bert; drummer Johnnie was six years younger. They were all skilled musicians, but it was Bert who had the leadership qualities and musical aptitude that eventually made him so well known across Canada for several decades.

For 18 glorious years, Bert Niosi led his orchestra at the Palais Royale, a dance palace along Toronto's lakeshore, whose name is almost as fondly remembered as Niosi's. The Palais Royale was built in 1921 as a boathouse; later, when it began to be used as a dance venue, it failed for some years for various owners. Not until 1932, after Bert Niosi was hired to bring in his band, did the Palais Royale make money – and dance music history.

Unlike his fellow Londoner, Guy Lombardo, Bert Niosi remained in Canada, except for one brief trip across the border. The same Lombardo, already a big name, offered the teenage Bert a spot with his band, who was then appearing in Cleveland.

Bert's mother was dead-set against his taking the job. She was convinced that the United States was full of crime. This was, after all, during the height of Prohibition and everyone had heard of hoodlums like Al Capone. But she reluctantly allowed 14-year-old Bert to take the summer job.

Young Niosi returned home from his Cleveland gig unscathed, but soon afterwards the papers were filled with the gory details of yet another gangland slaying in Chicago. Mama Niosi couldn't resist rubbing it in: "You see? I told you," she said, even though Bert's summer gig with Lombardo had been spent in Cleveland, some distance from Chicago.

It was in 1931 that Bert formed a nine-piece band to play at the Embassy Club in Toronto. The next year, he expanded the band and moved to the Palais Royale for what turned out to be a long stay. Bert's band and his own playing – no doubt aided by regular airings on CBC Radio – resulted in the growing popularity, as well as Bert's being acknowledged as "Canada's King of Swing."

Niosi also served as an inspiration to a young multi-instrumentalist named

Murray McEchern. "A Toronto fellow got me mixed up," McEchern told journalist Helen McNamara in 1974. "Bert Niosi. I was originally a violinist at 13, at 14 I played clarinet, then tenor sax, then trombone and trumpet. A teacher told me, 'You can't play all those.' Being a stubborn Scot, I said, 'If Bert can do it, I can do it.'"

And he did. After working in his teens in Toronto and Montreal, with various band leaders, including Luigi Romanelli, Rex Battle, Ronnie Hart, and George Watson, McEchern went to the United States and got a job with Benny Goodman as a trombonist in 1936. Two years later, he moved to the Casa Loma Orchestra.

Bert next embarked on a career with the CBC, first as a member of The Happy Gang from 1952 to 1959, and then as music director for such television series as *Four for the Show*, *Cross-Canada Hit Parade*, and *The Tommy Hunter Show*. At the same time, he continued to lead his band in personal appearances, returning again to the Palais Royale in 1979. About that time, the CBC aired a TV special about Niosi's career and the Palais. The show was hosted by singer Phyllis Marshall.

Niosi's professional association with his two brothers lasted for many years. On a CBC-TV showcase in 1957, Bert appeared with his brothers and he played four instruments (trumpet, trombone, alto saxophone, and clarinet) during that show.

327

Although he was primarily interested in the kind of music his own band played, Niosi also exhibited an interest in classical music. In 1950, he played Mozart's "Clarinet Quintet" with the Solway String Quartet for a CBC-Radio broadcast. He also made appearances as a soloist with the Albert Pratz Orchestra and with the Johnny Burt Strings, and his compositions have been recorded by Lucio Agostini and pianist Alexander "Ragtime" Read.

Bert's base remained Toronto throughout most of his half-century-long career. He rarely went outside the city; yet he was probably better known across Canada than any other bandleader. When he was at the height of his popularity, Bert had job offers from Jimmy Dorsey, Gene Krupa, and Glen Gray, but he never seriously considered moving away from Canada.

When Niosi died in 1987, pop culture critic Peter Goddard wrote: "He was likely listened to by more people who had more different interests than any other musician we have ever produced."

The Nylons

formed 1979 in Toronto: Paul Cooper (b. Tennessee, February 20, 1950) baritone; (replaced by Micah Barnes; replaced by Gavin Hope; replaced by Mark Cassius); Marc Connors (b. Ottawa, April 15, 1949, d. 1991) tenor; replaced by Billy Newton-Davis; replaced by Garth Mosbaugh; Claude Morrison (b. Toronto, October 11, 1952) tenor; Dennis Simpson, bass; (replaced by Ralph Cole; replaced by Arnold Robinson, b. North Carolina)

Canadian music did not experience the same kind of rhythm-and-blues explosion in the 1950s that the United States did. Audiences north of 49 did, however, hear the finger-snapping and four-part R&B harmonies of male groups such as the Four Lads singing "Moments to Remember," the Crew Cuts doing "Sh-Boom," or the Diamonds crooning "Little Darlin'." There was one notable addition to the Canadian ranks of a cappella singing that emerged in the late 1970s and remained popular into the 21st century – The Nylons.

In late 1978, the a cappella quartet emerged from the Toronto underground. Most of the original four – Cooper, Connors, Morrison, and Simpson – were out-of-work actors who rehearsed vocal harmonies, literally singing on Cooper's rooftop. To prevent becoming out-of-work singers too, the friends started out singing for their supper at a Toronto delicatessen. Their so-called "blue-eyed soul" material was one-third classic doo-wop, one-third contemporary pop music covers, and one-third original material.

By the spring of 1979, when they made their professional debut, Simpson

The Nylons, present lineup (l. to r.):
Claude Morrison, Mark Cassius,
Garth Musbaugh, Arnold Robinson

(who had won a part in a musical) had been replaced by Cole. Meanwhile, Connors and Cooper had chosen a name. On the basis of their appreciation of trailblazing "synthetic groups of the past, such as the Orlons and the Chiffons," the Canadians dubbed themselves The Nylons.

"People used to think we were punk because of our name," Morrison told *The Toronto Star*. "If anything, we're anti-punk, the antithesis."

Kidding audiences further, they defined their music as "25 per cent Rayon [Marc Connors], 25 per cent Darvon [Ralph Cole] 25 per cent Fabulon [Claude Morrison] and 25 per cent Come On [Paul Cooper]."

At their Toronto club appearances they polished their renditions of R&B standards from the 1950s and 1960s, such as the Rays' "Silhouettes" and the Tokens' "The Lion Sleeps Tonight." They even gave Bruce Springsteen's song "Fire" an a cappella treatment. They landed some television gigs, and by the time they hit the Ontario Place Forum in 1981, the Nylons had changed personnel once again – in place of Cole, they had hired a singer-songwriter-arranger formerly with the Platters, Arnold Robinson.

That year they also signed with Attic Records. Just 10 weeks after it was released, the group's debut album, *The Nylons*, went gold. Their second album, *One Size Fits All*, went platinum in Canada and won the International Chartbreaker of the Year Award (Holland's Grammy) and was voted Germany's Best Import Album. They made their concert debut at Toronto's Massey Hall in 1982.

"We really had something by the tail," Marc Connors said at the time.

Over the next seven years, the Nylons recorded six albums, which included single hits such as Steam's "Na Na Hey Hey Kiss Him Goodbye" (Number 12 on the *Billboard* chart in 1987), the Turtles' "Happy Together," and from their album ***Rockapella*** the song "Wildfire."

The Nylons were always quick on their feet too. During one of their numerous Ontario Place concerts, in front of 15,000 fans, the sound system suddenly failed. The group immediately shifted into a truly a cappella version of the Chiffons standard, "One Fine Day." The improvisation managed to hush the crowd all the way to the finale and earned a thunderous ovation.

The group found crossover opportunities as well. In 1986, it recorded the theme (written by Paul Cooper) for *Throb*, a TV sitcom that spoofed the youth-oriented record industry. The Nylons even appeared on the show several times. In 1987, the Disney producers integrated the Nylons' version of "That Kind of Man" into the soundtrack of the movie *Tin Men*.

The early 1990s brought more change. The Nylons lost two of their originals – Paul Cooper to retirement and Marc Connors (who had been the impetus for the group's multiple costume changes, its precise choreography, and its on-stage personality) to an AIDS-related illness. Within a month of Connors' death, the Nylons were back in business with three-time Juno Award–winning R&B singer Billy Newton-Davis helping to develop the group's new sound. They signed with BMG Music, released a seventh album, ***Live to Love***, in 1992, and began targeting a younger audience with rap and funk flavour worked into their act.

Again there were personnel changes – Garth Mosbaugh and Gavin Hope (replaced in 1997 by Mark Cassius) – came on board as the band went retro. They began "nylonizing" such 1960s tunes as the Beatles' "Because," the Zombies' "Time of the Season," and the Shirelles' "Will You Still Love Me Tomorrow." They recorded a Christmas album, ***Harmony***, which even included some original holiday songs.

"Originals are important," said Claude Morrison. "They give you credibility as opposed to just being another sound-alike group."

Proof they are not cookie-cutter is the fact that other 1990s vocal groups, such as the Backstreet Boys, Boyz II Men, Take 6, and Color Me Badd, have come on the scene borrowing many of the vocal stylings pioneered by the Nylons.

Billy O'Connor   *b. Kingston, Ontario, January 9, 1914*

Billy O'Connor was that rarest of all phenomena in Canada – a second-generation professional entertainer. And that was in the early 1920s.

His father, Tommy O'Connor, of Kingston, was working as a pianist and entertainer well before the start of the 20th century. In the late 1880s, O'Connor, Sr., had travelled with the famous Dockstadter's Minstrels in the United States. He was also once accompanist to Blackstone, the famed magician.

Billy got his first piano lessons from his father when the family moved from Kingston to Toronto in 1919. Billy was then five years old. By the time he grew up, Billy was already a seasoned veteran of show business, such as there was then in Canada.

"When the war broke out, I was playing in Kingston, in Lake Ontario Park, with a seven-piece band on Labour Day. I ended up with a two-piece band. All the guys had left. ... I ended up with a fiddle, a clarinet, a saxophone, and all this baloney, and they all hitchhiked back to Toronto. When I got back, in three days' time, they were all in the air force," Billy recalls.

O'Connor was then 28 years old and supporting his mother. Without a band, he made ends meet by playing at stags. "Guys would be getting their army calls, so they'd have these stags, with five or six strippers. And I'd play at four or five of those shows a night, in all the hotels on Jarvis Street and at the Royal York."

O'Connor tried to join the Royal Canadian Army Service Corps, hoping to get into the Canadian *Army Show*, then in rehearsal. But he missed the deadline. Two weeks later, he was called up to report for active duty. He was promptly assigned "with a bunch of guys with brooms and stuff" to go to the Victoria Theatre, in downtown Toronto, where the *Army Show* was going to rehearse. "Here I am dying to get into the *Army Show*, and my job is upstairs cleaning out the booth where they had the spotlight."

The rehearsal was about to be cancelled because the pianist hadn't shown up, when someone told the dance director that there was "a guy upstairs cleaning the booth, and he plays a little piano." Even so, Billy didn't get into the show. Instead he ended up in an infantry centre in Brantford and was

Billy O'Connor with Canadian Army Dance Band in 1942 at #20 Training Centre, Brantford, Ont.: Fred Faulkner on piano, Billy O'Connor, leader, Chester Towchyk, bass

asked to put together a little show in the drill hall. The program for that show listed this credit: "L/Cpl. BILLY O'CONNOR has written and produced the show, and many of the songs throughout are from his talented hand. He is a tireless worker, following in the footsteps of his father who was a showman for 40 years."

By the time the war ended, Billy had produced, written, directed, and appeared in countless army shows, often taking them to small towns like Delhi, St. George, and military installations like Camp Borden and the RCAF station at Hagersville.

After the war, Billy began working in such nightspots as the Club Norman (he was the first Canadian entertainer to appear there) and also on radio. He had shows both on CBC Radio and on the private station, CHUM. The latter was sponsored by Coca-Cola, and Billy enjoyed a relationship with that sponsor for years.

He later switched to television, first with *Four for the Show*, then *Club O'Connor* and *Saturday Date*. His popular program helped introduce such talented performers as Jack Duffy, Juliette, Peter Appleyard, Sylvia Murphy, Joey Hollingsworth, and Vanda King to the public.

O'Connor's breezy chatter and amiable performing style endeared him to Canadian TV viewers. He never pretended that he was a great "artiste," but he certainly had – in the famous phrase of Noel Coward – "a talent to amuse."

Billy always knew his audience, sensed that they wanted to hear him warble his "old chestnuts" and plunk the keyboard through his – and their – old favourite songs.

Even in his mid-eighties, although O'Connor had more or less retired as a performer, he still put together numerous shows – for seniors groups, for hospital patients and even prison inmates, and for private parties or business functions. And he usually acted as master of ceremonies for these shows. It was against his nature to avoid the spotlight altogether.

Born in Canada of Irish lineage, O'Connor retained a bit of the blarney. His banter, both on stage and off, was frequently spiced with Irishisms. Speaking of someone he admired and respected, Billy would say: "God never put a nicer man in shoes."

Walter Ostanek *b. Duparquet, Quebec, April 20, 1935*

The mailbox in front of his house is shaped like an accordion. Since he loves country music, the vanity licence plates on his truck read "EIO 1." The first LP he ever recorded was called *Gay Continental Dance Party* and was released in 1963 (when the adjective "gay" meant something completely different). He's a collector – of autographed pictures, of antique squeeze-boxes, and of Grammy Awards (he's got three of them). He'll also stop at nothing to introduce a few more citizens of the world to Slovenian Cleveland-style polkas and waltzes. He is Canada's polka king, Walter Ostanek.

"I have something cooking right now," he told Southam News. "I have a really funky blues band. ... We'll be getting serious on a recording ... [that] will have polka and blues and a little bit of polka-rap in there too."

Ostanek's Slovenian immigrant parents instilled a love of music in him very early. Walter's mother gave him his first piano accordion when he was 12. As a boy, Walter was inspired by accordion-playing polka artist Frank Yankovic. He assembled the Walter Ostanek Band in 1957 using the traditional Slovenian Cleveland-style in his polkas and waltzes. By 1963, he had recorded his first LP and won a guest spot on Johnny Carson's *Tonight Show* that same year.

Since the mid-1960s, Walter and Irene Ostanek have owned and operated a music emporium in downtown St. Catharines, Ontario, Walter's hometown. It's there in a basement where he has gathered rare accordions. They're not exactly Stradivarius models, but some of the 175 instruments are over 100 years old.

Adding a country and western flavour to accordion-playing has been Ostanek's passion almost from the beginning. His traditional C&W taste includes favourite artists such as Bill Monroe, Alan Jackson, David Kersch, Ricky Van Shelton, and even Randy Travis.

"People like Jim Reeves recorded a few polkas in their time," Ostanek said. "People who like country music also like polkas."

The accordionist has performed with some of the biggest names in country music – the Oak Ridge Boys, Brenda Lee, Roy Clark, Tommy Hunter, Mel Tillis, Ronnie Milsap, and Slim Whitman. At every opportunity, he promotes his favourite music genre.

Although his best-known titles are **The Joanne Polka**, **Lee and Ann's Polka**, and **Play Me an Old-Fashioned Waltz**, Ostanek's polka "ecumenism" has included such recordings as his Hands Across the Border series (incorporating famous Cleveland-style artists) and his recording *Polka-Stalgia*, whose proceeds go to the American-Slovenian Foundation and National Cleveland-Style Polka Hall of Fame.

In 2000, Walter Ostanek released his 60th album, *Yearning for Polkas and Waltzes*, and earned his 10th straight trip to the Grammy Awards. To date he has won three (an unbroken string between 1992 and 1994). No other Canadian has accomplished that feat.

Despite his apparent fame, Ostanek laughs when he remembers when Bo Diddley came into his music store to buy guitar strings for a performance in the area. Some time later, when Ostanek met him at a Grammy Awards ceremony and reminded him of the meeting, the rock 'n' roll idol still refused to autograph Ostanek's program.

Recognition for Walter Ostanek includes an honorary doctor of laws degree from Brock University, the Musician of the Year award from the Polka Hall of Fame in Cleveland, Ohio, and, in 2000, induction into the Order of Canada.

Seiji Ozawa

b. Manchuria, September 1, 1935

When Walter Susskind resigned from the Toronto Symphony Orchestra in 1965, after 10 years at its helm, he was succeeded by Seiji Ozawa, of Japanese parentage, and season subscriptions surged dramatically. His tenure lent a fresh flavour to orchestra music in Toronto.

His taste was daring, his style dynamic. He introduced music by such composers as Ives and Messiaen. His career with the TSO was launched with a symbolic concert at the opening of Toronto's new City Hall.

The following year, Ozawa took the TSO on a tour of Great Britain and France. Three years later, he and the orchestra went on a more extended tour of Ozawa's native Japan.

From this tour and from Ozawa's own emphasis on contemporary Japanese works (i.e., those of Toru Takemitsu) may be traced a marked influence on Toronto's musical tastes, especially in percussion performance and composition.

In 1967, Canada's centennial year, the Toronto Symphony introduced specially commissioned pieces by Otto Joachim and Luigi Nono. Though Ozawa's tenure was relatively brief, from 1965 to 1969, it had a stimulating effect on both the orchestra and the public. At his departure, he was named "musical director emeritus."

He was succeeded by Andrew Davis. It was first Davis and then the American conductor Erich Kunzel (presiding over the orchestra's pops concerts) who had asked Johnny Cowell, the skillful veteran trumpeter/composer with the TSO, to write something for the TSO's final concert at Massey

Hall (just before its scheduled move to Roy Thomson Hall). Cowell, while he was intrigued, hesitated, until Seiji Ozawa asked Cowell for an original composition to play as an encore piece for the TSO's tour of Japan in September 1969. Cowell's "Girl on a Roller Coaster," which featured the trumpet section executing a series of technically difficult passages, dazzled the Japanese audiences.

Then when Andrew Davis replaced Ozawa, he again asked Cowell to compose a piece for the orchestra's final concert at Massey Hall. The resultant "A Farewell Tribute to the Grand Old Lady of Shuter Street" (the Massey Hall location) thrilled the Toronto audience.

But Ozawa's connection with Toronto was not exactly over. Two years after he had left as conductor of the TSO, he was back. The regular conductor of the Symphony, Karel Ancerl, began a series of summer concerts at Ontario Place Forum, the outdoor amphitheatre on Toronto's waterfront. At one of the early events, Seiji Ozawa, as a guest conductor, drew an audience of more than 12,000 enthralled music lovers.

In 1991, the Toronto-based percussion group Nexus performed, with the Boston Symphony, the world premiere of Toru Takemitsu's "From Me Flows What You Call Time," which was commissioned by Carnegie Hall for its 1990–91 Centennial celebration.

Trombonist Murray Ginsberg, who played with everything from Dixieland bands to swing-era big bands, spent 18 years with the Toronto Symphony Orchestra. In 1998, he also proved himself an alert and articulate chronicler of Canadian popular music in his warm and revealing book, *They Loved to Play*, which offered readers a sweeping and amusing panorama of the many musicians whose careers had intersected his over the years. He was with the TSO when it toured Japan in 1969. Ginsberg wrote that nothing in his classical music career was quite like touring with Seiji Ozawa in the late 1960s.

He recalled that, prior to leaving on the long flight to Japan, Ozawa painted messages in Japanese on large three-inch buttons for every one of the more than 100 musicians to wear on his or her sweater or jacket. The messages announced the TSO's tour of Japan and asked every citizen to help the Canadians in any way they could. "All the citizens we encountered," reported Ginsberg, "responded gladly."

In Japan, Seiji Ozawa pulled enough strings to provide the visiting musicians with a guided tour of the grounds of the Imperial Palace, a place ordinarily closed to everyone except VIPs.

An especially memorable event of that period occurred during a tour of Florida in 1967. At Fort Meyer, because of the excessive heat, in the absence of air conditioning all the doors of the high school auditorium where they were playing were left open – even the stage doors. Ginsberg says: "Seiji had just started conducting Verdi's *I Vespri Siciliani,* when a small basset hound wandered through the [stage] doors onto the stage.

"Right after the opening drum roll in the introduction, there was a slight wavering in the orchestra as the dog sniffed his way from music stand to music stand. What could Seiji do? The show had to go on.

"He continued conducting as the hound proceeded to the podium and sniffed the conductor's legs, which caused the audience to break up with laughter. Finally the unconcerned dog made a slow exit stage left, but not before dropping a calling card against the last music stand of the cello section. The concert continued to a glorious finale."

P.J. Perry

b. Calgary, Alberta, December 2, 1941

It isn't often in Canada that you find musical dynasties – two generations of the same family – playing jazz. A few examples spring to mind: Alex Dean, one of the top tenor saxophonists in the country, and the son of trumpeter Ken Dean, who led a Dixieland band in Toronto half a century ago; Bernie Piltch and his two sons, Rob and David. (There's also a sister, Susan, a pianist.)

And then there's the Perry family – father Paul and son P.J. (for Paul John). The younger Perry grew up surrounded by music and took to it naturally.

The surname was originally Guloien. It was the father, Paul, who changed the name to Perry – actually his mother's maiden name – for professional

purposes, mostly to avoid the difficulties created by the unusual surname.

Paul senior was born near Regina of Norwegian parents, the second-oldest of eight children. He taught himself and several of his brothers to play saxophone and had a dance band (1939–40) in Medicine Hat. He moved to Calgary, where Paul John was born in 1941. After playing piano and clarinet as a child, P.J. joined his father's dance band at 14, playing baritone sax. For several years, he spent summers playing at Sylvan Lake, and winters in Vancouver, at various clubs.

P.J. developed into a vigorous alto player in the bebop style. Moving to Toronto in 1959, he played with Sonny Greenwich, Ron Collier, and Maury Kaye. In 1979, he moved to Edmonton and joined Tommy Banks.

After touring Europe, he moved again to Toronto, playing with Dizzy Gillespie, Slide Hampton, Woody Shaw, and Herbie Spanier, then returned to Edmonton to resume a long association with Banks.

P.J. Perry eventually developed into one of the most compelling alto sax players in jazz, not only in Canada but anywhere, a position he has maintained for the past two decades. By the 1980s, he was already being referred to as "legendary." In 1993, he won a Juno Award as Best Jazz Recording Artist, and also *The Jazz Report* Award for Alto Saxophonist of the Year. "Winning the Juno Award was a big thrill for me," P.J. told *The Jazz Report*'s Greg Sutherland. "I have been playing music for a long time and it hasn't been an easy road."

This was true. P.J.'s life had not been without its problems, some of them self-inflicted.

As mentioned, his father had brought him into the family orchestra when P.J. was 14. "At that time," Paul senior said later, "I thought it would be better for him to be in the band than running around the streets and getting into trouble. I don't know whether it worked out that way or not." Apparently it didn't. By the age of 15, P.J. had left home to play in the strip clubs and dives of Vancouver's east end, though returning to the fold each summer at Sylvan Lake. By the age of 20, he had acquired the habits and dependencies that were to plague him into his thirties. (Among his troubles was an incident in Germany, where he was sentenced to six months of solitary confinement in prison for possession of marijuana. On his release, after he changed his plea to "guilty," he was deported.)

Perry spent the early 1960s playing in Vancouver, Toronto, and Montreal. In 1963, he moved overseas for three years, living and working in London, France, and Berlin. For whatever reason, soon after he returned to Vancouver, he took six months off from the music business. He even sold his horns.

Tommy Banks proved to be a good and lasting friend. P.J. was newly married and not exactly rolling in money. Banks "sponsored" Perry's purchase of an alto sax and the dynamic saxophonist settled in.

Kris King

But by mid-1970, he was back in Vancouver and working outside the music business to support his family – now three, with the birth of a daughter.

Then bandleader Bobby Hales, an old Sylvan Lake associate, called P.J. to join Pacific Salt, a sextet with enough jazz-rock overtones to find favour with the CBC's *Jazz Radio-Canada* on a regular basis.

By 1973, Perry was back in Edmonton and resumed his association with pianist Banks. With his health stabilizing, he became the first-call lead alto saxophonist in Edmonton and played regularly in Banks' orchestras for numerous TV variety shows in both Vancouver and Hamilton, Ontario.

Perry also took assignments with the Edmonton Symphony for its recording of Jacques Ibert's *Suite symphonique Paris*, and with a rock band called Crowcuss for its *Running Start*. He also accompanied the Banks orchestra (in 1978) to the Montreux Jazz Festival. That band's double LP of its concert there won the Juno Award as best jazz recording of 1978.

P. J. Perry, now pushing 60, hasn't slowed down one bit. He seems to be ever on the lookout for new musical mountains to climb.

In the summer of 2000, he was an added attraction when Rob McConnell took his great Tentet to the Markham (Ontario) Jazz Festival. P.J.'s blistering alto work proved one of the standouts of their concert at the Markham Theatre. Perry was also added to the Tentet for the group's first CD, on Justin Time Records, late in 2000.

Perry's versatility continues to impress listeners and critics alike, as witness his 1999 CD made with the Edmonton Symphony Orchestra, which ranges from Gershwin to Ellington to Ravel to Mussorgsky to Jobim. The death of Moe Koffman in April 2001 left him the unquestioned Canadian alto sax champion.

Colleen Peterson

b. Peterborough, Ontario, November 14, 1950; d. October 9, 1996

Courtesy Canapress

In 1967, after the music industry heard her on a New York recording of the rock group Takin' Care of Business, *RPM* magazine recognized Colleen Peterson with the Most Promising Female Vocalist award. Nearly a decade later, in 1976, when Capitol Records released Peterson's first solo album, ***Beginning to Feel Like Home***, the Juno Awards voted her Most Promising Female Vocalist.

"How much promise does she have to keep showing?" a critic wondered.

Notice and awards were not the true measure of Colleen Peterson's career, cut short by her death from cancer in 1996. A summary of the material she created and the roads she travelled during her 30 years as a performer illustrates her contribution to the music scene. From the beginning, she was a perfectionist, always searching for that perfect song, that perfect performance, that perfect bit of instrumentation. It began at age 13, when she used Lucky Green stamps to buy her first guitar. Out came folk tunes, jazz licks, country twang, and imitations of R&B such as Aretha Franklin.

Still a teenager, Peterson hit the Toronto coffeehouses in Yorkville and met David Wiffen, Bruce Cockburn, Richard Patterson, and Dennis Pendrith who were the latest version of the Ottawa-based group Three's a Crowd. In 1966, she performed with the group at Mariposa Folk Festival and the next year at Expo '67 in Montreal. Shortly after, she worked with two other Ottawa groups, Five D and St. Patrick Street Rooming House and then the 10-piece rock band Takin' Care of Business in New York. Most fellow musicians raved about her versatility, both vocally and instrumentally, but in 1967 so did the industry with the most promising female vocalist title.

In fact, Peterson was just beginning to demonstrate her versatility. In 1970, she joined the Toronto cast of the rock musical *Hair*, and followed this by a stint in the road company of the musical *Love and Maple Syrup*. Next, setting up shop in Kingston, she teamed up with Mark Haines in the group Spriggs and Bringle. Colleen Peterson could easily slip in and out of any musical idiom. In the mid-1970s she decided to take a crack at country music.

"I'm not a country girl. I'm a suburban girl," she told the *Toronto Star*. "So what I sing has to have an edge of soul to it."

Her 1976 debut album with Capitol Records proved the point. *Beginning to Feel Like Home* demonstrated how comfortably she could make the transition to up-tempo country with songs such as **Don't It Make You Wanna Dance** as well as to country ballads with her song **Souvenirs**. She could cover material ranging from Willie Nelson to Willie P. Bennett. Her introduction to Nashville put her in touch with some of the day's best country artists; over the next few years she took time to tour with and write for Charlie Daniels, Roger Miller, and Waylon Jennings. Meantime, she recorded a second album, *Colleen*, which featured such backup performers as Emmylou Harris, Linda Ronstadt, Rick Nelson, Bette Midler, Barry Manilow, and (the album's producer) Lee Hazlewood.

Peterson's run in Nashville ended in 1988 when a publishing deal and a recording deal fell through simultaneously. She moved back to Canada and settled on a 40-hectare farm outside Lakefield, Ontario. In keeping with the quirkiness of her career, while she only rarely emerged from the farm to perform in the late 1980s, country radio stations began giving her version of Willie Nelson's song "Crazy" airplay. She had left country music behind, but suddenly this unreleased publisher's demo showcasing definitive "second versions" of famous country songs was becoming a national hit on radio.

The next twist of fate brought Peterson together with Sylvia Tyson, Cindy Church, and Caitlin Hanford on a stage at Toronto's Harbourfront Centre as the group Quartette. Intended as a one-time concert, the August 1993 performance proved to be the career jolt Peterson was looking for. In fact, the way Peter Goddard described it in a *Chatelaine* magazine piece in 1995, "[These] women's story could be a song in itself, some bittersweet country ballad. One verse would be about Tyson … big sister to the rest … then Church, the Albertan finding fame by coming east; Hanford, the schoolmarm with a passion for old country tunes … and Peterson, nearly famous since Expo '67, only now getting a break."

Quartette went on to become regular guests on CBC Radio's *Morningside* and NPR's *Prairie Home Companion*. Quartette's first self-titled album won a Canadian Country Music Award and a Big Country nomination; the second album, *Work of the Heart*, was also critically acclaimed in 1995, as was the third, *It's Christmas*, released in 1996, the year Colleen Peterson died.

"In 1967 I wanted two things," she told Peter Goddard. "to play the Royal

York Hotel in Toronto before I was 50, and not to be married before I was 26. I'm now 44 and neither has happened."

While there were no standing ovations at the Imperial Room nor storybook marriages in her life, there were memorable performances, including one in a television studio in Edmonton. In 1979, while videotaping an appearance on the syndicated television show *Rock It*, Peterson (backed by a 16-piece studio band) stopped the show with her song **Don't It Make You Wanna Dance**. It demonstrated the essence of Peterson live – soulful voice; upbeat and compelling personality; and so much more than a promising talent.

While a long list of awards was not in her all-too-short résumé, lifetime achievement is clearly acknowledged by her peers and her audiences.

Oscar Peterson *b. Montreal, Quebec, August 15, 1925*

Courtesy Canapress

Quite possibly the world's best-known jazz pianist, Oscar Peterson has long had one complaint – and he just might be wrong. Peterson has felt for years that he is taken for granted in Canada. As far back as 1969, he was expressing concern about "Canadiana."

"Everybody beats the drum for Canadian Consciousness," he told an interviewer in Rome, "but the French Canadians are more interested in splitting off from Canada and everybody else is interested in being English or American or what have you than in being Canadian – which is a shame. I want to see Canada live up to all it really could be.

"Like, I'm invited to a Command Performance for the Queen in England, President Nixon has asked that I do a concert at the White House. But I've never had any requests from Trudeau. It sometimes seems pretty hopeless getting through to Canadians that yes, we Canadian artists do exist."

Eleven years later, he was voicing much the same complaint. "I've achieved a funny kind of status in Canada," he told the *Globe and Mail* in March 1980. "Most of it comes because I went to the United States and other places, and as a result of Canadians having seen me repeatedly on the TV shows of people like Johnny Carson, Merv Griffin, Dick Cavett, Jonathan Winters, and André Previn, where I'm almost introduced as 'the Canadian pianist,' I think that has weighed heavily with Canadians.

"I've never had a series of my own on the CBC. That seems strange – everybody else has. Tommy Hunter, Anne Murray, Jack Kane – and yet I'm going back to England this summer for my third series in London. So you kind of wonder why."

(Somebody at the CBC must have read the article. He got a CBC series, *Oscar Peterson and Friends*, that fall. The "friends" were his weekly guests, such as Dizzy Gillespie, Mary Lou Williams, Buddy DeFranco, Roy Eldridge, and Jimmy Rowles.)

Peterson has always loved gadgets. For many years, he was addicted to photography. ("He didn't just buy a camera," said his friend, trombonist Butch Watanabe, "he bought a whole system.") He loved cameras and cars – and then synthesizers.

"Canada's best-known jazzman synthesizes his sound," read a heading in the *Toronto Star* on May 1, 1982. Roy Shields, who wrote the story, went on to describe Peterson's newest toy: "And his synthesizer is not the garden variety, either. His is a Synclavier H Digital Analysis/Synthesis Option. When seated at it, he resembles a mad scientist in a science-fiction movie. The console is huge with a background wall of connecting cables that might intimidate a Bell engineer.

"With his Synclavier, Peterson can compose music that is automatically transformed by a computer into written form on a video screen for other instruments. And these scores are then available as printouts or can be sent digitally by telephone to other musicians or members of his quartet around the globe."

When the Grammy awards were handed out there was a new category, synthesizer music, and Peterson rapidly rushed to the forefront of the creative form. "When they first came out," said Oscar, "I was leery of the sounds I heard because they were in their embryonic stage. But now they are valid instruments with voices and sounds of their own."

To those who still view them as weird electronic sound manipulators, Peterson replies with a smile and a shrug: "It's a little like somebody fighting the piano; it's a little late, they're here."

Peterson is not a great creator of jazz – he is a great executor, which is every bit as rare as a creator whose life has been spent immersed in the music of the jazz masters for whom he feels the most affinity.

And while others developed by changing the music, Peterson, more modestly, confined himself to the task of trying to become a better instrumentalist.

Over the past 10 years, in particular, perhaps because of all the concert work, he seems to have increased his control over the piano. His dynamics have improved, affording him greater range, and it seems easier for him to make the instrument sing (a mysterious business – the players themselves don't know how they do it).

In the end, Peterson's wisdom is evident. Aware of the nature of his gifts, he resisted strong pressure from those who wanted him to be an innovator and dedicated himself instead to celebrate jazz, with energy, honesty, intelligence, and obvious love. He's been doing it for 40 years, and he has prevailed. Noble work, to be sure.

In other words, he determined to become the best Oscar Peterson he could be. And he certainly succeeded.

The Poppy Family

formed 1966 in British Columbia: Terry Jacks (b. Winnipeg, March 29, 1944); Susan Pesklevits Jacks (b. Saskatoon, August 19, 1948)

Rock 'n' roll music exploded in Canada as the 1960s ended and the 1970s began. Among the energizers was the arrival of the CRTC radio music regulations (mandating at least 30 percent Canadian content in primetime hours). However, that boost was incidental to the kind of energy mustered by the two principal talents behind the Poppy Family – Terry and Susan Jacks. With little help from government, record companies, promoters, agents, or the media, they pushed their way to the top of the recording heap with three international hit singles and one big album.

The Poppy Family, photographed in 1969

James O'Mara

Terry Jacks was described by some as a rebel. Others said he was driven and a control freak. One of his contemporaries, Ronnie Hawkins, said Terry Jacks had been to the mountaintop and messed with the lions. Whatever the description, Jacks very much designed his own fate and saw nothing terribly complicated in succeeding.

"Simple music, simple lyrics, a melody people could remember, a simple performance, a lot of sincerity," he told Ritchie Yorke in *Axes, Chops and Hot Licks*. "If you've got good songs, you can do it."

The eldest son of a physician, Terry Jacks grew up in Vancouver under the expectation he might become an architect. The truth was he loved two things – going fishing and rock 'n' roll, in particular the music of Buddy Holly. When Holly died in 1959, Jacks said he bought a cheap guitar, joined a rock 'n' roll band and tried to drown his grief by performing. Despite being a poor guitarist, Jacks stayed on with the band and wrote **The Way You Feel**, which was a hit in western Canada. By the mid-1960s he was rhythm guitarist and singer for the Chessmen appearing regularly on CBC-TV's *Music Hop*.

That's how he met Susan Pesklevits. Together they worked in several Vancouver-based bands – Powerline and then Winkin', Blinkin' and Nod. Before long, Terry and Susan were married. They hit the road, and in the winter of 1966 appeared in a small coffeehouse in Blubber Bay, B.C., for the first time as The Poppy Family (a name Terry Jacks pulled out of the dictionary). They recorded (with London Records) in 1968 – first a song called **Beyond the Clouds** and then **What Can the Matter Be** – which both enjoyed some success in British Columbia.

Then came the miraculous third single.

"**Which Way You Goin' Billy?** was cut for only $125 dollars," Terry Jacks said. In order to keep costs to a minimum, he took only four musicians into the studio. In fact, Jacks gave the studio a one-third interest in the song to offset some of the costs. In any event, Jacks only intended **Billy** to be the B-side of a 45-rpm record. When he found out the song was suddenly number two on *Billboard*'s Hot 100 chart in the United States (he'd gone fishing at the time), Jacks immediately bought back the studio's one-third interest for $500.

"One day we can hardly make the rent," Jacks told *Canadian Magazine*, "and then there's a cheque for $98,000 in the mail."

When **Billy** was released in Canada, in 1969, it sold more than 100,000 copies. Susan Jacks became the first female Canadian singer to earn a gold record. The single also won two RPM Gold Leaf (later Juno) Awards and went on to rival the Guess Who's "American Woman," as one of the biggest Canadian singles of all time.

Which Way You Goin' Billy? was the top-selling single in New York for six weeks, preventing the Beatles' last single, "The Long and Winding Road," from reaching number one. The Poppy Family were offered a spot on the final

Terry Jacks, photographed in 1999

Ed Sullivan Show of the season, but had already committed to appearing at Expo '70 in Osaka. In the United States **Billy** sold more than one million copies. The Poppy Family's next single, **That's Where I Went Wrong**, generated nearly one million sales as well, and the group's debut album, *Poppy Family*, by 1970 was on its way to selling 150,000 copies.

Then, just as suddenly as the group rose to prominence, it disbanded. The Poppy Family had gone from making $30 a night to $6000. But at the same time expenses had risen. Terry Jacks – feeling the pressure to manage, book, and promote the Poppy Family's tour schedule, while finding time to write, produce, and perform the group's own material – decided to quit while he was ahead.

"We had enough money to retire," Jacks said. "But we were losing touch with our music. I was losing interest. So, I went off fishing."

Three months later, Terry Jacks changed his mind. He and Susan Jacks travelled to England for a recording with the string section of the London Philharmonic Orchestra. Then, after a New Year's performance at Disneyland with Blood Sweat and Tears, Terry Jacks wrapped up the band for good.

The co-founders of the Poppy Family began drifting apart professionally. Terry Jacks pursued his behind-the-scenes role, for a while producing the Beach Boys. He encouraged them to record an English treatment of Jacques Brel's song "Seasons in the Sun"; when they balked, he altered some of the

347

lyrics and recorded it himself. The Terry Jacks version sold over 10 million copies worldwide and earned him three Juno Awards in 1973. He was the first Canadian artist to reach platinum on a single (over 150,000 in sales) for "Seasons in the Sun."

By 1974, however, Susan and Terry Jacks' marriage had broken up too. Each pursued a solo career. Among Terry Jacks' later Canadian hits were **I'm Gonna Capture You** (originally written for Tommy Roe), **Rock and Roll (I Gave the Best Years of My Life)** in 1974, and **Christina** in 1975. He continued to write into the 1980s and produced such Canadian groups as Chilliwack.

Susan Jacks recorded "You Don't Know What Love Is" and "I Thought of You Again." In 1976, she worked with Cheese, a band with whom she recorded several minor hits, including "Anna Marie," "Dream," "You're Part of a Dream," and "Honey Love." In 1976, she also recorded a solo album, *Memories Are Made of You*; then her second solo album (through a series of corporate machinations) was eventually produced in 1980 by her ex-husband, Terry Jacks. Oddly, the album was titled *Ghosts*.

Prairie Oyster

formed 1974 in Peterborough, Ontario: Russell deCarle (b. May 31, 1953) bass, vocals; Joan Besen (b. June 12, 1951) keyboards, vocals; Keith Glass (b. February 4, 1952) guitar, vocals; Dennis Delorme pedal steel, banjo, dobro; John P. Allen fiddle, guitar, mandolin; Bruce Moffet drums (replaced by Bohdan Hluszko, replaced by Charlie Cooley)

Consider their diverse backgrounds – a bass player who once backed up George Hamilton IV, a guitarist who played in a Hank Williams retrospective, a fiddler who worked with The Great Speckled Bird, a keyboard player who considers reggae to be country music, and a multi-instrumentalist with a passion for pedal steel guitar – and it's not hard to see why one recording executive called Prairie Oyster "burlesque."

The music business can't seem to pigeonhole this six-piece band from Ontario. One reviewer called them "diehard country." A music industry profile described their sound as "rockabilly swing." And in 2001, most folk festival organizers slot them in the "roots music" section of their programs.

While their music may be hard to peg, however, Prairie Oyster's success over a quarter-century of touring and recording is not. To date, their 6 Juno

Señor McGuire

Prairie Oyster (l. to r.): Dennis Delorme, John P. Allen, Bohdan Hluszko, Joan Besen, Keith Glass, Russell deCarle

Awards, 12 Canadian Country Music Association (CCMA) Awards, 4 Society of Composers, Authors, and Music Publishers of Canada (SOCAN) Awards, and 13 RPM Big Country Awards speak pretty much for themselves. Yet even this notoriety falls short of defining what they're about.

"The fact is Prairie Oyster stands ... uniquely, distinctly alone," wrote Mitch Potter in the *Toronto Star* in 1994, "as a wonderfully subtle, seasoned country band with only a fleeting interest in conventional country fame."

Playing bluegrass was the initial musical motivation for at least two of the original members. Bassist Russell deCarle and guitarist Keith Glass were childhood friends and in the late 1960s performed in the King City Slickers. As well, deCarle worked in television and toured with George Hamilton IV, while Glass performed in the musical play *Hank Williams: The Show He Never Gave* with Sneezy Waters.

In 1974, deCarle and Glass joined banjo/dobro/pedal steel player Dennis Delorme for the first edition of Prairie Oyster (according to the anatomical definition, a prairie oyster is the part removed when a bull is castrated, and taking the analogy one step further, Prairie Oyster always delivered the delicacies of traditional country music).

"We tended to draw upon the golden age of country music," deCarle said, "honky-tonk, bluegrass and western swing ... they really are the roots and the soul of our music."

The trio broke up in 1979, but reassembled in 1982 when keyboard player

Joan Besen (who had left Sylvia Tyson's band) joined the Oyster's wildly successful reunion at the Horseshoe Tavern in Toronto. By 1985, part-time auctioneer and rest-of-the-time fiddler John P. Allen (who had formerly played for the Good Brothers, Ian Tyson's band the Great Speckled Bird, and Jesse Winchester) filled out the picture.

Prairie Oyster's debut independent recording (on 16th Avenue Records) was a single called "Juke Joint Johnny" (1984) followed by a second single, "Rain, Rain" (1984), which had originally been sung by George Jones and J. P. "The Big Bopper" Richardson in the 1960s. The choice of tunes and recording style were typical of Prairie Oyster – pick recognizable songs and update their treatment without losing the essence of the original. It was reminiscent but not retrospective.

"Retro is when a musician dusts off an old sound to show how clever he is for having rediscovered it," Keith Glass wrote on the band's Web site. "Roots is the sound musicians make when they mine the very soul of a genre and their own personal past, as a way to better convey their ideas."

In 1984, the band signed with Stony Plain Records and recorded its first album, *Oyster Tracks* (1986). That year, the band won its first Juno for Best Country Group of the Year and would recapture that category in 1987, 1991, 1992, 1995, and 1996. Meanwhile, airplay and a demo brought the band to the attention of producers and A&R reps in Nashville; the Oyster signed with RCA and was invited to record whatever it wanted. Several albums and singles followed: *Different Kind of Fire* (1990) and *Everybody Knows* (1991), which went platinum in Canada and spawned their hit single **Did You Fall in Love with Me?** Next were *Only One Moon* (1994) and *Blue Plate Special* (1996), which Judith Fitzgerald (of *Country Wave* magazine) called "undeniably the band's freshest."

Despite the recognition the band seemed to garner among audiences in Canada, Europe, and to a lesser extent the United States, the country music industry found it tough to pigeonhole Prairie Oyster. When their CD **What Is This Country?** (1999) was released, Glass called it "a career" album for its depth. DeCarle said the recording was like "going into the studio with our gloves off." The industry, however, had a tougher time defining it.

"It's a safe bet," Terry Pasieka wrote in the *Globe and Mail*, "that New Country programmers – their playlists filled with Nashville country-pop and the latest poster boys and girls – won't know what to make of the chronological journey Prairie Oyster takes over the album's 13 tracks – from satiny '50s country swing and '60s blues to heavily produced '70s countrypolitan, '80s urban-cowboy pop and steamy '90s swamp-rock."

The repertoire and the recordings continued to demonstrate what had brought the original members of the band together in the first place – a sense of fun and putting a different twist on grassroots country music. Prairie Oyster never aspired to have a Nashville career. As they told Stephen Cooke of the *Halifax Herald* in 1998, "We're a band that just never took itself seriously as being one particular thing, so we're quite willing to experiment with all different kinds of music and treat it all with equal respect or interest."

Raffi

b. Cairo, Egypt, July 8, 1948

While the audiences for certain genres of music – blues, jazz, and rock 'n' roll – ebb and flow with the temper of the times, child audiences remain constant. Particularly when the children of the baby boomers, the so-called "echo generation," came along in the 1970s, the impact of all those ears, hearts, and minds on the music industry was not overlooked by artists with a knack for singing children's songs. Few have been so dedicated to those young audiences as Raffi Cavoukian.

Courtesy Troubadour / Shoreline Records

"Finding one's true voice is a boon," he wrote in his autobiography, *The Life of a Children's Troubadour.* "When we help children make that discovery from an early age, we help them find a place in the world and a purpose in this life."

For Raffi, growing up in an Armenian family in Cairo, finding his own true voice was not immediately obvious. He was raised (with a brother and sister) by loving but authoritarian parents and taught in disciplined classrooms. When the family immigrated to Toronto, in 1958, Raffi began helping out his father, a professional photographer, with the expectation that son should follow in father's footsteps. At university he studied psychology and economics, but learned the songs of Dylan, Mitchell, Lightfoot, and Cohen and performed them for pocket money. In 1969, he left university to become a full-time singer-songwriter.

In the early 1970s, Raffi travelled (with guitar and backpack) across Europe, Canada, and the United States, performing at folk festivals, resorts, and coffeehouses. He honed his guitar-playing skills by catching Neil Young, Joni Mitchell, and David Rea at the Riverboat in Toronto and augmented his income by giving guitar lessons. Then, in 1974, he was invited to sing at a nursery school in Toronto. Not knowing any traditional children's songs, he turned to his wife, Debi Pike, a kindergarten teacher, for help. Then, he said he relied on a "make-them-laugh strategy to cover the awkward moments. … All in all, I had a good time and it seemed the staff and kids did too." That led to singing in the Mariposa in the Schools program, which at least supplemented his modest folk-singing income.

Without a recording contract in 1975, Raffi formed his own label, Troubadour, secured a loan, and recorded an album of contemporary folk songs called *Good Luck Boy.* The second album proved more a milestone in philosophy and return. **Singable Songs for the Very Young** had a simple concept – to fill the vacuum in the record stores between Disney cartoon soundtracks and educational records for kids. With the assistance of musicians Ken Whiteley (guitar), Chris Whiteley (harmonica), Bob Doidge (bass), Garnet Rogers (flute/fiddle), and Dan Lanois (mandolin), and an eight-track studio in the Lanois basement (Ancaster, Ontario), Raffi recorded a blend of traditional children's songs, such as "The More We Get Together," "Down by the Bay," "Must Be Santa," "Baa Baa Black Sheep," and his own composition **The Sharing Song**. Total cost $4000.

Critics raved. Interview and appearance requests flooded in. Sales went through the roof. However, Raffi still considered himself a folk singer who also sang for children. He produced another adult album, **Love Light**, and a second children's album, **More Singable Songs**, both in 1977; the next year his first album was certified gold (the first Canadian children's record to do so), then platinum in 1979. Raffi got the message. He put the adult singing career aside.

A visit to the Vancouver Public Aquarium in 1979 provided his next inspiration, because "Kavna, a beluga whale, stole my heart," he said, "and I set out to write a song about this beautiful creature." **Baby Beluga** was not a protest song, but a love song. Then he composed **All I Really Need**, as an anthem for the International Year of the Child. He added more children's songs to his repertoire and released two more albums (through A&M Records), *The Corner Grocery Store* (1979) and *Baby Beluga* (1980).

Raffi became a regular, performing every Christmas at the University of Toronto's Convocation Hall and every summer at the Vancouver Children's Festival. By 1981, television had come knocking with a CBC-TV special, and Troubadour celebrated 500,000 in album sales. That year, as well, Raffi was booked for his first concerts in the United States. The demand for tickets at the Portland, Oregon venue was so great that a second show had to be added. The trend continued in Dallas, Santa Monica, and Minneapolis with reviewers describing the phenomenon as "American Raffimania." The capacity halls, the gold and platinum albums, the television shows, and the adoration from children and adults continued. In 1983, Raffi was recognized for his work with children by being invested with the Order of Canada.

From the outset of his career, Raffi had staunchly refused to see his recordings entered in the annual Juno Awards, because "I didn't see much point in having a competition for 'best children's recording' when children knew what they liked and could care less about a subjective selection of 'winner' by an obscure process open to personal politics." Notably, following the release of his album *One Light, One Sun* (1985), which contained **The Bowling Song**, the American Bowling Proprietors Association acknowledged his contribution to youth bowling. Raffi rationalized the competitive aspect of bowling as something that didn't belong in the arts, but was best left to sports.

With nine albums recorded, two concert videos released, and several songbooks of his lyrics published, Troubadour and Raffi Cavoukian appeared to have achieved all they had set out to and more. But by the late 1980s he was burned out – diagnosed with chronic fatigue syndrome. He separated from his wife and dropped out of the children's entertainment business.

In the early 1990s, Raffi reinvented himself as an "eco-troubadour," writing and performing songs about the environment for children, adolescents, and adults. He moved to British Columbia and worked with such diverse groups as the Raging Grannies, David Suzuki, and U.S. Senator Al Gore promoting preservation of the planet. He attended the 1992 Earth Summit and the 1993 Kyoto Global Forum, and recorded songs to advance the cause – **Evergreen Everblue**, **Our Dear, Dear Mother**, and **Big Beautiful Planet.** The material was misunderstood, angering some parents and being mistakenly put in children's music bins at record stores.

A further reinvention brought Raffi back to his roots. In 1994 he recorded

Bananaphone, his first studio album in seven years. It included a variety of songs such as **Shake a Toe**, the Shaker hymn "Simple Gifts," "C-A-N-A-D-A" by Stompin' Tom Connors, **The Shmenge Polka**, a tribute to John Candy, and the title song, which managed to put to music every banana pun imaginable. The album earned Raffi a Juno Award for the Best Children's Album for 1995 (as well as a Grammy nomination) and the *Bananaphone* tour was a hit with audiences and the media. His album *Raffi Radio* (1997) mixed new songs, skits, and incidental music reminiscent of days when people gathered around a radio for entertainment.

As the new millennium arrived, so did new ideas for Raffi's continuing crusades. In 2000, he founded the Troubadour Institute in order to accelerate initiatives and support organizations promoting children's emotional, physical, spiritual, and mental well-being. To emphasize the point, he issued a Covenant for Honouring Children, in his words, "inviting us to seek a new partnership with our children, with each other and with our planet; redesigning society for the greatest good by meeting the priority needs of its youngest citizens."

Raffi had found his true voice.

The Rankin Family

formed 1989 in Mabou, Nova Scotia, disbanded 1999; John Morris Rankin (b. 1959, d. 2000) piano, fiddle, vocals; Jim Rankin (b. 1964) guitar, vocals; Raylene Rankin vocals; Carol Jean "Cookie" Rankin (b. 1965) vocals; Heather Rankin vocals

The Rankins all play music – all twelve of them. However, for a decade, the world knew the five of the them as the Rankin Family, a cross-over band that was as much at ease palying pop music as a Gaelic folk tune or a country ballad.

"Our music is distinct from American country music," Raylene Rankin told the *Toronto Star*. "The basis of our traditional music is Cape Breton Celtic, a mostly Scottish mix with touches of Irish. Music loses something when you ignore its roots, the place it comes from."

Kathleen (a pianist) and Alexander (a fiddler) Rankin raised 12 children in their family home along the northwestern coast of Cape Breton. The Rankin children got musical training by singing at weddings, at funerals, and in the church choir, but mostly during household *ceilidhs*, jam sessions in the family kitchen. The house was the social centre of the neighbourhood, often filled with friends and music. It seemed that, from the moment there were enough offspring to make up a band, every weekend the family was on the road to

The Rankin Family (l. to r.): Jimmy, Cookie, Raylene, John Morris, Heather

perform at dancehalls and taverns, playing traditional fiddle music for square dances and round-dance music.

Traditional fiddle music was not so popular then. When John Morris Rankin began playing old-time Celtic music as a schoolboy, he remembered often hiding his fiddle on the way to school. Celtic music crusader John Allan Cameron recalled a scene in the CBC-TV documentary *The Vanishing Cape Breton Fiddler* that showed John Morris Rankin (as a boy) walking along a Mabou back road with legendary fiddler Dan R. MacDonald.

"Dan R. had his hand on John Morris's shoulder," Cameron recalled. "That scene meant 'I am taking my traditions and passing them on to you. Take it and fly with it.'"

It was perhaps a calling. In the late 1980s, John Morris' siblings approached him about assembling a professional band to perform at a series of folk festivals. Raylene had tried her hand at solo performing, but in the meantime had just graduated from Dalhousie University with a law degree. Heather and Cookie had just graduated from Acadia University. Jimmy was graduating from the Nova Scotia College of Art and Design. John Morris (who had attended St. Francis Xavier) was the only full-time musician.

"We had a reputation for our singing," Cookie Rankin said, "but we hadn't taken it seriously, the idea of taking it beyond the level of pig-and-whistles."

The Rankin Family debuted in 1989, singing the songs of Cape Breton – of work, death, and departure. They drew much of their repertoire from traditional Gaelic tunes, which the brothers and sisters learned to sing phonetically. That same year, the group took just two-and-a-half weeks to make its first cassette recording, *The Rankin Family* (1989). That earned enough to record a second, *Fare Thee Well Love* (1990), which consisted of five original tunes, three traditional songs and two fiddle medleys. Together the two recordings sold 80,000 copies in Canada.

The group attracted national attention in the early 1990s when it began cleaning up at the East Coast Music Awards and through several appearances on Rita MacNeil's CBC-TV show *Rita & Friends*. Despite the following, the band stuck to its creative principles, writing and recording original "adult contemporary" pop tunes while continuing to pay close attention to traditional Celtic roots and harmonies. Their first Juno nominations were, appropriately enough, in the categories of Best Roots/Traditional, Best Country Duo/Group, and Most Promising Group in 1992.

"Both the arrangements and the material we do require unanimous consent," Raylene Rankin said. "That's reflected in the kinds of performances we give and in our ability to stay in sync with everyone on stage."

By that time, the group had signed with Capitol-EMI Records, who rereleased the Rankin Family's first two independent cassettes and their next recording, *North Country* (1993). It contained 13 songs, eight written by Jimmy Rankin and three Gaelic tunes with names such as "Oich U Agus H-Iuraidb Eile (Love Song)," "Ho Ro Mo Nighean Donn Bhoidheach (Ho Ro My Nut Brown Maiden)," and "Leis An Lurgainn (Boat Song)."

At the 1994 Junos, the Rankins broke through with four awards – for Entertainer of the Year, Best Country Group, Best Group, and Best Single (**Fare Thee Well Love**, written by Jimmy Rankin). Meanwhile, their worldwide record sales had topped a million, largely in Canada, but thanks in part to offshore tours in Britain, Australia, and New Zealand.

The band was hitting its stride. Reviewers didn't seem as attentive, however, and some (in particular, *shift* magazine) dismissed their music as "quaint." So the Rankins (as they were then known) added country-rock to their repertoire and recorded their next two albums in Nashville – *Endless Seasons* (1995) and then *Uprooted* (1998), created with George Massenburg (who'd produced Linda Ronstadt and Lyle Lovett).

"We experimented with more contemporary sounds," said Heather Rankin, "and even broke away from the [way] we approach the traditional material."

Strong as the material continued to be, the touring side of the business became too taxing. Cookie Rankin told the *Globe and Mail*'s Peter Feniak how "you'd spend all day getting psyched up for it. You're hanging around the hall and you're thinking about it. And then here it comes – that 90-minute set. You give it everything you have. Then you're back on the bus and rolling away."

"Trying to run a business and being on the road and living in confined spaces and night after night singing the same tunes," Jimmy Rankin told Brenda Bouw of the *National Post*, "it is not a natural way of life."

In 1999, with more than two million copies of their five albums sold, five

Juno Awards to their credit, and thousands of audiences more aware of Celtic music than ever before, the family members decided to break up the band so that each member could further his or her individual career. Raylene left after the birth of her first child; Heather decided to pursue acting; Cookie focused on her personal life (in July 2001 she married Nashville producer George Messenburg); Jimmy began assembling a solo album (*Song Dog* was released in July 2001); and John Morris wanted to play with musicians outside the family.

In January 2000, however, John Morris Rankin died in a road accident; he was driving his son, Michael, and two other teenagers to a hockey game when the truck went off the road and into the St. Lawrence River; the three boys survived. At his funeral, dozens of fiddlers, from children to octogenarians, collectively played some of John Morris Rankin's favourite fiddle tunes.

The Rankin tradition ended as it began. "The Rankins are a textbook example of how not to compromise ideals for the sake of simply selling records," said Halifax arts writer Ron Foley MacDonald in 2000. "The group ... prided themselves on maintaining themselves on the East Coast, preferring to stay close to family, friends, familiar landscapes and the musical taproot that provided continual inspiration."

Ginette Reno
b. Montreal, Quebec, April 28, 1946

"What a Colossus of the stage. What a magnificent performer, what a voice, what soul, what warmth she radiates. ... Ginette Reno is music pure and simple, music with no nationality, no boundaries, ageless beyond time." Thus wrote critic Pierre Beaulieu after attending Reno's 1977 recital at the Place des Arts in Montreal. This was just one of many rave reviews Ginette Reno has earned in her long and active career.

Unlike some Quebec musical artists who tend to restrict their activities to their native province, Reno has always reached out to find new worlds to conquer. Singing with equal ease in both English and French, she has won audiences on three continents. In 1970, she sang at London's Savoy Theatre; the following year, she hosted a series of programs with singer Roger Whittaker; and the year after that, she won first prize for performance at the Tokyo International Song Festival.

Reno has always gone against type. At five-foot-five, she once weighed 200 pounds (but later she managed to cut her weight by 40 pounds) and bore no physical resemblance to the svelte, sexy female singers that seem to roll off an assembly line and head for Las Vegas. Her singing is robust, her laugh is a roar. She is in many ways larger than life.

"I am a compulsive overeater," she confessed. "I eat when I am happy, and when I am sad. I eat when I am in love and when I am not in love. I am learning to understand the reasons why I eat … it's hunger for a lot of things which are not food. Affection, for example."

But it is mostly her work that saves Reno from despair. "I fill my audience," she once said. "I fill their bodies, their souls, everything." Almost anyone encountering Reno is disarmed by her earthiness and candour. She speaks the way she sings – with her heart, without guile.

This butcher's daughter from east Montreal has proven her talent and determination. "Some people need a kick in the ass to get going," she has said. "I was lucky. I have had a lot. … Being born and raised in a very poor family was my first kick."

At the age of two she was treated for scarlet fever in a hospital. The nurses taught her three songs, and when she got home she started to sing. "We knew then that she had talent," her sister Therese said later.

She worked three paper routes to earn money for singing lessons. She sang anywhere – church basements, local contests, and finally in Montreal clubs. Little by little, she built a career that has made her beloved both at home and abroad.

Reno's repertoire relies mostly on popular music, in both French and English, and her fans love her in both languages. In 1984, Mirielle Simard wrote of Reno in *Le Devoir*: "All somehow rests on that special timbre that a single breath is sufficient to unleash. She is there in her natural state, with a purity of unreal boundaries."

Her sister collects everything published about her. "Every time I go to listen to her sing, I cry," Therese said. "The way she sings, she puts so much of her soul into it."

But Reno's personal life has been darkened with sadness. "Men have hurt me a lot," she has admitted. "I would have to say it's my kids and career which have given me the greatest pleasure."

Her marriage to Robert Wattier, a former tailor who became her manager, broke up in 1973. After that she had an unhappy affair with one of Wattier's friends. More recently, she lived with a later manager, Alain Charbonneau, who fathered one of her children. But because of earlier bitter relationships, she could not even bring herself to tell Charbonneau she loved him.

Reno went to California in 1974 and eventually turned to famed drama coach Lee Strasberg to, as she admits, "see if I could do anything besides sing." But she didn't tell anyone in California that she was an established performer, but merely a housewife from Quebec. But Strasberg soon saw through her ruse. "When someone owns the stage," he said, "I know it. And you own the stage." Reno admits she cried at his words.

Despite her emotional ups and downs, Ginette Reno's strong personality allows her to keep her career going up and up. She was always a hard worker; in a sense, it has been the work that has kept her going in the face of so much personal pain. And Reno has gained a clearer understanding of her life, with all its roller-coaster swings: "There were times when I hated so many things that I went through, and yet when I am on stage and I start singing, I know darn well what I am singing about and I thank God because I have been through this. I used to envy other women thinking they have got everything. I forgot I have many things, too."

The Rheostatics
formed 1980 in Etobicoke, Ontario: Dave Bidini ((b. Toronto, September 11, 1963) rhythm guitar, vocals; Martin Tielli (b. 1966) lead guitar, vocals; Tim Vesely (b. Toronto, December 10, 1963) bass, vocals; Dave Clark (b. 1965) drums (replaced by Don Kerr)

Canada has produced its share of journeyman rock bands, the ones that always have a following, but don't necessarily generate frenzy. Stalwart among them, the four-man Rheostatics have been dubbed "the quintessentially Canadian band." They've written songs about Saskatchewan, Canada's Group of Seven painters, and hockey heroes; they've covered such Canadian artists as Jane Siberry and Gordon Lightfoot; and they've remained together, in their words, "longer than a lot of people have been married or at a job."

Making their longevity all the more understandable is the fact that none of the four members of the Rheostatics ever depended solely on the band's music for his livelihood. Of the originals, Bidini was first a writer and Tielli was a visual artist, while Vesely and Clark also made their principal livings outside the band, "so when we get together," said Tielli, "it's for the love of the music."

The band's earliest tapes were released under the name The Rheostatics and the Trans Canada Soul Patrol and its first official release was *Greatest Hits* (1987) on X Records, which contained the cult hit **The Ballad of Wendel Clark Parts I and II**, about the fiery Toronto Maple Leaf forward. They were regularly played by alternative radio deejays, most notably David Wisdom on CBC Radio's late-night program *Nightlines*.

The Rheostatics (l. to r.): Martin Tielli, Don Kerr, Dave Bidini, Tim Vesely

In 1992, the band fashioned an album, ***Whale Music***, around Desmond Howl, the principal character in Paul Quarrington's novel *Whale Music*; in it, Howl is a former rock star who accidentally writes a pop hit in his basement studio. Following their musical interpretation of the work, Quarrington hired the Rheostatics to compose a soundtrack for the motion picture adaptation of his novel. Consequently, the band was in the rare position of having two albums out with the same title; soon after, a hit single, **Claire**, emerged from the soundtrack.

Meanwhile, the group began getting favourable reviews. Mitch Potter, writing in the *Toronto Star*, claimed that "few bands anywhere dare impart the ideas-per-square-centimetre found in any one Rheostatics song. Too clever by half, the band has managed to synthesize from its four members a style of heart-wrenching, resonant pop that broadens exponentially with each subsequent release."

Following a fourth album ***Introducing Happiness*** (1995) on Sire Records, drummer Dave Clark left the band and was replaced by multi-instrumentalist and music producer Don Kerr. That same year, the National Gallery of Canada invited the band to mark the 75th anniversary of the Group of Seven by writing 40 minutes of music for a multimedia retrospective of the painters' history. The Rheostatics performed the ten-part piece during a national tour of the exhibit and then released it on CD as *Music Inspired by the Group of Seven* in 1996. Ultimately, the work revealed as much about the Rheostatics as it did about the Group of Seven.

"They weren't unlike a punk band," Dave Bidini told Chris Dafoe of the *Globe and Mail*, "in that they tried to smash things and turn everything upside down. And they succeeded."

With the release of their pop-oriented album *The Blue Hysteria*, the Rheostatics headed back out on the road (by then, Dave Bidini said they'd crisscrossed the country perhaps 20 times) as the opening act for The Tragically Hip. Among other things, this led to the Rheos covering Hip material and the groups became fast friends. The tour also generated an idea for another groundbreaking recording, *Double Live* (1997), a compendium of songs recorded in front of audiences at stadiums, pubs, and lounges across Canada. They even recorded a song in the lobby of the Uptown Theatre in Calgary.

"There's this tiny elevated platform next to the ticket window, where we had our stuff," Bidini told Matt Galloway of *Now* magazine. "As soon as we got there, the sound guy turned on the lights in the theatre. People left en masse and when they hit the entrance, they got us."

In addition, Bidini's diary from such a tour provided fodder for his book *On a Cold Road: Tales of Adventure in Canadian Rock*, in which he chronicles both the Rheostatics' experiences on tour and the touring folklore of Canadian rock bands dating back to the days of Trooper, Triumph, and the Guess Who.

The next year, 1998, the group released *The Nightlines Sessions*, another selection of live performance material, assembled in homage to the anything-goes spirit of David Wisdom's late-night CBC Radio show (on which their material had been regular fare in the late 1980s).

If recording in a movie theatre lobby weren't alternative enough, in 1999, the band released a children's concept album, *The Story of Harmelodia*. The project began as an antidote to the Barney phenomenon by telling the story of a boy and girl who, like *Alice in Wonderland*, disappear into the musical realm of Popopolous. Not unlike the merging of rock music with children's literature (reminiscent of Harry Nilsson's *Land of Point*, or the Beatles' *Yellow Submarine*), *Harmelodia* featured narration and full-colour illustrations created by the band's Bidini and Tielli respectively.

"I like to think it's an anti-rock album," Bidini told the *National Post*. "We'll always love to make rock albums, but what rock 'n' roll has become is something that we're not that interested in anymore."

Anti-rock, yes, but still popular enough to entertain their rock-solid fan base.

The Rhythm Pals (l. to r.): Mike Ferbey, Jack Jensen and Marc Wald

The Rhythm Pals

formed 1946 in New Westminster, B.C.: Marc Wald (b. Bismarck, N.D., 1922) baritone, accordion; Jack Jensen (b. Prince Rupert, B.C., 1925) tenor, guitar; Mike Ferbey (b. Saskatoon, Sask., 1926) tenor, string bass

The Rhythm Pals conspicuously patterned themselves after The Sons of the Pioneers, a western country group from the United States that dated back to the Gene Autry era of the 1930s.

The country and western trio lasted for four decades and never once took themselves too seriously. They made frequent appearances on CBC Radio's *Burns Chuckwagon* and other shows. They were one of the first Canadian groups to appear on U.S. television.

When the Rhythm Pals were performing on a radio station in New Westminster, a nurse from Vancouver's Children's Hospital visited them. She had written a song and she wanted their opinion. They rewrote the lyrics and the tune. The woman was so grateful she offered them half-ownership in the song's profits, but they graciously declined.

The song was called "There's a Bluebird on Your Windowsill." It was soon recorded by "everybody," according to the Pals, and sold "millions, millions.

You couldn't turn on the radio without that bird." (If this seems exaggerated, one must allow for the natural exuberance of performers.)

After touring with Nova Scotia–born country and western star Wilf Carter in 1950, they worked briefly in Hollywood, then moved to Toronto in 1958. After two summers (1958–59) of carrying their own CBC-TV series, they joined *The Tommy Hunter Show*, first on radio and then on television.

Hunter thought highly of them: "They are good fellas. When I was young and inexperienced on radio, I had them backing me up and I haven't forgotten the professional help they gave me."

When they reached their 25th anniversary, in 1972, they looked back comfortably on their career: "We make $25,000 to $30,000 each a year," said Ferbey. "Say $30,000," amended Jack Jensen.

"The secret of making money is to be commercial," said Marc Wald at the time of their anniversary. "Wherever music has gone, we've gone with it," Ferbey explained. "But we started out as a 'Sons of the Pioneers' sort of group," Jensen chimed in. "'Tumbling Tumbleweeds' sort of stuff. We still get more requests for that number than for anything else." "We were innovative," Ferbey added. "We sang cowboy songs 'purty.' That was the difference."

Their move to Toronto didn't result in sudden superstardom. Instead, they sat around for a few months. "We were nervous," recalled Jensen. "We were three country bumpkins who had changed horses in midstream. We almost went back."

But by the summer of 1958 they were on CBC-TV regularly, in their own series *Swing Gently* that was followed the next summer by *Swing Easy*. Then they joined Tommy Hunter and things began to look much better.

In addition to the Hunter series on radio and television, they performed as part of Hunter's CBC concert parties in Europe and the Far East. In December 1964 they accompanied a troupe that included Hunter, Gordie Tapp, and a small band that went to Cyprus to entertain Canadian troops stationed there.

The Rhythm Pals' view of themselves varied, seeming to depend on the mood of the moment:

High: We are better singers and instrumentalists in the sense of doing both together than anybody in Canada or the States.

Low: We go up there and act like fools; that's all we can do.

High: Our recording of "Never Ending Song of Love" hit number four on the Calgary Hit Parade and number eight in Saint John.

Low: We need a hit single. We don't go around whining about it, but gee it would be nice to get some good distribution.

Despite their occasional mood swings, wider recognition for the Rhythm Pals was inevitable. They won Juno Awards as Best Country Group in 1965, 1967, and 1968. In 1989, they were inducted into the Canadian Country Music Hall of Honour.

Although Marc Wald, the oldest member of the trio, retired at age 65 in 1987, Ferbey and Jensen continued to work into the 1990s, appearing at fairs, stampedes, and concerts.

Dal Richards

b. Vancouver, B.C., January 5, 1918

For more than a quarter of a century, Dal Richards led the dance band at the Panorama Roof of the Hotel Vancouver. But even when the band was playing at some other spot, or touring, they were always introduced as "Dal Richards and His Hotel Vancouver Orchestra" – with the added slogan: "The Band at the Top of the Town."

Dal & Lorraine, Panorama Roof, Hotel Vancouver, 1962

Courtesy Dal Richards

365

Dal's 11-piece band first featured a 13-year-old singer named Juliette, and later Lorraine McAllister, who had already performed with Art Hallman and other bandleaders. She became Mrs. Dal Richards in 1951. McAllister also starred on many CBC Vancouver radio shows and, later, on CBC-TV's *Holiday Ranch* from Toronto.

So firmly did Richards' name become associated with Vancouver that he also became music director for the city's CFL football team, the B.C. Lions, providing the music for the halftime show for some 30 seasons.

As a child, he was a member of Arthur Delamont's Kitsilano Boys' Band, playing clarinet and saxophone. "Arthur was thorough as a bandleader," Richards recalled many years later. "He was a disciplinarian. He taught you to keep your shoes shined, march in step, play with your horn held at the proper angle."

Dal's first professional job was at the city's Winter Gardens in 1938. Two years later, he played at the Palomar, at the Alma, and on Alaskan cruise ships. In 1940, he lied about his age to get the job at the Hotel Vancouver – which Mart Kenney had vacated to move east. Richards hoped the job would last for a year. It lasted for 26 – the longest-lasting gig by any Canadian dance band.

In that band, incidentally, were such top-drawer musicians as trumpeter Gordon Delamont and saxophonists Stan Patton and Lance Harrison.

During the Second World War, the ranks of most bands were decimated by the demands of the armed forces. "Starting in 1941, I guess," Richards remembered, "I had either 17-year-olds or 65-year-olds."

In 1965, with big dance bands a thing of the past and rock music dominating the scene, Dal Richards decided to switch careers. He returned to school, taking a two-year management training course at the B.C. Institute of Technology. His classmates were less than half his age. "It was terrible," he recalled. "I was the oldest student on campus. I'd never been up before 10 a.m. and here I had early classes. I couldn't afford to stop working, so I was playing the Holiday Inn six nights a week."

But his biggest problem was mathematics. Happily, one math teacher took an interest in Dal. "At Christmas time, he'd come down to the hotel and help me with my assignments," Dal said. After graduating from the Institute, Dal Richards held a series of jobs in hotel management, working in some of Vancouver's better hotels.

But the music never died in Dal's heart. Periodically, he has made attempts to recapture the glory of the dance band days. (He had limited success with an album he recorded called ***Dal Richards Plays the Songs of the Canadian Football League***.)

In 1982, a dozen years after his recorded salute to the men of the gridiron, Dal made another recording, this one titled ***Swing Is In – Let's Dance***. A year later, Dal made a followup record *Swing Is In – Let's Dance, Volume 2*. Both LPs sold comparably with the current rock band sales.

Leading a 14-piece band, Richards recorded such standard gems as "Dancing in the Dark," "Take the 'A' Train," and "Little Brown Jug." This was the same band at monthly dances at the Skyline Hotel – where he was also working as operations manager.

"The thought occurred to me," Richards explained, "that because these dances were more popular and because of the success of Larry Elgart's "Hooked on Swing," we should make a record." The album was recorded in two sessions at Vancouver's Pinewood Studio, with arrangements by Lance Harrison, Eddie Graf, and Harry Boon. One dollar from every $9.95 record and cassette sold went to the *Vancouver Sun*'s Children's Fund.

As of this writing, Dal Richards, aged 83, is still with us. Like most veterans of the Big Band Era, he is not optimistic about the likelihood of a big-band "revival." "There's not the real estate, as I call it, for big bands," he said, "meaning there aren't any ballrooms. Even the hotels: they have ballrooms for conventions, not for big bands."

Stan Rogers

b. Hamilton, Ontario, November 29, 1949; d. June 2, 1983

On a winter's night in 2001, a reporter for *Now* magazine in Toronto entered his favourite watering hole at the corner of Queen and Sherbourne Streets. Rod MacLean popped a coin in the jukebox to play a Jimmy Buffett song. Sitting down at the bar, he and a hulking man next to him were suddenly humming along with the song. The two struck up a conversation. It led to sharing names of favourite east-coast singers, such as the Rankin Family, Stompin' Tom Connors. Then, MacLean mentioned Stan Rogers.

Almost immediately the man next to him began to sing: "Oh, the year was 1775."

MacLean chimed in, "How I wish I was in Sherbrooke now."

At the back of the bar another voice was heard, "When letters of marque came from the king / To the skummiest vessel I've ever seen."

And half the bar added, "Goddam them all!"

The jukebox was turned off. The bartender, his wife, and most of the bar

Courtesy Cathy Jessup

patrons became a chorus, singing right through to its completion Stan Rogers' legendary tune **Northwest Passage**, "a song," MacLean wrote, that "could be the Canadian national anthem if 'O Canada' were to disappear."

The incident was significant testimony to the impact of Stan Rogers' song-writing, singing style, and powerful personality in the memories of his loyal fans. Though that instantly recognizable booming voice was stilled in the spring of 1983 during an aircraft fire at the airport in Cincinnati, Ohio, people who love songs that depict the Canadian experience always think of Stan Rogers.

While Rogers' family bloodlines can be traced to Maritime Canada, he was born in Hamilton. He grew to be a big man, six-foot-four and, in the words of his long-time producer, Paul Mills, "built like a fire truck and possessed of a voice that rumbled from his toes. He could bluff and bellow, yet was at heart a poet and intellect."

Rogers entered the musical world as a teenaged bass player in a rock band, but soon turned to folk music, turning professional in 1969. A suggestion from his Aunt June in Canso, Nova Scotia, that he write songs about the family's roots there helped the folk singer find his voice as a folk songwriter.

After a couple of singles and a self-titled album for RCA in the early 1970s, Rogers hit the coffeehouse circuit with Nigel Russell (guitar) and his brother Garnet Rogers (violin, flute, guitar, and vocals). Then the storytelling songs began to flow. Rogers assembled a demo tape in a basement in Hamilton before playing them back for Mitch Podolak, then the artistic director of the Winnipeg Folk Festival; in 1977, Podolak financed Rogers' first album,

Fogarty's Cove. It featured his signature low-register voice and the first of a hundred timeless narratives that spoke to so many audiences.

The songs offered timeless snapshots of the Canadian experience, of the survival of the human spirit despite the odds. They gave a new voice to ordinary people in fisheries (**Make-and-Break Harbour**), on farms (**The Field Behind the Plough**), and even in office towers (**White Collar Holler**). **The Mary Ellen Carter**, one of his classics, is a song of inspiration, or as Rogers himself puts it: "I really like the guy in this song. He's every person who ever had experts tell him that what he wanted to do was impossible (raising a sunken ship), then did it anyway."

"He was always on the road," wrote his widow, Ariel Rogers, "pursuing his dream of establishing a national identity for Canadian songwriting. It was a dream fulfilled. Through his constant soaring, dynamic performances and brilliant songs, he was known throughout most of the English-speaking folk music world."

Rogers wrote a song for Ariel in 1973, the very year he met her, called **Forty-Five Years**. It's the only love song he ever wrote and remarkably is the one song covered by more artists than any other Stan Rogers song. The chorus ends: "After twenty-three years you'd think I could find a way to let you know somehow / That I want to see your smiling face forty-five years from now."

Perhaps Stan Rogers' most loyal following came from the Maritimes. Every year, for example, he would include a one-night concert at the Rebecca Cohn Auditorium in Halifax. He would have no trouble packing 1200 people into the facility, every one in attendance because of his uncanny ability to capture Maritime life so perfectly in the space of a four-minute song. Audiences would invariably call for his other classics – the rousing **Barrett's Privateers**; the

Garnet Rogers, Stan Rogers and Jim Morrison in concert, Kerrville, Texas

Courtesy Ariel Rogers

369

song written about his father, **Working Joe**; and usually as a finale, an a cappella version of **Northwest Passage**. Edith Perth, the director of the centre that housed the auditorium, remembered those annual concerts fondly:

"Stan and I became good friends over the years and only disagreed on one matter – contracts. He didn't think that two old friends like us needed to sign a piece of paper. My accountant was, however, of a different opinion and it was more than once that I had to plead with Stan to sign a contract months after the concert."

Most of Stan Rogers' business dealings were down-to-earth and somehow out of step with modern music industry protocol. For example, after his early association with RCA, he never recorded for any but small-label independents. Said his producer Paul Mills, "They would try to change him and he'd just walk away. He was totally uncompromising when it came to his music."

On June 2, 1983, while returning from a folk festival to promote Canadian talent in Kerrville, Texas, the DC-9 on which Rogers was a passenger made a forced landing in Cincinnati, Ohio. Though the jet made it down safely, Rogers and 22 others died in the fire on the tarmac.

In the years since his death, Stan Rogers' presence has never faded. Not only is there the legacy of his nine albums (six during his life, three released posthumously), but in 1998 Theatre Orangeville (in Ontario) debuted a musical revue that celebrated his music. *A Matter of Heart*, conceived by singer Diane Stapley and Vince Metcalfe, got mixed reviews, but its strength – Stan Rogers' songs – rang true for most audiences. None could resist tapping, humming, or singing just as if the man himself had been on stage. The universality of his material ensures that Stan Rogers' music will live on.

Luigi Romanelli

b. Belleville, Ontario, Novemeber 29, 1885; d. 1942

In the history of Canadian dance bands, no other name conjures up such fond memories as that of "Romanelli," the family surname of this country's favourite musicians of their era.

The most famous among them, of course, was Luigi Romanelli. At one time in the 1930s there were three Romanellis leading dance bands in Toronto, appropriately enough, in the city's three leading supper clubs: Luigi's orchestra was at the King Edward Hotel's Oak Room, brother Don was at the Royal

York's Imperial Room, and Leo had his band at the Old Mill. Trump Davidson, who worked in Luigi's band from 1929 to 1936, commented: "If you didn't work for the Romanellis, you didn't work."

The Romanellis not only conducted their own orchestras but also sent out seven or eight bands under the Romanelli name to various dancehalls on Friday nights.

The three men were the sons of Joseph Romanelli, a harpist who was born in Italy. Their uncle (Joseph's brother) was Rocco, a violinist, known as "Romanelli the Great," who toured briefly with Enrico Caruso and accompanied Nellie Melba. In his youth, Luigi played the violin on Toronto street corners for a young dancer, George Weitz, who later changed his name to White. He became the famous producer of George White's Scandals.

At age 12, Luigi made his stage debut with Gladys Smith, who later became world-famous as Mary Pickford. In 1904 he joined a vaudeville troupe. By 1912 he was touring Canada as a violin soloist. Later he became music director for the Allen Theatre chain, following a period of study in 1918 in Europe. The Romanelli orchestra at Shea's Theatre (Toronto) is thought to have been the first in Canada to broadcast on radio, in 1922. Although he was not a jazz musician himself, Romanelli fronted a jazz band with some frequency in the downtown Allen Theatre from late 1921 through early 1923.

Murray Ginsberg, trombonist and author of *They Loved to Play*, did a lot of research about the Romanellis in preparation for his book. Among many other musicians, he talked to veteran saxophone player Lew Lewis, who remembers: "Luigi Romanelli was a man who made it his business to be impeccably dressed. In the morning he would wear morning clothes – tail coat, ascot tie, striped trousers, everything. He was immaculate, soft-spoken, and appeared the fine gentleman at all times. A remarkable man with a gospel background, Luigi was soft-hearted as well. If anybody was in trouble of any kind, he would always help as much as he could, quietly and graciously.

"When we were at the Manoir Richelieu he liked to go riding, I suppose to impress the hotel guests, but he liked the exercise as well. He'd wear the proper riding jacket, ascot tie, breeches, and the derby perched on his head at the proper angle. He looked absolutely stunning. At that time he was close to 60, but he was still quite athletic."

Ginsberg himself added more Romanelli data: "The King Edward Hotel directors knew what they were doing when they hired Romanelli. By this point, the King Eddie had supplanted the Queen's Hotel as the place in Toronto that catered to those who passed as visiting British and European aristocracy. In this atmosphere the man who led the orchestra in the Oak Room had to be a person of charm and integrity, who presented himself to the public at all times as a figure of refinement. Luigi Romanelli was such a man. He conducted the affairs of his orchestra like a business. He had an office in the hotel, with several secretaries, a manager and an assortment of personnel to attend to the business of his organization on a daily basis.

"Once he became established at the King Edward, it didn't take long before the maestro was in great demand by every corporation, institution and influential family in Toronto."

Rarely was the Romanelli dignity in as much jeopardy as it was on an occasion in the fall of 1938 at an automobile showroom in Oshawa, Ontario, when his orchestra was hired to play at the introduction of an auto manufacturer's spanking new 1939 models. All manner of corporate executives, politicians, dignitaries, and celebrities were on hand. So was trumpeter Ellis McLintock, then a Romanelli sideman. "Finally the house lights dimmed," McLintock related to Murray Ginsberg, "the orchestra started with a fanfare and the curtain – a roll-up curtain – slowly began to rise. On the stage Luigi was conducting, facing the orchestra, as the curtain rose, and as it did, his coat-tails got caught in the curtain as it rolled up. In no time Luigi was dangling about three feet above the stage in full view of the audience, as they roared with laughter while he struggled to get free. The stagehands immediately brought the curtain down, and poor Louie, embarrassed beyond belief, ordered the musicians to pack up and leave the theatre. The musicians, of course, did everything to suppress their laughter, each one moving swiftly out the stage door and into their cars in record time. What a shocker! He was lucky he didn't get killed." Luigi, ever the gentleman, was eventually able to laugh about it.

Ginsberg added this footnote: "The key to Luigi Romanelli was that he was a man of great integrity. He helped to set the standards for the music business in Toronto, and in Canada at large, that would go on to shape the future, long after he and his brothers … had left the scene."

Rough Trade

formed 1968 in Toronto: Carole Pope vocals; Kevan Staples guitar; John Cessine and Marv Kanarek percussion; Rick Gratton drums (replaced by Bucky Berger); Happy Roderman bass (replaced by Terry Wilkins); John Lang keyboards; Sharon Smith piano

When Carole Pope and Kevan Staples appeared at Toronto's Phoenix club in late winter of 2001, many anticipated the reunion might revive the duo's interest in Rough Trade as a regular performing and recording band. The appearance had been arranged by Toronto promoter Gary Topp, who had booked

Rough Trade for its inaugural 1975 gig at the Roxy, a repertory movie house renowned for its late night screenings of *Faster Pussycat! Kill! Kill!* The gig, however, was essentially a marketing vehicle for Pope to promote her autobiographical book, *Anti-Diva*. And as Staples put it, "We're not out to impress anybody. We're just out to play the songs, have fun, and entertain the troops."

For that one Phoenix appearance in Toronto (as well as one in Ottawa and Montreal) in 2001, bringing out a Rough Trade audience – a mixture of new wave music enthusiasts and gay camp followers – was easy. Conditions were far different during the group's earliest days in Yorkville. In 1968, when Carole Pope and Kevan Staples began singing as a folk duo in the village, finding their audience and sound was not so simple.

"We were doing original material," Pope said of the duet's early days. "We were singing about sexual or political subjects that people were thinking about but not saying."

Pope, Rough Trade's creative drive, went to high school with female impersonator Craig Russell, was pals with comedians Dan Aykroyd and Gilda Radner, and in her Yorkville hippie days roomed with Clive Smith, founder of Nelvana; for a time, she painted cels for the cartoon series *Rocket Robin Hood*. In 1969 Pope and Staples appeared as a band called O and even worked in the film shown at the Canadian pavilion during the world's fair at Osaka, Japan in

1970. In 1971 the two worked as The Bullwhip Brothers. The pair built up a following at Toronto's Grossman's Tavern and by 1974 were calling themselves Rough Trade.

From the outset, the band on stage focused on Pope's leather outfits, explicit lyrics, and provocative stage presence.

"When we first started I was wearing a bondage suit, whipping people, and masturbating on stage," Pope said on TV Ontario's program *Studio 2*. "The songs were satirical. … Some people got the humour and the campishness, but some people were getting aroused. We couldn't believe people were taking us seriously because I didn't think of myself as erotic."

Ultimately, Rough Trade took full advantage of this "clown erotic" image. The band appeared in such new wave clubs as Crash and Burn and the Colonial Underground. In 1976 it recorded a direct-to-disc LP for Umbrella Records called **Rough Trade Live!** Wider attention came to its 1980 album **Avoid Freud**, which eventually went platinum, thanks in part to such popular singles as **Fashion Victim** and **High School Confidential.**

"Shocking people – intellectually, politically and sexually in the years before the punk rebellion obscured artistic purpose in a frenzy of destruction – was Rough Trade's declared mandate," Greg Quill wrote in the *Toronto Star*.

The momentum carried Rough Trade through five more albums and into the mid-1980s. When she and white soul singer Dusty Springfield lived together, Pope had Dusty sing backup on her song "The Sacred and the Profane," while Pope and Staples contributed two songs to Dusty's album *White Heat*.

Carole Pope won several Junos – Most Promising Female Vocalist (1981) and Female Vocalist of the Year (1983 and 1984) – while Gene Martynec won Producer of the Year for **High School Confidential** (1981) and Gary Gray won Recording Engineer of the Year for **For Those Who Think Young** (1982).

In 1985, the act started to wear thin. Pope moved to Los Angeles and Staples began scoring music for films. The Rough Trade party was over.

Some music critics believe that Carole Pope and Rough Trade were underrated. "She's one of the very few people who I think should have been an international star," said the *Toronto Star*'s Peter Goddard. "If she had come along, there would not have been a Madonna … [Pope] is one person I wish the world had seen."

Jan Rubeš

b. Volyně, Czechoslovakia, June 6, 1920

"Being a Gemini, I think I lead many lives," Jan Rubeš once said in an interview. Then he smiled and added: "Of course, I don't believe any of that astrology crap." Whether he does or not, there's a certain amount of truth to the remark that he has led many lives.

Happily, neither his studies in Prague nor his budding career were affected by the wartime Nazi occupation of his country. He graduated from the Prague Conservatory in 1945 and made his opera debut as Basilio in *The Barber of Seville* and became a leading singer in the Prague Opera. He emigrated to Canada in 1948.

A founding member of the Canadian Opera Company, he had been a leading basso with that esteemed company in over 50 productions of 30 different operas between 1950 and 1985 and taken part in some 20 national COC tours. Then he won the key role of an Amish patriarch in the Peter Weir film *Witness*. The movie was a big hit and, suddenly, he was a film actor rather than an aging opera singer. Since *Witness*, he has appeared in more than 40 films and/or television series, in Canada, the United States, and Europe.

His burgeoning career as a screen actor didn't necessarily put an end to his singing, however. Even in one of his television roles (as a guest on *Due South* with Paul Gross) he did some singing. He played Mort, an opera-loving mortician.

"Whenever I work on dead bodies," he explained, "I sing. The writers created this part for me."

As if all this weren't enough versatility for one man, Rubeš also indulged his passion for tennis. He became the Canadian National Senior tennis champion. In 1991, he was ranked second nationally among senior tennis players.

While in his late seventies, he worked as much as he chose to. He played a Russian assassin on *The X-Files*, a Czech victim on *ER*, and a Viennese citizen in *Music from Another Room*. He went to Fiji to portray a refugee poet, husband of Margot Kidder, in *The Nightmare Man*. All this was in one year – 1996.

Once, in 1994, he had to choose between acting with Ann-Margret and Glenn Close. Happily married, he explained: "I was to play Ann Margret's husband and have three scenes in bed with her. It was about to be shot in Tennessee. I decided to be Glenn's father in Vancouver. It's based on a true story of a lady colonel in the U.S. army who was kicked out because she said she was a lesbian."

Rubeš recalls appearing with Peter Falk in a project called *Roommates*. "I play his Polish buddy," he remembers. "It's a true story. Our characters age 30 years, starting at 63. In one scene, I say to him, 'I've forgotten your name.' He says to me, 'How soon do you have to know?'"

Rubeš' credentials in his native Czechoslovakia were impressive. He made his operatic debut in 1940 in Prague, as Basilio in *The Barber of Seville*, and became a leading singer in the Prague Opera. He represented Czechoslovakia at the International Music Festival in Geneva in 1948 and was a first-prize winner.

That same year, he emigrated to Canada, where his limited knowledge of English was something of an obstacle. His first role was a minor one in an English production of Puccini's one-act opera *Gianni Schicchi*. The libretto called for Rubeš to call another character "you penniless imposter." Jan inadvertently changed it to "you penisless imposter." (And he didn't even realize he'd said it.)

Another early professional role in Canada was in a movie being made in Montreal with an actress named Susan Douglas, who had emigrated from Czechoslovakia to New York before the war. "I was infatuated," he recalled. "She wasn't."

Susan has her own version: "I didn't want to get involved with a European because they make lousy husbands – no cooking or cleaning."

He remembers their first meeting: "There was this bubbly lady. I said, 'This is the girl for me.' But she had a boyfriend. She flew to New York every weekend to see him. I was this Czech émigré who couldn't speak English. This Canadian wrote a script with flowery speech, and then there's me, a guy who couldn't even speak English."

Despite the language barrier, he wooed her and married her, but Susan continued to work in New York until 1959, when she settled in Toronto. Never one to be idle, she started the Young People's Theatre. "In 1964–65," Susan recalls with pride, "Dan Aykroyd was the stage manager. There was Marty Short, Saul Rubinek, Andrea Martin."

But for both Rubeš and his energetic wife, time and talent eventually paid off. Mrs. Rubeš still kept track of Jan's career and Rubeš was always quick to give Susan credit for much of his success: "Without Susan I'd be nowhere."

As they approached their 50th anniversary, Jan and Susan, their three sons all grown by now, still projected an easygoing, comfortable, love-filled relationship with room for gentle humour.

Rush

formed 1968 in Toronto: Geddy Lee (b. Gary Lee Weinrib, July 29, 1953) vocals, bass; Alex Lifeson (b. August 27, 1953) guitar; John Rutsey percussion (replaced by Neil Peart, b. September 12, 1952)

On a weekend early in the spring of 2001, hundreds of Rush followers gathered in Toronto for a fan convention. Nicknamed "Rushians," they came from Britain, Japan, the United States, and South America to share Rush memorabilia and memories in the group's hometown. Remarkably, the band, which was recording that same weekend across town, did not participate in the event. The phenomenon illustrated the band's loyal following, but also the band members' nonchalance about being Canadian.

"I can't really see what the Canadian sound is," Geddy Lee said to *Heart of Gold* author Martin Melhuish.

Canadian sound or not, the original trio of Lee, Lifeson, and Rutsey formed their group while still at Georges Vanier Secondary School in Toronto. They were loud. They were brash. They were honest about being heavy-metal and up-tempo. Singer Lee admitted the band's sound was raw and even that his Jimmy Page falsetto-style voice was irritating. By the early 1970s they had worked their way into Toronto bars and pubs and acquired a following. Even after it released its debut, self-titled album, however, Rush's music was rarely playlisted by Canadian radio stations.

Ill health forced drummer Rutsey to leave the band, and Peart, a former member of the St. Catharines band Hush, took his place. Peart's imaginative interest in fantasy and sorcery affected the band's creative direction. Peart's influence is best heard on the Ayn Rand concept album *2112* (1976) and on the space odyssey albums *A Farewell to Kings* (1977) and *Hemispheres* (1979).

While the group attracted some following in southern Ontario initially, it connected in the United States principally through WMMS-FM radio programmer Donna Halper, in Cleveland. From that came a record contract with Chicago's Mercury Records, who released Rush's second album *Fly By Night* in 1975, and eventually with agent Ira Blacker, who took Rush on as a full-time occupation. Blacker turned Rush into a touring band in Canada, the United States, and Britain, playing as many as 200 concerts a year.

A Rush live appearance (much like Loverboy, April Wine, and Triumph) offered a lot of the high-volume, high-energy, heavy-metal music that typified the late 1970s and early 1980s. However, in addition to the marathon, ear-piercing solos, Rush songs were accented with massive searchlight effects, special sound effects, and smoke bombs. In that sense they were trailblazers. They created heavy-metal rock 'n' roll theatre on stage as illustrated by their 1976 Massey Hall concert album *All the World's a Stage*. The next year, their managers – Vic Wilson and Ray Daniels – formed the band's own label Anthem (named after the Rand novelette) as an affiliate of Mercury in the United States.

Rush earned a Most Promising New Group Juno Award in 1974 and then Group of the Year awards in 1978 and 1979. They continued to record and tour in the 1980s and then began winning Junos again in the 1990s – Best Hard Rock/Metal Album *Presto* in 1991 and *Roll the Bones* in 1992 and the Hall of Fame Award in 1994.

Despite all the recognition at home, Rush drummer Peart insisted "the more I learn about the world, the less nationalistic I become. ... Nothing will stop originality ... it just is."

When it completed a tour in 1997, Rush retired with 22 albums recorded and 35 million in sales. Bass player Geddy Lee released a solo CD, *My Favourite Headache*, in the fall of 2000 and planned a studio reunion of the trio in mid-2001.

Buffy Sainte-Marie

b. Piapot Reserve, Craven, Saskatchewan, February 20, 1941

In the spring of 1980, just as the first colour of the season arrived on the Canadian prairies in southwestern Alberta, there was a gathering of Peigans on their reserve not far from Pincher Creek. The powwow attracted native families from across the West, a CBC television crew, and an array of entertainers – a rock band named Cree, Willie Thrasher (nicknamed "Bob Dylan of the Inuit") guitarist Vern Cheechoo, and, without much fanfare, singer-songwriter Buffy Sainte-Marie.

As guest host, the 39-year-old concert, recording, and television star made very little fuss. She shared change rooms with the rest of the cast. She was paid the same as the others. And she, like so many there that weekend, brought along family (her young son Cotie) to take part in the celebration. Buffy Sainte-Marie, whose show business world was half a continent and half a lifetime away, fit right in.

"Our tradition is to share," she said. "We may have little, but we give a lot. That's why ceremonies like this are so important to us ... to me."

From the beginning, Buffy learned to adapt to places and conditions and to

Buffy Sainte-Marie at a concert on the Piapot Reserve near Regina in 1975

make the most of each moment. Not long after her birth on a reserve in southern Saskatchewan, she was adopted by Micmac parents who moved the family to Wakefield, Massachusetts. There, Buffy taught herself to play the piano and, in her teens, the guitar. She learned love songs and protest songs while studying at the University of Massachusetts. Then, upon completion of a degree in Oriental philosophy, in 1963, she moved to New York's Greenwich Village.

A *New York Times* reporter caught her appearance at an open-mike night at the Gaslight Café in Greenwich Village and hailed her as "a promising new talent." Talent agent Herbert S. Gart helped her get a management contract and she immediately began touring around the U.S. east coast. In 1964 she made her first appearance at the Mariposa Folk Festival in Canada and that same year the Vanguard Recording Society released her first album, *It's My Way*.

"[This] debut album remains one of folk music's most chilling recordings," American music journalist Craig Harris wrote later. "Accompanying her tremolo-heavy alto on acoustic guitar and mouth bow, Sainte-Marie takes direct aim at U.S. society. … The opening track, **Now That the Buffalo's Gone**, is a haunting overview of Native American history. … The album helped to spread the word of her potent songwriting."

In 1965 she made her first appearance at New York's Carnegie Hall, the Newport Folk Festival, and Royal Albert Hall in London. Then in 1966 came perhaps her greatest success. **Universal Soldier**, a song she had written while at the Purple Onion coffeehouse in Toronto, was recorded by folk-pop singer Donovan; the song was an instant hit and became an anthem of the growing movement against the war in Vietnam. The song was also the first Top 50 hit for Glen Campbell.

Topical songs, however, represented only part of Sainte-Marie's repertoire. Another composition, **Until It's Time for You to Go**, was recorded by Odetta and Catherine McKinnon, and became a Top 40 hit for Elvis Presley. In 1967 she did an early interpretation of Joni Mitchell's song "Circle Game," while her 1968 LP, *I'm Gonna Be a Country Girl Again*, was recorded in Nashville and demonstrated Sainte-Marie's attraction to country music.

She toured and performed in Europe, Canada, Australia, Hong Kong, and Japan, and wrote more songs and essays. She also established a scholarship foundation to fund Native American study, and met indigenous people outside North America, received a medal from Queen Elizabeth II, and presented a colloquium to philosophers in Europe.

By 1975, she had settled in Hawaii with her son Dakota Starblanket Wolfchild, and the two began a five-year run of appearances on *Sesame Street*, teaching its young audiences that "Indians still exist." At the same time, she began composing music soundtracks for such films as *Starman, Jewel of the Nile*, and *9½ Weeks*. A song she co-wrote, **Up Where We Belong**, was recorded by Joe Cocker and Jennifer Warnes for the film *An Officer and a Gen-*

tleman, produced by her husband Jack Nitzsche. The song won an Academy Award in 1982.

Sainte-Marie returned to the musical world with her 14th album, ***Coincidence and Likely Stories***, in 1993. She resumed a concert schedule, with show venues as diverse as the Museum of Civilization in Ottawa and the Arctic tundra of Lapland. That year, France named her Best International Artist, and in turn she helped establish a new category at the Juno Awards for best aboriginal recording. In 1995, she was inducted into the Canadian Music Hall of Fame and also received the Award for Lifetime Musical Achievement from the First Americans in the Arts organization. In a move befitting her stature in the musical and aboriginal worlds, the award was then named after her.

Joe Sealy

b. Montreal, Quebec, August 16, 1939

It was Oscar Peterson's sister, Daisy Peterson Sweeney, who taught both Oscar Peterson in his youth and then Oliver Jones. Daisy was also responsible for teaching and mentoring another fine Montreal-born pianist, Joe Sealy, who is five years younger than Jones.

Joe said he didn't have a "strong" music teacher until he was 12, "when I was big enough to ride the subway from the suburbs into Montreal."

"She was the first dynamite teacher I had," Sealy later said of Daisy Peterson Sweeney.

Sealy began his playing career in the late 1950s in jazz groups and show bands with Bob Rudd, Benny Winestone, Walter Bacon, and others. Moving to Halifax in 1967, he served as music director or consultant for several CTV series (*Music Hop*, *Roundabout*, etc.) and was a pianist in local orchestras and hotel lounges.

In 1976, he moved to Toronto and served as music director for a succession of musicals throughout the 1980s, including *Spring Thaw*, *Ain't Misbehavin'*, *One More Stop*, and *Lady Day at Emerson's Bar and Grill*.

Joe also accompanied various U.S. jazz musicians in their Canadian appearances, including Buddy DeFranco, Milt Jackson, Sonny Stitt, and Joe Williams. Demonstrating considerable flexibility, Joe also accompanied Sammy Davis, Jr. and Anne Murray. In 1979 he toured the United States with David Clayton-Thomas and Blood Sweat and Tears.

In the early 1990s, Sealy was music director for Archie Alleyne's ambitious *Evolution of Jazz*, a credential of which he is proud. He also did another show, *Classical Cabaret*, a tribute to black Canadian entertainers. It featured Jackie Richardson and Dennis Simpson and was backed by a trio of Sealy, Alleyne, and bassist Paul Novotny.

At about the same time, Joe started his own record label, Sea Jam Records, on which was released a duo recording **Double Entendre** with Paul Novotny.

The two musicians got a gig at Café des Copains and taped their show. They edited it down to some six tunes and used it as a demo tape. This resulted in a two-year engagement at the Four Seasons Hotel in Toronto. "That really helped because we had a solid two years of very intense playing there," Sealy later told *The Jazz Report*'s Greg Sutherland. "People seemed to really like what we were doing. We had very receptive audiences with people like Billy Joel, Bernadette Peters, and Julio Iglesias attending."

In 1993, Sealy was the music director for the Harry Jerome Awards, which are the black achievement awards. The experience, Joe said, was "great."

There's another side to Joe Sealy, too, and that's as an actor. Over the years he has appeared in various television and film programs. "My acting career really started with an onstage appearance in Salome Bey's blockbuster hit, *Indigo*. It just sort of fell into place. Other opportunities presented themselves, so I took advantage of them."

These appearances involved working with the likes of Sammy Davis, Jr. and ballet star Veronica Tennant, as well as such jazz giants as Milt Jackson and Joe Williams.

Sealy won a Juno Award for his CD *Africville Suite*, which celebrated the role played by the black community in the early years in Halifax. And a followup CD titled *Blue Jade*, with his longtime musical partner, Paul Novotny, was nominated for a Juno in the spring of 2000.

In 2000, Sealy took his jazz quartet to the United States, and he also toured Ontario and the Maritimes with the Nathaniel Dett Chorale, Canada's only professional ensemble specializing in an "Afrocentric" repertoire.

The Sealy talents keep blossoming; the latest manifestation is Sealy the lyricist. In the spring he held the debut (at Toronto's Convocation Hall) of his work titled **And Still We Sing**, one of more than 60 Music Canada 2000 commissions celebrating the millennium.

The jazz suite is based on lyrics by Nova Scotia poet David Woods, but Sealy said: "Some of David Woods' words fit the music naturally, but others were more challenging and needed a lot of work. I had to take his poetry and make it into song." Sealy noted that Woods' poetry "comments on the realities of freedom and carries a powerful message with a strong religious element."

There are five songs in the suite and Sealy performed them at Halifax and Summerside, P.E.I., early in the year, where the work was very well received. Sealy later told the *Toronto Star*'s Geoff Chapman that this was his first such project. "I'd like to do more when the occasion arises. I've discovered the value of telling a story through music of the black experience in Canada."

More recently, Joe wrote and directed a new theme and music for TVO's *Imprint*.

Bernie Senensky

b. Winnipeg, Manitoba, December 31, 1944

"I could just sit and listen to him play all day," said Bill Evans. "The best of the Best," said Buddy DeFranco. They were both speaking of Bernie Senensky, as was Elvin Jones when he said, "One of the finest pianists I have worked with in my career." Senensky's keyboard work has been the envy of many a musician and critic over the years.

Senensky was blessed with parents who, though unmusical, recognized his

musical inclination early and supported it. After a brief (and unsuccessful) flirtation with the trumpet, he switched to piano, practising incessantly in the basement while school friends played ball.

"When I was 14 or 15," he told the *Toronto Star*'s Val Clery, "I used to watch the TV series *Peter Gunn*. There was a pianist playing in a club and the music was by Henry Mancini. That was my first exposure to jazz."

With the instructive help of Winnipeg jazz pianist Bob Erlendson – and in the company of such inspiring local colleagues as guitarist Lenny Breau and bass player Dave Young, Bernie edged toward a career in jazz by sitting in at a Winnipeg club called The Stage Door.

In 1964, when Senensky was just 19 (and had to pretend to be 21), he was steered toward a job in Edmonton, leading a trio for dancing and accompanying vocalists. "Tommy Banks was already the big name in jazz there," he told Clery, "and the Yard Bird Suite was open, so I used to go down there and play. That's where my jazz playing started. I was on my own, living the jazz life, playing all night long, sleeping all day long."

He returned to Winnipeg for a bit, then worked in Vancouver, Regina, and Halifax before settling in Toronto. Since then, he has worked with Art

Blakey's Jazz Messengers, the Elvin Jones Quartet, the Howard Ferguson orchestra and the Boss Brass. He also spent 10 years with the Moe Koffman Quintet.

One critic singled him out for praise when he was a sideman on a CD featuring the impressive singer Aura Borealis – along with such fine musicians as Ron Rully, Paul Hoffert, Michael Stewart, and Jack Long.

He led his own trio (with drummer Barry Elmes and bassist Kieran Overs) on a 1990 CD called *The Chalet Sessions* – a title, by the way, that is never explained in the liner notes. But that's Bernie Senensky: he plays what he wants to play and doesn't mind our listening, but he's not given to explaining things, except now and then.

"I feel comfortable playing piano in many different styles," he said in the Clery interview. "That may be one of my handicaps, that I'm too eclectic. ... When your style is eclectic ... it's difficult for people to categorize you. Booking agents hear me play with so many people that when they want a Bernie Senensky group, they don't know what kind of music it will play, don't know how to program me."

On the *Chalet* CD just referred to, Senensky plays mostly tunes of his own composition. But there are a couple of splendid versions of familiar tunes: "How Deep Is the Ocean" by Irving Berlin and "If I Should Lose You" by Leo Robin and Ralph Rainger – and both show his boundless creativity and technical skills to advantage. And there is also Don Manza's tune, "Steppin'," which is well worth a listen.

But Bernie Senensky is also an impressive composer. One of the more appealing tunes on this CD is a Senensky ballad titled **Pepper's Gone**, a heartfelt tribute to the great baritone saxophonist Pepper Adams, who had died a few years earlier.

Another successful tune on this CD is **White's Blues**, a simple but beautifully played 12-bar blues on which he gets stalwart support from Overs and Elmes. The *Winnipeg Free Press* wrote of this CD: "It's unlikely, I suppose, that we could persuade the city to officially honour one of its own for being a piano player. Fortunately, buying Bernie Senensky's latest [record] is an honour that plays in both directions at once."

Senensky the composer comes to the foreground on another CD titled *New Horizons*, recorded over several sessions in the latter half of the 1990s and issued in 1999, with liner notes by Hal Hill, the knowledgeable jazz aficionado (and virtual founder of the estimable Markham, Ontario, Jazz Festival).

Bernie is assisted here by drummer Jerry Fuller, bassist Neil Swainson, trumpet and flugelhorn player Eddie Henderson, and (on most cuts) tenor saxophonist Kirk MacDonald. All the tunes played here were written by Senensky. Henderson's trumpet is riveting, especially on **Eddie J**, a Senensky tribute to Edward Jackson Henderson, as is the Kirk MacDonald tenor sax work.

Another worthy item on the CD is **Don't Look Back**, a truly rewarding effort by all concerned. The best advice for any jazz lover is offered in Hal Hill's closing liner note line: "Listen and Enjoy."

Sharon, Lois & Bram

formed in 1978 in Toronto: Sharon Hampson (b. March 31, 1943); Lois Lilienstein (b. July 10, 1936); Bram Morrison (b. December 18, 1940)

Sharon Hampson learned of the relationship between music and social activism when she was a child. In her home, she was surrounded by the songs of Paul Robeson and Pete Seeger. As a teenager, she was naturally drawn to the folk music movement and made her stage debut as a folk singer in a Toronto coffeehouse. She was sitting in the audience when suddenly she heard her name being announced. Someone stuck a guitar in her hands and told her to sing. "What else could I do?" Sharon said. "There was no turning back." She didn't. That performance eventually led her to the Mariposa Folk Festival where she made several appearances. When she heard about the idea of bringing folk music into the schools, she helped organize the program called Mariposa in the Schools.

Lois Lilienstein was introduced to pop, jazz, big band, and American musical theatre by her father who sold insurance by day and played piano at weddings and bar mitzvahs by night. By the age of five she was singing contemporary songs with her father accompanying her. A serious music education followed and Lois earned a Bachelor of Music degree from the University of Michigan. When she and her husband Ernest moved to Toronto, her music turned in a new direction. She brought music to the children at her son David's nursery school and often used folk music to engage the children in singing, musical games, and creative movement. That led to organizing a broader program of uniting children with music and eventually to organizing the Music for Children program in the North York Public Library. Then she too joined the Mariposa in the Schools program.

Bram Morrison was always a bit of a clown and found the opportunity to explore his gift on the stages of his high school and university. A natural singer and musician, he teamed up with noted folklorist and singer Alan Mills and toured North America as his guitar accompanist and apprentice. Through this

David Cooper

association, Bram acquired an extensive repertoire of folk songs and began performing on his own for television and the Mariposa Folk Festival. Bram became interested in working with and performing for children, so he entered Teacher's College and became a teacher specializing in music. This led to Prologue to the Performing Arts and … the Mariposa in the Schools program.

Thus, in 1978, the three performers met and a trio was formed that was to change the sound of children's music in North America forever.

Upon discovering their common interest in music and children, the three decided to record their own album. They faced one stumbling block: money. So they went to friends and family and borrowed the $20,000 they needed to produce *One Elephant, Deux Éléphants*.

They didn't think beyond the album, not knowing how far it would go. How they underestimated the power and longevity of their union! *Elephant* became the fastest-selling children's album ever produced in Canada. Twenty years later, *One Elephant, Deux Éléphants* went triple-platinum.

Their immediate success led to fifteen gold, six platinum, and two double-platinum albums. They began touring and played to packed houses at Toronto's Hummingbird (O'Keefe) Centre, Broadway's Palace Theatre, Lincoln Center, and Carnegie Hall, and even headlined in the Easter Egg Roll and Hunt at the White House. Their two internationally sold television series attracted millions of fans. And along the way they picked up Juno Awards, an Ace Award, and a Gemini nomination, a spot in the Parents Choice Hall of Fame, and a lifetime achievement award from the Alliance of Children in Television.

The trio attributes its success to a combination of elements. First and foremost was the choice of music. They didn't select songs that were trendy, choosing instead songs that had proven themselves over time, from different genres and eras. They also didn't sing down to the kids.

As Lois Lilienstein puts it, "We shared a philosophy that children could enjoy the full range of music and they were entitled to the best culturally, just as they're entitled to the best food and the best care and the best education."

Another reason for their success, they claim, is that they had broad exposure, perhaps more than if they had come along later. "We and Raffi and Fred Penner all started around the same time," Bram Morrison says, "and we became the three best-known artists in this field of work. Although other highly talented children's artists have come along since, nobody has really achieved the same level of public acceptance."

The third contributor to their success was almost as accidental as their union. When they were asked to perform at Toronto's Young People's Theatre shortly after the release of their first album, they decided to borrow a Babar costume from the Toronto Dance Theatre and introduce an elephant on the stage. It was an immediate hit with the kids and Elephant ended up being a part of their concerts from then on.

Their first TV series was called *Sharon, Lois & Bram's Elephant Show* and they named their production company Elephant Records. Their second television series, *Skinnamarink TV*, featured a talking elephant named Ella. No wonder Bram Morrison's wife Ruth has a massive collection of lucky elephants.

The trio's commitment to children extended well beyond its music. They performed for countless charity events, promoting health, safety, nutrition, and education for children. In 1988 they became involved in UNICEF and went on to be the Canadian ambassadors for that organization for years, earning the Danny Kaye UNICEF Award in 1989.

Keeping a group together for over 20 years is a milestone in itself. Although the trio went through its trials (Sharon battled breast cancer twice and has become a spokesperson for the fight against that disease), one could say that, like many relationships, they stayed together "for the kids."

In late 1998, Lois Lilienstein's husband passed away and she decided it was time to retire. Sharon and Bram continued performing as Sharon, Bram and Friends, to the delight of children.

The trio's love and respect for children was always the foundation of its success. As Sharon Hampson put it, "I think we're pretty much fine-tuned to children because, basically, we like them. Sometimes they're better company than adults."

That fondness was expressed throughout and particularly at the end of every concert and show. That's when they sang their signature tune, "Skinnamarink," the traditional song they made their own. After the closing line "I ...

love … you!" the trio simultaneously sent out a huge kiss – "Mwa!" – to the audience. The kids accepted that kiss and have returned their affection – for generations.

Jane Siberry

b. Toronto, October 12, 1955

For some solo artists, the notion of also taking sole control of one's career makes great sense. In 1996, after being represented by Warner Brothers' Reprise Records for much of her professional life, Jane Siberry took advantage of contract renegotiation to make a change. With its head office in Toronto, she formed Sheeba Records to handle her management, her bookings, her recordings, her promotion – in short, her entire career. Jane Siberry became Jane Siberry's boss.

"I slept with myself right to the top of the company," she joked on CBC Radio.

The truth is, Jane Siberry has been very much the designer of her own fortunes since the beginning. Nearly all of her earliest song material sprang from her own poetry and prose. She even taught herself musical harmony; she explained that it was something she learned during schooldays, when she would sneak into the girls' washroom to smoke cigarettes; between puffs, she would sit on the floor and harmonize with the echoes of her own voice bouncing off the washroom walls.

While she studied for a microbiology degree at the University of Guelph, she learned to play the guitar and piano and began performing folk material with, among others, the Canadian group Tamarack. The money she saved from waitressing tips helped finance her first self-titled independent album, a collection of acoustic material released in 1981. A second album in 1984, *No Borders Here*, featured an underground hit song **Mimi on the Beach**, a seven-and-a-half-minute song about a woman floating on a pink surfboard, while her 1989 album, *Bound By the Beauty*, garnered rave reviews and included often-requested songs **Something About Trains**, **Everything Reminds Me of My Dog**, and **Hockey**.

While her first venues were Toronto coffeehouses in the 1980s, Siberry eventually moved to New York City, where, she said, "I really felt like a musician. There is a community of people to work with, a gathering of high-end talent who are always challenging themselves."

Jane Siberry in concert at the 1999 Edmonton Folk Festival

Jane Siberry concerts are generally different from most – reminiscent of less complicated encounters between folk performers and their audiences. They have often included screening self-produced videos, stream-of-consciousness recitations, and even question-and-answer sessions with her devoted fans. In a conversation about her creative process with *National Post* feature writer Rebecca Eckler, Siberry said that she hears music in her head all the time and "it can get pretty noisy in there."

When she first established Sheeba Records in 1996, Siberry ran the firm from a distance. That year, she released *New York Trilogy*, a CD box set of theme concerts recorded at New York's Bottom Line nightclub. The material intertwined new and old songs, including **Mimi Speaks**, a sequel to **Mimi on** the Beach. It soon became clear, however, that the company representing a unique talent needed that talent closer to home; Sheeba was losing money.

Siberry moved back to Toronto to take a hands-on approach to the label. She became Sheeba's sole employee. She didn't record any of her own material for nearly five years, while she learned computer programming and graphic design and then re-launched Sheeba as an Internet business. The Web site began to market Jane Siberry books, videos, pencils, and CDs, but it also invited fans to sign up for regular emails from her own *Museletter*.

"I have more peace of mind doing it myself," Siberry said.

In 2001, she released *Hush*, a collection of traditional songs including Irish folk tunes ("Pontchartrain"), lullabies ("All Through the Night"), spirituals ("Swing Low, Sweet Chariot"), and Americana ("O Shenandoah") for which she taught herself to play the harmonica. The album was nominated for a Juno in the category of best roots and traditional album.

Hank Snow

b. Liverpool, Nova Scotia, May 9, 1914; d. Nashville, December 20, 1999

More often recognized for his loud rhinestone suits, elegant presence, and distinctive yodelling style, singer Hank Snow should also be acknowledged (with Wilf Carter) as the father of country music in Canada. His record sales, in excess of 70 million, his nearly religious devotion to the traditions of country music, and his willingness to go anywhere on the globe to perform made him legendary. Nashville musicologist Chas Wolf called him "the first truly international country music star."

He was born Clarence Eugene Snow in a Nova Scotia fishing town. At the age of 12 he joined the crew of a Halifax fishing boat to escape a violent home life. For four years he stayed at sea, where he was often heard singing for shipmates with a distinctive "blue" yodel, a style he had heard on a Jimmie Rodgers recording of "Moonlight and Skies."

When he was 16, Snow spent $5.95 to buy a Hawaiian guitar (his first) from the Eaton's catalogue and started performing in small-town Nova Scotia. In 1933, Hank was spotted in a minstrel show at Bridgewater and offered his own radio show on CHNS in Halifax; he was billed as "Clarence Snow and His Guitar."

Three years later, Snow auditioned at RCA Victor in Montreal, recorded his

Hank Snow with Tommy Hunter

own compositions **Lonesome Blue Yodel** and **The Prisoned Cowboy** and signed a contract as "Hank, the Yodelling Ranger." In 1937, Snow spent four days at Victor again in Montreal and recorded eight more songs, including **The Blue Velvet Band**, one of his biggest hits, and that initiated his first cross-Canada tour. He was a regular voice heard on CBC Radio and from 1936 to 1942 was accompanied (as on a dozen 78-rpm recordings) by the Rainbow Ranch Boys and Anita Carter.

In the late 1940s, Snow was working extensively in the United States and by 1950 (thanks to the assistance of fellow Rodgers disciple Ernest Tubb) became a regular performer at the Grand Ole Opry and on WSM Radio in Nashville. About the same time, Snow went into the studio to record a new composition, **I'm Movin' On**. The song – about boarding a train to leave a wayward lover – went to the top of the country charts in July of 1950 and stayed there for 14 months. It was destined to become one of the most successful discs of the first 50 years of recorded country music. It also introduced Snow to a new venue and audience – servicemen and -women around the world – an experience Snow called "the most important part of my life as far as entertaining is concerned."

In 1953, in the last months of the Korean War, for example, Hank Snow led his backup band the Rainbow Ranch Boys, Ernest Tubb and his Texas Troubadours, vocal duet Annie Lou and Danny Hill, and Opry comedian Doc Lou Childre on a trip to South Korea. During his three-week tour, Snow performed **I'm Movin' On** everywhere – in theatres, on tailgates, and aboard hospital ships – and the soldiers sang along.

The United Nations troops (including soldiers from the United States and Canada) adopted the song as an anthem of their nomadic existence at the front. They sang it as they worked and particularly when they marched. In fact, the song became so engrained in the Korean War soldiers' lingo that whenever a unit was forced to make an unscheduled retreat or advance, to disguise the fact on radio sets, U.N. troops would say, "Let's pull a Hank Snow!" and few, if any, Communist Chinese eavesdroppers would ever know what it meant. Over the years, the song has been recorded in 36 languages.

Hank Snow formed a partnership with legendary promoter Colonel Tom Parker in the early 1950s. Their booking agency, Jamboree Attractions, promoted an unknown country performer named Elvis Presley; in fact, during the bidding war with Sam Phillips (Sun Records), at the request of RCA Snow drove to Memphis to persuade Presley's mother that Elvis should sign with Victor. He did, but Snow's association with Elvis ended when the young performer turned to mainstream rock 'n' roll.

Hank Snow's heyday spanned the next 15 years, when he regularly performed at the Grand Ole Opry and when he recorded some 40 songs that were in the Top 10 of the country music charts (including **Golden Rocket, Rhumba Boogie, Bluebird Island, I Don't Hurt Anymore**, and **I've Been Everywhere**). He released 140 albums in all. Snow was inducted into the Country Music Hall of Fame in Nashville in 1976, into the Juno Awards Hall of Fame in 1979, and (posthumously) into the Canadian Country Music Hall of Fame in 2000.

In an obituary in the *Toronto Star*, arts writer Greg Quill interviewed Nashville musicologist Chas Wolf, who summed up Snow's personality this way: "You could say he was parsimonious. In his bearing, Hank was very much like a reserved New Englander. He wasn't overly religious and he was painfully reserved and shy. … He was an elegant professional."

The Stampeders

formed 1963 in Calgary: Rich Dodson (b. July 1, 1947) guitar; Kim Berly (b. July 4, 1948) drums; Len Roemer (replaced by Ronnie King, b. August 1, 1947) bass; Brendan Lyttle; Van King; Race Berly

The Stampeders (l. to r.): Ronnie King, Rich Dodson, Kim Berly

Western Canada produced only a handful of nationally and internationally recognized talents in the late 1960s and early 1970s. Among the musical performing stars to emerge from west of Toronto were Bobby Curtola, Ian and Sylvia, Robert Goulet, Joni Mitchell, the Poppy Family, and the Guess Who. Were it not for their persistence and the arrival of the CRTC Canadian-content regulations in 1970, the Stampeders might never have joined that list. But those two factors helped deliver the trio a half-dozen years of success and at least two hit singles.

"The first few years were really tight," drummer Kim Berly told rock author Ritchie Yorke in 1970. "But it was a development period."

Berly originally got together with guitarist Rich Dodson, bass player Len Roemer, and Brendan Lyttle in a local Calgary band called The Rebounds. They met Mel Shaw, who worked both as a talent coordinator and coproducer for a Calgary television production called *Guys and Dolls*. Shaw booked the band on the show, became its manager, and renamed the group The Stampeders by the end of 1964. In 1965 Shaw brought in showman Van King and Race Berly, Kim's brother. That same year, Ronnie King replaced Roemer.

With Shaw at the helm, the band toured Canada during its centennial year, 1967, and managed to get them into an RCA studio in Montreal, where they recorded a single, **Morning Magic**; the song won a BMI certificate of honour and put the Stampeders on the map. Next was a one-record deal with MGM in New York; the single was called **Be a Woman**, which got little American play, but its flip side, **I Don't Believe**, got airplay on Toronto rock station CHUM-AM. However, by the end of 1968, Race Berly, Brendan Lyttle, and Van King had quit the band, leaving Rich, Ronnie, and Kim to carry on.

The new Stampeders stuck to touring – appearing at the Ottawa Exhibition with the Guess Who – and while they stayed out of the recording studio, they continued to work on new tunes. Over a period of eight months in 1970, the band recorded its first album, *Against the Grain*, and **Carry Me**, which became a national hit and then **Sweet City Woman**, which elevated the band's profile by hitting number one and selling over a million copies in 1971.

"The warmer climate of the [30 percent CanCon on radio] legislation era brought direct results," said Kim Berly.

Despite typecasting the band, **Sweet City Woman** brought the trio headliner status on the Canadian touring circuit. It even enabled them to stage

(l. to r.): Kim Berly, Rich Dodson, Ronnie King

Stampeders concerts outside Canada too – in London, Amsterdam, Paris, Rio de Janeiro, and various city venues in the United States. Their 1972 single **Wild Eyes** reflected the band's more hard-rock interest. Other singles in that vein included **Devil You** (1971) and **Hit the Road Jack** (1975), which were both successful in the United States.

The wave of popularity carried the band through the mid-1970s until Dodson (in 1977) and Berly (in 1978) both left to pursue solo careers. The band carried on in various forms, recording a dozen other singles and several albums. The original Stampeders reunited in 1992 on television and (appropriately enough) for a performance at the Calgary Stampede.

The band won two Juno Awards in 1972 – one as Vocal Instrumental Group of the Year and a second for producer Mel Shaw for Best-Produced Single of the Year on their signature tune, **Sweet City Woman**. In 1973, the Stampeders were honoured in the Netherlands with an Edison Award for their first overseas LP (a compilation of their first two Canadian albums).

Steppenwolf

formed 1968 in Toronto: John Kay (b. Tilsit, Germany, April 12, 1944) vocals, guitar; Michael Monarch (b. June 5, 1946) guitar (replaced by Larry Byrom, replaced by Kent Henry, replaced by Bobby Cochran); Goldy McJohn (b. May 2, 1945) keyboards (replaced by Andy Chapin, replaced by Wayne Cook); Rushton Moreve bass (replaced by John Morgan, replaced by Nick St. Nicholas, replaced by George Biondo); Jerry Edmonton (b. Oct. 24, 1946) drums

One of the earliest products of the Yorkville music scene didn't even come from Toronto, but was a refugee from East Germany. Joachim Krauledat arrived in Canada in March 1958. He entered high school in the city's west end, but because of vision impairment was transferred to the Canadian

John Kay and guitarist Danny Johnson of Steppenwolf perform in Moncton in July 1998

National Institute for the Blind, where to pass the time he taught himself to play the guitar imitating Hank Williams country songs. Soon after, he moved to the United States, where he got involved in folk revival music and the 1930s country blues of guitarist Robert Johnson.

He returned to Canada in 1965 as John Kay and began playing at such Yorkville clubs as the Half Beat and the Devil's Drum, where he jammed with a new rock band, Jack London and the Sparrow. Kay impressed the band members with his harmonica playing enough to get an invitation to join them.

"Two nights later," Kay told journalist Ritchie York, "we were scheduled to play our biggest gig up to that time – Waterloo Lutheran University – for $1000. We stayed up all night and learned 25 songs."

From September 1965 through May 1966, the Sparrow sustained itself by performing in a handful of clubs in the Yorkville village. While fees were minimal, at least the band had a place to rehearse during the day. They mimicked U.S. hit parade tunes occasionally slipping one or two of their own numbers into the Yorkville shows. What continued to elude them, however, was a contract and recording session.

They tried a move to New York, playing at Arthur's, then the Downtown Club in the west Village, and eventually a Long Island club called the Barge, where "one night there was a huge thunderstorm and water poured in onto the stage. There were three power failures in an hour. We were getting shocks from everything and there were only 20 people in the audience. We quit before we were all electrocuted."

They tried a move to California, playing at It's Boss Club and Whisky a Go Go in Los Angeles and then the Arc in Sausalito, where one night, for fun, the band performed a 15-minute version of the Hoyt Axton song "The Pusher." Suddenly, everything clicked. Steve Miller came to see the act. The Fillmore West and Avalon Ballroom booked John Kay and the Sparrow specially to have them do "The Pusher." With a light show they'd added, the number brought down the house. "It was the biggest success we'd had," Kay said.

Still without a recording deal in 1967, the band broke up. John Kay got married and settled in a Los Angeles apartment, which turned out to be the key to his future in the music business. It happened that a new neighbour in L.A. was married to Gabriel Mekler, a record producer in search of a saleable act. Kay reunited with Jerry Edmonton, Goldy McJohn, Michael Monarch, and Rushton Moreve. They recorded a demo tape of 10 songs, which Mekler took to Dunhill Records, and the label signed the band for two albums that year. All they needed was a new name. They chose the title of a Herman Hesse novel that Mekler was reading – *Steppenwolf* – and it stuck.

"The main character of the novel," said Kay, "was strangely representative of the same kind of alienation that people were going through at the time. The character drifts into a no-man's land – between the establishment and total isolation. The book had a great deal of relevance … despite the fact that people in Oklahoma still came up and asked which one of us was Stephen Wolf."

The first album came out and soon after a single, titled **Born to Be Wild**, which roared to the top of the charts, selling over two million copies. Steppenwolf's sound – a combination of electronic hard rock and white soul employing a guitar that was constantly on fuzz and a driving Hammond organ that never overwhelmed John Kay's grating voice – was its calling card. It also helped that Peter Fonda and Dennis Hopper chose to feature **Born to Be Wild** in their 1969 movie *Easy Rider* about two hippie bikers searching for the real America. Suddenly, Steppenwolf had "a larger-than-life mystique internationally."

The band went on to release six gold albums with other hit singles such as **Magic Carpet Ride, Move Over, Monster,** and **Who Needs Ya?** Everything went smoothly for Steppenwolf until 1970, when once again rifts between players, different opinions about the band's direction, and the trials of the road drove the group apart.

Several bogus groups using the name "Steppenwolf" emerged in the late 1970s; so, partly in angry response, Kay formed a new band, John Kay and Steppenwolf in 1982. Several years of writing and recording produced five more albums and rebuilt the band's hard rock reputation. In 1994, Kay took his band to the former East Germany, from which he had fled 36 years before.

John Kay and Steppenwolf accumulated sales of 20 million records and licensed their songs for use in 37 motion pictures and 36 television programs. In 1996, Kay was inducted into the Canadian Academy of Recording Arts and Sciences Hall of Fame.

Teresa Stratas

b. Toronto, Ontario, May 26, 1938

PAC/N1. 15339

In addition to a glorious lyric soprano voice and a salty tongue, Teresa Stratas also possesses an enduring flair for self-dramatization. She always likes to mention that her father was a shepherd in the mountains of Crete and makes frequent reference to having grown up in poverty. She rarely mentions that her father was later a reasonably successful Toronto restaurateur.

Early in her stormy career, she was nicknamed "the baby Callas." Later, she was referred to as "Miss Cancellation" because she had earned a reputation for cancelling scheduled appearances.

For quite some time, she and conductor Zubin Mehta had what is usually called a "relationship." But she was cynical about this. "To find a person in life who will accept all the facets of a person's personality is very difficult," she told a *Maclean's* interviewer. Franz Kraemer, then a CBC producer, remembered when he worked with Stratas on *La Traviata*. He said she would interrupt rehearsals frequently, either to take a phone call from Mehta or to call him.

"One minute she'd return from the phone in tears, the next sublimely happy. It went on and on like that," according to Kraemer. He also commented: "Teresa is never unhappy. Teresa is either in love or out of love."

After eight years, she left Mehta. Her reason? She didn't want to be known as "Mrs. Conductor."

Stratas once reflected: "People think it's very glamorous to be part of Stratas' life, to be part of the light that Stratas is. Let that light for a moment get black and no one wants you. To have to cope with Stratas in her depressions is something people don't want. They want to know about the glitter and champagne. The stress and what one goes through to give birth to a performance – no one really wants to know that."

Stratas showed an interest in music from the age of four. First she sang Greek folk songs. The first song she learned in English was "Pistol Packin' Mama." She sang for patrons of her father's restaurant.

Later she sang torch songs in nightclubs. "I had to keep the attention of all the drunks – an experience that pays off when I sing to the sometimes dozing opera audiences who come to listen for social reasons."

In her teens, she studied with Irene Jessner at the Royal Conservatory of Music in Toronto, and before she was 20, she was cast by Herman Geiger-Torel in a production of Vaughn Williams' *Riders to the Sea*. She made her professional debut as Mimi in *La Bohème* with the Canadian Opera Company. In 1959, she was co-winner of the Metropolitan Opera Auditions and made her debut with the Met in *Manon*. She quickly rose to major roles with the Met, appearing in *Turandot, Carmen*, and *Madame Butterfly*. She was soon an international star of opera, singing in Paris, Vienna, Munich, and Salzburg.

But she managed to find a dark side to her burgeoning career. "I don't do recitals and I'll tell you why," she pronounced. "I can't stand the format – the sequined gown, the lacquered hair, the clasped hands – and a good and acceptable program. … The cocktail parties and receptions, that sham which has nothing to do with making music, bugged the hell out of me. So now I say, 'If you want me, if you want Teresa Stratas the singer, then I'll do it.' But I won't show my face just for the sake of showing my face. I won't dress up. I don't get dressed up."

After scoring an international hit in Alben Berg's *Lulu* – first in Paris, then at the Met – she did Kurt Weill's *Mahagonny*, and met Weill's widow, Lotte Lenya, the world's leading interpreter of Weill's music.

Lenya had locked away in vaults a score of unperformed Weill songs. After hearing Stratas sing, Lenya gave them to her, saying: "You are the only one who has come along to sing Weill without making him sound vulgar."

Success never softened her tongue nor curbed her flair for being outspoken. Offered the lead in a movie called *The Diva*, she turned it down, referring to it as "a pile of shit."

She carries a black cloud around with her: "I would not have done what I have done and led the life I did had I not come from a background of poverty. I wouldn't be where I am – wherever that is – had I been born into a middle-class Canadian family. When you're terribly aware of the lack of things – though we had everything that counted in our family – well, you're goaded into going the distance. One more than compensates to make up for the void of knowledge that begins and ends at oneself."

By way of explanation, she refers again to Mehta, saying that he grew up on chamber music and she grew up on the *bouzouki* (a kind of Greek mandolin).

"Now that I've done just about what I've wanted to," she said, "I want to get back to where I came from. You kill yourself to escape from where you came from and then kill yourself to get back. It's a little absurd, isn't it?"

Ensconced in her lavish, Old World apartment in New York's Ansonia Hotel, she said she felt no urge to return to Canada. "I don't feel I belong anywhere. I'm first-generation and that's a problem first-generation children face. You never really feel at home anywhere. At some point in life, you realize that you've been at home all along – with yourself."

When her beloved mother died in 1963, Teresa Stratas said: "I still can't get myself to accept singing engagements in Canada. We were so close. The only thing that takes me back is her. I sneak into Toronto to visit her grave."

Walter Susskind
b. Prague, Czechoslovakia, May 1, 1913; d. Berkeley, California, 1980

In his decade as conductor and music director of the Toronto Symphony Orchestra during the years 1956–65, Walter Susskind had a considerable impact on the fortunes of the orchestra, as well as of the Toronto Mendelssohn Choir and Canada's National Youth Orchestra, the latter a passionate interest of his.

After studies at the Prague Conservatory – piano with Josef Hoffmeister, composition with Josef Suk and Alois Haba, and conducting with George Szell – he made his debut in 1934 as assistant conductor at Prague's German Opera House.

This urbane and witty man had amassed an impressive roster of credentials both in his native Czechoslovakia and elsewhere in Europe. He was an established conductor in Germany until the Nazis occupied his country in 1938. He moved to England, where he became a citizen and founded the National Youth Orchestra.

After the war, he conducted the Sadler's Wells Ballet on a tour of Germany. He also conducted the Scottish National Orchestra, the Victoria Symphony of Melbourne, and the Philharmonia Orchestra of London.

In coming to Canada, Susskind succeeded Sir Ernest MacMillan as conductor and music director of the Toronto Symphony Orchestra in 1956 and also became a frequent guest conductor of the CBC Symphony. He was conductor for various Canadian Opera Company productions, including Bizet's *Carmen*, Wagner's *Die Walkure*, Richard Strauss' *Der Rosenkavalier*, and Mozart's *Don Giovanni*. He also conducted the TSO in CBC Television productions of *Elektra* and *The Magic Flute*.

Susskind also appeared as a pianist with the TSO, usually performing Mozart concerts and in 1958 accompanied Teresa Stratas in recital. (There

were also rumours of a lively romance between conductor Susskind and diva Stratas.) After leaving the TSO in 1965, he became a freelance conductor in Europe and the United States, then was conductor of the St. Louis Symphony Orchestra. He became music adviser to the Cincinnati Symphony Orchestra in 1977 and taught at the University of Southern Illinois, returning occasionally to conduct the TSO.

After he moved to Canada in the early 1950s, he was active in featuring and promoting the works of Canadian composers, premiering John Weinzweig's *Wine of Peace* with the Vancouver Symphony Orchestra, Pierre Mercure's *Triptyque,* and Oskar Morawetz's *Symphony No. 2* with the TSO. He also conducted the Toronto Philharmonia in a recording called *Scored for Ballet,* which included works by Louis Applebaum, Robert Fleming, Morris Surdin, and Weinzweig.

An orchestral workshop which Susskind initiated at Stratford, Ontario, in 1960 led directly to the founding of the National Youth Orchestra in Canada.

Susskind, a particular favourite with women music fans, was usually very charming and gallant, but he was also capable of stinging comments when someone or something displeased him. At one concert, which was being aired live by CBC Radio, Susskind was leading the orchestra in the last, *pianissimo* notes of a beautiful piece of music. As the last quiet notes were still being played, the CBC announcer got ahead of himself and informed the audience (both in the hall and on the air) what the orchestra was going to play next.

Susskind gave the announcer a withering look and said: "Yes, but first, if you don't mind, we will finish *this* piece."

An equally famous story about Susskind concerns a Sunday afternoon in Toronto's Massey Hall, where he was conducting a concert. He had just conducted the Toronto Promenade orchestra in a performance of a Tchaikovsky piece – a performance with which Susskind was not especially pleased.

Over the applause, he left the stage and went to the wings. There, he was informed that on that same afternoon, a hockey game was being played in Europe between the Canadian and Russian national teams. It was suggested to him that since there were probably numerous hockey fans in the concert audience, they would probably be interested to be told the current score of the game.

Susskind returned to the stage, somewhat glumly, and made the following announcement: "Some of you may be interested to know that what we just did to Tchaikovsky, the Russians are now doing to our hockey team."

Tafelmusik

founded 1978 by Kenneth Solwey and Susan Graves, Toronto; music director Jeanne Lamon

The baroque chamber ensemble Tafelmusik was founded by oboist and recorder player Kenneth Solway and bassoonist Susan Graves on their return from a year of studies in the Netherlands. The group derives its name from Telemann's three volumes of table (banquet) music on instruments from the appropriate period (or modern replicas of them) and uses techniques and sensibilities appropriate to the instruments and styles.

The group gave its first concert in Toronto on July 29, 1978. In its early years it also performed some renaissance works, and contemporary compositions written for early instruments.

From its modest origins as a four-member chamber music collective with a six-concert season (and an $11,000 budget) it grew into an internationally acclaimed orchestra with a full-time core of 15 players, contracts with international recording companies, and by 1991 a full Toronto season with some 2200 subscribers and a $2 million budget.

Its composition was fluid during its initial years with a stable core of four players (oboe/recorder, bassoon, cello, harpsichord). Since at that time Toronto had very few period instrument performers, Tafelmusik hired interested modern instrumentalists and brought in guest soloists and directors who gave master classes and "on-the-job training." The emphasis in these initial seasons was on chamber rather than orchestral music.

In December 1980, Tafelmusik gave the first Toronto performance on period instruments of Handel's *Messiah*, and beginning in 1987 performed it annually to sold-out audiences in Massey Hall.

By the 1980–81 season, the orchestra had moved from the Church of the Holy Trinity to its permanent home at Trinity-St. Paul's United Church on Bloor Street.

Under the leadership of music director Jeanne Lamon since 1981, Tafelmusik has grown to 19 permanent members and has achieved international stature, now performing more than 50 concerts a year at home in Toronto, touring extensively around the world, and also recording.

In January 1995, Graham Lock (*BBC Music Magazine*) wrote: "Tafelmusik is now among the most pre-eminent of period-instrument ensembles, and already has several acclaimed discs to its credit."

Tafelmusik maintains a challenging schedule, spending an average of 12 weeks a year on the road with annual tours of Europe, Canada, and the United States. The orchestra is regularly invited to Europe's most prestigious concert halls such as Concertgebouw in Amsterdam, the Musikverein in Vienna, Symphony Hall in Birmingham, and the Barbican Centre in London. It has also performed in Belgium, the Czech Republic, Denmark, France, Germany, Holland, Poland, Portugal, Spain, Switzerland, and the United Kingdom.

The orchestra enjoys considerable popularity with the knowledgeable German public, and has been orchestra-in-residence at the Bavarian Klang and Raum Festival since 1993. In 1996, Tafelmusik received Germany's highest recording accolade – the ECHO Klassik award as Best Orchestra of the Year in a live-to-air television broadcast throughout Europe.

In June 1997, Tafelmusik made a much-anticipated debut at the Jerusalem Festival in Israel, and in Greece the orchestra performed in Athens and in Thessaloníki as part of the celebrations for that northern Greek city's year as Cultural Capital of Europe.

Tafelmusik performed in the inaugural season of Vancouver's Chan Centre for the Performing Arts, at the Bermuda Festival, and, while in the United States, made its debut at the Tanglewood Festival and spent two weeks touring eight states from New York to California. A highlight of the November 1997 United States tour was Tafelmusik's engagement at the newly renovated Orchestra Hall in Chicago.

As Marilyn Emerson wrote in *Musical Archaeologists* in June 1997: "The phenomenal success of Tafelmusik's playing lies in its unique sound, praised for its orthodoxy, polish and exuberance – a sound which has achieved world-class status for this orchestra, regarded by many as one of the best Baroque ensembles on the international stage. Tafelmusik's elegant sonority has achieved for the group various awards including multiple wins and nominations for the Canada Juno Award, the British *Penguin CD Guide*'s 1994 Rosette Award, and the Record of the Year award from *Absolute Sound* magazine in 1994."

Ms. Emerson also wrote: "Presently the most widely promoted and distributed Canadian artist on the Sony Classical label, Tafelmusik's recordings receive high critical acclaim internationally and its concerts have delighted audiences throughout the world."

The orchestra's continuing success in the last years of the past decade can be indicated by citing a few newspaper headlines regarding their various Toronto appearances:

Tafelmusik *Passion* a treat – The *Toronto Star*, April 3, 1998

Tafelmusik wraps up on rousing note – The *Globe and Mail*, May 22, 1998

Church is alive with sound of Tafelmusik – The *Globe and Mail*, December 16, 1998

Tafelmusik plays Handel with care – The *Globe and Mail*, May 31, 1999

Bach makes hot opener for Tafelmusik – The *Globe and Mail*, September 22, 2000

Tamarack

formed 1978 in Guelph, Ontario: Randy Sutherland (b. Simcoe, Ontario, October 27, 1950), James Gordon (b. Toronto, July 2, 1955), Jeff Bird (b. Whitby, Ontario, March 17, 1956) … other personnel included Alex Sinclair (b. Bassano, Alberta, October 26, 1952), Molly Kurvink (b. Detroit, Michigan, January 26, 1956), Shelley Coopersmith (b. Toronto, December 27, 1950), Daniel Lanois, Gwen Swick, Melanie Doane, Jane Siberry, etc.

If ever there was a musical aggregation that used the trial-and-error method of career trailblazing, Tamarack was it. The band was initially an ad hoc group. It grew and shrank depending on the interests and availability of its personnel. It chose its musical focus – like a chameleon – very much as a response to its immediate surroundings and audiences' tastes. Yet, during its roughly 20 years of touring and recording, Tamarack built a respectable library of work (14 albums) and an extraordinarily loyal audience across North America.

"The biggest reward for being in Tamarack," said James Gordon, a founding member of the band, "was that all across Canada I felt we had 'family,' people who shared their experiences with us and who were grateful that we gave their kind of lives a voice in song."

While it became known as perhaps Canada's premier acoustical band for traditional Canadian folk songs, Tamarack didn't start out that way. The original group of Randy Sutherland, James Gordon, and Jeff Bird "played anything, for anyone, anywhere." If Sutherland were playing his electric guitar, Gordon his trumpet, and Bird his double-bass, they called themselves a jazz trio. If the instrumentation happened to be mandolin, tin whistle, and bass, they were a Celtic group. If they were in a bar, they played country music. If they played a coffeehouse, they relied on their folk music repertoire.

"We had about 25 instruments among the three of us," Gordon said, "and that was a big part of our novelty appeal."

What appeared to be common amid all this eclecticism was an interest in

Tamarack (l. to r.): Jeff Bird, James Gordon, Randy Sutherland in 1979

Hart / Murdock Artists Management

405

Tamarack 2001 (l. to r.): Shelley Coopersmith, Alex Sinclair, Molly Kurvink

early Canadian music, that is, traditional European ballads adapted to folk songs about Canadian pioneers and settlement. Coincidentally, that kind of music tended to be a favourite among arts funding organizations in the 1970s and 1980s. As a result, various grants allowed Tamarack to make a living by travelling the country, gathering traditional stories and songs, and performing them to appreciative audiences that were hearing this music for the first time.

Tamarack (named after the tree whose lumber proved valuable to settlers because of its resistance to decay) began recording its material in the early 1980s – albums such as *Music of Canada* (1981), *A Pleasant Gale* (1983), and *Ontario: 200 Musical Years* (1984).

When Randy Sutherland left the band in 1985, another artist with strong performing and songwriting skills joined Tamarack. Alex Sinclair, who had worked with Gordon, Bird, and Sutherland in a band called Maple Sugar (1973–80), expanded Tamarack's instrumental complement (guitar, mandolin, harmonica, vocals) and drew raves from reviewers. What emerged in the mid-1980s, however, was a new emphasis on writing contemporary songs about Canada's past.

"Being history buffs, we were always collecting stories, legends, and anecdotes from fans about their ancestors," Gordon said. "We started writing songs in a traditional style, telling stories to audiences that seemed anxious to learn about their own heritage and culture. ... This is still the primary goal of the band."

This storytelling focus energized the band and increased Gordon's and Sinclair's output. Tamarack toured and recorded constantly. Among the albums in this period were *The Tamarack Collection* (1985); *Shave The Bear* (1989); and *Fields of Rock and Snow* (1991), which saw (bass player/singer) Gwen Swick replace Jeff Bird and was Tamarack's first album released on U.S.-based Folk Era Records.

The band's itinerary was like no other. Performing at a circumpolar conference in Inuvik, touring eastern Ontario's canal systems by boat and performing concerts at every lift-lock station along the way, and touring the Maritimes with luggage, musical gear, and personnel loaded in a Pinto station wagon were just a few of the group's unique touring situations. Clearly they were among the most inspirational too. Some of Tamarack's most evocative and most popular music emerged from these off-the-beaten-path locations.

What began as a song cycle – their boat trip and concert tour along the Rideau Canal – became a special on CBC-TV. Their album *On the Prairies* (1993) resulted from a prairie tour of 50 shows in 50 days. When Ontario's Grand River became a heritage river, Tamarack was commissioned to document its history in music; the result was their album *On the Grand* (1994), which also became a CBC-TV special. The commission opened a floodgate of historical creativity. Tamarack produced an album that explored the hardships endured by workers who built Canada called *Leaving Inverarden* (1996), then an album about the Muskoka area of Ontario called *Muskoka's Calling* (1996), and a Christmas album, *Blankets of Snow* (1998). Among their best-known works was the title song from their 1993 album *Frobisher Bay*.

"I remember playing a festival in New Jersey for a huge crowd," James Gordon recalled. "It was our first time to the state. I remember discovering that our song **Frobisher Bay** was already so well known by the audience that we let *them* sing it to us!"

A combination of their (Chicago) Folk Era recording contract, their regular airplay across Canada on the CBC, and a few tour stops at cross-border cities such as Seattle and Boston gave Tamarack a higher profile in the United States. They soon became one of the most-played Canadian acts on American folk radio.

"Tamarack's writing is in the same league as Stan Rogers, Gordon Lightfoot and James Keelaghan," said the *Victory Review* in Seattle. "All of the instrumental accompaniment and vocal harmonies are fantastic."

By the mid-1990s, Molly Kurvink had replaced Gwen Swick, and the band was touring not only North America but England and Scotland as well. It also performed more frequently in Canadian classrooms and conducted songwriting workshops. More recordings followed too, with *Spirit & Stone* (1999) and *Tree* (2001), commissioned by the Tree Canada Foundation.

A host of talented performers have come through the ranks of Tamarack.

Jeff Bird moved on to join Cowboy Junkies. Gwen Swick later worked on her own, but also performed regularly in Quartette (with Sylvia Tyson, Caitlan Hanford, and Cindy Church). Daniel Lanois worked as a guitarist and a producer for Bob Dylan, Emmylou Harris, and U2. Jane Siberry played with Tamarack in 1979 and Melanie Doane, who worked on Tamarack's first television special, for a while replaced Michelle Phillips in The Mamas and the Papas. Other Tamarack alumni included David Houghton, David Archibald, John Switzer, Anne Lederman, Andrea Barstad, and Carole Leclair.

Meanwhile, Alex Sinclair also wrote hundreds of topical political satire songs for CBC Radio and television, as well as material for other artists, film scores, and television production. James Gordon widened his songwriting career with his *Hometown Tunes* CDs and his regular CBC Radio appearances (*Ontario Morning* and Arthur Black's *Basic Black*). However, some of Gordon's Tamarack days are the most cherished: "There was a time in the 1980s when folk music was so unpopular," he said, "that our agency wouldn't use that word in our promo material. We were told so many times that we had to 'contemporize' our sound to survive. It was a pleasure proving a lot of those people wrong."

In 2001, Tamarack consisted of Alex Sinclair, Molly Kurvink, and Shelley Coopersmith.

The Band

formed as The Hawks 1960 in Toronto, as The Band 1967 in Woodstock, New York: Levon Helm (b. Marvell, Arkansas, May 26, 1940) vocals, drums; Jaime Robbie Robertson (b. Toronto, July 5, 1943) vocals, guitar; Richard Manuel (b. Stratford, Ontario, April 3, 1943, d. March 4, 1986) piano; Rick Danko (b. Simcoe, Ontario, December 28, 1943, d. Woodstock, New York, December 10, 1999) vocals, guitar, bass; Garth Hudson (b. London, Ontario, August 2, 1937) keyboards, horns

However loosely the term "big break" gets tossed about in the music business, no better description applies to the night in the summer of 1965 when folk troubadour Bob Dylan called the members of Ronnie Hawkins' band, known as The Hawks, with an important question:

"Wanna play Hollywood Bowl?"

They asked who else would be on the bill.

"Just us," said Dylan.

Courtesy Canapress

The Band play at "The Last Waltz" at The Winterland Auditorium in San Francisco on November 25, 1976. (l. to r.): Robbie Robertson, Rick Danko, Levon Helm. Garth Hudson is in the background.

So the five members of an unknown rock 'n' roll band from Canada joined a new, electrified Bob Dylan later that year and played across America, Asia, Australia, and Europe and into music history.

The story of The Band begins in Arkansas in the late 1950s, when aspiring rock 'n' roll singer, Ronnie Hawkins, discovered rockabilly music and experimented with several different band combinations to perfect the idiom and cash in on it. The first edition of his band, the Hawks, consisted of Jimmy Ray "Luke" Paulman and Fred Carter Jr. on guitars, Willard "Pop" Jones on keyboards, and Levon Helm (who had originally played guitar in a band called the Jungle Bush Beaters in Marvell, Arkansas) playing drums. A taskmaster and a maverick, Hawkins took the band on the road to gigs in the northern United States and eventually settled in Ontario. But as one after another of the Hawks retreated home to the United States, Hawkins searched out replacements.

To fill the gap left by Carter early in 1960, Hawkins recruited a guitarist who wasn't even 16. Jaime Robbie Robertson, although born in Toronto, was raised on the Six Nations Reserve near Brantford, where he spent his summers and learned to play the guitar. After stints in such bands as Robbie and the Robots, Thumper and the Trambones, and Little Caesar and the Consuls, Robertson joined The Hawks first on bass, then moved to lead guitar.

Rick Danko pushed his way into the Hawks. As a musician playing in bands in and around Simcoe, Ontario from as early as 1955, Danko was captivated by the Hawks' frenetic pace and by Ronnie Hawkins' unique camel walk, and approached them. He filled in on rhythm guitar the next time the Hawks came through Simcoe, in the spring of 1961. The next night he was invited to join the band permanently, initially playing rhythm but then moving to bass when Rebel Paine left the band.

Next, Ronnie Hawkins discovered another western Ontario musician to fill a gap in his band. Richard Manuel then worked as a pianist and singer with the Rockin' Revols, a heavy-duty rock 'n' roll band in Stratford. He had toured the southern United States through the same promoter that had booked Ronnie Hawkins into Canada. Manuel joined the Hawks in the summer of 1961.

Finally, the Hawks recruited Garth Hudson, although it took a little longer to sign him up. Raised in London, Ontario, and initially schooled as a classical pianist, the teenaged Hudson fell in love with both the accordion and the tenor sax and led a local band called Paul London and the Kapers. They even recorded a vinyl 45 with the Detroit-based label Checkmate in 1961, all of which made Hudson a valuable commodity for the Hawks. However, he agreed to join at Christmas that year on the condition that he be paid to give other members of the band music lessons while also being paid as a playing member of the Hawks. The deal was sealed. The band was complete.

"The boys must have worked for me for four or five years," recalled Hawkins. "And they were hard years. By God, I made them rehearse every damn day."

Hawkins meant it too. He was a virtual drill sergeant, rehearsing his five-man band seven days a week. He tolerated no distractions such as booze, drugs, or any outside life, and fined any of the five whenever he violated the rules. Together Hawkins and the Hawks became what rock historian Mike Jahn (in his book *The Story of Rock*) called "a tight, controlled ensemble playing a very rigid form of rock, not at all like the free-for-all improvisation rampant in the rock scene."

In the early 1960s, the Hawks met blues guitarist and singer, John Hammond Jr. (his father had first signed Bob Dylan to Columbia Records in 1961). Hammond hired the Hawks to come to New York to join Chicago blues pianist Mike Bloomfield and harmonica player Charlie Musselwhite as his backup band for an LP recording session. That experience led to a four-month engagement (without Hawkins) in New Jersey, where the group impressed more than just the patrons. A secretary to Albert Grossman, Bob Dylan's manager, suggested the Hawks would be a perfect backup for Dylan's upcoming electric tour of 1965. In what musicologist Rob Bowman describes as Dylan's "guerrilla-warfare attack on middle America's and eventually Australia's and Europe's consciousness," Dylan and his new backup band triggered ritual booing from folk purists who didn't recognize "music that was years ahead of its time in power and majesty."

Following a motorcycle accident in July 1966, Dylan retired temporarily to a farm with a big pink-coloured house in West Sugerties, New York, to put together a film documentary. His backup band joined him to work on the film as well as their own creations in the basement of Dylan's "Big Pink" house. There, in 1967, The Band and Dylan recorded *The Basement Tapes*. Then, in 1968, they signed with Capitol (the contract listed their name as The Crackers), gathered for two recording sessions, and released *Music From Big Pink*, their first collection of distinctly American short stories told in a musical language that bridged the growing generation gap. Not a smashing success right away, the album launched the group as The Band and gave them their first notable single, **The Weight**. In 1969, they released their album *The Band* (recorded in a pool house of a mansion in the Hollywood Hills) and then made their official debut as The Band at San Francisco's Winterland.

"While The Band's albums sold well," wrote fine arts professor and author Carl Belz in 1972, "the group's primary significance lay in their live performances. ... [The players], all first-rate musicians, gave the impression of enjoying their work. Without theatrics, they demonstrated that rock can fully accept its folk identity and can express itself richly within those limits." Belz credits The Band with generating renewed interest in country and western and so-called southern "mountain music" in the late 1960s, while influencing everybody from Johnny Cash to the Grateful Dead to Joan Baez (whose cover version of **The Night They Drove Old Dixie Down** angered some of her civil rights followers).

The Band's third album, *Stage Fright*, was recorded live at the Woodstock Playhouse in 1970; its fourth, *Cahoots*, was the first recorded in a real studio in 1971; its fifth, *Rock of Ages*, originated in a recording made live at the New York Academy of Music on New Year's Eve 1971; its sixth, *Moondog Matinee*, came out in 1973 and featured songs by those who had influenced them, including the Platters, Fats Domino, and Clarence "Frogman" Henry; its seventh, *Northern Lights/Southern Cross*, came out in 1975; and the final album, *Islands*, was released shortly before the group disbanded.

On a November night in 1976, the five members of The Band staged "The Last Waltz," an event described as its final public performance. The group wanted to finish in grand style, so it returned to San Francisco's Winterland (where it had debuted seven years before). More than 5000 fans paid $25 each to enjoy a buffet, a four-hour concert, and a gala party afterwards. The event was filmed by Martin Scorsese and recorded for a soundtrack release.

In addition to The Band, the show featured Ronnie Hawkins, Neil Young, Joni Mitchell, Eric Clapton, Van Morrison, Paul Butterfield, and, appropriately enough, the artist who had witnessed the birth of The Band, Bob Dylan.

Once The Band dissolved, its members pursued solo careers.

Robbie Robertson starred in the movie *Carny*, worked on the soundtrack of movies such as *Raging Bull* and *The King of Comedy*, and then began exploring his Mohawk heritage; in 1993 he created the soundtrack for *The Native Americans*, a six-hour documentary television series; and in 1999 he won the Juno Award for Best Music of Aboriginal Canada Recording for **Stomp Dance**.

Levon Helm continued writing music and acted in the film *Coal Miner's Daughter*, and when the group assembled some new album material, it was recorded at Helm's studio in Woodstock. Garth Hudson wrote and performed in *An Evening with Garth Hudson* at St. Ann's Cathedral in Brooklyn in 1989.

Richard Manuel appeared with The Band (minus Robertson) when it reunited and toured with Crosby, Stills and Nash in 1983, performing in Manuel's hometown, Stratford, in the fall of 1985. Manuel died in March 1986 at age 42.

Rick Danko recorded solo material and played on recordings for such artists as Neil Young and Ringo Starr. He died in 1999 just hours after turning 56.

In 1988 The Band attended the Juno Awards to be inducted into the Canadian Music Hall of Fame. In 1990 the group performed a live version of Pink Floyd's *The Wall* to celebrate the fall of the Berlin Wall. And in 1994 The Band became the first Canadian act to be inducted into the Rock and Roll Hall of Fame in Cleveland, Ohio.

Don Thompson   *b. Powell River, B.C., January 18, 1940*

He plays piano, drums, bass, and vibes. He composes and arranges. He has earned the admiration of George Shearing, Paul Desmond, Jim Hall, Ed Bickert, and Mel Tormé.

Born in Powell River, north of Vancouver, Don Thompson is innately modest and always seems uncomfortable when others praise him. A tall, rangy man who prefers to talk through his music, he began studying piano as a child – pretty much teaching himself – and then added string bass and vibraphone to his repertoire while in his teens.

He was already playing Glenn Miller and Stan Kenton stock charts in a school dance band. Then, Thompson recalls, a school chum returned from a trip to Vancouver with "all these jazz records." Young Don put on a Gerry Mulligan disc and "couldn't believe anyone could be serious about playing that kind of music. But I guess they were." It was a Terry Gibbs record that hooked him on vibes and he soon ordered a set and began playing.

By the early 1960s, he had moved to Vancouver and was working with Chris Gage and Dave Robbins. He also accompanied visiting musicians like Barney Kessel and John Handy. Along with drummer Terry Clarke, he joined Handy's quintet and toured in the United States, returning to Vancouver in 1967.

Two years later Thompson moved to Toronto, after working briefly in Montreal. He quickly became that city's first-call studio bassist, a position he maintained until he turned exclusively to jazz in the mid-1970s. He worked with Moe Koffman, Ed Bickert, Jimmy Dale, and other top-drawer musicians.

It was in 1975, while working at Bourbon Street and other Toronto clubs, that Thompson teamed up with guitarist Jim Hall and the great alto saxophone player Paul Desmond. Some of those sessions were recorded, and the perfectionist Thompson not only played bass but doubled as recording engineer. Later, he toured Japan, the United States, and Europe with Hall. In 1977 Thompson led his own band – and also played piano in it – at the International Jazz Festival in Laren, Holland.

It was in the 1980s that he attracted the attention of Shearing and Tormé. The blind pianist Shearing was so taken with Thompson that in many appearances he would invite Don to sit at the piano with him and play duets. He was the sole accompanist to Shearing and Tormé on *Top Drawer*, an album that won a Grammy award as the best jazz album of 1983. Earlier, in 1979, he and guitarist Ed Bickert shared a Juno award for *Jazz Canada Europe*, an album they recorded on the Sackville label in Toronto. It was named top jazz album of the year in Canada.

While working with Shearing, Thompson began to teach every summer at the Banff Centre for the Arts (and later also at Humber College, in Toronto). Thompson also spent some 13 years as a member of Rob McConnell's Boss Brass, from 1969 to 1982, playing bass or piano on several of their recordings.

Don still has a vivid recollection of a cross-Canada odyssey he and other members of the Boss Brass took: "We had a car with no muffler. We had to drive about 75 miles an hour just to stay ahead of the noise."

In 1987, Don resumed his activities in Toronto, playing piano in the Dave McMurdo Jazz Orchestra, accompanying Jane Bunnett and Trudy Desmond, among others, and teaching privately.

Despite his devotion to jazz, Don Thompson has long been an admirer of Glenn Gould's work. "Obviously, he was a master musician," Don once told interviewer Bill King. "It seems there wasn't one note, bar, or bridge that he didn't know why it was there. Actually, Oscar Peterson is like that, too. To me, they are the same. When you listen, they are so perfect, you ask yourself how anyone can be like him. It's not just the technical perfection, but their understanding of every aspect of the music."

Thompson could as easily have been talking about himself. But his lifelong modesty would never allow him to do that.

As a teacher, Thompson can be a hard taskmaster. He has little patience with students who want to learn and analyze particular solos recorded by various earlier musicians. "It seems a lot of the younger players go directly to the solo and try to figure out what someone did on a particular tune, never thinking about what they had been practising for 25 years before that. It's ridiculous. [Keith] Jarrett, for instance, has spent years learning how to play Bartok, Bach, Shostakovich, and other relevant music," Thompson said.

One of the marvels of Thompson's playing has been the ease with which he switches from bass to piano to vibes to drums, and just as smoothly from one musical idiom to another. On occasion, by overdubbing, he has played all his instruments on the same recording.

One critic described Thompson's piano playing this way: "There's a sense of peace in his touch – even when he falls into swirling passages – that is instantly identifiable."

By any imaginable yardstick, Don Thompson stands out as a master musician.

The Tragically Hip

formed 1983 in Kingston: Bobby Baker guitar; Gord Downie vocals; Gord Sinclair vocals, bass; Johnny Fay drums; Paul Langlois vocals, guitar

On a summer afternoon in 2000, fans began gathering in a parking lot outside a concert venue well in advance of the hall doors opening. Some reclined on blankets. Others gathered 'round open tailgates. A party atmosphere took shape as the music of their favourite band, the one performing that night, blared from car and truck radios. Canadian flags were everywhere. Remarkably, the venue was not Windsor or Saskatoon but Rochester, New York. The band was not the Stones or Bruce Springsteen's E Street Band. It was a Canadian band, The Tragically Hip. These fans have travelled from Canada overnight, on vacation time or playing hooky from work and will follow their heroes to Toledo, Cleveland, and other American stops on the Hip's tour.

The Tragically Hip (l. to r.):
Bobby Baker, Johnny Fay, Gordon
Downie, Paul Langlois, Gord
Sinclair

"For many Canadians of my generation," said one of those parking-lot faithful from Ontario, a 20-something John Zronik, "The Tragically Hip is a band of special significance. Their musical themes reflect our history, politics and the landscape that lives in Canadians' collective imagination."

The stories they tell in their songs are unashamedly Canadian – a prison break from Millhaven Penitentiary … the tragic story of Toronto Maple Leaf hockey hero Bill Barilko … the politics of language in Sault Ste. Marie … a song for author Hugh MacLennan … or a relationship in Bobcaygeon, Ontario.

A relationship is actually the genesis of the Tragically Hip. The band members had known each other in school in the early 1980s. They were friends before they were fellow musicians in the same band. Downie, Baker, and Sinclair were classmates at Queen's University in Kingston, while Fay was an acquaintance in high school. On the basis of lyrics in former-Monkee Michael Nesmith's video *Elephant Parts*, they named themselves The Tragically Hip and began performing in local clubs.

"We started the band because we needed a summer job," Gord Downie told *Network* magazine. "We want a long, healthy, satisfying, educational life and career."

The Hip's first major career boost occurred when the president of MCA Records saw them at Toronto's Horseshoe Tavern. Bruce Dickinson signed the band and their first, self-titled album was issued in 1987. With the release of their second album, *Up to Here*, in 1989, the Hip broke into the hit singles market with **Blow at High Dough** and what would become their signature tune, **New Orleans Is Sinking**.

While the studio provided a venue for their recording, the road provided

415

venues for their fan support to grow. From the outset, band members took the notion of touring seriously; they crossed Canada several times per recording. They even toured with two sets of instruments – those onstage for performance and a second set backstage for rehearsal.

"That's how we make our living, as performing musicians," Gord Sinclair told *Canadian Musician*. "The biggest test of any band is to take the show on the road."

Their touring paid off early. At the 1991 Juno Awards, the Tragically Hip were selected by audiences as Canadian Entertainers of the Year (they won the same Juno in 1991, 1993, and 1995, as well as Group of the Year in 1995). On the heels of those honours, the Hip released *Fully Completely*, which included their top 10 hit **Locked in the Trunk of a Car** and their tribute to hockey great Bill Barilko **Fifty-Mission Cap**. More touring and more recording (at the 19th-century Woollen Mill warehouse in Kingston) yielded their 1994 album *Day for Night*, which became the fastest-selling Canadian album in history. The media began describing them as "Canada's most popular band."

"We find that to be an odious term," Gord Downie said. "In a weird way, it's a dismissal. We're more than just Canada's most popular band, we're Canada's best band."

The following year, to prove the moniker, as they prepared for an American tour with ex–Led Zeppelin members Robert Plant and Jimmy Page, the Hip's overall album sales hit the three-million mark. Next, came albums *Trouble in the Henhouse* (1996), *Live Between Us* (1997), and *Phantom Power* (1998), which contained their hit song **Bobcaygeon**. It sold nearly half a million copies within the first weeks of its release.

Tours were not universally successful for the Hip. In Britain, the *Independent* newspaper described them as "relentlessly average." One-time Hip co-manager Allan Gregg said, "In Toronto, they're the biggest band in the world … bigger than U2 or the Rolling Stones"; but he went on to say that when he attempted to promote the band to American music business executives, "One guy asked me: 'Who is Bob Caygeon anyway?'"

Fan loyalty did not wane in Canada. Nor did it for the Hip's 2000 CD, *Music@Work*, which debuted at number two on the RPM chart. That year, during the MP3 and Napster controversy, a pirated copy of the new album leaked out on the Internet. Hip fans attempted to stop illegal downloading of the album, one (an Internet auctioneer) went so far as to bid US$676 for it on eBay Inc. to prevent it from falling into the wrong hands and having more free copies spread across the Web.

During a conversation between Gord Downie and Atom Egoyan (published in *shift* magazine), the filmmaker asked the musician about the Tragically Hip's strong relationship with its Canadian fan base. "Our so-called Canadian success is a debt we owe to Canadian fans," Downie said. "They've allowed us to build up a body of work. They've allowed us to concentrate on what we do, because they're interested in the whole process. We don't hide that process from them. If you come to our shows it's like going on a trip to the sugar bush. … The process is all wide open."

As a further illustration of the close relationship between the Tragically Hip and its audiences, a 19-year-old volunteer bouncer positioned between the band onstage and the 3200 fans in a gymnasium at McMaster University remembered a September 1991 concert with awe.

"[When] The Tragically Hip came on … the excitement exploded into a massive party that did not cease for two and a half hours," said Saied Ezzati. "The temperature in the room … got so hot we had to spray the crowd with ice water." At the end of the concert, the Hip came out for not one but four encores – 30 minutes of additional music. "This was one of the most generous gestures I have seen from any performer."

The Travellers

formed 1953 in Toronto: Jerry Gray (b. Toronto, October 3, 1933) tenor singer; Sid Dolgay (b. Winnipeg, May 17, 1923) bass singer, mando-cello (replaced by Joe Hampson, [b. Indianapolis, February 19, 1928]); Jerry Goodis (b. Toronto, June 25, 1929) tenor singer (replaced by Ray Woodley b. Copper Cliff, Ontario, September 2, 1935); Helen Gray (b. Toronto, September 7, 1931) soprano (replaced by Simone Johnston, replaced by Pam Fernie, replaced by Aileen Ahern); Oscar Ross (b. Toronto, December 8, 1930), replaced by Marty Meslin, who left and the group remained a quartet, later adding Ted Roberts (b. St. Boniface, June 7, 1933) guitarist; and Don Vickery (b. Halifax, August 16, 1938), drummer

The Travellers have been synonymous with summers in Canada almost as long as there have been campfires, blackflies, and folk songs. Their repertoire – drawn from immigrant roots, political activism, and folk music traditions – not only reflected images of Canada, but also became part of the country's musical lexicon. Canadians have hummed and mimicked their music for half a century.

Even before Canada had a music industry or had officially chosen a national anthem, the original five members of the Travellers – Jerry Gray and his sister Helen, Sid Dolgay, Jerry Goodis, and Oscar Ross – were waving the flag and singing an unofficial anthem, "This Land Is Your Land." A decade before politicians institutionalized multiculturalism, the group sang songs of Ukrainian, aboriginal, and French origin, such as "Envoyant de la vent." Long before it was popular at rallies and in the streets, the Travellers were

The Travellers on stage in Moscow in 1962 (l. to r.): Sid Dolgay, Simone Johnston, Ray Woodley, Jerry Gray

singing songs of social significance such as "Pastures of Plenty." "Simply put," writes musicologist Rob Bowman, "when the Travellers formed in late summer 1953 they were significantly ahead of their time."

In part, it was the summers spent at Camp Naivelt ("Camp New World"), a leftist cultural and community summer retreat northwest of Toronto, that inspired the young members of this folk group to sing together. From the mid-1940s, their parents had been members of the United Jewish People's Order (UJPO), which included singing in a community choir, the Toronto Jewish Folk Choir. Every summer, UJPO members and their families camped in tents and cabins at Camp Naivelt. They sang leftist tunes ("Solidarity" and "Hold the Fort") and enjoyed visits to the camp from such outspoken folk performers as Guy Carawan, Paul Robeson, and Pete Seeger.

Inspired by Seeger and his group the Weavers, the offspring of the Toronto Jewish Folk Choir – Jerry Gray, Sid Dolgay, Jerry Goodis, and (future Travellers manager) Marty Bochner – sang in support of striking workers at Ford and GM plants in Ontario. They called themselves the Youth Singers. However, once again at Seeger's suggestion, five members of the youth choir (including Helen Gray and Oscar Ross) organized themselves into a Weavers-like ensemble and considered a new name. One suggestion – the Beavers – captured the flavour of Canada while maintaining a connection with Seeger's group. Fortunately, they discovered the Weavers' song "Lonesome Traveller," and that sealed their decision. The Travellers debuted in September 1953 at the UJPO national convention. They sang their complete repertoire of three songs and when the audience called for more they sang all three songs again.

Television appearances began soon after the new medium came on stream in Canada. The Travellers appeared first on the *Haunted Studio*, then on *Holiday Ranch, Cross-Canada Hit Parade, The Jackie Rae Show, Junior Magazine, Summertime '57, Music Makers '58*, and *Country Hoedown*. However, the group's breakthrough came during the broadcasts of CBC-TV's *Pick the Stars* (an Arthur Godfrey–like talent show) in which winning contestants reappeared throughout the show season. The Travellers chose a crowd-pleaser for their debut.

"Both Pete Seeger and Woody Guthrie were blacklisted in the United States at the time," recalls Jerry Gray. "Guthrie's song 'This Land Is Your Land' had also been taken off the air. ... In 1954, we had rewritten the song with Canadian place names." They changed "from the Redwood Forest to the New York Island / From the snow-capped mountains to the Gulf Stream waters" to "from Bonavista to the Vancouver Island / From the Arctic Circle to the Great Lakes water, / This land was made for you and me."

The resulting version of the song propelled them to the finals of *Pick the Stars* and ultimately into Canadian folk music history. In 1958 the group incorporated **This Land Is Your Land** into an album, *Across Canada With the Travellers*. When it came time to assign the album's royalties, the group decided that, since one of its mentors, Woody Guthrie, was unable to work due to Huntington's Disease, it would deliver their portion of the profits to a trust fund for Guthrie's son, Arlo; to this day Travellers' royalties from the Canadian version of **This Land Is Your Land** fund Huntington's research through the Woody Guthrie Foundation.

Several more albums followed – *The Travellers Sing Songs of North America* in 1959; *Quilting Bee* in 1960 (which included Wade Hemsworth's humorous tune, "Black Flies"); *The Travellers On Tour* in 1963; and arguably their best album, *Something To Sing About* in 1964 (including traditional Québécois folk tune "Envoyant de la vent").

As Jerry Gray remembers it, the title song of the album, *Something To Sing About*, resulted when producer Sid Banks invited the Travellers to open his new television program *Let's Sing Out*.

"The host was Oscar Brand, who was living in New York at the time," recalls Gray. "Brand had a one-hour-and-10-minute flight from New York City to Toronto and he didn't have a theme song for the show. On the way up, he took out an Air Canada map and wrote the song based on all the place

The Travellers (1991; l. to r.): Don Vickery, Aileen Ahern, Ted Roberts, Joe Hampson, Jerry Gray

names on that map. It was like a travelogue from coast to coast of place names and all the things these names evoked."

Brand delivered the song the day of rehearsals. The Travellers taped it into the show the next day. It's been part of the group's Canadian repertoire ever since. The Travellers recorded a centennial album, an LP for the Canadian Labour Congress. They've performed for children, for British and Japanese royalty, and for Canadian troops stationed in Germany and Cyprus. They've done it all, never forgetting either their working-class roots or their nationalistic fervour.

As the Travellers approached their 50th anniversary, a National Film Board documentary was released in 2001, a national tour was planned for 2002, and they continued to perform at folk festivals and the national conventions of the CLC, CAW, CUPE, Communications Workers, OPSEU, Woodworkers Union, and at many other labour and peace-promoting functions.

In 1967, Parliament approved "O Canada" as the country's official national anthem. "That's okay," concludes Jerry Gray. "The songs we do are Canada's second and third national anthems. They don't have official status, yet everybody knows the lyrics and sings them louder and prouder than a national anthem."

Domenic Troiano *b. Modugno, Italy, January 17, 1946*

For some musicians, it's a living. For others it's a quest to be the greatest, the most successful, the one credited with the most hits. For a few, it's simply the joy of the experience, the satisfaction that comes from performing well and the camaraderie of being with like-minded players. The latter is the way Domenic Troiano might view his half-century as a guitar player. From his younger days playing rock 'n' roll and soul, through to his adult sessions, playing funk, jazz fusion, or R&B, Troiano never stopped loving the basic act of playing.

"I always wanted to go out and play," Troiano said, "and know that on our worst night, my band and I would still really be good."

Domenic Troiano discovered a lust for music early in life. Following his family's arrival in Toronto from Italy in the 1950s, young Domenic fell in love with rock 'n' roll music. His heroes were Jerry Lee Lewis, Little Richard, and Chuck Berry; he'd sometimes borrow a neighbour's acoustic guitar, listen to Chuck Berry records, and pretend in front of a mirror that he was playing "Johnny B. Goode." His first guitar was a $50 Harmony Patrician acoustic his father bought at Eaton's. Then Domenic discovered Ronnie Hawkins.

"I found out Ronnie was playing at the Concord club, where you could get in on Saturday afternoon if you were underage," Troiano said. "Even when I was playing in bands at high school, we'd go down there on Saturdays just to watch. It was a great learning experience. I saw Ronnie Hawkins play live and that just did it for me. I was hooked."

At the time, Toronto clubs were dominated by a handful of bands – Little Caesar and the Consuls, Little Anthony and the Road Runners, Johnny Rhythm and the Suedes. Troiano eventually won a spot playing guitar with Robbie Lane and the Disciples. Meanwhile, Ronnie Hawkins had arrived from Arkansas, assembled a new band called the Hawks (which then included Robbie Robertson, Leon Helm, Rick Danko, Richard Manuel, and Garth Hudson) and had become the house band at a Yonge Street tavern called Le Coq d'Or. In 1965, when the Hawks left to join Bob Dylan, Hawkins went looking for a new backup band and hired Robbie Lane and the Disciples, including Domenic Troiano.

"Inside four years," Troiano said, "I went from seeing Ronnie Hawkins on *American Bandstand* to playing in his band. It was amazing to me."

Just as quickly, Troiano got restless. He complained that Hawkins was going too commercial and not playing enough R&B and he left. Soon after, Troiano formed a nameless house band – with Joey Chirowski (keyboards), Don Elliot (bass), Pentti Glan (drums), and singer George Olliver – at another Toronto

Mandala in 1966 (l. to r.): "Whitey" Glan, Joey Chirowski, Don Elliot, Domenic Troiano, George Olliver (with guitar)

club, the Bluenote. They soon began appearing in matching pinstripe suits, playing R&B (aka "blue-eyed soul") and calling themselves The Five Rogues. As the house band, they accompanied American stars who visited, such as Stevie Wonder, the Supremes, and the Righteous Brothers, and local performers such as Shawne Jackson, Dianne Brooks, David Clayton-Thomas, and Eric Mercury.

Then the Rogues went through another transformation. In 1966, Troiano changed the name of the band to Mandala (suggesting a connection to Eastern religions and mystical properties). At his insistence, Troiano and the band adopted a rigid rehearsal schedule to the point of distraction.

"I was a perfectionist," Troiano said. "We would rehearse all the time. The guys used to kind of get sick of me. Matter of fact, in the early [days] of Mandala, the girlfriends had a strike. They demanded to have a meeting with me to discuss why the band was practising so much. They weren't able to spend enough time with the guys in the band. So I was sort of the bad guy."

Mandala also engaged Randy Markowitz, a media-wise manager, who aggressively promoted the band outside Toronto and into the United States by arbitrarily demanding an unprecedented $1000 per gig. They got the fees, played major clubs in L.A. and Hollywood, and built up their fan base. Their so-called "soul crusade" even caught the attention of blues performer Bo Diddley, who got Mandala a contract with Chess Records; that year they recorded their first single, **Opportunity**, but couldn't get the top rock radio station in Toronto, CHUM-AM, to air it.

"They couldn't ignore the number of fans we had built up over the previous four years," Troiano told writer Ritchie Yorke. "Those … kids … really wanted to hear our first record. When CHUM refused to play it, almost 200 Mandala freaks picketed the station. It shocked the hell out of them."

As Nicholas Jennings notes in his book *Before the Gold Rush*, the coffeehouse and club circuit in Toronto was among the busiest. In 1966, Mandala was one of more than 1400 bands working in the city, 400 of which were earning scale as union musicians. The irony, however, was that Toronto did not have the equivalent in recording studio facilities; nonetheless, that handful of studios managed to release more than 200 singles by those Toronto groups that year. Nor was there media interest in the local scene, because in Troiano's words "they refused to believe that a Canadian band could actually make music."

Despite all their efforts – Mandala's second single **Love-itis** (featuring their new singer, Roy Kenner) – didn't provide the breakthrough they expected in the United States. With lack of airplay in Canada, insufficient backing in American markets, and little media support, the members of the band reorganized as a California-based group called Bush. They recorded and released an album called *Bush* (1970) with ABC Dunhill Records. But it too suffered from bad timing.

"When our record came out," Troiano said, "Three Dog Night and Steppenwolf [also with Dunhill] sued the company for nonpayment of royalties. They were suing each other, but our record was coming out. So we became the football. … After six or seven months of that, Bush started self-destructing and we broke up [in 1971]."

Still, first and foremost a musician, Troiano pressed on, next touring and recording (two albums) with the American band the James Gang. In 1974, Burton Cummings hired Troiano to join the Guess Who for its last two albums. In 1976, after a half-dozen years based in Los Angeles, Troiano returned to Toronto to build yet another band, this time one he could call his own. Together with keyboard players Fred Mendel and Dave Tyson, bass player Keith Jones, and drummer Jim Norman, Troiano rehearsed his new band more than he put it onstage, just to create the desired sound.

"The cardinal rule in music," Troiano said, "is to surround yourself with good people. It always makes you look better and it makes life a lot easier. With those bands in the late '70s, we jammed all the time. To be able to improvise, you've got to have a foundation. I always wanted that foundation to be great."

Capitol Records released three of their albums in the late 1970s – **Burnin' At The Stake** (1977), **The Joke's On Me** (1978), and **Fret Fever** (1979).

Early in the 1980s, Troiano put together a trio called Black Market and worked as a sideman in the United States and Britain, but then settled comfortably into writing scores for motion pictures (such as *Gunfighters* and *Swordsman*) and television productions (such as *Night Heat*, *Diamonds*, and *Top Cops*).

Domenic Troiano was inducted into the Canadian Music Hall of Fame in 1996. It turned out to be the same night that David Clayton-Thomas (Blood Sweat and Tears), John Kay (Steppenwolf), Denny Doherty (the Mamas and the Papas), and Zal Yanovsky (the Lovin' Spoonful) were inducted.

"I got to be the only guy inducted who never sold any records," Troiano quipped. "It can't be because of my sales numbers."

To no one's surprise he has remained a working musician, composing music scores and operating his own recording studio in suburban Toronto. His guiding philosophy: "It's all about the music. For a lot of musicians today the goal seems to be to have a hit and be a star. But our thing was, 'Let's have a great band. Let's play some great music.'"

Shania Twain   *b. Windsor, Ontario, August 28, 1965*

In the summer of 1996, the northern Ontario city of Timmins experienced one of the biggest celebrations since the discovery of gold there in 1909. Its citizens honoured their own golden girl, country music singing sensation Shania Twain. The city renamed one of the highways into town Shania Twain Way and changed its entry sign to include a huge photo of the singer and the phrase "Home of Shania Twain." City council ordered a flower garden planted in the shape of a guitar and spelling out "Welcome Home Shania." And the city braced itself for the arrival of some 10,000 former residents and fans and 200 media people to cover the event. Timmins named the day – August 15 – Shania Twain Day and (for the first time in its history) gave away the key to the city. Remarkably, that day was just the first of many more celebrations in Shania Twain's fairytale career.

The singer, the second-oldest of five children, was named Eileen at birth; she later changed her name to Shania, an Ojibwa name meaning "I'm on my way." At home in Timmins, her mother encouraged Shania's interest in singing by placing her on the counter of a local diner to sing along with the jukebox. Of course, the material was country – Waylon Jennings, Dolly Parton, and Willie Nelson. By age eight, she was being paid to sing.

Courtesy Canapress

"I used to be dragged out of bed at one in the morning," Twain said. "They'd bring me to the local club to play with the band. ... They couldn't allow me in the premises before they stopped serving."

When she was 21, her mother and stepfather died in a car crash and Twain became sister and mother to her siblings. She worked at various jobs, sometimes singing at resorts, helping to get her younger brothers out on their own. With the help of a family friend, she recorded a demo and sent it to Nashville, eventually making a connection with Mercury Records. Her self-titled debut album was released in 1993; while it featured only one of her own compositions, the album enjoyed favourable sales in the United States and Europe.

Enter Robert John "Mutt" Lange, best known for his hard-edged, polished production work with Def Leppard and Bryan Adams. What began as a friendship soon became a working partnership and, by December 1993, a marriage. Lange, a Nashville outsider, worked to blend Twain's intuitive sensibility for country music and her flexibility to adapt other musical stylings. The resulting release in 1995, *The Woman In Me*, with cuts such as **Whose Bed Have Your Boots Been Under?** and **If You're Not in Love I'm Outta Here**, demonstrated Twain's mass appeal.

The album earned Shania Twain a Grammy for Best Country Album and a Juno for Entertainer of the Year. It propelled her to status as *Billboard*'s number one female country artist, and RPM's Entertainer of the Year, Female Vocalist of the Year, and Album of the Year, to name a few. The album sold over 12 million copies and every one of its single releases hit number one in the United States and Canada. The Twain/Lange touch appeared to be golden.

New York pop critic Jeff Breithaupt summed up their formula this way: "She is country music's Michael Jackson," he wrote in 2000. "Twain's music is a diabolical fusion of traditional country music elements, pop hooks and rock riffs. ... The little-bit-country-little-bit-rock-and-roll union of Twain and Lange may be the most significant factor in accounting for Twain's massive crossover success."

In fairness, Twain owed her widespread success to one other factor. By the mid-1990s, country music was hip. A music genre that had been in trouble in the 1980s had witnessed a rebirth that emphasized younger performers and looser ties to traditional country. The new country music of the 1990s, noted one critic, "sounded more at home in the suburbs than it did on the farm." Tom Tompkins, president of the Canadian Country Music Association, reported that country music product accounted for 18 percent of records sold in Canada in 1996, up from 6 percent a decade before. "Forget *Hee Haw*, forget Hank Williams and Patsy Cline," wrote *Globe and Mail* arts correspondent Chris Dafoe. "Country is the new music of the baby boom; youngish, sexy, sophisticated and with all of its own teeth."

The best was yet to come.

In 1997, Shania Twain released her third album, **Come On Over**, co-written with her husband-producer "Mutt" Lange. It immediately began challenging most music sales standards and became the best-selling solo album by a female artist in any genre in the history of recorded music in the United States. It also became the best-selling country album ever (17 million sold) beating out the then king of country Garth Brooks' album *No Fences* (16 million sold). It even tied sales of the Beatles' *White Album* as seventh best-selling album of all time.

"It's stratospheric," said Luke Lewis, president of her Mercury label, as he forwarded the information to the publishers of the *Guinness World Records*.

Once again, the accolades mounted. In 2000, Shania Twain won Junos for Best Songwriter and Best Country Female Artist and Grammys for Best Country Song (for her single **Come On Over**) and Best Country Vocal Performance (for her single **Man! I Feel Like a Woman!**). She earned US$48 million that year, was named (as No. 16) to the *Forbes* magazine list of top entertainers, accumulated nearly 10,000 press clippings, and made two magazine covers.

Twain seemed eager to share her success. She recorded a version of "God Bless the Child" with proceeds going to hungry children. She financed a scholarship at her alma mater, the Timmins High and Vocational School. And she donated $1 million toward a long-term tourist attraction in her hometown.

In 2001, the city of Timmins announced the creation of a $3 million Shania Twain Centre to honour its heroine. Like Opryville or Graceland, the 4000-square-foot centre, called "Shania Time," was designed to attract tourists (an estimated 50,000 a year) to see a collection of Twain personal mementos, memorabilia, clothing, and awards as well as other music industry exhibits. Among the attractions planned is a series of life-sized statues dubbed "The Great Wall of Shania," constructed, in the words of its creators, "to honour and forever stand proudly as a symbol of love and devotion from us, the fans, to Shania Twain."

On August 12, 2001, Shania Twain and John "Mutt" Lange announced the birth of their first child, son Eja.

UHF (Ulrich Henderson Forbes)

Shari Ulrich (b. San Rafael, California, October 17, 1951), Bill Henderson (b. Vancouver, B.C., November 6, 1944); Roy Forbes "Bim" (b. Dawson Creek, B.C., February 13, 1953)

The west-coast Canadian music scene has enjoyed a fluidity like few other music hotbeds in the country. The comings and goings of unique talents have given audiences a seemingly endless stream of talent – sometimes performing solo, but often in various musical combinations. The confluence of three B.C. performers known as UHF in 1989 was a perfect example of talent, temperament, and timing that created an experiment worth preserving.

His real name was/is Roy Forbes, but his late father was familiar with the song "Bimbo, Where You Gonna Goyo," and nicknamed the one boy of his seven children Bim. Like many teenagers in the late 1960s, Bim was attracted to the Beatles' *White Album*. The result was a rock band called Crystal Ship, in which Bim got to play a lot of his Fab Four favourites. Then, in 1971, he moved to Vancouver to pursue a professional musical career.

Courtesy Bill Henderson

UHF (l. to r.): Shari Ulrich, Bill Henderson, and Roy Forbes

A year later, a San Francisco native with a musical bent arrived in Vancouver. Shari Ulrich hooked up with a variety of rock and folk groups in Vancouver, including Rick Scott and Joe Mock in a band called Pied Pumkin. The group made an impact on the local folk circuit with its distinctive harmony and a unique marketing scheme. "To finance our recordings," Ulrich said, "Pied Pumkin would collect the names, addresses, and price of a future album from fans, go in and make the record, then mail it off to all those kind trusting souls who had prepaid."

Guitarist Bill Henderson was working on his second band in the Vancouver area by that time – first The Collectors by 1966, renamed Chilliwack by 1970. Henderson worked principally in rock 'n' roll circles. With bandmates – reeds and keyboard player Claire Lawrence and drummer Ross Turney – Henderson and Chilliwack chalked up their first hit, *Lonesome Mary*, in 1971.

"Live gigs are our most important method of communication," Henderson said in 1970. "If we don't enjoy ourselves, we might as well go home."

By the mid-1970s, Bim's innovative guitar work and songwriting were getting some notice, not to mention his "part Roy Orbison, part Billie Holiday" voice. The *Toronto Star* called him "one of the truest troubadours in the Canadian mosaic." In 1974, during an appearance on Terry David Mulligan's CBC Radio show, *Great Canadian Goldrush*, Bim met Chilliwack's Claire Lawrence, who then produced his first album *Kid Full of Dreams* (1976). He moved into the normal rhythm of touring and recording and released several more albums: *Raincheck on Misery* (1976), *Thistles* (1978), and *Anything You Want* (1982).

Ulrich, meanwhile, had become part of a western Canadian phenomenon known as The Hometown Band, which backed up Valdy. Ulrich sang with the cream of West Coast musicians – Claire Lawrence (from Chilliwack) as well as Robbie King, Doug Edwards, Geoff Eyre, and Edward Patterson (from the Hans Staymer Band). She got rave notices for her vocal work on the band's hit single "Flying" and won a Juno for Best New Group. When she subsequently went solo, she recorded several albums: *Long Nights* (1980), *One Step Ahead* (which earned her another Juno for Most Promising Female Artist for 1981), *Talk Around Town* (1982), and *Every Road* (1990), and once again worked with West Coast musicians, including Bill Henderson.

Henderson and Chilliwack began to hit their stride in the mid-1970s, when their LP *Dreams, Dreams, Dreams* produced three strong singles and became their first gold album. The production of the band's 1978 album *Lights From the Valley* yielded hit singles **Arms of Mary** and **Never Be the Same**, but also precipitated more personnel changes. Henderson and Brian MacLeod remained the nucleus of the band and (in 1981) generated another album *Wanna Be a Star* and Chilliwack's first Top 40 North American hit, **My Girl (Gone, Gone, Gone)**. The pair won a Juno for Producers of the

Year in 1982. The band appeared for periodic reunions through the 1980s.

Then came the onstage meeting of three remarkable careers.

In 1989, as he prepared the lineup for the year's Vancouver Winter Roots Festival, Steve Edge contacted Roy Forbes and Shari Ulrich (who had never performed together). Would they consider a duet or perhaps a trio in an acoustic concert? Forbes thought of Bill Henderson and invited him to a one-time performance at the festival. In spite of their disparate backgrounds and tastes, everything worked, even the name, UHF.

"Bill and I sort of rammed it down Roy's throat," admitted Ulrich. "He didn't like it. Still doesn't."

The one-time show expanded to several repeat engagements. They each brought their individual repertoire and comfortable patter to the shows. They each brought their favourite instrument – Ulrich her dulcimer and fiddle, Forbes his guitars and mandolin, and Henderson his guitar, accordion, and pennywhistle. Before long the idea of a debut album made sense and the CD *Ulrich, Henderson, Forbes – UHF* was recorded, then *UHF II* in the winter of 1994.

"When we're together, it's a real tripod," Forbes said. "We're each a leader and each a sideman. We can have our cake and eat it too."

The collaboration, however, was never a substitute for each member's solo career. Ulrich continued to perform on her own, compose music for film and television programs, and perform on stage (in the 2001 Vancouver Arts Club production *Tapestry*, a tribute to Carole King). Bill Henderson found time to write a tune, **When I Sing**, for the soundtrack of Anne Wheeler's film *Bye Bye Blues* (it won a Genie Award for Best Song in 1990) and worked as a producer for artists such as Long John Baldry, the Nylons, and Valdy; he was music director on Canadian segments of *Sesame Steeet* from 1990–1996. Roy Forbes kept busy, producing other performers' recordings (including Connie Kaldor and Susan Crowe), hosting his occasional radio show *Snap, Crackle, Pop* on CBC and recording his own (Juno-nominated) album *Crazy Old Moon*.

Each has a faithful following. It simply triples when they perform together.

Valdy

b. Ottawa, 1946

The folk music tradition, while rooted in England and most commercially successful in the United States, has some of its most loyal practitioners in Canada. Valdy is considered among the most original, versatile and continuously popular.

"Unquestionably the most public performer in Canada," Jeani Read wrote of Valdy in *Maclean's* magazine, and "where the insular Lightfoot inspires no more than awe – the most loved."

The son of Danish émigrés, Valdy (Valdemar Horsdal) studied piano for five years, learned orchestration from Prof. Robin Wood, the dean of a music school in Victoria, B.C., but also played guitar from the time he was a teenager. In the 1960s he worked in bands – the London Town Criers, in Montreal, The Prodigal Sons and then as a bass player for country singer, Blake Emmons. By 1972, however, he had signed with Haida Records (with A&M) and released his first album *Country Man* and his first single, **Rock and Roll Song** the same year. That year, he was recognized at the Juno Awards (it was the first year in which the award winners were not known prior to the awards ceremony) for outstanding folk music performance of the year.

In 1973, following the release of his album *Landscapes* and the single **A Good Song**, Valdy won his first Juno Award as Best Folk Singer of the Year. In the mid-1970s he represented Canada at the International Song Festival in Poland and also recorded with members of The Hometown Band. By 1976, Valdy had recorded five albums (each achieving gold record status) and was second only to Gordon Lightfoot in Canadian folk music record sales.

Valdy's music moved from strictly folk to rock and jazz flavour in the late 1970s. The material also shifted to environmental activism, particularly with his 1978 *Hot Rocks* album, which addressed nuclear power. He also recorded the material of other artists, some who were addressing social issues, including Bruce Cockburn, Bruce Miller and Joe White, as well as others whose work he enjoyed covering, such as Bob Ruzicka's "Ain't The Only way To Go" and "Easy Money" and Max Bennett's "Simple Life."

In the 1990s he joined a new label, Oak Street Music, recorded an album *Heart at Work* (in 1993) and released a single **Double Solitaire** soon after.

Rack-On-Tour records released his CD *Smorgasbard* (in 1996) and *Contenders* (with Gary Fjellgaard) was released by Stony Plain Records in 1999.

Most reviewers have referred to Valdy, at one time or another, as versatile without realizing that in addition to his dozen albums, 18 singles, two Junos, and CARAS Songwriter of the Year, he also acted on the CBC-TV series *The Beachcombers*, hosted CBC simulcasts, won music video awards, worked as a TV talk show host and guest and conducted countless music workshops.

Gino Vannelli

b. Montreal, June 16, 1952

He has enjoyed success at the box office. He has found favour in his recordings with sales. But Gino Vannelli's often unorthodox approach – in the business and his art form – has not always been acknowledged. That he did things differently probably accounts for his loyal following and respect among his peers.

Gino grew up with the sound of his father's voice around him. Russ Vannelli sang with the Montreal dance bands of Bix Belair and Maynard Ferguson. As a boy, Gino studied drums privately and (with his keyboard-playing brother, Joe) formed an R&B band called the Jacksonville Five. He started writing song material at age 15 and then took music theory at McGill University. By 1970 he

James Minchin

had actually recorded with RCA Victor (a single called **Gina Bold**) under the name Vann Elli.

The story goes that, on a trip to Los Angeles, Gino waited outside the A&M Records security gate for part-owner Herb Alpert to leave his office. When he did, Vannelli outran the security guard and pushed the tapes into Alpert's hands insisting that he give them a listen. Impressed by Vannelli's nerve, Alpert listened, liked, and signed the young singer with A&M a few days later. Alpert also produced the first album, *Crazy Life* (1973), on which the Vannelli brothers played all the instruments. Innovative, yes, but risky too, as he explained to author Martin Melhuish: "I played all the percussion and Joe played keyboard bass and all of the other keyboards," Vannelli said. "No matter how great a musician you might be, you are limited to your own capabilities."

Back in Montreal for the recording of his second album, *Powerful People* (1974), Vannelli restricted himself to vocals, while brother Joe Vannelli played keyboards, John Mandel played percussion, Richard Baker played the organ, and Graham Lear handled drums. The music itself was an extraordinary fusion of pop, jazz, soul, and funk. It was additionally remarkable because Vannelli did not use any guitars on the album, nor on the single **People Gotta Move**. The tour of Canada and a few American dates helped build momentum for the single. In 1975 he won the Juno for Most Promising New Male Artist and his first Grammy nomination.

Following the release of his album *Storm at Sunup* (1975), Vannelli earned another Juno as Male Artist of the Year and another Grammy nomination. Another departure album, 1977's *A Pauper in Paradise*, included Vannelli's four-part symphony recorded in London with the Royal Philharmonic Orchestra. His major commercial breakthrough came with 1978's *Brother to Brother*, which contained a single written by his brother Ross Vannelli, **I Just Wanna Stop**. It became a million-seller and earned another Grammy nomination. Vannelli and his brothers Joe and Ross had now won five consecutive Juno Awards as Male Vocalist, Producer, and Engineer of the Year respectively.

Calling his music intense, ambitious, and flamboyant, the press helped propel Vannelli into the limelight outside Canada too; the *Toronto Star*'s Steven Davey described Vannelli as "Canada's first export sex symbol since Robert Goulet."

By 1981, he had signed with Arista Records, taken a year off and come back with the album *Nightwalker*, which yielded another hit single, **Living Within Myself**, and another Grammy nomination. The next album *Black Cars* (1985) generated more hit singles and videos; BMI named the track **It Hurts to Be in Love** one of the most played songs worldwide in 1986.

Still stretching the boundaries of his own brand of popular music, Vannelli reflected on his time away from the touring circuit during the late 1980s in his album *Inconsolable Man* (1990). Then he signed with Verve Records and released a vocal-jazz record *Yonder Tree* and then an R&B album *Slow Love* in 1998. Not stopping there, in 2000 Vannelli completed the script and principal composition of an opera (set in post-medieval England), part of which he performed with several orchestras while on tour that year.

In a telling comment earlier in his career, Gino Vannelli explained that he had the opportunity to remain an opening act and to perform in front of larger audiences more often, but chose "to play in front of small audiences that were perhaps a part of a cult that was developing … maybe take a little longer and work a little harder."

That slow but sure path ensured constant sales, audience, and respect from his contemporaries.

Denny Vaughan
b. Toronto, Ontario, December 20, 1922; d. 1972

For a time, Denny Vaughan was one of the brightest stars on the Canadian musical scene. His career began when he was six years old, when he sang in a church choir.

By the time he was in his teens he was performing on radio station CFRB in Toronto and appearing with Horace Lapp's orchestra. Denny, who could play piano as well as sing, was seated high on the Lapp bandstand at a grand piano – as was Lapp at an equally impressive grand piano.

Vaughan studied music at the University of Toronto. During the Second World War he was a member of the Canadian *Army Show* and toured Europe.

The *Army Show* was split into two units for overseas performances and given the typically army-"inspired" names "Unit A" and "Unit B." Denny Vaughan was the pianist with Unit A, which had, among other blessings, Robert Farnon, trombonist Murray Ginsberg, bassist Murray Lauder, and violinist Jack Groob.

When the war ended, the handsome and personable Denny remained in England for a time and became something of a teen idol, with Denny Vaughan fan clubs springing up throughout England and Germany (where he had appeared with the Army show), and even in the British West Indies. In England, he was known as "the English Sinatra."

In the four years following the end of the war, Denny sang, arranged charts for, and recorded with the British dance bands of Carroll Gibbons, George Melachrino, and, for two years, Geraldo, probably England's most famous dance band of the time.

In 1950, he returned to North America, settling at first in New York. He played for a time with Lester Lanin, who then had perhaps the top "society" band in the area, being booked regularly to supply the music for society weddings, debutante debuts, and the like. Vaughan studied Lanin's approach and determined to make use of it.

During his time in New York, Denny worked as an arranger for such varied artists as Eddie Fisher, Kate Smith, and Ezio Pinza.

Denny decided to return to Canada and soon landed a spot with CBC Radio – a 15-minute show of his own. After three years of this, the CBC moved him to television, with his own weekly half-hour program, *The Denny Vaughan Show*, which also featured the talented blonde singer Joan Fairfax.

Denny also became a "name" recording artist in 1956, with his version of a song written by trumpeter Johnny Cowell. The song was "Walk Hand in Hand" and Denny's recording of it became a big hit both in Canada and in the United States.

The television series proved popular and went on for several seasons. Then, in 1957, an unforeseeable event proved to have a significant effect on Vaughan's career. In those days, variety shows – or "light entertainment," as the CBC preferred to categorize them – ran for 39 weeks and were then replaced for the summer by another program, usually a new one being more or less tested on the air.

That summer of 1957, while Denny took some time off, the program that replaced his was *Front Page Challenge*, which became such an instant success that it was continued in the fall – and for the next 35 years – and Denny Vaughan simply lost his spot on the network.

But the talented Denny was resilient enough to roll with the punch. The next year, he moved to Montreal, where he became orchestra leader at the Queen Elizabeth Hotel. The CBC carried regular broadcasts of the Vaughan band from the Queen Elizabeth and Denny even returned to Toronto from time to time to appear on one CBC program or another, including several appearances on *The Wayne and Shuster Show*. But the strained relations between the CBC and Denny never quite healed.

In the 1960s, Denny was working in New York and Hollywood. In the latter location, he served as choral director for such hit series as *The Glen Campbell Goodtime Hour* and *The Smothers Brothers Show*.

During all his years in England, New York, and Los Angeles, Denny kept his Montreal home, in hopes of someday moving back to Canada. He did just that in 1971 and again began working in and around Montreal. But he was stricken with cancer and died early in October 1972, at the age of 50. He left his wife, Helene, who nursed him during his final illness, and two children, daughter Corinne and son Kim.

Jon Vickers

b. Prince Albert, Saskatchewan, October 29, 1926

Jon Vickers as Otello

The sixth child in a family of eight, Jon Vickers recalls singing in a Christmas concert at the age of three. His boy's treble had become a robust tenor by the time he had finished high school, and he joined Baptist choirs in Prince Albert and Flin Flon, Manitoba, where he worked in stores during the day and sang leading roles in Victor Herbert and Gilbert and Sullivan operettas at night. In those days, he recalled, he sang "for anyone, anytime, anywhere."

By the time he was 20, Vickers was assistant manager of a chain store in Winnipeg, but soon the demand for his services as a singer began to occupy so much of his time that his employer ordered him to give up singing. Instead, he resigned and became a hardware salesman, but continued to sing.

Encouraged by singer Mary Morrison to study voice, he sent a recording of his material to Ettore Mazzoleni at the Royal Conservatory of Music at Toronto. Accepted as a scholarship student in the fall of 1950, he began training with George Lambert. During his first year in Toronto he sang in 30 oratorio performances for the Board of Education, was soloist in Handel's *Messiah* at the University of Western Ontario, was chosen by Mazzoleni as soloist for the Canadian premiere of Bruckner's *Te Deum* with the massed RCMT choirs, and in the fall of 1951 sang in *Messiah* at Massey Hall with the Toronto Mendelssohn Choir.

By 1955, despite wide exposure in concert and oratorio and some 28 operatic performances, including the Canadian Opera Company's productions of *Rigoletto* and *La Traviata*, he had received no offers from the United States or Europe. Finally, in 1957, he was invited (on diva Regina Resnik's recommendation) to sing in concert performances of *Fidelio* and *Medea*, the latter with Eileen Farrell in New York.

He was invited to audition for the Royal Opera House, Covent Garden, and soon had a three-year contract. After his debut tour with the Covent Garden company, Vickers received enthusiastic notices and subsequently enjoyed great personal success in *Carmen*, *Don Carlo*, *Aida*, and *The Trojan*. After his debut at Basy Reuth in 1958 as Siegmund in *Die Walküre*, Vickers was acclaimed as the world's leading interpreter of the role.

That same year he sang Jason to Maria Callas' Medea in Dallas, Texas. By the end of the 1959–60 season, having appeared in Vienna and Buenos Aires, and having sung in *Peter Grimes* and *Fidelio* at the Metropolitan Opera, he decided to become a freelance artist. Vickers' roles over the years represented most of the dramatic and heldentenor repertoire: Don José, Radames, Don Carlo, Canio, Otello, Tristan, Siegmund, and Parsifal, and his favourite, Peter Grimes.

One of his most significant associations was with the conductor Herbert von Karajan. He sang in Karajan's first three Salzburg Easter Festivals (1966–68), recorded *Tristan und Isolde*, *Die Walküre*, *Otello*, and *Fidelio* and filmed *Pagliacci* and *Otello* with the conductor. He also sang under Karajan's baton in the great opera houses, including La Scala and the Metropolitan.

In 1985, Vickers starred in Handel's *Samson* at Covent Garden in a joint production with the Lyric Opera of Chicago and the Metropolitan Opera to celebrate Handel's 300th birthday.

Although he has given occasional recitals in Canada, notably in Toronto and at the opening of the 1969 Guelph Spring Festival, Vickers in his mature years sang little opera in Canada. A combination of a busy schedule and his inevitably large fees can account for this. Nevertheless, there have been some stellar occasions: he sang *Otello* in four performances at Expo '67 in Montreal and he sang Act 1 of *Die Walkure* with the Montreal Symphony Orchestra at the opening ceremonies of the National Arts Centre in Ottawa in June 1969. During the 1970s and 1980s he made periodic appearances in various parts of Canada.

It was in 1976 that a *Newsweek* article described Vickers as "an austere, reflective Canadian goaded by the demands of a Protestant work ethic." The article also said: "He uses his rugged voice with a contemptuous disregard for musical or national boundaries and a compulsion to challenge the brutes of the repertory. ... The sound of his muscular, tireless voice is pitted and scarred as if hacked out of a Canadian quarry. But it is clearly made by hand, its imperfections redeemingly human and individual."

In his busy, decades-long singing career, Vickers has won numerous awards and honours, both inside and outside Canada. He has also recorded composers from Beethoven and Bizet to Vaughan Williams and, of course, Wagner. He has also given numerous lectures, including a series of three lectures titled *The Contribution of the Art of Music to the Civilizing Process.*

Moxie Whitney *b. Brockville, Ontario, June 3, 1919; d. 1989*

If Guy Lombardo had not left Canada, he might well have found Moxie Whitney breathing down his neck, vying for the title of leader of this country's most popular and successful dance band. For more than four decades, Moxie's name was synonymous with dance music. From Ottawa and Toronto to Lake Louise and Banff Springs and, later, Vancouver, Whitney and his smooth-sounding dance band packed them into the leading hotels that catered to the well-heeled diners-and-dancers of Canada.

Born George Eugene Whitney, he adopted "Moxie" as his name, from his mother's maiden name of "Moxam." He began his career in Toronto in his teens as guitarist and leader of the Pacific Swingsters, featuring Hawaiian music. He also played guitar for Stanley St. John's dance band, and was a trumpeter with the RCAF during the Second World War. In 1946 he formed his own band to play the Granite Club in Toronto.

It was essentially that band that became famous across Canada, playing at the Royal York Hotel's Imperial Room during the winters and either at Lake Louise or Banff Springs during the summers. He also spent 10 years playing at the Château Laurier in Ottawa.

So embedded in the minds of dance music fans was the name of Moxie Whitney that he was one of the very few bandleaders in Canada who could lead his musicians on a cross-country tour of some 40 one-night stands and draw crowds from one coast to the other. In the summer of 1986, for example, he played at the Quinte Music Festival, in Picton, Ontario, and shortly there-after he was at the Harvest Moon Ball in Nepean, near Ottawa. Then he raced back to Toronto's Royal York for a week, after which he went to Boston to lead a big band at the Maple Leaf Ball for the Canadian Consulate there. That winter he had a band at a Mardi Gras Ball in Ottawa and then played at the Tulip Ball, also in Ottawa.

In 1962, he opened his own booking agency in Toronto and for the next decade he was music director for the Canadian Pacific chain of hotels in Canada. But he still loved to lead a band. He didn't need the money, he said, but he liked the activity. "There's a lot of ham in me," he explained. "I like to reaffirm that people enjoy my music. I like to see people having fun."

The two key ingredients in a Moxie Whitney band were his comprehensive collection of arrangements and Moxie himself spearing the air with his baton and smiling at the happy dancers.

The Whitneys raised seven children – six of them boys. All the Whitney children either sang or played some instrument, but Moxie steered them away from choosing music as a career. "I discouraged all of them," he said, "because I felt there was no future in it. I think I'm one of the very few musicians fortunate enough to have made a fairly steady livelihood."

When he played at the CNE Dance Tent in Toronto during the summers of 1977 and 1978, he was pleased that some of the dancers would come up to him and tell him they remembered the band when they went out for special nights with their parents.

In November 1986, he brought a big band into the Royal York's Imperial Room yet again, but only for one week, because he had other bookings that prevented him from staying longer. That was his last appearance at the Royal York. Moxie Whitney died in July of 1989 at the age of 70.

David Wiffen

b. England, March 11, 1942

In the euphoric pop music explosion of the 1960s, it seemed if a rock band or a solo folk act could sing and play half decently, fame and fortune were just a club gig, a TV show appearance, or one recording session away. But hard as he worked to create it, David Wiffen often fell just shy of the big breakthrough. Truth was, he needn't have looked any further than his own vocal and songwriting ability for the quality of music that made his contribution so remarkable.

A "near-perfect album" is the way music reviewer Richard Flohil described David Wiffen's third and most successful album, **Coast to Coast Fever** (1973). In the liner notes of the 1993 CD re-release, Flohil went on to say, "its images are as bittersweet and accurate now as ever they were. The sadness is cathartic and it connects instantly."

Connecting instantly. That's exactly the way blues music came into David Wiffen's life in the first place. Growing up in England after the Second World War, David was fortunate enough to get three years of classical piano training, choir and band practice, and even music appreciation classes. When he was 14 or 15 he spotted country blues singer/guitarist Big Bill Broonzy on television.

"He just came on the screen with his guitar," Wiffen remembers. "I'd never heard anybody actually pick a guitar, other than strumming chords. He did a couple of tunes and there was all this music coming from the guitar. And I said, 'Right. That's for me. I've got to learn to do that.'"

Wiffen searched London record stores, found several 45-rpm extended-play records (one containing an instrumental version of "Saturday Evening Blues") which he played over and over and mimicked. Within a year, the Wiffen family had immigrated to Canada and in Toronto David found record stores with even more blues (Brownie McGhee) and folk music (Fred Neil) to emulate. He sang in the Yorkville coffeehouse scene – at The Village Corner and Purple Onion – for a while, but then hitchhiked across Canada.

In Calgary, Wiffen arrived at a coffeehouse called The Depression (which he managed for several months). That year during the Calgary Stampede, the club staged a huge folk jam session, at which Wiffen met Donna Warner and Brent Titcomb who were in town from Vancouver. Wiffen told them "how great it would be if we could all put a group together … because we all had the same sense of humour and musical ideas." Warner and Titcomb returned to Vancouver and in 1964 joined Trevor Veitch to form a folk trio called Three's a Crowd.

When Wiffen finally got to Vancouver, Three's a Crowd was indeed that, and had no room for a blues singer/guitarist. Wiffen moved to Ottawa, where he teamed up with the folk-rock group, The Children, which included a who's who of local musicians – Bruce Cockburn, Sandy Crawley, Neville Wells (later the founder of *Country Music News*), Peter Hodgson (later to perform as Sneezy Waters), and drummer Richard Patterson.

Reenter Three's a Crowd. This time the band was also playing folk-rock at coffeehouse Le Hibou in Ottawa and it was in need of another singer and a drummer. Wiffen and Patterson joined them in time to open in New York City and then play the Ontario pavilion at Expo '67.

"The gig was supposed to last two weeks," Wiffen said, "but we ended up being held over for seven weeks, during which time Cass Elliot and Denny Doherty (both of the Mamas and the Papas) came to Expo, saw us, and liked us. And we found ourselves in Los Angeles signed to Dunhill Records and making our first LP." The album, *Christopher's Music Matinee* (1968), featured songs by Wiffen, Cockburn, William Hawkins, and a new writer from Toronto, Murray McLauchlan.

Three's a Crowd remained a group for two years. During its run, Donna Warner became ill and left and was replaced by Colleen Peterson. In 1969, the group fell apart again, but was reassembled as the centrepiece of a CBC-TV show in Montreal; Three's a Crowd then included Patterson (drums), Peterson (vocals), Crawley (guitar, vocals), Cockburn (guitar, vocals), Dennis Pendrith (bass), and David Wiffen (guitar, vocals). Following the 26-week TV series, again the band broke up and everyone went separate ways. Wiffen next worked on CJOH-TV in Ottawa co-hosting (with Ann Mortifee) a variety show called *Both Sides Now*, then he disappeared.

"I sat for about six months," Wiffen remembered. "I did a lot of reading ... I drank a lot of beer and sort of kept to myself for quite a while. However, I did write most of the songs for my first solo album."

Fantasy Records released *David Wiffen* in 1971, which contained some of his most telling compositions to date. Wiffen was not happy with the production (done by musicians he didn't even know); he said that the tapes were damaged and his vocal tracks ended up "sounding like the Chipmunks." The album did, however, contain several of his best songs, many of which were later covered by a wide array of artists – **Mr. Wiffen** was recorded by Harry Belafonte; **Driving Wheel** was covered by Tom Rush, Roger McGuinn, and the Cowboy Junkies; and **More Often Than Not** was recorded by Eric Anderson, Ian and Sylvia, and Jerry Jeff Walker.

Wiffen's next album, *Coast to Coast Fever* (1973), was recorded for United Artists and certainly reflected his nomadic lifestyle. Once more, there were production problems, until producer Brian Ahern brought in Wiffen's onetime bandmate, Bruce Cockburn, who played acoustic and electric guitar as well as bass and celesta on several cuts. Again, it was the substance of the songs that transformed this album into what Richard Flohil called "a minor classic. ... This was a songwriter whose pain was severe, who found it hard to cope with the contradictions of adulation and relatively small financial rewards and who discovered that loneliness was a fact of life, even though he was surrounded by friends and lovers."

This third album earned a Juno Award nomination, but it appeared to be Wiffen's last. He left touring and recording behind. He successfully battled alcoholism and depression. He married and settled in the Ottawa area. He found other artistic outlets – painting, sculpture, and poetry (two volumes were published). Then in the mid-1990s, Wiffen reconnected with old friend Bernie Finkelstein (of True North Records), who talked to him about a fresh recording of both old and new Wiffen material. Ottawa bass player Phil Bova came on as producer, but the production took six years, several different studios, and difficult restarts before *South of Somewhere* was released.

"I've never written songs in large bunches," Wiffen said. "The songs come out one at a time and it's sometimes years in between each ... but it's still satisfying."

While not nearly as active in public appearances, in 1999 Wiffen was invited by the operator of Irene's, a local pub in Ottawa, to perform at and host an open stage every Thursday night. Each week Wiffen played a set and then emceed for people who wanted to have a crack at performing.

In a conversation after the release of his first solo album, Wiffen was asked what he wanted to become of his work. "Mainly, I'd just like to show as many people as I can, that I can sing. I'd love to have other well-respected people in the music business say, 'Hey, that David Wiffen, he writes good songs.'"

David Wilcox

b. Montreal, July 13, 1949

The popular music business does not encourage originality. There are more copy bands out there than originals. Some believe that artists have to earn the freedom to do their own material. Guitarist and singer David Wilcox has proven it the hard way. It took him more than 20 years, but where audiences once demanded he play Rod Stewart or Led Zeppelin material, today they shout for his originals – **Bear Cat**, **Bad Apple**, and **Hypnotizing Boogie**.

"I see myself as a singer and a writer," Wilcox said.

Getting to that point in his career, however, took some doing.

David Karl William Wilcox was born in Montreal and raised by his mother and her family in Toronto. At school David studied trumpet and clarinet. At home his family listened to classical music, while David was holed up in the basement listening to blues recordings of Robert Johnson and Bukka White.

But his first hero was Elvis Presley.

"Elvis frightened people because there was that overt sexuality and that sense of danger ... so I got a guitar because I wanted to be like Elvis," Wilcox said. "I remember I took an Elvis record to my grandmother's house. She wouldn't let me play it because she thought the vibrations might damage the needle on her record player."

Undaunted, at age 12, David gave his first public performance to a group of former prison inmates; one of them tossed a chair at him. At age 13, David was a paid professional and by 1963 he had dropped out of school, was working in a record store, and appeared regularly along Toronto's coffeehouse row playing folk and blues music. A devoted acoustic player, David bought an electric guitar, a Fender Telecaster, on impulse at a pawn shop, and though he hardly knew how to turn the amp on, it provided his first big break.

Wilcox got his break when he heard that Ian and Sylvia were looking for a guitarist (to replace Amos Garrett) in their country-rock band, The Great Speckled Bird.

"Ian and Sylvia were heroes of mine," Wilcox said. "I don't know why I got the job. I couldn't even turn the amplifier on at the audition. ... But I went

Andrew MacNaughtan

from a guy who was living in the suburbs of Toronto, who wasn't a good student and didn't know where his life was going ... to a guy travelling around North America meeting people like Waylon Jennings and playing Carnegie Hall. It was like life giving me a big kiss!"

For three years, he worked on stage, around the continent, and in and out of television studios with his heroes, Ian and Sylvia, and backing the big-name artists of the 1960s and 1970s – such as Jerry Reed, Anne Murray, Charlie Rich, Bobby Bare, Ray Price, and Carl Perkins – on Ian's TV show, *Nashville North*.

By the early 1970s, Wilcox had headed off on his own in more ways than one. He joined an anarchistic rock band called the Rhythm Rockets and was noted for his vaudevillian appearance – a Dali-like moustache, a top hat, silk tie, baggy suit, fake carnation on his lapel – and an extroverted personality to match. In 1975, he formed a rock trio called the Teddybears, which played everything from Otis Redding to swing to original material. But the world wasn't ready for Wilcox originals.

"Normally, when you start a band, you're encouraged to play and write original tunes," Wilcox said. "But we encountered an awful lot of prejudice against playing our own material. … One time in Hamilton, we went into a biker bar. The agent had told them we were a Top 40 band. So we went in there and I was playing Benny Goodman and black gospel *a cappella* tunes and my own tunes. The audience hated it and the owner hated it. I came very close to getting hurt."

With the encouragement of his friend, multimedia artist Sadia, Wilcox assembled enough of his own written material for an album, but not until 1980 did *Out of the Woods* get recorded and released by Freedom Records. The independent recording sold a respectable 30,000 copies.

Meanwhile, the stage persona of David Wilcox found a comfortable home on the college circuit, during the 1980s. He regularly performed 300 shows a year and was considered Canada's highest-grossing campus performer. His reputation for delivering upbeat, entertaining, and off-the-wall shows translated into packed houses on campuses and built a strong, young fan base for his subsequent recordings – *My Eyes Keep Me in Trouble* (1983), *Bad Reputation* (1984), and *Best of David Wilcox* (1985) which went platinum, selling more than 100,000 copies.

"The crazy David routine was something he switched on for the fans," wrote *eye*'s William Burrill. "Even while he's playing the part of the clown prince of rock 'n' roll, there was a darker side to the man. He had a brooding side that even he couldn't disguise."

In the late 1980s, Wilcox made an abrupt turn. On his album *Breakfast at the Circus* (1987), he worked with synthesizers and drum programs and sang songs with more abstract (and less party-oriented) lyrics. He got even more adventurous with his next album, *The Natural Edge* (1989), on which he experimented even further with a techno-sound and what Howard Druckman in *Canadian Composer* called "stylish production, catchy hooks, electric guitar textures and intriguingly idiosyncratic words."

By this time, Wilcox and his career were in desperate need of hiatus. Creatively, the next six years were spent recharging batteries, and staying off the road and out of the studio. In what he called "consciously letting go of my career," Wilcox only listened to music he liked, stopped writing and playing, and in addition took time to dry out from years of heavy alcohol and drug use. Wilcox emerged from his forced "sabbatical" with a back-to-basics CD *Thirteen Songs* (1996), that explored personal feelings, his lighter side, and even childhood remembrances; in 1997, he recalled for *Edmonton Sun* music critic Fish Griwkowsky the story behind the tune **Songs to Sell**:

"There was a knock on our door, one night," Wilcox said. "And it was an old man saying, 'Would you like to buy a song?' So my mother bought a sheet of paper with a song on it. When the guy went away, I made fun of him. ... My mother got angry with me, telling me I had it made. The ultimate irony, which I put into the song, is here I am with songs to sell. If only I had known."

At the end of 2000, David Wilcox completed an 11th album, **Rhythm of Love** (released through Stony Plain Records), which again featured more of his own material.

"I am going further with my art," Wilcox told the *National Post.* "I just try to take more chances."

Healey Willan

b. Balham, England, October 12, 1880; d. Toronto, Ontario, 1968

To those acquainted with classical, operatic, or symphonic music, James Healey Willan has long been regarded as Canada's greatest composer.

He was something of a child prodigy, considered brilliant. His mother had some musical ability and became Willan's first teacher when he was four-and-a-half. At eight years old he entered St. Saviour's Choir School in Eastbourne, England, and six months later he became a regular choirboy, something no other child of his age had achieved.

Willan studied piano and organ, harmony, and counterpoint, and by the age of 11 he began directing choir practice for boys older than himself and conducting for the evensong services at St. Saviour's. By the age of 18, he was a Fellow of the Royal College of Organists.

In 1905, he married Gladys Ellen Hall, also a musician. They were to have four children. (Mrs. Willan died in 1964.)

In 1913 Willan was invited to accept a post as head of the theory department at the Royal Conservatory of Music in Toronto. Willan said years later that the numbers 3 and 13 had always played an important part in his life. Since the invitation to Toronto arrived on the third day of the third month of 1913, he decided to accept. (His family joined him in Toronto the following year.)

Three weeks after his arrival in Toronto, he accepted a post as organist/choirmaster at St. Paul's Anglican Church, even though he was Anglo-Catholic. He found himself in a well-paid job among the city's social elite, but they were low church, not Anglo-Catholic.

Eight years later, a friend of Willan's sought his help in finding an organist/choirmaster for the small, and poor, Anglican Church of St. Mary Magdalene. Willan nominated himself (he said it was a birthday present to himself) and moved to the poorer parish, comprising mainly British immigrants. He exchanged a good salary for what he later derided as "my annual tip." He had to supplement his salary by extensive outside work to pay for his four children's private education.

Despite his devotion to his church, Willan also loved other forms of music. He composed some 700 works, including the full-length opera *Deirdre*, which he originally wrote for CBC Radio in 1946 as *Deirdre of the Sorrows*, plus a piano concerto, two symphonies, and numerous vocal pieces. He admired the work of Gilbert and Sullivan but never attempted to follow in their footsteps. "It's beyond me," he commented. "You've got to be bloody clever to write musical comedy."

But there was a lighter, almost elfin side to Willan. "He was a typical Anglican choirmaster," said a colleague at the University of Toronto. "He wasn't austere; he did it all by winks and nods."

He once set the constitution of Toronto's Arts and Letters Club to music. He wrote risqué limericks, sneaked musical jokes into his organ improvisations, and once described himself with these words: "I am English by birth, Irish by parentage, Canadian by adoption, and Scotch by absorption."

He was involved in several extramarital affairs that led to his suspension from St. Mary Magdalene in 1941, when he was 60 years old. But he apparently never considered leaving his wife. (A year later, he was forgiven by the parishioners of St. Mary Magdalene and returned to the church.)

He thought about going to Hollywood and writing film scores, or trying his hand at large-scale secular works that might expand his range; but, no doubt unfortunately, he didn't do either.

Willan was always a hardworking man who demanded the best of his students and choir members. He was given to extreme mood swings – he could be warm and entertaining or he could be a snob, the rudest person one could ever meet. In an article by Kildare Dobbs, Willan was described as follows: "Willan can be a holy terror; what saves him from fanaticism is his quite unholy sense of humour. That and a warmth and sympathy has made him as much loved as revered by the choirs he rules."

Various other quotations by Willan (or attributed to him) illustrate some of his views and his sense of humour:

> There are two things you can't buy: one is contentment, and the other is a dog's affection.
>
> Relative pitch is of absolute importance. Absolute pitch is of relative importance.
>
> The best committee consists of two persons with one absent.

I must go get my hair cut. I don't want to go around looking like a musician.

Willan's hobbies included collecting stamps and old books. He was also an animal lover and made donations to care for stray animals. "Anyone who doesn't love dogs," he once said, "can hardly be trusted."

Over his lifetime he received his share of honours. Leonard Brockington, the first chairman of the CBC, said of Willan: "He has brought forth more good music than any other man in our history."

He was the recipient of one of the first Order of Canada medals when the award was initiated in 1967.

In 1953 he wrote the 1953 homage anthem **O Lord, Our Governeur,** which was sung at the coronation of Queen Elizabeth II in London. It was the only anthem from the pen of a living composer at the ceremony.

Toronto is not noted for paying tribute to Canadian musicians. But two important parks were named for musicians. One is the Alexander Muir Garden named for the man who composed "The Maple Leaf Forever." The other is Healey Willan Park.

The latter would seem to be the realization of one of Healey Willan's fondest dreams: "If I can leave behind me some music which is good," he once said, "and if I can be held in memory for a while by a few good friends, I shall turn up my toes and willingly when the time comes."

Jesse Winchester

b. Shreveport, Louisiana, May 17, 1944

It's hard to say whether, if he'd stayed in his native southern United States, Jesse Winchester could have woven more of that culture and sound into his music. The fact that he moved to Canada didn't hurt his gentle, bluesy style, the richness of his storytelling, or his sense of humour at all. Nor did the distance from home make his music any less attractive to contemporaries who regularly sing his songs.

Raised in Memphis, formally trained on a music scholarship in Massachusetts and for a time abroad playing with a band in Hamburg, Germany, Winchester returned home during the Vietnam War. He became a conscientious objector and emigrated to Quebec in 1967. Early on, he played rhythm guitar

in a francophone band known as Les Astronauts. Then he went solo and worked the coffeehouse circuit around Montreal and occasionally Toronto. That's where Robbie Robertson of The Band saw him and offered to produce a recording.

In 1970 Ampex Records released his debut album, *Jesse Winchester*. The Robertson connection brought in a wealth of knowledge to the studio and a who's who of sidemen, including guitarist David Rea, fiddler Al Cherny, drummer Levon Helm, and Robertson on guitar, as well as talented musician and engineer Todd Rundgren.

Reviewers applauded the album. His self-imposed exile had clearly given poignancy to songs such as **Yankee Lady** and his finely edged country/folk style gave credibility to his **Brand New Tennessee Waltz** (which was covered by the Everly Brothers, Joan Baez, and Iain Matthews). Further endorsement came later when both Tom Rush and Jimmy Buffett recorded **Biloxi**, and when Brewer & Shipley also covered **Yankee Lady**.

David Sokol, editor-in-chief of *New Country* magazine, wrote that Winchester's first album "signaled the emergence of a sensitive and literate tunesmith with a lot on his mind."

Accordingly, Winchester recorded prolifically in the 1970s. Brian Ahern, Juno Award-winning producer of Anne Murray's "Snowbird," handled production on Winchester's second album, *Third Down, 110 To Go* (1972). The singer himself produced the next album, *Learn to Love It* (1974), on which he expressed some of the complexities of adopting a new home. In 1976, his album *Let the Rough Side Drag* came out.

About the time he began promoting his album *Nothing But a Breeze* in 1977, President Jimmy Carter announced an amnesty for draft resisters. The amnesty allowed Winchester to travel back to the United States to see friends and family. It opened up concert and recording possibilities, but by then he was a Canadian citizen and bilingual.

"When the amnesty happened," he told the *Toronto Star*, "I had already had 10 years of being a Canadian, raising a Canadian family. My life was in Montreal."

Winchester's 1981 album *Talk Memphis* was recorded and mixed in American production studios. It yielded his Top 40 hit single, **Say What**. Not until 1988 did he record again; his album *Humour Me* (notice the Canadian spelling) was recorded in Nashville and featured a dozen tracks of mostly laid-back material. As usual, other artists liked the songs too and quickly began covering them – **Let's Make A Baby King** (Wynonna Judd), **Thanks to You** (Emmylou Harris, Chris Smither), and **Well-a-Wiggy** (Weather Girls).

By the 1990s, Winchester admitted he was "burnt out ... I was discouraged. I was repeating myself. I felt I was saying the same thing in concert every night." He stopped appearing, but kept writing for other artists, including

Reba McEntire, Wynonna Judd, and the Mavericks, who made a Top 20 hit out of Winchester's **O What a Thrill**. Then, after a decade-long hiatus, he resurfaced in 1999 with his CD *Gentleman of Leisure*. It featured, among others, one of Winchester's idols – Booker T and the MGs' lead guitarist Steve Cropper.

"When I was a kid, he was my hero for a lot of reasons," Winchester told reviewer Nick Krewen. "Booker T and the MGs had two black guys and two white guys. That seemed to be what Memphis was all about, or what it could be until Martin Luther King got killed."

Political reality was never far from the artist's life.

Dave Young

b. Winnipeg, Manitoba, January 29, 1940

On the night of Dave Young's 60th birthday – January 29, 2000 – this fine bass player was doing what he loves. "I was working at the Montreal Bistro in Toronto with Norman Simmons, and he'd just turned 70, so I didn't feel so bad," Young commented.

He started young. His first instrument was the piano and then he learned violin, guitar, and finally bass. "I ended up playing the bass because, when I was 17, I was working as a guitarist in a dance band. One day the leader told me the bass player was leaving and he was cutting the guitar chair. My only choice was to learn bass," he told an interviewer.

By the time he was in his twenties, Dave had travelled to Boston to attend the Berklee College of Music. Then he returned to Winnipeg to attend the University of Manitoba, earning his bachelor's degree in business and commerce. He spent the late 1960s and much of the 1970s doing studio work during the day and then playing clubs at night.

Justin Time Records suggested he make a recording featuring himself with a variety of well-known pianists. Dave recalls, "I asked them who they had in mind as far as piano players went, and they said, 'Well, let's start with Oscar Peterson.' My reply was something like, 'Yeah, that's great but you must be dreaming.' Oscar was my first choice as well but initially I just didn't think he would do it. Of course, when I did approach him, he surprised me and said, 'Sure.'"

Thus began a close and fruitful association between Dave and Oscar. In the spring of 1997, Young was chosen Musician of the Year by *The Jazz Report*, the Toronto-based jazz quarterly. Oscar Peterson was at the awards ceremony to make the presentation. He was in a wheelchair, having suffered a stroke a few years before which caused partial paralysis on his left side.

In making the presentation to Young, Oscar spoke glowingly of the bass player and acknowledged his own debt to him. He recalled that Dave had phoned him one day and said he was heading for Oscar's house to play some music with him. Oscar told him he was no longer able to play, but Dave went anyway – with his bass. After some conversation, Dave suggested they go to the music room and play. Despite Oscar's objections, Young insisted. And so they played.

"It was Dave who gave me back my confidence," Oscar declared at the *Jazz Report* banquet. It was an uncharacteristic moment of candour for Oscar, who doesn't often talk about his stroke.

Later that same year, Oscar was asked to play at a benefit concert for the beloved (and ailing) jazz critic Helen McNamara. He readily agreed to this, but he wanted Dave Young as his bass player. Young was booked to play in Quebec City, but he managed to get to the benefit concert, thus not disappointing Oscar.

Young's stock has been high in recent times. In 1996 he was a two-time winner at the *Jazz Report* Awards. He won the magazine's Album of the Year award and was also chosen Bassist of the Year.

In 1975, he had moved back to Winnipeg to take the job as principal bass in the Winnipeg Symphony. Before that, he had been playing in the Edmonton Symphony "and doing various classical gigs in southern Ontario as well as the jazz stuff. Then I got the call to tour Japan with Oscar, so I quit the symphony."

Dave worked on and off with Oscar until 1986, "at which I went full-time for two years. In addition I was working with the Hamilton Philharmonic, so I was obviously very busy."

In the mid-1990s, he qualified for a Canada Council grant. "I've taken a one-year sabbatical from my teaching position at the University of Toronto to study with three New York bass players – Rufus Reid, Michael Moore, and a classical player named Dennis James. It was a chance to do a bit of practising. When I'm working as much as I do, there isn't a lot of time left over. It's been nice spending some time learning some new things before I jump back into the fire again."

His hunger for more knowledge seems insatiable. With degrees in business and architecture, he keeps exploring and learning. "I really want to do more travelling in this next decade on my own. I would like to work Europe in a much more definitive way," he said at the time of his 60th birthday.

"I want to play the bass until I die. Milt Hinton is a perfect example. It's got a lot to do with your physical and mental health. I'm going to keep on doing it."

He certainly kept on doing it by the end of the century. In 2000, Dave made his seventh Justin Time CD titled *Tale of the Fingers*. He headed a trio that had Cedar Walton on piano and Barry Elmes on drums and proved yet again what a great bass player he is – both bowing and plucking his way through such standards as "Sweet and Lovely," "Just in Time," and "Lost in the Stars."

Neil Young

b. Toronto, Ontario, November 12, 1945

In January of 1971, the day after federal government regulations went into effect requiring at least 30 percent of broadcast music in Canada to be Canadian, Neil Young arrived in Toronto for his first solo appearance in Canada at Massey Hall. Of course, the so-called "CanCon" rules made little difference to Young's rocketing career at that point. In the years since his departure from the Canadian scene in 1966, Young had participated in two of rock 'n' roll's most influential and popular bands, Buffalo Springfield and Crosby, Stills, Nash, and Young; made more than $100,000; bought a ranch near San Francisco; slipped a disc (giving him that patented forward-leaning stance); and received a hero's welcome wherever he performed.

"The applause which followed," reported rock reviewer Ritchie Yorke, "was unlike anything I had ever witnessed in three years of covering rock concerts at Massey Hall. ... Never had a Canadian been granted such enthusiastic acclaim by fellow Canadians."

The irony is that if Neil Young hadn't gone to the United States and had stayed in Canada to develop his folksy songwriting, his primordial guitar playing, and his high-pitched falsetto singing style, the radio programmers, record distributors, and public might have ignored him.

His history was not extraordinary. Born in Toronto, Young was packed off to Winnipeg in 1960 when his parents – Rassy and Scott – divorced. He learned to play guitar on a Christmas present ukulele, played guitar in a high school rock band called The Squires, and dropped out of school at age 17 to pursue a musical career. At a club in Fort William, Ontario in 1965, the Squires crossed paths with an American band, The Company, which featured a guitarist named Stephen Stills. In Toronto, Young and bass player Bruce Palmer assembled a group called The Mynah Birds, but later the two decided to try their luck in L.A. They travelled west in a 1953 Pontiac hearse.

"I loved the hearse," Young said. "Six people could be getting high in the front and back and nobody would be able to see in because of the curtains."

A hearse with Ontario plates on it was awfully conspicuous, however, and one day in the middle of a traffic jam on Sunset Boulevard in Hollywood, Palmer and Young were spotted by musicians Stephen Stills and Richard Furay. The four decided to form a group (including Canadian-born drummer Dewey Martin). They first chose the name the Herd, until they noticed the name "Buffalo Springfield" on a parked steamroller. With Atlantic Records the band recorded and released three albums, which, for the first time, blended folk, hard rock, and country music; the releases also contained

Neil Young in concert at Maple Leaf Gardens in Toronto in 1978

healthy portions of Neil Young material, songs such as **Mr. Soul, Broken Arrow,** and **Expecting to Fly**. Springfield disbanded in 1968; Young got married and went into seclusion outside L.A.

Nearby, at his home in Laurel Canyon, Stephen Stills periodically invited David Crosby (from the U.S. group The Byrds) and Graham Nash (from the British band The Hollies) to jam. Experimenting with electric folk material the trio soon released its first LP, *Crosby, Stills and Nash*, which contained hit singles **Suite: Judy Blue Eyes** (Stills' song about Judy Collins) and **Marrakesh Express**.

Neil Young would sometimes sit in. Since the demise of Springfield, he'd recorded and released his first solo effort and was planning a second with his new backup band Crazy Horse. The threesome approached Young about joining them in a loose arrangement allowing all members to work solo and as a group. The band called Crosby, Stills, Nash, and Young debuted August 16,

1969, opening for Joni Mitchell and then played at the historic Woodstock Festival two days later. They were instant favourites. In March of 1970, CSN&Y released their first album, *Déjà Vu*, which sold three million copies internationally and was the year's number-one album. The momentum continued with *4 Way Street*, recorded live at several U.S. locations in the spring of 1970; it included Young tracks such as **On the Way Home, Don't Let It Bring You Down, Ohio,** and **Southern Man.**

Sometimes referred to as "the American Beatles" and often compared to "juggling four bottles of nitroglycerin," the CSN&Y arrangement, however, brought out all of Neil Young's strengths. Crosby called him "a fine writer." Nash called him "very direct." Stills called him "my best friend ... with common understandings." Young modestly suggested his contribution was "a down home feeling ... I write songs. I consider myself more of a writer than a guitar player, but in this band, I think I'm more of a guitar player than a writer."

It was Danny Whitten, the leader of Young's band Crazy Horse, who best articulated Neil Young's persistently nomadic path; quoted in Ritchie Yorke's 1971 book *Axes, Chops & Hot Licks*, Whitten said, "Neil likes to play in groups, but basically he's a solo artist. I don't think he'll ever stay with any group for very long. Deep down, he knows that he has to do the gig himself." While there would be periodic reunions in the coming decades, by 1972, CSN&Y was no more.

American music critic David Menconi describes Young as "an extremist who never sticks with any one extreme for very long, not to mention that he's a brilliant artist ..." He points to Young's 1970 release of *After the Gold Rush*, again featuring Crazy Horse with guitarist Nils Lofgren, as one of his best. It was both a sales and a critical success and featured such hit singles as **Southern Man** and **Only Love Can Break Your Heart**, which reviewers called "smooth" and "powerful." His 1972 album *Harvest* is considered his most popular. It's considered a landmark for its 1970s-vintage West Coast folk-rock and because it included his first number-one hit, **Heart of Gold.**

During the 1970s, Young seemed to be everywhere. He composed music for movies – a song for *Strawberry Statement* and entire scores for *Landlord* and *Journey Through the Past*, which he also assembled into a double album of the same name. Periodically, Young dropped in on solo shows of his friends Crosby, Stills, and Nash, and in 1974 the foursome, as CSN&Y, did a summer stadium tour. He continued work on solo projects as well: *On the Beach* (1974), *Homegrown* (produced in 1975 but not released), *Zuma* (1975), *American Stars 'n' Bars* (which included appearances by Linda Ronstadt and Nicolette Larson and The Gone with the Wind Orchestra in 1977), and *Rust Never Sleeps* and *Live Rust* (live recordings in 1978–79).

Events offstage also affected his writing. His marriage broke up in 1971 and in 1973 Bruce Berry (a roadie with CSN&Y) and Danny Whitten (guitarist with Crazy Horse) both died of drug overdoses. A tour to promote Young's eighth solo album, *Tonight's the Night*, some say, featured him at his best because of its haunting images of death and its honky-tonk sound from a revamped Crazy Horse.

In 1976, Young also joined a roster of all-star performers in The Band's "Last Waltz" concert at Winterland in San Francisco. No wonder both *Rolling Stone* and *The Village Voice* named Young "Artist of the Decade."

Rock 'n' roll's most intriguing chameleon revealed an even broader spectrum of musical colours in the 1980s. He seemed to ricochet between a number of different genres, performing and recording with an ever-revolving collection of old and new musician friends. He threw himself into country music on *Hawks & Doves* (1980) and *Old Ways* with Willie Nelson and Waylon Jennings (1985), and his voice acquired a perceptible twang when he was touring with the band International Harvesters. He experimented with techno (computers and synthesized music) on *Trans* (1982) and *Landing on Water* (1986), with retro on *Everybody's Rockin'* (1983), and with a revitalized Crazy Horse band on *Re-Ac-Tor* (1981). Young even fulfilled a promise to David Crosby that he'd perform as CSN&Y if Crosby beat his drug addiction on their 1988 album *American Dream*.

In 1986, Young began an autumn tradition by presenting the first Bridge School Benefit at the Shoreline amphitheatre in Mountain View, California. Hosted by Young and his wife, Pegi, the series of acoustic concerts were created to raise funds for a school where children (such as Young's youngest son) with cerebral palsy learn to communicate through computers and other technology.

There were more movie soundtracks, a foray into blues with a 1988 album *This Note's For You* (whose video was first banned by MTV for criticizing corporate sponsorship, then voted video of the year at the 1988 MTV Music Video Awards), and, when he performed **Rockin' in the Free World** (from his 1989 album *Freedom*) on *Saturday Night Live*, a clear demonstration he was still very much a vital rock 'n' roll artist.

In the 1990s, Young continued to defy musical pigeonholing. His early-1990s albums (*Arc* and *Weld*) and live shows with Crazy Horse experimented with extended, feedback-laden, guitar instrumentals, which earned him the moniker "Godfather of Grunge" from Generation-X audiences. His release of *Harvest Moon* featured some of the Stray Gators as well as Linda Ronstadt and James Taylor (reminiscent of his *Harvest* album from 20 years earlier). In 1993 he toured with Booker T. and the MGs and composed the Academy Award–nominated title track for the film *Philadelphia*. His 1994 release *Sleeps with Angels* became one of Young's most critically and commercially acclaimed albums and was nominated for a Grammy.

In 1995 Neil Young was inducted into the Rock and Roll Hall of Fame as one of modern music's pioneers, but, true to form, when it came time for the induction a new Neil Young CD *Mirror Ball* was previewed at the ceremonies. With the three CD releases since then, Young's output to date is more than 35 albums.

"No other boomer rock star," wrote David Browne in *Entertainment Weekly* in 2000, "not Dylan, not the Stones, not the ex-Beatles, has matched this son of a Canadian sportswriter for prolonged vitality. ... (He) has become the Mark Twain of rock – a craggy, folkloric figure restlessly striding the musical landscape."

Acknowledgements

No singer, band member, conductor, or soloist can take a bow onstage without acknowledging those behind the scenes. Similarly, before accepting any applause, the authors wish to offer a heartfelt thanks to those who've helped get us here.

We are grateful for the full cooperation of the National Archives of Canada, particularly Peter Robertson and Dan Somers, for their help in tracking down biographical information and photographs on many of the artists included here.

Others have provided numerous photo stills to accompany our words. Many of the artists profiled here and other industry-watchers have dug into personal collections and provided images from today and yesterday. For the freedom to borrow from their collections, we especially thank Fred Phipps, Holger Petersen, Jim Lynch, Geoff Roberts, John Zronik and Richard Flohil.

We also acknowledge the valuable resources of the CBC archives/library and the Toronto Reference Library; despite an era of cutbacks and downsizing, their stacks continue to provide valuable assistance to authors such as ourselves who regularly research Canada's musical heritage.

At HarperCollins we are also indebted to Don Loney, our editor, for his patience and for helping to steer us away from the pitfalls of inaccuracy, to Roy Nicol, who designed this book, and to our copy editor, Rodney Rawlings. An additional thanks to our interview transcriber, Braunda Bodger.

Most of all, we want to express our gratitude to the many musicians and performers who gave of their time in talking with us about their lives and careers. Their memories, anecdotes, and insights about the Canadian music industry are the gift that made this book possible.

Finally, a word of thanks to Kate Barris for her assistance and to our respective wives – Kay Barris and Jayne MacAulay – for their constructive criticism and support throughout the creation of this opus.

Artists' Birthdays

Joe Rockman (Jeff Healey Band) – Jan. 1, 1957
Benjamin Darvill (Crash Test Dummies) – Jan. 4, 1967
Dal Richards – Jan. 5, 1918
Archie Alleyne – Jan. 7, 1933
Mike Reno (Loverboy) – Jan. 8, 1955
Billy O'Connor – Jan. 9, 1914
Gisele MacKenzie – Jan. 10, 1927
Ronnie Hawkins – Jan. 10, 1935
Brad Roberts (Crash Test Dummies) – Jan. 10, 1964
Art Hallman – Jan. 11, 1910–1995
Johnny Cowell – Jan. 11, 1926
Bill Reed (Diamonds) – Jan. 11, 1936
Long John Baldry – Jan. 12, 1941
Wray Downes – Jan. 14, 1931
Ben Heppner – Jan. 14, 1956
Domenic Troiano – Jan. 17, 1946
Don Thompson – Jan. 18, 1940
Molly Kurvink (Tamarack) – Jan. 26, 1956
Rudi Maugeri (Crew Cuts) – Jan. 27, 1931
Bruce Good (Good Brothers) – Jan. 27, 1946
Brian Good (Good Brothers) – Jan. 27, 1946
Susan Aglukark – Jan. 27, 1963
Sarah McLachlan – Jan. 28, 1968
Lois Marshall – Jan. 29, 1924–1997
Dave Young – Jan. 29, 1940
Joyce Hahn – Jan. 31, 1929
Ofra Harnoy – Jan. 31, 1965
Tom Stephen (Jeff Healey Band) – Feb. 2, 1955
Keith Glass (Prairie Oyster) – Feb. 4, 1952
Kate McGarrigle – Feb. 6, 1946
Stompin' Tom Connors – Feb. 9, 1936
Bert Niosi – Feb. 10, 1909–1987

Jim Creeggan (Barenaked Ladies) – Feb. 12, 1970
Roy Forbes "Bim" – Feb. 13, 1953
Scott Smith (Loverboy) – Feb. 13, 1955–2000
Wally Koster – Feb. 14, 1923–1975
Rob McConnell – Feb. 14, 1935
Loreena McKennitt – Feb. 17, 1957
Joe Hampson (Travellers) – Feb. 19, 1928
Sheila Henig – Feb. 19, 1934–1979
Paul Dean (Loverboy) – Feb. 19, 1946
Larry Evoy – Feb. 19, 1946
Buffy Sainte-Marie – Feb. 20, 1941
Paul Cooper (Nylons) – Feb 20, 1950
Eugene Watts (Cdn Brass) – Feb. 22, 1936
Ashley MacIsaac – Feb. 24, 1975
Hagood Hardy – Feb. 26, 1937–1997
Horace Lapp – March 3, 1904–1986
Paul Weldon – March 4, 1936
Carroll Baker – March 4, 1949
Mart Kenney – March 7, 1910
Matt Frenette (Loverboy) – March 7, 1954
Richard "King Biscuit Boy" Newell – March 9, 1944
Tommy Hunter – March 10, 1937
David Wiffen – March 11, 1942
Boris Brott – March 14, 1944
Jeff Bird (Tamarack) – March 17, 1956
Donnie Walsh (Downchild Blues Band) – March 24, 1947
John McDermott – March 25, 1955
Jeff Healey – March 25, 1966
Jann Arden – March 27, 1962
Terry Jacks – March 29, 1944
Céline Dion – March 30, 1968
Sharon Hampson – March 31, 1943
Louis Applebaum – April 3, 1918–2000
Richard Manuel (The Band) – April 3, 1943–1986
Victor Feldbrill – April 4, 1924
Percy Faith – April 7, 1908–1976
Fraser MacPherson – April 10, 1928–1993
Travis Good (Good Brothers) – April 10, 1968
John Kay (Steppenwolf) – April 12, 1944
Norman Amadio – April 14, 1928
Mike McKenna – April 15, 1946
Marc Connors (Nylons) – April 15, 1949–1991

Bobby Curtola – April 17, 1944
Walter Ostanek – April 20, 1935
Doug Riley – April 24, 1945
Ginette Reno – April 28, 1946
Walter Susskind – May 1, 1913–1980
Terry Dale – May 2, 1926
Goldy McJohn (Steppenwolf) – May 2, 1945
Maynard Ferguson – May 4, 1928
Don Messer – May 9, 1909–1973
Hank Snow – May 9, 1914–1999
Connie Kaldor – May 9, 1953
Ralph Cole (Lighthouse) – May 13, 1947
Catherine McKinnon – May 14, 1944
Tom Cochrane – May 14, 1953
Ted Kowalski (Diamonds) – May 16, 1931
Sid Dolgay (Travellers) – May 17, 1923
Jesse Winchester – May 17, 1944
Dan Roberts (Crash Test Dummies) – May 22, 1967
Dallas Good (Good Brothers) – May 22, 1973
Teresa Stratas – May 26, 1938
Levon Helm (The Band) – May 26, 1940
Bruce Cockburn – May 27, 1945
Rita MacNeil – May 28, 1944
Russell deCarle (Prairie Oyster) – May 31, 1953
Corey Hart – May 31, 1961
Alanis Morissette – June 1, 1974
Moxie Whitney – June 3, 1919–1989
Phil Nimmons – June 3, 1923
Dan Hill – June 3, 1954
Michael Monarch (Steppenwolf) – June 5, 1946
Jan Rubeš – June 6, 1920
Ted Roberts (Travellers) – June 7, 1933
Larry Cramer – June 7, 1955
Joan Besen (Prairie Oyster) – June 12, 1951
Chris O'Toole (Carlton Showband) – June 14, 1927
Ian McDougall – June 14, 1938
Gino Vannelli – June 16, 1952
Guy Lombardo – June 19, 1902–1977
Anne Murray – June 20, 1945
Steven Page (Barenaked Ladies) – June 22, 1970
Myles Goodwyn (April Wine) – June 23, 1948
Jerry Goodis (Travellers) – June 25, 1929

Robert Charlebois – June 25, 1945
Frank Mills – June 27, 1942
Murray McLauchlan – June 30, 1948
Rich Dodson (Stampeders) – July 1, 1947
James Gordon (Tamarack) – July 2, 1955
Ralph Fraser – July 3, 1925
Kevin Hearn (Barenaked Ladies) – July 3, 1969
Kim Berly (Stampeders) – July 4, 1948
Andrew Creeggan (Barenaked Ladies) – July 4, 1971
Robbie Robertson (The Band) – July 5, 1943
Raffi – July 8, 1948
Phil Levitt (Diamonds) – July 9, 1935
Tony Nolasco – July 9, 1950
Lois Lilienstein – July 10, 1936
Kim Mitchell – July 10, 1952
Liona Boyd – July 11, 1950
Charles Daellenbach (Cdn Brass) – July 12, 1945
David Wilcox – July 13, 1949
Ellen Reid (Crash Test Dummies) – July 14, 1966
Boyd Neel – July 19, 1905–1981
Robert Farnon – July 24, 1917
Maureen Forrester – July 25, 1930
Stan Fisher (Diamonds) – July 26, 1935
Jim Galloway – July 28, 1936
Gary "Geddy" Lee Weinrib (Rush) – July 29, 1953
Paul Anka – July 30, 1941
Joe Mendelson – July 30, 1944
André Gagnon – August 1, 1942
Ronnie King (Stampeders) – August 1, 1947
Garth Hudson (The Band) – August 2, 1937
Lenny Breau – August 5, 1941–1986
Bobby Hales – August 9, 1934
James Campbell – August 10, 1949
Ruth Lowe – August 12, 1914–1981
Oscar Peterson – August 15, 1925
Don Vickery (Travellers) – August 16, 1938
Joe Sealy – August 16, 1939
Colin James – August 17, 1964
Sir Ernest MacMillan – August 18, 1893–1973
Susan Jacks – August 19, 1948
Stuart Laughton (Cdn Brass) – August 19, 1951
Mario Bernardi – August 20, 1930

Juliette – August 26, 1927

Peter Appleyard – August 26, 1928

Alex Lifeson (Rush) – August 27, 1953

John Perkins (Crew Cuts) – August 28, 1931

Shania Twain – August 28, 1965

Seiji Ozawa – Sept. 1, 1935

Ray Woodley (Travellers) – Sept. 2, 1935

Helen Gray (Travellers) – Sept. 7, 1931

Graeme Page (Cdn Brass) – Sept. 8, 1947

Oliver Jones – Sept. 11, 1934

Dave Bidini (Rheostatics) – Sept. 11, 1963

Neil Peart (Rush) – Sept. 12, 1952

David Clayton-Thomas – Sept. 13, 1941

Pat Barrett (Crew Cuts) – Sept. 15, 1933

Mitch Dorge (Crash Test Dummies) – Sept. 15, 1960

Sylvia Tyson – Sept. 19, 1940

Leonard Cohen – Sept. 21, 1934

Tyler Stewart (Barenaked Ladies) – Sept. 21, 1967

Paul Hoffert (Lighthouse) – Sept. 22, 1943

Glenn Gould – Sept. 25, 1932–1982

Ian Tyson – Sept. 25, 1933

Jack Duffy – Sept. 27, 1926

Guido Basso – Sept. 27, 1937

Randy Bachman – Sept. 27, 1943

Dave Somerville (Diamonds) – Oct. 2, 1933

Jerry Gray (Travellers) – Oct. 3, 1933

Murray Ginsberg – Oct. 4, 1922

Charles Dutoit – Oct. 7, 1936

Frank Busseri (Four Lads) – Oct. 10, 1932

Claude Morrison (Nylons) – Oct. 11, 1952

Healey Willan – Oct. 12, 1880–1968

Jane Siberry – Oct. 12, 1955

Elmer Iseler – Oct. 14, 1927–1998

Shari Ulrich – Oct. 17, 1951

Tommy Ambrose – Oct. 19, 1939

Jane Bunnett – Oct. 22, 1955

Jerry Edmonton (Steppenwolf) – Oct. 24, 1946

Bobby Gimby – Oct. 25, 1918–1998

Ed Robertson (Barenaked Ladies) – Oct. 25, 1970

Alex Sinclair (Tamarack) – Oct. 26, 1952

Randy Sutherland (Tamarack) – Oct. 27, 1950

Jon Vickers – Oct. 29, 1926

David Foster – Nov. 1, 1949
k. d. lang – Nov. 2, 1961
Judy Loman – Nov. 3, 1936
Phyllis Marshall – Nov. 4, 1921–1996
Bryan Adams – Nov. 5, 1959
Bill Henderson – Nov. 6, 1944
Joni Mitchell – Nov. 7, 1943
Shirley Eikhard – Nov. 7, 1955
Neil Young – Nov. 12, 1945
Colleen Peterson – Nov. 14, 1950–1996
Michael Harrison – Nov. 15, 1949
Gordon Lightfoot – Nov. 17, 1939
Ellis McLintock – Nov. 18, 1921
Ray Perkins (Crew Cuts) – Nov. 24, 1932
Holly Cole – Nov. 25, 1963
Trump Davidson – Nov. 26, 1908–1978
Robert Goulet – Nov. 26, 1933
Amos Garrett – Nov. 26, 1941
Luigi Romanelli – Nov. 29, 1885–1942
Jack Kane – Nov. 29, 1924–1961
Ed Bickert – Nov. 29, 1932
Stan Rogers – Nov. 29, 1949–1983
P.J. Perry – Dec. 2, 1941
Anna McGarrigle – Dec. 4, 1944
Andy Kim – Dec. 5, 1952
Oscar Ross (Travellers) – Dec. 8, 1930
Tim Vesely (Rheostatics) – Dec. 10, 1963
Russ Little – Dec. 13, 1941
Howard Cable – Dec. 15, 1920
Galt MacDermot – Dec. 16, 1929
John Allan Cameron – Dec. 16, 1938
Tommy Banks – Dec. 17, 1936
Wilf Carter – Dec. 18, 1904–1996
Bram Morrison – Dec. 18, 1940
Richard "Hock" Walsh (Downchild Blues Band) – Dec. 19, 1948–1999
Doug Johnson (Loverboy) – Dec. 19, 1957
Denny Vaughan – Dec. 20, 1922–1972
Larry Good (Good Brothers) – Dec. 25, 1952
Shelley Coopersmith (Tamarack) – Dec. 27, 1950
Danny Marks – Dec. 27, 1950

Moe Koffman – Dec. 28, 1928–2001

Rick Danko (The Band) Dec. 28, 1943–1999
Lucio Agostini – Dec. 30, 1913–1996
Bernie Senensky – Dec. 31, 1944
Burton Cummings – Dec. 31, 1947

Index

479

485

486

487

494